By Louis R. Harlan

BOOKER T. WASHINGTON

Volume I   The Making of a Black Leader, 1856–1901
Volume II   The Wizard of Tuskegee, 1901–1915

BOOKER T. WASHINGTON

Booker T. Washington, 1906
Photograph by Frances Benjamin Johnston

Booker T. Washington

THE WIZARD OF TUSKEGEE

1901–1915

Louis R. Harlan

OXFORD UNIVERSITY PRESS
New York   Oxford

Oxford University Press
Oxford New York Toronto
Delhi Bombay Calcutta Madras Karachi
Petaling Jaya Singapore Hong Kong Tokyo
Nairobi Dar es Salaam Cape Town
Melbourne Auckland

and associated companies in
Beirut Berlin Ibadan Nicosia

First published in 1983 by Oxford University Press, Inc.,
200 Madison Avenue, New York, New York 10016
First issued as an Oxford University Press paperback, 1986

Oxford is a registered trademark of Oxford University Press

Library of Congress Cataloging in Publication Data
Harlan, Louis R.
Booker T. Washington: the wizard of Tuskegee,
1901–1915.
Includes bibliographical references and index.
1. Washington, Booker T., 1856–1915.
2. Afro-Americans—Biography.
3. Educators—United States—Biography. I. Title.
E185.97.W4H373 1983 378'.111 [B] 82-14547
ISBN 0-19-503202-0
ISBN 0-19-504229-8 (pbk.)

Printing (last digit): 9 8 7 6 5 4 3 2

Printed in the United States of America

To Sadie

PREFACE

THIS book begins in 1901, when Booker T. Washington at the age of forty-five was approaching the zenith of his fame and influence, and ends with his death in 1915. It is a biographical study in the sense that its focus is on the complex, enigmatic figure of Washington, the most powerful black minority-group boss of his time. It also recounts the inner life and struggles of the small black middle class in that generation once removed from slavery, as a coterie of college-bred black men and women challenged Washington's powerful coalition of northern white philanthropists, southern white paternalists, black businessmen, and such members of the black professional class as he could attract to his side.

Washington was born in 1856, a mulatto slave on a small Virignia farm, and spent the early years of freedom in West Virginia working in the salt furnaces and coal mines and as a houseboy, and attending a Freedmen's Bureau school.* After graduating from Hampton Institute, then a secondary normal and industrial school, he founded Tuskegee Institute in 1881 in the Black Belt of Alabama. During the next fifteen years he was engrossed in building his institution, mollifying the local whites, and raising money in the North.

A single speech in 1895 catapulted Washington into national fame and recognition as a black spokesman. In what became known as the

---

*For a detailed account of Washington's early life, see my earlier book, *Booker T. Washington: The Making of a Black Leader, 1856–1901* (New York: Oxford University Press, 1972).

Atlanta Compromise Address, delivered before a southern commercial convention, he proposed a triple alliance between northern capitalists, the New South white leadership class, and blacks. Washington offered to trade black acquiescence in disfranchisement and some measure of segregation, at least for the time being, in return for a white promise to allow blacks to share in the economic growth that northern investment would bring. He captured the formula neatly in the phrase: "In all things that are purely social we can be as separate as the fingers, yet one as the hand in all things essential to mutual progress." It was a compromise that whites of both sections hailed with enthusiasm and blacks generally accepted as the best they could negotiate in the age of segregation that had already begun. Washington further elaborated his social philosophy of accommodationism and black self-help in his best-selling autobiography, *Up from Slavery,* in 1901. From his southern base at Tuskegee he gradually built what became known as the Tuskegee Machine, an all-pervasive control of every avenue of black life. His accession to power was crowned in 1901 by dinner at the White House with President Theodore Roosevelt and his family. This mark of official favor began a close collaboration in black patronage politics and added another arm to the octopus-like Tuskegee Machine.

The subtitle dubs Washington "the Wizard of Tuskegee," partly because many blacks of his day, both friendly and unfriendly, referred to him privately as "the Wizard," though never to his face. It was customary in the early twentieth century to refer to Luther Burbank as "the plant wizard," Thomas A. Edison as "the wizard of Menlo Park." But Booker T. Washington's wizardry owed a debt also to L. Frank Baum's wizard of Oz. Tuskegee was his Emerald City in the worn-out cotton lands and pine barrens of the Black Belt. There was magic and seeming miracle in Washington's secret maneuvers against his white and black enemies, both those who defended white supremacy and those who thought Washington too conservative.

Washington's wizardry—his skill of maneuver and ability to make the most of bad circumstances—was his strong point as a leader. His greatest failing was his inability to reverse the hard times for blacks during what whites called the Progressive Era. What was for Washington personally the best of times was for most blacks the worst—the most discouraging period since the freeing of the slaves. The loss of voting rights in the South, segregation, economic exploitation, and a nationwide atmosphere of white racial hatred and violence made the turn of the century what the historian Rayford Logan calls the nadir of Afro-American history. Washington, the era's most prominent black man, found it impossible to accommodate to the system of white supremacy and at the same time to challenge or change it.

This book does not claim to offer a "final" explanation of Washington's social philosophy, in so far as he had a coherent one, nor to expose to the core his very complex personality, nor to thread through the labyrinth of the Tuskegee Machine to the monstrous minotaur therein. Booker T. Washington had no quintessence. At the center of his intellectual maze was a hall of mirrors reflecting endlessly the platitudes and dubious social science of the late nineteenth century. Like most other historical figures, and particularly politicians, Washington can be best understood not by studying his presumed ideology, but by learning what he did.

Washington had multiple personalities to fit his various roles. Along with the Washington who cozied up to the white paternalists of the South and philanthropists of the North and who rigorously fought the civil rights champions of his day, there was another Washington who worked unceasingly for black pride, material advancement, and every kind of education. He also, in his own way, fought against lynching, disfranchisement, peonage, educational discrimination, and segregation. He did these things more by private action than by ringing declaration. Most of his public utterances on civil rights contained weasel words that his critics said vitiated his purposes, but he contended these were necessary to gain any hearing at all from whites. He saw his own unique role as the axis between the races, the only black leader who could negotiate a social peace with the whites, but whose influence could be destroyed by an instant of self-indulgent flamboyance.

Washington never forgot, however, that it was the blacks whom he undertook to lead. He could not lead the whites; he could not even divide them. He could only exploit the class divisions the whites created among themselves, working in the cracks of their social structure. As a guide for the black community, on the other hand, he had a concrete program of industrial education and the promotion of small business as the avenue of black advancement "up from slavery" and into the middle class. This program may have been anachronistic preparation for the age of mass production, urbanization, and cor-

porate gigantism then coming into being; but it had considerable social realism for a black population which was, until long after Washington's death, predominantly rural and southern. It gave purpose
and dignity to black working-class lives of toil and struggle, and also
was well attuned to the growth and changing character of black business in Washington's day. He championed the emerging black business
class as the leaders of black communities, and they in turn, through
the National Negro Business League, became the backbone of Washington's following.

There was also a more feral, more power-hungry Washington, in-
ordinately involved in politics, and particularly the politics of patronage. Washington built the Tuskegee Machine by rewarding friends
and punishing enemies, and political plums were his chief means for
winning over individual members of the college-bred professional class,
the Talented Tenth, his chief critics. A presidential appointment for
a lawyer or a Republican party subsidy for a black editor were powerful solvents of opposition. Against the intransigent black critics of
the Niagara Movement, headed by W. E. B. Du Bois, Washington was
ready to employ ruthless secret methods of espionage, provocation,
and sabotage that seem utterly at variance with the Sunday-school morality he publicly professed. Washington never tried to reconcile his
secret machinations with his public life, perhaps because, being secret,
they did not pragmatically require justification.

W. E. B. Du Bois, Washington's most eloquent critic, spent much of
his long life puzzling over the phenomenon of Washington, a man
who did not seem to have an abstraction about him. Toward the end
of his life, in an oral history memoir in 1954 at Columbia University,
Du Bois said of his old rival, then dead almost forty years: "Oh, Washington was a politician. He was a man who believed that we should
get what we could get." Du Bois himself found the political part of
his race work the least agreeable, and went on to say of Washington:
"It wasn't a matter of ideals or anything of that sort. . . . With everybody that Washington met, he evidently had the idea: 'Now, what's
your racket? What are you out for?' " Du Bois was a shrewd observer,
but what he saw in Washington as a lack—of ideals, principles, vision—was actually Washington's great and almost unique gift as a black
political leader. He could immediately and intuitively, without formal
questioning, see through the masks and intellectual superstructure of
those he met to the mainsprings of their behavior. Then he imagina-

tively bent their purposes to his own. Washington did not always get his way, of course, politics being merely the art of the possible, but the surprising thing was the number and diversity of those he enlisted in his coalition.

Readers who expect to find in this book a treatise on Washington's role in the history of education may be disappointed to find that his educational administration at Tuskegee Institute and his speeches and writings on education receive relatively brief attention. In view of the greater detail on this side of his life in the published *Booker T. Washington Papers*, and because I feel that he played an important but not remarkably innovative role in educational history, I have stressed what seems to me more important: the sources, nature, uses, and consequences of his power.

In 1901 Washington was married to his third wife Margaret. Portia, his daughter by his first wife, was almost ready for college, and he had two sons by his second wife, Booker T. Washington, Jr. and Ernest Davidson Washington (Dave). Though Washington was clearly a conscientious parent in the years when his children were going to school, maturing, and moving out in their own directions, his private and family life remains something of a mystery. The approximately one million documents in Washington's private papers include only a few hundred letters between him and his children, and even fewer personal letters between him and his wife during the twenty-three years of their marriage. Either his letters to his wife were removed from his papers or else he never wrote them, though the two were apart more than half of the time. Her letters and telegrams often complained of his failure to write. With the personal rewards of a rich and varied public life, and also with the peculiar satisfactions of a secret life unrestrained by the social and racial conventions, perhaps Washington felt no need for the homey comforts, leisure, and indirection of a private life. At any rate, he had no time for it, for his sense of mission and his demon of ambition filled his days and allowed him repose only in sleep.

An indispensable element in Washington's uniquely personal leadership of the black minority group was the help, advice, and devotion of his private secretary, Emmett J. Scott, the only person who knew all of Washington's secrets and the full range of his public and private affairs. Almost twenty years younger than his chief and always in his shadow, the meticulous Scott surrendered himself to Washington's will and worked to give expression to every nuance of Washington's thought and purpose. He supervised an office staff of a dozen members, including Nathan Hunt who was Washington's traveling secretary and companion. Remaining at Tuskegee whenever Washington traveled, Scott was his spy among the faculty, his press secretary, the voice at his ear, and often his ghostwriter. When Washington had to be at Tuskegee, Scott frequently traveled as his emissary on confidential errands. As more lucrative opportunities came to Scott, including the presidencies of two colleges, he turned them down to remain near the seat of power, not only because he relished his Iago-like role but because Washington had become dependent on his services as the general manager of the Tuskegee Machine. Scott bore a resemblance to Iago in his penchant for the whispered calumny, the planted anonymous editorial, secret messages, code names, and spies. In none of his activities, however, did Scott intentionally betray Washington's interest. The worst that could be said of him is that he prompted or initiated many of Washington's underhanded maneuvers, but in all of these Washington was a knowing and willing participant.

After Washington's death in 1915, many observers assumed that Scott would be the logical person to run Tuskegee, but the trustees, perhaps recognizing the limitations which a lifetime of subordination had fostered in the faithful secretary, chose instead Robert R. Moton. Moton proved an adequate head of the institute but allowed the Tuskegee Machine to fall into disarray. Washington's little empire ended with his death.

College Park   L. R. H.
November 1982

ACKNOWLEDGMENTS

IT HAS taken me a long time to write this book since the appearance of my earlier work on Booker T. Washington's early life. I hope that readers will find it worth the wait, and offer as my explanation that my gifted co-editor Raymond W. Smock and I have been hard at work on the thirteen volumes of the *Booker T. Washington Papers,* the last volume of which will be published by the University of Illinois Press at about the same time as the present book. Though the editorial enterprise has demanded much of my time, I consider it a great boon to this biography. Editorial staffs are better and more persistent ferrets of telling detail than most monograph writers, and I appreciate the labors of all the assistant editors, editorial fellows, and research assistants who contributed to the richness of evocation of a buried life, not only in the edited volumes but in this biography. I am grateful also to the National Endowment for the Humanities, the University of Illinois Press, the University of Maryland, and the taxpayers for supporting our effort to give a broader focus to the study of the American past.

In order to write, however, I needed leisure, stretches of time free from the daily demands of editing and teaching. A fellowship of the John Simon Guggenheim Foundation, sabbatical leave and a summer research grant of the University of Maryland, and a joint fellowship of the Center for Advanced Study in the Behavioral Sciences and the Andrew Mellon Foundation gave me this relief and opportunity.

Though I claim sole authorship and responsibility, I owe a large debt to the three other persons who know Booker T. Washington best through years of study of his personal papers. Sadie Harlan, my wife and co-worker on the editorial project (our "mom and pop store"), has read the manuscript piecemeal several times and saved me from many errors. Ray Smock and August Meier also read the manuscript and gave me good advice. For criticism of portions of the work in an earlier form, I thank Pete Daniel, Elliott Rudwick, David Lewis, the history department seminar of the University of Maryland, and the Wednesday evening seminar at the Center for Advanced Study in the Behavioral Sciences. For editorial criticism of articles in their journals I thank Henry R. Winkler, Robert K. Webb, and Nancy Lane of the *American Historical Review* and Sanford W. Higginbotham of the *Journal of Southern History*. I thank Sheldon Meyer and Leona Capeless of Oxford University Press for their aid and guidance. One would think that with help of this quality the book would write itself, but I did hard labor over the problems of selection, structure, interpretation, and style. It still needed the editorial skill and judgment of Sallie Reynolds. The only clichés she allowed me were the ones that could stand on their heads.

L. R. H.

CONTENTS

Illustrations between pages 270 and 271.

BOOKER T. WASHINGTON

CHAPTER 1

Partners of Convenience:
Washington and Roosevelt

But alas for good intentions,
And such democratic ways!
For there came a cry from Dixie
And a fire was set ablaze.
"You insult us, you outrage us!
You commit an awful sin!
When you welcome to your table
That—er—man with a dark skin."*

THE White House Social Calendar, a regular column in the news-papers of the national capital, reported in small print that on October 16, 1901, Booker T. Washington had been President Theodore Roosevelt's guest at dinner. Overnight, the dinner became a sensation. The southern newspapers, ever since Washington's famous Atlanta Compromise address in 1895, had held him up as an example of "the good Negro," the very model of discretion, the man who had promised that black and white people could remain "as separate as the fingers, yet one as the hand in all things essential to mutual progress." Now they felt betrayed, and vied with each other in frothing denunciation of both Washington and Roosevelt. The level of white

* Mobile *Weekly Press*, Dec. 1901, clipping.

supremacy rhetoric in the South had risen steadily over the preceding decade of lynchings and disfranchisement, but the southern press and political leaders abandoned all restraint now, and the cry from Dixie resembled the howl of a mob. Men who had never supported Roosevelt swore they would never vote for him again. As for Washington, they would never trust him again.

Both Roosevelt and Washington refused to give any interviews or otherwise break public silence to either apologize or explain. The newspaper war went on, however, growing by what it fed on, the exchanges with other newspapers, until it became a paper tiger. Both men must pay for their sin. Roosevelt could never win reelection in a white man's country; and Washington, like Humpty Dumpty, had fallen and all the Rough Riders couldn't put him together again. One rustic southerner, believing that somewhere in this affair a joke was imbedded, sent the President a 'possum with a card around its neck bearing the name "Booker Washington."[1] In Lincoln, Nebraska, William Jennings Bryan saw a chance to seal his alliance with the South. He devoted a page and a half in *The Commoner* to the White House dinner. "It is to be hoped that both of them," he wrote, "will upon reflection realize the wisdom of abandoning their purpose to wipe out race lines, if they entertain such a purpose."[2]

Many white southerners, however, sought a way out of their dilemma. They excused Washington, saying that he could not disobey the invitation of the President, which was in effect a command. After all, Washington was the only Booker T. Washington they had. And Roosevelt also was personally popular with many southerners who would not think of voting for him. He was an outdoorsman, a Rough Rider, a gentleman. He could have been a professional southerner but for the accident of birth. Within two weeks after the dinner with Roosevelt and his family, the Washington, D.C., correspondent of the Louisville *Courier–Journal* began to circulate a myth that became part of southern folklore, that the dinner was only a luncheon in the midst of work and "not premeditated."[3]

Reason soon reasserted itself even in the South, a region not noted for thinking things through, and this was in no small part due to Washington's home town newspaper, the Tuskegee *News*, whose editorial was widely reprinted:

Prof. Washington's life for twenty years has been an open book in this community and the South, and it is hardly the part of fairness to judge a man by one act with which we may not agree rather than by his twenty years of wise living. It is perfectly well known in this community that for fifteen years Prof. Washington's business in securing the money to carry on his work has thrown him into contact with the Northern white man both in the South and the North in a way that does not often fall to the lot of the average colored man. . . . There has been scarcely a week during the last ten years when the Associated Press has not told us of his speaking and dining at some banquet in the North with governors, etc. We all know that it was widely reported in the press dispatches three years ago that he lunched with President McKinley and his party during the Peace Jubilee in Chicago. Nothing has been hidden from the South.

The editorial expressed "the highest confidence" in the great man in their midst, and said: "Surely if Principal Washington were engaged in preaching a propaganda of 'social equality' we believe we should see evidences of such teaching in this little community where his school of 1200 students and teachers is located. Until we do we shall be slow to pass condemnation for one incident." [4]

When the tumult and the shouting died, it became clear that the White House dinner had not hurt him among white southerners not already blindly hostile, and that it had greatly strengthened his claim to leadership of blacks. The fiery young editor William Monroe Trotter of Boston called him a hypocrite for going to the White House dinner after all his public accommodation to segregation in the South, and in Alabama the rival black educator William H. Councill tried to use the "accident," as he called it, to undercut Washington's white following.[5] But other blacks saw that Washington, knowing the personal risks, had been brave enough to go to the White House as the representative of his race. Bishop Henry M. Turner, putting aside his own ideological disagreement with Washington, wrote him: "You are about to be the great representative and hero of the Negro race, not withstanding you have been very conservative. I thank you, thank you, thank you."[6] More blacks were now willing to acknowledge Washington as the leader of their choice, even though initially it had been white favor that had thrust him upon them. And Washington's partnership with President Roosevelt in the federal patronage put the final rivet in the Tuskegee Machine that made it fully operational. Ironically, the very black leader who had denied the efficacy of politics in solving the race problem became the black politician without a peer in his time.

Roosevelt's official reason for taking Washington as a counselor was that Washington knew the South so well that he could help him build up the Republican Party into a real contender with the Democrats by choosing for federal office and hence for party leadership the whites and blacks who had real standing and respect in their own communities instead of the venal professional politicians of both races who had been buying their appointments by selling their votes at Republican national conventions. Though Roosevelt was sincere in this desire to elevate the public service, he also wanted as soon as possible to replace the appointees of President McKinley and his political manager Mark Hanna with his own men before 1904, when Hanna might be his challenger for the presidential nomination.[7]

Washington had many purposes in his limited entry into politics that neatly dovetailed with Roosevelt's aims. He made it clear from the start and maintained throughout that he wanted no office himself and would refuse it if offered. When the Chief Magistrate asked his advice, he simply did his duty in giving it—a double duty since southern disfranchisement had brought to an end the presence of any elected representatives of the black people in Congress. That foot dragging was only a pretense, however. Washington actually entered patronage politics with gusto and with a remarkable talent for its trivial details. He did not always wait until the President asked for his advice, he persistently pushed for his favorite candidates for presidential appointment, and he used his influence with Roosevelt, and later with William Howard Taft, to build his own personal Tuskegee Machine.

During Roosevelt's first term, Washington had several particular goals, in addition to the reelection of the Chief Executive. He tried to replace the black professional officeholders, particularly those wedded to Hanna's interest, with men of the Booker Washington type, men who had made their mark on their own in private business or a profession. He made many exceptions, however, and a seasoned and possibly venal black professional politician could be miraculously cleansed by a promise of loyalty to Washington and to Roosevelt. Another of Washington's goals was to drive from office and party leadership the "lily white" Republicans, those who in the wake of disfranchisement tried to purge the Republican Party of blacks in order to make it "respectable" in the South. In order to keep the Republican party biracial, he encouraged Roosevelt to replace these lily whites with Gold Democrats, those whiggish, upper-class white southerners alienated by Bryanism who were also Tuskegee's allies in the social politics of the South. Washington's third and overarching goal was to enhance his own power by getting Roosevelt to appoint the men he wanted, so that he could reward friends and punish enemies among the black leadership. If this raised the quality of the federal service or changed the character of southern Republicanism, so much the better.

In the pursuit of his own goals, it was easy for Washington to ignore the fact that the Roosevelt administration steadily reduced the number of black presidential officeholders, appointing whites to replace some and abolishing the offices of others. To some extent this was due to the fact that blacks had often held marginal offices to begin with, and the federal government, as it sold or distributed the public lands in the South, could consolidate and reduce the land offices. A more important reason was the loss of black voting power. A disfranchised people obviously had no votes to trade for political appointments. Washington accepted this fact of political life and simply sought to make the most for his own machine out of the few black offices that remained. "When it gets down to hard pan," he wrote his closest northern black adviser and friend, T. Thomas Fortune of the New York *Age*, "it is hard to give an individual or race influence that it does not intrinsically possess."[8]

Washington forgot his own truism, however, when he saw the lily white Republicans with swift savagery take advantage of the black misfortune of disfranchisement. Seeing the black Republicans absent from the polls, the lily whites tried to expel them also from the Republican Party. Washington fought back against this effort not only in Alabama but also in Mississippi, Louisiana, and Texas. He was inhibited in this effort, however, by the necessity of working through agents. In the wake of the dinner at the White House, he did not want to appear openly as an office-broker. His faithful secretary, Emmett Scott, emphasized the danger by passing on an editorial in the Atlanta *Constitution* warning Washington that if he went regularly to the White House as "a general factotum and purveyor of patronage in the south at large" this would jeopardize his standing with southern whites "for a few messes of pottage to favorite negro politicians."[9]

Roosevelt and Washington found a way around this problem that promised to serve both Roosevelt's interest in securing delegates for the 1904 national convention and Washington's need to use the federal patronage to combat the lily whites. Roosevelt appointed as sur-

veyor of customs of the port of New York a veteran political spoils-
man, James S. Clarkson, and informally put him in charge also of
black Republican affairs. Though Clarkson and Roosevelt had once
locked horns over civil service reform, Clarkson also claimed descent
from abolitionists, believed in civil rights, and had known Washington
for a decade. "He is one of the finest men I have ever met," Washington wrote Fortune.[10] Clarkson seemed to be the ideal go-between for
the petty problems of southern Republican politics, while Washington
would still have recourse to the White House whenever it was really
necessary.

The lily whites completely controlled the party in Alabama when
Washington began his work there. U.S. District Attorney William
Vaughan, a Hanna-appointed lily white, was chairman of the state
Republican Party, and white men held all the other party offices in
the state. In the summer of 1902, Vaughan called together the state
executive committee, ostensibly to submit his resignation because
President Roosevelt was ignoring all his recommendations for appointments. The executive committee, all white, refused to accept his
resignation and called for a party convention that fall admitting only
registered voters, which meant the exclusion of all black delegates denied registration under the new Alabama constitution of 1901.[11]

A white man, the ex-Populist Joseph C. Manning, tried to challenge
Vaughan's rule by calling for a counter-meeting to form an interracial
Alabama League of Republican Clubs. Manning called Vaughan's followers "office-holding thugs" and "old political prostitutes," but the
Vaughan forces were better organized. They held their convention,
far outnumbered Manning's following, and barred black delegates
from entering the hall. Even one of Roosevelt's appointees, the collector of internal revenue, Julian H. Bingham, sided with Vaughan.[12]

Washington watched these developments from the sidelines, and a
month after the convention Roosevelt suddenly removed Vaughan
from office, charging neglect of official duties.[13] As the question arose
of Vaughan's successor, Washington confided to T. Thomas Fortune,
"I cannot bring myself to the point where I feel like recommending
any white republican in the state as all of them are more or less tainted
with 'lily whitism.' "[14] Washington did not trust Manning, but another
white challenger of Vaughan at the 1902 state convention was the
Tuskegee postmaster, Joseph O. Thompson, Washington's longtime
personal friend and a Republican ever since he was old enough to

vote, though his own brother was a Democratic congressman. Washington had the idea of pushing Thompson to the front, along with two other white men new to active Republicanism. They were Captain Charles H. Scott of Montgomery, son of a Confederate soldier and himself a participant in the Spanish–American War; and Thomas R. Roulhac, a Gold Democrat in the past, but now willing to join the Republican Party. Scott was a wealthy realtor and hotelier who saw the Republicans as the party of business, and offered to found a Republican newspaper in Montgomery and to raise money for candidates to actually challenge Democrats for office.

Washington wrote to Clarkson that the recent state convention posed the direct question of "whether or not the national republican party will recognize a party in any state based upon color. There is no getting around this point." The issue was not only of loyalty to Roosevelt but of racial justice, and he foresaw defections of black Republicans in the North if the issue was not met.[15] Washington went to New York for two long interviews with Clarkson, taking Captain Scott with him. Clarkson, thoroughly aroused, reported to the President that Washington had spoken of a possible "stampede of colored men in the North from the Republican party," which would mean the loss of thousands of votes in closely contested states.[16] Washington, Scott, and Clarkson all urged Roosevelt to appoint Roulhac as district attorney in Vaughan's place. "He is a discovery," Clarkson wrote of Scott to Roosevelt, "a man of intelligence, character, wealthy, beyond any ambition in politics, an enthusiastic admirer of yours and eager to follow your flag and help you in whatever way he can." As for Washington, Clarkson described him as "modest and in a certain degree, as you know, timid."[17] Scott would later turn out to be less than a lion, and Washington more than a mouse, but Clarkson correctly gauged the deference of Washington's manner toward whites in authority.

Roosevelt agreed to appoint Roulhac; and Washington suggested other steps to deal with the party crisis in Alabama. Since Julian Bingham had been a "prime mover in organizing this white party," Washington suggested removing him as internal revenue collector and putting Joseph O. Thompson in his place.[18] Just as he was pressing the cases of these white men, however, and trying to calm the suspicions of both southern and northern blacks that he was so busy helping whites get into office that he was neglecting black candidates, the local newspapers somehow secured and published a letter he had written the President in 1901 recommending the Gold Democrat Thomas G. Jones for the federal judgeship that Roosevelt appointed him to. The letter not only embarrassed Jones, who did not want to be known as the recipient of a Negro's favor, but embarrassed Washington because it seemed, as a Democrat put it, "making Booker Washington's will, the law of the Republican party in Alabama."[19] Washington wanted Roosevelt to "concentrate matters in Mr. Thompson's hands," but Roosevelt instead chose a trio of referees on all presidential appointments in Alabama, Thompson, Captain Scott, and the north Alabama ex-congressman William F. Aldrich.[20]

Washington felt, after the publication of his private letter to Roosevelt, that he needed to explain his political brokerage, to reconcile it with his Atlanta Compromise by minimizing it. He waited until after the mid-term elections of 1902 to issue a public statement for the newspapers. "My life work is the promotion of education of my race," he began, and the inculcation of "habits of thrift, skill, intelligence, high moral character, and the gaining of the respect and confidence of their neighbors." That had not changed, he said, but his new political role grew out of the need for a black voice in the national councils at a time when not a single black man sat in Congress. He promised not to push political candidates nor volunteer endorsement of either men or measures, but when public officials asked him for information or advice about matters concerning blacks, he would simply do his duty as a citizen and respond to the questions. He continued to warn young blacks against careers in "mere political activity," but some public questions had such an importance to black interests that they transcended politics, and he would make his position known on these questions. He made the Delphic statement: "Every revised constitution throughout the Southern States has put a premium upon intelligence, ownership of property, thrift and character." Did this mean that Washington endorsed those constitutions that actually put a premium on a white skin? He would have denied that, and presumably meant that southern restrictions on voting would spur blacks to get more education and property in order to qualify. He did not explain himself, however, except to urge whites to allow blacks "inspiration and hope of reward."[21]

In nearby Mississippi the lily whites were likewise in control of the Republican Party when Washington, with encouragement from Roosevelt and Clarkson, found a near-counterpart of J. O. Thompson to be the sole presidential referee for Mississippi. Edgar S. Wilson of Jackson was a Gold Democrat and the Mississippi correspondent of the New Orleans *Picayune*. His wife was the sister of the incumbent Democratic governor, Andrew H. Longino, and he had aided Longino's successful campaign for the office. Some Mississippi blacks, particularly unsuccessful office seekers, later accused Wilson of racial bias, but he denied the slightest taint of it.[22] Washington arranged for Wilson to have several interviews with Roosevelt at the White House, and at their conclusion Roosevelt offered him the post of referee. "We must handle it wisely and well," Wilson wrote Washington. "The happiness of posterity, perhaps is involved. I think with a Mississippi governor and a republican president working to a common end, much may be accomplished along your life-work and mine."[23] Roosevelt allowed Wilson to choose one of the federal offices in the state for himself, and after some hesitation he chose that of federal marshal.

Washington was delighted with the Wilson appointment, and though Wilson's optimism about Roosevelt and Longino collaborating was unfounded, he worked well with Washington and remained loyal to Roosevelt. Washington called him "one of the finest, truest white men I have ever seen."[24] Wilson took Washington's advice and made Isaiah T. Montgomery, the successful black businessman and town-developer of Mound Bayou, the federal receiver of public monies for Mississippi. "I fully concur with you about places for colored men," Wilson wrote Washington. "I shall be the same friend to the colored people that I have all my life, and merit, will be the touchstone to my endorsement, and not color." He also left no room for doubt that his heart was with Roosevelt. He ended a letter to the President, "Yours as ever, more than ever and for ever."[25]

Though Wilson apparently tried to walk a straight line, Mississippi politics meandered like its great river. Some Republicans accused Wilson of trying to get his brother-in-law a federal judgeship, which was true, but at Washington's suggestion he quickly dropped the matter. He took pride in not removing any black officeholders, and even added blacks as collector of the port of Vicksburg, postmaster of Dry Grove, and so on. He was working closely with the black politicos John R. Lynch and W. E. Mollison, he wrote Washington, to ensure black representation and a pro-Roosevelt commitment in the delegation from Mississippi in 1904. "This is my thought and aim, by day and by dreaming night," he wrote.[26] He promised Washington that he would keep their political collaboration a deep secret. In case they should have to telegraph one another, he suggested, "I will sign 'W.' Your answer can be signed 'W' also." Wilson arranged for two white men and two black men, a majority of the state Republican executive committee, to be deputy collectors of internal revenue, and thus bound them to him.[27] Washington predicted to Roosevelt that by the time of the 1904 convention Wilson would be in complete control of the Mississippi Republican Party.[28]

Two black appointments in Mississippi caused Washington and Wilson considerable trouble but did not upset their control over party affairs in that state. At Indianola, Mrs. Minnie M. Cox had been postmistress since McKinley days. She was a model of black middle-class respectability, a graduate of Fisk, rated highly efficient by the postal inspectors. Her husband, an Alcorn graduate, was in the railway mail service. They owned their house and business property, and handled their affluence with quiet dignity. But in 1902 James K. Vardaman, running for governor against Longino, spoke in Indianola and jeered at the whites for "tolerating a negro wench as postmaster," all at the behest of Edgar Wilson and "the saddle-colored philosopher of Tuskegee." A white mob demanded and received her resignation, but Roosevelt refused to accept it and closed the post office until her term expired in 1904.[29] After several years in Birmingham, the Coxes returned to their house in the white section of Indianola and opened a successful bank with a substantial white clientele. "It is a curious circumstance," Washington wrote President Roosevelt, "that while objection was made to this black family being at the head of the post-office no objection is made to this black man being president of a bank in the same town."[30]

No comforting homily could be drawn from another departure from federal office, that of Isaiah T. Montgomery in 1903. Montgomery had become receiver of public monies not because he needed the job but because Washington hoped thereby to raise the quality of the public service in the South. A special federal agent found evidence in 1903 that Montgomery had put public funds in his own private bank account. A distressed President and Secretary of the Interior asked Washington to arrange for Montgomery's voluntary resignation.[31] Washington got his secretary Emmett Scott to meet Montgomery not in Jackson, Mississippi, but in New Orleans. "If M. hesitates resigning," Washington wired, "hold him in New Orleans till communicating with me."[32] Unfortunately, Montgomery had immodestly shown Scott's telegram asking for the meeting to his office force and others. Arriving in New Orleans, he refused to admit guilt or resign. But Scott would not parley with him. "I have told him that he cannot now seek 'to save his face,' that he ought to feel mighty glad 'to save his neck,' " Scott wrote Washington. Montgomery finally agreed to resign, and Washington and Roosevelt rushed to find a first-class black replacement before the whites had a chance to make an issue of it.[33] Edgar Wilson was outraged, called Montgomery "a traitor to his race," and wondered, "Where shall I look for another when I have endorsed him as the best, and the ideal man?"[34]

In Louisiana also the lily whites were entrenched in control of the Republican Party at the beginning of the century, after the constitution of 1898 had disfranchised most blacks. Whites were particularly strong in the party in that state because many of the Carpetbaggers of Reconstruction had remained in Louisiana and prospered, among them ex-Governor Henry C. Warmoth, and because sugar planters wanted protection for their sugar and therefore supported the Republican high tariff policies. Washington had come to know the Louisiana black Republican leaders around 1899, when he began to help local leaders challenge the Louisiana grandfather clause. The most venerable of the black Republicans was Colonel James Lewis, a weary veteran of Civil War and Reconstruction battles, now surveyor of the federal land office in New Orleans. The active leader, however, was a middle-aged black Catholic named Walter Cohen, receiver of the New Orleans land office. He was too young to have been part of the old venal political ring, and those in charge of raising money for the grandfather clause case received more help from Cohen than from anyone else.[35] It was one of Cohen's liabilities, however, that he had begun life as a bartender and reputedly as a brothel keeper.[36]

Cohen and Lewis became Washington's main lieutenants in Louisiana. In addition, Washington had an opportunity to place a black man in a third federal office when the naval officer at the port of New Orleans died. At Washington's suggestion, the President appointed the Reverend Isaiah B. Scott, editor of the *Southwestern Christian Advocate*, a black Methodist journal.[37] Soon thereafter, Dr. Scott became the only black bishop in the Methodist Episcopal (northern) church, and his church promptly despatched him to Africa as a missionary.

Washington hoped to wrest the Louisiana Republican Party from the lily whites with this combination, but he first had to arrange for the reappointment of Lewis and Cohen, both of whose terms were due to expire early in 1904. Roosevelt at first agreed to do this, but then said he would wait until after the vote on the Panama Canal Treaty. "He fears just a little to do anything that might arouse any of the Southern senators just now," Washington wrote reassuringly to Cohen.[38] While Roosevelt was waiting for this vote, early in 1904 the lily whites excluded all blacks from membership in the Republican state executive committee. This appeared to foreshadow an all-white delegation to the national convention. At this juncture, however, Mark Hanna, Roosevelt's only serious rival for the presidential nomination, suddenly died. This took much of the urgency out of efforts to reform the party in Louisiana. As soon as the Panama Canal Treaty was approved, Washington reminded Roosevelt of his promise to reappoint Lewis and Cohen.[39] But Roosevelt began to drag his feet. A lily white delegation appeared in Washington and made grave accusations against Cohen; Washington elaborately documented his defense of Cohen that he was a loyal party man and no longer was in the saloon business, and Roosevelt finally said he would not remove Cohen but also would not give him a reappointment. Roosevelt started to reappoint the noncontroversial Lewis, but Washington persuaded him to withhold it until he could appoint both men together.[40] The outcome of the intraparty struggles in Louisiana remained in doubt.

The lily whites of Texas carried black exclusion even further, if possible, than in the other Gulf coastal states. Their leader, Cecil Lyon, had a personal bond with Roosevelt because he had been one of his Rough Riders in Cuba in 1898. The Texas lily whites swore absolute loyalty to Roosevelt, who dealt directly with his friend Lyon rather than through Washington. Roosevelt did not seem to care whether the Texans were lily white or not as long as they supported him. Washington confined his efforts in Texas to securing an office for one man, Robert Lee Smith, to break the monopoly of the lily whites.

Smith was an outstanding example of that "better class" of black men, successful in other lines, whom Washington wanted to place in office and into participation in southern Republican politics. Born in Charleston, South Carolina, an Atlanta University graduate, Smith had founded in 1889 the Farmers' Improvement Society, a black agrarian organization for self-help that survived through the 1890s and into the twentieth century and spread through Texas and adjoining states.

It engaged in many cooperative enterprises and for a while even had an agricultural college. Smith was an early and frequent participant in the Tuskegee Negro Conferences. He served a term in the Texas legislature in the 1890s.

In his earliest meetings with Roosevelt, Washington alluded to Smith as "the type of a colored man to be recognized . . . strong and clean and not in the hands of your enemies." When Roosevelt refused to appoint Smith without lily white approval, Washington wrote the President: "It will seem like a recognition of the worst element of our people and a throwing down of the best."[41] Roosevelt had his secretary reply: "The President requests me to say that the objection is not on the ground of color, but it would be accepted as a humiliation by Mr. Smith's factional opponents if their wishes were disregarded."[42] In 1902 Roosevelt let another opportunity to appoint Smith pass, and Washington's friend Whitefield McKinlay remarked that it seemed to take more moral courage to appoint this obscure man than to invite Washington to dinner.[43] The 1904 election passed without any appointment for Smith, and when Roosevelt finally insisted on a black appointment in 1905, the Lyon faction slyly proposed a man not susceptible to Booker T. Washington's influence.[44]

In other southern states Washington had even more limited and uncertain influence. In Arkansas he took a McKinley black appointee, John E. Bush, receiver of the land office in Little Rock, and made him over into a Washington and Roosevelt man, and in 1902 he persuaded Roosevelt to appoint Bush for a second term.[45] Similarly in Georgia he took another McKinley black holdover, Henry A. Rucker, collector of internal revenue 1897–1910, and made him informally a lieutenant of the Tuskegee Machine. Rucker was an active member of the National Negro Business League.[46] He also had another black lieutenant in that state, William A. Pledger, who had held several federal offices and the chairmanship of the Republican state executive committee. In the 1890s Washington had hired him as a lobbyist for a federal land grant to Tuskegee, but for some reason in the Roosevelt era Pledger fell out of favor. "It used to be my job to aid in keeping up the 'Wizzard's' fences," he complained to Emmett Scott, but the Wizard had found "new friends that take my place."[47]

The thousands of hours and great expenditure of energy that Washington and Scott put into the struggle with the lily whites produced nothing better than a deadlock. The only justification for it was that, without that effort, the lily whites would have made a clean sweep of the blacks out of the party from Texas to Virginia.

More important for the building of Washington's Tuskegee Machine as a dominant force in the black minority group was his use of his influence with Roosevelt and national Republican leaders to reward key lieutenants in the North and in Washington, D.C. Some of them he won away from previous allegiance to his critics. In their individual cities and in a network of power, they came to dominate black life beyond the sphere of politics, even though urbanization was gradually undercutting the rural southern base of their boss down in Tuskegee.

Since Washington's obscurity in the early 1890s and for many years after he became famous by his Atlanta Compromise address in 1895, T. Thomas Fortune, the premier black journalist of his day, had been Washington's only intimate adviser in the North. He coached and groomed Washington for leadership, and defended him in the New York *Age* with a fierce loyalty and wit that gradually effaced Fortune's own natural bent toward social protest. As Fortune slipped from king-maker to lieutenant, as he lost his own identity in the errand-running for his chief, as he played a smaller and smaller role in Washington's growing empire, Fortune took to heavy drinking. A fiery orator, he now sometimes slurred his words or became incoherent. He always got out his weekly paper on time and usually made it home from late-night parties, but his friends sometimes had to carry him aboard trains after conventions. From a great asset to Washington he became a slight embarrassment.

Meanwhile, Washington found other allies in the North. The earliest and perhaps most important of these was William H. Lewis of Boston, whom Washington with Roosevelt's help snatched from the very camp of his black critics. It was actually Roosevelt who first suggested Lewis, in one of his earliest conversations with Washington. Originally from Virginia, Lewis had been a Dartmouth football hero, then Harvard's football coach while attending Harvard Law School, then a young Boston attorney with a bright future. Brainy, brawny, and handsome to boot, Lewis was nearly everything Roosevelt admired, and while governor of New York he had entertained Lewis and his wife as overnight guests at the governor's mansion.

Roosevelt was probably puzzled by the chill that fell over his conversation with Washington when he mentioned Lewis as a good man for a federal office in Boston. The reason, however, was that, several years earlier, Washington had met a group of Boston Afro-Americans at dinner at Young's Hotel. After dessert and Washington's bland after-dinner speech minimizing the extent of the worsening southern race relations and emphasizing economic self-help and group solidarity, William H. Lewis arose to reply in behalf of the college-educated elite blacks of Boston. In effect he told Washington to go home where he belonged, to continue his constructive educational work, but to "leave to us the matters political affecting the race."[48]

Washington responded to Roosevelt's suggestion of Lewis by promising to think it over. Since the President seemed determined to appoint Lewis, Washington apparently decided he might as well take credit for it, for he hastened to write Lewis. "The main point of this letter," he wrote, "is to say I believe that both you and I are going to be in a position in the future to serve the race effectually, and while it is very probable that we shall always differ as to detailed methods of lifting up the race it seems to me that if we agree in each doing his best to lift it up the main point will have been gained, and I am sure that in our anxiety to better the condition of the race there is no difference between us, and I shall be delighted to work in hearty cooperation with you."[49] Lewis enthusiastically agreed. Washington endorsed Roosevelt's appointment of Lewis as an assistant district attorney in Boston. Lewis became Washington's tower of strength in the intraracial struggles in Boston.

In Washington, D.C., the Tuskegean already had many adherents, mostly out of office, but early in the Roosevelt term in 1902, he placed two loyal friends in presidential appointments. Robert H. Terrell, a young Virginian, had been principal of the prestigious black M Street High School in Washington and also had a law degree. He was the husband of Mary Church Terrell, Oberlin graduate and heiress to a Memphis real-estate fortune. Washington arranged for R. H. Terrell to become the District of Columbia's first black judge. He also put John C. Dancy of North Carolina into the traditionally black office of recorder of deeds of the District of Columbia. Dancy, an old ally of Washington and a loyal member of the National Negro Business League, had been collector of the port of Wilmington, North Carolina, off and on, for a decade, but after the Wilmington race riot in 1898 killed several blacks and ran the black officeholders out of town, and after the state disfranchised black voters and elected lily white

Republican Jeter C. Pritchard as Senator, Dancy was glad to find a safe haven in a Washington office. Washington did not invite either Terrell or Dancy into his inner councils, but he found them both useful, Terrell for prestige and Dancy for small errands. Dancy, as editor of the *A. M. E. Zion Quarterly Review,* defended Washington, tried to keep Fortune sober when he came to the national capital for a speech, and carried Washington's bribe money to editor W. Calvin Chase from time to time in payment for favorable editorial treatment.[50]

In New York City political and racial affairs, Charles W. Anderson was the man Washington increasingly counted upon as his dependence on Fortune declined. One of the things Washington admired most about Anderson was that he could get and hold his own political office without any need for Washington's help. A dapper, dark, witty man in his thirties, Anderson had secured what formal education he had in the public schools of Ohio, a business college in Cleveland, and the Berlitz School of Languages in Worcester, Massachusetts. Moving to New York, he became a gauger in the customs house in 1890, private secretary to the state treasurer for two years, chief clerk in the state treasury for three years, and from 1898 to 1905 supervisor of accounts of the state racing commission. Anderson was a thoroughly professional politician, knew every political figure in the state, white or black, was absolutely loyal to Washington, and had the energy and skill to organize Colored Republican Clubs not only in New York City but elsewhere in the state. He became the chief lieutenant of the Tuskegee Machine in New York.[51]

It was largely through Anderson that the Tuskegee Machine also captured another important prize of war from the ranks of Washington's professional-class critics. This was James Weldon Johnson, the black poet, novelist, composer with his brother Rosamond of the Negro National Anthem, "Lift Ev'ry Voice and Sing," and, after Washington's lifetime, chief administrator of the National Association for the Advancement of Colored People.[52] Anderson got Johnson to help him organize the Colored Republican Club of New York City and saw to it that Johnson became its president. As a reward for this party service, Anderson overcame Washington's suspicion of Johnson as an Atlanta University graduate, and persuaded Roosevelt's Secretary of State, Elihu Root, to appoint Johnson to consular posts at Puerto Cabello, Venezuela, and Corinto, Nicaragua. As Anderson explained to Washington, "His appointment will do much to convince the brethren hereabouts that our forces are really potent." It would "convince the weaklings that our friends are 'at court.' Thus, you see, it will serve two purposes: to take care of Johnson, and, at the same time give the enemy a black eye."[53]

Washington found it impossible, however, to land a federal office for his chief Chicago lieutenant during Roosevelt's first term. His efforts to create a place for S. Laing Williams were unsuccessful partly because of Williams's weak local support. Chicago was not a Booker T. Washington city, the more militant blacks were entrenched in the favor of white Republican leaders and determined to block the Tuskegean from securing a toehold there. Furthermore, Williams lacked personal force, bordered on incompetence as a lawyer, according to some, and was overshadowed by his wife, the journalist Fannie Barrier Williams. Not until after the 1904 election, when he did yeoman service in getting out the black vote, did he have a serious chance for the reward of office.[54]

By 1904, however, Washington had the nucleus of a political network in the North, with Lewis in Boston, Anderson and Fortune in New York, Whitefield McKinlay and his circle of officeholders and ex-officeholders in Washington, and Williams in the wings in Chicago. They and lesser lieutenants would serve him in his most exhaustive political effort of the Roosevelt first term, an office for Dr. William D. Crum of Charleston, South Carolina.

The appointment of William D. Crum as collector of the port of Charleston, South Carolina, the cradle of the Confederacy, was the most symbolically important appointment of a black man in the Roosevelt administration. This was not because Crum became a powerful leader. Indeed, he shrank from power and from the limelight that his office brought him. His importance stemmed from the stubbornness of Roosevelt in keeping his nomination before Congress, and from Washington's political skill and persistence in lobbying for his confirmation.

Crum's name was one of the earliest that Washington brought up in his first conversations with Roosevelt about southern appointments. A light-skinned man of mixed black and German descent, born free in 1859, Crum attended Avery Institute in Charleston and the University of South Carolina, and took his medical degree from Howard University. He practiced medicine in Charleston beginning in the 1880s, played an active part in local Republican politics, and attended every national convention of the party from 1884 to 1904. President Harrison had appointed him postmaster of Charleston in 1892 but had hastily withdrawn his name in the face of white protest. He ran as a Republican for the United States Senate in 1894.

When the incumbent customs collector of Charleston died suddenly in 1902, Washington immediately began to urge Roosevelt to appoint Crum. He had known Crum for fifteen years, he wrote, "and he is as far different, in my mind, from the old irresponsible and purchasable Negro politician as day is from night." The Charleston whites themselves, he pointed out to Roosevelt, had chosen Crum to be the black assistant commissioner of the Charleston Exposition the preceding year.[55]

Roosevelt appointed Crum, and to his surprise a raucous outcry arose in Charleston and spread through the South in the same way as a year earlier after the dinner at the White House, reopening the earlier wound. White southerners apparently thought that disfranchisement had settled the issue of black officeholding. There was also a misunderstanding involved, for Roosevelt had visited Charleston early in 1902 and apparently agreed not to appoint a black man to any "important office," but said he would have to appoint one black man to some office in the state for the effect it would have on black voters in the North, and the white Charlestonians unanimously recommended the discreet Dr. Crum for this token office. What Roosevelt apparently remembered of the agreement was the endorsement of Crum, whereas the Charlestonians remembered agreement on no important office.[56] Probably Roosevelt viewed the collectorship as less important than the white Charlestonians did.

Once challenged, Roosevelt defended his appointment with bulldog determination. He rejected the demand "that the door of hope—the door of opportunity—is to be shut upon all men no matter how worthy, purely on the grounds of color."[57] That would not be a square deal. But the hullabaloo in the South did not die away as it had after the White House dinner, for an appointment to office had no folded napkin to signify its end. The South Carolina Senators delayed confirmation for years, and Roosevelt kept reappointing Crum. But it was Booker T. Washington who finally whipped up the President's courage, propped up the sagging Crum, and lobbied until victory was won.

At the first Senate hearings on Crum, the South Carolinians unearthed an old charge that he had sold his vote in 1892 to Benjamin Harrison in return for the Charleston postmastership.[58] Washington, anticipating this, had already reassured Roosevelt that it was "hardly possible for any man from the South to go to one of these conventions without some stories being circulated regarding his vote."[59] The attacks were so vehement, however, that Crum wanted to resign then and there. Washington sent Emmett Scott to a hasty conference with Crum in Atlanta to stiffen his back. Crum timidly sent his own private secretary to the meeting in his place, but he did agree to remain in the post.[60]

Many of Roosevelt's close friends thought the appointment a mistake, and he himself almost immediately had a siege of doubt. Roosevelt asked Washington again if he was personally sure of Crum's probity and character, and Washington again pronounced him "a clean, upright man."[61] Crum was the only black man Roosevelt had appointed to a place not previously held by another black man, and Roosevelt was two men short of McKinley's total of black appointments. "You have increased the quality of Negro officials in the South and reduced the quantity," Washington pointed out.[62]

Senator Benjamin R. Tillman of South Carolina invoked senatorial courtesy and the Senate commerce committee voted against Crum's confirmation, two western Republicans, Perkins of California and Jones of Nevada, voting with the Democrats. Roosevelt expressed his regret of the appointment to his friend Owen Wister, and Washington's own white friends Lyman Abbott of the *Outlook,* the Tuskegee trustee William H. Baldwin, Jr., Robert C. Ogden, and Edgar Gardner Murphy all thought Roosevelt was pointlessly inflaming southern white opinion and thus interfering with the educational and economic progress of blacks that they associated with Washington's leadership.[63]

Washington never wavered in his insistence on the Crum appointment, because he realized its symbolic importance to blacks all over the country. He sent word to the White House by Whitefield McKinlay that there was "no alternative but to fight it out."[64] As one of Crum's fellow black officeholders said, "if a man like Crum gets out of the way, it means that the idea of Tillman will prevail, and it would take us 20 years to overcome it."[65] So in March 1903, when Congress began a short session, Roosevelt resubmitted Crum's name.

Washington enlisted McKinlay as his chief lobbyist at the capitol, while he himself mobilized black constituent pressure on key Senators. Neither the "big stick" of Roosevelt nor the Republican leaders of the Senate gave him much support. Senator Jacob Gallinger of New Hampshire told McKinlay, who remembered it vividly a decade later, that he was sympathetic to Crum but "when he attempted to speak in the Senate on any question in behalf of the Negro his coat tail was pulled by the leaders." The Senate floor was open to Tillman and other white supremacists to rant against Crum without rebuttal.[66] A particular target of the black lobbyists was Perkins of California, who had voted against Crum in committee, but after an hour with Perkins, McKinlay's delegation "came away convinced that he was a sneaking hypocrite."[67] The session ended without a vote on Crum, and Roosevelt made a recess appointment. Crum, however, felt like a hollow man when he entered office in March 1903. He had spent several preceding days in bed with the shakes.[68] To make matters worse, he would receive no pay until confirmed, so he had to continue his medical practice in his off hours.

President Roosevelt sent Crum's nomination back to the Senate in the summer of 1903 and again that December, and Washington once again used his Tuskegee Machine to orchestrate constituent pressure on the Senators. He brought a black friend from St. Paul to Washington to persuade Senator Knute Nelson to get out of his sickbed to vote for Crum.[69] He brought similar pressure on Chauncey Depew of New York and Stephen Elkins of West Virginia. He insisted to his black followers that "their home constituents" were "the only kind of influence that they pay much attention to."[70] Washington's campaign was only one of the factors in the balance, but apparently it was effective. Even Senator Perkins said he could not vote against Crum once he understood the nature of the fight.[71] Dividing strictly by party, the committee voted eight to five to recommend confirmation.

Committee approval was only the first step in a tortuous process, but Washington let Crum know what he had done for him. "I do not mind telling you," he wrote, "that most of the money I have had to take out of my own pocket, although I feel it was a good cause in which to spend money." Washington seemed to wish that Crum would muster more personal force in his own behalf, but at the same time warned him to avoid doing anything to excite the white Charlestonians into returning to the capital.[72]

Ignoring the Democrats, Washington prepared for the floor fight by assigning each of his lieutenants to a particular Republican Senator.[73] Senator Tillman thwarted all efforts to bring the appointment to the floor, however, by feigning illness and returning to South Carolina. By the tradition of senatorial courtesy, the body would take no action on an appointment in his state in his absence. "I am about disheartened and sick," Crum complained.[74] But the sickness was more than that of hope deferred. "Dr. is broken in health and spirit," his wife Ellen wrote; "he has been quite sick this week having to go to bed. I am afraid it is the beginning of the end with him should this senate neglect to confirm him." She added a bitter afterthought: "Better be dead than an Afro-*American*. Still we trust in God."[75]

Tillman returned to Washington briefly but said he was too ill to engage in debate. Roosevelt tried to get around this ingenious form of filibuster by a chiding letter to the Republican leader Nelson W. Aldrich and by threatening a special session.[76] Washington, abandoning all pretense of aloofness, came to the capital and called on about a dozen Senators. He urged his lieutenants to send a new flurry of telegrams "intimating unrest among the Negro people because of nonaction & the possible effect of failure to confirm at this session."[77] But the Senate once again adjourned, and Roosevelt made another recess appointment.

The Crum case played a small part in the political rhetoric of the election of 1904, but its most important political effect was intangible: it helped to weld the Tuskegee Machine, to make its scattered lieutenants a team. It unified the previously divided South Carolina Republicans behind Roosevelt at the 1904 convention. It helped to give Roosevelt the overwhelming support of northern black voters in 1904. And when Roosevelt sent Crum's name back to the Senate again in January 1905 he was confirmed without fanfare. The President's stubbornness and Washington's persistence had finally succeeded. Crum collected his back pay, served in office for Roosevelt's second term with quiet efficiency, lengthened the pier and deepened the channel, and won a grudging respect from white Charleston as a tolerable black officeholder.

The question remained whether or not Washington could play an effective role in politics while refusing to hold office and remaining aloof from Republican conventions. The events of 1904–5 put this question to the test, in the struggle over seating of black delegates and over the platform planks in the Republican convention, in the passing out of subsidies and marshaling of the black vote in the election campaign, and in the spoils of office after the election. In this cycle of events, Washington and his Tuskegee Machine did not demonstrate the mastery that they showed in other aspects of black life. Considering the time and energy that Washington, Scott, and their scattered lieutenants were devoting to politics, the rewards were small. And yet the political connections enhanced their power in other spheres of life.

As the Republican national convention approached, Washington wanted to make certain that Alabama, his home state, did not send and seat an all-white delegation. His agents therefore compromised with the lily whites by an exactly equal division of delegates. He insisted, however, that J. O. Thompson, his friend, become the state Republican chairman and head of the delegation. Roosevelt at first objected, but Washington insisted. "Mr. Thompson is really the man who has taken off his coat," he wrote, "gone down among the masses, and done the work."[78] The state convention in 1904 ratified this arrangement. The lily whites were on their good behavior, and a black delegate reported that "at this convention very few 'yaps' were in evidence, but old 'Cuffy' [the black man] was there in all his Sunday clothes and he behaved with the dignity of a judge."[79]

The Louisiana factional dispute was so irreconcilable that two rival delegations appeared in Chicago, each claiming to be the legitimate one. After strenuous behind-the-scenes efforts, Washington persuaded Roosevelt to endorse Cohen's integrated delegation instead of the all-white one, and the Republican credentials committee so voted. Washington claimed a large share of this success, saying privately that he had had to talk so plainly to Roosevelt that "I feared at one time that there might be a break between our friend and myself."[80]

Washington did the best he could without being present by sending Emmett Scott to Chicago to be his eyes and ears, and Charles Anderson to be his right arm. Anderson had earned his own way to the convention by organizing the Republican Club of the City of New York, which had some 500 members in March 1904, and he was a duly elected delegate from New York. Anderson had built his club by a house-to-house canvass all over the city, even finding black voters in the top floors of Wall Street banking houses where they worked as janitors.[81] He established rapport with the Henry Highland Garnet Club in Brooklyn and met with or organized similar groups in a dozen New York cities.[82] Washington sent the word to other blacks at the convention to follow Anderson's lead. Anderson was the main speaker at a black mass meeting of about 1000 on the eve of the convention to honor the black delegates. This would be the ideal time, Washington wrote him, "to speak out boldly telling just what the President has done in the face of great odds in standing up in behalf of the colored race." Anderson did as Washington had suggested, saying that Roosevelt was the first president of recent times who had even bothered to consult with blacks.[83]

Because he was an officeholder, however, Anderson had to yield to a Baltimore lawyer, Harry S. Cummings, the honor of being the black seconder of Roosevelt's nomination. Cummings was not Washington's first or second choice, and not really a Washington man, but he was a moderate and Washington was generally if erroneously credited with selecting him. Furthermore, to achieve a balance of sorts, a Georgia lily white made another seconding speech.[84]

Washington was also unable to shape the Negro planks of the Republican platform from a distance. Through Emmett Scott he sent to James S. Clarkson "the plank or planks that should go in the platform relating to the interests of the Negro," with the note to Clarkson: "These have had the full consideration of the best minds among the race."[85] What Washington proposed was the statement:

The Republican Party avows its unalterable opposition to the establishment of the color line in Republican Party councils, state or national; it condemns unreservedly the policy of any state in so far as it discriminates, on grounds of race and color, against its citizens in the matter of the elective franchise. Equal protection to every citizen in his civil and political rights is demanded and should be guaranteed. Color is no condition precedent in the payment of taxes, and should not be made a condition precedent in the holding of public office.[86]

Washington asked Clarkson to pass this plank to Henry Cabot Lodge, chairman of the platform committee, adding: "Of course I do not desire that my name shall be used in any way in presenting these planks to Mr. Lodge or that my efforts in the matter shall be known at all."[87] That anonymity was a serious handicap.

Washington also privately sent a copy of the proposed plank to Andrew B. Humphrey, the white secretary of a civil rights group, the Constitution League, and added another plank: "Murder in the form of lynching or burning should have no place in a civilized country, and to this end we condemn these practices wherever they exist and contend that all men of whatever color should have the full protection of the law." He once again asked for secrecy, writing, "I am sure I can trust entirely to your discretion to get them in without the use of my name in any way."[88]

Not only was Washington unable to push his planks personally, but with the moderation of an accommodationist he had failed to suggest any specific remedy for the lynching and disfranchisement the planks condemned. These two points of vulnerability provided an opportunity for William Monroe Trotter, the bitterly anti-Washington editor of the Boston *Guardian,* and his black militant National Negro Suffrage League. They met in Chicago but had no delegates in the convention. Somehow, through some delegate acting in their behalf, they inserted their plank into the platform. "The fact is," Washington later wrote, "the Negro plank at Chicago, was slipped into the platform without the knowledge of the President, or that of his friends on guard there." Only after the convention had approved the platform did the party leaders discover this plank.[89]

What might appropriately be called the Trotter plank called for Congressional legislation to carry out the enforcement clause of the Fourteenth Amendment by reducing the number of congressmen in states that unconstitutionally reduced their electorate by depriving blacks of voting rights.[90] Reduction of southern representation was a recurrent proposal throughout the era of disfranchisement. Henry Cabot Lodge's Force Bill in 1890 failed of passage, and after the turn of the century every congressional session saw bills introduced, all of them dying in committee. The remedy became known as Crumpackerism, after its chief sponsor, Congressman Edgar D. Crumpacker of Indiana. On Fortune's advice, Washington had opposed it from the beginning because of the danger that some border states would be willing to give up a congressman in return for federal sanction of disfranchisement. Robert C. Ogden had won a debate in the New York Union League Club in 1903 by opposing it, but when some northern blacks threatened to organize "silence clubs" that would refuse to vote, the club reversed itself.[91] Lodge himself, despite his sponsorship in 1890, opposed southern reduction in 1904 and so informed Roosevelt.[92]

Washington was chagrined by the plank, and he urged Roosevelt not to mention it in accepting the Republican nomination. "As a matter of righting wrongs in the South," he said, "you of course know that I have never felt that reduction of representation was a remedy." Instead of legalizing disfranchisement by reduction, he advised, Congress should take up each individual case of election fraud and punish it.[93] Roosevelt saw a simple way out of his dilemma. Since the plank "calls for Congressional action, and not action by the President," he wrote Washington, he would say nothing at all about it during the campaign.[94]

The Republican campaign of 1904 offered rich opportunities for the Tuskegee Machine to win new adherents and strengthen old ones in the northern states through subsidies to black newspapers and politicians for turning out the black vote in the close races there. Washington was new to this game, however, and had the same inhibitions as he did in the South about playing a direct part. His idea was to install Charles W. Anderson as head of the Negro Bureau of the Republican Party in New York City, and to send Fortune to Chicago to run a similar but subordinate western bureau. Such an arrangement would signify to black men all over the country that Washington and the Tuskegee Machine were in charge of matters political for the race.

The trouble with Washington's plan was that it ran counter to other interests. General Clarkson, who had been all smiles when he and Washington were partners against the southern lily whites, now began to avoid Washington. Clarkson became busy trying to woo the more militant blacks of the North who hated Booker T. Washington, and who themselves wanted to be in charge of the Republican campaign among blacks. When Washington asked Fortune if he wanted to be in charge of the Chicago bureau, Fortune replied, "I want it, and it will make the Chicago hyenas wild."[95] But Ferdinand Barnett and his wife Ida B. Wells-Barnett, who had run the Chicago bureau during the two preceding presidential campaigns, wanted to do so again, and they mustered some strong Chicago resentment against a New Yorker being sent to take charge. Washington countered with the suggestion of S. Laing Williams, but he was the weakest of Washington's main men in local support. Furthermore, the Barnetts made common cause with Bishop Alexander Walters of the A. M. E. Zion Church, who coveted the New York bureau. An unseemly scramble threatened.[96]

Washington hoped General Clarkson would help him control the rival politicos and get the campaign for the black vote underway, but he discovered that once Roosevelt had been nominated the political kaleidoscope turned slightly and produced an entirely different relationship between him and Clarkson. About a month after the national convention, in late July 1904, Charles Anderson called at the New York custom house, and to his surprise found waiting outside the radical suffragist James H. Hayes, while inside, closeted with Clarkson, was Bishop Walters in quest of the Negro Bureau. When Anderson managed to get in to talk with Clarkson, however, he learned that Clarkson had "been 'dropped' out of this work."[97]

In the end the white Republicans decided not to have a national Negro Bureau, but to put Anderson in charge of an eastern bureau and Barnett in charge of a western one.[98] Washington confined his own part in the campaign to advising Anderson on which black newspapers to subsidize in return for supporting the Republican candidates.[99] He also kept President Roosevelt informed of the intimations of black political attitudes that he picked up as he traveled on speaking tours through West Virginia, Indiana, and other doubtful states. His only fear in Indiana, he wrote Roosevelt, was that the Democrats would pay some blacks not to vote, "sending them off on an excursion or something of that kind."[100]

Toward the end of the campaign Washington increased his involvement somewhat, making sure that Republican subsidies went to the black newspapers most loyal to him.[101] He arranged for several of his southern Republican adherents to tour the black communities of close northern states at party expense.[102] A few days before the election he placed in the *Outlook* an editorial he had written but did not sign, defending Roosevelt's southern policies. Roosevelt had replaced the leftover Carpetbaggers with clean native southern whites and the "horde of ignorant and characterless colored politicians" with black men who had established their character by achievements outside of politics, said the editorial. Roosevelt had "not only decreased the quantity, but improved the quality. He has not only tried to do so, but has actually done it." Washington anonymously promised that the South, black and white, would learn that it never had had a warmer or more consistent friend than Theodore Roosevelt.[103]

Just before election day J. Thomas Heflin, the Democratic congressman for the district that included Tuskegee, gave a speech in the town. He revived the memory of the dinner at the White House and bitterly assailed both Washington and Roosevelt. Perhaps, in addition to the demagoguery that characterized his whole political career, Heflin's particular object was to frighten Washington out of casting his ballot, but if so he was unsuccessful. Washington voted for Roosevelt and Fairbanks within thirty minutes after the polls opened, and he felt sure that his vote was counted, for there were two Republican poll watchers at his polling place for the first time in twenty years.[104]

What were the rewards of Washington's labors in the Augean stables of southern and black Republican politics? Certainly not another dinner at the White House. Washington was not a guest at any of the inaugural festivities of March 1905. His reward, if indeed there was any in the uncertain game of politics, would be in added political appointments for his personal Tuskegee Machine, particularly of his proconsuls in the national capital and the northern cities.

Charles W. Anderson was clearly the outstanding black contributor to the Republican victory, and the Republican boss of New York State, Senator Thomas Platt, first suggested that Anderson's reward should be promotion to a federal appointive office.[105] It required a while to find a suitable political plum, but in 1905 the President appointed him collector of internal revenue for the district that included Wall Street. This was a prestigious and lucrative appointment and a demanding one, as he would have to represent the government in dealings with some of America's most powerful men. The financier August Belmont, who had known Anderson for years as a member of the racing fraternity, undertook to ease his confirmation by persuading Democratic Senators not to oppose him.[106] Anderson now became the captain of Washington's lieutenants.

Washington cleared a place for another adherent by persuading the President after the election to remove one of his black enemies, Judson W. Lyons, as register of the U. S. Treasury. Lyons, an old-line Georgia politician, had been on Washington's secret blacklist for two years, ever since he had expressed sympathy for the leader of the Boston Riot against Booker T. Washington, which occurred in 1903. This was not the reason that Washington gave the Roosevelt administration, however; he brought out evidence that Lyons, while holding his federal job, had given W. Calvin Chase of the Washington *Bee* some ammunition for anti-administration editorials.[107]

The registership was the highest traditionally black-held position in the District. Washington made a strategic mistake in recommending for the vacancy S. Laing Williams of Chicago, as "one of the few colored men I have relied on to create public sentiment among the colored people in the direction you and I believe in," as he wrote President Roosevelt.[108] But Williams as in the past came up short in local support. Edward H. Morris, who despised Washington and his faction, said the appointment would be "distasteful to both factions of the colored Republicans in this State, and especially in this City." He accused Williams of having once been a Democrat and an Independent, and added, "Booker T. Washington most likely favors Williams, but we do not need any advice from Alabama, when it comes to putting colored men in office from Illinois."[109]

Washington hesitated, while Scott urged him to fight for supremacy in black affairs in the Roosevelt administration, and Williams scurried about Chicago getting affidavits that he had worked for the Republicans for ten years. Roosevelt ominously chose a man not even recommended by Washington, a political unknown, William Tecumseh Vernon, the president of Western University in Quindaro, Kansas. Vernon was the candidate of Bishop Abraham Grant of the A. M. E. Church, with headquarters in Kansas City. Bishop Grant was an active Republican in the midwest, and a friend of Washington of long standing. Vernon's chief qualification, which Williams could not match, was the backing of both of his Senators. Vernon did not represent any political or ideological opposition to Washington, did not in fact represent anything at all. So Washington acquiesced in his appointment.

Privately, Washington hoped that Vernon would stumble. He urged Laing Williams to cultivate Senator Albert J. Hopkins of Illinois, saying, "Let him feel that in case Vernon does not succeed that he will be running no political risk in favoring you or even in aiding you."[110] In the meanwhile also, he arranged for two of his lower-echelon lieutenants to receive minor posts in the Treasury Department, where they could keep an eye on Vernon. Ralph W. Tyler of Ohio, formerly a reporter for the white daily Columbus *Ohio State Journal*, received appointment as auditor of the Navy Department accounts, and Peter Smith, Washington's errand runner in Boston, became Tyler's secretary. Richard W. Thompson, who had secretly been in Washington's personal pay as a syndicated columnist for a number of black newspapers, received a succession of minor federal clerkships through Washington's influence, in order to supplement his writing income and better serve "the Wizard."

At the beginning of 1906, Washington could see nothing but good resulting from his partnership with Theodore Roosevelt over the preceding five years. He had not really won the battles with the lily whites or had much impact on Republican administration policy toward the South, but he had greatly strengthened his machine through Roosevelt's patronage. He could agree with the words of the campaign song, "Hurrah for Teddy, He's all right!"

CHAPTER 2

Black Intellectuals
and the Boston Riot

Is the rope and the torch all the race is to get under your leadership?
WILLIAM MONROE TROTTER

IT WAS inevitable that Booker T. Washington's leadership would face bitter challenge from within the black minority group and a denial of its legitimacy, for he rose and prospered at a time of deep depression for blacks, the worst since emancipation. The great majority of black freedmen remained in the rural South, exchanging slavery for another exploitative system of sharecropping, and most of them had to mortgage their share of the crops to a merchant—often also the landowner—who would furnish them the necessities until the harvest. Some even slipped over the edge into peonage, or involuntary servitude for debt. Just as Washington was establishing his rule over this empire of poverty, southern whites in the 1890s began a movement of several decades duration to take back the rights that the Civil War and Reconstruction had established for blacks. They took away the voting rights of most blacks, extended segregation to virtually every walk of life, justified this by a verbal assault that denied human status and dignity to blacks, and punctuated these changes by lynchings and race riots. Northern whites also adopted white supremacy in attitude and deed, particularly by occupational and residential segregation.

Washington shrugged off any blame for these developments, and spoke for the segment of blacks who somehow succeeded despite these odds in advocating accommodation, at least for the time, to what blacks could not change, and gathering strength through education, economic struggle, and black solidarity as a surer foundation for progress.

Washington had set the stage for debate over black leadership in 1892, when he called the black clergy unfit to lead and proposed secular goals and leadership.[1] In 1895 he proposed his own Atlanta Compromise with whites that, he promised, would allow blacks to progress through self-improvement and economic means. His was a conservative social Darwinist proposition that whites everywhere readily accepted. Most blacks acquiesced at first, then a chorus of critics murmured and grew louder and more articulate. By 1903 Washington faced a well-considered alternative and a bitter challenge to his leadership and strategy. Most, though not all, of his critics were of the younger generation born after the end of slavery.

The way that Washington's critics confronted him in 1903 and the way he responded to them polarized black leadership into warring factions during a time when white aggressions were sweeping away what remained of the human rights of blacks. The deep factional division continued until Washington's death more than a decade later. Washington would continue to be the dominant figure in black America, ruling as a monarch or political boss. His fear of losing his power, however, made him prize loyalty above talent, drove talent to the opposition, and forced him to rely heavily on white advisers and black yes-men. His panicky overreaction to his critics in 1903 established his behavior pattern for the remainder of his career. He used ruthless means against black critics, accepted too readily the promises of white men, and grasped at every straw to justify his public optimism about the success of his own formula for black progress. Some features of this behavior had appeared earlier, but events of 1903 fixed and exaggerated them.

As the black criticism mounted early in the new century, Washington's close adviser T. Thomas Fortune counseled calm. "Let the whole gang, white and black, howl," he wrote. "The people, black and white, are with us, and we shall win."[2] Fortune's advice seemed justified when Washington spoke in May 1900 at the Bethel Literary and Historical Association in Washington, D.C. The national capital, with its small army of black government clerks and professional-class blacks, rivaled Boston as a center of discontent, as the loss of southern black voting power weakened the claim of blacks to federal patronage. Washington spoke, however, to an overflow crowd, despite such counterattractions as an illuminated parade downtown and a house fire a block away. The black elite of the capital attended, as usual, the Bethel Literary, and "Mr. Washington's appearance upon the rostrum was the signal for a storm of handclapping and the fluttering of ladies' dainty handkerchiefs." In an elaborate metaphor comparing the race to a ship in stormy weather, Washington offered himself as the cool-headed captain with whom all on board must cooperate if they were to weather the storm. He met every criticism of industrial education, his economic emphasis, and even his compromises with whites, saying of the latter that he practiced the charity that Christ taught and symbolized, and that he denounced as vigorously as anyone the black man who cringed or debased himself in order to gain the favor of a white man. A friendly newspaper reported that the audience responded with a "rapturous applause which followed every significant utterance and punctuated every paragraph."[3]

Washington frequently had to joust with the ghost of Frederick Douglass, whose life and doctrines had symbolized the preceding half-century of black experience. The escaped slave, abolitionist orator, self-taught intellectual, Reconstruction leader, and champion of political and civil rights had died in 1895, the year that Washington's career as leader was born. Washington argued that Douglass's era had been a political one, now succeeded by a commercial age in which Washington's doctrine of economic priority was more appropriate and the black businessman was the logical social arbiter. There was a call for "a New Negro for a new century." Washington was ready to wipe the slate clean and sketch his own silhouette on the new age, but there was continuity of Douglass's tradition and nostalgia for his leadership. Douglass had been unanswerable because he told the truth, said Harry C. Smith of the Cleveland *Gazette,* whereas Washington seemed to have the whole world to command but "teaches subordination of his own race to another."[4] A sympathetic image of Washington, on the other hand, appeared in a cartoon in the influential Indianapolis *Freeman.* It showed a giant, serene Washington seated at his desk, pen in hand, while his black critics depicted as pygmies clambered toward the desk top.[5]

Washington's white admirers in the North believed absolutely in the truth and statesmanship of his doctrines, and when they occasionally heard black critics characterize him otherwise, they dismissed these persons as cranks. "I was shocked the other night to hear a reference to your policy in a meeting of colored men, hissed," Edward H. Clement, editor of the Boston *Transcript*, wrote Washington in 1898. "Turning to my neighbor in the pew, I asked, 'Is he not hitting at Washington?' and the answer was 'Yes; there is much and growing opposition to his counsels among blacks.'" Clement could see justice in the critics' protests against southern injustice and said he would have to take account of dissent against Washington's nonchallenging strategy, but he wrote Washington in sympathy: "I confess that I wonder at, and admire, your reserve and am not at all sure that yours is not the course of wisdom in the thickening difficulties which beset the upward path of your race."[6]

Rabbi Charles Fleischer of Cambridge had a similar shock a few years later when he appeared before the black Boston Literary and Historical Association. He compared the debate among the Jews over Zionism with the differences between Washington's meliorist doctrines and the Back-to-Africa movement of Bishop Henry M. Turner. To his astonishment, at mention of Washington's name "a frost fell upon the audience which had been warmly sympathetic." In the question period excited men and women sought to "prove" that Washington was "playing into the hands of their enemies," was "a selfish timeserver and what not." No amount of Fleischer's expostulation that Washington placed the race problem in longer perspective than they did made the slightest impression, the Rabbi informed Washington. "I was astounded at this discovery that you were without honor among your own people though it serves negatively to prove you the prophet and the emancipator." Fleischer urged Washington to put himself on record unmistakably for "the Negro's rights and privileges."[7] But Fleischer and many others failed to understand how Washington's role as interracial diplomat was based on ambiguity, how Washington had license to criticize but not to challenge the white supremacy system, since his own position of preeminence rested on his accommodation to the system.

Washington complacently responded to Fleischer that the black masses supported him, that his critics were limited to small bands in Boston and the capital and some scattered individuals. With only slight exaggeration, he said that of 200 black newspapers, only three, in Boston, Washington, and Chicago, opposed him. As for their criticisms, "These people have not the least foundation for the main charges which I understand they now keep prominent, that is that I endorse the Jim Crow cars and the unjust election laws in the South." The opposition was healthy for him, he said, but showed spite and jealousy on their part. "The mere fact that I know there is a group here and there watching for mistakes on my part makes me more valuable I think to the race."[8]

Behind the mask of self-confidence, however, Washington knew that a small but growing coterie of college-bred blacks was scoring points against him. He feared this group the more because he did not quite understand it, did not always follow the verbal footwork of its ideas. He felt the challenge to be a personal one and prepared to deal with it in ruthless ways he had somehow, off the record, learned during his struggle up from slavery and poverty. The center of this opposition was a new black weekly newspaper, the Boston *Guardian,* founded in 1901 as his personal mouthpiece by William Monroe Trotter, Washington's most relentless Boston critic. A recent Harvard graduate, Trotter built his career around the defense of black civil and political rights and the inexorable denunciation particularly of Booker T. Washington but also of Presidents Roosevelt, Taft, and Wilson, and anyone else who fell short of his expectations, including most of his friends.

"Trotter has been calling the President names for having *you* to dine with him," Washington heard from a Boston friend in 1901, who added that the co-editor of the *Guardian,* George W. Forbes, also "so lost himself at a public meeting [as] to say, 'it would be a blessing to the race if the Tuskegee school should burn down, etc.' "[9] Generally, however, Forbes gave the literary polish to the *Guardian* and left the racial politics to Trotter. Trotter's objection to the dinner at the White House was simply that the President had invited the wrong Negro, one who "advised his race to keep out of politics and . . . criticised what use they made of the franchise."[10] Trotter's criticism of Washington, however, extended to his subservience to whites, his silence before racial injustice, his advocacy of second-class education for second-class citizens, his repression of dissent, his southernness, his personality. Trotter sought to close every discussion with *"Washington est delenda."*

Robert W. Taylor, Tuskegee's young financial agent in Boston, wanted to silence the *Guardian* by a libel suit. Roscoe Conkling Bruce, however, suggested a shrewder plan. The son of a Mississippi Senator of the Reconstruction period and of Tuskegee's dean of women, Bruce was a Harvard student preparing himself to become the head of the academic department of Tuskegee Institute. Trotter was too fanatical to be restrained, he concluded, but Forbes was another matter. "Forbes delights in writing the editorials," Bruce reported. "He is not so hard to deal with as is Trotter. Just one word from the Librarian would in my opinion shut Forbes's mouth. Trotter can't carry on the paper alone—& no conceivable coadjutor could equal Forbes!"[11] The Librarian Bruce alluded to was James L. Whitney, head of the Boston Public Library, under whom Forbes drew his principal income as assistant librarian of the West End branch. Washington may have given Bruce the nod, or Bruce might have simply thought well of his own idea. In either case, Bruce spoke privately to Whitney and reported the conversation to Washington: "Doctor Whitney is of course enthusiastic in his admiration for you & Tuskegee. I let him understand the situation created by the Guardian—I spoke as far as Doctor Whitney knew, entirely on my own responsibility. He promised to do whatever he could to shut Forbes' mouth. Under the Civil Service rules it would hardly be possible to dismiss Forbes." On second thought, Bruce wrote, it would be just as well for Forbes to "remain at the beck and call of Whitney." If he were out of the library he would be beyond restraint. "With Forbes in the Library, we have a constantly effective check upon his audacities."[12] This was undoubtedly one of the stresses that eventually broke up the partnership of Forbes and Trotter.

Trotter developed a network of opposition to Washington, centering in the *Guardian* but spreading out in Boston and elsewhere in New England. He and others organized the Boston Literary and Historical Association as a forum of racial militancy, and soon afterward the Massachusetts Racial Protective Association, which put him in touch with anti-Washington sentiment all over the state.[13] Other black newspapers also took up the hue and cry against Washington's leadership, notably the Washington *Bee,* the Chicago *Conservator,* and the Cleveland *Gazette.* None of the others, however, pursued him with the unremitting, obsessive ardor of the *Guardian.*

The Trotterites sent forth a missionary, William H. Ferris, a recent Yale graduate who lived intermittently in Boston and New Haven.

Early in 1903 he spoke at the Bethel Literary and Historical Association in the capital on "The Boston Negro's Idea of Booker Washington." Ferris aped Trotter in attacking Washington personally as well as his program, but the main burden of Ferris's criticism was that Washington's promotion of industrial education and his ridicule of the black college man was schooling the race for subordination and blunting its higher aspirations. "The interesting feature of the occasion, to me," a Washington admirer wrote, "was the evidence of a number of people here who, from their applause, indicated a feeling of hostility to Mr. W. In studying these malcontents I felt that I could account for each of them by reason of interest in rival institutions, Howard, Atlanta, &c. and the others under the not very elegant term of 'sore-heads' who have succeeded wonderfully in doing nothing themselves and hence have a grievance against any man who is doing something."[14]

Interest in the subject ran so high that a few weeks later the Bethel Literary sponsored a full-scale debate between the anti- and pro-Washington spokesmen. Ferris led the attack again, with the support of some local citizens, while defenders of Washington included the lawyer Jesse Lawson, newly appointed municipal judge Robert H. Terrell, W. Bruce Evans of the District public schools, the newspaper columnist Richard W. Thompson, and Washington's sometime critic, Bishop Alexander Walters. Each of these men had some sort of obligation to Washington. Both sides claimed to have won the debate. "The antis did a great deal of talking and earned some applause," Thompson wrote Scott, "but the force of the argument presented by the friends of the Wizard went to make up for lack in numbers and the hearty encores showed the spirit of the audience to be in sympathy with Dr. Washington. It was only the political phase that gave the opposition a chance to score." Thompson also reported to Tuskegee the beneficiaries of Washington's favors who failed to attend or "maintained a *silence* rivalling that of the tomb."[15]

Factional skirmishes in Boston were often equally petty, with personal dignity the chief victim. When black students at Harvard rented a meeting room on whose walls Washington's portrait hung, Trotter and associates tried and failed to induce the students to cancel their engagement. They also approached several young women who had been invited and tried to persuade them not to attend. When the Boston branch of the National Negro Business League arranged for a

banquet in Washington's honor, the *Guardian* group busied themselves "buttonholing those invited to attend the banquet, beseeching
them to stay away." Pulling out all stops, they sent letters to the Atlanta *Constitution,* Montgomery *Advertiser,* and other southern white
papers giving news of Washington's social life in the North in an effort to embarrass him.[16] Meanwhile, Washington negotiated with his
lieutenants in Boston for the establishment of a black newspaper there
which could only have nuisance value in undercutting the *Guardian's*
small circulation.[17]

The annual meeting of the Afro-American Council seemed to the
Trotterites the logical place to confront Washington. It was the only
national meeting place of all the elements of Afro-American leadership, and its very reason for being was civil and political rights. And
yet, ever since its revival in 1898 out of the ashes of the earlier Afro-
American League, Washington and his followers had dominated the
meetings, even though he himself was not a member. Washington's
adherents held most of the offices, and consequently the council resolutions were seldom the ringing declarations of protest that the age
of white supremacy should have called forth. Even the legal bureau
of the council fumbled indecisively for years with its only case, the
testing of the Louisiana grandfather clause. The Afro-American
Council mirrored the divided mind of the race.[18]

An effort to censure Washington in the 1899 council meeting failed.
In 1902 Washington's critics made a more concerted effort to wrest
control of the council from him and his friends. One of his Boston
lieutenants warned him that "the 'Guardian' folks are going to use
every effort to have the Afro American Council *Denounce* you."[19] A
friend in St. Paul, where the meeting was to be held, advised that
"there will probably be some effort made to have some expression go
forth from the Council with respect to your position as given in your
speeches and lectures, it being claimed that it is harmful and detri-
mental to the race."[20] Washington's lieutenants promised to squelch
the criticism, but he decided to attend the meeting himself. "It was
wonderful to see how completely your personality domiominated everything at St. Paul," Emmett Scott wrote afterward. "From the moment
you reached there you were the one center of interest. . . ."[21] The
Washington *Bee* sourly confirmed this, remarking: "The 'Wizard of
Tuskegee' was there. . . . His satellites were in the saddle. . . . They
trotted and pranced as he pulled the reins and his ticket was elected

and his namby-pamby policy . . . was incorporated into the address, which was nothing more than a pronouncement of his nibs, the boss of Negro beggars."[22]

To cap Washington's victory, Fortune replaced Bishop Walters as president, and the militant Ida B. Wells-Barnett was removed as secretary. Trotter grumbled in the *Guardian* that "Fortune is only a 'me too' to whatever Washington aspires to do. These two men have long since formed themselves into one twain in their dealings with the Negro race, Fortune furnishing whatever brain the combination needs, and Washington the boodle." Trotter laid part of the blame for his failure at St. Paul at the unlikely door of W. E. B. Du Bois of Atlanta University. "We might have expected Prof. Du Bois to have stood in the breach here," Trotter wrote, "but like all the others who are trying to get into the band wagon of the Tuskegeean, he is no longer to be relied upon."[23]

Washington's continued dominance of the council, however, masked some weaknesses of his own position. He could repress the council into a pattern of accommodation while his own program of economic and educational progress and his interracial diplomacy was supposed to do its work, but black discontent was reborn daily because of white aggression against the rights of blacks. Furthermore, because he bound his faction to him through mutual interest more than through ideology, this generated personal rivalries among his lieutenants. Bishop Alexander Walters, for example, unhappy at being ousted as president of the council, joined forces at its next executive committee with James H. Hayes of the National Negro Suffrage League and began to ridicule Washington's doctrine that education and economic advancement would solve the race problem. Walters hastened to reassure Washington that he was just as anxious as the Tuskegean to "defeat the Trotter 'gang,'"[24] but Washington could see that Walters was scheming to replace Fortune as president and was "laying a great deal of stress on the opposition which he seems to have found throughout the country against Fortune."[25] Washington's friends spread the word that "Fortune had not tasted liquor since the St. Paul meeting,"[26] and Fortune had indeed sworn off alcohol, but his friends were embarrassed a few months later by newspaper reports that, while in Manila on a government mission of inspection he got in a brawl with police.[27]

Many months before the 1903 meeting of the Afro-American Council at Louisville, Trotter made new plans to seize control in the name of militancy. Peter J. Smith, a Washington footsoldier in Boston, warned that the *Guardian* folk were trying to win over Bishop Walters. "Those fellows are working like trojans to influence people white and black against you North and South," he reported, "and Trotter has said he will spend all his own money and everybody's else he can get to kill you."[28] Learning that the Trotterites planned to use the celebrations of Lincoln's birthday in Boston and New York to condemn his conservatism on the suffrage issue, Washington undercut them by publishing a strong pro-suffrage statement. At the same time, however, when President Roosevelt became worried that a too enthusiastic endorsement of him by blacks might hurt him among white voters, Washington conveyed Roosevelt's concern to Bishop Walters and urged him to keep the Lincoln's birthday resolutions "very mild so far as they refer to him and his interest in the colored people."[29]

Washington made his own plans for the Louisville meeting. He had a feeling that the ideologically oriented Trotterites might form a coalition with the more opportunistic Walters and Hayes. He sought to organize the Tuskegee Machine to meet the onslaught. Fred R. Moore, editor of the *Colored American Magazine* and a New York lieutenant, wrote to Scott: "A line from Mr. W. to Fortune to refrain from drink would I believe be in order."[30] Meanwhile, Washington wired Scott from somewhere in New England: "perhaps dozen Boston and New England men opposed to us will attend Council. Must take no chances."[31] On the same day he sent Fortune a resolution he wanted passed as soon as the first day of the meeting began. "It is one which will protect us, and prevent the other people from getting in their work," he wrote. It is not clear what the resolution was, but Washington also warned Fortune: "Be careful not to rile the Bishop or Hayes, and thus give them an excuse for going against us."[32] He sent urgent calls to lieutenants to be sure to attend.[33] General Clarkson, in the interest of Roosevelt Republicanism, furnished two free round-trip tickets to Louisville. He offered one to Anderson, who was unable to attend, but Anderson suggested that he give one ticket to the indigent Bookerite Peter J. Smith and the other to the influential Baptist leader, the Reverend Charles S. Morris of New York, who "ought to be instructed to support Fortune before supplying them with transportation." According to Anderson, Clarkson also "read the riot act" to John E. Bruce for joining forces with Trotter.[34]

Washington's machine overwhelmed the opponents at Louisville by superior numbers but also by superior political skill. This was clear from the beginning, when Trotter and his followers considered a rump meeting but at the last minute decided to come into the meeting to dissent and disrupt as much as possible. At the resolutions committee meeting the night before the convention, the Trotterites won approval of only one of their resolutions, to ask the President to support the reduction of congressional representation in states that had disfranchised blacks. On the first morning, President Fortune denied Forbes and Trotter permission to rebut a paper on black literature that praised Washington's writings. That afternoon Ferris caused "almost a riot" by dramatically pointing to a huge picture of Washington on the stage and saying, "I object to that picture being on the platform, unless placed opposite is some other negro who stands for the higher life and intellectual development. Booker Washington's propaganda has given color to the opinion that the negro is mentally inferior, and his doctrine has been the most powerful argument to the country in favor of the disenfranchisement of the negro, Washington arguing that the colored man should confine himself to labor and forego the ballot." Ferris and Trotter continued their disruption until, as a concession, a portrait of the late Joseph C. Price adorned the other side of the stage.[35] Price, the president of Livingstone College when he died in 1891, was often hailed by Washington's critics as a marginally more outspoken southern black educator.

While Washington's critics won this symbolic victory, however, he asserted his own power. He arrived in Louisville in the company of his Boston convert William H. Lewis, who took his seat in the Massachusetts delegation and, at Washington's instance, on "important committees."[36] Washington's own arrival at the meeting hall was a triumph. "The convention was electrified," a local newspaper reported. The cheering lasted so long that Washington was obliged to repeat his acknowledgments before business could resume.[37] That night he spoke optimistically to the convention, calling the Gold Democrats whom Roosevelt had appointed "a class of brave, earnest men at the South, as well as at the North, who are more determined than ever before to see that the race is given opportunity to elevate itself." He urged blacks not to become discouraged, for a race would be judged in the end by its creative will. "An inch of progress is worth more than a yard of complaint."[38]

W. H. Lewis had an opportunity to address the convention, and was even elected a vice president. Trotter was the only radical placed on the executive council, where he was surrounded by Washington's lieutenants and allies. Washington took a complacent view of the failed putsch. "I am used to attacks," he told reporters. "I have no ill feeling against Trotter or Ferris. I think that they misunderstand Southern conditions, however. If they had been through my experience I do not think that they would express the views that they do."[39]

Trotter's position continued to deteriorate, and on the last day he sought to regain ground by a heated denunciation of President Roosevelt. "Sit down. Sit down," yelled half a dozen delegates. "No, sir; I am going to have my say," insisted Trotter. "We Northern negroes are not going to sit supinely by and let the whites put their feet on our necks." He continued through a storm of hisses: "What has President Roosevelt done for the race? He has only appointed one negro in every hundred appointments—just one per cent." "Throw him out," several delegates shouted, while others laughed uproariously. It was a humiliating moment for Trotter; and as he continued the indignation of his audience turned to ridicule and mock applause until he desisted.[40] The Washingtonians had the last word in press interviews at the end of the meeting. Wilford H. Smith said: "The sentiment of the Boston crowd found no response in the delegates to the council." Charles S. Morris, present on Clarkson's free pass, said: "Sampson slew the Philistines with the jawbone of an ass. The little crowd from Boston has the same weapon, but doesn't know how to use it." "The shallows may roar," he added, "but the great deeps of negro manhood believe in Booker Washington and are proud to trust and follow him."[41] General Clarkson took perhaps too much credit for Washington's triumph, but white political favor was a key element in the outcome. "I found that there was a very strong and active effort being made to have the body turn a cold shoulder to the President," he wrote Roosevelt's private secretary. "Booker Washington was here the first of the week, and he and I had two meetings to devise plans for making the convention go right without any public disclosures of our movements. He told me the men who ought to be there and hold it straight—five or six of the strongest men of the race—and who had not intended to go and were not able to go; I reached them all and sent them all there, and the result was all right." The only anti-Roosevelt people at Louisville, he wrote, were a few Bostonians who were "against the President because he is for Washington."[42]

Washington's victory at Louisville was so sweeping that he could dismiss his opponents as "three colored men from Boston." He wrote a white newspaper editor: "In reality, these men make such asses of themselves, and every one knowing that their object is to gratify a mere personal spite, the colored people in conventions do not take them seriously and for that reason pay little attention to them in the way of opposing or giving notice to what they say."[43] Moving on to his summer home at South Weymouth in the Boston suburbs, however, he heard disturbing rumors of new plots to embarrass him. "In case the Boston crowd persist in advocating the holding of another Afro-American Council," Washington wrote Scott, "I should like you, so far as you can exercise influence, to exert it in the direction of causing the colored Press [to] pay absolutely no attention to this undertaking."[44]

Trotter planned another confrontation on his home ground in Boston that he hoped would end forever Washington's monarchy, his one-man spokesmanship for the black race. Learning that the Boston branch of the National Negro Business League had invited Washington to speak at the black Columbus Avenue A. M. E. Zion Church, Trotter prepared a list of embarrassing questions to ask Washington from the floor. Trotter had been jeered and laughed down at Louisville, but in a black church before a black audience in his home town he could count on a greater number of sympathetic listeners, particularly if he quietly packed the hall with supporters.

Most of Trotter's nine questions were simply accusatory requests that Washington explain some of his unfortunate public statements, of which Trotter had a large file. They accused him of advocating disfranchisement, peonage, the Jim Crow car, and black submission. Trotter's last two questions were more sweepingly rhetorical: "Can a man make a successful educator and politician at the same time?" and "Is the rope and the torch all the race is to get under your leadership?"[45]

Anticipation of trouble at the meeting brought forth a squad of eleven policemen. A crowd of about 2000, the absolute capacity of the church, filled the aisles, made movement difficult, and raised the temperature on that hot night of July 30, 1903. The meeting opened with a prayer by the pastor of the church, the Reverend James H. McMullen, an admirer of Washington at least since the dinner at the White House.[46] As usual, there were preliminary speeches. William

H. Lewis, in introducing T. Thomas Fortune, favorably referred to Washington. This brought hisses from scattered Trotterites in the crowd. "If there are any geese in the audience they are privileged to retire," Lewis remarked, but the crowd continued to murmur. Taking the center of the stage, the volatile Fortune opened with expressions of loyalty to Booker T. Washington, and provoked the audience by saying: "I took the Boston delegates to the Louisville convention . . . and virtually spanked them across my knee." "That was indiscreet," muttered a deputy sheriff who was present.[47] As Fortune continued his harangue, he was interrupted by Granville Martin, a Trotterite still dressed in his butler's uniform, who tried to move toward the front of the hall to be heard. Ushers moved to his side to dissuade him, and when he persisted three or four policemen ejected him from the hall. Fortune tried to begin again but began to cough violently. He reached for the accustomed water pitcher only to find it had been emptied in the confusion of the interruption. His coughing became so marked, and the sneezing of others on the platform so prevalent, that it was clear something was amiss. During Granville Martin's disruption, someone had sprinkled cayenne pepper over the platform. The meeting paused until Fortune caught his breath and began anew. Granville Martin, who had returned as soon as the police released him outside, once again made himself heard in the back, bellowing an inarticulate question, hissing, and stamping his feet. On Lewis's order the police removed and arrested Martin, and Fortune completed his speech.

The crowd quieted somewhat as Harry Burleigh sang and Edward Everett Brown, a Boston black lawyer, spoke. When Lewis tried to introduce Washington, who had sat calmly through all the earlier excitement, pandemonium broke loose again. "We don't want to hear you, Booker Washington," someone shouted from the back of the church. "We don't like you. Your views and aims are not what we sympathize with or think best for our race." That, at any rate, was what the Boston *Transcript* reported. Scuffling and fist fights broke out all over the hall. Bernard Charles, one of the fighters, was stabbed and then arrested. This precipitated further rioting, and William Monroe Trotter stood on a chair and read off his list of questions, but few could hear even his shrill voice above the hubbub. A crowd of screaming women surrounded the policemen and impeded their movements until they threatened to use their clubs. Trotter's sister

Maude was arrested and at first charged with stabbing a policeman with her hatpin, but the charge was dropped. Washington's supporters were on the whole the more dignified, but Dr. Samuel E. Courtney, Washington's friend and former student, shouted: "Throw Trotter out the window!" The police led Martin, Charles, Trotter, and Maude Trotter to the police station, where they were booked and she was released.

Meanwhile back at the church, when order returned, it was nearly ten o'clock. Washington gave a bland account of his leadership and social philosophy with only one interruption. He said the disturbance was the work of only a few individuals who opposed free speech. He dwelt upon "the gospel of thrift and saving," "the dignity and beauty of labor," "the disgrace of idleness, and the mastery of some special trade or calling."[48] In his remarks to reporters after the meeting, Washington tried to make light of the incident and even to turn it into a triumph of the silent majority who supported him. "Just as a few flies are able to spoil the purity of a large jar of cream so three ill-mannered young men were able to disturb the good order of a large and otherwise successful meeting of our people in the city of Boston," he said.[49] He left Boston for other engagements in Illinois.

The Boston Riot was not actually a riot, and from a superficial standpoint Washington was the victor, because he was able to complete his speech while Trotter was led off to police court and charged with disturbing the peace. But Trotter achieved his purpose of breaking through the pro-Washington news screen. The next day the event appeared in the headlines of daily papers all over the country, proclaiming a riotous assembly questioning the leadership and spokesmanship of Booker T. Washington. Many whites learned for the first time that it was possible for blacks to disagree with that paragon Booker T. Washington. The press made much of alleged razor wounds and hatpin stabs. "Education vs. razors" was the Montgomery *Advertiser's* oversimplification of the issue.[50] "In no case is the old text, that a prophet is not without honor save in his own country, better exemplified than in the case of Booker T. Washington," wrote the Boston *Transcript*, "whose work is appreciated and applauded even by the Negroes' hereditary oppressors, and whose person is persecuted only by his own race."[51] A Boston *Traveller* cartoon showed Washington and a hardworking crew crossing the Delaware, despite black hatred, prejudice, and envy.[52] There was a general disposition of Washington's supporters of both races to rally to his side, and Emmett Scott carefully shepherded the flock. The Alabama Baptist state convention, meeting at Tuskegee, resolved that Washington was "a conservative, worthy and safe leader" and that the attack on him was "without provocation and severely to be deprecated."[53] The Atlanta *Constitution* called the riot "a direct and logical outcome of the unnatural and undivine maleducation that Boston has crammed into the undiscriminating heads of its negro population."[54] Even as far north as New England, the Hartford *Times* claimed that Washington's gospel of work was unpopular among blacks because they were black, whereas Washington, "although a mulatto by birth, resembles the late Frederick Douglass in being much more a white man than a negro. Mr. Washington sees the need that the negro shall work as hard and as persistently as the white man, if he would make his way in the world."[55]

In contrast to the unanimous condemnation of the rioters in the white press, the black press reaction was mixed. The *Bee* spoke of Washington's "political dictatorship" as the ultimate cause, and the Chicago *Broad Ax* said rebellion would continue as long as Washington refused "to answer these questions which are of vital importance to the Negro."[56] But Washington had many defenders in the black press, including the Washington *Colored American* and the nationally influential Indianapolis *Freeman*. The most sweeping indictment of the rioters was an anonymous press release datelined at Boston but actually prepared by Emmett Scott. It asserted that Trotter had "become insane" in his opposition to Washington. "The plan to break up the meeting was deliberately precipitated, and was of the coarsest, most vulgar sort, such as is employed everywhere by the hoodlum, rowdy elements to create riot and confusion. Trotter was backed up in his rowdyism by a half-dozen women of the street, whose vulgar services were obviously purchased." But behind Trotter were five other men, who "have more brains, if no more character, than he." The release named Forbes, Ferris, Archibald H. Grimké, Clement G. Morgan, and W. A. Shaw, "a democratic soldier of fortune, who has always been down at the heels." The only reason Ferris was not present to assist his fellow-rioters was that his friends had left him stranded "completely on his uppers in Louisville."[57]

The charges against Maude Trotter were dropped, but Boston Bookerites, including the Reverend McMullen, pressed charges against Martin, Charles, and Trotter. They employed a white lawyer, G. R.

Swasey, while each of the three defendants had his black lawyer. The defendants tried to argue that they were merely exercising their right of free speech, but William H. Lewis, the chief witness for the prosecution, testified that Trotter had disrupted an orderly assembly and prevented Washington from speaking, forcing him at one point to sit down, and that after Trotter's arrest Washington was able to speak without hindrance.[58] The charges against Charles were dismissed by a jury at the appeals court, but Trotter and Martin were convicted, and the judge gave them the maximum sentence of thirty days in jail. "There is no doubt that these men were present at the meeting and that they went there with the intention of preventing Booker T. Washington from speaking until he answered certain questions which they desired to ask," said the judge. "These men might have thought Washington was unwise, but they had no right to disturb the meeting. They were found guilty in the lower court and the jury convicted them in this court. I do not see how a jury could have come to any other conclusion." The judge added that he might have been more lenient if Trotter and Martin had apologized or indicated that "if Booker T. Washington were to speak here tomorrow night we might [not] expect a similar disgraceful scene."[59]

Trotter and his fellow participants brought no credit on themselves by their conduct, but neither did the Tuskegee Machine. There is no evidence in Washington's private correspondence that, as Trotter intimated in the *Guardian*, Tuskegee money paid for the expensive white prosecutor. Nevertheless, the sentence was unduly severe, and Washington's Boston friends pressed for it and were gleeful at its severity. Washington himself joined in the vindictiveness. Soon after the riot he wrote to a friend: "You will be glad to know that Trotter, Forbes, Grimké, and two or three others, have by their actions completely killed themselves among all classes, both white and colored, in Boston. Trotter was taken out of the church in handcuffs, yelling like a baby. They are to be tried in Court tomorrow, and every effort is being exerted by the citizens of Boston to secure their conviction."[60] He sent similar glad tidings to William H. Baldwin, Jr., chairman of the Tuskegee trustees, who was then meeting with the Southern Education Board at Lake George. Baldwin replied: "I am tremendously interested in the suit against Trotter. Your message was received at Lake George and gave intense satisfaction to the members of the Board present. They feel that your work will be materially helped in the

South by reason of the attack upon you. I should watch carefully for a revulsion of feeling in Boston, and not have it appear that there is any persecution of 'free thought,' but that the position of your friends is held simply because of the vicious interference with the meeting." [61]

Though Washington stayed aloof from the court case against Trotter and his co-defendants, he did manipulate the news reporting of the affair. A few days after the first trial he wrote to Scott from Shelbyville, Illinois: "Please let the enclosed appear in two or three colored newspapers which you can thoroughly trust, as coming from a correspondent at Boston. The facts of course, can be used from time to time as editorial squibs, as you may think best. You may be interested to know that the whole crowd are thoroughly scared, and are on their knees, begging for mercy." [62] It is uncertain what that enclosure was, but in September 1903 Washington wrote Scott again: "I wish whenever you can you would get a short note in the colored papers about the late arrest of Forbes and Trotter." [63] This probably led to a typescript, corrected in Scott's hand, datelined at Boston under the pseudonym of Amos Joy. It purported to represent the black people of Boston who "almost unanimously . . . condemn the riotous acts, and are determined to see the guilty ones punished." "Amos Joy" said of Trotter: "From Harvard College to the gaol—the distance is great; but Trotter has travelled it in short order." [64]

Washington's reversal from victim to persecutor, his loss of moral authority in the eyes of many blacks, was largely the result of his own vindictiveness and that of his friends, at least some of whom acted at his personal instigation. He began with Scott's help a blacklist of those expressing sympathy for Trotter, including the Reverend Francis Grimké of Washington, D.C., and Judson W. Lyons, register of the Treasury. It also included two Atlanta University faculty members, George A. Towns and W. E. B. DuBois. DuBois wrote a letter praising Trotter's earnestness and expressing regret that he was made "the object of petty persecution & dishonest attack." His letter appeared in the *Guardian*, as did that of Professor Towns, a 1900 graduate of Harvard, who had written directly to the jailed Trotter a more radical letter of endorsement. [65]

Whatever hot anger Washington may have felt at these endorsements of his enemy he cooled down to a reasonable complaint to a key philanthropist who might influence the northern financial supporters of Atlanta University. Sending Robert C. Ogden clippings of the Towns and Du Bois letters, he said of one of them that there was not "a word of truth in any statement made in this letter."[66] "I am beginning to think," Ogden replied, "that the toleration of such men as Towns and Du Bois is deeply injuring Atlanta University."[67] George Foster Peabody and perhaps others joined Ogden in their protest. Hoping to fend them off, President Horace Bumstead wrote first a mild and then a sharp reprimand to Towns: "The publication in the Guardian of your letter to Mr. Trotter is making serious trouble for me and I fear will work considerable injury to the University and its cause." Subsequently he wrote: "When you told Mr. Trotter that he was going to jail for a principle, you obscured the fact that he had done anything worthy of punishment." Bumstead reported to Washington a severe reprimand of Towns by the executive committee of Atlanta University.[68]

It was Du Bois whom Washington wanted to humiliate, however, for he was convinced that Du Bois was not merely a sympathizer but a co-conspirator with Trotter in staging the disturbance. He wrote his moneyed friend Ogden: "I think I ought to say to you that I have evidence which is indisputable showing that Dr. Du Bois is very largely behind the mean and underhanded attacks that have been made upon me during the last six months. This, of course, is for your own personal information."[69]

Du Bois had indeed come a long way from that day in 1895 when he congratulated Washington on his Atlanta Compromise address and expressed the view that it might form the basis for an equitable racial settlement. He had once applied for and once considered teaching positions at Tuskegee in the nineties, but when Washington at the turn of the century tried to hire him as director of research, Du Bois backed away, perhaps out of fear that Washington would try to dominate him as he did all the faculty at Tuskegee. Meanwhile, Du Bois was drifting ideologically away from Washington, becoming increasingly a reformer rather than a detached social analyst. In his review of Washington's autobiography *Up from Slavery* in 1902 Du Bois deplored the Mammonism of Washington's educational and social programs under the influence of the millionaire philanthropists. More important was the appearance in the spring of 1903, months before the Boston Riot, of Du Bois's greatest book, *The Souls of Black Folk*, a passionate evocation of the inner experience of blacks. One of its essays, "Of Mr. Booker T. Washington and Others," was the most persuasive intellectual critique ever written of Washington's racial strategy—both his industrial education and accommodationism. The burden of Du Bois's rejection of Washington was that his materialism and his compromises with white tyranny denied blacks their right to dream, to aspire, to master the world around them. The very restraint with which Du Bois presented his case, conceding Washington's genuine fostering of black self-help and acknowledging that he often opposed racial injustice in his own way, rendered Du Bois's arguments more persuasive than the *ad hominem* attacks of Trotter, and made Du Bois clearly the intellectual leader of the anti-Washington faction.[70]

Though Du Bois was not even in Boston when the riot occurred, he was a house guest of the Trotters for the rest of the summer. And he wrote Trotter a letter of sympathy for his inordinate punishment by the friends and agents of Washington. Washington, assuming that this was evidence that Du Bois was part of the conspiracy to riot, warned Ogden, who in turn wrote Horace Bumstead. Bumstead informed Washington's powerful friends of his reprimand of Towns and Du Bois in the hope of protecting his school from the loss of funds from the foundations that Washington's friends controlled. George Foster Peabody was inclined to consider the reprimand sufficient, but Ogden warned him: "If it be true that Trotter is an unprincipled agitator, Du Bois must meet the issue. He cannot serve God and Mammon. In my judgment, there is a great deal of moral responsibility for that Boston riot chargeable to Dr. Bumstead himself." Ogden had no evidence for that, however, and he considered it unwise to charge publicly that Bumstead was harboring agitators on his faculty. "But do not trust Bumstead," he warned. Washington initiated the misconstruction of Du Bois's letter of sympathy, but Ogden carried the chain of non sequiturs further to make Atlanta University itself responsible for riot in Boston. For more than a decade Atlanta University felt a chill wind from the North, partly the result of growing northern coolness toward black higher education but partly also directed specifically at the institution that gave Du Bois employment.[71] "Too many of our colored friends are bumptious," punned Ogden, "for much of which we may thank Bumstead." As for Du Bois, Ogden wrote, "I do not believe him intellectually honest."[72]

Du Bois felt compelled, after the chaplain and the president of Atlanta University had spoken to him, to explain to Peabody his actions in relation to the Boston Riot. Trotter's wife was an old school friend, he said; he had known Trotter himself not so long nor so well but had met him in college. They had often argued over racial policy and over Washington's leadership, but Du Bois said he viewed Trotter as "a clean-hearted utterly unselfish man whom I admired despite his dogged and unreasoning prejudices." Du Bois denied by implication any conspiracy with Trotter. He was teaching at, of all places, the Tuskegee Summer School when Trotter planned his "riot," and had "absolutely no knowledge" or inkling of suspicion of the matter. He had arranged months earlier to spend the vacation after Tuskegee summer school with the Trotters, and was traveling north on a coastal steamer when the Boston Riot occurred. He denied any correspondence with Trotter "save in regard to the boarding place." After the riot, he told his host that he thought the confrontation would do harm rather than good. Though unable to defend Washington's policies as he once had, he addressed a meeting at Trotter's house on "the vast difference between criticising Mr. Washington's policy and attacking him personally."

Nevertheless, Du Bois wrote Peabody, after carefully sorting out the various elements of the issue, he found himself drifting from his earlier neutrality. In close contact with Trotter after the riot, he said, "my admiration for his unselfishness, pureness of heart and indomitable energy, even when misguided, grew." He thought that it was Lewis's conduct as chairman of the meeting that had provoked the riot. He considered Lewis an unprincipled man who once wanted to "burn down Tuskegee," but after Du Bois brought the two men together so that they might understand each other, "[t]hey evidently came to understand each other so well that Mr. Lewis got a political appointment and turning around proceeded to abuse his former comrades—a conversion in which I had as little faith as I had in his former radical stand." While he came to admire Trotter on closer acquaintance, Du Bois also observed "things that made me have less and less faith in Mr. Washington." He felt the threat of authoritarianism in Washington's lieutenants' pressing for Trotter's jail sentence to an excessive extent, and hence wrote the open letter to the *Guardian*. He repeated to Peabody that while he condemned the disturbance of the meeting, "I nevertheless admire Mr. Trotter as a man and agree with his main contentions." A man of unpurchasable soul was needed "when Mr. Washington is leading the way backward."[73] Thus the Boston Riot precipitated what was slowly evolving anyhow, the polarization of black leadership into two warring camps, one led by Washington and the other led not by Trotter but by Du Bois, the most distinguished intellectual and champion of higher education among blacks. If Washington had brought this to pass by his harsh retribution for the Boston Riot, he had made a serious mistake.

Washington and Trotter had declared a private war on each other, the Boston Riot being but a skirmish in that war. Scott was compiling at Tuskegee his blacklist of those who expressed sympathy or support for Trotter. Almost a year after the riot, Scott noticed in the *Guardian* an editorial reference to Judson W. Lyons of Georgia, the register of the Treasury, whom Washington had approved for reappointment as a holdover from the McKinley administration. The editorial said that Lyons's "repugnance to our being jailed by the Tuskegeean we shall ever appreciate." Filing the editorial "for future use," Scott wrote his chief: "Little by little, the names of the persons who have stood behind Trotter are being revealed."[74] The word went out among the Bookerites that Lyons was slated for removal when his term expired in 1905. R. W. Thompson soon spoke of an alliance between Lyons and the Tuskegean's enemies in Washington, D.C., Lafayette M. Hershaw and W. Calvin Chase. "He doesn't care a rap about the industrial policies of the Wizard," Thompson wrote of Lyons, "but he is skittish of the Doctor's supposed incursion into politics."[75] One of Scott's anonymous press releases early in 1905 charged that Hershaw, "bosom friend of Judson W. Lyons," had used Lyons's office in the Treasury Department to write anti-Roosevelt editorials for the *Bee* and the *Guardian*. The release stated ominously: "We have heard from reasonably good authority that something is likely to drop after March 4th."[76] When Roosevelt soon afterward removed Lyons, Washington and his lieutenants denied that Washington had had anything to do with it, though conceding that the President had consulted Washington about it.[77]

A delegation of Boston supporters of Washington took a more direct tack a few days after the riot. Led by the Reverend McMullen, they called on the mayor of Boston and asked him to remove Napoleon B. Marshall from the city tax office and George Forbes from the West End library.[78] There is no evidence that Washington directed this effort, and apparently it was unsuccessful.

Washington and Scott, however, were directly if secretly involved through Washington's personal lawyer, Wilford H. Smith, in an effort to further punish Trotter by a libel suit filed by William Pickens. An ambitious southern black, born in South Carolina and educated at Talladega College, an attendant at the Tuskegee Negro Conference in 1902, Pickens had asked Washington for help in the spring of 1902 when he learned that he had won a scholarship to Yale. "You see, I am wholly self-depent [sic], and will have to earn all my support and at the same time do the work of the college," he wrote. Pickens did not directly ask for money, but apologized for interrupting a man busy with "matter of far more consequence than the education of one Negro boy—but can you offer a suggestion or a bit of advice?"[79] Pickens was somehow enabled to attend Yale, and in 1903 he won the Yale oratory prize for a speech on Haiti that raised questions about its capacity for self-government, an echo of Washington's own graduation speech on Cuba a quarter-century earlier. Trotter was so outraged on hearing of the speech that he not only chided Pickens for "surrendering his self-respect" but attacked his personal appearance as "the little black freak student at Yale . . . with his enormous lips, huge mouth, and a monkey grin co-extensive with his ears."[80] When Washington himself had been the butt of similar racial stereotyping in the *Guardian,* he had remained silent,[81] but he was on the lookout for a *Guardian* libel not involving himself.

Since February 1903 Washington, Scott, and Wilford Smith had been scanning the *Guardian.* "I have taken out my subscription to the Guardian, and am examining the criminal statutes of Massachusetts," Smith wrote Scott under an assumed name.[82] A month later he expressed disappointment that the *Guardian* had been silent on Robert W. Taylor, the Tuskegee financial agent in Boston. "They seem so circumspect here of late I am beginning to fear that they suspect something," Smith complained.[83] When the Pickens libel appeared, it seemed made to order. Washington and Smith approached Pickens with an offer to help him sue. "Pickens hesitates about matter," Smith telegraphed Scott under a pseudonym. "Have written again urging him."[84] Washington pressed Smith to persuade Pickens.[85] Washington himself wrote Pickens on the day before the Boston Riot suggesting a meeting. With his eye on the future, Pickens answered: "Thanking you for yours of 29th July, I am glad to reply that it is my one unaltered and unalterable purpose to engage in some form of educational work. Doubtless you remember my writing you just before coming to Yale; and acting upon your kindly suggestion, I chose among my courses one in 'Systematic Pedagogy,' which I have pursued with pleasure and profit."[86]

The Boston Riot caused a speed-up in the timetable of the Pickens case. "By all means Trotter and Forbes must be muzzled, and at once," Smith wrote Washington. "Just as early as possible, I shall go to New Haven and exert my best endeavors to bring it about through the matter there."[87] Washington urged him to go there immediately and to telegraph the results of his meeting with Pickens, adding: "Both white and colored opinion now ripe for action."[88] A few days later Smith reported that Pickens had taken the bait: "Pickens was in to-day and he consents to do what we wish."[89]

Smith enlisted a white Boston lawyer in September 1903 for the prosecution of Trotter and Forbes for libel of William Pickens. Pickens meanwhile bound himself further to Washington's ideas and faction by a speech at a black church in Hartford. He said: "There can be no possible reason for doubt that the vast majority of our race must devote themselves to intelligent and useful manual work. This is Booker Washington's opinion, an opinion sadly misunderstood by many of his own people. He has been accused and assailed as if he had said that no negro, however capable, should lift his aspiration above the plow and the anvil; whereas his sayings from beginning to end disclose no excuse for the accusation."[90] Pickens said he would be willing to drop the suit if the *Guardian* apologized. From jail, where he was still serving his Boston Riot sentence, Trotter refused. He wrote his friend George Towns that his partner Forbes "is badly scared in this and wants me to join him in an abject apology, which I should almost rather die than agree to."[91] Forbes published an apology and retraction in the *Guardian* while Trotter was in jail, however, and Trotter was helpless to stop it.

Washington wrote Pickens that he had been wise "in permitting these men to make an apology and thus teaching them a lesson which I hope will be a benefit to them in the future." He denied even the slightest feeling of resentment of the continued attacks of the *Guardian* editors, having only pity for them.[92] A clearer glimpse into Washington's heart, however, is his letter to Smith after the apology: "I note, however, that nothing is signed on the part of Trotter. What about that side of the case?"[93] And he privately crowed to R. W. Thompson over "the apology made by Trotter and Forbes so as to prevent wearing stripes." The apology had been written by Smith and inserted without change in the *Guardian*. "I send this information as you may care to use sometime as rebuttal of their story that they have been glad to make the apology because Pickens has recanted or some such drivel as that."[94] As a reward for his suit, Washington offered Pickens a place in Tuskegee upon his graduation from Yale. Pickens was undecided for a month, insisted that "I have preferred your work to all others," but finally decided "that there is a greater need at my own College, Talladega."[95] In later years Pickens became an outspoken critic of Booker T. Washington and eventually a field secretary of the NAACP.[96]

T. Thomas Fortune, observing the success of the Pickens lawsuit, considered a libel suit of his own, but Scott quickly warned him against it. Trotter and his coterie were eager to have the public believe that they were being hounded, he said. "You may of course expect the cry to be set up that you are being influenced by the Wizard to bring this suit," he wrote Fortune, "and while I believe the dirty gang needs to be thoroughly repressed, I think just now an inopportune time for the suit to be brought."[97] Fortune responded that his suggestion had simply been a tease, but a month later Washington himself warned Fortune to say no more in the New York *Age* on the subject.[98]

Washington had other methods for harassment of the *Guardian*, including attempted purchase of a share of the paper, espionage on Trotter and his associates, and the founding of a rival newspaper. News soon came to Washington, after Forbes had apologized to Pickens, that the two editors of the *Guardian* had had a falling out. Forbes put his half of the *Guardian* stock in the hands of William H. Lewis to be disposed of without Trotter's knowledge.[99] Word came from Boston that a half-interest in the paper could be had for $100 down and $300 in notes.[100] "It would certainly be very interesting for Trotter to wake up some morning and find that the other half interest is in the hands of some special ones of our friends," Scott wrote his chief.[101] Trotter discovered and publicized, however, that Washington's lawyer Wilford Smith was trying to make the purchase, and this spurred Trotter's friends into raising the money to keep the *Guardian* under his control.[102]

Even before the Boston Riot, Washington had considered espionage as a weapon against Trotter, and the riot settled for him the issue of its appropriateness. In May 1903 a friend of Scott from his

Texas days, Melvin Jack Chisum, arrived in New York and began publishing a shortlived monthly, *The Impending Crisis,* in partnership with John E. Bruce. Passing a copy of the magazine's prospectus on to Washington, Scott wrote: "I know Chisum well. He will be amenable. . . ."[103] "I do not think Chisum is a very brainy man, but I do know he is resourceful and I think at the same time honorable," Scott further commented. "Our New York friend [Wilford H. Smith] can use Chisum in any way that we desire. Chisum formerly lived in Texas and I know him very well."[104] At a meeting in Trotter's house on September 1, 1903, some two months after the Boston Riot, "M. J. Chisholm [Chisum] of New York" was in attendance to help form the Boston Suffrage League, no doubt worming his way into the Boston radical's confidence by the extremeness of his rhetoric. One of the resolutions stated:

> Inasmuch, therefore, as Booker T. Washington has glorified the revised constitutions of the south, has minimized the Jim Crow car outrage, has attacked the wisdom of the 14th and 15th amendments to the constitution, has deprecated the primary importance of the ballot, has preached to the colored people the silent submission to intolerable conditions, and makes his people a by-word and laughing stock before the world, he is not a fit leader for the colored race and no President who recognizes him as a political leader should receive the colored vote of the north.

The body urged Roosevelt to "dispense with Booker Washington as our political spokesman."[105]

More significantly, Chisum was also present at a secret gathering at Trotter's house later that month. If Chisum may be believed, the Trotterites planned to go beyond the methods of the Boston Riot in a conspiracy for "disorder and possibly murder" at a meeting where Washington was to speak in a Cambridge black church. Chisum's report disappeared from Washington's office files at Tuskegee in 1906, but it is possible to partially reconstruct it through Emmett Scott's account of the meeting two years later:

> . . . it was finally decided in Trotter's home that when the meeting should be in full sway one of their number would light a bonfire in a near-by vacant lot, that another in the church should yell 'fire' and that a third should cut the electric wire, thereby throwing the church into darkness and confusion. This program of wrath, disorder and possibly murder, which Trotter and his gang had planned came near succeeding. At their

final meeting to perfect their arrangements a colored attorney of Boston, who had learned of their scheme, threw open the door, walked into the midst of the band and gave them to understand in no Sunday-school language that he had the names of every man and knew all the details of their plans. He further told them that if a single one of them attempted to carry out the plan, he would have them all in jail in a few hours. At this revelation the little gang was thunderstruck and scattered in every direction; not one of them dared to show his face at the meeting.[106]

On learning of this conspiracy, Washington said he was "most anxious that the last dastardly attempt on the part of that Boston crowd to disgrace the race be made public in some way."[107] But William H. Lewis, the Boston lawyer who had burst into the meeting, advised against it, saying: "I rather prefer to hold it as a club over their heads." He warned that Chisum's unsupported affidavit would be insufficient safeguard against a libel suit, which Trotter and his friends would be only too anxious to file in retaliation for the Pickens suit. "Besides," Lewis wrote, "I am not inclined to believe absolutely the story of our confidential friend. I think he has overdrawn it somewhat, and I am not sure that he did not himself make some of the propositions purporting to have been made by others."[108] Fortune independently reached a similar conclusion.[109] And the Trotterites denied the existence of such a plan. "I talked it over with Grimke but he knew nothing of it," Lewis reported. "I afterwards talked with [Clement] Morgan, who claimed that our man Chisholm set up his own man of straw and there was nothing in his story at all."[110]

Even as he tried to silence or intimidate Trotter, Washington was also attempting to put him out of business by sponsoring a rival newspaper that would share the small black readership and advertising clientele of the *Guardian*. Two members of the Boston branch of the National Negro Business League, William H. Moss and Peter J. Smith, began publishing the Boston *Advocate* in 1902. When it failed in 1903, they founded another at Washington's suggestion, the *Enterprise*.[111] Smith was among the lowliest of Washington's errand runners. At various times a job printer, government clerk, and podiatrist, Smith at this time made his living principally by providing a janitorial service for several downtown office buildings. Smith and Moss dedicated their paper to Washington's cause. "I should have it thoroughly 'Booker T. Washington,' and 'Theodore Roosevelt,' " wrote Smith.[112] When the

Enterprise collapsed two weeks before the Boston Riot,[113] Washington as a temporary expedient paid the editor of the Washington *Colored American* to send his paper to a list of Bostonians for three months.[114] In the fall of 1903, however, Washington subsidized Smith and J. Will Cole in establishing a third pro-Washington weekly, the Boston *Colored Citizen.*

"From time to time when anyone in the office has time to do it, I wish you would have editorial and other notes written out for the paper to be published in Boston by Mr. Peter J. Smith," Washington wrote Scott.[115] He also bought subscriptions for the entire Tuskegee faculty.[116] Smith was an inept journalist, however, no match for Trotter. He pleaded with Washington for a direct subsidy, saying: "all the editor wants is the kind of encouragement that greases the wheels of the machinery in a substantial way so as to have them run along smoothly."[117] Washington's response was that no black man in the country had been so well started off in the newspaper business. Smith replied, pleading the special circumstance that liberal Boston was a poor field for a conservative black newspaper.[118] For a loan of $300, Smith gave as security his half-interest in the newspaper.[119] In 1904 Scott began sending Smith regularly $65 a week.[120] When Smith said he needed even more, Scott answered indignantly: "You know there are no inexhaustible stores from which to draw these checks."[121]

Meanwhile, Washington and Scott made plans to replace Smith with someone more competent. Charles Alexander, a Tuskegee graduate and former employee in its print shop, was then teaching printing at Wilberforce University. He had once lived in Boston, and he agreed to take over the Boston *Colored Citizen* with the promise of a Tuskegee subsidy.[122] "Of course this arrangement is strictly between you and Mr. Washington," Scott explained, "and he expects that his name will not be used by you even in private conversation with any one."[123] Washington wrote Alexander that Smith would be too expensive to retain in any capacity and must gradually be let go.[124] Washington wanted to hold the reins of the *Colored Citizen,* but at the same time he was obsessed by the fear that Alexander would slip up and make certain what was already a suspicion in the *Guardian* office. He was alarmed to learn that Alexander had given his name as a reference to a type foundry company.[125] "I hope that you will let my name appear in the paper just as little as possible," he wrote, and later: "You will note that my name is mentioned twice in the correspondence and I hope you will see that it does not appear anywhere else in your paper this week."[126]

Washington had explained to Smith that he was making the change to Alexander because he could not afford to subsidize a paper from week to week.[127] But Alexander, though a more competent journalist, found it impossible to operate without a subsidy, and he soon applied for the $65 a week that Smith had received. "I am sure, Mr. Washington," he wrote, "that if you will have a little chat with some of your generous friends, and explain to them the necessity of *having a strong colored newspaper in Boston* that will advocate your cause with dignity and decency, I am convinced that you will be able to get the money necessary to run the paper in the way it ought to be run."[128]

Alexander asked for a capital investment of $5000, but Washington carefully limited his involvement to a weekly subsidy. "He feels and I feel," Scott explained, "that there is a great opportunity for the planting of a newspaper there, and where moral support can be given, and financial support to the extent already indicated, you will find him willing, but I do not think his disposition is at all in the direction of being led to go beyond the understanding already reached."[129] Trotter charged on the circumstantial evidence that Washington had "virtual ownership" of the *Colored Citizen*,[130] and even the friendly Francis J. Garrison, one of Washington's chief white defenders in Boston, inquired about his relationship with the paper. Washington replied with literal accuracy but with something less than candor: "The fact is, I do not own a dollar's worth of interest in a single Negro publication in this country."[131] The fact also was that without Washington's money there would have been no Boston *Colored Citizen*.

Along with their subsidy, Washington and Scott bedeviled Alexander with advice and direction, telling him that "a two and one-half column editorial would kill any paper in the world," that he should lift news of interest to blacks from the Boston dailies, that he should employ men to conduct a house-to-house canvass for subscriptions. They paid him for job printing of pamphlets and leaflets and wrote him letters of introduction to Boston business firms that might advertise in his paper.[132] Despite further business difficulties, Alexander found favor with Washington as a journalist. "Under all the circumstances," Washington wrote Scott, "I cannot see how he could have done better than he has."[133] Alexander was now part of the Tuskegee

Machine. "I think the idea of making Alexander president of the local [Business] League a very good one," Washington confided to the still-loyal Peter Smith.[134] Alexander became, instead, its secretary, a fact in which Trotter quickly saw sinister implications.[135] When the *Colored Citizen* collapsed in spite of its subsidies in about a year, Alexander converted it into the monthly *Alexander's Magazine,* which struggled along until 1909, drifting gradually toward an independence from Washington that ended in Alexander's last-ditch offer of the magazine to the newly formed NAACP.

Meanwhile, Boston became to a large extent Trotter territory. The next time Washington's friends in the area sought to honor him, in Cambridge in the fall of 1904, they chose to do so at a banquet for which tickets had to be purchased rather than in an open meeting. Not to be thwarted so easily, Trotter and his group schemed to hold an anti-Washington indignation meeting on the same night. They hired a hall and secretly printed circulars advertising their rally. Once again, however, they had an unsuspected Washington spy in their midst. This time it was Clifford H. Plummer, who had been the defense lawyer for Bernard Charles in the Boston Riot trial, and even that early had been negotiating with Washington.[136] Forewarned by Plummer, Washington's friends went to the owner of the hall and persuaded him to cancel their enemies' reservation. Meanwhile Plummer quietly gathered up and destroyed their circulars. He even succeeded in concealing his clandestine partnership with Washington. "I informed 'the gang' that I do not expect to attend the dinner," he wrote Washington, "which declaration by me made me eligible to any office within their gift, from the presidency of the United States, to a member of the common council from any ward in Boston or Cambridge."[137]

After this fiasco, Trotter went briefly into eclipse. Late in 1904 he was on his good behavior when Oswald Garrison Villard came to address the Boston Literary and Historical Association. Villard was the grandson of the great abolitionist William Lloyd Garrison, the son of a railroad baron, and a power in his own right as editor of the New York *Evening Post* and the *Nation.* He supported both Tuskegee and the civil rights cause, and both black factions hoped to capture him exclusively. Plummer, who was at the meeting, reported to Washington: "In all the history of this association we have never had a paper to equal it. No one there could help indorsing all that was said by him, other than a few who were there who must have felt a pang when he made reference to you several times in glowing terms, using words of this kind: 'That able and noble statesman, Booker T. Washington'; 'That courageous man of your race, Booker T. Washington'; and terms of this kind he brought in at intervals when he had made some most striking point."[138] Trotter made no attempt to reply, and Washington was amused to tell his friends "that the persons having in charge the Literary Society, have forbidden Mr. Trotter to use my name."[139] He knew too much of human nature, however, to believe that would last.

Washington's hope was to minimize in the eyes of others the importance of his Boston critics and to confine the revolt against him as far as possible to Boston. He insisted that the rank and file of black people in the country and even in Boston were behind him and his program, and his critics were only a dozen, or even a half-dozen soreheads. "What their ground of opposition is, is hard for me to understand," he wrote a white sympathizer. "I think it is largely jealousy or personal ill-will."[140] His critics were simply spoiled young men who had been educated beyond their intelligence, he explained to President Roosevelt. "In most cases, someone has taken these men up and coddled them by paying their way through college. At Tuskegee a man works for everything that he gets, hence we turn out real men instead of artificial ones." The appeal of his critics he explained partly by circumstances. "When a people are smarting under wrongs and injustices inflicted from many quarters," he wrote Roosevelt, "it is but natural that they should look about for some individual on whom to lay the blame for their seeming misfortunes, and in this case I seem to be the one."[141]

Despite his seeming complacency, Washington recognized that the Boston Riot and the whole Trotter campaign had weakened his claim to be the sole racial spokesman and leader. To combat this, he needed first of all to separate Du Bois, with all his distinction and dignity, from the Boston mischief-maker.

CHAPTER 3

Conference at Carnegie Hall

I am quite sure that several of the members, perhaps the majority of those who have been in opposition, are either silenced or won over to see the error of their way.*

BTW, 1904

A S HE saw black opposition to his leadership and his policy of compromise mount toward the Boston Riot, Washington knew that his best hope was not the leadership of a faction but spokesmanship for a unified black community. He understood the problem, but he did not know how to deal with it. Instead of meeting his critics halfway, he invited only some of them to a summit conference, and then packed the meeting to overshadow them with his numbers. His use of the methods of a political boss rendered his effort at black unity, or at least the isolation of Trotter, abortive. The New York Conference, held in secret in Carnegie Hall, January 6–8, 1904, is nevertheless instructive because it reveals that Washington's whole purpose was not to persuade or treat with his critics but to outmaneuver and overwhelm them.

As early as 1900 Washington had vaguely considered calling a gathering of twelve to fifteen prominent black men to discuss concerted action for racial advancement.[1] In early 1903, while he had Du Bois at Tuskegee to discuss a position he had offered him as director of

*BTW to William H. Baldwin, Jr., Jan. 22, 1904.

research, the two men disagreed about the job offer but agreed on the desirability of a jointly sponsored conference of leading Afro-Americans. Washington delayed action, however, until he could consult T. Thomas Fortune, then on a government mission in the Philippines. He wrote Du Bois: "I am very anxious that the meeting be not confined to those who may agree with my own views regarding education and the position which the race shall assume in public affairs, but that it shall in every respect represent all the interests of the race." Washington found Clement G. Morgan of Boston, a Trotterite whom Du Bois proposed, acceptable as a substitute for Trotter. He asked Du Bois to write Morgan the letter of invitation, however, saying, "I do not know him very well and then besides I rather have the idea that he has some feeling against me and would not perhaps under the circumstances be inclined to consider favorably anything that I might say."[2] Next he asked Fortune's opinion of "a two or three days private and quiet conference concerning the present condition and future of the race."[3]

Similar letters went to nineteen other prominent black men, most of them thoroughly committed to Washington's outlook and his leadership. "It is important that this matter be kept entirely private at present," stated each of the letters.[4] Washington himself broke security, however, in a speech. He referred to a possible gathering of a "group of representative southern white men, and northern white men, and Negroes" to "meet and consider with the greatest calmness and business sagacity the whole subject [of voting rights] as viewed from every standpoint." Trotter, knowing or sensing something of the plans for a conference, asked editorially: "What Does Booker Want With a Conference?" The black suffrage question had already been decided by constitutional amendments thirty years earlier, said Trotter, and needed no review by a self-appointed conference.[5]

Du Bois wrote confidentially to Kelly Miller, a mathematics professor of Howard University, that his own "judicious pressure and insistence led to your invitation and that of Morgan of Cambridge." He said he thought this conference would afford a good chance for "a heart to heart talk with Mr. Washington," and proposed a platform:

Full political rights on the same terms as other Americans
Higher education of selected Negro youth
Industrial education for the masses

Common school training for every Negro child

A stoppage to the campaign of self-deprecation

A careful study of the real conditions of the Negro

A National Negro periodical

A thorough and efficient federation of Negro societies and activities

The raising of a defense fund

A judicious fight in the courts for civil rights [6]

After a month or so, when Du Bois inquired again about the plans for the conference, Washington pleaded the difficulty of choosing a date when so many busy people could meet.[7] In the fall of 1903, after Andrew Carnegie had assured him of a subsidy to pay the expenses of the conference, Washington revived the plan and set the date at January 6–8, 1904, in the meeting rooms of Carnegie Hall in New York. He modified the original plan to include an invitation to some of his white philanthropist friends to meet with the black participants during one afternoon. It is not clear that Du Bois was consulted about these modifications, but he apparently drifted into acceptance of Washington's unilateral planning of the conference.

Washington tried to limit the number of black participants to twenty, but the number gradually grew to twenty-eight, most of whom accepted the invitation. In the last few days, the Reverend Francis J. Grimké decided not to go and suggested his brother Archibald as a substitute. Washington accepted this after some argument about geographical and occupational balance. The prospect of the conference evoked enthusiasm, particularly in the Booker Washington faction. Blacks faced "troublous and stormy times," said the Reverend Isaiah B. Scott of New Orleans, and resistance to the tide of white aggression should begin without delay. "God bless you in all your efforts for the race and for humanity."[8] Kelly Miller as usual found his place somewhere between the two factions of the black leadership dispute. "We have invited two worlds (white and black) to come and reason together," he wrote a friend at Tuskegee. "It is indeed a momentous undertaking, and I am almost overawed at the audacity of it. The effort, however, must not prove abortive, if so, it will serve to estop future movements of like character."[9]

Friction and cross-purposes appeared among the black delegates. "I

have not told you before," Washington wrote Fortune, "but some of
the parties who have been asked to meet in the conference have made
a special fight against your being invited. . . . For you not to be present would place me in rather an awkward position."[10] The Georgia
politician Judson W. Lyons, register of the United States Treasury,
also at first declined to come, on the ground that it would do some
unspecified harm to the Republican Party. Washington pleaded with
him to change his mind. "I cannot understand how a private conference, composed of a few of our leading men, could in any way endan-
ger party success," he wrote Lyons. "Practically every man who will be
present is a worshipper and supporter of Mr. Roosevelt, and none
more so than myself." Washington said he was sure the President
would approve of the conference if he knew of it.[11] This invitation
was some months before Washington learned that Lyons had expressed sympathy for Trotter after the Boston Riot and Trotter's trial.
Both Fortune and Lyons consented to attend.

Events arising after the first proposal of the conference were giving
Du Bois pause, however. He had declined a job at Tuskegee. *The Souls
of Black Folk,* trenchantly criticizing Washington, had been published.
The Afro-American Council imbroglio in the spring and the Boston
Riot in July had brought Du Bois to the decision to join the radical
dissenters against Washington's compromises. Du Bois at first failed
to reply in November 1903 when Washington wrote him for advice in
reactivating the plans for a conference. "Of course the main object of
the New York Conference," Washington wrote, "is to try to agree upon
certain fundamental principles and to see in what way we understand
or misunderstand each other and correct mistakes as far as possible."[12] Du Bois was waiting to see the final list of those invited before
he would agree to participate.[13] Washington telegraphed Du Bois six
days later asking for a reply at once.[14] The next day Scott informed
Washington: "DuBois in letter today, testily refuses further advice in
conference matter."[15] What Du Bois wrote was: "I do not think it will
be profitable for me to give further advice which will not be followed.
The conference is yours and you will naturally constitute it as you
choose."[16]

Faced with the possible collapse or irrelevance of the conference if
Du Bois refused to attend, Washington urged William H. Lewis to
second the invitation to Clement Morgan, to tell him: "If he really
wants to help the race, this is his opportunity."[17] Morgan responded

with some cogent questions, possibly on prompting from Du Bois: "I should be glad to know who will make up the conference, what the scope of it, and what, if any, the plan of procedure."[18] Procedure, Washington replied, would be decided when they met. He sent a list of those invited. "I should think, however," he wrote, "that all the subjects we would want to take up might be comprehended under the following heads: Educational, political, moral and religious, and sociological, but that will be a matter for the conference to determine."[19] The breadth of Washington's agenda for the conference suggested his consensus view of its purpose. What Du Bois feared was that it would amount to nothing more than a "BTW ratification meeting."[20] Washington's concern, on the other hand, was that if many of Du Bois's sympathizers in the North were invited, "we should be very sure that there is a large element in the conference who actually know Southern conditions by experience and who can speak with authority, and we should not have to depend too much on mere theory and untried schemes of Northern colored people."[21]

Washington made a special plea to Edward H. Morris, a Chicago lawyer thoroughly alienated from his leadership. Washington offered to pay "all your expenses of travel and board" and urged Morris to keep the whole matter "absolutely confidential" and to "speak on the subject to no one else." He emphasized what he believed to be the importance of the conference to the future of the race, saying: "I do not believe that there has ever been a meeting so fraught with value and seriousness."[22] Washington also urged S. Laing Williams of his own faction in Chicago to urge Morris to accept. Williams promised to see Morris and remarked shrewdly: "It is a good stroke of policy to put him in a position where he must 'either fish or cut bait.' "[23]

The personnel problems continued to plague Washington. Lewis suggested that, if Morgan should decline, George Forbes be invited. Forbes had recently quarreled with Trotter and resigned from the *Guardian,* but Washington vetoed inviting him. "Du Bois is very sensitive on the question as to who shall be invited," he wrote Lewis, "in fact I very much fear he is trying to find an excuse to absent himself, and I have the feeling rather strongly that if Forbes is invited since he has made a break with Trotter that Du Bois will object, for he does not object to saying that we are trying to pack the conference with people who are thinking in a certain direction."[24] When Francis Grimké, who was not even going to attend the conference, proposed several persons to be invited, perhaps at Du Bois's instigation, Washington wrote to Du Bois objecting that this would make the conference too large to accomplish its objects.[25] The only one Washington singled out for special objection was Grimké's brother Archibald. Two others had already been invited from Boston, Washington pointed out, and said, "in politics I understand that he is a Democrat, and you will note that we have already invited one prominent Democrat from the West."[26] Meanwhile, Washington himself made sure that his own faction in Boston would have a representative. He arranged that, if W. H. Lewis had to be absent on official duties during part of the conference, Samuel E. Courtney would be his alternate.[27] Francis Grimké meanwhile demolished the objection to his brother by saying, "my brother is not a democrat and never has been. He is what is known as a Mugwump or Independent in politics."[28]

All through December 1903 Washington worked to weave the web of his conference without losing his control of its membership. He wrote Morris a second letter and also asked his Philadelphia friend John S. Durham to urge Morris to attend, "and explaining some of my views."[29] He wrote second letters to Judson Lyons, Clement Morgan, and Fredrick L. McGhee.[30] One by one the members of the anti-Washington faction accepted. Two weeks before the conference, Morgan was the only hold-out. He asked that "the enclosed names" be added to the list, "that I may disarm some criticism, already brewing and sure to increase."[31] The list is no longer attached to his letter. It probably included Archibald Grimké, however, for in an eleventh-hour meeting with Francis Grimké, Whitefield McKinlay speaking for Washington persuaded him to accept P. B. S. Pinchback as a substitute for his brother, or actually for himself.[32] Washington then "yielded to the earnest solicitation of various parties" and invited Archibald Grimké.[33]

Privately, Washington was thoroughly out of sorts over this family politics and the necessity of inviting Archibald Grimké. He sent his friend McKinlay a copy of his telegram of invitation and said: "I confess to you I have sent this telegram very much against my own personal wishes and sense of what is right and proper, because I do not feel that Archibald Grimke has ever done anything to entitle him to membership in such a body. In the second place, he represents a noisy, turbulent and unscrupulous set of men to such an extent that I cannot feel that he would enter into the serious and far-sighted deliberations of such a conference in the way that we plan to enter into it. I wish, however, directly or indirectly, you would say to Mr. Grimke that the conference is called for a serious purpose and not for the purpose of airing personal grievances or entering into a scramble, and that if he attempts to have the same kind of 'nigger meeting' that was had in Washington a few days ago, it will be much wiser for him not to go to New York."[34] That was certainly not a warm invitation, but it covered up the fact that in general it was the Washington and not the Du Bois faction that got its way in the choice of conferees.

It proved impossible to keep secret the fact that the New York Conference was occurring. Even before the meeting the Boston *Guardian* and the Chicago *Conservator* both carried editorials that could only have been written with inside knowledge. Fortune called this "a rank betrayal of confidence on the part of some one of the invited," and suspected Du Bois and Morris. "Neither of them is above such conduct," he charged.[35] Washington himself wrote to Theodore Roosevelt telling him confidentially of the conference, "composed of those who agree as well as those who disagree on important matters." He said he would call on Roosevelt on his way to New York "with the hope that you may have some suggestion to put before the conference."[36] Washington also informed his philanthropic friends, particularly Carnegie and William H. Baldwin, Jr., whom he planned to invite into the conference at the appropriate moment. He thus applied a double standard of secrecy, one applying to the other delegates and another applying to himself.

When Washington first consulted his white associates prior to the conference, their reaction was so negative that apparently something like a quarrel took place over the telephone. "I think that I owe you an apology for the manner in which I spoke to Mr. Baldwin over the telephone concerning the conference," Washington wrote Wallace Buttrick, secretary of the Rockefeller-funded General Education Board. "Judging from what Mr. Baldwin said, I thought that objection was made to the conference on the ground that it would be displeasing to the Southern white people. If this had been the cause of the objection, I should feel, (and I am sure that you would share the feeling with me) that we have already gone as far as decency permits in our attempt to avoid stirring up Southern feeling." He said he was glad to hear that the objections were on other grounds.[37] Whatever their initial objections, however, Baldwin and several northern members of the Southern Education Board agreed to visit the conference, which, incidentally, would strengthen Washington's hand there by showing what powerful white allies he had. Fortune suggested that Washington further control events by making Emmett Scott the secretary of the conference. "You would then be sure of the accuracy of the report of the proceedings for future reference," wrote Fortune.[38] Scott did attend, but the conference chose, instead, the compromiser Kelly Miller as secretary.

Du Bois must have realized as soon as he saw the list of those invited that Washington had outmaneuvered him. While he had been considering the issues to be discussed, Washington had been gathering the manpower. Du Bois estimated the factional division of delegates at sixteen to nine in Washington's favor. In a confidential memorandum to his faction on the eve of the conference, he divided the conferees into six classes: "Unscrupulously for Washington"; for Washington "without enthusiasm or with scruples" (Robert R. Moton and others); "Uncertain, leaning to Washington" (Bishop Walters and others); "Uncertain, possibly against Washington"; "Anti-Washington"; and "Uncompromisingly Anti-Washington." He warned:

The tactics of the pro-Washington men will take one or more of the following forms—a. Conciliation and compromise. b. Irritation and browbeating. c. Silent shutting off of discussion by closure methods. Come prepared therefore in case of a. to be firm and hammer at the principles and Washington's record. b. to keep good temper and insist on free speech. c. to protest against closure or underhand methods even to the extent of leaving the meeting. Bring every speech or letter or record of Washington men you can lay hands on so that he can face his record in print. The main issue of this meeting is *Washington*, refuse to be sidetracked.[39]

Trotter, doubtless irked at being excluded from this gathering of black leaders, publicized every rumor or leak he could get wind of. "But why not let us know who are to be invited?" asked the *Guardian*. "Why have it a secret? And above all, let both sides be equally represented. No tricks, Mr. Washington."[40] This editorial a week before the conference gave Washington reason to distrust the good faith of the Du Bois faction and he wrote to Du Bois at once: "I find that some of the men invited have such a low sense of honor that one or two have deliberately given out to the press the substance of the correspondence which I have had with them. It is impossible for one to feel at ease when in conference with men who have no sense of honor."[41] Trotter went so far as to go to New York and try to crash the conference, but he was not allowed inside.[42] Nevertheless, he was there in spirit, for Morgan at Du Bois's request brought to the conference the nine questions Trotter had tried to get Washington to answer at the Boston Riot.[43]

In such an atmosphere of mutual distrust, it is surprising that the conference met at all, and even more surprising that it ran its full course. Few details survive, for the conferees were enjoined, in the interest of secrecy, against even taking notes. According to Du Bois's memory three years later, the Du Bois faction told Washington "frankly behind closed doors with the other men present, the things we objected to in his program. We did not object to industrial education, we did not object to his enthusiasm for its advancement, we did object to his attacks upon higher training and his general attitude of belittling the race and not putting enough stress upon voting and things of that sort."[44]

What Du Bois remembered best and longest was the chilling presence of Washington's white friends near the end of the conference, just when it could have been expected to begin resolving the factional conflicts among the blacks. The white delegation included Andrew Carnegie and three members of the Southern Education Board, William H. Baldwin, Jr., Robert C. Ogden, and George Foster Peabody. Also on hand were three of Washington's white journalist allies, Oswald Garrison Villard of the *Nation* and New York *Evening Post,* Lyman Abbott of the *Outlook,* and William Hayes Ward of the *Independent.* That the whites acted on Washington's cue is suggested by a letter Baldwin wrote Washington during the conference: "If you have any special points that you want me to refer to, send them to me."[45] "There was considerable speaking," Du Bois remembered years later, "but the whole purpose of the conference seemed revealed by the invited white guests and the tone of their message. . . . Their words were lyric, almost fulsome in praise of Mr. Washington and his work, and in support of his ideas. Even if all they said had been true, it was a wrong note to strike in a conference of conciliation."[46]

After the white visitors had left, tempers grew short and the disagreements became more personal. Lewis at one point noticed Morgan writing and accused him of taking notes of the meeting, contrary to agreement. Morgan angrily replied that he was writing a letter to his wife.[47] The conference ended with speeches by Washington and Du Bois and the passage of resolutions. While the Du Bois faction later recalled most vividly how they had talked up to Washington, his own faction remembered Washington's "wonderful speech" at the end that sent the delegates home "knowing you better and appreciating you more for your great work for the race and mankind." A few days after the conference Courtney sent to Tuskegee his impression of Archibald Grimké's conversion as a result of the persuasiveness of Washington's final speech: "Wish you might have heard him tell how he and Morgan were completely overcome by your frank and most convincing address. He admits that they had never measured you correctly, and he tells me how Morgan told him that he could scarcely refrain from weeping when you gave your experiences after that 'White House Dinner.'" Courtney believed that Washington's critics present were "completely overwhelmed by your big heartedness and wonderful calmness and modesty."[48]

Courtney, however, was a blind partisan, incapable of judging the extent of remaining disagreement. Washington had anticipated and possibly hoped that Du Bois and his faction would decide at the last minute not to attend the conference and thus expose themselves to criticism for fearing to confront Washington. Du Bois sensed that possibility and urged his faction to attend, but Washington's candor and reasonableness in the face of criticism may have caused Du Bois to regret his participation in the meeting.

The "Summary of Proceedings" that Kelly Miller prepared contained "the sense of this conference" rather than the exchange of views. The conferees agreed that the bulk of the black people should remain in the South and struggle there for political and civil equality, but at the same time individuals might properly be encouraged to pursue opportunities by migration to the North or West. Second, there was a Du Bois point: "that in a democratic republic the right to vote is of paramount importance to every class of citizens and is preservative of all other rights and interests." Third, the conference opposed all restrictions of civil rights in travel and public accommodations and urged court suits to enforce these rights, and stood for "no compromise, or equivocal statement, respecting our civil rights." This was an indirect reference to Washington's frequent equivocations on civil rights, the subject of Trotter's shrill questions during the Boston Riot six months earlier. The resolution on education endorsed all its forms, elementary, industrial, and collegiate. The conferees denounced lynching; and while they condemned rape they were certain that "skillfully exaggerated reports of rapeful assault" were being used to discredit blacks. The conference agreed that blacks should cooperate with southern whites whenever they could "without compromise of manhood." A future conference of northern whites, southern whites, and blacks to consider means of solving the race problem was endorsed. Finally, it was the "sense of the conference" that an effort should be made "to disseminate a knowledge of the truth in regard to all matters affecting our race."

By unanimous vote the New York Conference approved the establishment of a "Committee of Safety with twelve members" to be a bureau of information and to "seek to unify and bring into cooperation the action of the various organizations" and sections of the country. Washington, Du Bois, and Hugh M. Browne, head of a state industrial school for blacks in Pennsylvania, were made members of this committee and authorized to select the other nine members. Why Du Bois acquiesced in this arrangement is not clear, but it may have been because he mistakenly regarded Browne as an uncommitted delegate rather than a Washington partisan. A final resolution expressed gratitude to Booker T. Washington for his "thoughtful initiative" in calling the conference and his "helpful address delivered before the closing session of the conference."[49]

Rumors began to fly even before the conference disbanded—some of them wild and without foundation. At Tuskegee, because of the unusual absence of both Washington and Scott, Washington's brother John reported: "For the last two days there have been numerous rumors on the school grounds, in town, and inquiries have come from Montgomery and other places in the State." Among the rumors were that Scott had been shot in Washington, that Scott was confined to his room there very sick, and that Booker T. Washington himself had been shot.[50] Washington quickly put these rumors to rest, but there were others that contained more truth. Two days after the conference Washington wrote Courtney in Boston: "It is persistently repeated that Trotter has a plan for giving out later on, either in his own paper, or in some white paper, the entire proceedings, real or imaginary, of our conference." Since Archibald Grimké had promised to prevent this, Washington asked Courtney to "see that Mr. Grimke keeps his hand

on Trotter." He added: "Do not use my name."[51] Washington's telegram found Courtney out of town, but his wife immediately called
Lewis on the telephone and he took care of the matter. By the time
Courtney reached the office of the Associated Press, they had already
agreed to suppress Trotter's revelations. Courtney also spoke to
Grimké, who renewed his promise to see that Trotter dropped the
matter and promised to call a conference of all factions in Boston to
try to moderate their differences.[52]

Despite these efforts, Trotter tried to get a pretended account of
the New York Conference into the New York *Sun,* and nearly succeeded. Hearing of it, Charles W. Anderson and Emmett Scott "re-
paired to the Sun office . . . and going directly to the managing editor succeeded in holding it out." Washington apparently knew the
contents of Trotter's manuscript, for he described it as one that anyone could have written and "not based on information directly given
respecting the conference."[53] An editorial in the *Guardian,* however,
showed that Trotter had somehow gained direct information from a
participant. He referred, for example, to Baldwin's offer to finance a
suit that Du Bois and Washington discussed at the conference, to be
undertaken against Pullman car segregation. This "must have been
the result of information given by some one who was a member of
the Carnegie Hall Conference," said Anderson.[54]

Anderson and Scott did not succeed in getting a copy of Trotter's
manuscript article sent to the New York *Sun,* but Trotter apparently
thought they did. He angrily accused the editor of the *Sun* of handing
it over to his "most inveterate enemy in New York." Anderson was
delighted that Trotter was "laboring under the impression that it is
carefully tucked away in the pockets of my old gray gaberdine."[55]
Washington asked Anderson to continue to try to secure a copy for
future use against Trotter. Meanwhile, Scott said: "I think it would be
well to have Trotter feel that we have this copy, or rather think it well
not to disabuse his mind of the thought that it is in our possession."[56]
Finding the *Sun* reporter who had written a story on the manuscript,
Anderson told him that he "would gladly pay him for the copy if he
would secure it for us. He looked high and low at the office, but could
not find it, and thinks it must have been destroyed." The editor also
promised to search for the manuscript and give it to Anderson if
found, but it apparently had vanished.[57]

In the aftermath of the New York Conference other Bookerites, as

Washington's faction was coming to be called, had more encouraging news. Robert R. Moton, who was more clearly in Washington's camp than Du Bois believed, wrote that Archibald Grimké had said to him that "Washington's speech is unanswerable and he is undoubtedly working for the best interests of the Negro," and that "there is simply a difference in method and lack of understanding." Moton wrote that he also planned to invite Du Bois to spend a few days at Hampton on his way south, in order to soften the impact of Hollis B. Frissell's harsh review of *The Souls of Black Folk* in the *Southern Workman*. Moton wrote Washington: "I think we can, in a quiet way, change the whole front of that band of Negroes who seem to be opposing everything that does not coincide with their narrow and I fear in many cases selfish ideas."[58] Washington, however, persuaded Moton not to issue the invitation to Du Bois. He said that some months earlier Baldwin had invited Du Bois to his house for "a frank conference," and Du Bois "afterwards said that it was the purpose of Mr. Baldwin to try to bribe him or change his opinion regarding Hampton and Tuskegee and myself." In fact, Du Bois had vaguely referred to this at the New York Conference. Washington warned Moton that his own invitation might be interpreted by the hypersensitive Du Bois as a bribe.[59]

Looking back on the conference, Washington decided that it had on the whole been a success. He wrote to William H. Baldwin, Jr.: "I am quite sure that several of the members, perhaps the majority of those who have been in opposition, are either silenced or won over to see the error of their way. There were others of whom this cannot be said, but will have to be watched in the future in order to determine how they should be classed. All of them, however, I am sure, were overwhelmed by the general sentiment of the conference and by the high character of the men present. I feel that it was a very helpful meeting from every point of view and among the most important efforts that I have ever had part in."[60]

Acting in the spirit of the conference, J. C. Asbury, editor of the *Odd Fellows' Journal,* urged his fellow-conferee James H. Hayes to diminish his criticisms of the Republican Party, on the ground that "the man who attempts to secure [his] rights by 'menacing' the only friend he has ever had is a very poor tactician." He urged Hayes also to try to understand Washington better. "I regard him as thoroughly sound upon every question affecting the progress of the Race. He is just a little more diplomatic than the rest of us and consequently more successful; and as you know in times of peace diplomacy rules the world. As Lewis of Boston wrote me a couple of years ago 'he is trying to get the wooden horse inside the walls of Troy.' " [61]

Many of Washington's contemporaries doubted his Trojan horse role, however, because his self-help and solidarity preachment seemed an uncertain remedy for white persecution, and because his compromises and humility seemed to encourage further humiliation by arrogant whites. The factional fighting continued unabated. At the Bethel Literary and Historical Association in Washington, D.C., only a few days after the New York Conference, one of the conference participants, Edward H. Morris, gave a lecture on "Shams," a scathing attack on Washington as though the uneasy truce of the conference had never been agreed on. The attack was especially exasperating after Washington had so carefully maneuvered Morris into attending the conference. Morris's bitter tone shocked Moton, who had just talked with Morris at a banquet in Morris's honor before the lecture, where "he took as liberal views on the situation and Mr. Washington as one could wish." Moton concluded that Morris had "prepared his paper before leaving Chicago and felt obliged to get it off." [62] That may have been the case, but Washington's feeling was that Morris was simply "a hard and difficult creature without any sense of honor." As usual, Washington saw only a personal attack in what was essentially an ideological criticism. "If he wanted to attack me he had an opportunity during the three days we were together face to face in a manly, straightforward way," Washington complained, "but he was too big a coward for that, but waited until he got an opportunity to do so behind my back." [63]

Washington took this criticism more seriously than it deserved, and arranged for accounts to be gathered in order to answer them at some appropriate time without calling Morris's name. Roscoe Conkling Bruce reported that, by adroitly quoting from Washington's writings and speeches, Morris "built up a proposition made up of half truths, as would any small lawyer, in order to win his case." Another witness wrote: "His speech was, all in all, about the cleverest piece of sophistry I've ever heard. He made skillful use of extracts from your books and speeches, which, taken out of their original settings, were twisted and construed to make you a sham and a traitor to the best interests of the Negro." [64] Bruce illustrated this style of presentation: "His case was simply this—quoting from Dr. Washington he said, 'I recently saw a young colored man reading or studying a French grammar' and very adroitly failed to finish the sentence which described the squalor and dirt by which he was surrounded and which to any intelligent reader would say that before we take up the books of classic culture, let us have clean homes." Bruce gave several other examples of quoting out of context.[65]

Cyrus Field Adams in his report to Washington paraphrased Morris as saying: "It is generally believed that Booker Washington believes in the natural inferiority of the Negro, that he should have a special place in American civilization, separate and distinct from other peoples and that he should consider the suffrage as of secondary importance." Morris also allegedly objected to Washington's "funny stories showing up the weaknesses of the race," and even his standard "gospel of the toothbrush" in that it gave whites a wrong idea of blacks.[66] One Bookerite even charged that Morris in a church pulpit "three times declared his non-belief in Christianity preferring nature and her wonderful teachings."[67] Actually, this naturalistic view was probably the one point at which Washington's and Morris's ideas may have joined, but Washington carefully kept his liberal theology quiet.

There was some disagreement as to how Morris's audience responded to his speech. One estimate was that the audience of about 1500 persons was about evenly divided, but another said four-fifths supported Morris. So forceful was the speaker that at first only a lowly government clerk, John Ewing, would speak in defense of Washington. Soon, however, Judge Robert H. Terrell, J. C. Napier, and P. B. S. Pinchback gathered courage to speak. "Pinchback's was such a slobber that it probably did more harm than good," Bruce Evans reported. He himself claimed to have "made two efforts for recognition but soon found that the preference of the President was for anti-Bookerites." S. Laing Williams also defended Washington, but the presiding officer called time on him after three minutes.[68] John C. Dancy lamely explained afterwards: "I declined to speak lest my remarks should have taken a course which would have appeared personal, which I always try to avoid."[69] Having the last word and "being skilled in coarse sarcasm by long practice," Morris held up to ridicule those who had defended Washington's leadership and his race program.[70] The currently anti-Washington local editor, W. Calvin Chase, challenged Terrell's claim that nine-tenths of blacks in the nation's capital favored the Tuskegean's leadership, and Chase proposed a resolution that Morris's speech expressed the sentiments of District blacks. "For God's sake don't let it pass," shouted Pinchback. The chair ruled the resolution out of order, but Chase was sure it would have passed by four to one.[71] Even Washington's strongest advocates conceded that Morris's speech had inflamed the already hotly debated question of the wisdom of Washington's methods of race leadership.[72]

"Although the Doctor does not intend to categorically dignify the small fry by directly referring to them," Scott wrote confidentially, "I think he will clean up the ground rather effectively with the whole batch before he is through with them. You will remember how he whipped them in his speech at the New York conference, and I have [no] doubt that he will go after them in much the same way at Washington."[73]

In short, the New York Conference had not succeeded at all in its main objective of laying factional differences to rest and unifying the leadership of the race. Washington himself was soon referring to "smoking out the opposition" as a legitimate activity.[74] Charles Anderson thoroughly approved of a return to aggressive methods. "A good thrashing would convince these young upstarts," he wrote the Wizard. "My experience in politics is, that he is whipped oftenest who is whipped easiest, and I long ago made up my mind to give my opponent the best I have in my shop, when he sets himself the task of fighting me."[75] On the other hand, this return to factionalism as usual was an admission that Washington's conference had failed.

Carrying out the mandate of the New York Conference, Washington, Du Bois, and Hugh M. Browne undertook to organize the standing Committee of Twelve for the Advancement of the Negro Race. "Even before our committee is formed," Washington wrote Du Bois, "I think there are one or two matters that we might attend to effectively. He suggested that they ask his lawyer, Wilford H. Smith, to prepare a leaflet of instructions to blacks on how to qualify for jury service. "If the facts and proper instruction as to methods of procedure are put before the colored people and they do not secure representation upon juries they will have no one to blame but themselves," Washington wrote. He suggested also a pamphlet on requirements for voting in the various southern states. Surely many blacks would be able to vote if they would remember to pay their poll taxes by the deadline.[76] That last remark could not have been very persuasive to Du Bois, who refused on principle to pay his own poll tax.

A conference resolution also authorized the committee to reprint and distribute an article on the Negro and the South which the white veteran libertarian Carl Schurz had recently published in *McClure's*.[77] Du Bois agreed with Washington that "both the matters you suggest are important and should be attended to immediately."[78] It was harder, however, to arrange for an organizational meeting of a committee of three that was to choose the Committee of Twelve. They decided on a meeting in New York in March 1904, two months after the conference. Meanwhile, Washington and Du Bois collected from their friends suggestions for members of the expanded committee and proposals for the structure and functions of the committee. Washington proposed simply a secretary and a "working committee of five" to act between meetings. He proposed "Turning the attention of the race to the importance of constructive, progressive effort," calling attention to examples of black success, emphasis on "the points upon which the race agrees," campaigns for voter registration, and the correcting of errors and misstatements about the race in white publications. As Washington saw it, the aim of the committee should be, above all, "the unification of the race in the near future."[79]

Du Bois proposed a more elaborate, even grandiose program that in many features foreshadowed his later Niagara Movement. He proposed that a "Committee of Safety" of twelve meet quarterly, a "General Committee" of 120 meet annually, and "Committees of Correspondence" be organized in every black community. Du Bois proposed an annual "relief fund" of $12,000. The Committee of Safety he wanted further divided into six sub-committees of two members each to keep watch on the various concerns of the race—political action, defense and information, legal redress, social reform, economic cooperation, and organization and finance. Du Bois would have "the Committee of Safety," as he insisted on calling it, concern itself with matters ranging as widely as political action, petitions for kindergartens, consumers' leagues, and a crusade against tuberculosis among blacks.[80]

"I think the plan of Dr. Du Bois has some good points in it toward which we should work," Washington privately confided to Browne, "but I have the feeling that it is rather large and complicated for our present purposes." Washington's own greater political experience led him to "the feeling that the smaller the number, the more effectively one can work." He wrote Du Bois and Hugh Browne that perhaps if they could succeed with a simple committee of twelve members for a year or two, then perhaps they could enlarge the structure.[81]

The committee of three, following its parent body, met in secret without minutes, but clearly the voting was consistently two to one against Du Bois. He, Archibald Grimké, and Charles E. Bentley of Chicago were the only ones chosen to represent the anti-Washington faction. All the others were moderates leaning toward Washington or unambiguously Washington men. Though these proportions did probably reflect the relative power relationship between the factions and was about the same ratio as the New York Conference member-ship itself, that was small comfort to Du Bois. He might believe that the ratio did not represent proportionally the brainpower of the two factions, but Washington in this situation had again shown himself the master politician who had outmaneuvered the black intellectual once again. Even Bentley, one of Du Bois's choices for the Committee of Twelve, had some obligation to Washington, for he was a substitute at Washington's insistence for Edward H. Morris, who had been Du Bois's first choice. Anderson told Bentley and then reported it to Washington that "*I thought* you regarded him as a man, who, while not altogether approving of your course, was at the same time willing to endorse the large part of your work, and a man who was not an insane and irrational opponent." Anderson also learned that Bentley already knew what had gone on at the meeting. "Du Bois has evi-dently told his cohorts all," Anderson wrote Washington. "*I was careful to remind him that you had not done so with yours.*"[82]

Washington scheduled the first meeting of the Committee of Twelve to be in St. Louis at a black church on July 1, 1904, when he was to be in town for a speech at the St. Louis Exposition. Du Bois did not respond to this call, however. At a late date, his wife wired Washing-ton: "Du Bois ill, probably cannot attend St. Louis meeting."[83] Wash-ington postponed the meeting until a week later in New York. Again Du Bois absented himself. He had apparently decided that the com-mittee was so thoroughly in Washington's control that it would not accomplish any of his own ends. He was also disturbed that its funds came from an undisclosed source through Washington, and correctly surmised that the money came from Andrew Carnegie. For about a decade Carnegie gave the Committee of Twelve the same amount he gave the National Negro Business League, $2700 á year.[84] "For my part," remarked Emmett Scott, "I am all but glad that Du Bois was not present. To my mind he has all but decided to flock by himself. I think he will be practically harmless from now on."[85]

Lacking Du Bois's counterpoint, the Committee of Twelve unanimously adopted all of the recommendations that Washington presented. Scott, whose loyalty often outran his judgment, declared it "the only sane program that has been offered during the whole of the conferences and meetings of these various men."[86] Its moderation in the face of the worsening race problem probably confirmed Du Bois's suspicions. Washington's suggestions were that the committee's work should be mainly directed in certain channels: "Turning the attention of the race to the importance of constructive, progressive effort, and the attention of the country to Negro successes. Emphasizing and keeping before the public, points of agreement rather than points of difference amongst us. . . . Correcting errors and misstatements concerning the progress and activities of the race, as well as making known the truth regarding the acts of the white race affecting us."[87]

Washington must have realized that he had driven away the very men he had hoped to encompass through his conference, by his immoderate use of power and his overly moderate goals. He wrote to Archibald Grimké soon after the meeting: "I have been thinking a good deal of your suggestion that we ought to have in our general directions to the secretary something bearing more directly upon the franchise, and the more I think of it the more I agree with your view." He proposed the following additional suggestion: "And to keep constantly before the people through the medium of the press, pulpit and platform the importance of registering and voting at all elections, both state and national, and the prompt and regular payment of all taxes, especially that class of taxes that are a condition for voting."[88] Grimké, following Du Bois's lead, had already sent in his resignation from the Committee of Twelve,[89] but he now changed his mind, withdrew his resignation, and even in time wrote a pamphlet for the Committee of Twelve series. Du Bois, however, stood by his own resignation, and his departure rendered the committee insignificant as an institution for bridging the growing rift in the leadership class of the black minority group.

The Committee of Twelve for the Advancement of the Negro Race became largely a paper organization, conducted from the office of Hugh M. Browne, its secretary. Its members corresponded with Browne or with Washington and Scott rather than meeting as a body, and their work consisted almost entirely of a succession of pamphlets. Some of these were original writings, others were reprints of speeches or magazine articles by Washington, Carl Schurz, Archibald Grimké, and one even by the committee's angel, Andrew Carnegie, who relied on Emmett Scott for his parade of statistical evidence to prove the steady progress of the Afro-American.

In only one instance did the Committee of Twelve act in a way that promised the advancement of blacks. This was in the Maryland disfranchisement contest in 1905. Black men were effectively barred from voting by one means or another in the ex-Confederate states, and the Maryland case raised the question whether the movement would spread to the border states that had remained in the Union. The Poe Amendment to the state constitution, designed to disfranchise blacks, passed the legislature and was submitted to the people.[90] Harry S. Cummings, a black attorney and Baltimore councilman who had seconded Roosevelt's nomination in 1904, organized the Colored Voters Suffrage League in 1905 to fight the Poe Amendment, and appealed to Washington and the Committee of Twelve for help.[91] The committee met with the Maryland leaders, gave them some money, counseled them on political strategy, and published and distributed copies of a pamphlet on the right of suffrage that Archibald Grimké prepared.[92] Washington also invited the Constitution League to assist in the Maryland campaign.[93] The Poe Amendment was defeated by nearly 25,000 votes, and Cummings gave considerable credit to the Committee of Twelve for stopping the wave of southern disfranchisement at the Potomac. "I cannot thank you too much for your interest in us and your practical assistance," Cummings wrote Washington.[94] Four years later, however, history began repeating itself, and Cummings wrote: "I know what you did in our last fight and it was confidential. Can you in anyway help us in this struggle? Whatever you may do will be as you know 'within the Lodge.' "[95] Washington girded up his committee for another effort of advice, encouragement, and perhaps direct assistance in 1909 and 1910; but this time it was mainly local campaigning with Washington's quiet enlistment of support from President Taft and Cardinal James Gibbons that kept the disfranchisers at bay.[96]

The Committee of Twelve was really a still-born racial organization, but it made a feeble effort to come to life at one point, when it proposed in 1906 a private conference between southern blacks and whites to work for a change in harsh southern practices of racial discrimination. The southern members of the Southern Education Board vetoed it.[97] The Committee of Twelve for the Advancement of the Negro Race moved offstage toward oblivion, dropping a few pamphlets in its wake.

CHAPTER 4

Damming Niagara

I am, Your obedient humble servant, Chisum, to use as your Eminence desires, absolutely.

T HE summit conference of black leaders at Carnegie Hall in January 1904 was not only a logical response to the fragmentation of Afro-American leadership symbolized by the Boston Riot, but its failure to achieve any unity or even truce among the factions pointed inevitably toward the Niagara Movement a year later. The times themselves contributed to this polarization, as white aggression took the extreme forms of lynching and race riot, and the slower but continuous forms of segregation, disfranchisement, and exclusion from one avenue after another of black advancement. Black dissatisfaction took the form not only of protest against white oppression but disillusionment with the compromising, temporizing leadership of Booker T. Washington.

The Niagara Movement reflected the personality of W. E. B. Du Bois rather than Monroe Trotter, for Trotter's talents lay in stirring controversy, whereas Du Bois was an intellectual system-builder. He fashioned a black self-advancement movement that in every feature was a contrast to the Tuskegee Machine. Where Washington proposed to improve the racial climate through conciliation, the Niagara Movement proposed to clear the air by frank protest of injustice. Where the Tuskegee Machine stood for the up-and-coming black businessman and farmer and such professional allies as these classes could attract, the Niagara Movement centered on the college-graduate professional class and spoke of its membership as the Talented Tenth. Where Washington emphasized economic means and self-help, the Niagara Movement depended on universal suffrage, civil rights, and an intellectual elite to bring about the promise of black opportunity in America. The Niagarites saw Washington as the greatest obstacle in their path, and one more vulnerable to their protest than the white majority. Washington saw in his critics a collection of impractical visionaries and personal failures who lacked the capacity to lead and were jealous of his own constructive achievements and legitimate leadership. Naturally, seeing one another in this extravagant light, the two factions spent their energies fighting each other, leaving only a small part of themselves free to bring about the noble ideals and meliorative goals that each professed.

The Niagara Movement was clearly the brainchild of Du Bois, but it is harder to fix the moment of its genesis. Perhaps it began with Washington's easy success in controlling the membership, structure, and functions of the Committee of Twelve. Du Bois had by that time become convinced that protest against the loss of civil and political rights was the first order of race business, and he would insist on a membership of ideological purity in the pursuit of these rights. His organizational plan for the Committee of Twelve, which Washington found hilariously grandiose, became the structure for the Niagara Movement. But the Niagara Movement was also born of frustration and humiliation, as Du Bois found it harder than ever to influence the cause of racial justice or even to bastinado Booker T. Washington from his ivory tower.

In the January 1905 issue of *The Voice of the Negro,* summing up the "Credits and Debits" of the past year in race relations, Du Bois placed in the debit column the charge that "$3,000 of 'hush money'" had been spent "to subsidize the Negro press in five leading cities."[1] No mention of Washington's name was necessary; the meaning was clear. Emmett Scott retaliated by persuading a black businessman to withdraw his advertising from the magazine.[2] More significantly, however, Du Bois was challenged to prove his case by Oswald Garrison Villard. Du Bois labored hard to assemble the evidence, and came forward with an elaboration of his charges, much circumstantial evidence, and twelve "exhibits" appended to his letter.[3] Although, as we shall see,

Du Bois was essentially correct in his charge, Villard replied: "I must say frankly that it will take a great deal more than the evidence you have presented to shake my faith in Mr. Washington's purity of purpose, and absolute freedom from selfishness and personal ambition." All he would concede was that Scott's "literary bureau" at Tuskegee had been "extremely injudicious." [4]

If even the most liberal white Americans refused to find Washington at fault, Du Bois thought the times called for an all-black organization as close-knit as a cabal to champion black liberty. So he secretly gathered a band of brothers to meet in Buffalo, New York, in the summer of 1905. Washington somehow heard advance rumors of it, however, and he unhesitatingly used the same tactics of espionage and repression he had employed against the Boston *Guardian* and its editor. In response to Washington's telegram, S. Laing Williams sent the names of ten Chicagoans invited to Buffalo and of three others from farther west observed at the Chicago train station on their way through to Buffalo. He could learn nothing, however, about the character of the meeting.[5] Washington sent a member of his secretarial staff, Julius R. Cox, on a sudden vacation to Niagara Falls. "I assure you I have enjoyed my outing up to this time and I know I shall enjoy the rest," Cox wrote back to Tuskegee.[6] Apparently Cox had arrived at the meeting place a week early, and he returned to his regular work in Boston. Washington telegraphed him there: "See Plummer at once. Give him fifty dollars. Tell him to go to Buffalo tonight or to-morrow morning ostensibly to attend Elks convention but to report fully what goes on at meeting to be held there Wednesday and Thursday. Get into meeting, if possible but be sure name of all who attend and what they do. Answer when you have completed this matter."[7] Cox replied: "All arranged. Drew personal check for fifty. Plum leaves this morning. Will look after all also press reports. Most of crowd to leave here financially unable."[8]

Clifford Plummer, the lawyer who had spied for Washington in the Boston troubles, reported from Buffalo that there were few delegates to the secret meeting, "Nothing serious so far. Will try to stop their declaration of principles from appearing." Plummer went to the Associated Press office in Buffalo to arrange as far as possible for the newspapers of the country to ignore the meeting.[9] This maneuver was so successful that of all the white daily papers outside of Buffalo, only the Boston *Transcript* carried a detailed report. It was sent in by Trot-

ter immediately on his return from the meeting.[10] The *Transcript*
quoted in full the declaration of principles, listed the twenty-seven
participants, and announced the group's ambitious plans for propaganda and lobbying for civil rights.

Plummer at first called the Boston *Transcript* report a pack of lies,
for he had completely missed the real meeting of the Niagara Movement, which had moved from Buffalo to Niagara Falls, Canada, after
discriminatory treatment in the Buffalo hotel. Plummer insisted that
there had been no conference. "I was located near 521 Michigan Avenue from Wednesday morning until Friday," he wrote his chief, "and
I can state positively that none of the men named in the report were
present except Du Bois. Notwithstanding the fact that the conference
amounted to nothing, the local editors informed me that some colored man did bring in a report such as appeared in the Boston papers; but no reporter was assigned to the seat of the conference."[11]

Washington decided to extend to the black press the silent treatment he had been able to manage with the white newspapers. He
wired Scott: "Telegraph [Richard W.] Thompson and other newspaper men that you can absolutely trust to ignore Niagara movement."[12]
Scott did so. "The best of the white newspapers in the North have
absolutely ignored it and have taken no account of its meetings or its
protestations," he wrote Thompson. "I think, then, as I have intimated, if we shall consistently refuse to take the slightest notice of
them that the whole thing will die aborning." He named several newspapers Thompson should influence.[13] Scott's telegram reached
Thompson too late, however, to prevent a reference to the Niagara
Movement in his newsletter— "In *sarcastic* vein, however, which will
do no harm," he reassured Scott. He agreed in the near future, however, to a strategy of silence. "To advertise the movement by opposition even, would be to magnify it."[14]

Washington's strategy was largely successful. Surveying the entire
black newspaper coverage of the Niagara Movement's inaugural
meeting, Scott wrote Washington complacently that aside from the
Atlanta *Age,* which straddled, he did not find "that any papers that
have been heretofore favorable will be deflected from support of the
great principles for which you have been laboring."[15] But Washington
could not tolerate even one defection. "On your way North," he instructed his secretary, "I wish that you would stop and have a conference with the Atlanta *Age* man, I forget his name, and show him the

true inwardness of Du Bois. Perhaps it would be better to have him come to Tuskegee, at our expense, for a conference, without you letting him know the exact reason. I am very anxious that we lose not one of our friends on the account of this new movement." [16]

The black journalist George W. Cable of the Indianapolis *Freeman* also balked. He wrote Thompson: "I see no reason why The Freeman should become a party to any petty jealousies and it is quite impossible for me to conceive of Mr. Washington's being vindictive to the point of wishing that this or any other matter be treated otherwise than on its merits." [17] Washington had to accept this response with a shake of the head. "Mr. Cable's views are all right when dealing with gentlemen," he commented to Scott, "but not scoundrels, whose purposes are wholly known." [18] But who were the gentlemen and who the scoundrels in this instance of attempted repression of free speech and assembly?

Scott was ever ready at Washington's elbow to stir his chief into baleful suspicion, and to pass on to friendly black editors any derogatory information or turn of phrase about the Niagarites that came his way. [19] Each faction increasingly regarded the other as "the enemy," against whom any tactics that worked were justified. Washington's chief concern was to keep the Niagara Movement weak and small. As Scott explained Washington's view of the Niagarites to a black college president: "In communities where they do not think it prudent to do so they conceal its position toward him in every way they can. Whenever they think it prudent to do so they openly state their position to him and their intention to 'destroy him.' My frank opinion is that the movement exists for the sole purpose of opposing Mr. Washington and the work he is trying to do, since its declared principles represent the already declared principles of the Afro-American Council and other organizations of that character." [20]

The Niagara Movement was only a trickle at the end of its first year, so successful had been the silent treatment of Washington and his Tuskegee Machine. There were only 170 members, and most of its activities were in cooperation with other, larger organizations. Its second annual meeting was at Harper's Ferry, West Virginia, a place rich in symbolism for a people recently out of slavery. The meeting celebrated the centennial of the birth of John Brown, the white man who attempted almost singlehandedly at that spot to begin a slave rebellion and end the institution of slavery. [21] The meeting place was also well located for drawing a crowd, for the round-trip railroad fare from Washington was only a dollar. This meeting received more publicity than the one at Niagara Falls the preceding year, and many daily newspapers carried its address to the country.

Washington had his spy at the Harper's Ferry meeting also. Richard T. Greener, the first black graduate of Harvard and once professor of law at the University of South Carolina, was down on his luck and in need of Washington's help. During the McKinley era he had secured a consular post with Washington's help. The State Department sent him to Bombay, but when he complained of the heat there, they reassigned him to Vladivostok, Siberia. Suddenly in 1906 he was removed under circumstances that involved racial discrimination.[22] He wrote, while visiting at Storer College in Harper's Ferry, asking for Washington's help in getting him reinstated. "Here is a good chance to get a good friend into the inner portals of the Niagara meeting," Scott wrote on the margin.[23]

Washington tried to arrange a meeting with Greener before the Harper's Ferry convention, but Greener wired: "Think best not to see you before the meeting."[24] "There are some facts which I wanted to put before you before that meeting," Washington explained. The circumstances forced him to put them in writing: "You will find, in the last analysis, that the whole object of the Niag[a]ra Movement is to defeat and oppose every thing I do. I have done all I could to work in harmony with Du Bois, but he has permitted Trotter and others to fool him into the idea that he was some sort of a leader, consequently he has fritt[er]ed away his time in agitation when he could succeed as a scientist or Soc[i]ologist." Washington urged Greener to "spare no pains to get on the inside of everything" at Harper's Ferry.[25]

To Greener's credit, it is not certain that he actually passed on any information to Washington, though it is obvious that Washington was ready to exploit Greener's personal troubles and need for his influence. Greener was to attend the National Negro Business League meeting in Atlanta soon after the Niagara Movement meeting, and he wrote Washington: "The details, as well as some points of mutual interest, I hope to have a chance to go over with you either at Atlanta, or while *en route* there."[26] Washington invited Greener to Tuskegee after the league meeting, and the two went on a Sunday train excursion in New York two months later.[27] On one of these occasions, Greener may have passed on information of the Niagara Movement meeting. Washington, however, did little to help Greener, who was eventually exonerated of charges against him, but Secretary Elihu Root decided Greener was not in the class of officers who had the right to have cause given for dismissal.[28] At Greener's request Washington arranged, or thought he did, for Greener to see President Roosevelt on the matter.[29] When Greener appeared for his appointment, however, he found that the President was on vacation.[30] Years later, a Washington spy reported that Greener was "about on the fence. He is just a little irritated at Dr. Booker T. Washington because he did not take him up and give him a job in or since 1906, during which year Mr. Greener lost his political post."[31]

Washington employed other spies also against the Niagara Movement's leaders. "Let me know . . . by Saturday in what way the wife of William Monroe Trotter . . . is employed," he wired a white detective agency in Boston. "If in domestic service, state the nature of it and for whom she is working. Don't say for whom information is wanted."[32] Washington was probably disappointed to learn that Trotter's wife worked every day at the *Guardian* office.[33] Washington abandoned use of this detective agency when one of its agents was exposed as a Washington spy by the man he was shadowing.[34]

Washington had better success with black agents. His most active spy was Melvin J. Chisum, whose success in infiltrating Trotter's inner group after the Boston Riot in 1903 brought him to Washington's mind again in 1905 when the Niagara Movement presented a threat. "Could you not secure a man in New York," Washington wrote his friend Charles Anderson, "who would get right into the inner circles of the Niagara movement through the Brooklyn crowd and keep us informed as [to] their operations and plans?"[35] Chisum's first important assignment, however, was in Washington, D.C., where the Tuskegean felt badly the need for a sympathetic local newspaper. The *Colored American,* which had been pro-Washington to a fault, had collapsed in 1905, and Washington's efforts to launch a new paper in the District had failed.[36] He decided, therefore, to use Chisum in a scheme to capture the *Bee.*

The plan was for Chisum to seek employment on the *Bee,* worm his way into the confidence of its editor, W. Calvin Chase, and persuade him to take actions that would transform him from a Trotterite into a Bookerite. It was just the sort of challenge that appealed to a man of Chisum's temperament. "Most of the day has been spent with my newly made cantankerous friend," Chisum reported to Washington soon after arrival. "The cat got clearly out of the bag today. He is 'busted.' " Chisum undertook to convince Chase that, though they both hated Washington as any upstanding lover of the race should, the best way out of the *Bee*'s financial crisis was to accept some of Washington's money. At the strategic moment Robert H. Terrell and John C. Dancy, Washington's lieutenants, proffered money for the *Bee*'s extensive news coverage and favorable editorial treatment of several Washington speeches. "But, rest perfectly sure, that my plan is so surely carefully lain that he will not see," Chisum wrote Washington. "The 'Guardian crowd' to the contrary notwithstanding, I have him Doctor, I have him." Chisum ended on a further reassurance: "But will in no way connect your Excellence with my plans. For I do not trust a soul with any real fact that touches my visit here."[37]

A few days later Chisum reported his best day's work on this assignment. Editor Chase was going to print two of Washington's speeches, a favorable editorial, and an endorsement of Washington's candidate for register of the Treasury who would oust a Niagarite. The editorial, wrote Chisum, would be "such an one as will bring the break we want." This was the break with Trotter; for the cream of the jest was that Chase had such a pugnacious temper that when his militant friends criticized him for his editorial, he would cantankerously defend himself by attacking them. Chisum wrote his Excellence, as he called Washington: "Now! The Bee will be a surprise to everybody that knows it the forthcoming week and the war is on between his highness bub Trotter and bub Chase. Are you willing that I remain here for a couple of weeks and make shure [sic] of Chase's broadsides being properly directed so as to put them beyond the point of repair, or reconnection? I know Trotter will fire on the Bee, and I think I ought to be in the con[n]ing tower with Chase when he does." Chisum confided that he considered Chase "at heart, a vile, malicious, jealous—heartless 'cuss,' " but he was careful not to reveal his true feelings to Chase. "To him I am constantly pounding you," Chisum wrote Washington, "but always with the added 'confidential,' 'Mr Chase, I would let no one but you hear me say this.' "[38]

Chisum's scheme worked perfectly. Trotter and the other Niagarites read Chase out of their organization and drove him into dependence on Booker T. Washington. "Chisum seems to be doing good work in Washington," commented Anderson. "He has his valuable points." [39] Washington let Chisum know that he was "most grateful to you for what you have done." [40] Washington now had a major newspaper in the nation's capital in his pocket. The only problem was that Editor Chase, whose impulses were on the other side, was loyal to Washington only when recently paid. [41]

Chisum returned to New York, where he ran a Harlem realty business largely as a front. "Relative to our man Chisum," Charles Anderson complained to Washington, "I want to advise you that you have left an awful load on my hands." Chisum had asked Anderson five times for money, and had got it four times. There was a faint suggestion of blackmail in Chisum's importunities. "The trouble with him," said Anderson, "is that he has made up his mind not to work, and expects to live by borrowing." He warned that he might break with Chisum before Washington returned to New York. [42] "I hope you will not worry about Brother Chisum," Washington replied. "I hope that he will be fat and with a full purse by the time I reach New York City." [43]

Chisum took obvious delight in his role as the genie in Washington's bottle. "I am, Your obedient humble servant, Chisum, to use as your Eminence desires, absolutely," he roguishly ended one letter. Again: "From one who will always deem it a very great honor to serve you in the ways that please your Eminence most." [44] If it ever seemed to Washington incongruous for himself, the conventional and conservative black leader, the Baptist layman, the public purveyor of conventional morality, to be in league with this plump little rogue in a bullet-proof vest who made his living by invading the privacy of others, he never committed such an attitude to writing. His resort to his humble servant Chisum is a measure of a certain moral insensitivity in Washington that one does not find in the private lives of his opponents such as Du Bois or even Trotter. Those Harvard graduates started near the top. Washington, having started in slavery and poverty, would gag at almost nothing that promised dominance.

Chisum offered to "do the Chicago work," whatever that was to have been, under an assumed name while working part-time as a waiter. "No one would have any interest in Jack Cameron a waiter, just doing what he could to move in decent society and keep soul and body together with the aid of the pan," he wrote. [45] Washington decided, however, that Chisum would be more useful to him spying on the Brooklyn branch of the Niagara Movement. It was Chisum who learned in advance the date and place of the second annual Niagara meeting at Harper's Ferry. "I attended a meeting last night in Brooklyn where I learned this," he informed Washington. "That much and that much only is *settled*. Another meeting Wednesday night next. . . . I am almost sure I will be able to attend the secret conference at the Convention, if you desire me to go please notify me."[46] Apparently the Niagarites were aware of leakages of information that they could not locate, and were increasingly secretive.

Chisum shuttled nightly between his Harlem residence and the Niagara meetings in Brooklyn Heights, often getting home long after midnight. His reports to Washington were usually oral, the letters between them recording only the times and places of meeting, usually on a park bench in Manhattan. "I sat in the park today from 12:45 to now," Chisum wrote Washington one day at 3:30 P.M., "and will be there near where we sat again tomorrow Friday at 1 sharp."[47] A few weeks later Washington wrote him, "I plan to be in New York about the 13th and shall hope to see you at the usual place at that time."[48] Sometimes the messages were too cryptic for an outsider to understand. Chisum wrote, for example, just before Washington gave a New York speech: "I have *Chase* in leash. Questions are to be asked you tonight. I will, I think, succeed in stopping them. I shall see Mr. [Fred R.] Moore and get him to talk to the Captain of the Police and get plain clothes men."[49]

After 1906 Washington found less use for Chisum, who became involved in a series of small business enterprises in real estate, banking, and journalism in several states, and his spying for Washington ceased. He stood ready to be again Washington's "obedient, humble servant," but the master no longer rubbed the lamp. Not long before Washington's death, Chisum sent his former employer a copy of the Baltimore *Afro-American* and of his own paper, *The Colored Man,* inviting comparison of the rival paper's compromise with the NAACP with "how religiously I am hewing to the Tuskegee line." Chisum added: "Please don't become impatient because of my asking that I be not forgotten when the 'pie' is to be passed around."[50]

Though Washington dropped him, Chisum continued spying for the rest of his life. During World War I he was a labor agent for northern manufacturers seeking cheap black labor and strikebreakers from the southern farms. In the 1920s he served Robert R. Moton, Washington's successor at Tuskegee, as an undercover man at the time of the Ku Klux Klan march beside the campus to threaten black control of the Tuskegee Veterans Hospital. In the 1930s he worked secretly for the railroads and the Pullman Company against the organizing efforts of the Brotherhood of Sleeping Car Porters.[51]

The Tuskegee Machine's most effective means of struggle against the Niagara Movement, however, was the informal organizational work of Washington's lieutenants in every major northern city. These were a varied lot—businessmen, lawyers, editors, physicians, and officeholders. They did not have in common even an ideology. Some of them championed Washington's social philosophy of economic self-help and undertook to put it into action in their own lives. Others, however, never really subscribed to the Tuskegee gospel. The one thing that tied the lieutenants to each other was that they were all beholden to Washington for favors past or in prospect. They were aboard the same ship, and he was the captain, who ruled by mutual interest rather than by an abstract code of ideology.

Washington, D. C., as the nation's capital, gradually became a strong Bookerite center. It was a city where possession of a white collar and a minor government clerkship conveyed instant middle-class status and the possession of a presidential appointment gave its holder an elite status that even followed him out of office and clung as an aura to his descendants. The Tuskegean pointedly did not disturb the chief black officeholders who had gained their appointments during the McKinley administration, such as Judson W. Lyons in the most prestigious black post of register of the Treasury, but he put the old-line politicians subtly on notice that they served on good behavior, and he waited until their four-year terms expired.

One by one the Booker T. Washington men found places in the federal bureaucracy. Robert H. Terrell secured with Washington's help a municipal judgeship in the District of Columbia in 1902. In the same year Washington made his loyal but none-too-courageous friend John C. Dancy of North Carolina the recorder of deeds of the District of Columbia.

A large cluster of pro-Washington notables formed in the District of Columbia during Theodore Roosevelt's presidency. No one of them could claim to be the Tuskegean's chief lieutenant in the capital city, but they generally worked together as a coterie. Some were longtime residents of the area, such as the realtor Whitefield McKinlay, originally from South Carolina, and P. B. S. Pinchback, formerly lieutenant-governor of Louisiana, who had spent decades of exile in Washington. Somewhat below these men in rank and distinction were Richard W. Thompson, holder of a succession of clerkships and on Booker Washington's payroll as a syndicated columnist for black newspapers; former Tuskegeans such as the realtor Thomas J. Calloway, who had been on the faculty, and W. Sidney Pittman, a Tuskegee graduate, an architect trained at Drexel Institute who had married Washington's daughter Portia. On the periphery of the Bookerites were some fence-straddlers, such as the Grimké brothers, at a certain stage of the intraracial struggle; Professor Kelly Miller of Howard, who could not make up his mind into which camp to jump; and Mary Church Terrell, wife of the judge but a strong-minded woman whose inclination and background as an Oberlin graduate prompted her to run with the opposition, the civil rights protesters such as Trotter and Du Bois.

Mary Church Terrell was, in fact, suspected in 1906 of spying for Washington's enemies. Anderson learned of a leak of some sort through a white informant and warned Washington: "I am quite confident that our Washington 'judicial friend' passed the story along to his wife, and she passed it on to the gentleman here. One never knows how to deal with families when one member poses as a friend, and another member trains with the opposition."[52] This continued to worry Anderson, who said a few days later that somehow or other "everything that they know about our program, has already reached the enemy."[53] Washington promised to be more careful what he said around either of the Terrells.[54] Anderson's suspicions were heightened late in 1906 by a report that in a lecture in New York "she devoted considerable time to drastic criticisms of that sort of race leadership, which holds up the seamy side of the race, tells dialect stories at the expense of the race, advises the race not to retaliate, but to seek the approval of those who approve of negroes, only as subordinates and inferiors, and counsels the race to acquire only an inferior sort of education." It was clear whom she meant, and Anderson's informant said: "why, she did everything but call his name. She told me she was going to unshirt him, and she did."[55] Washington nevertheless kept his amicable relations with both the Terrells for the rest of his life, and even prevented an editorial attacking her from appearing in the New York *Age*.[56]

Washington never really liked the city of Washington, but at least he could people it with his lieutenants in positions of influence. The

Bookerites were stronger there than in Baltimore and Philadelphia, where Washington had friends but never a faction. His closest Baltimore friend was Ernest Lyon, who spent the crucial years of black factional struggle as minister to Liberia. Washington exchanged occasional favors with the lawyer and politician Harry S. Cummings, Episcopal clergyman George F. Bragg, and the principal of the city's black high school, J. H. N. Waring, but not always his liberally educated faculty. The Baltimore *Afro-American Ledger* and its editor, John H. Murphy, generally supported Washington, but with occasional assertions of independence.

Similarly in Philadelphia the Tuskegee Machine had talented professional men but no mass following. John S. Durham, an economist of many practical talents, spent years away from Philadelphia as an official of the U. S. Spanish Claims Commission, as manager of a Cuban sugar plantation, and in self-exile in Europe where it was more comfortable to live with his white wife. Two superior black journals were on Washington's side, the *Odd Fellows Journal* edited by J. C. Asbury and the *A. M. E. Church Review* edited by H. T. Kealing. But Washington had no weekly newspaper there.

Black New York was a Booker T. Washington town. It was in transition, as the scattered blacks of lower Manhattan moved uptown and the population pressure of southern migrants and the entrepreneurship of black realtors such as Scott's and Washington's friend Philip Payton began to create black Harlem.[57] The Harlem of the future Renaissance was only in the bud, and the businessmen and politicians held sway. Over in Brooklyn was another sizable black enclave that leaned toward the Niagara Movement. In Harlem the spirit of business enterprise was more congenial to Washington's social philosophy, and the arrival of southern migrants to Harlem tempered its urban attitudes with first-generation rural ones. And many blacks, like Washington himself, found self-help and a strong insistence on civil rights compatible with each other rather than mutually exclusive.

Though Washington gradually discarded Fortune as his "man in New York" in the early years of the century, his machine dominance of black New York was closely involved in his control of the New York *Age*. For many years Fortune had employed his newspaper to defend Washington against the vitriol of Trotter and the rapier thrusts of Du Bois. But Washington was too conservative and materialistic to satisfy all the needs of the ambivalent Fortune. Fortune showed signs of wanting to be a protest leader again, decrying the loss of civil rights and the indifference of Republican Party leaders. Occasionally he yielded to impulse, threatened black retaliation against the white South, attacked the Roosevelt administration, and earned a reputation for undependability.[58] Washington, the pragmatic and phlegmatic and often enigmatic leader, found an unevenness in being yoked with the passionate Fortune. He turned gradually for advice and help between 1904 and 1906 to Charles Anderson. Anderson was reliable without surrendering his independent judgment. He did not seem to feel the grand passions of Fortune, but kept a cool head in a crisis and turned away wrath with humor or wry sarcasm. When Fortune, as editor and publisher, in a weak moment offered to sell the *Age*, Washington unhesitatingly bought it. He kept his ownership secret, Emmett Scott and other agents holding the stock, and he installed the more tractable Fred R. Moore as the new editor.

Also in New York were Washington's personal lawyer, Wilford H. Smith, and a number of sympathetic black businessmen such as Philip A. Payton; John B. Nail, the restaurateur, saloonkeeper, and father-in-law of James Weldon Johnson; and in Brooklyn, Samuel R. Scottron and others. Among the clergymen who backed Washington in New York were the Reverend Charles S. Morris of the Abyssinian Baptist Church, and his successor in that church, the Reverend Adam Clayton Powell, Sr. Though Washington never felt completely at home in any city, his Tuskegee Machine dominated New York City black politics, and he felt as comfortable there as in any other city.

The major black centers of the Midwest all had black communities divided in sentiment between Washington and his critics, though in many an isolated city the blacks were more deeply involved in the rivalries and activities of the churches and fraternal lodges. In Cleveland the editor of the leading black newspaper, Harry C. Smith of the *Gazette*, was a Niagarite, but like his friend Charles W. Chesnutt the lawyer and novelist, he did not personalize his racial politics. A wealthy barber with a white clientele, George A. Myers, the local Republican boss, favored Washington. Kenneth Kusmer has shown for Cleveland what was probably true in many other black communities, that the old leadership of Smith, Chesnutt, and Myers "began to be challenged by a new group of black businessmen and politicians who relied primarily upon Negro patronage for their success." This new elite, less educated and articulate, were self-made men with an implicit faith in

Washington's doctrines of self-help, economic means, and racial solidarity.[59]

In the substantial black community of Indianapolis was one of the
most influential black newspapers in the country, the *Freeman,* which
was next to the New York *Age* in overall importance. Controlled at
various times by George E. Knox, A. E. Manning, and George W.
Cable, it generally followed a pragmatic, self-help philosophy similar
to Washington's, and never crusaded against him. Other influential
friends of the Tuskegean there were Seymour A. Furniss, who with
aid from Bishop Abraham Grant and Washington, himself, tried in
1905 to purchase the *Freeman* from the Knoxes.[60] The plan was unsuccessful, but it would have made little change anyhow. As a Washington lieutenant reported: "There is much silent ill-feeling between
the Knoxes and the Furnisses, and Manning is not enamored of either
crowd, while Cable is a *rank outsider*—new man—as they look at it.
. . . All are loyal to the Wizard, but simply jealous of each other."[61]

Even before the Great Migration from the South began in 1915,
Chicago had a large black population, mostly of the inarticulate, the
unskilled working and servant class. But it also had substantial elites
of professional and business men, large churches, hospitals, newspapers, and other black institutions. The Chicago branch of the National
Negro Business League was a source of strength to the Tuskegee Machine, and Washington's alliances also invaded the professions. He
had friends in several Chicago pulpits. His personal physician, George
Cleveland Hall, was the head of the black Provident Hospital in Chicago, and he also maintained a private collaboration with Hall's bitterest rival and the most distinguished of black physicians, Daniel Hale
Williams. Though D. H. Williams did many private errands for Washington, the chief Tuskegee Machine lieutenant in Chicago was S. Laing
Williams, a lawyer. He and his journalist wife, Fannie Barrier Williams, however, were overmatched by another couple in the militant
faction, Ferdinand L. Barnett, a lawyer and legislator, and his wife
Ida B. Wells-Barnett, the antilynching crusader. The black press in
Chicago also was more militant than anywhere else except Boston,
perhaps because Chicago blacks had had a longer taste of freedom
than most northern blacks, including seats in the legislature and in
the councils of the state Republican Party.[62]

In Chicago as in other large black centers, Washington felt strongly
the need of a black newspaper to sing his praise and support his ac-

commodationist racial strategy. The city's leading black paper, the *Conservator,* edited by D. Robert Wilkins, was aligned if not identified with the Niagara Movement. To compete with it, Washington and Scott subsidized the *Leader,* a small weekly run by the veteran journalist W. Allison Sweeney.[63] In return for his repeated rescue from bankruptcy, Washington asked Sweeney to publish an unsigned editorial saying of the Niagara Movement newspapers in Chicago: "Never an issue of one of these papers comes from the press without the most vile slanders and abuse of Mr. Washington and his work." Though the Niagara Movement claimed to represent freedom of expression, said the editorial, its leader Trotter had been in jail "for attempting to break up a meeting in Boston in order to prevent free speech, the very thing for which the leaders of this 'movement' say it was brought into existence."[64]

When Sweeney published the editorial, the *Conservator* denounced Washington for buying up "crippled Negro newspapers" to use against the Niagara Movement.[65] This led Sweeney to plead for further subsidies to keep his paper alive. Washington finally, after many entreaties, sent Sweeney an almost insulting $50 payment for an advertisement of Tuskegee, but the Chicago *Leader* soon suspended publication.[66]

Meanwhile a rumor reached Washington that the *Conservator* itself was up for sale. In February 1906 Washington had a friend wire S. Laing Williams: "If possible be in New York Sunday morning to confer with friends Stevens House. All expenses paid. Get full information where stock Conservator is and what can buy it."[67] Two weeks later Williams wrote Washington that he had met with the stockholders twice and that they were anxious to sell the paper for about $2500. "They dislike Wilkins," he reported, "opposed to his policy in reference to you and your work, but they have no backbone." Wilkins, it turned out, owned only one-fourth of the stock.[68]

For some reason now obscure, the purchase of the *Conservator* held fire, perhaps because it was Washington's plan to install his friend H. T. Kealing in the editorship, and Kealing would not be free for a year.[69] Suddenly, in April 1907, to the surprise of many in Chicago, Wilkins carried an editorial favorable to Booker T. Washington and his policies. Washington hastened to invite him to Tuskegee, hoping that he had found at last his journalistic voice in Chicago. "As a matter of fact, there is no difference between your position and mine,"

Washington wrote Wilkins. "The only difference being that you are working to secure certain ends by traveling perhaps a different route. Since we all are aiming at the same thing, there is no earthly reason why there should be bickerings, jealousies and cursings. . . ." Washington described his critics, to a man who had lately been numbered among them, as members of the "upper ten" who "very seldom mingle with the masses, who in fact think themselves and their families too good to even touch the hem of the garment of the ordinary man and woman."[70] Wilkins came in for some bitter criticism by his former friends. As Dr. Daniel Hale Williams reported to Washington after a visit to Wilkins's office: "He said that his office had been stormed by the enemy but asserted that he was firm in the conviction that he had done the right thing."[71]

Wilkins wanted Washington to meet him in Chicago, but Washington was wary. Instead, he and Scott arranged for D. H. Williams to be their middleman, receiving and passing on to Wilkins weekly items of news and editorials from the Tuskegee news factory, and possibly money. Williams was careful to persuade Wilkins not to overdo the conversion of the *Conservator* into a pro-Washington paper, and when "fool friends" submitted several Tuskegee news items within a week, Williams quietly "pencilled them all."[72] Scott commended this good judgment, saying that "Quiet effort is much more satisfactory in every way than that which carries around a 'brass band' to accomplish its results."[73]

After a few months passed, however, Wilkins was ousted as editor in January 1908 and J. Max Barber, a refugee from the Atlanta Riot and a member of the Niagara Movement, became the editor of the *Conservator*.[74] Barber had been the chief editor of the influential magazine, the *Voice of the Negro*, 1904–7. When Washington felt alarm over this development, he was reassured by the largest stockholder in the paper, Sandy W. Trice, department store owner and member of the National Negro Business League. Trice wrote Washington that "I will see to it that it will not be antagonistic to you."[75] Barber soon afterwards took his first opportunity to publish an anti-Washington editorial, but Trice reported to Washington that "I had this gentleman understand that if anything like that happened again he could no longer hold that position."[76] Washington replied that Trice had Barber completely at his mercy, that he was "wholly dependent upon the position which he now holds. I happen to have information that he was to the point of nearly starving when you gave him something to do."[77] Soon afterward, as if in response to Washington's unspoken wish, Trice telegraphed: "Barber no longer editor Conservator."[78] When Barber then sued Trice for damages, he appealed to Washington for "some immediate financial assistance."[79] Washington apparently helped Trice. "I have already wired to party who saw you last, and asked him to see what he could do for you," he wrote cryptically to Trice.[80] Trice secured as the new editor a Washington supporter.[81] Washington then arranged for Republican party funds to go to the *Conservator* during William Howard Taft's election campaign in 1908.[82] Just as Washington seemed to finally have a favorable Chicago newspaper without having to buy one, the *Conservator* failed—this time for good—in 1909.[83]

Besides building local bastions of strength in the various urban black communities in the North, Washington also worked to influence as many of the nationwide black institutions as possible. He had, of course, the unquestioning allegiance of the members of the National Negro Business League that he had founded in 1900, but the league itself did little beyond meeting once a year, and in many cities there were bitter factional struggles in the local branches. There was also the Committee of Twelve, founded in 1904, but of course it was little more than a paper organization.

Washington found further allies in the secret black fraternal orders. This was largely through Emmett Scott's knowledge and suggestion, for Washington was too rationalistic to have an interest in the hocus-pocus aspect of the secret orders that figured largely in black middle-class life. But Washington was aware that the fraternal orders were open to the majority of black strivers rather than just the college-educated elite. He also recognized that the fraternal orders sustained black group life and racial solidarity. They could be valuable allies in his struggle for power.

Washington's machine lieutenant J. C. Asbury came up in 1906 for reelection as editor of the *Odd Fellows Journal*. A fellow Odd Fellow of Chicago, Edward H. Morris of the Niagara Movement, challenged Asbury for the post. Needing Washington's help, Asbury asked him to say to John C. Dancy, currently recorder of deeds of the District of Columbia and "a big Odd Fellow in North Carolina," that Asbury was Washington's friend and that "you would regard it as a favour if he would work with me."[84] It was Scott rather than Washington who wrote to Dancy in that vein. Dancy replied that "my friendship for our friend and his interests will always find in me a certain and ready champion. I will not submit to J. C. A.'s undoing on that account. There must be something more far reaching as we must inculcate the teaching of 'Love' as well as the other links in the mighty chain."[85] Whatever else that meant in the rhetoric of odd-fellowship, it clearly signified that Washington could count on his lieutenants to carry his racial politics even into the inner sancta of the secret orders. In further support of Asbury, Washington also enlisted a prominent Georgia Odd Fellow, Benjamin J. Davis. In an editorial in the Atlanta *Independent*, Davis predicted that at the Richmond skating rink where the nation's Odd Fellows would hold their 1906 meeting, "It will be a fight to the finish between the friends of Mr. Washington inside the Order and his enemies for the mastery. At Richmond Booker T. will be the issue and his friends have accepted the challenge and will whip the enemy on his own platform."[86]

Davis was so confident of victory that he told Washington there was no urgent necessity for urging friends to be on the ground, "to cause them to feel that any interest or desire of yours was so much at stake as to make their visit to Richmond the basis of favors expected."[87] As the 1906 convention approached, however, Washington and Scott became nervous about the outcome and sent telegrams to as many of their friends as possible to "strain a point, if necessary, and attend the meeting at Richmond."[88] At the convention, however, Dancy in a surprise move joined forces with Morris. "Wire him to quit, not mentioning my name," Asbury wired Washington.[89] Washington did as requested, reminding Dancy of his many obligations to him. "Morris of Chicago has been our bitterest enemy," he reminded Dancy, "opposing everything I have tried to do for you and others. Would be deep disappointment to me if you give him any comfort. Have done all I could to serve you and expect to continue to do so and in this crisis hope you will stand by my friends. If Jones or Asbury are defeated Morris will claim it as defeat of myself and friends."[90] Washington asked lieutenants to send similar telegrams to Dancy.[91] Asbury was reelected. In congratulating him, Washington said he was less interested in the details of the contest than in the results. "You and Mr. Davis were editors of papers which have been generous toward this work and toward myself (that was known to every member of the organization) and yet, notwithstanding that fact, you were both elected to important positions, almost without opposition. That kind of thing, it seems to me, is the important thing."[92]

When Asbury came up for reelection again in 1908, Dancy again pledged support, and the pro-Washington Odd Fellows were so well organized that they not only reelected Asbury but raised his salary. Asbury wrote, however, that "Dancy left before the fight came off; whether [because] he believed there would be no fight or to dodge the issue purposely, I cannot say."[93] In 1910, however, the convention met in Baltimore near several anti-Washington cities, and "the Steam Roller" of Edward H. Morris crushed Asbury's bid to become Grand Master of the order.[94]

In other secret orders also, Washington sought support or tried to neutralize opposition to his race leadership. Perhaps the reason why Washington had refused earlier invitations to membership in the secret orders was because his teachers at Hampton had disapproved or because of his own no-nonsense personal philosophy. When the opportunity presented itself to join the oldest and most prestigious of them all, the Prince Hall Grand Lodge of Masons in Boston, Scott persuaded him to become a member in order to deliver its centennial oration in the home of his bitterest enemies.[95] Several months before he was scheduled to speak, however, the lodge had a bitter internal dispute. At a special meeting it voted: "That Dr. Washington be officially notified by the Grand Secretary, in a courteous and fraternal letter, that his selection as Centennial Orator has created such serious discord in this and other jurisdictions, that the M. W. [Most Worthy?] Prince Hall Grand Lodge finds it imperatively necessary in the interests of harmony to withdraw the invitation extended to him by the Executive Committee."

Just as it was clear that the invitation had come to Washington through the friendship of Samuel E. Courtney, it was also clear that the enmity of Monroe Trotter's friends was behind the withdrawal of the invitation. The Grand Secretary so worded the withdrawal letter, however, as to claim that the dissension was not personal to Washington but was simply an expression of a deeply rooted feeling of the brethren that they should be represented on this important occasion by a Massachusetts Mason, identified by years of association with the Grand Lodge.[96] The Grand Secretary, who was a well-known Trotterite, suggested that Washington withdraw his acceptance of the invitation, but Washington refused. One of the things the "grand order" stood for, Washington wrote, was truth, and to make it appear that he was withdrawing something which in fact was withdrawn from him would be a deception. "For a number of years I have been a teacher of youth," he wrote, "and have always taught that short cuts and pretenses never pay, but in the long run it pays to be square, frank and open, even though by so doing one may seem to meet with momentary defeat and embarrassment."[97]

Washington's most devastating action against the Niagara Movement was his repression and then suppression of a black magazine, *The Voice of the Negro*, after it became increasingly the voice of the Niagara Movement. Washington had encouraged the founding of the journal in January 1904. He saw to it that the publishers, who also published several of his own books, put Emmett Scott on the staff as an associate editor and made his longtime friend J. W. E. Bowen a sort of senior editor. But J. Max Barber, a recent graduate of Virginia Union University, was the real editor. He was an idealistic hater of injustice, a champion of civil rights, and brash enough to take on the old minotaur Booker T. Washington himself if he thought him wrong.[98]

The first number of *The Voice of the Negro* showed a split personality, with Bowen promising in one editorial to "steer clear of the prophets, seers and visionaries" and Barber writing in another that "There may be times when literature we publish will rip open the conventional veil of optimism and drag into view conditions that shock."[99] Scott and Barber soon quarreled bitterly over editorial policy, and Scott resigned in protest against criticisms of Washington and Tuskegee.[100] Barber fell increasingly under the spell of Du Bois's thought and personality. In January 1905 he published Du Bois's charge of Washington's "hush money" to the black press.[101] Washington and Scott retaliated not only by persuading advertisers that the magazine was unfriendly to the National Negro Business League, but by complaining to the publishers.[102]

In the spring of 1905 Barber attended the founding meeting of the Niagara Movement, and after that threw off all restraint in publicizing the movement and praising Du Bois. He also featured a cartoon satirizing Washington's opposition to the reduction of southern representation as a means of combatting disfranchisement. In a lengthy account of Tuskegee's twenty-fifth anniversary, Barber scathingly criticized the speakers and recommended Washington's retirement as a race leader. Washington wrote the *Voice's* publisher warning that "they will attempt to use your magazine as a propaganda, and if permitted, you will find that Barbour will show his hand more fully in the September number."[103] The publisher promised that he would "keep an eye on the magazine," that he would do everything short of censorship and would "be on the alert and endeavor to put in the proper word at the proper time."[104] Nevertheless, *The Voice of the Negro* became not only the best edited black magazine of its brief time but increasingly the unofficial journal of the Niagara Movement. While Barber continued to solicit articles from Washington, Scott, and others of the Tuskegee faction in an effort to make his magazine a forum of all viewpoints, his editorials clearly reflected his own commitment to the militant protest of the Niagara Movement.

It was the Atlanta Riot in 1906 rather than Booker Washington directly that brought Barber down, but his own nature and Washington's contributed to making his fall a permanent one. Barber telegraphed from Atlanta to a New York newspaper an accurate anonymous report of the riot that blamed white leaders and newspapers. A telegraph operator leaked to the whites the authorship of the telegram, and they frightened Barber into fleeing to Chicago, where he stutteringly tried to continue his *Voice.* Either Washington or Scott anonymously wrote for the New York *Age* that other black Atlantans who stood their ground were "disappointed in Mr. Barber's bravery and sense of loyalty to the race if he deserts us in this trying hour."[105] They published it under a bogus Atlanta dateline. Scott justified such tactics by saying privately that "there was no reason whatever for Barbour to get scared and leave Atlanta as he did."[106]

Barber in Chicago in late 1906 and 1907 made frantic efforts to revive the *Voice,* and Washington privately considered purchasing it. Barber used T. Thomas Fortune's money to get out a few numbers of his magazine before it failed. After briefly editing the Chicago *Conservator* until Washington found out about it, and after another newspaper effort with help from Du Bois had failed, Barber moved to Philadelphia to teach in a manual labor school. Then a trustee of the school asked Washington about Barber, and Washington declared him a failure, a troublemaker "teaching colored people to hate white people," and "about as unfitted for such work as is needed to be done in Dr. Anderson's school, as any man that I can think of."[107] Barber lost the position. In desperation, he worked his way through dental school and set up practice in Philadelphia. He had found a profession in which he had only to satisfy his patients and was safe at last from Washington's baleful influence.[108] It was he, not Washington, who retired from race leadership.

Barber's decline as a voice of black aspirations and Washington's relentless pursuit of him to the dental office door is the story in exaggerated form of the failure of the Niagara Movement. The Niagara Movement was part of a black protest movement that went back to the black abolitionists and Reconstruction leaders, but its disdain of alliance with whites, its exclusiveness within the professional class of blacks, and its secrecy and rigorous ideological tests for membership made it inevitably small and powerless. Washington's Tuskegee Machine, by contrast, was broadly based throughout the black middle class, had powerful white allies and many recruits even from the Talented Tenth, made rewards and punishments a central feature of its recruitment and retention of its followers. So the Tuskegee Machine flourished and the Niagara Movement barely survived until new events in 1908 and 1909 brought them new allies among the whites.

CHAPTER 5

Family Matters

God setteth the solitary in families. . . .

PSALM 68:6

BOOKER T. Washington in his prime had a tremendously active public life, which went with his role as the most famous Negro in the world. He also had a multichambered secret life, full of spies, whispered confidences, false datelines, and "personal and confidential" correspondence. But he never had much of a private life. Living his adult life far away from the places of his birth and youth, he maintained close touch with only one friend of his youth, Dr. Samuel E. Courtney of Boston. His co-workers all called him Mister or Doctor. Even his third wife, Margaret, had a hard time saying his first name, and so virtually the only persons who used it were his former teachers at Hampton Institute and some of his enemies. Just as in his youth he had never had leisure and knew no childish games, in his adulthood he was too busy meeting the demands of public life to have time for a private life. The only exception was his family, and particularly his three motherless children on whom he and their stepmother lavished care and warmth, in spite of the press of his public affairs and her duties as head of Women's Industries at Tuskegee Institute.

Washington's relationship with Margaret presents the student of his life with a mystery because, for one reason or another, there is no intimate correspondence with her, or with his earlier wives, for that matter. Perhaps such letters were removed from his files after his death, but perhaps not. While he was away from Tuskegee for about half of every year, Margaret was busy at her headquarters in Dorothy Hall and as hostess at "The Oaks" to a steady stream of white and black guests from afar. She played a central role in extending the educational and home economics role of the institute into the surrounding region, holding mothers' meetings in the town and doing missionary work at the black schools and plantation settlements of rural Macon County. She made women's club work an important part of her life, heading the local black woman's club, serving as president of the state federation, and twice as president of the National Association of Colored Women's Clubs. She usually spent summers with her husband at his northern fund-raising headquarters, first in Massachusetts and later in New York, but she seldom traveled with him on his busy lecture tours and hard all-night train rides. There is no evidence in the written record that she played a major role in Washington's decisions in public affairs. At Tuskegee, however, she was a power. As one of the school's chief divisional officers and member of the executive council, she had a moderating influence on the ultra-strict code of personal conduct that many of the faculty tried to impose. She also tried in the fullest sense to be the mother of Booker T. Washington, Jr., and Ernest Davidson Washington, and did her best with the willful eldest child, Portia.

Portia M. Washington had found it difficult to share her father with her stepmother after his marriage in 1892, and she spent three years in Framingham, Massachusetts, living and studying with a classmate of her first stepmother, Olivia. She returned to enroll at Tuskegee Institute, graduating in 1900. After teaching music and reading at Tuskegee for a year, she went North again to study music and prepare herself for college.[1] She entered Wellesley College in the fall of 1901, but as a special rather than regular student because of the haphazard nature of her preparatory education. She had planned to live in a dormitory, but either because some southern students objected, as some newspapers reported, or because she was a special student, as officially reported, she moved into a boarding house near the campus and took her meals nearby with three of the professors. In an interview in the Boston *Globe,* Portia said her reason for going to Wellesley was to make herself more useful to her father and to Tuskegee as a teacher. "Besides," she said, "my father has been very anxious to have me attend college. He believes in the college education of girls where it is possible for them to have it, and my mother, you know, is a graduate of Fisk University. But for most of the girls at Tuskegee father sees that the industrial education and that which emphasizes the household arts is most needed. None the less, he encourages further study whenever it is possible for the student to get it. One Tuskegee girl, whose father is a rich Jew in Mobile, Ala., has just entered Columbia university, and is doing very well there. Another is at the German conservatory in New York City." [2]

A letter from one of her instructors, Alicia Keyes, provides an insight into Portia's experience at Wellesley. She wrote that the year had been a hard one for Portia because of loneliness and homesickness. The teachers were more cordial than the students, and Professor Keyes hoped that Washington would send his daughter to "some more musical place. It is too lonely for her here, living as a special student must, in the village. She sees too little of the people of her own age. She's been spending this evening with me, but my interests are so much older ones that I feel I cannot give her the gayety that she needs with her temperament." [3] Katherine Coman, another professor with whom Portia took her meals, wrote the concerned father as mid-year examinations approached: "Portia's status in college will depend upon her passing in harmony and Bible. I hope that she may pass both, but in case she does not, what am I to do for her? I think it would be a mistake for her to remain in College even if the authorities could be induced to make an exception in her case. If she fails after all the help that has been given her, she is evidently not prepared for work of college grade." [4]

Wellesley College did not permit Portia Washington to continue beyond the first year, a decision that must have been particularly galling to her because it disappointed her father's expectations of her. She idolized him. She did not stand in awe of him, however. As she said in a newspaper interview, "We joke at home about father's silence. I suppose he is thinking always of the work when he is at home. But the public sees him at his best. When he loses himself in his subject he is much more animated than in the family circle." [5]

The official reason Wellesley gave was "deficiency in music," but the skeptical Montgomery *Advertiser* said that was "merely an excuse, not a reason," and that it was "mainly, it seems, because the numerous young Southern white women there refused absolutely to associate with her," and this antagonism was increased by her writing signed articles for publication about Wellesley. Because northern students took her side, the school divided into two hostile camps.[6] There was so much newspaper comment that Caroline Hazard, the president of Wellesley, sought to set the record straight. Portia Washington, she said, was treated exactly as other special students were treated, and "left entirely of her own accord, having never intended to pursue a regular college course." Wellesley had always admitted qualified black students, and two had graduated.[7]

Many northern as well as southern newspapers took an inordinate interest in the matter. "He has always warned the negroes in the South against the folly of forcing themselves into the company of the whites," said the New York *American*. "That is good advice for others and is really good counsel for Booker Washington."[8] The Boston *Guardian*, a year before its editor, Monroe Trotter, clashed head-on with Washington in the Boston Riot, took Portia's misfortune as an opportunity to needle her father, remarking that his children "are not taking to higher education like a duck to water, and while their defect in this line is doubtless somewhat inherited, they justify to some extent their father's well known antipathy to anything higher than the three Rs for his 'people.'"[9] Washington was livid with rage that the *Guardian* would stoop to attacking him through his daughter. "For over a year," he wrote privately, "they have been trying in all kinds of ways to force me to note the mean things that they have said, but thus far I have been silent and that has hurt them worse than anything I could say."[10]

T. Thomas Fortune came to Washington's defense against "the Boston skunk," saying that Trotter had his facts wrong, that Portia had told him that she had never intended to return to Wellesley but hoped to enter the Boston Conservatory of Music instead because at Wellesley "restrictions imposed on her in the matter of domiciliation were objectionable."[11] The whole truth probably did include Portia's inadequate preparation for work at one of the nation's elite colleges. At any rate, Washington asked Fortune not to prolong the controversy, saying, "I dislike exceedingly to discuss private affairs in the papers."[12]

Portia found a less challenging, more congenial atmosphere at Bradford Academy, in the Boston suburbs, a secondary girls' school headed by Laura A. Knott, a longtime friend of Washington and of Tuskegee. "Miss Knott is very kind to me and has me up in her room so often to play to her," Portia wrote her father. "One night she asked me to play her to sleep." The students at Bradford were friendly and interested in Tuskegee; they collected small donations to provide a scholarship for one female student. "I like Bradford more and more and the girls too," she wrote home. "I have some very good friends among the best girls here." [13] Laura Knott promised to do her best to protect Portia from newspaper reporters, and did so by invoking the school rule that no person from outside could see any student without a teacher's permission.[14]

When the New York *Times* persisted in keeping the Wellesley dismissal in the public eye by questioning Washington's judgment in sending his daughter to a college in the first place, since he believed in industrial rather than higher education, Washington could not resist replying to this distortion of his position. "I sent my daughter north to take some special studies after she had finished two regular industrial courses at the Tuskegee Institute," he wrote, "in the same way that I have sent at least a dozen of our students to other institutions in order to better prepare them for work at the Tuskegee institute. I never lose sight, and never intend to, of the fundamental ideas of our institution, and they are always kept in view." [15] The Boston *Guardian* crowed: "Thus is our 'greatest' man compelled to excuse the education of his children." [16] When William H. Baldwin, Jr., the Tuskegee trustee, first learned of the controversy, he asked Washington for an explanation. It was all started by the scurrilous *Guardian*, said Washington. "I have never attempted to set any limit upon the development of our race and shall never attempt to do so. The only thing I insist upon, and shall continue to insist upon, is that they lay the foundation in the more fundamental things and grow in a natural rather than an artificial manner, and just in proportion as they do this their children will be given advantages which the first generation did not possess. I confess that the editorial in the Times seems to me very contemptible." [17]

When Portia decided she was happy enough at Bradford to become a regular student there, Emmett Scott sent a transcript of her Tuskegee courses to Miss Knott.[18] She hoped that another black student would attend, and at her suggestion Washington made arrangements for admission of the daughter of George H. White of North Carolina, the last southern black congressman for many decades.[19] Meanwhile Portia felt isolated and lonely, though her grades were good and she was popular enough to be elected an officer in the student government.[20] She was particularly lonely during vacations, and Tuskegee was too far for her to visit before summer. During the spring vacation in 1904 she proposed that she board at Wellesley, near where her brother Booker was in Wellesley School.[21] Her father persuaded her instead to visit his friend Fred R. Moore and his family in Brooklyn.[22] Washington himself saw her briefly on his way through New York on a business trip.[23] She remained rather lonely and uncomfortable, however, and wrote her parents that "while I really love Bradford I shall not be sorry when I graduate because of the nervous strain I feel nearly all the time."[24] She wrote wistfully of the weekend some other girls were to spend in the White Mountains. Her report to her father on her course of study in her final year indicates the college preparatory character of Bradford. It included "Ethics with Miss Knott, History of Art with Dr Von March of Harvard, Eng Lit. studying such poets as Milton, Browning, Tennyson, Burns, Byron and Shelley, Composition, Bible, taking up the History of the early Christian Church, Hist of Christianity, Economics and Sociology." She wished her brothers well in their own boarding schools and reassured her parents, "I am in splendid health now—never felt better. I sleep better than ever before."[25] A highlight of her last year was when her father gave a lecture at Bradford in the spring of 1905.[26] She graduated that June a few days after turning twenty-two.

Far more mature and self-assured than she had been at the time of her plunge into college four years earlier, Portia Washington also knew better what she wanted. She and her father decided she should go to Germany for further music study. He received a rebuff from the first school he tried, the Willard School for Girls in Berlin, where he thought he had a friend in Alice H. Luce. She replied to his letter: "It gives me more pain than I can express to have to say that your daughter could not be other than extremely unhappy if she were placed here, under these conditions. And much as I might long to do so, I should be powerless to change these conditions to such an extent as to really protect her from the most painful experiences."[27]

They made arrangements for Portia to board with a German family and to study piano under Professor Martin Krause, an instructor at Stern's Conservatory in Berlin. Jane E. Clark, Tuskegee's dean of women, accompanied Portia to Europe. They spent the summer in

England and France before settling Portia in Berlin for the academic year.[28]

Meanwhile Booker T. Washington, Jr., nicknamed Baker within the family and called Booker at his schools, was having a different kind of adolescence from that of his half-sister. Whereas she was always eager to please her father and all in authority, almost too earnest in her effort to follow in his footsteps, Booker was a handsome, willful youth who seemed to bring most of his problems on himself. His insouciance troubled his busy father. After attending the practice school on the Tuskegee campus with the other faculty children, in 1902 he entered Rock Ridge Hall in Wellesley Hills, Massachusetts. Portia, of course, was still a student at Wellesley College and very close by. Their occasional visits together relieved their homesickness.[29] Soon afterward, however, Booker transferred to Wellesley School for Boys, and Portia went on to Bradford Academy.

Edward A. Benner, principal of Wellesley School, was a warm admirer of Booker T. Washington and hoped to be of service to him in bringing up his son. At first he described Booker's behavior as exemplary, but he soon had to report his "playing with the truth," "smoking in his room," and neglecting his study hours. Benner even wrote that "one night he came into his room by the window after hours." Neither principal nor parent found that amusing.[30] Finally Booker committed the unpardonable misdemeanor of visiting his sister in Boston during school hours, and Benner asked Washington to remove his son from the school.[31] Washington somehow mollified Benner, for Booker was still at Wellesley School the following fall. Benner wrote to the anxious father: "I am very glad to report a great improvement in Booker's spirit and way of going to work. He seems to have acquired more manliness and feeling of responsibility." But the principal had to qualify his praise by saying, "It may be that he will not do brilliant work, but if his industry and loyalty hold out, he will make such an advance as will gratify you more than a large pile of brick and mortar for Tuskegee."[32]

Washington was a conscientious if somewhat humorless father, and he worked closely with Benner to try to shape his son's character development. He wrote the headmaster that he had just urged Booker to work hard in his carpentry course rather than go into Boston for drum lessons. Furthermore, he was "asking his mother to write him also as she puts things a little more persuasively and perhaps a little more softly than I do."[33] Washington brought Booker home for the Christmas holidays in 1903 but later decided that had been a mistake, for Booker's grades slipped and "his mind is considerably on matters at Tuskegee."[34] Booker seemed to live for vacations. "I am going to buckle down to business and hope that when Easter vacation comes I shall not be disappointed about being in New York, with you," he wrote his father in the spring of 1904.[35]

"We are so anxious to have these children grow up to be useful and good," Margaret Washington confided to Emmett Scott.[36] The very nature of their work, however, forced them to neglect the children of their own family, to relinquish to others much of the responsibility for their guidance and environment. They did the best they could under the circumstances. Washington urged Benner to correct his son's posture, saying "He has a tendency, I have noticed, to stoop over when he sits, and to stand not at all erect when he walks."[37]

Benner was only one of a series of headmasters sorely troubled by Booker's adolescent combination of lassitude and high spirits, his truancy, and his fast motorcycle, which his father in some weak moment indulged him with. Removing Booker from the Wellesley School in 1904, Washington arranged for his admission at the Institute for Colored Youth in Cheyney, Pennsylvania,[38] but then changed his mind and enrolled him in the senior class at Tuskegee, where he graduated after one year. While Booker was actually enrolled at Tuskegee, the New York *World* published a story that Booker was "captain of the football team at Phillips–Exeter and on equal social footing presumably with the sons of leading white men of the country." This was alleged evidence that Washington did not practice the industrial education that he preached and that "if his school is not good enough for his own family there must be something wrong."[39] The author of this story was the Birmingham *Age-Herald*'s Montgomery correspondent, whose purpose was to compare Tuskegee Institute unfavorably with the Negro Normal and Industrial School in Montgomery headed by a white man, Washington's inveterate rival William B. Paterson, who furnished all the misinformation in the article.[40] The Washington *Post* published another false story, reprinted with alacrity in the Montgomery *Advertiser,* that Booker had applied for a government job as an army paymaster. This was too much for Washington, who protested to the editor of the *Advertiser* that his son was only sixteen, had been

all year a student at Tuskegee, and was taking not only academic subjects but bricklaying.[41] Washington's son was the victim of an effort
on the part of southerners to force Washington into affirmation of a
mutual exclusiveness of industrial and academic education. The effort, of course, was unsuccessful.

During the year at Tuskegee, Washington took Booker to a New
York physician, whom he later thanked for "the almost miraculous
cure which you brought about in the case of our son. . . ." Both the
nature of the ailment and the cure remain mysteries, but Booker was
reported "completely relieved of the trouble which has been such a
serious handicap to him for years. He seems entirely like a new boy."[42]

In the fall of 1905 Booker entered Dummer Academy, in South
Byfield, Massachusetts. He began to show more ambition to "go
through college," according to Thomas and Lexa Calloway, old Tuskegee friends of the family whom he visited during the Thanksgiving
holidays. "So few sons of famous men have ambition to do anything
more than be sons of their fathers," Lexa Calloway wrote Margaret
Washington, "and I feared that the unnatural life which they have
had at Tuskegee—among the masses and yet not of them, a class alone
to themselves—would make them less ambitious than boys who were
not so situated."[43]

Booker complained, however, of "a thumping in the head or dizzi-
ness whenever he concentrates his mind on a given study for any
length of time," and Washington removed him from Dummer Academy for a semester in the open air of the Tuskegee Institute farm.[44]
On his return to Dummer, however, he began to excel both in his
studies and in football. His parents visited him several times in Boston, and during his last year his roommate was his old friend Juan E.
Gomez of the Tuskegee class of 1906. Booker played left halfback on
the football team, caught for the baseball team, and reportedly was
"making good" along academic lines.[45] Washington apparently hoped
that Gomez would have a steadying influence on his son, as apparently he did for a while. In the fall of 1907 they both transferred to
Phillips Academy in Exeter, New Hampshire, with good recommendations from Dummer.[46]

Exeter's headmaster, Harlan P. Amen, was another longtime admirer of Washington, and the school had a tradition of liberal admission policy. There were already three other Afro-American students.[47] The two Tuskegeans, however, lasted for only three weeks

there. When a teacher spoke sharply to Gomez, he left class in a rage; Booker also left, cut his other classes, and was dismissed.[48] Amen wrote Washington mildly after the two young men had enrolled elsewhere that he hoped they were doing "profitable work in their respective schools. We shall not lose our interest in them, because they are no longer with us."[49] To one of the many newspapers that gave inordinate attention to the dismissal, Washington wrote: "My son has kept me fully informed about his actions and movements. I consider his leaving Exeter nothing more than a boyish huff, perhaps growing out of his not understanding the rules and requirements of the Academy. . . . The whole matter has been settled to my satisfaction."[50] It was not too late in the year for Booker to enroll at Fisk University.

Washington's youngest child, Ernest Davidson Washington, familiarly known as Dave, was not as robust as the two older children. He was the last to leave home for boarding school after attendance at the Tuskegee Institute practice school until 1904. The Washingtons chose for him Oberlin Academy, connected with the college of the same name in northern Ohio. John Fisher Peck, the principal, wrote to Margaret Washington, "We are finding that Dave has many things to learn, but are hoping that steadiness and patience will do for him what he needs."[51] His report card at the end of the first term, however, was a disappointment, and Washington wrote Peck that he hoped that under his guidance Dave would get down to harder study. "We wish very much that the marks had been higher," he explained, "but, as Mrs. Washington has already stated to you, the boy has never learned to study and he has been made a pet and a baby of by every one in our family and on the school grounds. He has always impressed me as being a boy who above all things likes to have a good time, he is not bad nor stubborn, but in some way he has always been able to ingratiate himself into the good graces of the teachers to such an extent that they have never really come down hard upon him like the other students."[52] For a man earnestly dedicated to self-help, Washington showed a remarkable understanding and tolerance of this son's youthful hedonism. Perhaps he had learned something from his difficulties with his older children.

Whether Dave would respond to the demands of the Oberlin Academy was a question never settled, for in December 1905 he developed an inflammation of his left eye so severe that the physician forbade any close use of his eyes for six months.[53] He took an extensive trip with his mother to the west coast and Mexico that winter.[54] Eye troubles plagued Dave for the rest of his life, but he entered Tuskegee Institute, and Washington wrote Portia in Berlin in 1906 that "Davidson is not very strong this winter, but is managing to keep up with his studies."[55] He graduated in 1907, and spent several years teaching penmanship at Tuskegee, while studying college preparatory subjects part time.[56]

Portia Washington meanwhile had gone to Berlin for her musical studies. At Paris she and Jane E. Clark met Edward W. Blyden, the Liberian minister to France, Germany, and England. He took them sightseeing all over Paris, and the black men connected with the American embassy also took a great interest in the young Miss Washington and the beautiful Miss Clark.[57] Washington had already arranged with the Colonial Economic Committee, which owed him a favor for sending Tuskegee graduates to Togo, West Africa, to teach cotton-growing, to act as his daughter's bankers in Berlin.[58]

Portia's first test was an audition for admission to piano instruction by Professor Martin Krause, who had once been a student of Franz Liszt. After playing some European classical pieces, she ended with a work of the Anglo-African composer Samuel Coleridge–Taylor, an arrangement of "Sometimes I Feel like a Motherless Child." She undoubtedly played it with feeling, for her own mother was dead, and it was a piece both unfamiliar and moving to Professor Krause. She passed her examination.[59] She studied for two years under Krause, whom she called "one of the greatest teachers now living," and developed a good command of German.[60]

In one of her letters home Portia apparently expressed some reluctance to return to the hostile racial climate of the United States, for her father urged her to put aside such thoughts. "I think you will make a mistake," he wrote, "if you will let your mind dwell too much upon American prejudice, or any other racial prejudice. The thing is for one to get above such things. If one gets in the habit of continually thinking and talking about race prejudice, he soon gets to the point where he is fit for little that is worth doing. In the northern part of the United States, there are a number of colored people who make their lives miserable, because all their talk is about race prejudice."[61]

At the end of her first year Portia wrote her father: "I thought you would be interested to know how successful I was in my examination before Professor Krause. He expressed himself as being very much satisfied with my work and the great progress I had made during the year. He said that my work showed that I had been very industrious. I was so frightfully nervous over this examination that now I really am completely run down. I took it yesterday (June 28th) and it was one of the hottest days I have ever known. I shall be so glad to get out of Berlin for a while and have a complete rest."[62] She had already made plans for a summer vacation in England and Scotland, and promised her father to visit his friends the T. Fisher Unwins and Samuel Coleridge–Taylor when in London.[63] Margaret Washington visited her in the summer of 1907 and Portia accompanied her home.

Meanwhile Portia must have been relieving her loneliness also by another correspondence, for in December 1906 the Boston *Guardian* had maliciously announced the impending engagement of Portia and William Sidney Pittman of Washingon, D.C., who had been a student at Tuskegee. R. W. Thompson promised Emmett Scott that he would set the record straight. "I shall get up a Washington letter this week," he wrote, "denying the cock-and-bull story . . . and discrediting the rumor of Pittman's engagement to Portia Washington. The Guardian is a modern Ananias, aged in the barrel, and stamped 104 proof by the Internal Revenue department."[64] The *Guardian* was truthful, however, if premature, for Portia had hardly returned home in 1907 when the engagement announcement appeared in the *Tuskegee Student,* and the wedding followed about a month later.[65]

Sidney Pittman was a Tuskegee graduate who owed much to Washington's favor but also had earned by drive and ambition his professional status as an architect. The son of Alabama slaves, he had grown up in Montgomery and Birmingham. He entered Tuskegee at seventeen and graduated after five years while earning all of his expenses. He graduated as a wheelwright, but he also had three years of mechanical drawing under the tutelage of an M. I. T. graduate architect, Robert R. Taylor, the superintendent of buildings and grounds. Washington helped pay Pittman's expenses to study at Drexel Institute in Philadelphia until its faculty voted him a scholarship. He graduated with honors in 1900 and returned by prior agreement to teach at Tuskegee. He designed five of Tuskegee's buildings. Quarreling with Taylor, he left for Washington, D.C., where he quickly became a leading architect. He designed the Garfield School, the segregated black YMCA, and other buildings in the city, and elsewhere, including a hotel in Norfolk, campus buildings at Voorhees Industrial School

and Kentucky Normal and Industrial Institute, and the Negro Building at the Jamestown Exposition of 1907. He organized the Fairmount Heights Improvement Company in the Washington suburbs
and was a leader of one faction of the National Negro Business League
in Washington.[66]

The wedding of Portia Washington and Sidney Pittman was the chief
social event of the season at Tuskegee Institute. On the evening of
October 31, 1907, the electrical division of the school transformed the
entire grounds of "The Oaks" into a blaze of colored lights festooned
on the trees, rose bushes, and shrubs. Booker T. Washington led his
daughter down the aisle, and the Reverend John W. Whittaker, chaplain of the institute, performed the ceremony before a large crowd.
The wedding cake was "a particularly formidable looking affair," which
was served with elaborately molded ice cream.[67]

The couple left for a house that Sidney Pittman had designed in
Fairmount Heights. All of Portia's three children were born in Washington, D.C.: William Sidney, Jr., Booker T., and Fannie Virginia.
Her father kept in close touch and did all he could to help make the
marriage a good one. Among the early presents he and Margaret gave
Portia was a piano, for Christmas 1907.[68] Washington also helped his
son-in-law in his usual quiet way to find clients. "I suppose you have
seen by the papers that Mr. Carnegie is likely to give Howard University a building for a library," he wrote. "Perhaps you might see President Thirkield regarding the plans for this building. Do not mention
my name in connection with this information."[69] Over the years
Washington did Pittman many similar favors.

Washington arranged for the Pittmans to have two reserved seats
in the reviewing stand opposite the White House for the inaugural
parade in 1909.[70] The *Tuskegee Student* reported in detail Portia's first
American piano recital, at the Metropolitan A. M. E. Church in Washington. The highlight of her performance was a moving rendition of
"Sometimes I Feel like a Motherless Child."[71] When his first grand-
child became seriously ill and the mother was near a nervous breakdown with worry, Washington canceled his busy schedule for two weeks
to spend the time with the Pittmans, arranged for Dr. A. M. Curtis,
head of Freedmen's Hospital in Washington, to take the case, and
gave help with the hospital and medical bills.[72] Years later, Portia Pittman recalled that, during one of his many visits with her, she and her
father decided to ascend the Washington Monument. Just after he

had signed the guest book the white man in charge snatched the book and officiously said something to the effect that "niggers" were not allowed to sign. Then, seeing the signature, he sought to apologize. Washington accepted with an indifferent shrug.[73]

The Pittmans moved to Dallas in 1913, and Portia took a position as a music teacher in the Booker T. Washington High School there. Sometime in the 1920s she separated from her husband, though she never divorced him. In 1928 she returned to Tuskegee Institute, where she taught music and directed the choir for more than twenty-five years. Her son Booker Pittman was a jazz saxophonist who played with several of the big bands and later moved to Brazil.[74] Portia outlived all of her children, dying in Washington, D.C., in 1978.[75]

Booker T. Washington, Jr., after leaving Phillips Exeter Academy so abruptly in 1907, was not too late to enroll at Fisk University, and did so. This appealed to his father, who was a trustee of Fisk and a frequent visitor; he also had many friends in Nashville who could check on his son and report on his progress or any difficulties. Washington also made special demands on the Fisk faculty. He urged a faculty member, for example, "without using my name," to require his son to commit to memory "good specimens of literature, either poetry or prose, and also have an opportunity to speak before his class or some other body once a month, or something like that."[76]

Washington furnished his son with the tennis racquets and motorcycle requisite to his college experience, and Booker in response showed that he had matured. He studied more diligently but kept his high spirits. In 1909 he developed a strong desire to attend the Taft inaugural festivities. "Personally I do not wish him to go," Washington wrote to Dean Herbert H. Wright. "I have not told him yet that he cannot go as I found it better policy to gradually lead him and guide him. I wish very much, if you take my view, that you might talk with him with a view of persuading him out of his notion."[77] Washington did not want his son to interrupt his class work when he was doing well. Soon afterwards, a Nashville friend reported: "I saw Booker last night after the mid-week prayer meeting. I found him well and in good spirits and reconciled to remaining at school rather than going to the inaugeration [sic]. He was anxious to go, but sees that it is best to put in his time at the university."[78]

Washington's new policy of giving his son more power of decision seemed to work. He became known as "a chip off the old block," and began to speak on "character building," saying that "all work is honorable and all forms of idleness [are] a disgrace."[79] As usual, he tired of school by spring, but wrote his father, ". . . whenever I have these tired feelings I always look at that little 'motto' that you sent me, and get from it new vigor to continue. 'The World Honors the Sticker, Never the Quitter.' "[80] When he had trouble with Latin, his father insisted that he hire a tutor.[81] When Washington rented a summer place on the beach on Long Island, Booker spent much of his vacation there. "I am spending the greater portion of my time out on the water," he wrote his father, "rowing, swim[m]ing, etc. so as to be ready for hard study the coming year."[82]

Booker was always in difficulty with one or another academic subject, Latin one term, algebra another. In the summer of 1911 Washington made arrangements for Booker to get his textbooks in advance so as to get a head start on the next year's classes.[83] Washington was pleased with his son's growing self-reliance, however, and wrote to Harlan P. Amen of Exeter that his son's crisis there had been a turning point in his life. "He is as settled and thoughtful as a man many times his age," the proud father wrote. "He does not give a single bit of trouble or cause us any anxiety whatever. He is a completely changed boy, and promises to make a strong, good, useful man."[84] He graduated from Fisk in 1913.

As Booker returned home from Fisk, Washington confessed to Dean Wright that "he and I both are somewhat puzzled as to what he ought to undertake for the future." In spite of Booker's mediocre grades, his father thought he should take a year or two of postgraduate training of some kind before launching a career.[85] He enrolled that fall in the Northwestern University School of Pharmacy in Chicago. During the Christmas vacation he went to Houston, Texas. There on New Year's Eve of 1913, apparently to his parents' surprise, he married Nettie Hancock, whom he had known in college. She was a graduate of Fisk and a teacher in the black institution for the deaf, dumb and blind in Austin. Her mother was a faculty member at Prairie View State Normal and Industrial Institute.[86]

After some indecision, Washington decided to increase Booker's allowance so that his bride could live with him in Chicago. Washington wired his son, "Think good plan for Nettie to take lessons in domestic science at some of [the] institutions there."[87] Booker finished the year at the pharmacy school but apparently did not do well. After a talk with his son while passing through Chicago, Washington wrote the secretary of the school that Booker "realizes keenly that he is not making the record that he wants to make or should make in all of his studies, but I think he is doing his best. He realizes now that he made a great mistake when in college in not taking the course in chemistry."[88]

Washington did what he could to settle Booker in Tuskegee. He had a house built for the couple in Greenwood, the faculty village, in the summer of 1914. He also financed his son's construction of a business building on the courthouse square in Tuskegee.[89] Booker remained for some years at Tuskegee, and Washington lived long enough to hold Booker T. Washington III in his lap for a photograph. Booker worked briefly in connection with the establishment of Baldwin Farms, a farm-purchase community experiment near Tuskegee.[90] Then the Rosenwald Foundation program for building black rural schoolhouses employed him as an agent. In 1918 he became a federal claims adjustor for the 9000 black employees of the Muscle Shoals nitrate plant in northern Alabama. Then he moved to Los Angeles, where he was a successful real estate broker and his wife a teacher in the California State School for the Deaf.[91] He died in 1945.

Davidson Washington was less successful in college, partly because ill health continued to plague him. He enrolled at Talladega College in 1910–11 but did not take a full load of courses. "Be sure to take plenty of good open air exercise every day," his anxious father wrote. "Do not try to take more than two studies, otherwise your health will break down."[92] Davidson apparently had a successful college year,[93] but decided to move on to the Leonard Medical School, a branch of Shaw University in North Carolina. He studied there from 1911 to 1913 but did not complete the course, possibly because of continued eye trouble. He earnestly tried to live up to what was expected of him, but he was blind in one eye and had only partial vision with the other.[94] He had to live with the frequent reminder, as a friend of his father put it, to "remember, people expect so much of you because of the greatness of your father."[95] Dave was popular among his fellow-students at Shaw, and several of them urged him not to drop out. One wrote, "I believe with your ability you could be alright by the time school opens, and if it is too lonesome for you to study alone write me and I'll come down and put more medicine in your head this summer than you can tell in a year. . . . You know best though but I think you are wrong this time."[96]

Dave enrolled in the fall of 1913 in the New York School for Secretaries, taking stenography and typing, a field of employment not yet dominated by women. While in New York he met and married Edith Merriweather, a Washington-born teacher in Atlantic City. He continued his secretarial course in New York, while his wife moved to Tuskegee and taught in the practice school. Soon after her arrival on campus she first met her father-in-law when he knocked on her door and graciously presented as a wedding present the deed to a house in Greenwood. Meanwhile, Davidson passed all of his courses except shorthand, in which he did not achieve the required speed of 100 words a minute. The school's director, however, allowed him to meet the requirement at Tuskegee if he would send a notarized statement that he had reached the required speed. She called him "a very pleasing and intelligent student."[97]

After working for a short while in the principal's office under the guidance of Emmett Scott, Davidson Washington became a northern fund-raiser for Tuskegee, and for the last ten years before his death in 1938 he was a public relations officer of the institute. He edited a compilation of his father's major speeches, published in 1932, and a short volume of his quotations.[98]

Being the principal's children often made life difficult for the younger Washingtons. Though often away in boarding school rather than in a normal family environment, they never lacked their father's attention and devotion. Washington gradually learned to trim his expectations of his children to fit their abilities, and though they never achieved his fame or distinction they never embarrassed him by wrongdoing. They led useful, ordinary lives. Indeed, they seemed to do everything better as soon as they ceased to depend on him.

Washington's strong family sense embraced also his extended family. This he had shown in his early career by bringing his half-brother John and his adopted brother James to Tuskegee Institute as officers of the school, and he took a fostering interest in their numerous children as well as his own. He also maintained a lifelong interest in the welfare of his sister Amanda, back in West Virginia, whose limited education kept her on the edge of poverty. Washington himself had been deprived during his childhood of family stability, and he seemed to compensate for this by a strong interest not only in his own kinfolk but in the in-laws of his three marriages and in a few people, such as Aunt Sophie Agee and Cousin Sallie Poe, whose genetic relation to him was vague and uncertain but who had shared the early experiences of slavery and struggle.[99]

As all of the Washington children left home for boarding school, in 1904 Margaret Washington's nephew and niece came from Mississippi after the death of their parents to live in Tuskegee. The nephew, Thomas J. Murray, was almost grown and lived on his own, working as a cashier of the Tuskegee Institute savings bank.[100] Laura Murray the niece, however, was a pre-school child, and the Washingtons adopted her and brought her into their house. "Your mama and Booker and Laura send love," Washington wrote Portia in 1904 while she was at Bradford. When the photographer Frances Benjamin Johnston made her second visit to Tuskegee in 1906 to add to her portfolio of photographs taken in 1902, she took a group photograph of Washington with his family. He was seated, with his two nearly grown sons in the background and on his knee in a white dress was Laura Murray Washington, as she now called herself. She bore a strong resemblance to her Aunt Margaret, whom she now called "mama."[101]

The Washingtons treated Laura in every way as part of their nuclear family, and in 1914 they sent her to Spelman Seminary (later Spelman College) in Atlanta. Her "papa" kept her supplied with good reading matter as well as the necessities and the news. "We all want to see you very much and are longing for Christmas time to come so you can come home," Washington wrote in a more openly affectionate way than he had shown to his other children.[102] He had not been excessively severe with the other children, but he indulged Laura. She felt free to ask for extra Christmas money to buy presents for Booker, Dave, and their wives, signing her letter "Your loving daughter."[103] After she had returned to Spelman for a second year, one letter from Washington apologized for not having written recently. "I have thought of you constantly, as all of us have," he reassured her. "I hope very much that you are well and enjoying your studies and life at Spelman. We are all well." That was less than a month before his death. He sent her a book and her "Mamma" sent a Bible.[104] Laura later graduated from Spelman, moved to Chicago, and married a lawyer named Cyrus whom she later divorced. Margaret Washington on her death in 1925 left her several houses she owned in Tuskegee, Chicago, and Lincoln Heights, Maryland.[105]

Washington kept continuous touch with his sister Amanda Johnston, particularly after her husband died in 1902, and arranged for her children to attend Tuskegee. The eldest, George Washington Albert Johnston, known as Albert or G. W. A., graduated from Tuskegee Institute in 1893, and worked as Washington's personal business agent and cashier of the campus savings bank for several years. Beginning in 1901, he was part of Washington's personal political machine, working in Birmingham as the clerk of Joseph O. Thompson, the collector of internal revenue and presidential political referee for Alabama. Clara Johnston, who graduated in 1901, returned to Malden to raise chickens, help her mother run a restaurant, and engage in other small enterprises. In 1908 she married John S. Cheatham.[106] The marriage did not last, however, and she soon returned to live with her mother. The two younger Johnstons, Scoville and Benjamin, also attended Tuskegee but did not graduate. Scoville remained in Alabama after leaving school, but Benjamin returned to West Virginia.[107]

Amanda Johnston had a harder and harder struggle as Malden declined; the salt works were abandoned, and the nearby coal mines closed. She worked long hours in a restaurant, and she and Clara raised vegetables and livestock.[108] Washington helped his sister to make hers "the prettiest house in Malden," but she was so poor that when her husband died in 1902 she had to borrow $20 from Washington for the funeral expenses. "Clara has thirteen young chickens," she wrote. "Hope we can do well with them." Of her own situation after the funeral she said, "Well Bro Im alone in this world. If I keep Restrant Ill not get up all Hours of the night Im afraid that Will Caus trouble. I dont know what to do."[109]

Washington helped his sister in 1903 by paying for construction of a separate restaurant building.[110] He sent her about $20 every month for many years.[111] He paid her expenses and those of several old Malden friends to attend the Tuskegee commencement in 1905.[112]

Clara relieved some of the financial strain by taking a job in Charleston in 1906 cleaning and pressing clothes.[113] To give Amanda more room for a market garden, Washington rented one or two acres of bottom land from Ernest H. Ruffner, son of Viola Ruffner whom he had known as a child. She also with his help expanded her restaurant to include a boarding house with about five occupants.[114]

Amanda was always able to turn to her affluent brother for help, which he always gave without stint or chiding. He visited her about once a year, whenever his journeys brought him nearby. In 1914 her health began to break, despite frequent visits from the black family doctor in Charleston at Washington's expense. "I had two doctors Tuesday," Clara wrote, "they decided she is suffering with mental melancholy."[115] After a few months' rest she was up and about again, but in the spring of 1915 she had a stroke.[116]

Washington rushed to Amanda's bedside, but he had to leave for a speaking engagement. It was obvious that this was to be her final illness, but Washington as usual had no room to fit death into his schedule. He arranged for Margaret, Albert Johnston, and other family members to go to Malden to her deathbed and the funeral. He telegraphed his nephew, "Before you leave Malden be sure arrange for good iron fence to be put around grave. See that suitable tombstone is erected, also see that suitable arrangements are made for Clara. Sorry cannot be with the family today."[117] To Byrd Prillerman, an old friend near Malden who had often helped his family, he wrote: "I cannot find words with which to express the deep gratitude which all of the members of our family feel to you and Mrs. Prillerman and others there for your very great kindness to my sister during her illness and in connection with the funeral and burial. We shall never forget you."[118]

Though Washington was the boss of everything he undertook—Tuskegee, the National Negro Business League, the Tuskegee Machine, and his family—in all of these he took care to meet all of his obligations and to encourage and sustain others. He gradually learned to give his children freer choice as they matured, and mutual help rather than individualistic self-help was the social principle that guided his relationship with both his immediate and his extended family. He managed, without any evident abuse of nepotism, to gather as many of his family members around him as possible and to help them without selfish calculation as to how they might repay the obligation. He was a good family man, but too busy to enjoy the good of family life. In the same way he had a good house, but no intimate friends to entertain there of a leisurely evening. Washington was one of the most admired Americans of his time, but somehow the satisfaction of his many good deeds eluded him, and instead his satisfactions in life generally came from overcoming his enemies in some underhanded maneuver.

CHAPTER 6

Other People's Money

The modern Moses, who leads his race and lifts it through Education to even better and higher things than a land overflowing with milk and honey.

ANDREW CARNEGIE, 1903

BOOKER T. Washington was a materialist. He believed that strong black institutions would bring forth strong black men and women, and he undertook to build such a tower of strength in an unlikely place, the worn-out cotton fields of the Alabama Black Belt. He started with nothing but the piddling state appropriation of $2000 a year, that and the sheer numbers of his black clientele. He would never lack for students, but he needed money, and by his willpower, cajolery, and compromise he built his school. Beginning in the 1880s with the sponsorship of Hampton Institute and the old wealth of New England and the waning zeal of its Congregational and Unitarian church folk, he sensed around the turn of the twentieth century the coming of a philanthropic revolution. The swollen fortunes of American industrialization and financial capitalism rolled out of the Midwest into New York City and were ready to be disgorged. Washington seized the moment and in 1905 moved his northern headquarters from Boston to the new philanthropic capital, New York, soon after the moguls of oil and steel, John D. Rockefeller and Andrew Carnegie, moved from Cleveland and Pittsburgh to live in mansions in the money capital. Washington's money-raising headquarters was not in a mansion, but in a first-class midtown hotel, about halfway between the millionaires' houses and their offices. He made forays to Boston and Chicago, and eventually acquired a summer place near Northport, on Long Island Sound, but he found his chief partners in philanthropy in New York, and he directed their interest not only to Tuskegee but to other black schools, including the colleges and the public schools.

Washington had a community of interest with the millionaires chiefly because they had the money he needed to build the ever more factory-like buildings at Tuskegee, to meet current expenses, and in a mysterious way the record does not show to build his personal empire. But he also had a business-oriented social philosophy. The businessman, white or black, was his model citizen. Furthermore, he himself was a large employer of the non-union labor of students and faculty. It did not take a conspiracy with the old union-busting steel magnate Carnegie or even the president of the Long Island Railroad, William H. Baldwin, Jr., chairman of the Tuskegee board of trustees, to cause Washington to give assurance in the Atlanta Compromise address in 1895 that blacks would work "without strikes or labor wars." Washington had no use for unions, and his bread was buttered on the non-union side, but he also observed and complained that most of the unions of his day were for whites only, that they segregated or excluded blacks from the more lucrative blue-collar jobs.

Washington also had unstinted admiration for the success that great wealth symbolized. In an era of much social criticism, he never spoke of "tainted money," "frenzied finance," or "malefactors of great wealth." The closest he ever came to criticizing the "Christ-like philanthropists" was in an addresss to students at Hampton Institute. Persons of great wealth, he said, had a choice between "the higher and the lower life." The man who used his wealth to ride over others chose the lower life. "On the other hand, the world is full of men who get hold of large wealth, of beautiful homes, of large farms, of fine business establishments, not as ends but that they may have these possessions as means through which to serve their fellows."[1] The admiration was mutual. Wealthy men and women gave him their gold partly because he spoke their language to others, but also because he spoke a more ingratiating language to them. In addition the reason that many other American whites, many blacks, and many foreigners favored him was because they considered him a sage, the only man with a handle on the American race problem.

Washington was never an intimate of John D. Rockefeller, a man whose personal coldness matched his shrewdness. Nevertheless, Rockefeller was among the earliest and steadiest large contributors to Tuskegee. He began in the 1890s to give $10,000 a year to Tuskegee, and when the General Education Board was formed in 1902 to dispense his educational philanthropy, he turned his commitment to Tuskegee over to it. Rockefeller avoided personal contact with objects of his charity, never visited Tuskegee, and never showed any particular interest in it. John D. Rockefeller, Jr., on the other hand, visited the school in 1901 on Robert C. Ogden's annual Pullman train excursion from New York to southern educational institutions, and he came again on his own in 1903. Only a few days after Washington's dinner at the White House, young Rockefeller invited the Tuskegean to address his Bible class, and not long afterwards invited him to supper after tea at his parents' New York house.[2] Out of these contacts money came in 1902 for Rockefeller Hall, a three-story brick building, the largest on campus. When Washington in 1903 sent back $249 not needed to cover the cost, young Rockefeller refused to accept it, saying: "My father is gratified to know that the building has been constructed so well within the estimated cost, the more so since it so frequently happens that the opposite is the case."[3] The prestige of receiving Rockefeller's contributions probably opened other doors to Washington, but the General Education Board, when it made its first report to the public in a book published in 1914, revealed that, compared with the millions it had awarded to white colleges and universities, in its first twelve years it had given only a pittance to black education, mostly to Hampton and Tuskegee.[4]

Washington's popular autobiography, *Up from Slavery* (1901), inspired a number of gifts to Tuskegee. The camera manufacturer George Eastman wrote Washington in 1902: "I have just been re-reading your book 'Up from slavery' and have come to the conclusion that I cannot dispose of five thousand dollars to any better advantage than to send it to you for your institute."[5] This was the first of many contributions from Eastman, who let Washington apply his money to whatever the school needed at the moment. His usual annual contribution after 1910 was $10,000, and after Washington's death he gave $250,000 to the memorial fund.

In London E. Julia Emery, a wealthy expatriate of seventy, read *Up from Slavery* in 1903 and felt the stirring of mixed emotions. Miss

Emery had been born in Cincinnati but had lived in idleness abroad since before the Civil War. The story of Washington's life of struggle and service caused her to feel vaguely guilty that she herself had done nothing to relieve the national guilt of slavery or to uplift the black people once they were free. "Oh! How wondrously has God appeared on your behalf!" she wrote Washington. "Over-ruling all the sadness and bitterness and disadvantages of your early life! And has in the end recompensed you a thousand fold, in blessing you to others. And in causing your own heart to sing for joy that such a useful life, as is your present, sh'd have been the outcome of all yr early sufferings." To make some small amends for her half-century of neglect, she sent Washington $1000, the first of many thousands. "You are at liberty to use it for the various branches, most needing help," she wrote, "and let me know when you write, how wisely you have disbursed it."[6] Washington used this money as wisely as he could, by raising the salaries of Tuskegee faculty members.[7] It developed, however, that Miss Emery wanted a more permanent memorial to herself, and through negotiations with her and her brother in Cincinnati, Washington persuaded her to finance a succession of small, Spartanly plain brick dormitories for men, known simply as Emery building No. 1, Emery building No. 2, and so on. A half-century later they were in use as warehouses.

Henry H. Rogers, one of the earliest partners in the Standard Oil trust, redoubled the fortune made in oil by investments in railroads and other enterprises. A typically ruthless entrepreneur in all of his business affairs, Rogers showed a radically different personality in his private life. He was a Santa Claus to those he liked and admired, and Washington was at the top of his list. Rogers began to donate small amounts to Tuskegee in the 1890s but, mesmerized by hearing Washington speak in New York in 1903, he became Washington's personal benefactor. The next day after the speech he invited Washington to his office. "When I entered," Washington later recalled, "he remarked that he had been present at the meeting the night previous and expected the 'hat to be passed,' but as that was not done he wanted to 'chip in' something. Thereupon he handed me ten one-thousand-dollar bills for the Tuskegee Institute. In doing this he imposed only one condition, that the gift should be mentioned to no one." Rogers finally consented to letting one or two Tuskegee trustees in on the secret.[8]

Rogers enjoyed watching the play of emotions on the faces of recipients when he opened his desk drawer and forked out cash in large denominations. He was a cheerful giver, and especially enjoyed doing good by stealth. He aided not only Tuskegee in this way but other small southern black schools, giving Washington about $500 a month to distribute to them. At the time of his death in 1909 Rogers was anonymously aiding about sixty-five schools. Rogers once took the black educator on a trip through Long Island Sound on his yacht, the *Kanawha*. Washington later recalled: "During the course of the trip I had abundant opportunity to tell him more in detail than I had hitherto done about the good that his money was accomplishing for the uplift of the people in the South. It seemed to me that his face fairly radiated with happiness as, through the account I gave him, he was able to enter fully into the situation and realize the good that he had been able to do." [9]

Under any circumstances it would have been hard to dislike a cash giver, or ask whether his money was tainted, but Washington did not try. He saw in Rogers's smiles and tears all the emotional involvement of the tooth fairy. "Of all the men that I have ever known, intimately, no matter what their station in life," Washington wrote, "Mr. Rogers always impressed me as being among the kindest and gentlest. That was the impression he made upon me the first time I ever met him, and during the fifteen years that I knew him that impression was deepened every time I met him." [10] Only once did Washington violate the secrecy he had promised Rogers. This was occasioned by the visit of a leading magazine editor to Tuskegee. Hearing mention of Rogers, the editor began to denounce him not only for the way he had gained his wealth but for his selfishness and stinginess. After hearing all he could stand, Washington pointed out that the building they were sitting in had been a gift of Rogers. "He seemed perfectly amazed, had no idea that you were interested in such matters," Washington wrote Rogers. "I think I have changed his attitude somewhat for the future. He certainly is an astonished man, if not a converted one." [11] As Rogers's latest enterprise, the Virginian Railroad from Norfolk to West Virginia, was nearing completion just before his death, he arranged for Washington to tour the little towns along the line preaching his gospel of black self-help and cooperation with whites, and incidentally creating good will for the railroad. After Rogers died, Washington fulfilled his commitment in 1909, using a special train provided by the railroad. Washington made many such tours in other parts of the South, but this was the only one in direct partnership with a railroad. Washington was perhaps insensitive to the conflict of interest involved, but he saw the journey as a way of encouraging his hearers and of repaying some of Rogers's kindnesses in the only way he could.[12]

One of Washington's other major partners in philanthropy was Andrew Carnegie, almost a dwarf in size but with none of the other kewpie qualities exhibited by Rogers. The immensely wealthy Carnegie was charmed by Washington's philosophy and example as a self-made man. Carnegie was an irascible, egotistical man who demanded effusive gratitude and public recognition, but Washington was equal to such demands. Having retired from active business after selling out to U. S. Steel in 1901, Carnegie had little to do and no son to inherit his swollen fortune. He sought impulsively, intuitively, and toward the end desperately, to give it all away, but not in such a way as to do any particular person any good, for he feared the generosity that would sap the self-reliance of the poor. Born poor himself, a child laborer in the textile mills and a telegraph messenger boy before he got his business start, Carnegie believed in poverty as a spur to the Darwinian struggle out of which the fit, the natural leaders like himself, survived. He even wrote a book about it, *The Gospel of Wealth* (1890), a rich man's version of social criticism.

Washington had little success at first in stalking Carnegie in search of a donation. When Washington, on his first trip to Europe in 1899, learned that Carnegie was vacationing in the castle he had bought near his birthplace in Scotland, Washington tried to pay him a visit. He received in reply to his overtures a curt, unsigned note: "Mr. Carnegie's Secretary begs respectfully to say that Mr. Carnegie does not wish to take up any new work at present. He has come here for a much needed rest and would like a holiday until 1900."[13]

Soon after *Up from Slavery* appeared, however, its publisher Frank Doubleday, between shots in their golf game, regaled Carnegie with anecdotes from Washington's book. These piqued Carnegie's interest in the man he had refused for years even to see, a man whose life uniquely exemplified his own "gospel of wealth." His impulse was to say to his secretary, "Bertram, give the man a library." A Carnegie library, as the comic character Mr. Dooley described it, was architecture, not literature, a big brownstone building with all the dead authors inside, and outside all the living authors wishing they were dead.

Learning of Carnegie's interest, Washington and R. R. Taylor, the school's architect, "spent hours and hours of time in scrutinizing every detail to bring the cost down to the smallest possible figure consistent with an adequate result."[14] They knew the way to a Scotsman's heart. The final cost to Carnegie of a two-story brick building using student labor was only $20,000. Carnegie was so impressed by this evidence of Tuskegee ingenuity that he began in 1902 to donate a sum of $10,000 a year to Tuskegee's current expenses. This was fine, but Washington eagerly awaited some more substantial sign of favor. "His income before dinner would set you up for a whole year," wrote a friend of Tuskegee.[15]

It was both Washington's obligation and his gift as a fund raiser that he understood the foibles of the wealthy and played upon them. One day W. E. B. Du Bois and Washington found each other aboard the elevated train in New York. Washington was on his way to call on Andrew Carnegie. He asked Du Bois if he had ever read *The Gospel of Wealth* and Du Bois replied, no, he had never thought it worth his while. "You should," answered Washington, "*he* sets great store by it." As Du Bois understood him, Washington simply applied to Carnegie one of his own traits of character: "He had no faith in white people, not the slightest, and he was most popular among them, because if he was talking with a white man he sat there and found out what the white man wanted him to say, and then as soon as possible he said it."[16] Du Bois was wrong about Washington's faith in white people, but he had insight into how Washington manipulated a cantankerous man of wealth such as Carnegie.

The highlight of Washington's funding campaign in the spring of 1903 was a huge gathering at the Madison Square Garden concert hall in behalf of Tuskegee. Former President Grover Cleveland presided over the meeting, arriving there from dinner at the Carnegie mansion, and Mrs. Cleveland sat with Mrs. Carnegie in her box. Cleveland actually made a bad, insensitive speech in introducing Washington, referring to "racial and slavery-bred imperfections and deficiencies" of blacks, who he said burdened the South with "a grievous amount of ignorance, a sad amount of laziness and thriftlessness."[17] Lyman Abbott also indulged in such racial condescension that one of Washington's old friends wrote him: "I laughed when Mr. Abbott spoke of the superiority of the white race—for I remembered your having told me that it happened every time you had a white man to speak at a meeting."[18] Washington, however, restored dignity to the occasion. "The most fundamental and far-reaching deed that has been accomplished during the last quarter of a century," he said, "has been that by which the Negro has been helped to find himself and to learn the secret of civilization—to learn that there are a few simple, cardinal principles upon which a race must start its upward course unless it would fail, and its last estate be worse than its first." After recounting the principles of work, thrift, property ownership, mutual help and patience, all of which Tuskegee taught, Washington made an appeal: "You of the North owe an unfulfilled duty to the Negro, and equal duty to your white brethren in the South in assisting them to help to remove the load of ignorance resting upon my race."[19]

According to the later recollection of George McAneny, who had helped to organize the meeting, the audience received slips of paper for pledging a contribution to Tuskegee Institute. Discovered after the meeting was a note from Andrew Carnegie pledging the astonishing sum of $600,000, and providing that $150,000 of this be used to finance Washington's speaking tours.[20] McAneny's memory may have failed him as to the details, but however Carnegie phrased the slip, he sent a more formal letter of gift three days later to William H. Baldwin, Jr., giving $600,000 in U. S. Steel bonds for the Tuskegee endowment, with the condition that the revenue from $150,000 of the bonds was to go to Booker T. Washington personally "to be used by him for his wants and those of his family during his life or the life of his widow." Carnegie said of Washington in his letter: "To me he seems one of the foremost of living men because his work is unique. The modern Moses, who leads his race and lifts it through Education to even better and higher things than a land overflowing with milk and honey. History is to know two Washingtons, one white, the other black, both Fathers of their People. I am satisfied that the serious race question of the South is to be solved wisely, only by following Booker T. Washington's policy which he seems to have been specially born—a slave among slaves—to establish, and even in his own day, greatly to advance."[21]

Washington hurriedly sent his letter of acceptance. "Your action will make me dedicate my life anew to the cause," he wrote. "As for the very generous provision which you make for Mrs. Washington and myself, it is so foresighted that my heart is so full that I can only say that we will try to repay you for what you have done in hard earnest work." [22]

Washington continued, however, to turn over in his mind the implications and probable public reaction to the gift. When George McAneny called on Washington, he found him "very perplexed about the personal settlement clause in particular." McAneny warned that the amount would seem a fortune to southerners and to blacks particularly, that Washington might lose some of his standing as a fund raiser, and that if he became the beneficiary of a single man he would lose some of his independence and moral authority. Washington agreed that these were serious concerns, and on that same day McAneny and another trustee, William J. Schieffelin, accompanied Washington to Carnegie's baronial mansion. [23] Many years later McAneny recalled the scene: "Carnegie listened to us in silence while I explained the situation to him, then he answered, 'You go back there into my library, re-write my pledge to suit yourselves, bring it back to me and I'll sign it.' So we changed it to provide for Washington's tour in an unspecified amount, and Carnegie signed it." [24]

According to the way Carnegie remembered it, Washington himself proposed the changes in the terms. After expressing his personal gratitude for the donation, he said, "Some might feel that I was no longer a poor man giving my services without thought of saving money. Would you have any objection to changing that clause, striking out the sum, and substituting 'only suitable provision'? I'll trust the trustees. Mrs. Washington and myself need very little." Carnegie agreed to the changes Washington suggested, but when Baldwin asked Washington to exchange the original letter of gift for the substitute, he refused. He wanted to keep the original letter as a souvenir to pass on to his children, as marking his place in history. [25]

"I suppose he had in mind that I should spend more time at the institute than I do," Washington said modestly of Carnegie's gift in a newspaper interview. [26] The trustees by a resolution set aside the $150,000 as an endowment of Washington's salary, and Washington gave up his regular Institute salary. [27] These efforts to head off criticism and preserve Washington's public image of modesty, however, did not obscure an important change in his private circumstances. Rather than actually confining him more to the school, the Carnegie gift enabled him to do many things he had not been able to do before, including a trip to Europe that summer, his first vacation in four years. It opened the door also to new extramural enterprises, for Carnegie a year later began annual subsidies to two agencies of the Tuskegee Machine, the Committee of Twelve and the National Negro Business League. It may have been out of the Carnegie funds also that Washington suddenly at this time seemed to be able to finance more secret activities than in the past, hiring spies on his black enemies and paying costs of the court case against the Alabama grandfather clause, both undertaken in 1903. "The 'Modern Moses' Strikes Rocks" was the caption of a cartoon on the Carnegie gift that half-unconsciously captured the essence of Washington's new power through the Carnegie connection.[28]

When Washington returned to the Tuskegee campus after the announcement of the Carnegie accolade, all work ceased and the entire population gathered at the Lincoln gate. Washington rode between long lines of wildly cheering men, women, and children. The band played "See the Conquering Hero Comes." The crowd followed Washington to the chapel, decorated with palms, tree branches, roses and wild flowers, American flags, and giant portraits of Washington and Carnegie. With Emmett Scott in the chair, Lewis Adams, Charles W. Hare, and others extolled Washington and expressed their pride in his success "in gaining the approval of the best business men of the whole country."[29]

Washington made his role as intercessor with the steel magnate a significant element in his Tuskegee Machine. The detailed evidence of his private correspondence shows that he used his influence with discretion, so as not to seem too importunate, but always benignly. He privately advised the presidents of colleges and the proponents of black public libraries as to the timing and manner of their applications to Carnegie, even initiating proposals when the time seemed ripe and discouraging others until the time, purpose, or amount of the request was more appropriate. As in his orchestration of black political appointments, Washington preferred not to write formal endorsements. He preferred, in the first place, for the college or other institution to approach him for advice on the grant application. He then recommended that the application be made independently of him, while he waited for Carnegie to ask his advice. There were many variations of this pattern according to circumstances, but in one way or another Washington helped at least twenty-two black educational institutions applying for Carnegie libraries, other buildings, or operating funds. In almost every case the application was successful. The roster included Howard, Fisk, Livingstone, Biddle, Wilberforce, Wiley, Prairie View, Atlanta Baptist College—practically the whole list of leading black colleges and universities, with the exception of a few outstanding ones such as Atlanta University and Talladega and Tougaloo, which did not apply. Maybe the heads of these institutions sensed a coolness in Washington, but how he would have responded is problematical. In addition, at least nine black community efforts to secure Carnegie branch libraries for blacks, in southern cities where the public libraries excluded blacks, received Washington's advice and support; and several Carnegie pipe organs and Carnegie pensions went to black people through Washington's efforts.[30]

Washington and Carnegie belonged to a mutual admiration society that knew no restraint. In contrast with the matter-of-fact tone of most of Washington's correspondence, he wrote extravagantly to Carnegie in reference to one of his gifts, calling it "your crowning act for the benefit of humanity," and added: "The world bows in gratitude to you."[31] Washington sensed Carnegie's hunger for recognition. And Carnegie often sought the ultimate compliment of Washington, in hope of a reciprocal one. Thanking Washington for a copy of one of his minor works, *Putting the Most into Life,* Carnegie said: "One who has made so much out of life, (more than any man living as far as I see, taking into account the lowly start) must surely be able to tell us how to put the most into life." Washington replied that he would cherish this letter and leave it "as a precious legacy to my children as being an expression from one of the dearest and best friends I ever had."[32]

Washington was nothing if not sensible, and he knew better than to make any other demands on Carnegie for Tuskegee or himself for many years after the big gift of 1903. Part of the secret of his success in supporting the applications of others came from this self-restraint and his careful avoidance of intrusion on Carnegie for trivial reasons. But flattery was the other key. Washington joined Carnegie's American Peace Society and became one of its numerous vice presidents. He praised the Carnegie Hero Fund heroically. He sent shoes made by Tuskegee students to Carnegie. He cultivated the favor of Carnegie's secretary James Bertram in ways he would not dare with Carnegie himself. When Bertram asked Washington to find him a good domestic servant at Tuskegee, he did not send him the usual form letter denying that Tuskegee trained students to be servants, but found a suitable person for him in New York through the Armstrong Association.[33] He even introduced Bertram to the 'possum, shipping a Tuskegee 'possum and sweet potatoes to the Bertrams one year for their Christmas dinner.[34]

Carnegie's only visit to Tuskegee, apparently, was in 1906, when he was one of the principal speakers at the twenty-fifth anniversary celebration. "Money may be the root of all evil in some sense," Carnegie said, "but it is also the root of all Universities, Colleges, Churches and libraries scattered thru the land." Without money, he said, there would have been no Tuskegee Institute, and with it and its educational contribution black suffrage would some day be restored through the increased capacity of blacks to perform the duties of citizenship. He ended: "I say to our colored friends, seek ye first education and all rights will soon be added unto you in this country."[35]

Washington was well aware of Carnegie's foibles and learned to maneuver around them. He described Carnegie to John Hope of Atlanta Baptist College as "a very curious proposition. He gets ideas into his head in his own way, and when they once get there, it is very hard to get them out. Almost impossible by direct methods."[36] The problems increased as Carnegie grew older, became exhausted by his morning golf game, and found the mounting requests for money exasperating. Washington consoled one disappointed applicant by saying, "Mr. Carnegie has become rather enfeebled and aged, and it is an increasingly difficult thing to get his personal attention given to any subject."[37]

It may have been this growing querulousness that doomed to repeated rejection one Tuskegee proposal, first presented by Emmett Scott in 1910 and later revised and resubmitted by Robert E. Park and Booker T. Washington, for a Carnegie Endowment for the Negro. Scott described such an agency as "for the special purpose of stimulating and directing the constructive efforts of the Negro people, in so far as that can be accomplished by the publication and distribution of the authentic records of what has been achieved for and by the Negro in the direction of his moral and material up-building."[38] When Washington wrote Carnegie in 1913 that, because of the growth of the school it was necessary to enlarge the Carnegie library and asked for money for the purpose, he received the tart reply from Carnegie: "Don't you think Tuskegee has had its share from your humble servant, and that Hampton has prior claim on anything I have to give for Negro education? Just think this over my friend. Take part of the revenue from the six hundred .thousand dollars given Tuskegee & extend Library & it will still be all Carnegie Library." [39]

The work and worry of fund-raising for Tuskegee eased somewhat as the years passed and Washington's successes mounted, but he continued to put much of his imagination and ingenuity to work on the task. He discovered, for example, that there were Jews with money and with empathy, men whose own history paralleled in many ways the black experience of exclusion and discrimination. Lillian Wald, director of the Henry Street Settlement for the poor Jews of the East Side, introduced him to the investment banker Jacob Schiff in 1903, [40] and soon he received support from Schiff, Paul Warburg, Isaac Seligman, the Goldmans, the Sachses, and the Lehmans. He often found that when one wealthy Jewish businessman contributed to Tuskegee, he enlisted his relatives and his business partners. "The more I think of it the more I am favorably impressed with the idea of inviting Mr. Warburg or some Hebrew of his standing to be a member of our Board of Trustees," Washington confided to William H. Baldwin, Jr. It would put new life into the board and provide also an excuse to get rid of its two New England clergymen. "I think neither of them are of very much value to us." [41] About a month later the trustees unanimously elected Paul Warburg a member. New England philanthropy was by no means extinct, as witness the funding in 1912 of John A. Andrew Memorial Hospital at Tuskegee, an up-to-date medical and nursing facility provided by Elizabeth Andrew Mason, daughter of the Massachusetts Civil War governor. Nevertheless, the day of major Jewish philanthropy in the mainstream of American life had arrived.

Jacob Schiff not only made several major contributions to Tuskegee but developed such confidence in Washington's judgment that he put him in charge of all his donations to black schools. He was receiving constant appeals, he wrote. "I feel entirely at a loss to know where to contribute properly and justly. Considering this, I have thought it would be best if I placed annually a given amount at your disposal, of which a part might go to Tuskegee and the balance be appropriated towards other Southern educational institutions for colored people, such as under your advice may be entitled to support from me." [42] Schiff had quadrupled his annual amount by 1915, and he continued to aid Tuskegee by gifts and a bequest.

The greatest American Jewish philanthropist of his day, however, was Julius Rosenwald, president of Sears, Roebuck, and Company. There was nothing in Rosenwald's background, education, or business experience to foreshadow the merchant prince, but once he was irreversibly wealthy Rosenwald turned his keen intelligence and commitment to doing good. He was more ready than most philanthropists to take risks. The Chicago millionaire was one rich man, at least, whose interest in Tuskegee was *not* kindled by reading *Up from Slavery*. He first became interested instead through reading a biography of William H. Baldwin, Jr., the chairman of the Tuskegee trustees who died in 1905. But it was not until 1911 that Rosenwald first visited the Tuskegee campus. He was greatly impressed by the contrast between the decadent rural surroundings and the energy and achievement he saw at the institute. A few months later he accepted an invitation to become a trustee.[43]

Rosenwald immediately launched imaginative projects for winning new contributors to Tuskegee. He brought a private railroad car full of wealthy and prominent Chicagoans to see Tuskegee for themselves, and used the railroad journey to imbue his guests with his own enthusiasm.[44] He began an aggressive fund-raising effort in Chicago to support Tuskegee's five-year endowment plan, which the trustees devised as Washington's health and vigor began to decline. Each subscriber pledged a certain amount each year for five years, not really for endowment but to meet the annual expenses of Tuskegee Institute, in order to take the pressure from Washington of meeting current bills.[45]

Rosenwald never seemed too busy to give some thought to Tuskegee, and in this he was ably abetted by his private secretary, William C. Graves. Rosenwald made Tuskegee a sort of pet project. He sent down a lot of shoes and hats from Sears, Roebuck to be given to any students who needed them. Washington thought it wise to charge a nominal amount, "so as to make them not get into the habit of accepting something for nothing."[46] To celebrate his fiftieth birthday, Rosenwald offered Washington $25,000 "for the colored schools that have grown out of Tuskegee Institute, or are doing the same kind of work as Tuskegee branch schools," provided each school raised a matching sum.[47] And to mark their twenty-fifth wedding anniversary, the Rosenwalds gave bonuses in varying amounts to Tuskegee teachers and officers who had served the school for fifteen years or more.[48] Equally with Carnegie and with a much gladder heart, Rosenwald became a principal benefactor of Tuskegee. Having won such a staunch friend in Chicago, Washington at the end of his life was reaching further into the Midwest for support. Not long before his death he secured a letter of introduction to Henry Ford, which he planned to use on a trip to Detroit that he did not live to make.[49]

Washington's correspondence with the large donors to Tuskegee does not reveal a conspiracy, either large or small, to prepare Tuskegee's students to become wage-workers in the corporate structure. The typical donor sent his check rather than his advice, and as we shall see, Washington's efforts at Tuskegee Institute were to train students to become independent small businessmen, farmers, and teachers rather than wage-earners or servants of white employers. At the same time, it is clear that Washington flattered and cajoled the very rich and never challenged the appropriateness of their status at the peak of the American success pyramid. Washington also inculcated in his students the work-ethic, self-help, and self-improvement that the millionaires liked to believe were more important to their success than their acquisitive behavior. The wealthy loved Washington because he seemed rather like one of them, a self-made man with a big physical plant to prove it. But for his color, he could have belonged to their club.

CHAPTER 7

Tuskegee's People

I find that the school offers advance courses equivalent to any High School courses, and the notion that Tuskegee teaches A, B, C's is another joke for the Boston joke-book. There is plenty of work to do here; no one is a drone, but everybody works and the greatest worker is Mr. B. T. Washington.

G. DAVID HOUSTON, 1904

Mr. Washington's scheme is to have such a control over his teachers that they will tremble at his approach. Most teachers like to see the train puff out with him and dread to hear the engine whistling his return.

G. DAVID HOUSTON, 1906

F OR nearly half of every year Booker T. Washington was far from Tuskegee Institute. He spoke from nearly every rostrum in the land, drew up a chair at the President's desk at the White House, traveled abroad, or battled with the black college-bred men, using methods they had not learned in college. Students and even faculty at Tuskegee heard of his role in public affairs almost in fable form, after careful screening in the *Tuskegee Student* or else in the garbled style of the Montgomery *Advertiser,* which followed the Wizard of Tuskegee closely but seldom saw him clearly. Even when he was generally believed to be on campus, Washington would often be at the Chehaw station boarding an early morning train on some urgent appointment.

On other mornings, however, he saddled up his riding horse just as students began their early morning chores, and rode over the institute farms. Or he would appear without warning at the student dining hall to check the cleanliness, service, and quality of food, or at dormitories to see if discipline was maintained and the straw was regularly changed in the beds. Sometimes he walked the streets of Greenwood, seeing which faculty member's chickens were loose and whether the trash was cleared from the yards.

Tuskegee Institute changed somewhat in the new century, but more in size than in character. It stabilized the size of its student body at somewhat more than 1000, and throughout Washington's lifetime remained at his insistence a secondary school. Did it represent progressive education in the manner of John Dewey and his associates in this same period? Or was it a trade school, preparing its black students of both sexes for the occupations the new industrial age demanded, shaping up round people to fit into square slots? Was it the instrument for achieving a black man's dream of self-sufficiency through a marketable skill, or was it a white man's dream of preparing black people to fill the subordinate places, the only ones available to them in the new order of white supremacy? Perhaps the best answer is that Tuskegee was none of these abstractions, but an amalgam of parts of each, with a predominance of intense desire for racial progress through self-help. Washington as the spokesman for Tuskegee frequently played upon the desire of southern whites to have a docile, subordinate black population and the desire of northern capitalists to have a skilled, tractable, and hard-working black laboring class. The Tuskegee curriculum, however, was clearly centered on self-help, and on a greater flexibility than the term industrial education suggests.

From the earliest years of the school, there was a tension between the industrial and the academic faculty. Washington himself tried to bridge the gap both through his own governance of the institute and through the weekly meetings of department heads in the executive council. But the tension remained. The great majority of students was always in the lower classes, and most of these students did not graduate. Their class curricula were weighted toward the industrial courses and toward overcoming the inadequacies of the southern black public schools through training in the literacy skills. The higher students progressed, however, into the junior, B middle, A middle, and senior years, the broader the academic training. Many of those who survived the sifting and winnowing of Tuskegee to graduate, went to college, and into the professions of the Talented Tenth. Most of the teachers in the academic department were college graduates, who felt a sense of superiority to the typical industrial or agricultural teachers, self-taught or half-taught men and women whose particular skills had earned them faculty status. Robert R. Taylor, the head of buildings and grounds, was an architecture graduate of M. I. T., but he was the exception. George Washington Carver, Tuskegee's resident genius and agricultural chemist, had some rare gifts, but spelling and punctuation were not among them. By contrast, the academic faculty had graduates of Harvard, Oberlin, Fisk, and Atlanta, men and women who read novels, wrote poetry, and played in Shakespearean drama. The tension was inevitable, and though Washington wanted the college graduates on his faculty and frequently boasted that Tuskegee hired more black college graduates than any other institution in the country, he searched for ways to bring them into line with the industrial character of Tuskegee.

Washington took a bold step toward improving the standards of the academic department but at the same time bringing about harmony between the two halves of the faculty in 1903 when he appointed Roscoe Conkling Bruce, a Harvard graduate, as head of the academic department. Bruce's father was Blanche K. Bruce, a Reconstruction-era Senator from Mississippi and panjandrum of black Republican politicos in Washington until his death in 1898. His mother had once been lady principal, or dean of women, at Tuskegee. At Washington's suggestion, in his third year at Harvard he began taking education courses. While still in college, also, he made plans to upgrade the Tuskegee faculty by bringing in his friends at Harvard, Oberlin, Cornell, and the University of Michigan.[1]

Bruce arrived at Tuskegee in the fall of 1903 at the age of twenty-four and began to order about white-haired teachers who had been at the work since before he was born. They seemed to accept it well, however, either because his Harvard degree conveyed instant maturity or because of Tuskegee's authoritarian tradition inherited from General Armstrong's Hampton that orders were orders. The first flare-up of rebellion came not from faculty but from students.

The only serious defiance of the school's authority in Washington's lifetime was the student strike or "rebellion" in the fall of 1903, soon after Bruce's arrival and during Washington's absence. Had Washington been on campus to provide both authority and mediation, the strike might never have occurred or might have been more quickly settled, but it did deal with a fundamental concern of the students, the schedules of the work they did to earn their way through school. For years, at Tuskegee as at Hampton, night students had worked at their trades throughout the day, but the day students, who were the large majority, attended their academic classes all morning and worked in the farms and industrial shops all afternoon. In the late spring and through the summer of 1903 John H. Washington and a special committee planned a drastic change that would rationalize the production process, make labor more efficient, and more fully utilize the school's resources. What the committee was doing, whether it realized it or not, was to join a nationwide movement in industrial plants, business offices, and elsewhere toward the gospel of efficiency.[2] The committee mandated that at the beginning of the 1903–4 term students would be divided into two groups, preparatory and academic. Monday through Friday, academic students were to be in academic classes in the mornings and in industrial and agricultural "classes"—actually employment under tutelage—in the afternoons, and preparatory students, vice versa. Both groups would work alternately on Saturday mornings. Students were to be paid "on the average not more than two and one-half cents an hour."[3]

The students would probably have accepted this new system, as eventually they did, if the reasons for it had been fully explained to them, if Washington had not left for a desperately needed rest just as the new system began, and if there had not been intense rivalry between academic and industrial teachers. As Washington on his return to campus explained to the chairman of the board of trustees, "the students were crowded pretty hard both in their studies and in their industrial work. The attempt was made on the part of the heads of the literary department to get as much out of the students as possible, and the same was true regarding the heads of the industrial departments, and between the two, the students had little time left."[4] Just before his departure for a vacation in France, Washington called the teachers together to ask how the new system was working, and they said it had not been tested long enough to judge, or for any modifications to be made.

About a week after Washington had left, and after student petitions and complaints had been rejected,[5] student dissatisfaction became so general that it was easy for a few leaders to bring about "an open rebellion." The men students marched from the breakfast table to the chapel, locked themselves in, and after some haranguing voted not to work or study until changes were made. Hastily calling a special meeting of the executive council, Acting Principal Warren Logan allowed a committee of students to appear and state their grievances. The students said that until the authorities made concessions they would refuse to work. The council asked the student delegation to put the complaints in writing and to report to the strikers "that the Council will consider their grievances, provided they return to work by one o'clock." This demand seemed like strikebreaking tactics to the students. When the executive council met again at 3:15 that afternoon, they faced the continued refusal of students to return to work after the deadline the council had set. Roscoe Conkling Bruce expressed the view that "the leaders in the revolt should be sent home." The council, however, decided on delay, "to make no concessions until students had obeyed."[6]

The little "rebellion" lasted through a second day and then collapsed. Tuskegee, after all, was like a company town, with housing, food, education, everything at the pleasure of the authorities. The executive council then debated their response to this act of defiance, many of them no doubt inwardly groaning that Washington was not there to make their decision for them. The "royal family" was more outspoken than most others. John H. Washington agreed with R. C. Bruce that "unless the leaders in such rebellions are dealt with, the troubles will grow worse." The majority, however, agreed with Margaret Washington that "the feeling is so general that it would be difficult to locate the leaders." In view of the complaint of students that too much of their time was taken up in organized activities, the council considered but ultimately rejected a proposal to reduce the frequency of chapel services from every night to two nights a week. On Bruce's suggestion, the council forbade general meetings of students without the principal's permission, "but in the present state of things, it was decided that it was better to say nothing of this regulation at this time."[7] Two faculty members stood accused of open expression of sympathy for the students. One denied it; the other "acknowledged having expressed sympathy, but he did not intend to actively abet a rebellion. Mr. W. is to see him."[8]

"The student body is now quiet and satisfied," Washington wrote

William H. Baldwin, Jr., after his return, "but I am taking up the whole system with a good deal of care, with a view of still further perfecting it." Washington knew that Baldwin as a railroad president had a passion for efficiency and a studied opposition to strikes. Of the forty-seven students who had left the school in anger during the week of rebellion, he wrote Baldwin, most had already been doing unsatisfactory work. "In studying the whole matter," he concluded, "I do not see how our teachers could have acted more wisely under the circumstances than they did. I think if I had been on the grounds, I could have nipped the matter in the bud, and there would have been no outbreak, but since I was not here, I do not see how anyone could have managed the affair more carefully, wisely and patiently."[9] Thinking and investigating further, he wrote Baldwin a few days later that "there is no feeling against any form of labor," that "the students felt that they were required to devote too much time to both industrial work and studies with too little time for preparation." He thought there was merit to the students' case from the standpoint of efficiency and adjusted the schedule accordingly.[10] The student pay rate remained one dollar for forty hours' work.

Washington spent more time on campus in the 1903–4 school year than he had done for years, possibly because of the student strike, but also because he sensed a need for a more drastic revision of the curriculum.[11] This effort carried over into the following year, and early in 1905 Roscoe Conkling Bruce announced the revisions he and the Principal had developed for "a first class industrial school rather than a second class academic." In order to relieve the higher classes from excessive demands of the academic department, they eliminated Bible and music. Bruce also announced other changes: "Instead of eliminating another academic study—History or Literature or Education or some other—the Principal agreed to this arrangement: *Every Academic teacher is appreciably to diminish the amount of time required of his students for the preparation of his subjects. This arrangement goes into effect at once.*"[12] This was a blow to the heart of academic teaching and learning at Tuskegee, where poetry and scholarship had often crept quietly into the classroom to coexist with the industrial function of the school. Leslie Pinckney Hill, whom Bruce and Washington had recently brought from Harvard to establish a division of education, complained that "this means a positive crippling of the work in our department."[13] But the Principal's will prevailed.

Washington believed the new regulation equally divided the academic and industrial work of each student, and he reported to the trustees: "Serious effort has been made to render the Academic Department more effective for the special purposes of the Institution. Thoroughness in book studies, rather than scope is sought. The student arrives at general principles after and through ordered observation and painstaking analysis of concrete cases." Washington asserted in his original draft but deleted in the final version of his report: "This process is slow and laborious, it secures no glib facility in the declamation of rules and definitions; but it is thoroughgoing and sound and sure. The desideratum is power rather than knowledge, for not all knowledge is power." [14]

What Washington called "correlating," or sometimes, more colloquially, "dovetailing," was the essence of his educational philosophy. He began systematic efforts to institute this approach in the 1890s, but in the early twentieth century he redoubled his efforts. As Washington elucidated this concept to the trustees, dovetailing meant, as in dovetail joints in carpentry, "blotting out differences between the literary department and the industrial department." The idea was that students would practice mathematics in the carpentry shop and write essays on plowing a field in the English class. Thus, "the training on the farm, in the blacksmith shop, the cooking division will be given due credit in the academic department for all work in arithmetic and English that [the student] does in those departments, and that the industrial processes shall be made the basis of the academic department wherever possible for the lessons in the academic department." [15]

This view prevailed because it represented Washington's sovereign will, but not without some protest from academic teachers who loved their discipline or the beauties of literature. Even Bruce, who was at first Washington's chief agent in imposing the system, began to complain of a steady reduction of the time allotted to academic studies and said the encroachment by industrial departments was not warranted by the argument that "this is an industrial school." He said the real reason was the school's increasing demand for student labor, and because "the trades and industries, despite 'theory classes,' are really taught by the apprenticeship and not by the instructional plan, and the apprenticeship plan wastes time." He suspected that the registrar assigned green students to trades and industries not because of interest or aptitude but "in accordance with the demands of labor."[16] Washington replied that Bruce's concept of education was too narrowly literary, whereas Tuskegee offered "a rare opportunity to strike out in the educational world, and do that which our people and our situation demands, rather than yield to the temptation of following too blindly some one else." He noted that in Bruce's own annual report on teachers in his department, "Out of the eight persons whose names you give me, as not desirable for re-appointment, or whose ability you question, six of them have been trained in institutions where all of their time has been devoted to purely literary and professional methods."[17]

Bruce was to prove in his later career as head of the black schools of Washington, D.C., that he did not differ fundamentally with Washington. Others in the academic department, however, including paradoxically several whom Bruce himself had attracted to Tuskegee, rebelled against the dovetailing of their humanistic discipline with carpentry or agriculture. Ruth Anna Fisher, who came to the Tuskegee faculty immediately after graduation from Oberlin in 1906, lasted less than two months because of her absolute refusal to dovetail. J. R. E. Lee, who succeeded Bruce as head of the academic division, reported to Washington: "Miss Fisher said that she was unwilling to cooperate with us in correlating our work and that we need not expect her to do so; she said that I might so inform you."[18] In reply, Washington informed her: "We cannot change the policy of the school, nor can we permit you to be an exception to the rule followed by the majority of the other teachers; therefore I see nothing for me to do but ask that you hand in your resignation." Another count in the indictment against her was that the head of the Sunday school said that she "absolutely refused to have any part in Sunday School work."[19]

Washington sought to inculcate correlation by requiring academic teachers to make one visit a week to some industrial department.[20] In the fall of 1906 he instituted a system whereby each student received full credit in the academic department for work in English composition in the industrial department. "For example," Washington explained to Ella Flagg Young, at that time principal of the Chicago Normal School, "when a student in one of the shops is required to write a composition for his industrial instructor, this instructor examines the paper and marks it as to its technical correctness; the paper is then sent to the English Division of the Academic Department where it is examined and marked upon the grammar, etc., used."[21] According to one English instructor, the aim in English instruction was in complete harmony with the Tuskegee idea, "to teach to do by doing." It was more important that a student learn to write a clear exposition of the principles underlying his trade than to compose a sonnet or describe a sunset, though the school did not wish the student to be "unresponsive to the beauty in the world about him."[22] Washington complained to that same English instructor, however, of a group of his students' essays. "There are too many big words in some of them," he wrote. "The sentences are too long and involved. Nothing is stronger in the teaching of English than to teach the students to use the smallest words possible, and the shortest and most simple sentences. Let them use the same kind of language in writing that they do in talking."[23] The theory on which Tuskegee's policy rested had obvious merit, but in practice it meant the subordination of the academic side of the instructional program. A generation of Tuskegee graduates, not to mention the larger number who left before graduation, murdered the King's English in their letters back to the school.

Washington had a lifelong hatred of the abstractions and generalizations in the discourse of college-educated men. Part of the reason, no doubt, is that he did not always understand their arcane language, but also because he sensed that much of it was nonsense. After a tour of observation of the academic classrooms he wrote to J. R. E. Lee: "I am quite sure, judging by the teaching which I saw last night, that there is a decided tendency back to the old abstract and general methods of teaching rather than carrying out the idea of articulating the classroom work into the life of the people and into the life of the school."[24] Perhaps Washington was following the vogue of Deweyite progressive educational theories, but it is more probable that he was simply following his own preference for the unpretentious and the down-to-earth. These were the qualities of his own speaking and writing style that won him responsive audiences and devoted followers among both blacks and whites, and he sought in the Tuskegee instructional program to universalize them. Washington spurred his teachers into requiring agriculture students to write essays on how to prepare a field for turnips, while women students were expected to

write on the various ways of cooking greens. Chemistry classes analyzed the local clay, while an arithmetic class figured the amount and
cost of plastering the recitation room.[25]

Washington made all the important decisions at Tuskegee, within
his own interpretation of "the rules of the school." As he spent more
and more of his time in the North and on the road, however, and as
age brought a decline in even his tremendous energy, he delegated
more of the supervision and the minor decision-making to the executive council, an oligarchy of fifteen to twenty officers and department heads. He and two other Washingtons, Margaret and John, were
members, as were his secretary Emmett Scott, the treasurer Warren
Logan, the auditor, the dean of women, business agent, experiment
station director, and commandant. The other members were senior
teachers in charge of major departments. They generally enjoyed the
best salaries on the faculty. The highest ten salaries in 1903 were above
$1000 a year and board.[26] In 1908 twelve were making more than
$1000 a year.[27] This was in contrast to junior faculty members, who
made as little as $250 or $300 a year and board. When some of the
ablest academic teachers took employment elsewhere, Roscoe Conkling Bruce believed that the fundamental reason was the low salaries
at Tuskegee in comparison to even those of elementary school teachers in Washington, Indianapolis, and other cities. Urging salary in-
creases, he warned: "We can't afford to let the Academic Department
be utilized as a temporary resource for indigent teachers out of a job,
and as a training school."[28]

Washington insisted on holding faculty salaries down to a lower level
than at other black schools, and said that he wanted only teachers so
dedicated to Tuskegee's ideals and mission that they would work there
at a lower salary than they could command elsewhere. When he and
the department heads decided any teachers were incompetent, he
usually notified them in the early spring that they would not be re-
employed in the fall. There was no such thing as tenure, though
teachers who had been there for many years could presume that they
would be renewed. Dismissal for insubordination or some other grave
offense, however, was often peremptory. The school took no responsibility for those too ill to work; if they could not work they were not
paid, though in some cases a leave of absence without pay was granted
when there was expectation of recovery. When teachers found and
accepted other positions during the summer, after signing a statement

of intention to return, Washington charged them with unethical conduct and hounded them in their new jobs. There was more than one such incident.[29]

The case of G. David Houston illustrates in an exaggerated form the predicament of the college graduates on the Tuskegee faculty. They performed vital services to the institution but posed a standing threat of subversion of the industrial emphasis. Houston came straight from Harvard in 1904 at the age of twenty-four. He had been in the class behind R. C. Bruce. Emmett Scott had warned that Houston was a "particular friend" of one of Washington's bitterest enemies, Edward H. Morris of Chicago, but Bruce stood by his college friend and he was hired as Bruce's secretary and teacher of English.[30] Washington liked Houston, and Houston reciprocated. He wrote back to his pastor in Cambridge that he found Tuskegee "far above the Boston criticism," and that "the notion that Tuskegee teaches A, B, C's is another joke for the Boston joke-book." As for Washington, the hardest worker at Tuskegee, "we have a second 'father' of a country of people, and with the same name—Washington."[31] Washington somehow came into possession of a copy of this letter within two weeks, and the only reason he did not try to have it published was, as he told Bruce, "because it would be suspected that he had been inspired to write it."[32]

Two years later, having lost his enthusiasm for Tuskegee, Houston became interested in an opening in the Washington, D.C., black high school, but Washington refused to give him leave to take the examination, and then refused to accept Houston's resignation in midsummer. Houston wrote his pastor again, saying that while Washington had no legal power to claim his services, he felt he could not defy him. "He could easily reach me in any government position in that city," Houston wrote, "so when he told me not to go, I obeyed the edict, for I fully realized the folly of any attempt to defy him at this time. I am determined not to be held in such a modified form of slavery." Washington had no love for college men, said Houston, but kept them on the faculty only so that he could boast of them. "Mr. Washington's scheme is to have such a control over his teachers that they will tremble at his approach. Most teachers like to see the train puff out with him and dread to hear the engine whistling his return. Relying upon his absolute power, he reserves the right to discharge a teacher at any time. . . . This is not all, he haunts that teacher forever."[33] These were damning words and one-sided, and insubordinate if publicly uttered, but they were, after all, in private correspondence to his pastor.

Houston bided his time, even negotiated a raise in salary, but he pleaded with his pastor to help him find a school situation where he might escape the eye of the Tuskegee wizard.[34] Just after Houston's resignation in the spring of 1907, word came to Washington from his old friend and former student, Dr. Samuel Courtney of Boston: "Dave Houston has been writing some letters to Boston that are not becoming a true and loyal subordinate."[35] The very next day, the Reverend J. Henry Duckrey wrote to Washington: "I miss some important papers from my desk, and after just having a conference with Dr. Courtney." He suspected that either Courtney or Paul L. Wootton, another Bookerite, "in his over zealousness has taken them to you."[36] Courtney apparently tried to persuade Duckrey to let him see other compromising Houston letters, but had no success. Courtney wrote Washington: "I have hired our friend Wootton to get them by any means. It will take a little time but [he] feels quite certain he can get them long enough to make a copy."[37] A few days later Washington heard from his secretary: "Courtney wires he has letter."[38]

Learning that Washington had read his letters, Houston began to try to explain them away, writing to Washington that he had never had anything to do with "the anti Tuskegee party" and had always been guarded in his remarks about the school and its chief. He could only deduce that his private letters to his pastor had been stolen.[39] Washington, ignoring his own complicity in the purloining of private letters, replied simply: "Letters have been placed in my hands which make it clear that during a portion of the time while you were at Tuskegee you were disloyal to the Institution, which you were paid to serve; second, that you were making efforts to get away from the institution at any time in any manner without regard to your promise or contract to remain through the year; third, the statements made in these letters are false to the extent of being almost ridiculous." Washington said he would withdraw his favorable recommendation of Houston that had enabled him to secure a position in the Baltimore schools for the following year unless Houston made a satisfactory explanation or acknowledged his wrong action.[40]

Houston wilted in the heat of Washington's righteous indignation. "I beg leave," he wrote, "to admit the guilt of the charges that you bring against me, and to state that I regret very much my action. I thank you heartily for the assurance of your renewed confidence in me."[41] Having humiliated Houston as an example to any other teacher who might be tempted to do the same thing, Washington quickly according to his promise reaffirmed his original recommendation in a letter to Houston's principal in Baltimore, adding: "I very much hope that you can give him the place which you had in mind. I think he is thoroughly repentant and has learned a lesson."[42] The Houston incident is significant because of its revelation of Washington's excessive fear that his own college-trained teachers would catch the Niagara spirit. It did not adversely affect Houston's career, for while Washington was a trustee of Howard, Houston joined its English faculty with Washington's blessing.

If Tuskegee's teachers often felt overworked, underpaid, and unappreciated, this was doubly true of the office force. Washington and Scott had a standing order that all correspondence be answered on the day it came in from the post office, even "if it is necessary to remain at the office until twelve o'clock at night to do it."[43] Furthermore, the office force had to screen its confidential work from outsiders on the campus. Washington ordered that "(1) office boys be allowed to have nothing to do with any of the correspondence that comes into the office—(2) that everything be removed from the desk when you are not present yourself & that this be kept as much in mind at twelve o'clock, as at 5 o'clock."[44] Washington even pronounced gum chewing "against the rule of the office." One office worker defied the rule, however, for he had been chewing for fifteen years on a doctor's advice and considered chewing gum not "a pernicious habit, a vicious practice or an immoral act, but rather one within the rights of personal privilege."[45]

A Victorian code governed all matters of conduct of Tuskegee's people, one partly inherited from the prudish school teachers of Hampton a half-century earlier but compounded by upward striving. The code bound Booker T. Washington as well as the lower ranks. When Washington suggested about 1902 that, as times were changing, dancing might be permitted, the Dean of Women warned him that if he aired that opinion he would open a Pandora's box. She would be unable to control the students, who already wanted to dance. "With the prevailing opinion that dancing is not permissible, the matter is easily controlled," she wrote. "Otherwise we could have no order in the dormitories. I am impressed that it would be a serious menace to good order, if not to the well-being of the institution itself, to permit dancing. What the students most need is restraint; they come for the most part from undeveloped homes where there are no standards. This being true we must take an extreme position in order to counteract the tendencies of their lives before coming here."[46]

A class principle was clearly involved in the Tuskegee social code. The force that bound college-bred and self-made teachers into a social unit was their common middle-class status, whereas the students were either lower class or déclassé, as in the army. If dancing would shake the social purpose of Tuskegee, this purpose would collapse in the presence of whiskey, beer, tobacco, firearms, cards or dice, or walking girls home from chapel even on Sunday evenings. The institute catalog forbade these activities. No student could leave the grounds without permission. Male students had to wear the school cap, and a woman teacher had to chaperone women students off the grounds. The rules governing students generally applied in a looser way to faculty members, particularly in places where students might observe. George Washington Carver rather prissily complained of the use of loose language by teachers. "The matter of teachers calling each other by their given names—such as 'Hetty,' 'John,' 'Bill,' etc., should be corrected," he said. "Also, their addressing each other thus: 'Hello! How are you?' etc."[47]

The rules were much the same at Tuskegee as in other schools and colleges in the period, but at Tuskegee they were particularly oppressive because the discipline there was so rigorous that it allowed few safety valves in its restraint of natural impulse. Time also added the weight of tradition to some rules, for they seemed to be more generally obeyed than in the early days of the school. Law and order prevailed on the grounds. Washington would call periodically for a crackdown on card playing, secret alcohol consumption, or teachers fraternizing with students. On the crucial subject of dancing, however, he remained more liberal than many of his faculty. "As you perhaps know," he wrote the Dean of Women in 1913, "social dancing among girls is now indulged in in many parts of the country as a great means of giving the girls better carriage and appearance in every way." He sent her a pamphlet describing such dancing classes at Hull House, Jane Addams's famous settlement house in Chicago where so many immigrant girls were gently "Americanized." This ray of enlightenment led to an all-girls dancing class once a week. "Of course," Washington explained, "I mean for this to be done among the girls alone not with boys."[48]

Human nature found outlets, however. Senior men drank beer on a country picnic on the eve of graduation. The punishment was suspension of their diplomas for a time. Faculty men sometimes left Gamlin's store, across from the campus on the Montgomery highway, with alcohol or sen-sen or mints on their breath. After Carver had chemically analyzed the beverage they drank there, the executive council warned Gamlin, who rented his store from Booker T. Washington, that if he continued to sell alcoholic drinks he would be liable to prosecution.[49] Some seniors celebrated New Year's Day, also known among blacks as Emancipation Day, by climbing dangerously up the domed roofs of campus buildings to plant their class flag there. Instead of the total liberation they expected from such an experience, however, they were dismissed from school for the remainder of the year.[50]

Because of its strictness, Tuskegee Institute was almost entirely free of the scandals that wracked many other boarding schools. Scandal could not be eliminated entirely, however. Early in 1905 a scurrilous little book appeared and was eagerly read within a hundred-mile radius of the institute and even beyond. It undertook to insinuate that "social equality" was taught there, but all it presented was a succession of true, half-true, and imaginary stories of sexual improprieties among faculty and students. Dr. S. Becker Von Grabil, the author, a German-born music teacher in the town, had *Letters from Tuskegee, Being the Confessions of a Yankee* privately printed in Montgomery under the pen name Ruperth Fehnstoke. He hawked the book himself. The source of his rancor against Tuskegee was that, finding his salary as a music teacher at the Alabama Conference Female College inadequate, he offered to give a concert at Tuskegee Institute at what the school considered the exorbitant fee of $200. He agreed to lower it to $100 but broke off discussion when the school offered what he considered an insulting amount, $15.[51]

Washington refused to read the book. He had Emmett Scott read it and list its main points. When asked by persons in widely scattered parts of the country if there were any truth in the book, his standard reply was: "I have never read the book because I feel that I could not afford to do so. I have heard the book discussed by some of the teachers here, but the majority of the teachers here feel that the book is written on too low a plane for them to spend time at it. Personally, I never read anything that does not help me to be a better and stronger person."[52] In a community of some 2000 persons over a period of twenty-four years, he said, Von Grabil could discover only one true instance of immorality, that of a widow with four children who "fell." She was dismissed and sent from the campus, but before she went she was forced to marry the man involved, and "was made so unhappy in the community, she left the town."[53] No one could say honestly that Tuskegee Institute was not a community of virtue.

Not to be denied his hearing, Von Grabil hired persons to throw advertising circulars on the book into the yards of white and black residents of Montgomery. Washington, however, quickly rallied to his support respectable Tuskegee white citizens. John Massey, head of the Alabama Conference Female College in the town, threatened to suspend any of his students caught reading *Letters from Tuskegee*.[54] "While I concur in the sentiment of all the better class of Southern people," Massey wrote to the Tuskegee board of trustees, "I wish to express my unqualified dissent from the conclusions drawn in 'The Confessions of a Yankee.' " Far from fostering immorality, he said, "I believe that your management has endeavored to do the best possible, under the circumstances, for the moral development of the negroes." Massey sent his letter also to the Tuskegee *News* for publication.[55] Washington, however, persuaded the editor not to publish it, on the ground that it would only give Von Grabil the publicity he craved. "As you and other prominent citizens of Tuskegee well know," he wrote Massey, "it is impossible to conduct an institution of any character or of any size without weaknesses appearing and without mistakes. . . . one policy I have always pursued and that is I have always gotten rid of any individual, whether student or teacher, who brought disgrace on the school. The wonder is that there have not been more instances of wrong doing than there have been."[56]

Von Grabil's screed appealed to prurient interests, however, and it surfaced from time to time in embarrassed letters of inquiry as to its truth. Washington answered these by quoting Massey and discrediting the little German who pretended to be a Yankee.[57] Von Grabil had to move his headquarters from Tuskegee to Montgomery when local whites found that he was using for his book the signatures of endorsement they had given him for organizing a company to manufacture

horse medicine.[58] Perhaps Charles W. Hare spoke for most Tuskegeans in saying, "my contempt for such hyenas is beyond expression."[59]

Nevertheless, despite Washington's vigilance, pecadillos and acci-
dents occurred that Von Grabil never knew about, and the pressure
to maintain a front of respectability led Washington sometimes into
unfairness to those in trouble. Not surprisingly, a woman student occasionally went home pregnant. A faculty member's wife gave birth
after only five months of marriage. The committee investigating this
case concluded that the husband was not the father and was therefore
not "guilty," and offered its sympathy. The school physician improp-
erly collected a fee for medical service to a student and was dismissed.
The business agent, caught accepting favors from suppliers to the
school, was removed from that position, but in view of his long service
to the institution was given a less sensitive office in the school. None
of these affairs, however, transcended ordinary human frailties or
caused a disruption of the institute.

The dismissal in 1907 of Edgar J. Penney, however, shook the institution to its foundations. It was of a different order, not only because of the outside publicity it evoked but because of the moral authority Penney had exerted and his long service as dean of the Phelps
Hall Bible Training School at Tuskegee, and also because of the ques-
tionable grounds for his dismissal. The charge against Penney was
that he had sexually molested a young woman student boarding in his
house. The stenographically recorded testimony against Penney consisted entirely of the girl's accusations, all of which Penney categorically denied. It was her word against his, but somewhat damaging to
Penney's credibility was that some years earlier another student had
made similar unsubstantiated charges. On that earlier occasion Penney had been cleared of all charges. Somehow the benefit of the doubt
on the earlier occasion weighed against the benefit of the doubt a
second time. Devastating to the girl's claim of injured innocence were
love letters to her from a white physician in New Orleans, clearly indicating their intimacy and the deception of his wife.[60] The young
woman was in fact sent home in disgrace, and Washington wrote her
father that his parental neglect had been partly responsible for his
daughter's disgrace, as she had been led into ways of thinking and
acting that she would not have if properly reared.[61] The evidence of
the girl's sexual experiences, however, increased rather than dimin-

ished the doubt about Dean Penney, by making her testimony more credible. Penney was trapped in a paradox.

Washington offered Penney the choice of resignation rather than dismissal, but threatened that if he did not do so by a certain date, "I shall have to take a different course to bring about the desired result."[62] Penney bargained endlessly on the details, asking for half-salary until the end of the school year and the use of his house for at least thirty days, conditions that Washington grudgingly granted.[63] Rumors brought newspapermen from Montgomery and Birmingham to the campus, and Washington frankly stated to the press that Penney's resignation "had been asked for on grounds that the reports and gossip which were going the rounds concerning him had in the opinion of the trustees brought his usefulness as a member of the Tuskegee Institute faculty to an end." Washington, however, "made it plain that he was not passing upon Penney's guilt or innocence."[64] In other words, he was merely bringing Penney's career to an end.

Penney resigned under pressure, but he urged Washington to remember that he was "admitting no guilt in this affair." Being innocent and not responsible for the affair, he said, "I can not plead guilty. I am poor, helpless and *alone,* therefore I, to this extent yield. . . . But you have treated me, in this case, as though I had had a fair trial and had been found guilty and dismissed in disgrace. That is the news that has gone out to the country. I have heard of it from several states already, and it has hardly begun to travel. You could not have planned better to do me and my family the greatest human injury, and all, because you would not listen to but one side and acted prematurely and hastily in not granting me the asked for interview; and in demanding my resignation & in taking my work from me before knowing all the facts."[65]

Horace Bumstead, president of Atlanta University where Penney was a graduate and a trustee, wrote Washington a letter of inquiry, saying that if Penney was unfit to teach at Tuskegee he would also be unfit to be an Atlanta trustee. Bumstead said, however, that he had heard the charges were "based solely on the testimony of a young girl student whose own character and testimony have been impeached by letters found in her trunk, the discovery of which has resulted in her own dismissal from Tuskegee. If there has been any corroborative evidence of her testimony, it would seem important for us to have it."[66] Washington replied rather evasively after nearly a month's delay. He merely sent Bumstead a copy of the letter he had sent to Penney and added: "We have already taken the position that a school is not a court of law, that it is the duty of the court to prove a person guilty; in the case of a school we take the position that whenever a student or teacher gets into a position where his influence is hurtful that the school has a right to part with such an individual."[67]

Bumstead differed with Washington on educational policy issues and also probably had found that Washington's best friends among philanthropists were his worst critics, so there may have been some relish in his lecture to Washington about his denial of academic freedom. He wrote: "You say you take the position that a school is not a court of law and not bound to prove the guilt of a teacher. But is it not bound to be governed, in dealing with him, by the ordinary laws of evidence which prevail among men even outside the courts? You say when a teacher gets into a position where his influence is hurtful the school has a right to part with him. But has it a right to do so in a way to besmirch his character? And is it not bound to consider whether he 'gets' into such a position or is *put* into it by no fault of his own?"[68] There was clearly merit to Bumstead's charge that Penney had been sacrificed unfairly to Tuskegee's respectability. Washington, however, took the position that he was not answerable to Bumstead for his executive decision. He said to another questioner, "I cannot without a request or order from our Trustees, think of going into detailed defense or exposition of our action."[69]

Tuskegee was a nice place to visit if not always a nice place to teach. It was a showcase of "the Tuskegee idea" of industrial education, self-help, and black self-sufficiency. A steady stream of prominent visitors, white and black, northern, southern, and foreign, came to see and admire. They came in largest numbers on Commencement Day and to the Tuskegee Negro Conference, but they came by twos and threes in all seasons. John D. Rockefeller, Jr., and his wife Abby arrived in 1903, with a maid and valet, to inspect the school and particularly the huge Rockefeller dining hall. When young Rockefeller rose to speak in the chapel, the senior men also rose and gave a yell involving the spelling of his name. "I think the scholar who can spell my father's name without mistake should receive a diploma without further examination," said Rockefeller.[70] Susan B. Anthony and a half-dozen other woman suffragists stopped by on the way home from their annual convention in New Orleans. The welcome accorded Anthony was

"a sea of snowy handkerchiefs greeting her with the 'Chautauqua salute.' " Since it was Sunday, the students were forbidden to use the
usual school yell.[71] Equally dramatic was the arrival of General John
B. Gordon to give his stock lecture on "The Last Days of the Confederacy." He stated an article of faith of a certain class of southerner:
"Standing in this presence, and measuring well my words, with the
fear of God upon me, I declare to you that the Southern white man
is the best friend the negro in the South has." The students cheered
him to the echo.[72]

One of the most publicized visits to Tuskegee was that of a large
party of northern congressmen brought by Tuskegee's Democratic
congressman, Charles W. Thompson. His purpose was to demonstrate to them that disfranchisement of blacks was having a benign
effect. Thompson took his party first to his plantation six miles out in
the rural part of Macon County, where he spread an authentic southern barbecue on improvised tables. While the visitors ate, 1000 field
hands given a holiday for the occasion provided entertainment. They
engaged in the plantation pastimes of fiddling, shooting craps, and
dancing. After the guests were finished but in their sight, "the entire
crowd of darkies were let loose on the remains of the feast and furnished one of the great spectacles of the day. . . . The negroes were
greasy from chin to eyebrow and from finger tip to elbow."[73] This, to
a southern reporter at least, showed bestiality rather than hunger and
justified white supremacy. The following day at Tuskegee Institute,
the Thompson party witnessed a sharp contrast to the degrading parody of black life they had seen on the plantation. Students took charge
of the party and guided visitors to the departments. In the chapel
ceremony, Washington referred to his graduates with pride as successful men and women, and "made the observation that not one of
his students had ever broken into jail or Congress."[74] Thompson's
object lesson apparently had the desired effect on some of the congressmen, for when they visited a black church in Mobile and the
preacher made a disparaging reference to disfranchisement, two of
the congressmen took exception and endorsed an educational qualification.[75]

"I felt all day that I was watching a sort of drama that would reach
its climax," said one white visitor to Tuskegee, "that the curtain would
fall and the play be ended; that I would go home with a subdued
sadness that one feels after witnessing the Passion Play; but thank

God; it was all real, and if the men and women be actors the world is their stage and life their drama, and the curtain will never fall." [76] Nearly all the visitors, white or black, northern or southern, felt an aura about Tuskegee Institute, heightened by the contrast with the desolate countryside and the woebegone little hamlet it adjoined. The spectacle of Tuskegee's brick buildings and industrious campus citizens stunned the critical faculties of visitors and challenged all their stereotypes of blacks and black communities.

An Illinois normal school professor found the correlation of industrial and academic work at Tuskegee the best he had ever seen. He wrote to Wallace Buttrick of the General Education Board: "The very minimum of the 'make believe' and superficial and the maximum of the real, the genuine, the education." His only criticism of the institute was that some academic classes seemed poorly taught. [77] Others also balanced their general praise of the school with some specific criticism. A Hampton donor compared Tuskegee's grounds unfavorably with those of Hampton. Washington considered that criticism unfair because at Tuskegee the students maintained the grounds, whereas outside laborers did some of this at Hampton. Furthermore, "We are 'subsoiling' at Tuskegee," he wrote, "and in doing so, while we may not present to the public such a finely finished picture as some other institutions, I do think that we are doing work that is needed to be done in this generation and in this section of our country." [78] When visitors complained of lack of neatness in the boys' rooms, however, he took this to heart and wrote the commandant: "Nothing can hurt us so badly as filth and disorder of any sort whatever." [79] Charles W. Eliot, the president of Harvard, gave Tuskegee an incisive critique from his own unique perspective. He doubted that the programs for training ministers and nurses were adequate. He wondered whether the agricultural and industrial shops were absorbing too much of the school's revenues. He urged Washington to get onto his board of trustees some younger men. Finally, he wondered whether the industrial side was overdeveloped out of all proportion to the academic. Without a taste for reading, the isolated black farmer or mechanic would not prove capable of progress, he said. "The world changes so fast nowadays that the man or woman who does not read will be left behind, no matter what the calling." [80] W. E. B. Du Bois could not have said it any better.

Many foreign visitors came on their own random schedules, rather than on Commencement Day. Sir Horace Plunkett of Ireland, interested in land reform, Jules Huret of *Le Figaro*, Lord Eustace Percy, the British ambassador, and the sociologist Max Weber were but a few of the foreigners who braved the journey into the South to visit Tuskegee. Their amazement at its physical plant, its amenities, its good order and its sense of purpose was an index of their white supremacy assumptions and consequent low expectations of an institution conducted by blacks.[81] Most of the black visitors of distinction came either as commencement speakers—one each year—or on summons from Washington to discuss a matter of racial politics. Most of them, therefore, were preselected for sympathy with Washington's goals, though critics such as J. Max Barber and W. E. B. Du Bois were occasional visitors. Kelly Miller of Howard University was there in 1903, and explored not only the campus but the town and surrounding countryside, and what struck him most vividly was the problem the institute faced. "The soil is generally thin and well exhausted," he noted. "It almost makes the heart bleed to see those hard-working, honest, ignorant men wearing out soul and body upon a barren hill-side, which yielded up its virgin strength a half century ago, and whose top soil has been washed away, and can be restored only by another geologic epoch." He found the plantation system had broken down, and renting of small tracts the general rule among black farmers. "A careful and dispassionate analysis of all the facts and factors," Miller concluded, "leads plainly to two conclusions, (1) the Tuskegee idea alone cannot solve the race problem, and (2) the race problem cannot be solved without the Tuskegee idea." Miller, as usual, came down firmly on both sides of the issue.[82]

Commencement Day at Tuskegee in Washington's day was too rococo an affair for brief description. Suffice it to say that all Tuskegee was a stage, and all the men and women merely players. The songs for the occasion were a serious enough matter for executive council action. In 1906, as always, spirituals and other plantation songs predominated. They began with "Reign Massa Jesus" through "Balm in Gilead" toward a mundane conclusion with "Auld Lang Syne, Star Spangled Banner, Kentucky Home."[83] Everything else was carefully ordered in advance, even the spontaneity. Instruction 5 on the 1903 Commencement list was: "When the Principal is brought to the platform, young men are asked to instantly come to their feet, while all give the regular Tuskegee yell; the young women are asked to instantly come to their feet, give the Chautauqua salute & vigorously clap their hands. The teachers, of course, will heartily join in the demonstration."[84]

Two Presidents of the United States, McKinley and Roosevelt, visited Tuskegee during their terms of office, but undoubtedly the climactic public ceremony of Washington's career as principal was the Twenty-Fifth Anniversary of Tuskegee in 1906. On the platform with Washington as principal speakers were three symbolic figures of white America, Charles W. Eliot of Harvard, the quintessential capitalist Andrew Carnegie, and Secretary of War William Howard Taft, heir apparent to the presidency. These cultural, economic, and political leaders all found Washington's accommodative and meliorist leadership to be the congenial and sensible way to adjustment of America's race problem. These represented, as J. Max Barber said, "the three classes which run this country; and they all joined in the praise of Booker Washington and pledged him their support."

Barber, who was no friend of Tuskegee or Washington, had nothing but praise for Washington's address on the occasion, which "rebuked the country for its political treachery to the Negro, sounding a warning note to the effect that free government was losing ground thereby; pointed out the impossibility of a community rising while at the same time trying to keep down an integral part of itself; rebuked the mob and declared that he desired that the Negro have free scope to develop himself to the limit." What deeply disturbed Barber was Secretary Taft's address on the "Three War Amendments." He found the Thirteenth and Fourteenth Amendments right and just, but said that the many movements for Negro education were misguided, declared that "the only hope of the Negro race was economic independence," and praised Washington for finding and moving along this line of "least popular resistance." He declared blacks "a people not fit to enjoy or maintain the higher education," as they needed primary and industrial education.[85]

Washington always had to work in rural Alabama along the lines of least resistance, and even his very successes awakened hostile criticism. To some whites Tuskegee itself was an affront, its big buildings, neatly dressed students, air of bustle, and affluence were a contrast to the shabby downtown and the flaking paint of the old mansion houses. Tuskegee town needed the institute payroll, and the Tuskegee merchants who had taken over from the old plantation elite were themselves accommodationists to the dominance of the institute in the economic life of the town. Underneath the smooth business relations, however, were jealousy and fear, bred anew whenever the school's industrial shops sold a wagon or a load of brick, whenever the campus orchard's surplus peaches went to market in town. Merchants often felt, whether it was true or not, that a tax-free institution was unfairly competing. Even worse, when school officers bought tracts near the school to resell to teachers and small farmers as a land reform measure, townspeople saw this as "trying to buy up the whole county" and drive the whites away. Washington never missed an occasion to say that the white people in his home town and county were the best on earth, and certainly the Negro's best friends, but if so some of them had a habit of forgetting it. Washington had to respond to outbreaks of hostility and jealousy with his usual resourcefulness.

Washington was aware that Tuskegee's sales and services off campus were a potent source of trouble, for he instructed the business manager: "When we do sell, it should be to merely accommodate people who could not get material elsewhere." Nothing should be sold at less than cost, for then merchants would complain of being undercut.[86] It was no surprise, therefore, when the town marshal in 1903 demanded payment of the privilege tax on all of the school's mechanical departments. Washington was away, and Logan delayed until he could ask him what to do, pay the tax or take the issue to court.[87] Washington decided to resist, and soon afterward J. Richard Wood, the Macon County legislator and recently mayor, retaliated by a bill to take away the state grant for Tuskegee's agricultural experiment station.[88] Washington was out of town throughout the time the bill was considered, but Tuskegee's white friends successfully defended the school. Charles W. Hare set up lobbying headquarters in Montgomery. The Tuskegee *News* flatteringly described the experiment station and noted that Wood had been one of the original petitioners for it.[89] J. O. Thompson contacted his Democratic congressman brother and other influential Tuskegeans, and a petition quietly circulated in town. "I think we shall have Mr. Wood pretty well cornered," Scott wrote;[90] and Jodie Thompson promised, "We will make Mr. Wood 'look like 30 cents' before he is through with the bill."[91] During the three hours of debate on the subject before the House education committee, Wood made the mistake of attacking all black education, thus losing focus. The committee unanimously rejected the bill and that was the end of the matter.[92]

Three years later, however, J. O. Thompson's own nephew Ernest won a seat in the House by a campaign denouncing Tuskegee Institute's ownership of too much untaxable land, thus reducing the property tax revenue in the county, and its unfair competition with local businessmen, and he vowed to end the tax exemption of the institute land. Washington first tried to head off Ernest Thompson by explaining the facts. He wrote that the school held no land not used for the institution's purposes, that it had no financial interest in the Southern Improvement Company, which did pay taxes, and that he and the trustees were anxious to do their share to support the county. He valued the good will of the people of Macon County more than of anybody else, he wrote, and believed their differences ought to be settled at home.[93] Next Washington enlisted the legislator's uncles, J. O. and W. W. Thompson, to try to dissuade him.[94] Washington asked his own brother John to enlist prominent Tuskegee whites in visiting Ernest Thompson "on different days." John talked with the young man's hunting companions, but they told him that, having made up his mind, Ernest Thompson would go ahead regardless of advice. Perhaps the Tuskegeans went too far, for Thompson accused the school of trying to buy him off. When asked what bribe had been offered, however, all he could come up with was that his wife had got some cream from the dairy and the institute refused to accept pay for it.[95]

Ernest Thompson suddenly changed his tactics and secured passage of a resolution requesting the governor to send an auditor to Tuskegee to inquire into the entire financial affairs of the institute. "I am humiliated and feel that our whole family has been betrayed by that youngster," moaned J. O. Thompson.[96] But Washington concentrated his attention now on the new governor, Braxton Bragg Comer, a man born in the Black Belt but now a millowner representing the industrial and predominantly white north Alabama. Charles Hare took a train ride to Birmingham with Comer in order to tell him of all the "other audits & examinations of the school."[97] Washington wrote a flattering letter to Comer, thanking him for the racial references in his first message. "I have always found that persons who were raised in the Black Belt right among our people are those who possessed the deepest sympathy for the race and knew best how to help it," Washington wrote soothingly. He invited the Governor to visit Tuskegee and see for himself how the school encouraged blacks to stay in the country and progress rather than flock to the cities.[98] He followed this up two days later by writing that he had not been to see the Governor about the Thompson resolution because "I have implicit faith in your sense of absolute justice towards the Negro race, and I do not believe that anyone would be appointed to come here by you who is prejudiced to the Negro and especially prejudiced against his education."[99] The Governor reassured Washington: "I do not think the State intends any persecution of your school."[100] Even Ernest Thompson reportedly said that he had no animosity against the school but was simply doing what his constituents had requested of him.[101]

Washington took no chances of misunderstanding, however. He arranged for Seth Low, chairman of the trustees, to write a letter to Robert C. Ogden predated the previous December, saying that the late William H. Baldwin, Jr., had organized the auditing "on a railroad basis," with an auditing department at the school and an independent auditor, Daniel Cranford Smith, responsible to the trustees.[102] The arrival of the governor's special examiner, William W. Haralson, was something of an anticlimax. Washington had canceled all his appointments to be on campus for the week, and he found Haralson "a high-toned, broad-minded gentleman" who seemed well-disposed. He wrote Low of Haralson: "He has never, I think, come into contact with colored people before in the capacity that he is now meeting them and it is rather interesting to study him in this capacity." Haralson expressed astonishment "that it was possible for a perfectly black unmixed man of our race to keep books."[103]

Haralson gave every indication of approval, and the Governor when he received the report announced that it was favorable but did not release it.[104] Thompson resisted great pressure at this point from family and neighbors to withdraw his bill to tax Tuskegee's lands, still swearing that he was going to beat Tuskegee in the end.[105] As the Thompson bill came before a committee for hearings, Washington sent paid and unpaid lobbyists to Montgomery to work against it, but the release of the Haralson report at the critical moment was decisive. It found Tuskegee, "looking at its purely business side . . . a model of perfection." No transaction took place without record, every detail was readily accessible, everything balanced. Haralson added unstinted praise of the condition of the grounds, the good order, and "the general air of earnestness and industry that seemed to pervade the entire establishment."[106] The committee voted evenly on the Thompson bill and the chairman broke the tie to report the bill adversely.[107]

That adverse recommendation crippled the bill's chances, but it was still possible for Thompson to call the bill up on the floor if he could stir up enough white fear that the Institute would "buy up the whole county." Washington left the remainder of work against the bill to Scott and Charles Hare. Hare sought to counter the scare campaign by a long article in the *Advertiser*. He pointed out that Tuskegee had located in its first year in a district where no whites had lived for a quarter-century, on a farm known as "The Big Hungry." As for the charge that the school was speculating in lands by developing the community of Greenwood, Hare said the purpose was to help teachers and others live close to the school and to own their own homes and pay taxes on them. "Again," he added, "this segregating of the negro families is the best for the school, and best for the white community of Tuskegee."[108] Thus, a central argument in behalf of Tuskegee Institute was that it was promoting segregation, though Washington himself did not make that argument.

After intense lobbying, heated floor debate, and the availability of Haralson's favorable report, Thompson's bill lost by more than two to one. This was not, however, until after floor debate had brought expressions of fear that Tuskegee and Washington were subverting white supremacy. Samuel Will John of Birmingham said: "Now the Tuskegee Institute has more income than the University of Alabama, the Polytechnic Institute and the Girls' Industrial School combined, and they are educating them how? To hate us." He presented no real evidence of this, but race relations were worsening, for John had once been a Tuskegee supporter. Another representative said: "I believe Booker Washington and his gang would prove to be the curse of the South, and if I had my way I would wipe his institute off the face of the earth."[109]

Greenwood village figured in the Thompson bill debates as an accommodation to white desire for segregation, but the community had another meaning to Booker T. Washington. It was, in the words of a promotional pamphlet, "a Model Negro Village," a residential counterpart of the institute. The school bought the 200 acres north of the campus, and Washington and other school officers took the lead in the building and loan association that laid out the village and arranged for financing the purchase of lots beginning in 1904. Lots 70 x 210 feet sold for $50, corner lots for $60, purchasable at six per cent. To demonstrate that blacks could live in the clean, orderly, middle-class way, the Village Improvement Association governed and patrolled the town. No whiskey was sold or allowed; streets were paved, lighted, and tree-lined; there was a city park. Children of residents were admitted to the campus model school, the "Children's House." Greenwood filled up rapidly, and in 1906 had some 2100 inhabitants.[110] Greenwood invited local farmers and laborers, but most of the residents were faculty, and this led over the years to some tension between the institute people and the black townspeople. Washington insisted that when, from time to time, the school laid off outside laborers, preferential treatment be accorded to Greenwood residents.[111]

Washington gave Greenwood the same paternal attention he bestowed on the institute. It was, after all, part of the standard tour of visitors. He frequently fired off memos to his brother John to keep his chickens in his own yard, or to another property-owner to pick up the paper strewing his lawn. "I very much fear that a mistake is being made in Greenwood in having too many dances," he wrote one resident. "I shall have to take some strong and definite measures if the matter is not controlled."[112] When a Greenwood storekeeper opened his shop on Sunday, Washington threatened to forbid students to enter his store until he obeyed the blue law.[113] There was a purpose behind this authoritarianism, however. If Tuskegee was a preparation for life, and for assimilation into the mainstream of American life, as Washington strongly believed, then Greenwood was that life in miniature.

The graduates, however, were the pride and concern of Washington's Tuskegee. Their careers and daily lives would be living symbols of the success or failure of the institution. So, as at Hampton, there was perhaps one graduate for every ten ex-students. There were others who received industrial certificates testifying to their mastery of their trade, but only those who proved their all-round worthiness became seniors and finally graduated. Graduation was almost an ordination as a minister of the Tuskegee gospel. It was Washington's frequent boast that not a single graduate of Tuskegee had been in jail. He did not say that no ex-student had been to jail, or even rarely a resident student whose crime went beyond the limits of the commandant's authority. He simply asked that Tuskegee be judged by the world on "its finished product rather than the raw material which sometimes spends a week, a month, or even a year at the school."[114]

All over the South, and the North as well, were white skeptics of Washington's methods and true intentions, and they often focussed on what sort of people they imagined the graduates to be. In some, white supremacy doctrine was so ingrained that they could not believe education could make of a black person anything other than an inferior human being. Gordon Macdonald, for example, a white lawyer in Montgomery, created a stir when he claimed in 1903 that Tuskegee was miseducating its students. Though he later admitted under close questioning that he had never been on the Tuskegee campus, he wrote as though from certain knowledge that "for one genuine, hardworking husbandman, or artizan sent into the world by Washington's school, it afflicts this state with twenty soft-handed negro dudes and loafers, who earn a precarious living by 'craps' or petit larceny, or live on the hard-earned wages of cooks and washerwomen whose affections they have been able to ensnare." The women students, he asserted, learned to scorn hard work "while their poor mothers toil over the wash tubs and cook stoves that their daughters may be taught music and painting—God save the mark!—and to rustle in fine dresses in a miserable imitation of fine ladies." What really rankled Macdonald was Washington's dinner at the White House, which he said taught by example "that social equality is a possibility and that it is near." Washington's industrial education was merely "a blind"; his example was the real teacher.[115]

Washington might have ignored Macdonald if his allegations had not appeared in the Washington *Post* and spread to many other papers. Washington assigned his white ghostwriter, Max B. Thrasher, to confront Macdonald with a demand for evidence. Macdonald offered to give Thrasher a court record of Tuskegee ex-students' misdemeanors and a list of Tuskegee girls who had studied music and painting while their mothers washed clothes, but he failed to produce either list and finally admitted that his informant on Tuskegee was William B. Paterson, Washington's longtime bitter rival as the white head of a black state college in Montgomery.[116] Thrasher died of appendicitis in the midst of his interviews with Macdonald, but before he died he made a personal investigation of each ex-student living in Montgomery and concluded "that Mr. Macdonald has failed to substantiate his statement that Tuskegee graduates are living by their 'wits' rather than by work."[117]

Washington was both blessed and cursed by ambiguity, and a large part of the white public persisted in mistakenly believing that Tuskegee prepared its graduates or students for housework and other menial jobs. When scores of letters arrived each year asking for domestic servants, Washington's standard reply was that Tuskegee education was to "prepare them to be of service to their own people in the South." Girls in advanced classes, he wrote, "receive instruction in various branches of housekeeping, the expectation being that they will go back to their communities and by example, as well as by precept, aid in making their homes and those of their neighbors more nearly what they should be."[118] The demands, however, continued, particularly from the South. "If it be claimed that the whites are benefited by educating the negroes, then let us see some cooks come into white kitchens from the Tuskegee schools," one newspaper demanded.[119] Clark Howell of Atlanta also asked Washington: "Do you think sufficient attention is being paid to the education of negroes for housekeeping and domestic work?" The places were "ready and waiting for competent workers of this kind."[120] Washington made a few concessions. He sent Howell a servant from town, not a student. He once offered to send any white lodge or other organization in town planning a party a few students to serve without charge.[121] He even responded to a request for "a full negro, 'as black as possible,' " to go to France as a servant.[122] He considered but abandoned a plan to set up a domestic training school in Montgomery, and in 1914 as an extension service a domestic science teacher gave lessons to the black domestic servants of Tuskegee.[123]

Though Tuskegee graduates almost without exception brought credit to their alma mater and themselves, one exception proved the rule. Albert G. Davis of the class of 1889 came to be listed in the catalogs as "present occupation unknown." Davis was "simply a drinking, worthless character," according to Washington's nephew, who frequently saw him in Birmingham.[124] He was always in some kind of trouble. The state superintendent of education accused Davis of impersonating another man at a teachers' examination and revoked his certificate. Davis denied the charge, claimed he had been denied due process, and asked Washington to help pay his legal expenses for a test case. When Washington refused but wished Davis well, Davis threatened to denounce Washington in the Boston *Guardian,* and to write a letter there every week until Washington relented. "Your New England friends and worshippers can form an idea of what many of your graduates think of you," he wrote his former principal. "All of my energies are now bent on tearing away your mask."[125] Washington ignored this attempt at blackmail, but when he gave a speech in Birmingham soon afterward his friends kept "a sharp lookout on Mr. Albert Davis."[126]

In 1906 Davis was accused of impersonating another man at a letter carriers' examination. "No graduate of your school is a convict," he wrote Washington, "and I cannot bring myself to believe that you will instead of helping me get out of jail write me a nice unctious letter with sugar-coated words."[127] The charges were dropped, maybe through Washington's influence.[128] Soon, however, Davis was convicted on another charge and sentenced to thirty days in the coal mines, plus court costs. The prison chaplain urged Washington to pay the court costs, but Washington said, "he has been doing wrong and acting carelessly for a long while, and I cannot help but feel that perhaps the lesson he learned in prison will help him rather than hurt him."[129] Washington soon relented and tried without success to intercede, and Davis had to work out his $58 court costs at 30¢ a day.[130] After this, Washington had to modify his boast of Tuskegee graduates to say: "With one exception, no graduate of Tuskegee Institute has ever been lodged in jail."[131]

CHAPTER 8

Other People's Schools

While Mr. Washington has of late thrown in a parenthetical expression about higher education, his main influence has been on the other side and has at times poked fun at the college-bred Negro. How far a word from Mr. Washington goes!

J. MAX BARBER, 1906

This matter of defending and explaining these so-called higher institutions makes me tired. The sooner these institutions can learn that they are simply making a contribution to the general education of the people, the better it is going to be for all concerned.

BTW, 1910

THERE were major differences of social philosophy and racial strategy that polarized Booker T. Washington and W. E. B. Du Bois and the Bookerites and Niagarites who followed them. Higher education versus industrial education, however, was not one of those polarizing differences. Just as Du Bois recognized the need for industrial training and a class of black artisans, Washington acknowledged the appropriateness of higher education. Sharing honors with the president of Harvard at a black banquet in Cambridge, Massachusetts, in 1904, Washington stated a truism about black education: "We need not only the industrial school, but the college and professional school as well, for a people so largely segregated, as we are, from the main body of our people must have its own professional leaders who shall be able to measure with others in all forms of intellectual life. It is well to remember, however, that our teachers, ministers, lawyers and doctors will prosper just in proportion as they have about them an intelligent and skillful producing class."[1]

Though the differences were not fundamental, they were considerable. Du Bois and his coterie of college men who somewhat hyperbolically called themselves the Talented Tenth of the black race—more accurately the one-hundredth—scathingly criticised the materialism and incompleteness of industrial education. They also blamed Washington for the decline of northern white philanthropy for black colleges, though Tuskegee, Hampton, and other industrial schools had no direct responsibility for this except by being themselves. Washington, as we shall see, actually steered philanthropic funds toward rather than away from the black colleges. Nevertheless, from time to time, he could not resist the urge to poke fun at the airs of black college graduates, an urge that may have stemmed from his own lack of a college degree, as well as from the fact that these jibes played into the caricature his white listeners and many of his black ones wanted to hear. One of his faculty members at Tuskegee, a Harvard graduate, took issue with his remarks to Tuskegee students that, so far, the college men of the race had not shown themselves successful in "economic, constructive work." Washington said: "I make that statement, first, because I consider it a fact, and, second, because I hope to spur that class of men to that kind of endeavor." He wanted men to judge themselves by what they did rather than what class they belonged to, and illustrated this by saying of Robert E. Park, his white ghostwriter, that he did not know "whether Dr. Park is a graduate of any college or what college." His only consideration in collaborating with Park was "that he is a broad, sympathetic, strong, helpful man."[2]

Though a bad experience at a theological seminary in his youth had warped Washington's attitudes toward the more abstract and less functional aspects of higher education, he directed his ablest graduates and his own children to colleges. He supported the principle of the career open to talent, while at the same time, living in the poverty and quasi-illiteracy of the rural South, he believed both industrial school graduates and college graduates had obligations to the unskilled masses. Yet, he felt trapped in the world's stereotype of him. T. Thomas Fortune proposed to Washington in 1903 that he simply put himself on record unequivocally as supporting higher education. Washington replied that he had already done so. "Would it be possible for me to place myself on record in any more forceful and plain manner than I have already done in my books, 'The Future of the American Negro' and 'Up from Slavery'? I have discussed fully every one of these questions in these two volumes, and . . . in the October number of the Atlantic Monthly. You will note that not one of the papers that are opposing me has dared to print a single line from the Atlantic Monthly, neither did these papers print my Louisville address. They systematically avoid publishing anything that defines my position on all these vital questions." [3]

What Washington said on higher education in *The Future of the American Negro,* his most systematic statement of his views on many subjects, was: "I would say to the black boy what I would say to the white boy, Get all the mental development that your time and pocketbook will allow of,—the more, the better; but the time has come when a larger proportion—not all, for we need professional men and women—of the educated coloured men and women should give themselves to industrial or business life. The professional class will be helped in so far as the rank and file have an industrial foundation, so that they can pay for professional service." Nevertheless, his endorsement of higher education for blacks was often studiedly ambiguous. In this same book he also said: "Boys have been taken from the farms and educated in law, theology, Hebrew and Greek,—educated in everything else except the very subject that they should know most about." He said: "It is little trouble to find girls who can locate Pekin or the Desert of Sahara on an artificial globe, but seldom can you find one who can locate on an actual dinner table the proper place for the carving knife and fork or the meat and vegetables." And he cited the southern white man's idea of black education in a way that might have been misread as his own, that it was merely "a parrot-like absorption of Anglo-Saxon civilisation, with a special tendency to imitate the weaker elements of the white man's character; that it meant merely the high hat, kid gloves, a showy walking cane, patent leather shoes, and all the rest of it." So, while it was Washington's purpose to exhort the educated to contribute to the improvement of the lot of all blacks, it is easy to understand how his words could be construed as indictment. [4]

There is a certain irony in the fact that Booker T. Washington, the man so many black college men considered their enemy, became a trustee of two of the leading black universities, Howard and Fisk. The irony cuts even deeper in the case of Howard University, where he became a trustee in 1907 at the behest of its white president, Wilbur P. Thirkield, for Thirkield owed his position to the fact that his predecessor had two years earlier tried to introduce industrial education and had been ousted by a near-revolt of students and faculty.[5] Thirkield came from a different tradition, of liberal arts and home missionary activity, but he was hardly installed in office when he showed a willingness to embrace Washington for both his practical help and his ideas. After a long interview with Washington and Frissell, Thirkield wrote the Tuskegean that he had drastically revised the Howard curriculum: "Manual work is required of all our students and the course for A. B. can be completed with honor without either Greek or Latin." He projected Howard's future development in civil, mechanical, and sanitary engineering. Then he mentioned Washington's half of a tacit bargain, "I trust that you have borne in mind my suggestion, in which you concurred, that you write to Mr. Carnegie with reference to a library for Howard University."[6] Soon afterward, Washington was unanimously elected a trustee, and he accepted the offer as an opportunity to "build up a great Negro university," one "abreast with the best institutions of the kind in the country."[7]

As news spread of Washington's election, not all of the letters were congratulatory. The black radical William A. Sinclair wrote from Philadelphia that Washington should decline. He had heard from other alumni and said: "I notice that your selection has already divided the graduates and friends of the University into hostile camps. I fear that the struggle will be even more bitter and acrimonious than that of two years ago, and thus the peace of the University will be undermined and its prosperity imperilled."[8] "This fellow is a cheeky cuss," Scott noted on the margin of the incoming letter, and he himself answered it.[9] Whitefield McKinlay, Washington's friend and lieutenant, however, saw the invitation as "an end to the foolish 'higher education' criticism."[10] As matters turned out, Washington's appointment was neither the beginning nor the end of strife.

Washington as a trustee managed to serve both Howard's needs and his own political purposes. He helped Howard get its Carnegie library building,[11] and was the school's liaison with the General Education Board and the U. S. Congress. His greatest service to the university, however, was during the hostile, southern-oriented atmosphere of the Wilson years, when in 1915 a southern congressman removed from the appropriation bill the entire Howard appropriation which had been regularly approved for the past quarter-century. Washington enlisted the trustees of Tuskegee Institute in an appeal to the President and key members of Congress for fair treatment for Howard University.[12] Guided by the larger mind and campaign promises of President Wilson, the White House interceded with the Democratic leadership in the Senate, which restored the cut and gained concurrence of the House.[13]

Despite Thirkield's early gestures toward industrial education, there is no evidence that Washington as a trustee succeeded or even tried to change the character of Howard. In his inaugural address, Thirkield took the middle ground. He emphasized that, "while efficient, industrial training alone is not sufficient for the rounded and complete life of any people," and that "there must be a body of elect men and women trained to large knowledge" to lead the people—"But may this 'elect tenth' never forget that education involves obligation; that their election is not to privilege alone or to mere place and power above men, but rather to service and sacrifice for the downmost man."[14]

Washington used sparingly but significantly his powers as a trustee, most notably in 1909 when Du Bois made plans to leave Atlanta University to join the NAACP staff and begin editing its journal, the *Crisis*. Du Bois was reluctant to leave the academic world altogether, since it had been his home for his entire adult life, and a movement developed at Howard to try to attract him there as a professor of sociology. The movement was led by Kelly Miller among the faculty and by John R. Francis among the trustees, and it had considerable support. Thirkield asked Washington his opinion in a private interview, and Washington advised against it, as did two other trustees. Thirkield then put the quietus on the appointment on the ground that Washington objected to it. The last thing in the world Washington wanted was to be exposed as exercising a veto on Du Bois, so he hastily sent a letter to Thirkield stating his own version of their interview. He had, he conceded, opposed Du Bois as more a hindrance than a help to Howard, and as unlikely anyhow to come at the salary Howard could afford, but he had promised to stand by Thirkield if he decided in favor of the appointment. It was the kind of question, he insisted, that only the president should decide. "In the last analysis," he said, "he [the president] bears the burden and should have the credit or censure for success or failure."[15] Trustee Francis tried to save the situation by eliciting from Du Bois a statement that his organization, the NAACP, was not "an organization for personal abuse."[16] Washington meanwhile covered his own tracks by sending Francis and others copies of his letter to Thirkield as a vindication of his own behavior and thrusting the burden of judgment on Thirkield. As Emmett Scott explained to a friend, Thirkield had "sought to block the selection *on the ground of the Doctor's opposition.*" Instead, Thirkield should have had the backbone to decide for himself, and not "take refuge behind somebody else."[17]

In a final effort to persuade Washington himself to nominate Du Bois, Francis wrote to the Tuskegean: "A recent interview with him has convinced me that his location at Howard will do more to eliminate from his efforts the offensively abusive & unscrupulous fellows who contaminate his career than anything else in sight."[18] In other words, as another commented, the appointment would be "a good way to squelch him."[19] Washington stood firm, however. Howard did not make the offer, and in view of Washington's letter to Thirkield it could not be said exactly that he had vetoed the appointment.

Learning a year later that a local candidate for Howard trustee had "a part of the Du Bois crowd working for him," Washington took steps to interfere.[20] He wrote to Thirkield that, being a national institution, Howard needed a broad-based board of trustees. "I have noted in connection with several institutions," he wrote, "that wherever they have a large number of local Trustees, trouble is likely to brew sooner or later." Local trustees would be influenced in their votes and actions by personal friends. As for the local candidate in question, if his name should come up, he was not the right man for the place. "Aside from his vile habit of getting intoxicated, he has other qualities which wholly unfit him for being a Trustee."[21] The local man was passed over in favor of Washington's lawyer-banker friend from Nashville, J. C. Napier, recently appointed to the high Washington post of register of the Treasury.[22] Washington also helped his lieutenant, Judge Robert H. Terrell, become a Howard law professor over "tooth and toe-nail" opposition.[23]

Washington missed an opportunity, however, to participate in the choosing of the first black president of Howard. Thirkield resigned suddenly in 1912 after becoming a Methodist bishop. Washington's first thought was of Thomas Jesse Jones, a white Hampton faculty member, as a suitable president. The two men were in close agreement on many questions confronting blacks at that time. Kelly Miller, however, wrote Washington that in his opinion "the time has now arrived for colored men to be put in control of activities intimately connected with the racial life and uplift," and offered himself as a candidate.[24] Washington could hardly argue with Miller's general point, since he had been the president of his own all-black faculty for a quarter-century. In a "highly confidential" reply, "not to pass from your hands," Washington was favorable but tentative. Had the time really come for a black president? "Without committing myself on this point, I would say I believe it has, still I confess I am open to argument." If a black man was to be put in charge, Washington endorsed Miller as "the logical man."[25] Perhaps he had some second thoughts on learning that a committee of trustees had narrowed the list to two white men, for he wrote Miller, "I think it just as well that you do not let anyone know what my position is regarding the presidency as my support might hurt more than it would help in certain directions."[26] So another white clergyman became the president of Howard, and Washington let pass a chance to give history a nudge.

Another direction that Howard might have gone is indicated by a letter received from his friend and fellow-trustee Napier in 1915. Napier wrote that he had had an extended conversation with a professor at the University of Tennessee "about the line of Agricultural work we wish to get on foot at Howard University." He reported of the professor: "The first thing he asked me was why I did 'not go to Dr. Washington, the best posted man in the entire country on such matters, for advice and suggestions as to a method of procedure.' He insisted that you were the man to take the lead in the matter. I tried to explain to him how you felt and just what your position of modesty was when I heard from you. He regretted it; but promised to furnish me, within the next few days, some suggestions which may be of benefit to us."[27] This letter strongly suggests that Washington, while perhaps in favor of the introduction of agriculture in the Howard University curriculum, preferred that some other trustee take the lead, not out of modesty but with the certain knowledge that his own sponsorship of such a proposal would cause a storm of protest from the liberal-arts oriented faculty, students, and alumni. On the other hand, it is possible that Napier was in fact the only sponsor of the agricultural program and that what he thought was "modesty" was actually disapproval.

Washington was also a trustee of Fisk University for the six years from 1909 until his death. Here if anywhere was his opportunity to prove his benign attitude toward higher education and his ability to turn his administrative talent and fund-raising genius to the aid of a faltering institution. Washington seemed to genuinely like Fisk, where he had been for twenty years a frequent visitor and occasional commencement speaker. He had drawn on Fisk for many of Tuskegee's teachers. Margaret Washington had graduated from Fisk in 1889, and young Booker attended Fisk from 1907 until his graduation in 1913. In addition to these considerations, Washington was predisposed to favor Fisk because, though Du Bois had graduated there, Fisk as a whole took less part in the polarization of black social thought than other leading black universities such as Atlanta.

A crucial element in Washington's ever closer relations with Fisk University and particularly with its administrators was his effort, finally crowned with success, to persuade Andrew Carnegie to give to Fisk. At first Fisk asked for a music building, but Washington decided the time was not ripe for this particular request, for Carnegie had recently given to several other black schools at Washington's behest, and Washington had the impression, as he wrote President James G. Merrill, that "he [Carnegie] was feeling just a little that he ought to do a little more for the white people in the South before going further in the direction of helping colored institutions."[28] As many months passed without any action, Merrill wrote in exasperation: "Now of course if Mr. C. won't give any thing but a library 'beggars should not be choosers,' but if he could see the uniqueness of our case and give the music building . . . it would be a very great mercy."[29] Washington explained that the crotchety old Scot would probably refuse to give a music building out of fear that if it became known that he had begun a new line of giving there would be an avalanche of letters asking for music buildings. At Washington's suggestion, therefore, the Fisk authorities asked for a library and planned to use the second floor for musical purposes.[30] Washington soon reported success, though Fisk would have to raise a nearly matching amount. "Mr. Carnegie will give the building," Washington wrote, "and one of the reasons, that made him especially pleased to do so is the fact that Mrs.

Washington was educated there."[31] Washington sent copies of this letter confidentially to his lieutenants, saying, "you might show it to some of my . . . critics."[32] "The Morris, the Dubois and the Grimpke adherents will now have to take a new tackle," replied J. C. Napier, "for this one thing which you have done for Fisk University and the cause of higher education is more than *they* and *their kind* have done in all their lives."[33] Washington would find his critics, however, on other grounds than money or bricks and mortar.

President Merrill certainly valued Washington's friendly services, and almost immediately he invited the Tuskegean to speak at the Fisk commencement. When Washington pleaded a prior engagement, Merrill invited him to address the anniversary celebration the following winter.[34] When Washington learned, however, that without telling him Merrill had also invited Du Bois to speak, he withdrew from any such confrontation. As Scott explained to Merrill, "since the point of view of himself and Dr. Du Bois might differ, he does not think that it will be wise to have anything in the way of a seeming controversy."[35] Merrill reported soon afterward that Du Bois had also declined, and then Washington agreed to speak.[36]

Carnegie had offered Fisk $20,000 if it would raise an equal amount, but after two years its earnest but tired old president still had not matched the sum. Washington proposed a plan: "Mr. Carnegie is very fond of Mrs. Washington, and I am quite sure if she were to make a personal appeal to him on the grounds that she is a Fisk graduate, to leave off the condition and to give you $25,000 straight for the erection of the library that he would accede to her request."[37] Margaret Washington presented to Carnegie the case for Fisk, and her husband followed it by explaining that, while Merrill was a poor fund raiser, he was an excellent educator and administrator, and that the Fisk faculty could be trusted to take good care of the library.[38] Carnegie yielded to the Washingtons' request and made his grant outright. His secretary could not resist pleading, however: "As it would not take many of these 'waivers' of endowment to embarrass us dreadfully please have the President keep the circumstances to himself."[39]

Another development at Fisk accompanied Booker T. Washington's increasing presence there. Du Bois discovered to his alarm that in the 1906–7 Fisk catalog a new department of "Applied Science" was added, including courses in agriculture, animal husbandry, plant breeding, structural botany, and rural engineering, and in addition courses in mechanical arts and domestic science. Du Bois's address to the graduating class in 1908 was a jeremiad against this development and, according to his own account, brought about the hasty disappearance of the new department and the resignation three months later of President Merrill.[40] The history of Fisk by Joe M. Richardson (1980), however, tells a more complex story, that Fisk had accepted money for vocational instruction since 1884 but was careful not to let this work, mainly in the preparatory division, interfere with the commitment to liberal education. In 1905 it accepted $5000 from the Slater Fund for a department of applied sciences, but this applied to secondary and normal pupils only.[41] At any rate, there is no evidence that Washington had anything to do with these developments.

When President Merrill wrote to Washington of his intention to resign, and of his regret that he could not have any further part in the education of Washington's son, he said of his reason: "How I wish that I had been enough of a money getter to have felt justified in staying."[42] Merrill enlisted Washington in the search for a successor. The field soon narrowed to Washington's own candidate, George A. Gates, ex-president of Grinnell and, later, Pomona. Gates, however, gave no promise of improvement over Merrill, for he was said to have resigned at Pomona "because he could not raise the money for endowment."[43] Washington defended the choice, however, on the basis of his own favorable impressions of Gates's educational administration at Pomona. More important than fund raising, he wrote, was keeping Fisk up to its current academic standard. "If the college does good work the money will come in some way."[44]

It is hard to believe that Washington wanted to see Fisk take a weak president, but he apparently believed that his own golden touch would help the school raise the funds it needed. He got Gates off to a brisk start by sending a check he had persuaded Jacob Schiff to give Fisk.[45] Soon invited to become a trustee, Washington accepted with alacrity.[46] At the first opportunity he visited the campus and gave Gates his own earthy view of the priorities in running an educational institution, three points that "dwell constantly in my mind." First was the condition of the boys' outhouse. "I am sure," he wrote Gates, "that no boy ever goes to the closet and comes away with any added respect for the University. I am also sure that no boy goes there unless he is absolutely forced to do so. When this is true, it does not add to the health of the students." Second, Washington noted that the basements were not clean and orderly. Third, arrangements should be made so that students could bathe, for at the current stage of civilization regular bathing was "no longer considered a luxury but a necessity, especially where large numbers of people congregate."[47] Washington also objected to the failure of Fisk students to rise to recite.[48] He thought that colleges taught too little English, and in the English courses neglected composition in favor of literature. Even where composition was taught, he thought, "too much stress is put upon the abstract, and too little upon the concrete."[49]

Washington mentioned none of these private misgivings about the way higher education was conducted in his detailed and persuasive article praising Fisk, "A University Education for Negroes," which appeared in the New York magazine *Independent* in March 1910. The appearance of the article coincided with the formal inauguration of Gates as president. Washington spoke of the widespread black "love and even reverence for Fisk University." He remarked that during a recent tour of the campus he was surprised "that any institution, with so little means, could do so much work and such good work, and care for so large a body of students." He had nothing but praise for the dedicated faculty and earnest students, and pointedly deplored the fact that, while so much philanthropic wealth was going into white colleges, so little went to good black higher institutions such as Fisk.[50]

Neither Washington's private letters nor his magazine article revealed much understanding of the nature of higher education, but he so clearly supported it that he was embarrassed that the editors of the *Independent* felt it necessary to preface his article with a note declaring "how mistaken is the idea that he is concerned only in the industrial training which will fit the race to support themselves in a humble station of life." To his friend Robert R. Moton, commandant of cadets at Hampton Institute, Washington grumbled privately: "This matter of defending and explaining these so-called higher institutions makes me tired. The sooner these institutions can learn that they are simply making a contribution to the general education of the people, the better it is going to be for all concerned."[51] Gates himself touched a sensitive spot in his inaugural address at Fisk when, perhaps too anxious to overcome criticism of his alliance with Washington, he invidiously compared Fisk and Tuskegee, saying that graduates of Tuskegee needed four years of additional study to graduate from a higher institution such as Fisk. Washington protested that, like most people who had no knowledge of it, Gates undervalued industrial training. One might reply "that it would require at least two or three years for a graduate of Annapolis to complete the course at West Point" or for an M I T student to get through Harvard and vice versa.[52] Gates could only lamely reply that he was merely saying that Tuskegee and Hampton were secondary schools, whereas the general public believed they were "doing the same kind and grade of work that Fisk is doing and in addition to that carrying on the superb work in the industrial and manual education and training." He left the controversial passage out of the printed version of the address.[53]

Despite these differences of outlook, perhaps inevitable, Washington worked as hard and effectively for the financial rescue of Fisk University as though it were part of his Tuskegee Machine. In October 1910 the Fisk board of trustees voted to undertake an ambitious campaign for $300,000. A committee consisting of Harvey L. Simmons, a New York trustee, and a Fisk teacher got nowhere until sometime in 1911, when Washington and Paul D. Cravath, New York corporation lawyer and son of Fisk ex-president E. M. Cravath, replaced the committee and took charge of the campaign. Washington and Cravath persuaded the General Education Board to grant $60,000 if Fisk raised the remaining $240,000 from others. By 1913 Washington and Cravath secured the matching amount, much of it from Washington's friends Julius Rosenwald, Andrew Carnegie, and J. P. Morgan, as well as from the more traditional sources of support for the school. Fisk alumni pledged $45,000 of the total.[54]

President Gates played so small a part in the fund raising that it must have seemed to outsiders that Booker T. Washington was in charge of Fisk. But Gates held the administrative reins firmly in hand and continued the liberal arts tradition at Fisk until a brain concussion suffered in a train wreck forced his sudden resignation in 1912. There was a two-year interregnum as two Afro-Americans, Dean Herbert H. Wright in 1912–13 and Dean Cornelius W. Morrow in 1913–14 administered the university while the trustees searched for another white president. Whereas at Howard, Booker T. Washington had at least considered a black president, as a Fisk trustee he unambiguously opposed such a move as untimely. The insistence of some blacks in and out of the university on a share of the governance of the institution was unfortunate, he wrote George E. Haynes, sociology professor and Urban League officer. "Now you and I both know," he went on, "that this kind of agitation is most harmful and unwise. I am sure that the white people who during all these years have given of their money and of their time, and have suffered much in the way of ostracism, have done so for the sole purpose of helping. . . . The very worst thing that we could do is to indicate that we do not appreciate what has been done and is being done for us." Haynes agreed that the time was not ripe.[55]

The trustees first offered the presidency to Thomas Jesse Jones, who turned it down, possibly because he sensed that his longtime connection with Hampton and industrial education would provoke controversy at Fisk.[56] The trustees next considered Fayette A. McKenzie, a Ph. D. from the University of Pennsylvania then teaching sociology at Ohio State University. He had taught in an Indian boarding school in Wyoming for several years and also had done research on Indians. McKenzie made the requisite pilgrimage to Tuskegee so that Washington might look him over. Washington was enthusiastically for McKenzie, and the doubters among the trustees came around to his support after Cravath threatened to resign unless they joined in the recommendation.[57]

McKenzie turned out to be one of Washington's worst mistakes. He was a good fund raiser, but abetted by Isaac Fisher, a Tuskegee graduate and ex-employee, as editor of the *Fisk University News,* McKenzie gradually secured better relations with Nashville whites at the price of humiliation and alienation of the blacks. In 1925 a student revolt precipitated his resignation.[58]

At the other end of the black educational ladder from the colleges were the wretchedly underfinanced black public schools, and Washington took a fostering interest in them, particularly the ones in the South. By 1912 he was urging Tuskegee's graduates not to found any more little industrial schools in imitation of Tuskegee, but instead to work at improving the public schools.[59] His chief agency in this work was the Southern Education Board, the executive body of the Conference for Education in the South, but also linked by interlocking directorate with the General Education Board and the Peabody and Slater Funds. The Southern Education Board, also known as the Ogden Movement, would appear to be the ideal instrument for the improvement of black as well as white education in the South, filled as it was with friends of Tuskegee and Hampton. Its stated purpose was to stimulate popular campaigns for better public schools for every child in the entire South. But Washington's relationship to the SEB proved one of the most frustrating of his life. He had close connection with the northern members of the board, including William H. Baldwin, Jr., chairman of the Tuskegee trustees; Robert C. Ogden, another Tuskegee trustee; George Foster Peabody, contributor to both Hampton and Tuskegee; Walter Hines Page, Washington's publisher and admirer; and Wallace Buttrick, executive secretary of the General Education Board. Hollis B. Frissell was also a member, as was Edgar Gardner Murphy, Washington's old ally in Montgomery, Alabama, and J. L. M. Curry of the Peabody and Slater Funds. Washington was himself a paid agent of the Southern Education Board, but his duties were never clearly defined and his appointment seemed almost a gesture of apology that he was not invited to be a member of the board.

The problem with the Southern Education Board was that its purpose was really the promotion of white public education. The southern white college presidents who formed the southern contingent of the board insisted on this. They also insisted that no black person, even Booker T. Washington, could meet with the board. It was the understanding of Charles W. Dabney, president of the University of Tennessee, that for the first two years at least "we would not emphasize the *negro* too much. In the excited state of public sentiment, this was considered wisest."[60] Another of the southern members, Edwin A. Alderman, president of Tulane and later of the University of Virginia, stated frankly in a national magazine article that in his view the education "of one untaught white man to the point that knowledge and not prejudice will guide his conduct . . . is worth more to the black man himself than the education of ten Negroes."[61] Charles D. McIver, president of the State Normal and Industrial College of North Carolina, was in some respects more democratic than his southern colleagues on the SEB, but he believed that disfranchisement of southern blacks by educational qualifications had a salutary effect on black education. "The less the Negro has to do with politics the more cheerfully will his white neighbors help him to work out his educational and industrial salvation," McIver wrote.[62] These men and Murphy, an anguished southern paternalist, prevented the northerners on the Southern Education Board from doing anything effective for black education on the ground that it would jeopardize the board's alliance with southern white moderates.

Throughout the thirteen-year duration of the Southern Education

Board, Washington was kept on the sidelines. He could influence policy only indirectly through Baldwin, Frissell, and Ogden. Even before the board was formed, Washington urged Frissell in 1901 to "keep in close and constant touch, in order to guide matters wisely."[63] A few months later he warned Frissell that "you and others will have to watch carefully to see that nothing is done that would give the impression that Negro education is being shoved aside for white education, I mean that it is much easier to drift in the direction of least resistance. Of course Negro education means to those who are engaged in it a certain amount of trial, difficulty and ostracism that does not obtain in white education and for this reason the average man would yield to the temptation to go in the direction where there is least hardship to be endured. The recent outbreak in the South regarding my dining with the President convinces me more than ever of the importance of broad liberal education for all the people regardless of race."[64] Frissell reported to Washington a few days later on the organizational meeting of the Southern Education Board: "I spoke to Dr. Curry and Mr. Buttrick first about your appointment on the Committee. They both approve of it. I wanted to wait until to-night's meeting before formally having your name presented, in order to get enough atmosphere created so that a Southern representative will suggest your name, say Walter H. Page." Page had been born in the South, but he lived in New York. Apparently part of the atmosphere Frissell referred to was J. L. M. Curry's testimonial to Washington. He said: "In twenty years laboring and associating with him under all kinds of trials and conditions, I never heard him say or do an imprudent thing."[65] Baldwin also wanted to see Washington voted onto the Board, but neither he nor any of the other northern members could bring himself to chill the atmosphere by proposing his membership.[66] Frissell tried to reassure Washington by writing: "The fact that it is controlled by Mr. Ogden & Peabody will make it necessary for it to devote much thought to Negro as well as white education."[67] Ogden and Peabody footed the small expenses of the board, but on this crucial question of black representation it was clear from the beginning that the southerners were in control. Washington was appointed from the start as an agent of the SEB. Ogden wrote him: "I am not quite ready to express an opinion as to the precise form that this latter office may take."[68] It turned out to consist largely of touring the South urging blacks to improve their own schools and to conciliate their white neighbors.

Washington took the initiative in planning the SEB's Alabama public educational campaign in 1902. He arranged for the cooperation of the governor and the state superintendent. It was the white men, however, who took charge of the campaign, beginning with a mass meeting of whites in Montgomery.[69] This educational movement, a Tuskegee graduate pointed out, "means a very little to the Negro. The Negro teachers are very poorly paid now, because the persons in authority have a general understanding to cut their (Negro's) pay and augment the white teachers' salaries. If it is decided to help any rural schools, it must come thro' the medium of the Co. Supts, Trustees, etc., in just the ways they say. They say, educate the white boy first and then the Negro boy. This was the common consent among them."[70]

Washington continued to search for a meaningful role in this educational movement that meant "a very little to the Negro." Under the sponsorship of President Alderman of Tulane, Washington went to New Orleans in the fall of 1902 to address an all-day meeting of the black teachers of Louisiana. He stressed the need for pressure on the white school officials to provide better salaries and longer terms and adequate schoolhouses for blacks. Many whites attended, either out of interest in the subject or to see Washington the celebrity. Alderman came as close on this occasion as he ever did to a public stand for equal opportunity, and he believed the meeting marked an epoch in the history of New Orleans. "There was a tremendous lot of nervousness about it," he confessed to Baldwin, "and a slip-shod sentence from either of us would have had power to raise a good deal of trouble, but I am glad to say that much good was done, and absolutely no criticism *after* the meeting. There was much doubt expressed by certain people as to the wisdom of my going into it, but I made up my mind that I had not worked eighteen years for nothing, and that if I could not afford to stand up for the education of all people, I may as well find it out."[71]

Despite these brave words, Alderman remained one of the southern members of the SEB who would exclude Washington, its own agent, from its meetings in New York. All blacks were also excluded from the public platforms of the Conference for Education in the South in various southern cities. Ogden did make a feeble attempt to include Washington on the conference program in 1903, but he yielded to southern white protests out of fear that his shaky intersectional partnership would collapse.[72] Particularly irked that even the private northern meetings of the SEB excluded him, Washington wrote to Ogden in 1902 that his conscience would compel him to resign as an SEB agent unless his duties were defined and he was permitted to report personally to the board as the white agents were. "When this proposition was made and when I first began receiving it [his salary]," he wrote, "I was under the impression that I was to see the Southern members of the Board and that some kind of definite, systematic and organized plan was to be agreed upon by which I could work, but this has not been done. I cannot see that I am doing anything now for education in the South which I was not doing before I began receiving this money, and under these circumstances I cannot feel that it is right, I repeat, for me to continue receiving it."[73]

It must have occurred to Washington that he was in effect being bribed to stand out of the way while the SEB did its work of promoting white public education. But his lifetime habits of interracial diplomacy gained the upper hand, and instead of sending the letter to Ogden he sent it to Baldwin to deliver to Ogden. Instead of delivering it, Baldwin merely talked with Ogden about the problem Washington presented, as he thought the letter as phrased "would seem like a criticism."[74] Washington realized that he would have to state his complaint more bluntly, and wrote Baldwin in 1903: "I have found it difficult to bring myself to the point where I could feel it proper to make a written report to a body which did not feel that it could afford to have me personally present at a meeting in order that I might make a report in the same way that the other officers made theirs. . . ."[75]

Baldwin, though the chairman of the Tuskegee trustees, simply ignored Washington's complaint, for it challenged the intersectional compromise at the heart of the Southern Education Board. There was an undercurrent of disagreement between the northern and southern members of the SEB, but whenever disagreement reached the surface it was the northern members who yielded to the adamant southerners. Dabney wrote home to a Tennessee colleague after an SEB meeting, referring darkly to a "partisan feeling, at least a disposition to consider the negro's educational interests as separate from the whites," which "aroused intense anxiety in the Southern men."[76] The south-

erners in the movement preferred to use the term "universal education," which in practice meant the universal education of white children in the South. On the very day that Washington protested his
exclusion from board meetings, a North Carolina educational campaign agent wrote the director of that state's campaign that in an eastern North Carolina town he had visited "they are hot for the tax, if
they can leave the negro out." He sounded the dominant note of the
Ogden Movement.[77]

Occasionally Baldwin, before his death in 1905, nudged his southern partners and timid Robert Ogden toward comparative racial liberalism, as when he persuaded Edgar Gardner Murphy and some
other southerners to lunch with him and Carl Schurz in 1904 after
the old Reconstruction warhorse had scathingly attacked southern racial injustices in a national magazine. Murphy, full of "sensitiveness
and Southern blood," had to be talked into the luncheon, then told
Schurz his article would make southern whites "hate the negroes." In
reporting to Washington, Baldwin commented: "I wanted to say to
him it ought to make the Alabama people hate themselves, but there
is no use in stirring up bad blood."[78] But it was Ogden's movement,
and he was overwhelmed by the gothic complexities of southern white
supremacy and sectionalism. "The relation of the races has involved
real complications quite aside from prevailing injustice," he wrote
Baldwin. "We are doing great good but can destroy it in five minutes."[79] What they were actually doing was steadily widening the gap
between the educational provisions and hence the life opportunities
of the two races.

Washington persistently argued for the presence of blacks in the
southern educational conference programs. "The whole question is
very difficult for me to understand," he wrote Baldwin. "For example,
I have just received a most hearty and earnest invitation from a white
Chautauqua in Louisiana inviting me to deliver an address there in
August."[80] The more Washington privately complained, however, the
more remote grew the southern contingent of the SEB. Their theme
was that Washington, though seemingly popular among white southerners, was actually unpopular, and that the SEB could not defy public opinion. "Tuskegee and Mr. Washington were never so intensely
unpopular," Murphy wrote Ogden in 1904. "Poor fellow! I am glad
he does not see—and cannot see—the situation as it is. It is partly the
unjust resentment at his success, partly the just resentment of the

'showiness' of so large an institution, partly the effect of the national & state campaigns, partly the old old feud between black and white." [81] When Washington urged upon Murphy the need for southerners of both races to deal directly with each other, Murphy shied away. "The worst elements of both races cannot be expected to get together," he answered, "but it is especially saddening to me to find the increasing suspicion between those on both sides who ought to understand each other better. This is due in large degree to the instinctive feeling among the masses of our white population that there has been in your own leadership a distinct change of emphasis, if not of direction. I confess quite frankly that I think this feeling not wholly unreasonable." [82] Murphy warned Ogden with deep pessimism that southern demagogues lay in wait for a confrontation on race policy that "would 'drive to cover' men . . . on whom we—and the negro—*must* depend for fairness and patriotism." [83]

The Southern Education Board reached its crisis at its New York meeting in the summer of 1906, as the lowering clouds of impending race riot hung over Atlanta and as the racial imbalances created by its own educational campaigns were becoming more apparent. The very appetite for educational opportunity that the educational campaigns generated tempted whites all over the South to seize the school funds of the disfranchised blacks, to gerrymander school districts so as to exclude blacks from local tax benefits, and to develop an anti-black ideology to justify unequal treatment. Washington wrote urging the northern members to take "a strong stand in reference to Negro country schools." He charged that the southern members "do not put themselves on record in a straight and frank manner as much as they should," and that as a result the educational movement "means almost nothing as far as the Negro schools are concerned." In one Alabama county, for example, the black schools had been reduced from thirty to three; in many cases black teachers' pay was as little as $10 a month; and he had seen a contract between a black teacher and a white school official for a salary of $1.40 per month. [84]

George Foster Peabody tried to force consideration of the state of black public education on the southern members, but they suggested delay until the South was calmer. Alderman said he had not felt comfortable about southern racial attitudes since Booker T. Washington's dinner at the White House five years earlier. "We should avoid anything like a crusade," Alderman spoke for the other southerners;

"guard against going into it with heat"; avoid "touching a sore tooth." Peabody replied that it was "about time for a crusade of the right kind," but none of the others took up the theme, and the Southern Education Board continued to skirt the whole subject of black education.[85]

Charles L. Coon, who had become superintendent of schools of Wilson, North Carolina, after several years as a Southern Education Board agent, undertook to disprove the frequent southern white claim that the whites were heavily burdened to pay for the black public schools. Coon demonstrated in the North Carolina state school report for 1905–6 by an array of statistics that, counting indirect taxes, more tax money was paid by blacks than the black schools expended. In 1909 he elaborated this argument with statistics from other southern states and presented his findings in an address at the Conference for Education in the South. The conference and the SEB continued to ignore the implications of Coon's study, but Washington immediately recognized its significance. He arranged for the Committee of Twelve to publish and disseminate it in pamphlet form.[86]

Washington continued to press the case for the black public schools. In 1909 he sent the SEB members evidence that in Lowndes County, Alabama, $20 per capita went to white schoolchildren and 67¢ per capita to black schoolchildren.[87] He pointed out that all nine of the Alabama teachers' institutes were for whites, and that Georgia had established an agricultural school in each congressional district for whites, but none for blacks. Nearly every southern state had appropriated legislative funds for building schoolhouses, but none of this money went for black schools.[88] Washington wrote to Peabody in exasperation that much of the advancement of white education "is being made at the expense of Negro education, that is, the money is actually being taken from the colored people and given to white schools." The southern whites who attended the Ogden conferences, he warned, "do not, I think, always state the truth."[89]

Washington also tried to badger the General Education Board into doing something to correct the inequity of public high school provisions, for whites only. He wrote to its chief executive officer, Wallace Buttrick, in 1910: "I very much fear that if the General Education Board continues to employ people to encourage white high schools, and does nothing for Negro high schools, the southern white people will take it for granted that the Negro is to have few if any high schools.

. . ."[90] Buttrick neatly sidestepped the suggestion by replying, "The professors of secondary education in the Southern States are not under our control or direction. All of our work is done through existing institutions." Though the GEB had provided the salaries of these professors, the fact that they promoted only white high schools in their states was to Buttrick simply a matter of policy of the state universities that employed them.[91]

Just as it was becoming clear to Washington that the Southern Education Board and General Education Board were structurally incapable of helping the black public schools, he was fortunate enough to find more directly committed philanthropic agencies which he could more directly control in ameliorating the disadvantages of the black schools. It was not enough, and white public education steadily gained ground on the provision for black schools, but it was better than nothing at all.

The first of these new agencies for black public schools was the Anna T. Jeanes Foundation, generally known simply as the Jeanes Fund. Anna Jeanes was a wealthy Quaker woman in her eighties living in Philadelphia. When in 1905 Washington approached her for a contribution toward a new dining hall at Tuskegee, he had known her for a decade. She asked Washington the same question that she had recently posed to Hollis B. Frissell when he had called on her on a similar errand for Hampton. She asked: "Is not aid for 'Rural Schools' more desirable and important than the Tuskegee dining room, (to cost $54,000)? that might benefit the few while the influence of Rural Schools might benefit the *many*." [92] Taking a large view of his educational mission, Washington agreed with her: "I could use to the very greatest advantage $10,000 in the way that you suggest. There are few greater needs than that, especially if the money is used in a way to stimulate self-help, and that would be the manner in which I should like to use it." He thanked her for the opportunity to serve her purpose and said that he would find some others to help with the dining hall.[93]

Washington apparently realized from the beginning that more than $10,000 was at stake, and at an early stage he and Frissell went into partnership and kept one another informed about negotiations with Miss Jeanes. Washington at first suggested that the money be made to do double duty, being lent at six per cent to black patrons building their own schoolhouses, and using the interest to pay part of the cost of schoolhouses. Miss Jeanes frowned on that suggestion.[94] A few weeks later, while Washington and Frissell were still considering various alternative uses for the money, Washington visited her again and she decided to enlarge the amount to $200,000, placing it for fiscal purposes under the General Education Board.[95] From the beginning, however, it was clearly understood that Washington and Frissell would make the policies and spend the money.[96] They began by giving matching grants for the building of black schoolhouses to communities in the immediate vicinity of their institutions.

Sensing her approaching death, Anna Jeanes in 1907 gave a million dollars to Washington, Frissell, and such other trustees as they would select, for an independent agency for black rural schools. In delicate negotiations concerning the terms of the gift, Washington and Frissell sought to satisfy Miss Jeanes's wishes but also tried to get the best terms for blacks and to disassociate themselves from the General Education Board, whom they did not inform until they had completed their negotiations with Miss Jeanes.[97] The two men then selected a board for the new fund modeled on the Tuskegee board of trustees. It included the most liberal white southerners available, Samuel C. Mitchell, president of the University of South Carolina; David C. Barrow, chancellor of the University of Georgia; and Belton Gilreath, a Birmingham coal operator and Tuskegee trustee. Among the northerners were Washington's collaborators in the Southern Education Board, Ogden, Page, and Peabody, along with Andrew Carnegie and William Howard Taft, then Secretary of War. The black members were all trusted lieutenants of the Tuskegee Machine: Robert R. Moton of Hampton Institute, Robert L. Smith of Texas, J. C. Napier of Nashville, and A. M. E. Bishop Abraham Grant.

Anna Jeanes lived until November 1907, long enough to see her agency's work underway but not before it had chosen an executive officer. James Hardy Dillard, a classics professor and dean at Tulane who had been active in the Ogden Movement, at first refused the offer of appointment as general agent because he had only three more years of teaching before he could qualify for a Carnegie pension. This was a coveted award in that day when universities had no pension programs. But the Jeanes trustees persuaded the Carnegie Foundation for the Advancement of Teaching to count Dillard's years with the Jeanes Fund toward his retirement, and he accepted.[98]

The trustees of the Jeanes Fund debated the best use of its limited resources for the improvement of the black rural schools. Washington's first suggestion was that it be used "in changing and kneading public sentiment, so far as the white people are concerned, as to the question of Negro education in the public schools." Just as the Southern Education Board had stimulated interest in white schools, he reasoned, the Jeanes Fund could promote a concern for the development of black schools. "Of course, a man to do this work would have to be very discreet," Washington recognized. "It might not appear wise for him to be too bold in his utterances or in his activities."[99] Dillard, however, proposed a more direct program, one that could show tangible results in black schools rather than be dissipated in an uncertain white sentiment about black education. Beginning in 1908, he used the Jeanes Fund to employ the first supervising teacher. She was Virginia Randolph, an able and experienced black teacher in Henrico County, Virginia. She served, in effect, as a county superintendent for the black schools of her county, improving teaching methods, introducing simple forms of manual training that did not call for expensive apparatus, learning at first hand about conditions and problems in the scattered country schools, and guiding their development.

Randolph and Dillard developed a network of Jeanes supervising teachers, using Randolph as the model, first in other counties in Virginia and then in other southern states. In some counties the supervising teacher was on the faculty of some intermediate normal or industrial school such as Hampton and Tuskegee graduates had founded by the score; in other cases the Jeanes Fund agents simply searched out the best teacher in the county and set him or her to work visiting the other schools. Dillard took care "that nothing we might do should tend to lessen the responsibility of the regular school officials," and the Jeanes Fund never entered a county without authorization and assurances of good will.[100]

As chairman of the Jeanes trustees, Washington insisted that the fund should not only stimulate the black teachers to self-help but somehow prod white school officials into more equitable provision for black schools from the public funds. He sent Dillard a copy of Coon's pamphlet on "Public Taxation and Negro Schools" to be given to the South Carolina state superintendent, John E. Swearingen. He wrote to Dillard: "Mr. Swearingen's attention might also be called to the fact that Negro education is not primarily for the benefit of the Negro, but is for the benefit of the South, in order that it may have the fullest development." When a black man was hanged for a crime, he noted, "one does not go around seeking to find how much of the expense of hanging was contributed by white people and how much by Negroes. Both races pay for the hanging in order that society may be protected, and both races pay for the education of all the people so that society may be protected."[101] Such negative arguments were the only ones that had any appeal in South Carolina, where the ratio of school expenditure for the white and black child was eleven to one.[102]

By 1915 the Jeanes Fund, with help from the General Education Board, had placed black supervising teachers in 134 southern counties; in 110 of these counties part of the salary, from one-fourth to one-half, was paid by the county school board.[103] These achievements were statistically insignificant, as compared with the great and growing gap of educational opportunity between white and black. The typical black school was a black country church full of barefoot children of tenant farmers, children allowed to go to school for three or four months in the off-season, taught by a teacher barely more knowledgeable than the pupils. But at least it was a beginning.

Meanwhile the Rosenwald program to provide more adequate school buildings began to supplement the Jeanes Fund program to improve the quality of teaching for black schools. Rosenwald, the most imaginative of the American philanthropists of his time, began on a small scale in 1912, when he gave Booker T. Washington $25,000 to distribute to schools that were offshoots of Tuskegee, thus continuing programs along the same line funded earlier by Henry H. Rogers and Jacob H. Schiff. Washington next persuaded Rosenwald to allot $2100 of this money to the building of six model schoolhouses near Tuskegee Institute.[104] Rosenwald wanted these houses to be constructed "at the lowest possible cost without sacrificing quality. By this I do not mean a cheap building, of course, but a good building at a low price." Though his own firm offered prefabricated houses of a score of designs for sale by mail order, Rosenwald gave explicit instructions not to consider Sears, Roebuck in the purchasing "except as a factor toward reducing the cost."[105] In each construction contract the people of the community were to contribute as much in money, materials, or labor as they could.

Washington's report on the construction of these first Rosenwald schools was so satisfactory that Rosenwald decided to continue the experiment on the larger scale of a grant of $30,000.[106] It was Washington's plan at first to build Rosenwald schools only in Macon County and a few surrounding ones until they were thoroughly supplied, and then to move on to other counties. He soon realized, however, that such a strategy would be unpopular in the depressed South, so he decided to open the program to a wide territory and build in counties where such schools were requested rather than in more apathetic ones.[107]

Washington worked closely with the Jeanes Fund board of trustees and with Dillard, who became the agent of the Slater Fund as well as the Jeanes Fund, in carrying out the Rosenwald campaign. Though Rosenwald had insisted that his own company should not be given preference, Washington wrote to Rosenwald's secretary that "in connection with the building of schoolhouses we are using as far as we can Sears and Roebuck material; we not only show our appreciation to Mr. Rosenwald but save money at the same time."[108] He did not buy the Sears prefabricated buildings, however, because he found that local construction with the patrons donating their labor was far cheaper and also involved the parents in the education of their children. He had to be conscious of costs in another sense as well. "I think we will have to be very careful," he wrote the Alabama state rural school supervisor, "not to put so much money into a building that it will bring about a feeling of jealousy on the part of the white people who may have a schoolhouse that is much poorer."[109]

A few months before his death in 1915, working through Tuskegee's extension department and in harmony with a state rural school supervisor, Washington decided to extend the school-building program to five additional counties in Alabama that were "thoroughly ripe for such a movement." He wrote Rosenwald that by October 1, 1915, they could expect construction of a total of fifty schoolhouses.[110] Thus began the program basic to the quality of black education that was later conducted, after Washington's death, by the Rosenwald Foundation. "It is impossible for me to describe in words the good that this schoolhouse building is accomplishing," Washington wrote W. C. Graves, Rosenwald's secretary, "not only in providing people with comfortable school buildings, who never knew what a decent school building was before, but even in changing and revolutionizing public sentiment in the South, as far as Negro education is concerned."[111] To Rosenwald he wrote: "I often wish that you could have time to hear and see for yourself some of the little incidents that occur in connection with this work. I wish you could hear the expressions of approval that now come from white people—white people who a few years ago would not think of anything bearing upon Negro education. I wish you could hear the expressions of gratitude uttered over and over again by the most humble classes of colored people." [112]

In his role as an educational statesman, Washington challenged the stereotype of mere accommodation and self-seeking. In a skillful and broad-gauged way he brought the money of the philanthropists into conjunction with the areas of need at every level of black education. He took care of the needs of his own institution first, of course, and did not scruple to play upon the foibles of the rich to gain his ends. But he also helped to channel philanthropy into a great number and variety of black higher educational institutions. As a dispenser of the philanthropy of Andrew Carnegie and as a trustee of both Fisk University and Howard University, he showed himself to be a friend rather than an enemy of black higher education. There were limitations to his grasp of the concept of liberal education that limited his usefulness to it, but there was no such limitation on his work of rescue of the black public schools through the Jeanes Fund and the Rosenwald school-building program.

Washington had dreamed for decades, since the earliest days of Tuskegee, of an independent survey of the black private schools and colleges that competed for funds in the North. Such a study could separate the fraudulent claimants from the large majority of legitimate ones, and perhaps also establish some objective standards for the earnest but not equally efficient school enterprises for blacks. He saw a great opportunity in 1911 when Anson Phelps Stokes, treasurer of Yale University, wrote him of the founding of the Phelps-Stokes Foundation with a million dollars from the will of his aunt, Caroline Phelps Stokes, for many years a generous donor to Tuskegee. Stokes asked Washington, among others, to suggest a method for using $5000 to $10,000 "to the special advantage of negro education of the type that you are now doing at Tuskegee." [113] Washington replied that many of the denominational schools were trying to do the same kind of work as Tuskegee but failing because they did not know how. "If a person of tact and ability is selected," he suggested, "this individual could go to one of these schools and spend, say, a week or two showing them, in the first place, how to clean up the premises, what cleanliness and order mean, and above all, how to make out a course of study that would actually mean something to the people in the community where the school exists."[114] Such a program would in effect duplicate for the private and denominational schools what the Jeanes Fund teachers were doing for the public schools. The first thing to be done, however, should be "a pretty thorough study of the entire field with a view of selecting schools that are physically located in the right place, and secondly, those that have such backing as to insure them a reasonable future." But Washington warned that "to kill out a poor school" was the hardest task, saying: "The killing out of the poorer schools would have to be done very gradually and through a process of placing emphasis upon the efficient ones rather than any direct attempt to have the poorer ones disappear."[115]

What Washington proposed was perhaps too ambitious for the initial project of the Phelps-Stokes Fund, and in 1911 and early 1912 he endorsed the Phelps-Stokes Fellowships, one each at first at the University of Virginia and the University of Georgia, granted to young white college students who would spend the year researching some aspects of the race problem.[116] These Phelps-Stokes fellowship papers later appeared in pamphlet form as part of a growing social-science literature on the race problem. Washington also persuaded the fund to contribute to the costs of the Tuskegee Negro Conference and his speaking tours of the various southern states.[117]

Washington nevertheless continued to write and converse with Anson Phelps Stokes about his proposal of a survey of the roughly 600 black schools in the South classed as "above the ordinary public schools," that is, high schools, industrial schools, colleges, universities, and professional schools. "It would be a matter of the greatest help to have these schools thoroughly examined with a view of letting the public know just what they are doing," Washington insisted. "This has never been done. For example, there are many so-called industrial schools that have the reputation of giving industrial training, but in fact the work is a mere sham. There are not a few institutions with the name 'college' and 'university' that are in fact mere local schools pretending to do college work when in reality the majority of their students are in the primary or public school grades with no college work whatever being done." He suggested that the Fund employ someone with a salary and travel expenses, and strongly recommended his own ghostwriter Robert E. Park, who had degrees from

Michigan, Harvard, and Heidelberg, and who had traveled widely in the South and knew conditions there among both whites and blacks.[118]

The Phelps-Stokes Fund adopted Washington's suggestion, but rejected Park as the researcher, though Washington gave Park the credit for first suggesting the idea to him and called Park "by far the best qualified white man in any part of the country to have charge of this work." He conceded that the candidate put forward by Hampton Institute, Thomas Jesse Jones, was "a good man" but "a professional statistician," whereas Park "has the knack of meeting all classes of people in a way to get from them valuable information and at the same time not offend them."[119] The rejection of Park was probably fortunate for him, for he went on in 1913 to the University of Chicago to begin a distinguished career in sociology. Thomas Jesse Jones, a Welshborn former teacher at Hampton, took this opportunity to move into a key position in the bureaucracy of educational philanthropy. His study of the black educational institutions, published by the U. S. Bureau of Education in 1916, was important not only for its information but because it gave the philanthropic foundations the initiative in reorganizing black higher and secondary education according to initiatives and standards of the foundations rather than of the black institutions affected. Jones moved on to Africa in the 1920s with a Phelps-Stokes survey that reached the sinister conclusion that industrial education was the type best suited to the distinctive racial nature of black Africans.[120] This was a position Washington never endorsed, and it was Park rather than Jones whom Washington proposed to the Phelps-Stokes Fund. Nevertheless, once Jones began his work, Washington loyally promoted it and worked to keep Oswald Garrison Villard and his allied black militants from forming a counter-organization.[121] In the area of education, as in other aspects of black life, Washington left an ambiguous legacy, despite his earnest labors in behalf of every form of black education.

CHAPTER 9

Up from Serfdom

I are sho' ready to lef' dese lowgrounds. I has hearn Booker T. . . . I has seen de ile mill, de big wheels an' all dat.*

WHATEVER else the Wizard of Tuskegee was in his many guises, he was always indelibly a southerner. He blended into his time and place like an old tree in a woodland landscape: of medium size and medium brown color, at home in a rumpled business suit, unexcitable, a master of understatement, modest but too dignified to be humble. In the many photographs taken of him at Tuskegee in company with northern dignitaries, the Yankees generally stood in stiff pose while he lolled relaxed with a thumb in each side pocket of his trousers. When he dressed up for public occasions it was as a prosperous peasant, wearing a brown derby instead of a top hat. The same rural southernness showed in his speech, never salty but always earthy and direct. He abhorred abstractions as he lived among people to whom mathematics was a foreign language and polysyllables a Yankee invention. He was southern also in his closeness to nature, the out-of-doors, in his pleasure in working with animals, in his fear and distrust of cities and city-dwellers, whether white or black.

Southernness came naturally to Washington, for he was born in the South, chose to remain there, achieved the zenith of his fame there

---

*An old black woman, attending the dedication of the Mound Bayou Cotton Oil Mill, November 25, 1912.

in his Atlanta Compromise address. And, when his time came, he chose to die there. It was a southern professor at a southern college, John Spencer Bassett of Trinity College, North Carolina, who called Washington "the greatest man, save Robert E. Lee, born in the South in a hundred years."[1] Bassett's southern neighbors made it so uncomfortable for him after that heresy that he left for the North, but Booker T. Washington stayed.

Washington knew the harsh injustices of southern society, but he was sentimentally fond of the southern physical environment. From the crowded cities and coal-burning trains of his northern speaking tours, he loved to retreat to the outdoor life of the south. He rode horseback all his life, hunted and fished when he could, and derived psychic healing from cultivating his own garden. "When I am at my home at Tuskegee," he once wrote, "I usually find a way by rising early in the morning, to spend at least half an hour in my garden, or with my fowls, pigs, or cows. As far as I can get the time, I like to find the new eggs each morning myself, and when at home am selfish enough to permit no one else to do this in my place." Other early risers found him in his overalls. "The pig, I think, is my favorite animal," he said, running through a list of the varieties he kept. "I do not know how this will strike the taste of my readers, but it is true . . . and it is a real pleasure to me to watch their development and increase from month to month."[2] Like the prosperous peasant the world over, Washington's garden was vegetables, not flowers. Compared to them, the food in the most expensive restaurants seemed tasteless. "One feels," he said, "when eating his own fresh vegetables, that he is getting near to the heart of nature; that is, not a second-hand, stale imitation of something, but the genuine thing."[3]

Though he was well aware that many southern whites were proclaiming their region a "white man's country," he insisted repeatedly that he and the other blacks who were born there were loyal sons of the South and devoted to the region's best interests. He endorsed the New South doctrine of Henry Grady, who had said in the 1880s that, while northern capital investment would be welcomed as an aid to southern modernization, the southern people of both races should settle their racial differences among themselves. However Washington accommodated himself, and by implication his fellow-blacks, to the exclusion, segregation, and discrimination in the South, he insisted that it was merely the price of admission and that he was just as much a southerner, an insider, as the white man. He was an assimilationist above all else, and his quarrel with the blacks who left for the North or who talked of emigration was with their giving up the struggle in the land of their slave forefathers, with their self-alienation. He himself did all he could to wear the badge of the southerner, though it was not honored everywhere, and never said in the North anything about the South that he would not say at home. "I believe I have grown to the point," he said in 1898, "where I can love a white man as much as I can love a black man. I believe that I can sympathize with a Southern white man as much as I can sympathize with a Northern white man. To me 'a man is but a man for a' that and a' that.' "[4]

Washington was more complex, however, than his public statements suggest. Where necessary he found secret means to fight directly against the meaner forms of southern white supremacy, and his ultimate goal was not a separate sphere for the black man but the opportunity and means to do all that the whites considered part of a full life. This was similar to the dreams of the European immigrants who poured into America by the millions during Washington's lifetime to begin the struggle upward into middle-class life, but with differences caused by Washington's being southern and black. Unlike the typical southerner of either race of his day, Washington was not ill-educated, poor, or provincial in his range of experience. He was a widely traveled man of the world, a man who hobnobbed with millionaires, with political leaders and heads of state, with the leading editors and authors who made opinion, and with those who ran the United States. And yet there clung to him the air and attitudes of a country bumpkin. He distrusted the immigrants who shared his dream of assimilation because of their foreignness and because they were labor competitors with blacks and lived in the cities he abhorred. He had the fear of strangers that coexisted with hospitality in all southerners.

Washington was a southerner also in his suspicion of the black intellectuals who dwelt in the northern cities or at the southern colleges he had never attended. He dismissed their arcane knowledge as too much from books and too little from life. "My experience," he wrote, "is that people who call themselves 'The Intellectuals' understand theories, but they do not understand things. I have long been convinced that, if these men could have gone into the South and taken up and become interested in some practical work which could have brought them in touch with people and things, the whole world would have looked very different to them. Bad as conditions might have seemed at first, when they saw that actual progress was being made, they would have taken a more hopeful view of the situation." But their environment had isolated them until all they could do was "insist on the application of the abstract principles of protest." At first, he said, the intellectuals protested against the South, which rarely heard them, then began to attack nearer home, until they "made me a frequent and favourite object of attack."[5]

Washington was, however, a southerner with a difference. A lifetime of experience with white southerners gave him, and most other blacks in the region, an ability to see through the white stereotypes to the realities of southern society. When he himself employed the white stereotypes in his utterances, one assumes that he did so deliberately, to further a purpose of his own. Sometimes that purpose was his own influence and security, but it was more often an effort to buy social peace at the cost of concessions to the southern social order of segregation. In the Atlanta Compromise in 1895 and on other occasions he reassured whites that blacks would not demand an abstract "social equality," or intrude into private gatherings where they were not wanted. But he tried to distinguish between segregation and subordination, conceding separation for the present if blacks were to have "a man's chance in the commercial world" and equal educational opportunity. His approach was bound to fail, however, because it accepted the structural framework that stultified blacks' efforts at progress. The chief purpose of segregation was subordination. How could blacks make educational and economic progress without status as citizens and voters? How could blacks get their share of school funds without votes? How could black farmers struggle out of tenancy when whites refused to sell their land on the open market, banks refused to advance credit, and whitecap mobs—an informal, local Ku Klux Klan—drove black merchants out of small southern towns? And yet Washington was not wholly wrong, for Reconstruction experience had shown in the preceding generation that the power to vote could not be sustained by an impoverished and uneducated people.

Washington sought to make of Tuskegee Institute a mighty engine of black self-help, not only through the formal educational program for the students enrolled there, but through its many and varied extension activities. The earliest of these was the Tuskegee Negro Conference, which he had founded in 1892. It consisted entirely of a gathering of as many black farmers as possible from the surrounding counties, as many as 2000, for a day of exhortation. The agricultural faculty also addressed the crowd, but the principal speaker and perennial president was Washington himself. In a typical address, delivered in 1904, Washington painstakingly told the sharecroppers and small owners how far short they were from "a great successful and progressive race." He offered an immediate remedy: "You could change all of that if you would take some of the money you spend in candy and help the school—that is build a schoolhouse for your children. I say candy, because one of the most disgusting sights to me is to see a man, a great big man going around the streets eating a red stick of candy on Saturdays." The money spent for that candy could buy seats for the schoolhouse, paint the building, extend the term, and pay the poll tax. "We disfranchise ourselves nine cases out of ten because we do not exercise enough forethought to pay our polltax. We should pay our polltax whether under the law we are allowed to vote or not. Every time you pay your polltax that much goes in the education of your children."[6]

At the Negro Conferences, the poorer farmers heard from the more successful ones how they had managed to gain and hold their own land, build and furnish their houses, and educate their children. A second day was devoted to a Workers' Conference, when the country ministers and teachers addressed the social problems of rural black people. But one of the rules of these self-help conferences was accentuation of the positive. It was considered bad form to complain or protest, though occasionally a discouraging word would be heard, as when a farmer reported that the tax collector had said he was "not collecting poll taxes from colored people." The conference concluded that that was because the poll tax was "part of the qualification for voting," but it offered no remedy.[7] Occasionally a well-meaning white man would address the conference. Benjamin F. Riley of Birmingham said in 1910: "Those who are favorable to your race are the original slave owners and their descendants." The unfavorable ones were the "poor white trash." His remedy for the race's problems was "a mediator in the form of a Southern white man."[8] Washington used the conference as a forum to plead with the farmers to work hard, give up hurtful habits, avoid patent medicines, and acquire possessions. The twentieth annual Negro Conference in 1911 was much like the first, but there was one new element: "Prepare to meet the boll weevil by improving your methods of cotton raising."[9]

A more direct service to the local farmers was the Jesup Wagon, a sort of agricultural school on wheels designed by Washington and George Washington Carver. The idea was probably Washington's, for Carver wrote him in 1904: "I think your idea of fitting up a wagon to serve as a traveling agricultural school is a most excellent one. Germany, Canada and other countries, I understand, do this with success." Carver then detailed the paraphernalia of such an undertaking.[10] Money for outfitting the wagon and the mule and harness came from Morris K. Jesup, a New York banker, Slater Fund trustee, and longtime contributor to Tuskegee. According to the early announcements, Carver was to take the wagon on the road, but the honor went to George R. Bridgeforth, Carver's bitter rival in the Tuskegee agriculture department.[11] Avoiding the idlers at the crossroads country stores, Bridgeforth took his wagon directly to the farmers at work in the fields, particularly the landowners on the Southern Improvement Company land near the campus.[12] The wagon's mobility made it convenient not only for demonstrating improved farm implements and methods but as a means of recruiting for Tuskegee's other extension services, the weekly farmers' institute, and the "short course" in agriculture open to non-students. For many years the Jesup Wagon served as Tuskegee's most visible sign in the nearby countryside. It was a sight that would make a man chopping cotton drop his hoe and approach for a closer look. This moving schoolhouse was twelve feet long and twelve feet high. The roof, according to Bridgeforth's description, "was covered with canvas and shaped like an electric car. The sides and ends were made of movable canvas, so that in case of rain they could be fastened down to protect the materials and apparatus which the school carried with it for the purpose of making its demonstrations."[13] Later, Washington persuaded Jesup to fund a similar wagon operating out of Mound Bayou, Mississippi, and both received a grant from the Slater Fund for operating expenses.[14]

Of more far-reaching importance in Tuskegee's extension program were the pamphlets that George Washington Carver produced as a result of his work at the agricultural experiment station at Tuskegee. One of his pamphlets, "How To Build Up Worn Out Soils," attracted the attention of Frederick T. Gates, who wrote to Washington in 1905:

"I wish you would please send me half a dozen more copies of that rich work by your Mr. Carver."[15] A few weeks later Gates pursued the matter further, and the Tuskegee executive council minutes reported: "Mr. Gates, Mr. J. D. Rockefellow's confidential man wishes a report on agricultural conditions in the south, with an eye to carrying on work in reclaiming the soil at Mr. R.'s expense."[16] This was part of the genesis of the General Education Board's partnership with the U. S. Department of Agriculture in organizing what was then called the Cooperative Farm Demonstration Movement, later relinquished to the federal government as the county agent system. Dr. Seaman A. Knapp had begun a demonstration farm in Terrell, Texas, in 1903 for the Department of Agriculture to show local farmers that cotton could be raised despite the boll weevil by better methods of cultivation. Gates's investigation in 1905 was preparatory to the General Education Board's supplementing the federal effort by sponsoring demonstration farms in states where the boll weevil had not yet reached. About a month after Gates's expression of interest, Knapp asked Washington to recommend a Tuskegee graduate who "is well posted in agriculture, knows how to mix with men, is a good practical farmer, and can make a good talk on agriculture." Washington recommended three such men.[17] Negotiations took about a year to reach a signed agreement between the Agriculture Department and General Education Board to share Dr. Knapp's direction but to work in separate territories. Then Knapp paid Tuskegee a visit in 1906 and discussed with Carver and others his tentative plan for demonstration work using black agents for black farmers in Alabama. Knapp proposed that one black man be placed on the Farm Demonstration staff, and that in addition they would use Tuskegee's Jesup Wagon to reach each month about 150 demonstration farm plots. If Jesup would continue his aid, the Department of Agriculture would supplement the salary of the agent. Knapp thought Bridgeforth the best choice, for he had had experience with the Jesup Wagon.[18] In the agreement Washington ultimately signed with Knapp in the fall of 1906, however, Thomas M. Campbell became the demonstration agent, and the agreement was with the General Education Board rather than the Department of Agriculture.[19]

Washington took an early opportunity in 1907 to try to persuade Knapp to expand his commitment to black demonstration agents elsewhere, at Mound Bayou and in Texas, but Knapp replied: "In fact,

Mr. Washington, I am trying to manage this colored work in the Gulf States as an extention of the Tuskegee work. From my knowledge of conditions I think it will work better to keep it as an attachment and extension of your work than to consider it as something inaugurated by us. We can manage it just the same and I believe we shall run against fewer snags to handle it in this way." Knapp was seeking to compliment Washington and his school, but he also thus avoided giving black farmers an equal share in his agency's services.[20] There was apparently hostility among whites to any federal payment of black demonstration agents, and, in response to the power imbalance between the races, most of the benefits of the federal program went to white farmers through white agents. Thomas Campbell wrote in 1910 that "there are some sections in the South that Negro agents doing work under the auspices of the government would be subjected to bodily harm."[21] In 1911 Washington asked Knapp's son, who took over the demonstration program on his father's death, how many black agents there were. Bradford Knapp reported twenty-three: seven in Virginia, one in North Carolina, six in South Carolina, one in Georgia, five in Alabama, two in Mississippi, and one in Oklahoma.[22] Though these were outnumbered by the hundreds of white agents, thousands of white demonstration farms, and hundreds of thousands of white visitors to demonstration farms, it does indicate that blacks were not entirely left out. They simply received the separate and unequal treatment they experienced in education and other aspects of life.[23]

In addition to Tuskegee Institute's formal extension work, Washington singled out occasional Macon County white plantation owners with many black tenants for individual arrangements for cooperation that combined agricultural improvement with public relations. He persuaded Morgan Russell in 1910, for example, to accept eight pounds of lime sent from the institute to be used in whitewashing the tenant houses on his plantation. A few weeks later he visited the Russell plantation and its black community, Fort Hull, and used it as an illustration that whites who treated their tenants well would suffer no "labor famine." He noted that the community had a good, painted schoolhouse, well taught and open for eight or nine months in the year. At the church building, also painted and attractive, was an exhibition of the vegetable crops grown by the tenants on their garden plots, and exhibits also of sewing, canning, and the school work of the children. "Right in the midst of it all," wrote Washington in the Wash-ington *Post*, "was Mr. Morgan S. Russell himself with his son and clerks and helpers. He sat upon the platform, he spoke to the people, he welcomed our party, he was as proud in showing to our party the evidences of progress of the colored people in that community as any father could have been."[24] If this was paternalism, it was in Washington's view a benign variety that he hoped other whites would emulate. About the same time he sent the Tuskegee marching band out to play at a picnic that William Watson Thompson, brother of his Republican friend J. O. Thompson, gave to his tenants. Like Russell, Thompson encouraged his tenants to raise all of their vegetables and livestock, and told Washington he did all he could to help them get out of debt. Here also was a good schoolhouse and church, tenant houses of two or three rooms, and school in session seven to eight months.[25] Margaret Washington also continued the work she had begun in the 1890s through the Tuskegee Woman's Club of improving the conditions of black home life within a day's ride of the institute, supplying both the missionary spirit and the technical knowledge to promote what later came to be called home economics.

Many of these schemes of rural self-improvement came to a focus during the Woodrow Wilson administration. Congress in 1914 passed the Smith–Lever Act, providing federal funds to the states for agri-cultural extension services through county agents. In the Congres-sional debate over distribution of the funds some advocated the allo-cation of a definite proportion of the funds in each state to black agents for black farmers, but one of the sponsors of the measure, Senator Hoke Smith of Georgia, stated that no graduate of Tuskegee Institute had ever been sufficiently trained to be a scientific farmer. This silenced objection in the all-white Senate, and the bill left allo-cation of the funds to the states. Washington knew that, in most if not all southern states, this would mean the same sort of racial discrimi-nation that blacks had suffered in the public school allocations, land grant colleges, and experiment stations. He began, therefore, an en-ergetic campaign to try, at least in Alabama, for an equitable distri-bution.

Washington appealed to Governor Emmet O'Neal in the summer of 1914 to designate Tuskegee Institute as recipient of the Smith–Lever funds for blacks, on the ground that it had the requisite expertise because of its twenty years of agricultural extension work.[26] The Governor sent to Tuskegee a blue-ribbon commission of white men to investigate the school's suitability. The chairman was Reuben F. Kolb, an old agrarian reformer who had been for many years the commissioner of agriculture. The committee recommended that thirty per cent of the Smith–Lever money be allocated to blacks, to be divided equally for programs at Tuskegee Institute and the Agricultural and Mechanical College for Negroes, at Normal, in the northern part of the state.[27]

Thirty per cent was fair in that it represented the black proportion of the state's population, and Washington appealed to the Governor to carry out the committee's recommendation. "I am anxious to have it demonstrated to the world," he wrote, "that the distribution of such a sum of money is left to our Southern white people and that they will do justice to the Negro without such appropriations having to be restricted at the original source by Congress or any other organization out of the state."[28] One may assume that Washington was appealing to state pride rather than expressing his true feelings, for he sent to Governor O'Neal statistical evidence of discrimination against blacks in the other agricultural funds.[29]

Washington finally had to settle for a compromise. The state assigned the entire administration of the fund to the white agricultural college at Auburn, but the officials at Auburn agreed with the two black schools to furnish about thirty per cent of the amount to them for black agricultural agents.[30] "The people at Auburn seem deeply interested and want to do the fair and just thing," Washington wrote a white friend in Washington, "in fact at present they are rather priding themselves on the fact that they are going to do more than any Southern state south of Virginia."[31] Washington feared, however, that in most of the South and in the future most of the money would ultimately go to white agents for the aid of white farmers. A lifetime of experience with "separate but equal" as an avowed policy had bred a distrust even in such an eternal optimist as he was. His hope was that David F. Houston the Secretary of Agriculture, who had once been a member of the Southern Education Board, would exercise "a veto power on the use of the fund," or at least a suggestion that white agricultural colleges give blacks their fair share of agricultural agents. "Without any some such suggestion," he wrote privately in December 1914, "I fear that little or nothing will be done." He thought once or twice of approaching President Wilson on the subject, but apparently put the thought aside.[32]

School extension work was another service that Tuskegee Institute sought to render to the surrounding community. Its effectiveness is even harder to judge than agricultural extension. From the beginning Tuskegee Institute extended its educational program beyond the bounds of the campus, through the teachers' institutes, the Workers Conference during the second day of the Negro Conference, and tours by faculty members to the schools of Macon and surrounding counties.[33] Margaret Washington began what she called a plantation school in 1898 at the Russell Plantation, about eight miles from the institute, adapting some of the methods of the settlement houses of northern cities to the rural conditions of the Black Belt. Tuskegee's school extension program began in an abandoned one-room cabin, when Annie Davis moved in and set up a school based on what she had learned at Tuskegee. At first the effort was subsidized by money from Tuskegee, but eventually it was, at least in part, supported by the patrons, with the state contributing $15 a month for the teacher's salary. The Russell Plantation settlement became "an oasis of thrift and comfort" in a region of "thriftless fields and unwholesome little cabins."[34]

In the fall of 1905 Clinton J. Calloway took charge of all Tuskegee school extension work. He and an assistant undertook to persuade the Macon County farmers to raise money for lengthening the school term and building schoolhouses. In 1906 he founded a monthly magazine, *The Messenger,* published at Tuskegee Institute, to combine exhortation for school improvement, thrift, and temperance with information on improved farming methods.[35] Washington kept a close eye on the magazine, writing Calloway: "In the Messenger keep constantly before the people the advantages of buying homes in Macon county and settling there. Hold out the advantages of the school, cheap land, good race relations, etc. Emphasize constantly before the teachers the importance of teaching agriculture and other industries in the public schools."[36] When the philanthropic agencies and federal government began to turn their attention to similar concerns in the first decade of the twentieth century, they found Washington and his school already at work. Washington supplemented the efforts of the extension agents by his own speaking tours through Macon, Wilcox, and other nearby counties. When in 1913 Joseph L. Sibley became state supervisor of rural schools under subsidy by the General Education Board for his salary, he soon realized the enormity of his task and relied heavily on Washington's advice and Tuskegee's experience. Naturally, he made Macon County one of the three he selected for an intensive study of rural school conditions and needs.[37]

Another constructive effort Washington made to change the dismal cycle of black farm tenancy was a series of schemes for black farmers to buy farms and houses at low interest. The earliest such effort at Tuskegee Institute was the Dizer Fund, established about 1892 by a small grant from Silas C. Dizer of Boston, which provided $1500 as a revolving loan fund to black tenant farmers to buy or build a farm or a "model Christian home" among the surrounding tenant shacks.[38] Later other amounts for a similar purpose came from Ellen Collins, John E. Milholland, and W. Bourke Cockran. Hard times among the borrowers soon dissipated these funds through failure to repay. A more ambitious and businesslike plan along the same lines was actually started at Hampton and then extended to Tuskegee. This was the Southern Improvement Company, founded and directed by the white treasurer of Hampton Institute, Alexander Purves, who was also Robert C. Ogden's son-in-law. The chief financial backers were Ogden, W. H. Baldwin, Jr., and other supporters of the two industrial schools. The Southern Improvement Company bought 4000 acres adjoining the Tuskegee Institute farm and sold small plots of it on long-term credit to black farmers. One strength of this plan was that it was sufficiently capitalized to provide a house on each plot of forty to eighty acres of farm land. Though the company lost momentum after the death of Purves in 1904, it was on the whole a success.[39]

Borrowing on the experience of the Southern Improvement Company, Washington established Baldwin Farms in 1914 as a memorial to his most helpful trustee, William H. Baldwin, Jr., who had died in 1905. Tuskegee trustees and friends were the financial backers. The plan permitted Tuskegee graduates in agriculture who had no land of their own, who would otherwise have to work for someone else, to purchase forty acres and a $300 house planned in such a way that rooms could be added as the family grew. A sawmill and a railroad spur line offered Baldwin Farms a chance to survive economically. The Tuskegee Farm and Improvement Company, which held the land, also mortgaged crops and equipment at eight per cent, whereas mortgage on the land was at six per cent. In the tradition of the Southern Improvement Company, the company was on a business rather than a charitable basis, and Washington thought that "the idea of getting the experiment located far enough from the school so that the graduates will not depend upon Tuskegee too much is very good."[40] As Washington explained to a local newspaper, he believed this method of helping the graduates "would inspire enthusiastic work, since the result of their struggles and sacrifice is a home and a farm paid for and clear of debt."[41]

Washington urged the superintendent of Baldwin Farms, himself a Tuskegee graduate, to stress five practical rules of conduct: to pay as much as possible on the debt; to use rainy days to improve the interiors of the houses; because of the nature of the soil, to keep it stirred all the time so as to conserve moisture; to can and preserve everything possible; and to raise as many pigs and fowls as possible. He sent copies of the rules to every colonist.[42] A month later, however, just before reaching Baldwin Farms on the train with a group of teachers coming to the summer session, a Tuskegee faculty member proudly invited the group to note the contrast between the farms on either side of the railroad, and to his shock, discovered the conditions were the same. "I must confess," he wrote Clinton Calloway, "that I have never been more embarrassed by the poor crops, weeds, and grass along the colony." He did not get the impression that the colonists had yet caught the spirit of freedom, "and it seems that they are getting the spirit of looking for a hand-out from somebody rather than dig it out of the ground."[43] Miracles did not occur overnight, even with a "wizard" about.

The most ambitious black land-purchase scheme of the era was that on Hilton Head in the South Carolina sea islands, a joint effort of Washington and W. T. B. Williams of Hampton Institute. Because of his distance from the site and his busy schedule, however, Washington depended on Williams for detailed supervision of the enterprise. The largest of the sea islands, Hilton Head was some ten miles south of Beaufort at its north shore and twenty miles from Savannah on the south. The shipping magnate William P. Clyde owned about half the island, four white men owned between them another fourth, and about 1000 black inhabitants owned the final fourth. Clyde used his 10,000 acre tract as a hunting preserve. Sometime after Washington had secured a small contribution from him for Tuskegee in 1904, perhaps because of something Washington said to him or simply because he was getting too old to enjoy hunting, Clyde asked Washington for suggestions about a settlement on his tract. As Washington explained to a Tuskegee worker, Clyde was "thinking of trying to make an ideal settlement, as an illustration of what Tuskegee graduates can teach the people to accomplish. He is thinking of financing the scheme, in case we care to undertake it." [44]

Once a producer of high-grade sea island cotton, Hilton Head had lost its entrepreneurs after the Civil War, and life went on at a lower level and a slower pace induced by poverty, the subtropical climate, and widespread malaria. The plan worked out by Washington and Williams, and approved by Clyde and his son William P. Clyde, Jr., was to divide the Clyde tract into one-horse farms of about thirty acres each. They would build on each tract a frame house of two or more rooms, with a shingled roof, provide an outhouse and a well, and sell each farm at $520, to be paid over a seven to ten year period. [45] Clyde agreed to commit 1000 acres to the experiment, reserving the rest until the plan had been tested. Stephen T. Powell, a Tuskegee graduate with some practical farming experience, became the superintendent of the colony. He could rely for advice on another Tuskegee graduate nearby, Joseph S. Shanklin, principal of the Port Royal Agricultural School in Beaufort, or on Williams, a black Harvard graduate on the Hampton staff, who soon became a traveling agent of the General Education Board. As a last resort he could ask Washington's advice, but it was many years after the colony began in 1906 before Washington found time to visit. He could only urge from a distance that Powell "stick to that work until you make it a great success." He urged upon Powell the use of whitewash and paint, improvement of the school, and production of some long-staple cotton for sale. [46]

When the colony was two years old, Washington sent J. R. E. Lee, head of the academic department at Tuskegee, to assist and advise Powell for two or three days. "I am very anxious that the industrial, moral and religious condition of the people be improved as fast as possible," Washington instructed Lee. "For example, I want them to begin the whitewashing of their houses and fences, planting better crops and making better farms. They are a very primitive, backward people and cannot take ideas on very fast." [47] Lee reported at length on his visit. He found Powell setting a good example of farming methods on his plot, and that some neighbors who had cultivated exclusively with hoes were going to use plows after seeing him do so. Powell had whitewashed his school and all the houses of those who had taken up land in his colony. Lee recommended more industrial instruction in the school that Powell and a Hampton graduate were conducting. He also suggested that another school be built five or six miles away, to be taught by a Tuskegee graduate. Lee believed the islanders needed an example in the use and preparation of food and in house furnishings. "The people need to know how to live," he wrote.[48]

Washington reached Hilton Head for his first visit to the colony in the summer of 1908. He found the land better than he had expected, but the people were poorer and more primitive. "We shall have to, in my opinion, greatly interject a little new blood into the island," he wrote Clyde. "The people are about as run down as the animals, but there is a foundation for a good work here."[49] During the following year, some of the islanders were replaced as colonists by Tuskegee students, and the Tuskegeans added another two-teacher school.[50] Clyde and his son, in addition to furnishing the land, had been from the beginning of the colony contributing $500 a year to the salaries of four teachers not on the state payroll, as well as a small sum for a conference modeled on the Tuskegee Negro Conference, designed to encourage the islanders "to adopt the improved methods of living and farming that it is the purpose of the colony scheme to teach them."[51] To infuse that "new blood," Washington placed a letter in the *Tuskegee Student* apprising Tuskegeans of this excellent opportunity to put Tuskegee principles to work, "to either buy or rent land and settle down as successful farmers on Hilton Head." He was eager "that a first-class, up-to-date Tuskegee colony be located there."[52]

With one exception, the Tuskegeans who took up the challenge prospered in their first years on the island, but W. T. B. Williams reported a serious social problem: "The islanders, it seems, will not help the men of the colony." The one Tuskegean who failed did so because he could not get help in harvesting his crop. "His cotton was late in maturing. It was just ready for gathering about the first of December when according to custom all the horses, cows and hogs on the island are turned out to go where they will. Stanfield's crop of cotton was actually eaten up by the stock before he could get it in without assistance."[53] Washington and Clyde had hoped that, in addition to revival of sea-island cotton production, winter truck farming for the eastern cities could be developed. This was impossible as long as the hogs ran loose. They also talked of the construction of a cotton gin for the island, but Clyde hesitated to invest more in an enterprise with already so many other problems. He decided to put the whole colony on one more year of trial, with the threat of abandonment if it did not begin to surmount its problems.[54]

Powell took every precaution to avoid reporting one of his biggest problems until disclosure was unavoidable. This was the "general dishonesty" of the colonists. "It seems impossible to get in a full set of tenants who will not fall into the hands of the islanders," he wrote Washington; "and when ever they do that means a loss to us. And it seems that every body is in favor of the man who steals. I have found that even the people who are suppose[d] to administer the law have received cotton which was thrown over in their yard by night. That is the system of delivering it. Just throw it over in the yards and who ever calls for pay for the right number of sacks will get the money." Powell began to question whether it was worth while to remain to bring order and modernity out of this traditional disorderliness.[55] Washington also privately concluded that "the work there has not panned out as we hoped it would. This is no fault of Powell's, however."[56] Even the weather conspired against the self-help utopia by a drought, and Clyde decided to discontinue his outlays. "Please notify all of the teachers," Washington wrote Powell, that Clyde would no longer pay their salaries.[57] Washington brought Powell to Tuskegee for discussion of a plan for gradually closing down the Hilton Head colony. "Please be careful to see that all property is carefully locked until after formally turned over," he wired Powell. "See nothing is lost. Let men understand what they can depend on."[58] Washington suggested that it would please Clyde if, in dismantling the schools, the school furniture be given to the islanders.[59] By April the colony was no more. Washington wrote the younger Clyde, "we have done the best we could under the circumstances I think," and Clyde must have agreed, for that year he made a $1000 contribution to Tuskegee.[60]

For a few individuals, those charged with the work-ethic and the desire for self-determination, the land purchase schemes succeeded. As group enterprises, however, they failed. The whole system of racial subordination and labor exploitation on which the cotton growing economy rested went counter to such efforts. White supremacy in political control reinforced the whites as landlords, the whites as bankers, the whites as merchants, and relegated the blacks to tenancy, sharecropping, the crop lien, and, sinking deeper into subservience, to the forced labor of debt peonage and convict lease. As the dream of the self-sufficient peasant, of "Uncle Tom in his own cabin," faded, Booker T. Washington dreamed another dream, the all-black town, where not only would the black farmers own their land, but the merchant, the banker, and the mayor would be black.

Washington put great faith in the self-segregated economy and polity of the all-black town, seeing it as a positive sign of black enterprise rather than as a negative result of white exclusion. Indeed, he probably thought of Tuskegee Institute, with its all-black faculty and student body, and the surrounding families of Greenwood Village as an example of the all-black town. What he said of Boley, Oklahoma, in a magazine article captures his attitude toward all such communities. "Boley," he wrote, "like the other negro towns that have sprung up in other parts of the country, represents a dawning race consciousness, a wholesome desire to do something to make the race respected; something which shall demonstrate the right of the negro, not merely as an individual, but as a race, to have a worthy and permanent place in the civilization that the American people are creating. In short, Boley is another chapter in the long struggle of the negro for moral, industrial, and political freedom."[61]

Washington took a fostering interest in Boley and in Allensworth, California, and Wilberforce, Ohio, but it was Mound Bayou, Mississippi, that captured his heart. He was devoted to this small town in the Yazoo–Mississippi Delta that seemed to embody the values, methods of self-help, and priorities of his own social philosophy. If any all-black town in the middle of a white-dominated America could satisfy all the needs of its citizens, it would be Mound Bayou. Yet a thoughtful historian, August Meier, has concluded that the Mound Bayou attempt at a segregated economy was a failure, even with strategic help in its critical moments from northern philanthropy. Self-help and racial solidarity in the substandard status that blacks held in America were no basis on which a viable economy or a genuinely independent community could develop. The white supremacy atmosphere of the surrounding region choked the life out of the isolated and struggling town.[62]

Mound Bayou demands a close look as a test of the viability of Washington's priority of the economic over the political approach. Isaiah Montgomery, the founder, went into partnership with a railroad company to clear the underdeveloped area where the town was located in 1887. Three years later, as the only black delegate to the state constitutional convention, he supported the constitution that disfranchised the state's blacks. His whole faith was in economic progress. As he wrote in 1901, "a colored man may successfully conduct almost any kind of business in an average town; he must, however, have tact, grit, and sufficient backing to hold on till his business is well understood; experience proves that he can secure fair patronage from the public generally."[63]

By the early twentieth century, Montgomery was relegated to the role of patriarch of the town, and Charles Banks, a native of nearby Clarksdale, became its leading businessman. In 1904 he moved his mercantile business to Mound Bayou and founded the Bank of Mound Bayou, becoming its cashier.[64] Tuskegee took an active interest in the bank, Scott investing in its stock and becoming a director.[65] Washington arranged for Mound Bayou to receive a Carnegie library and a General Education Board farm demonstration agent,[66] and Banks in turn became an officer in Washington's National Negro Business League, a Republican politico in partnership with Edgar S. Wilson, and sponsor of Washington's speaking tour through Mississippi in 1908.

Banks and his bank saved the town from financial crisis when the railroad company that had originally sponsored Mound Bayou changed hands and the new owners threatened wholesale foreclosure of mortgages it held against most of the farmers in the community. Banks and his associates persuaded the railroad to renew the loans, and at six instead of eight percent, and founded the Mound Bayou Loan and Investment Company to gradually take over the mortgages.[67]

Recognizing the need for a broader economic base in the town, Banks in 1907 began to raise money for a cottonseed oil mill. He asked Washington to find a northern capitalist willing to cooperate with the bank in advancing money to local farmers and establishing the oil mill.[68] Banks was a mixture of romantic black nationalism and the business ethic, and he vacillated between pleading for a white angel and building a model town "owned and controlled by Negroes."[69] He tried to persuade Emmett Scott to ask Andrew Carnegie for the money to buy out the railroad and other white owners and sell the land around Mound Bayou in forty-acre plots. "You have an idea what it would mean for us to ultimately control this corner of the county as we now control Mound Bayou," Banks wrote. "Talk this over with the Dr. and let us know what can be done."[70] Washington himself was somewhat captured by the mystique of black territorial expansion, and wrote a white friend about the Yazoo Delta: "There, if anywhere, I believe, the black man is going to finally get on his feet, or finally perish."[71]

Banks grew ever more solicitous of Washington's help in securing outside white capital for the oil mill. He and his black associates had by 1910 practically completed the buildings without borrowing from outside, but they needed machinery and working capital. If he could market ten or fifteen thousand dollars of oil mill stock, he wrote Washington, with someone who "really wanted to help us, but wanted to do so on a business basis, some one who was in easy circumstances, and could afford to wait three or four years, with the interest paid annually, I should be glad to be put in touch with them as I want to operate this fall."[72] His original deadline for opening had been two years earlier, and it would be two years later before the machinery actually turned.

Meanwhile Banks used the bank and the mill to promote race pride. The Mississippi State Business League met in Mound Bayou, and according to Banks's report "race consciousness, race confidence struck a new note many keys higher in the scale" as the assembled black business leadership of the state walked about *their* city and for the first time in their lives "felt that they were welcome, truly welcome to the city they had entered." They walked in the shadow of their oil mill "now nearing completion by all Negro capital." "They lodged and feasted in Negro homes . . . bought what dry goods they needed from Negro merchants; rode in Negro carriages, ate in Negro hotels, drank their soda water from the bottles of a Negro bottling firm; bought their tickets from a Negro ticket agent; cashed their checks at a Negro bank, and went and came in perfect security under the rule of a Negro Mayor and a Negro Marshal."[73]

Such was the dream but only part of the reality of Mound Bayou under the leadership of Charles Banks. It is unclear how much the black businessmen of Mississippi invested in the oil mill, but it was clearly not enough to turn the wheels of the enterprise. Banks continued to hope that Carnegie would be the angel of the all-black town, but Robert E. Park the sociologist, at this time Washington's ghostwriter and adviser, was skeptical of Banks's grasp of reality. "The real trouble," he wrote Emmett Scott, "is that Banks hasn't got a definite scheme to pursue to philanthropic people and he hasn't any one with sense enough and persistence enough to take it up and hammer it into the heads of the Northern people."[74] Besides, Banks had failed to carry out his part of contractual obligations in his earlier dealings with philanthropists. As Scott himself reminded Banks, Washington had persuaded Andrew Carnegie to donate a library to Mound Bayou on condition that the city council provide $400 a year for books and upkeep, but reportedly there were no books in the library and "it is not at all being used for that purpose, and instead is the headquarters of the Masonic Beneficent Association." If Carnegie should learn how his library grant had been abused, the canny Scot would resent it and take no further interest in the town.[75]

Banks nevertheless somehow reached Andrew Carnegie, who asked him to arrange for letters of recommendation from those who knew about the Mound Bayou enterprises at first hand. Banks asked Washington to write, but the Tuskegean preferred to wait, and told Banks: "If Mr. Carnegie desires my personal opinion on the project he undoubtedly will write me, and I shall then be very glad to write him at such length as may seem wise."[76] Nothing was forthcoming from Carnegie, perhaps because he heard of the neglectful treatment of his library. In 1912, however, Julius Rosenwald began to take an active interest in Mound Bayou and its symbolic importance as an all-black enterprise. This was undoubtedly through Washington's suggestion, and the first Rosenwald "investment" in the town was a Rosenwald school.[77]

Of all the philanthropists of his time, Rosenwald was the most accessible to black people and the most easily touched in heart and pocketbook by blacks who undertook to match his generosity with their own self-help. Isaiah Montgomery, who happened to meet him in New York where he had gone to a memorial service for a friend who had died on the *Titanic,* secured from Rosenwald an offer to buy some of the cottonseed oil mill bonds and also to supply funds to the Bank of Mound Bayou to take mortgages on surrounding agricultural lands and thus "supplant all of the foreign loans existing there now."[78] A month later Banks made this informal agreement somewhat more definite by a meeting with Rosenwald to persuade him not to make his loans contingent on funds from other sources.[79] Still in general terms, and in consultation with Washington, Rosenwald indicated that he might lend the Bank of Mound Bayou as much as $250,000 for buying up local mortgages held by whites, draining swamp land, and financing agricultural improvements.[80]

With the prospect before him of Rosenwald's backing, Banks decided to formally open the oil mill in 1912 with a community ceremony with Washington as the principal speaker. Banks informed Washington that *opening* the mill did not mean operating it, but he did not disclose how far the mill actually was from readiness to operate.[81] Standing on a platform of cotton bales, with the mill building looming behind him, Washington addressed a crowd of 15,000, an enormous one for a small town that was not even a county seat. The Wizard of Tuskegee saluted black enterprise without frightening the whites into opposition:

> At this late date, it requires no argument to demonstrate the fact that white people and black people in this state are here to remain for all time and in my opinion side by side, and the building up of an enterprise of this kind in the commonwealth of Mississippi does not mean that it is anything that will threaten or jeopardize the white man's civilization or power, but it means that which will enhance the white man's prosperity and civilization, for if one race goes down the other in the same degree goes down. If one race goes up, the other in the same degree goes up.

He was proud that it was in the South that such a monument of black enterprise rose, and promised blacks that it would mean both black capital gains and black employment.[82]

A tremendous yell went up when Washington pulled the cord that stretched through the trees for 200 yards and sounded the factory whistle and set the wheels in motion for a few rounds inside the Mound Bayou Cotton Oil Mill. A white reporter for a Memphis newspaper thought an old black woman in the crowd epitomized the meaning of the ceremony and recorded her words: "Well, Lord, here I is. I are sho' ready to lef' dese lowgrounds. I has hearn Booker T. . . . I has seen de ile mill, de big wheels an' all dat. But what was ain't now, fer us cullud folks is gwine ter see de cotton after it's done picked in de fiel' and 'fo' we buys it back 'cross de counter."[83]

The opening really proved, however, that Banks's supreme talent was that of the promoter. He claimed, for example, both publicly and to Julius Rosenwald, that the oil mill represented an investment of $100,000 entirely by black people, principally through fraternal orders in the state. But the $100,000 figure was actually the capital stock of the company, not all of which had been sold. At a meeting with Banks that Washington staged at Tuskegee, in February 1913, Rosenwald agreed to buy $25,000 of an issue of six per cent bonds if Banks could sell another $15,000 of them. Rosenwald bought the bonds on Banks's representation that the plant cost about $100,000 and had no other indebtedness, and he secured a first mortgage on the plant as security for his loan.[84]

Banks put Montgomery to work trying to sell the remainder of the oil mill stock, while he himself tried to market the $15,000 in bonds to match the $25,000 Rosenwald was buying. This effort led both black men into quagmires. It turned out in 1915 that an agent of the oil mill company had sold stock under false pretenses and pocketed the money.[85] Meanwhile with Washington's help Banks tried to market the bonds among oil mill machinery companies.[86] Meeting with no success, he finally sold the bonds to B. B. Harvey, a Memphis white man with a cottonseed oil mill of his own. Harvey secured a lease on the Mound Bayou mill and became in fact its manager, but Banks obscured that fact from both Washington and Rosenwald. He sent Washington the news: "MOUND BAYOU OIL MILL BEGAN MANUFACTURING TODAY."[87] A visitor from Tuskegee saw "the big oil mill, standing there with its shadow outlined against the stars" and dreamed dreams of the expanding spirit of black enterprise: "the lone puffing of an engine, the opening and shutting of a boiler door . . . the glare of red fire in the distance."[88] That was the poetry, but the prose of the oil mill was that it became Harvey's enterprise, and this unscrupulous white man milked it into disaster.

Particularly after the depression of 1914 brought about the bankruptcy of his Memphis mill, Harvey used Rosenwald's money for operating purposes but refused to submit a financial statement, and forced Banks and Montgomery at first to pay the interest, taxes, and insurance required by their agreement with Rosenwald, and finally when the mill suspended operation in January 1915 its attorney revealed to Rosenwald the true state of affairs.[89] Rosenwald apparently never reaped the six percent return on his quasi-philanthropic loan. In the fall of 1915 Banks sent to Tuskegee a somewhat farfetched explanation of the failure to operate the mill. He said he was baffling the efforts of "designing White men including our late lessee, Harvey, to confiscate the plant. . . . We have taken possession and rather than let Harvey operate to our financial detriment as well as wear and tear to the plant, we have refused to let it run this Season, and are aiming to fortify ourselves for the coming Season when we will have a plant owned by Negroes, operated by them in its entirety."[90] This was black enterprise in reverse gear.

Washington also persuaded Rosenwald to become financially interested in the Bank of Mound Bayou. He first asked Frank J. Parsons, vice president of the United States Mortgage and Trust Company, in 1913 to consider investing in the bank. Parsons agreed to discuss the matter with Charles Banks, but he concluded that the bank's affairs had "gotten to the point where it was rather a matter for philanthropic interest than a strictly commercial proposition." Any investor, he thought, would be wise to insist on putting "an experienced and competent party in charge of the mill and bank operations until they were on a firmer footing."[91] Even before the outbreak of World War I brought depression, the Bank of Mound Bayou was in trouble in early 1913 because of overextension of credit to neighboring black farmers, and Banks's trip to New York at that time was unsuccessful.[92] He managed to borrow $5000 in May 1913 and another $10,000 in April 1914.[93] By June 1914, however, he was pleading to Tuskegee for rescue, and Washington met him in Chicago to visit Rosenwald, who agreed to lend the bank $5000.[94] Despite this, the state bank examiners closed it in August 1914.

As soon as the white-owned banks in the surrounding towns learned that they were free of the Mound Bayou competition and low interest rates, they raised their own interest rates, insisted that cotton be brought to their towns for sale and ginning, and even dictated to landowners how much they should charge for rent. The people of Mound Bayou felt the full severity of the white retribution against their effort to run their own affairs. "These conditions set our people to thinking and resulted in a few get together meetings recently," Isaiah Montgomery reported to Washington; "as a result we shall have cash capital for a $10,000 Bank safely subscribed within the near future, Mr. Banks as usual takes a large share."[95] The crisis brought at least a temporary end to the rivalry that had developed between Montgomery and the more aggressive and younger Banks, and Washington found "comfort and happiness" in that news. He wrote to the grizzled founder of Mound Bayou: "I am so glad that the people of Mound Bayou are realizing the importance of getting together and working together. Outside of Tuskegee, I think I can safely say that there is no community in the world that I am so deeply interested in as I am in Mound Bayou." Above all else, he hoped harmony would lead to a reorganized bank.[96]

Mound Bayou needed all the unity it could muster for the further storms ahead. The state bank examiners sought to indict Banks and other officers of the failed bank, but the grand jury decided that since the bank's accounts were in good order and no shortage or irregularities were evident, the officers had committed no criminal act, and so turned down the examiners' recommendation of indictment. Banks wrote to Washington that the examiners' complaint that the bank's securities were worthless was based on the fact that they were in a black settlement. Whites would not buy the securities as long as the blacks of Mound Bayou insisted on controlling their own institutions, and the blacks lacked the money to take over the securities.[97]

As in the case of many another small-town bank, the Bank of Mound Bayou died, its threnody was sung, and out of its ashes phoenix-like a new bank appeared, the Mound Bayou State Bank, organized in the spring of 1915 to be opened in June. The state authorities delayed the granting of its charter, however, and Banks complained to Tuskegee: "Besides their carrying out a policy to eliminate Negro banks wherever possible it is an effort to handicap me." Banks sought a national charter, and also withdrew as an officer of the new state bank. Then the state authorities relented and allowed the bank to open in October 1915. Though not an officer, Banks furnished according to his account $11,000 of the $12,000 the state required.[98] Since Rosenwald was soon to visit Tuskegee, Banks asked Scott, if he got a chance, "in that characteristic tactful way of yours [to] tell him how well we have worked out of our difficulties here, in the face of all kinds of opposition and discouragement."[99]

Mound Bayou was the vessel of many of Washington's hopes for a successful and expanding empire of black enterprise, racial solidarity, and self-determination. Yet it was the opposition and discouragement that was most striking. There was a gap between the rhetoric of black capitalism and the reality of exploitation by grasping white capitalists and rescue by more benign ones, a gap between the ideology of black solidarity and independence and the practice of shoddy compromises and petty quarrels. Nevertheless, Mound Bayou was a temporary refuge for enterprising blacks elsewhere in the state who were being literally run out of town.

Whitecapping flourished in Mississippi all through the early twentieth century. The very blacks whose respectability and usefulness to the community Washington had promised would lead to their acceptance and the restoration of their rights were driven out of towns where their prosperity excited the envy of whites. A sort of informal Ku Klux Klan of hooded men enforced the rule that no black person be accorded human dignity in that neighborhood.

Isaiah Montgomery in 1904 gave Booker T. Washington a detailed description of the impact of the whitecaps on black business in West Point, Mississippi. "Thomas Harvey runs a neat little Grocery, he kept a Buggy and frequently rode to his place of business, he was warned to sell his Buggy and walk. Mr. Chandler keeps a Grocery, he was ordered to leave, but was finally allowed to remain on good behavior. Mr. Meacham ran a business and had a Pool Table in connection therewith, he was ordered to don overalls for manual labor." A hackman was ordered to sell one of his two hacks. A black printer named Buchanan owned a piano and allowed his daughter, who was his cashier and bookkeeper, to ride a buggy to and from work, until "a mass meeting of whites decided that the mode of living practiced by the Buchanan family had a bad effect on the cooks and washerwomen, who aspired to do likewise, and became less disposed to work for the whites." A mob forced Buchanan's wife and children to flee during his absence from town, and refused to let him return even to collect his belongings.[100] The economic means and hard work that Washington's social philosophy proposed for blacks in the face of the political, social, and economic problems they faced as a minority group were clearly not a remedy that the blacks could in all circumstances employ.

Could technological change cut the Gordian knot of black subordination? Washington pinned his main hope for black progress on the work-ethic and its inculcation through industrial education, but he gave his provisional blessing at least to the mechanical cotton-picker that seemed in his day most likely to succeed. Theodore H. Price in 1911 claimed to have invented a cotton-picker that would be commercially successful, organized a company, and asked Washington for an endorsement. The machine already had the enthusiastic recommendation of Walter Hines Page, Charles W. Dabney, Robert C. Ogden, and other advocates of a modernized South, but Price frankly wrote Washington that he wanted to use Washington's name because others "have thought that possibly the effect of the Machine upon the financial condition of the negro would be injurious."[101] Washington, after some hesitation, spoke at a Boston meeting in favor of the machine. There is no record of Washington's words, but he later remarked to Price: "It will be a happy moment for our country when the colored people and the white people in the South can get nearer together and let the world see that in actual daily relations there is little friction between them. I am sure that the launching of this cotton picking machine will go far in this direction, and whenever I can serve in the slightest manner I hope you will not fail to command me."[102] The Price machine failed commercially, however, and Washington turned a deaf ear four years later to the promoter of a rival machine, the Kotton King.[103]

The southern cotton mills offered another limited avenue of black advancement, if only the total exclusion of blacks that had been their hallmark since their burgeoning in the 1880s could be broken. The wages among the "lintheads" in the mills were among the lowest in the United States, and use of child labor was rampant, but Washington explored every possible crack in the "door of opportunity." Though a low-wage industry, cotton manufacturing was the South's leading industry, and Washington's effort to get black-owned and black-operated mills was part of his quiet campaign against labor segregation and exclusion. He encouraged every black entrepreneur who wanted to start a cotton mill and every white millowner willing to take the risks involved in hiring black workers in defiance of the unwritten law.

One possible way of promoting black entry into cotton mills would have been to train Tuskegee students for such jobs, but the pay was so low, the requisite skill so low, and the prospect of employment so poor that Washington saw no point in doing this. For a brief time in 1900 the Tuskegee trustees seriously investigated the possibility of setting up a cotton mill as one of the campus trade buildings.[104] Several philanthropically inclined whites, notably Henry C. Davis of Philadelphia, Elkan Naumburg of New York, Richard P. Hallowell of Boston, and B. Frank Mebane of Spray, North Carolina, considered establishing cotton mills with black labor, but nothing developed from any of their plans. A Charleston cotton mill used black labor for a short while in the 1890s. In general, however, poor whites had a labor monopoly, for whatever that was worth.

In 1897 a black grocer named Warren C. Coleman finally grasped the nettle. He established in Concord, North Carolina, a black-operated cotton mill with 140 looms and 5000 spindles, which lasted for a number of years. He offered Booker T. Washington the presidency of this company; Washington did not accept it, but he encouraged the enterprise from the beginning, glorified it as a model business during the meetings of the National Negro Business League, visited the mill, and gave it an enthusiastic description in a magazine article. Coleman's own spirit was an essential element of the enterprise, however, and when he died in 1904 the company immediately collapsed, and its property was sold to whites at public auction.[105]

Washington's only active involvement in promotion of an all-black cotton mill began in 1902 and continued for a decade with the New Century Cotton Mills of Dallas, Texas. Washington put its black founder, Joseph E. Wiley, in touch with two Bostonians of wealth who were sympathetic with the desire to end the white monopoly in this field of enterprise. Richard P. Hallowell and Henry Lee Higginson raised some $30,000 in the Boston area for bonds of the New Century Cotton Mills.[106] Though the capital for the enterprise was largely white, the management and labor were black. Wiley boasted that "we have completed the entire work done, of every character, without calling in the help of a single Machinist, or other Mechanic except our own People."[107] Some $2000 of Tuskegee's own endowment funds from a Boston legacy were in bonds of the New Century Cotton Mills.[108] Wiley was a hard worker and a persuasive promoter, but apparently financially inept, for by 1906 the company was losing money and was on the verge of bankruptcy. The largest of the Boston bondholders offered to give the company's up-to-date mill machinery to Tuskegee Institute if the school wished to use it in its industrial training.[109] For some reason, however, the proposition never materialized; the company was reorganized, still under Wiley's management, as the Mill City Cotton Mills. When Wiley asked the Tuskegee trustees to invest in his new enterprise, trustee William G. Willcox blocked the move. He wrote to Washington: "I can quite realize its importance as an experiment in the interest of the progress of the colored race but, on the other hand it is always a mistake, I think, to mix up philanthropy and business. . . ."[110] Washington himself reduced his commitment to Wiley's enterprise. He questioned whether a cotton mill could succeed "where the lands are rich and producing cotton in great abundance," as around Dallas, because in the very season when the mill most needed labor, the workers went cotton-picking.[111] Washington refused in 1912 to give Wiley a letter of introduction to businessmen, saying that if he recommended investment in an enterprise that subsequently lost money, he would be blamed and would lose a potential supporter of Tuskegee Institute. He urged Wiley "to place the matter before the men who have money to invest and let them take the proposition upon its face value."[112]

"I do not think that it can be said that the Negro is a failure in the cotton mill," Washington wrote in 1904. "A sufficient trial has not been afforded him." He believed the various black-labor efforts had failed because the machinery was old, the capitalization insufficient, or the labor supply "a miscellaneous city population." He took a tough-minded position, saying: "The only way, in my opinion, to control colored labor in a cotton factory is to pursue the same policy that is pursued with white laborers, and that is colonize them at some distance from a city in houses owned and controlled by the factory operators."[113]

Washington's many efforts and indirect encouragement to black economic means for racial and individual advancement make clear that he gave this approach equal priority with education, though it was also clear that his own Tuskegee Institute remained his prime responsibility, and that he restrained himself from direct involvement or investment in the savings banks, landownership schemes, cotton mills, and all-black towns. Over all of this class of black striving he held the umbrella of the National Negro Business League and tried to maintain a cadence of onward march through the reiteration of his rhetoric of self-help, mutual aid, racial pride, and racial solidarity. For those who faltered on the march, he was often censorious. He rebuked the idler, the alcoholic, and the unhealthy, but he was not without compassion. He sought to clean up their messy lives by involvement in efforts for a state reformatory, for prohibition, and for public health.

The reformatory movement in Alabama originated with others, but Washington helped to encourage and coordinate it. Sometime in 1903, the progressive city judge Noah B. Feagin of Birmingham, exasperated by the necessity of sentencing adolescent boys to the chain gang, put 175 black youths on probation and established a temporary reformatory farm for them on land donated by a black man, Samuel Daily, at Foster in Tuscaloosa County. "The wayward boy can and should be saved from a criminal life," Feagin vowed, but he needed a black partner in this rescue work and asked Washington in 1904 to locate a suitable superintendent. Washington recommended a Tuskegee graduate who had also graduated from Talladega College and was a successful farmer and carpenter.[114] The Negro Women's Clubs of Alabama, in which Margaret Washington took an active part, assumed a fostering interest in aiding the reformatory and petitioning for state support, as did the Tuskegee Negro Conference. Washington informed Feagin that a similar movement was underway in Montgomery, where Washington and Warren S. Reese, the U. S. district attorney, had persuaded Judge J. M. Carmichael, president of the board of inspectors of the state convict bureau, to consider separating the juvenile convicts from the hardened adults at the black state prison in Speigners, Alabama. Though Alabama and most of the other southern states had reformatories for white boys and girls, only Virginia of the southern states provided reformatory services for black youth. "The subject . . . has weighed heavily upon my heart for several years," Washington wrote Reese, "and I longed to see the time come when something would be done in Alabama resulting in a change in the present policy."[115]

Washington attended a meeting of the state convict board in the summer of 1904 to testify in behalf of a black reformatory.[116] Through Robert C. Ogden, he put Feagin and Carmichael in touch with a Boston penologist for advice on the needs of a reformatory.[117] His black lieutenant in Birmingham, the banker Ulysses G. Mason, organized a mass meeting of black citizens at the A. M. E. Zion church in Birmingham to support the reformatory and give Judge Feagin the expression of community support that he needed to overcome local white resistance.[118] Seeing the movement well launched, Washington confined his efforts thereafter to suggesting to supporters in Birmingham and Montgomery, "instead of a number of reformatories, that all of them be put in the direction of cooperating for the larger good."[119]

Prohibition of the sale or consumption of alcohol was one of the many movements that passed for social reform during the Progressive Era, and it was widespread all over the United States. It was particularly powerful in the South, where it had to compete with fewer other schemes for the improvement of mankind. Not surprisingly, enthusiasm for prohibition evolved in Booker T. Washington at about the same rate that prohibition developed as a regional social and political issue. Tuskegee Institute, like many other schools where minors resided, had strict sumptuary regulations from the beginning that banned the use of both alcoholic beverages and tobacco by students and that confined smoking by faculty to their private quarters.[120] The institution was wise to protect itself by these rules, for the mention of wine and cigars on the menu of a dinner on campus honoring Emmett Scott brought cries of outrage from a Chicago trustee who heard of it.[121] Washington himself was completely silent for many years, however, on the subject of prohibition as a public issue.

The year 1906 was a turning point. Just as in Georgia prohibition rivaled the disfranchisement of blacks as a campaign issue, and the rest of the South girded itself to do battle over the saloon, Washington invited a prominent black temperance lecturer, Rosetta E. Lawson of Washington, D.C., to spend several weeks at Tuskegee preaching, as it turned out, not temperance but abstinence. She organized fourteen chapters of the Loyal Temperance Union and addressed not only students but local churches and Sunday schools and even the prisoners in the county jail.[122] Washington had believed in earlier times that restrictive laws would do no good, that reform must come from within, but in all probability he became convinced, by the heavy emphasis of Atlanta white leaders after the race riot there, that they at least believed in a causal chain from liquor to black crime to white riot. At any rate, when the issue came to Macon County in the spring of 1907, he opposed the state dispensary, the local compromise on the saloon question, as a "harmful influence . . . over the growing lives of young men."[123]

Once committed to prohibition, Washington grew steadily more sanguine about its "miraculous" power to reform. He predicted to a northern magazine editor in 1907 that within five years "no liquor will be sold in any of the Southern states legally, except perhaps Louisiana and Texas."[124] He hailed prohibition as a boon to black and white alike, in a speech at Hampton and in articles in several magazines. He denied that it was a scheme to deny alcohol to blacks while allowing whites to obtain it illegally. Prohibition, he asserted in 1908, was "based upon a deep-seated desire to get rid of whiskey in the interest of both races because of its hurtful economic and moral results." He cited arrest records before and after prohibition in Birmingham and Atlanta as "a sort of barometer of the conditions among the poorer classes," and found not only fewer drunk and disorderly arrests but fewer murders, shootings, knife and razor fights, and other acts of violence. Because prohibition enlisted not only the white male voters but the disfranchised blacks and women and children, Washington said, it was more than a political maneuver. It was the broadest-based public issue in the South, "an intellectual awakening and a moral revolution."[125]

Washington wrote Ray Stannard Baker in 1909 that prohibition was both effective among blacks and regenerative in its effects. "True, some get liquor," he wrote, "but my observation is that where one man gets liquor, ten are prevented from getting it." Under prohibition conditions blacks worked harder and put more money into the bank or into property.[126] His principal argument, however, was that prohibition prevented crime. He told a white reformer that strong drink was "productive of more crime among the people of my race than any other one factor."[127] He objected, however, when Alabama Congressman Richmond P. Hobson, notorious for his white supremacy expressions, proposed in 1912 a constitutional amendment to prohibit the sale of alcoholic beverages to persons of African descent. This, he wrote to the congressman's secretary, would be objectionable to blacks as "class or race legislation."[128]

The most systematic effort Washington made to study the relationship between liquor and black crime was a questionnaire he sent in 1912 to Alabama county sheriffs. He concluded soberly from the responses in an article in a criminological journal: "It appears that where prohibition has really prohibited the Negroes from securing liquor their crime rate has been decreased. On the other hand, it appears that where the prohibition law did not prevent the Negroes from securing whiskey there has been no decrease in the crime rate, in fact the introduction of a cheaper grade of liquor has apparently had a tendency to increase the crime rate."[129]

Washington explained the rise in shootings and murders in black communities during the Christmas holidays by the heavy consumption of liquor during that season.[130] He also blamed liquor for "a good portion of the lynchings that take place in the Southern States as well as the crimes that give an excuse for them." While he conceded that laws could not change human nature, he also asserted that habits of temperance were hard to develop "so long as there exists a great, powerful, highly organized and enterprising business engaged in stimulating the desire for this dangerous kind of stimulants." He was ready in 1914, therefore, to "put whiskey in the class with dangerous drugs" and forbid its sale or consumption.[131]

The promotion of better public health among blacks was a meliorative movement that Washington sponsored with his customary vigor and organizing skill, most notably through his founding of National Negro Health Week. From the beginning of his long tenure as head of Tuskegee Institute, he had concerned himself with matters of sanitation and preventive medicine and healthful personal habits. He devoted much attention to the details of the earth closets, the night cart, and the purity of the water supply of the campus. He provided ample bathing and swimming facilities for students, programs of physical culture, and careful inspection of living quarters. But he realized that Tuskegee was an oasis amid the squalor and neglected pathology that was the lot of the majority of poor blacks. In 1908 he held a five-day conference at Tuskegee Institute on the study and prevention of tuberculosis with the help of the National Tuberculosis Association's traveling exhibit and stereopticon lectures.[132] In 1911 he proposed to the newly founded Russell Sage Foundation that it cooperate with Tuskegee Institute in a nationwide effort to improve the sanitary and health conditions of blacks. Recent newspaper discussions of the general health hazards arising from unsanitary conditions of black settlements in southern cities had aroused white interest, he said, and blacks were also "becoming aroused to the need of sanitary conditions." Black women's clubs, secret societies, insurance companies, and nearly every other black organization were giving some attention to the improvement of black public health, and he proposed coordination of these efforts through a special conference connected with the annual Tuskegee Negro Conference, a "Conference on Improvement of Health Conditions Among Negroes."[133]

The Russell Sage Foundation did not respond favorably, but the idea remained in Washington's mind, and it was reinforced and modified by his experiences at a Conference on Race Betterment he attended at Battle Creek, Michigan, sponsored by the health-food magnate J. H. Kellogg. Washington turned one day of the Tuskegee Negro Conference in 1914 into a public health conference. Tuskegee's dairy instructor contrasted sanitary and unsanitary milking and butter and cheese making. Dr. John A. Kenney, head of the newly completed John A. Andrew Hospital at Tuskegee, and his nursing staff presented an exhibit on sanitation, nursing, and patent medicine frauds. George Washington Carver, the institute's chief agricultural expert, gave an exhibit of pure and impure water. Others talked on the proper care of teeth, of babies and children, or warned of the baneful effects of cheap whiskey and gin.[134] This conference was a valuable public service, but it was too makeshift and localized to satisfy Washington's growing sense of the importance of public health and preventive medicine.

Washington tried to broaden the 1914 conference by arranging for the head of the Alabama state board of health to be present, and several black doctors attended. But the highlight of the conference and the guidepost to the future was the Louisiana Health Car, a traveling exhibit designed in 1912 and brought to the meeting by Dr. Oscar H. Dowling, president of the Louisiana state board of health. Louisiana, long in struggle against epidemic disease, had developed this ingenious method of informing the public about health hazards. Dowling's Health Car was the public-health equivalent of Tuskegee's Jesup Wagon. The thousands of black attendants at the Tuskegee conference had an opportunity to learn its message.[135]

In his address to the conference, Washington said the health question was of urgent concern to the 9,000,000 southern blacks but also to the white people. He estimated that 200,000 blacks in the South at that moment had easily preventable diseases, "and the time has come to emphasize prevention more than cure." He called on whites to concern themselves also "from a money point of view as well as from a humanitarian point of view," for the economic losses from disease were substantial. "The life of the humblest black person in the South in some way touches the life of the most exalted white person in the South," he warned. But he disagreed with a noted physician who was "preaching the doctrine that the Southern white women are weak in body and mind because of the presence of the Negro in the South." Nevertheless, whites did have a stake in the health of those who laundered and cooked for them. "To my own race," he said: "We must remember . . . in every city of this country . . . the death rate among our people is much higher than it is among the white people. Perhaps in the country districts the large birth rate overbalances in a large measure this increased death rate in the cities. Certainly, except for the fact that the race in the city is replenished by those who move in from the country to the city, our race would decrease in numbers very fast." He urged all black ministers, business leagues, and fraternal orders to make prevention of sickness their motto.[136]

Washington planned earlier and more systematically for the 1915 campaign for black health. He wrote to Anson Phelps Stokes in the fall of 1914 asking for $600 from the Phelps-Stokes Fund for promotion of a Negro Health Day throughout the country. He promised that the money would be used largely in keeping up an interest in the day through circulars, newspaper advertisements, and other reminders. "Our people have remarkable ability to help themselves," he wrote Stokes, "but they have got to be educated as to how to help."[137] The Fund granted $500 for the purpose but asked that its name not be used.[138] Washington also loosely coordinated his plans with those of Robert R. Moton, whose Negro Organization Society of Virginia scheduled a meeting with the Virginia state board of health in planning for a "cleaning up week."[139]

Washington also enlisted the aid of the National Negro Business League in sponsoring what became not just a day but National Negro Health Week, March 21–27, 1915. The National Urban League also gave minor support, but Washington and Emmett Scott were the driving personalities behind the promotion.[140] The climax of the week was Washington's address at the Bethel A. M. E. Church in Baltimore, sponsored by the Maryland Colored Health Association and the Medical and Chirurgical Faculty of Maryland. About 3000 persons crowded the auditorium and thousands of others, turned away, "waited in the vicinity for two hours, vainly hoping for a chance to get on the inside." According to the report of the black journalist R. W. Thompson, whose syndicated writing had once been subsidized by Washington, "The eagerness to hear the message of Dr. Booker T. Washington, displayed by the best citizens of both races on this occasion, testifies significantly to the personal popularity of the Negro's natural leader in Baltimore, and to the enthusiastic interest all are taking in his campaign for better health conditions for the people of the entire country."[141] The crowd's size probably reflected a curiosity about Washington himself, who did not often speak in Baltimore, rather than a consuming interest in public health. Nevertheless, the campaign drew large crowds also in New York City, New Orleans, and other centers of large black population. Washington took justifiable pride in the widespread interest his campaign had generated and what he called "the whole-souled cooperation of the Southern State Health Officers."[142]

No revolution in black public health resulted from Washington's efforts, but they do show him imaginatively promoting the welfare of the "men farthest down" in the minority group he led. Washington was such a sponge of the conventional wisdom of his day that he sometimes appeared callous in using the language then in vogue of Social Darwinism and "the survival of the fittest." He frequently boasted, for example, that there were no black orphan asylums because black people took care of their own without the need for such institutionalized charity. He noted that in the city streets one almost never saw a black beggar, whereas importunate whites were plentiful in the streets of America and Europe. Actually, as recent scholarship has shown, blacks were not receiving public charity in the South generally because they were victims of public policies of exclusion rather than segregation.[143]

When Washington sponsored National Negro Health Week in 1915 he was only six months away from his own death, but he was determined that this movement would not die with him. He saw Anson Phelps Stokes at New Haven just before the public speech there that brought about his collapse, and he wrote Stokes from the hospital a week before he died to say that he had forgotten to ask him for "the same appropriation toward health week this year as last year."[144] National Negro Health Week did continue. Another campaign along the same lines occurred in 1917 under the National Negro Business League and Tuskegee sponsorship, when Washington's cohort J. C. Napier was president of the league, Moton head of Tuskegee, and Scott secretary of both. The program continued as the wartime influenza epidemic and the crowding and sanitation problems brought on by the Great Migration of 1915–1919 compounded the health crisis among blacks. Fortunately by that time the National Urban League, of which Washington was somewhat a godfather, joined in the public health campaign on a more continuing basis.[145]

It is evident that Washington's leadership of myriad efforts at self-help, independence of white bosses and landlords, enterprise and material progress, went beyond rhetoric, beyond the "gospel of the toothbrush," and beyond what would please whites bent on subordination of blacks. Furthermore, he had welfare programs for those who stumbled or fell on the march. Washington was no Moses, and bootstraps could not lift an oppressed people far off the ground. The burden of his compromises and accommodations to a repressive system of white supremacy often vitiated his efforts to advance the interests of blacks, and indeed the history of his years of black leadership in America illustrates the impossibility of reforming a system while at the same time accommodating to its institutions and spirit. Nevertheless, that was the impossibility that Washington sincerely and doggedly tried.

CHAPTER 10

A White Man's Country

. . . take him all in all the greatest man, save General Lee, born in the South in a hundred years; but he is not a typical negro.

JOHN SPENCER BASSETT, 1903

A fraud & a liar; a smart man; training social parasites; you never heard of a student of his school who ever did anything useful except teach school. BTW has one practice in South another in the North—showing him a hypocrite.*

JAMES K. VARDAMAN, 1907

EVEN before he had become a leader and spokesman of other blacks, Washington had built his own personal career as a southern black educator out of his ability to survive and even thrive in the South, a region that white men unanimously, but with varying degrees of raucousness, proclaimed a white man's country. Washington survived through deliberate compromises with the white men who owned and controlled the South; his compromises were reflected in the social philosophy he espoused and in the way he conducted Tuskegee Institute. But the most important feature of his interracial politics and diplomacy was the personal relationship he established with whites in power. He constantly and cannily cultivated the friendship

* Notes of an interview of Vardaman by Ray Stannard Baker.

and good will of whoever would serve his needs, suppressing what must have been his private feelings about their racial expressions and condescensions, dilating whatever he could find to praise in their utterances and deeds. He did all this with specific as well as general purpose, however, to exploit the class divisions within southern white society, and to seek out and cultivate those southerners with whom blacks could make common cause. First he joined forces with the conservatives of the planter and employer class, who failed him miserably in the crisis of disfranchisement and segregation laws, and then with the minuscule and isolated southern liberals, dissenters, and renegades who appeared in the southern professional class in the early twentieth century and found in Booker T. Washington a black ally more congenial than the northern black militants.[1]

From the first day Washington stepped on Alabama soil in 1881 he began to establish a relationship of mutual interest with the conservative whites, and as his larger ambitions for national leadership became more central to his life, he continued to tend the garden of good will he had already planted. Washington remained careful to keep the merchant elite of Tuskegee and the larger planters out in Macon County on his side and ready to defend him against the jealousy and outright hostility that the success and growth of Tuskegee excited among the poorer whites. It was a condition of Tuskegee Institute's affiliation with the state that three trustees were state-appointed commissioners from within the state, and Washington skillfully maneuvered to make certain that these included a black man, a member of one of the leading families of Tuskegee, and a sympathetic white from elsewhere in the state, such as R. O. Simpson of Furman or Belton Gilreath of Birmingham. He employed the prominent local lawyer and editor Charles W. Hare as the institute's lawyer, and cultivated members of the Campbell, Drakeford, and Thompson families, the Varners who had sold part of their land to form the Tuskegee campus, and John Massey, president of the Alabama Conference Female College. Washington could not abolish town–gown tensions, but his partnership with the white oligarchy of Tuskegee held them in check.

It was a mark of Washington's skill in human relations that he charmed every successive governor of Alabama throughout his thirty-four years as principal of Tuskegee, and the state superintendents of education, though seldom actually helpful to the black institute, took no hostile action. The blessings of these governors and state superintendents were vital to the security of Tuskegee Institute, for the state legislature and the white voters of Alabama were deeply divided along sectional lines, and Tuskegee could have been caught in the crossfire between north Alabama and the Black Belt if it had not had shelter under the wings of officials representing the entire state. The state also guaranteed the certification of most Tuskegee graduates and other former students as teachers.

Two of the ex-governors especially favorable to Washington who continued to be active in state affairs in the early twentieth century were William C. Oates and Thomas G. Jones. Both of them crumbled miserably after trying to stop the disfranchisement of blacks in the state constitution of 1901. Washington arranged for Jones to become a federal district judge, however, only to find that Jones used his office to support strikebreaking with state militia and let peonage masters off with a slap on the wrist. The governor from 1901 to 1907 was William D. Jelks, another Black Belt conservative like Jones and Oates; then from 1907 to 1911 the Birmingham millowner and "business progressive" Braxton Bragg Comer was governor. Because Comer represented the white counties of north Alabama, Washington feared that he would be hostile to Tuskegee and to blacks, but his administration changed race relations little for either better or worse. From 1911 to 1915 power shifted again to the Black Belt with the governorship of Emmet O'Neal, the son of an earlier governor who had befriended Washington in the early days of Tuskegee. Washington accepted the challenge of each new administration as it came.

Washington thought he had found in Governor W. D. Jelks the kind of white leader he hoped to duplicate in the South. In his inaugural speech of his second term in 1903 Jelks condemned lynching, and Washington rushed copies of the speech to his northern friends as a sign of changing times. While Jelks did assume that some blacks were guilty of the crimes alleged, he argued that many other lynch victims were innocent, and that one crime did not justify another. "It is false, absolutely false," said Jelks, "to assert that this evil spirit is merely anticipating the action of the Courts."[2]

A few years later, in 1906, however, Washington discovered the less benign side of Jelks's racial paternalism when he invited the Governor to share the platform with him on Negro Day at the state fair. Washington sought to satisfy all elements of his audience by dividing blacks into two classes, the peaceful, hard-working ones and the idle and immoral. He pleaded the case for better provision for black education as an encouragement of one class and a deterrent to the other.[3] To his great surprise, however, the Governor denounced black education, including that at Tuskegee, as luring black labor from the fields. Jelks's view, probably heightened by a pro-white interpretation of the recent Atlanta Riot, he expressed privately to a friend: "If we can not work the idle loafers and thieves, we can not escape a race war."[4] Since blacks unfortunately could not be deported, they would have to mend their ways, and he believed that "we will have to put white teachers over them in the schools."[5]

Washington recognized a crisis of confidence, and he tried to mollify Jelks by sending a detailed report of Tuskegee graduates at work in Montgomery County, most of them in agriculture, the trades, and teaching.[6] But the Governor stubbornly reiterated what he had said at the fairgrounds, that "the number of vagrants and crimes attributed to your race are larger in numbers than ever before and that an education in your school educates the boy away from the farm. I expressed regret at this. However, I may say to you that an education in the higher white schools is having the same effect."[7] He had said nothing of the white students in his speech, however, nor called them boys. Washington puzzled over how to regain the Governor's good will, then sent to see him a man, not a boy, who had graduated from Tuskegee sixteen years earlier and "now owns 1100 acres of land right in the community where he lived before coming to Tuskegee."[8] Jelks's dudgeon began to subside after a few weeks. He changed the focus of his indictment from race to the lure of the city.

Jelks approved of the Jesup Wagon—he could hardly do otherwise—but he still grieved at the flight of the educated from the farm. "I am sure it would be better if we had no larger schools," Jelks suggested to Washington, "so far as the State is concerned, but depend upon high schools—very high—in each county. A boy who gets his education upon his native heath will probably remain at home."[9] There remained a blend of white supremacy in Jelks's agrarianism. He said he had little interest in black schools to turn out doctors, lawyers, or even teachers. "Our general wealth is in our soil," but brick masons were also useful. "Blacksmiths we need next to the farmer, and above all and before them all, we need to educate men who are to be lovers of the soil."[10] When the mainspring of his rhetoric finally ran down and Washington allowed him the last word, Jelks exhibited no direct animosity toward Tuskegee Institute, but his administration did nothing to improve the black public schools.

Braxton B. Comer, because of his manufacturing connections and north Alabama residence threatened the partnership of railroad lobbyists and Black Belt leaders who had long run Alabama politics, and the new imbalance of power also threatened redistribution of state school funds from the white schools of the black counties to the white schools of the predominantly white counties.[11] Comer's supporters in the campaign had also called for a state investigation of Tuskegee Institute's tax exemption. The auguries were unpromising for black institutions generally. Washington's friend Jody Thompson sat next to the governor-elect on the train from Birmingham to Montgomery as he worked on his first message to the legislature, and Thompson reported to Washington that he "could see from his expression that he was not inclined to be as liberal in his views as had been hoped for." Comer volunteered some demagogic comments on Tuskegee Institute, and Thompson told Comer that the school owned only 2500 acres, which Comer said was "not so bad as he thought."[12]

When Washington next spoke in Birmingham, he arranged for the officers of the Colored Citizens Club of that city to invite the governor-elect to attend. Afterward, Comer wrote in a public letter that Washington's was a "sound, logical and well made address" that would allay black discouragement and unrest, but he denied that there was any cause for unrest. "Any colored man who is obeying the usual principles which should control the conduct of any well-meaning citizen, should have cause to be thankful that he is now living in our midst," he wrote. Washington also literally buttered up the Governor. He had George Washington Carver take to the Governor's Mansion six pounds of butter from the institute dairy.[13]

In his valedictory message in 1911 Comer claimed that in his term fewer interracial murders, assaults, and lynchings had occurred than ever before, and credited prohibition and the rise in cotton prices for this. Self-revealingly, he said he did not consider education of blacks to be bad, but he also denied that blacks in the Black Belt had inadequate schools. It must be remembered, he said, that black schools "surpassed" the white ones there, in enrollment. "In the precinct where I was reared," he said, "near my father's old home there is a negro school which had 105 pupils last year, while the white school in the same locality had only 5 pupils." This proved nothing, of course. Enrollment was no measure of educational quality or support, and the reason for the disproportion was that more blacks resided in the neighborhood and many white planters sent their children to private schools.[14]

Washington did what he could also to cultivate the state school superintendents. He sent a Tuskegee officer to the office of Superintendent Harry C. Gunnels to measure him for a suit of clothes. "I have told Mr. Gunnels," Washington wrote, "that the school would present him with this suit of clothes to be worn to the meetings of the various (county) superintendents of schools."[15] A few months later, when another state superintendent took over, Washington asked for an appointment to discuss a joint effort to get the legislature to appropriate money for teachers' institutes, but apparently did not offer him a suit of clothes.[16]

When Emmet O'Neal became governor in 1911, Washington made haste to send not only butter but peaches from Tuskegee Institute. "It was my privilege to know your father when he was Governor," Washington wrote, "and I remember his many acts of kindness to me as an individual and to our race."[17] Rhetorically, at least, O'Neal endorsed black education, saying that agricultural progress depended on modern scientific methods, and "the colored man must be trained and fitted by education to adopt similar methods. Moreover, none can deny that education tends to lessen crime and to fit every man to perform more efficiently his duties in life."[18] Such sentiments had their reward in the form of a Thanksgiving turkey from the institute, surrounded by Macon County sweet potatoes, tomatoes, parsley, and autumn leaves.[19] In 1914 Washington varied the peace offering by sending the Governor fifteen fryers and the state superintendent of education twelve.[20]

Of the three early twentieth-century Alabama governors, O'Neal was the only one who approached Washington's ideal. Soon after his inauguration some whites asked O'Neal to pardon a white murderer on the ground that the victim had been "only a Negro." O'Neal reportedly replied: "The open season for killing Negroes closed when I became Governor of Alabama." In 1914 he commuted to life imprisonment the death sentence of Ervin Pope, a black man five times sentenced to death for one alleged murder. The state supreme court had reversed the decision four times. O'Neal detailed to Washington his careful investigation and said that the commutation was because the most incriminating evidence was a pair of blood-stained shoes found in Pope's outhouse, shoes two sizes larger than Pope's feet.[21] In 1915 Governor O'Neal and a large party of state officials toured the Tuskegee campus and rounded out the day with an elaborate, whites-only dinner at Dorothy Hall.[22] This was only two days after a lynch mob took two black prisoners from the Elmore county jail and shot them to death. O'Neal publicly announced that all the power of his office would be used to establish the guilt and guarantee the punishment of the lynchers.[23] Brave words, but blown away by the wind of passion. This was the year of rebirth of the Ku Klux Klan.

Washington's ritual offering to successive governors of the fruits of Tuskegee's labors had a medieval quality of subservience, an accommodation to the structure of white supremacy. Less systematically but frequently Washington did similar favors to newspaper editors, Tuskegee merchants, Black Belt landlords. In most cases these were peace offerings to those whose outlook radically differed from his own but whose personal good will he hoped to win. None of these reciprocated with gifts of their own, seeming to accept the Tuskegee offerings as fealty. When Washington sent a gift to one of his true friends, it was often a 'possum, and these friends reciprocated with good whiskey or Havana cigars.

Unquestionably, Washington was one of a class of black leaders and spokesmen who in many respects and on many occasions accommodated themselves to the conditions imposed by the more numerous and powerful whites. Rather than protest against injustice with utter frankness and rebuke the perpetrators, Washington sought to disarm the whites by conceding what mattered least to blacks or most to whites, and then to persuade the whites to behave better by gentle rebuke, flattery, and inordinate public praise for every act of decency he could find among them in the age of white supremacy. In this he was typical rather than exceptional, however, particularly of black spokesmen residing in the South. What made him exceptional were his skill in manipulating the whites, his zeal in exhorting blacks to strengthen themselves through self-help, his constant search for allies among the whites, and his deeply secret civil rights campaign through financing test cases in the courts.

The manifest racial discrimination in voting rights under the new southern state constitutions was what drove Washington to his first secret resort to the courts. Though he accepted and even endorsed a suffrage limited to the literate and property owners, if administered without racial discrimination, Washington denounced the grandfather clauses in the southern constitutions as patently unjust and also objected to the boards of registrars with broad discretion to deny applicants for registration. As early as 1899 Washington initiated a test of the Louisiana grandfather clause, bringing together the strands of a New Orleans committee, the Afro-American Council's legal committee, the monetary and legal contributions of white liberal friends, and his own funds and leadership, with assurances from all parties that his role would be secret and his contributions recorded as "from X. Y. Z."[24]

When disfranchisement came to Alabama in 1901, Washington joined with a group of black petitioners against it and in a private interview with the chairman of the suffrage committee of the convention continued to object to the plan for a board of registrars and to the grandfather clause. By a local understanding, Washington and many of his Tuskegee faculty registered, received lifetime voting certificates, and voted.[25] But this was not the pattern of the rest of the state. Governor Jelks reassured U. S. Senator John T. Morgan early in 1902: "The Board of Appointment spent thirty days selecting these Registrars and in every instance we were assured positively that the appointees would carry out the spirit of the Constitution, which looks to the registration of all white men not convicted of crime, and only a few negroes."[26] The first black man allowed to register in Montgomery County was a veteran of the Spanish-American War who had his discharge papers with him.[27] All over the state only blacks who had served in the army or navy were allowed to register, and blacks of the standing of Bishop J. W. Alstork and the businessman Henry A. Loveless in Montgomery were refused.[28]

Some of the blacks denied registration formed the Colored Men's Suffrage Association of Alabama, centered in Montgomery, and its president Jackson W. Giles became the plaintiff in two Alabama suffrage cases, *Giles* v. *Harris* (1903) and *Giles* v. *Teasley* (1904), both of which reached the United States Supreme Court. Giles had a federal job as a mailman, and was thus less vulnerable than other possible plaintiffs. Not even Giles and the other members of his association apparently knew that Wilford H. Smith, the lawyer they employed and paid a pittance, was actually paid by Washington to litigate these cases. On his arrival in Montgomery, Smith wrote to Emmett Scott to arrange for a private meeting. "It is understood," he wrote, "that I am sent from New York by the Citizens Protective League, from whom I hold credentials."[29] Washington doubly guarded his secrecy by having Scott handle all the correspondence with Smith. Fearing a breach of security, Scott began addressing Smith's letters by the code name "Filipino," and in telegrams, particularly, Smith adopted the code name "McAdoo," the last name of his secretary.[30]

Washington, however, warned Scott: "It seems to me in case any of these communications were found, it would be less suspicious should some real name, such as 'John Smith' be found on the letters."[31] Scott could do better than "John Smith." He kept up a lively correspondence with Wilford Smith using the names R. C. Black and J. C. May respectively. Through these go-betweens Washington passed on money, news, and cogent advice on the Giles cases as they made their way through the court system. Within the letters were other code words, referring to Washington as "His Nibs" or "the Wizard"; "M" stood for Montgomery, "C" for a hundred and "D" for dollars.[32] References to "D" were frequent, for Giles's association could raise only a few hundred dollars whereas the legal expenses were in the thousands of dollars.[33] Washington apparently contributed most or all of this himself, for there is no record that he took the risks involved in even a private fund-raising effort.[34]

The Giles cases took arms against a historical trend of white supremacy that not only swept through the South but permeated the North even to the high bench itself. Washington met disappointment at every level. The Giles cases attacked not merely the grandfather clause but the refusal to register blacks solely on account of their race or color. When the case was defeated in the state courts, Washington hoped for a favorable decision from Judge Thomas G. Jones, whom Washington himself had persuaded President Roosevelt to appoint, but Jones ruled that his court had no jurisdiction and refused to comment on the merits of the case.[35] During the long course of litigation and appeal, a leader of the Colored Man's Suffrage Association lost his job, and then Giles himself did.[36] Some local blacks blamed Smith for carelessness or incompetence as the courts at each level found technical grounds for ruling against Giles.[37] Undoubtedly there was some truth to this, for Smith was no Ivy League law graduate, but every time he plugged a leaky loophole the opposing lawyers or the courts would find another. The United States Supreme Court threw out both of the Giles cases on technicalities. In the first case Justice Holmes for the Court found that Giles had attacked the validity of the state constitution under which he sought to register and that the case presented a political rather than a constitutional question. The Court rejected the second case because the plaintiff failed to claim in the state courts that his rights as a United States citizen were denied, although that became the basis of his appeal.

Wilford Smith wrote defensively to Washington: "To my mind the Supreme Court took advantage of the only loop-hole in sight to get around the decision of a question fraught with so many important political consequences. We will have to find a way to hem them in as they do in playing checkers. . . ."[38] Washington urged Smith to press a new case, to "at least, put the Supreme Court in an awkward position. We must not cease our efforts."[39] He suggested a new plaintiff, Charles O. Harris, a clerk who "has been practically conducting the Montgomery Post Office for many years," and a new strategy. "A case based upon the refusal to allow an unregistered Negro to vote for a Member of Congress, or for Presidential electors," he proposed, "seems to me to offer another opportunity and one which I think it well for us to follow up."[40] Washington continued for some months to try to mount a fresh legal assault on Alabama disfranchisement.[41] But Smith had lost heart. "I have had a bad case of the blues ever since the Supreme Court sat down on me," he confessed to Scott. "I have been doing a great deal of thinking against the Supreme Court, which I am unable to express."[42] Smith and other legal advisers persuaded Washington that it would be useless to continue.

Washington and Smith collaborated more successfully in a test of the exclusion of blacks from jury panels. With secret money from Washington, Smith carried the Dan Rogers case from Alabama to successful issue before the United States Supreme Court in 1904. They overturned the conviction of a black man in a criminal case because qualified blacks were excluded from the jury.[43]

The Jim Crow railroad cars presented a dilemma for Washington. Ever since the 1880s he had publicly acquiesced in separate but equal transportation, but challenged at every opportunity the fiction of equality by pointing out publicly and in private correspondence with railway officials the crowded and often filthy condition of Jim Crow cars and segregated station facilities and the unimpeded invasion of the black cars by white drunks, smokers, and rowdies.

When Georgia in 1900 and then other southern states segregated sleeping cars, however, Washington sought behind the scenes to take more militant action. He urged Georgia black leaders to protest and also sought the help of his confidant and Tuskegee trustee William H. Baldwin, Jr., himself a railroad president. Through Baldwin, Washington secured a private conference for himself and a black delegation with the president of the Pullman Company, none other than Abraham Lincoln's son Robert Todd Lincoln.[44] When Lincoln refused to support the black group in protesting against the Georgia law, Baldwin advised Washington to seek "a light mulatto of good appearance, but unquestionably colored," for a test case.[45] But resort to the courts is not a philanthropist's way of achieving an object, and Baldwin's enthusiasm soon flagged. He urged Washington to "let the matter drift a little longer" on the dubious ground that "if a test case is not made it will soon become a dead letter."[46]

Washington for once ignored Baldwin's advice. He and Wilford Smith secretly assisted W. E. B. Du Bois in a case he contemplated against the Georgia law in 1902, and though Du Bois publicly broke with Washington in 1903, the two were cooperating as late as December 1904 in an effort to test the Tennessee Pullman segregation law. Emmett Scott later took occasion to criticize the militant Du Bois for not pushing these cases vigorously enough.[47] Washington persuaded Giles B. Jackson of Richmond to begin a similar suit against the Virginia railroad segregation law.[48] He talked his friend and lieutenant James C. Napier of Nashville into a challenge of the Tennessee sleeping car segregation law. When the man chosen as plaintiff for the Tennessee case lost his nerve, Washington tried another round of conferences with the Pullman officials. This time the son of the Great Emancipator refused even to reply to the letters of the Great Accommodator.[49]

There was always an element of artful dodging in Washington's actions, even as a secret militant, but in 1906 he was impaled on both horns of the "separate but equal" issue. During the Senate debate on the Hepburn railway rate bill, Senators William Warner of Missouri and Joseph B. Foraker of Ohio proposed amendments that would guarantee equal railroad passenger facilities for blacks. Washington through secret agents lobbied at first for the Warner–Foraker amendment, apparently being as insensitive as its sponsors to the implicit federal approval of separate facilities that such a guarantee carried. Though the Supreme Court's Plessy decision in 1896 had sanctioned separate but equal, this would give congressional sanction as well. Through a pair of black friends in Washington, the Tuskegean paid $300 to Henry W. Blair, former Senator from New Hampshire, to lobby for the amendment. Then Washington learned that more militant northern blacks sensitive to the implied segregation were on their way to Washington to lobby against the amendment. Washington nimbly reversed himself, sent word to Blair to lobby now against the amendment, and urged his black go-betweens to claim credit for the defeat of the amendment.[50] But he was still personally undecided about the merits of the amendment. As against the abstract and theoretical opposition to segregation, he weighed the more concrete advantages of a more comfortable ride in a decently equipped Jim Crow car. As he wrote to one of his secret collaborators, "In fact the more I think of it the more I am convinced that the Warner Amendment would have been a good measure, and very helpful."[51]

Washington also worked privately to champion the rural black poor in their enjoyment of the most basic of all rights, the right to live and to labor in their own behalf. He responded warmly and effectively, for example, to the predicament of Pink Franklin, an illiterate South Carolina farmer. Franklin shot and killed two white men in 1910 when they broke into his cabin before daylight without announcement of their purpose to arrest him for violating a state peonage statute already declared unconstitutional by the state supreme court. After the United States Supreme Court refused to reverse Franklin's conviction for murder, Oswald Garrison Villard recruited Washington's help in seeking a commutation of the death sentence. Washington suggested two alternative courses: to employ a leading South Carolina white lawyer to go directly to the governor, or to ask the Reverend Richard Carroll to intercede with a plea for clemency. An ultra-conservative and rather sycophantic black man often referred to as "the Booker T. Washington of South Carolina," Carroll had, as Washington wrote Villard, "many qualities that neither you nor I would admire." But he also had "tremendous influence with the white people of South Carolina."[52] Villard replied that he had no money to pay a lawyer, but he urged Washington to do all he could through Carroll. It is not clear what tipped the balance, whether it was Carroll's influence, a persuasive letter from Washington's friend and trustee Robert C. Ogden, or possibly a letter from President William Howard Taft, but the South Carolina governor did commute Pink Franklin's sentence to one of life imprisonment.[53]

The most significant example of Washington's secret aid to southern black victims of peonage, however, was the Alonzo Bailey case, which Washington secretly aided and shepherded all the way, from 1908 to its success in the United States Supreme Court in 1911. A farmworker in Montgomery County, Alabama, Bailey had signed a year contract with a corporate farm to work for $12 a month. When he borrowed $20 against his future wages and then left the farm without repaying, he was tried and convicted under the Alabama peonage statute, not in a civil suit for debt but in a criminal suit for signing a contract with intent to defraud. Washington and some of his upper-class southern white friends had long sought such a test case providing opportunity to demonstrate the benevolence of their leadership, as had agents of the Justice Department under Theodore Roosevelt's attorney general, Charles J. Bonaparte. Washington sent a discreet Tuskegee instructor, Ernest T. Attwell, to contact his secret collaborators in the Bailey case, Judge William H. Thomas of the Montgomery city court and U. S. District Judge Thomas G. Jones. The two judges secretly gave legal counsel in the case without charge, but because of their judicial positions they were barred from being the lawyers of record. With Washington's secret encouragement and financial assistance, therefore, they persuaded two local white lawyers to defend Bailey without fee. Washington quietly raised the other legal costs from northern liberal friends, and Attorney General Bonaparte submitted an *amicus curiae* brief. Washington may have viewed the Bailey case as evidence of the viability of the bargain he had made with the southern white upper class in his Atlanta Compromise address, but if so he never explained it thus, for his circumstances required him to keep his participation in the case hidden from view. The Supreme Court in 1911 declared that peonage was involuntary servitude and that the Alabama law was therefore unconstitutional. As a recent scholarly study has shown, peonage continued illegally in Alabama but became less common there than in other southern states where similar contract labor laws were enforced. Alonzo Bailey was now free, except for the chains of ignorance, poverty, and racial discrimination, and was soon

"slinging hash" at a local country club. Washington took private satisfaction but no public credit for this rare legal victory for civil rights
in an era of reaction.[54]

Washington's secret stiletto thrusts at the huge body of institutionalized white supremacy did not substantially change its shape or force,
but they were clues, to the few who knew about them, of Washington's thought and feeling, and of a stouter heart than his bland public
manner suggested. Another indication of the inner man was his close
watch through the clipping services of his private secretary and his
encouragement of every faint marsh-light glimmer of white liberalism
he could find in the South. Washington had no direct connection with
the Andrew Sledd case, for example, when in 1902 this professor lost
his job at Emory College after publishing a mild rebuke of southern
racism in a northern magazine. But he and Scott followed the case so
closely in the press that Francis J. Garrison, the abolitionist's son, was
amazed. "You seem to keep as closely in touch with the Southern press,
and as close an eye upon it, as if you were an editor," Garrison wrote.
"I am constantly surprised by the way in which you sweep the field
and the horizon North and South with your telescope, and keep in
touch with events affecting the great question."[55]

Washington found frequent occasion for disappointment with the
southern conservative allies on whom he depended to hold the radical
anti-Negro whites in check; and as the white supremacy storm mounted
in statute, word, and deed, Washington swept the horizon in search
of a southern liberal. He thought for a while in 1903 that he had
found such a champion in William N. Sheats, superintendent of education of the state of Florida. Sheats invited Washington to address a
conference of county school superintendents, all of them white, in
cooperation with Wallace Buttrick of the General Education Board.[56]
Sheats had not always seemed so friendly toward blacks. In 1896 he
had said that blacks were getting "all the educational advantages they
are capable of appreciating" and should be "let alone by their over-
zealous friends."[57] In fact, so ambiguous was Washington's image in
the South that Sheats apparently thought he was inviting a fellow conservative. The county superintendent in Gainesville where the meeting was to take place, however, coveted Sheats's office, and he raised
the issue of "social equality inconsistent with the ideas, customs and
institutions of the South" if Washington were allowed to speak. He
declared the auditorium "unavailable for the use of Booker Washing-

ton, or any other colored person, during the convention of Superintendents, or upon any subsequent occasion."[58]

Washington wired Sheats offering to withdraw his acceptance if he was not welcome, but Sheats urged him to wait, and three days later wired: "Reason has asserted itself. Speak here Thursday night without fail." Sheats, the mayor, and the county superintendent who had raised the original objection sent a joint telegram renewing the invitation.[59] Washington cannily waited until his ghostwriter Max Thrasher and Wallace Buttrick in Gainesville reassured him about the atmosphere there before he accepted.[60] Washington's speech itself was a rousing success, "with as many of the white and colored people as could crowd into the room," some 2000 inside and hundreds turned away. Washington privately praised Sheats "for the manner in which he stood up; the mere fact that he had stood by his guns resulted in bringing even the opposers over to his side."[61]

Sheats said in his introduction that he could not name the greatest white American, but he knew that Booker T. Washington was the greatest Negro American. The crowd and the Florida newspapers cheered.[62] Washington's friends in the Southern and General Education Boards misread the meaning of the Sheats affair, however, for Washington's speech in the heart of "crackerdom" did not halt the trend toward greater discrimination against black schools even in Florida, and Sheats lost his office in the next election, his opponent using Washington's visit as his only campaign issue.[63] Sheats asked the General Education Board to do something in his behalf, but the cautious Buttrick would not even express a preference in the election, lest southerners resent this as northern interference in their affairs.[64]

A few months after his speech in Gainesville Washington addressed a large crowd on Negro day at the North Carolina state fair in Raleigh. "The white people here are completely carried away with your speech," one of his black sponsors wrote, "especially the women, who read it in the papers and are open in their praise of it. I need not tell you that the colored people liked it, you saw that for yourself."[65] One white who either heard or read the speech was John Spencer Bassett, a North Carolina-born history professor at nearby Trinity College in Durham, fresh from a doctorate at enlightened Johns Hopkins. As it was his turn to write an article for a little academic magazine on campus, the *South Atlantic Quarterly*, Bassett took the opportunity to encourage moderation and reason in race discussion and entitled his essay "Stirring Up the Fires of Race Antipathy." It was baseless optimism, he wrote, to assume that all blacks were or could be Booker T. Washingtons. "Now Washington is a great and good man," he wrote, "a Christian statesman, and take him all in all the greatest man, save General Lee, born in the South in a hundred years; but he is not a typical negro. He does not even represent the better class of negroes. He is an exceptional man. . . ."

Bassett's moderate voice was immediately drowned, however, in the outcry against his comparison of a black man with the sainted Lee. The outburst of press criticism would be astonishing but for the similar noise over the White House dinner two years earlier. Trinity College, already tainted by money from the hated tobacco trust, had now joined hands with blackness. Did Bassett turn toward Tuskegee to pray, asked a local editor, who began to spell the professor's name "bASSett." The more Bassett tried to explain, the more he stirred the fires of race antipathy, and he finally offered to resign. As the trustees considered his letter, Walter Hines Page wrote from New York to James B. Duke himself urging a rebuke to demagogues and a blow for free thought by refusing to accept the resignation. Duke apparently then said privately that Bassett was a fool and should not have been hired, but "must not be lynched." The trustees followed his lead and announced, "Candor impels us to admit our regret that Professor Bassett has expressed certain opinions"; but they unanimously declined the resignation. Bassett stayed on for three years before heading north to a distinguished scholarly career.[66]

Washington persistently sought "constructive" cooperation with southern liberals as they appeared, but they too were isolated, "exceptional men," and became pariahs in the South as fast as they revealed themselves. One of the more interesting of these liberal fish to swim into Washington's net was the Reverend Quincy Ewing of Greenville, Mississippi. Ewing's first heresy was a religious one. While in Greenville in 1903, he performed the marriage ceremony of a fellow Episcopal priest while the man's divorced wife still lived. Ewing's own congregation tolerated this, but when he was invited to a rectorship in Birmingham the Bishop of Alabama at first refused to accept him, though he finally relented.[67]

Ewing in 1905 prepared a book manuscript on "The Criminality of the Negro," and Washington tried unsuccessfully to induce several northern friends in the book trade to publish it. Walter Hines Page, whose firm had published *The Clansman* and other racist novels of Thomas Dixon, Jr., rejected Ewing's manuscript but offered to take an article for *The World's Work*. Houghton, Mifflin, where Francis Garrison worked, decided the book would not sell, and Washington also failed to interest Macmillan and S. S. McClure. Garrison summarized the main propositions of the manuscript: "that the negro is not only not more criminal than the white, but less so, all things considered; that the country is deluded and deceived by the false and misleading statistics, and the wholesale asseverations constantly thrust upon the country by the Southern malignants; that there is a deliberate and systematic attempt made to decry the colored people of the South and to keep them under heel; and that equal justice is not meted out to them in the courts."[68] Washington was intensely interested in finding a publisher because of the uniqueness and ring of truth of these propositions, which, coming from a southerner of standing, would at least attract attention. Ewing was willing to risk the probable loss of his position in a large-city church in order to do what he conceived to be his duty to write the truth. Garrison wished Ewing well, but he did not run his publishing firm, he only worked there.

Washington hated, except as a last resort, to have the salient points of Ewing's manuscript compressed to article length without all the supporting data. "I think the object of it would be largely lost," he wrote Garrison. "In the first place, the *World's Work* circulates very little in the South and is very little known among the Southern people. In the second place, it would take perhaps five or six months for the South and the country generally to get interested in the statement that the manuscript contains." By that time the magazine issue would be out of circulation.[69] Garrison suggested that Washington rather than he send it to other publishers he named, so they would "not get the impression that the book had been hunting around for a publisher, and been declined by other houses."[70]

Washington wrote enthusiastically to McClure, Phillips, and Company, but it turned out that Ewing had already sent his manuscript there and been rejected.[71] As a consolation, Washington invited Ewing in 1906 to give the Tuskegee commencement sermon. Ewing gratefully declined. "Nothing would give me more genuine pleasure than to preach your Commencement sermon," he wrote, "but I am far from certain that it would be well for me to do so, regarding the matter from *the standpoint of Tuskegee's welfare*. It is probable that, within

a few months, I shall be vigorously condemned in certain quarters for
my attitude toward the Negroes of the South, and I am not willing
that Tuskegee should be put in the position of honoring a Southern
white man who may be at the time of its Commencement under considerable fire as a 'traitor to the traditions of his race, a slanderer of
the Southern people, etc., etc.' I am sure you will see my point and
fully appreciate its importance." He suggested that Washington pick
a white man friendly to blacks but not conspicuously their champion.[72]

Washington had the Committee of Twelve for the Advancement of
the Negro Race consider publishing Ewing's entire manuscript in a
cheap binding, but they concluded that "the circulation would fall flat
unless some reliable and well known firm of publishers, or magazine,
would first publish the article."[73] Ewing never published his book, but
he published dissenting articles and letters to the editor that alienated
both congregation and hierarchy of his church, and led to his exile in
a small parish at Napoleonville, Louisiana. In 1914 Washington wrote
him there to thank him warmly for his published criticism of the white
supremacy leader James K. Vardaman. "It is all the more deplorable
that a man of the type of Vardaman should be misrepresenting the
South," wrote the Tuskegee optimist, "when in my opinion there is a
very friendly feeling existing between the white and colored people
of the South." It is doubtful that Ewing was as sanguine as Washington after his experiences, but he shared his contempt for Vardaman,
who he was sure knew better than what he said, and thought "the
great work of Tuskegee under your leadership makes the Vardamans
of to-day ridiculous."[74]

Washington believed other mildly liberal utterances to be heralds of
a new dawn in the South. In 1904 U. S. District Judge Emory Speer
of Georgia rendered a decision critical of the chain gang system that
used conviction for crime as a means of providing forced and unpaid
labor, mostly of blacks. This was the same man who had proclaimed
at the Atlanta Exposition in 1895 that there was no race problem, but
Washington distributed his judicial opinion to a number of newspapers.[75] Similarly, Washington raised more than $1000 in New York
for the white Law and Order Clubs that ex-Governor William J. Northen of Georgia organized after the Atlanta Riot in 1906.[76]

The Reverend John E. White of the Atlanta Baptist Tabernacle was
another straw in the southern wind that Washington briefly clutched.

In his apprenticeship days in North Carolina White had been one of those sectarian leaders who had hated the state university so much that they joined the Democratic white supremacy campaign of 1898 after promises that the university would be curtailed.[77] In Atlanta, however, he worked as early as 1904 to bring about closer relations between the white and black Baptist conventions.[78] He led in church efforts after the Atlanta Riot to heal the wounds and build better race relations through more frequent joint meetings. At the Conference for Education in the South in 1907 he announced a plan to persuade southern governors to appoint delegates to a southern commission on the race problem. Finding no support from the governors, he turned to the college presidents. President Edwin A. Alderman of the University of Virginia tried to divert the proposal into a southern version of the National Civic Federation, but White had meanwhile written some eighty southern college presidents, most of whom replied favorably. They formed the University Commission on Southern Race Questions in 1912.[79] Washington followed White's efforts closely, though he took no direct part, and he invited White repeatedly to give addresses and sermons at Tuskegee Institute as a means of keeping in touch. In 1915 White went about as far as he could go in addressing the National Negro Business League on what was described as "the encouraging side of Negro life in the South" and "the fact that the New South has decided to encourage the Negro People who are in their midst."[80]

Washington was always hungry for evidence that the Faustian bargain he had made for black leadership and regional influence was worth the cost. It would be an exaggeration to say that he was ready to see liberalism in any white southerner who did not wear a sheet, but he found accommodation under the roofs of Tuskegee for the benevolent paternalists as well as the dissenters. There was the earnest Reverend Benjamin Franklin Riley, a former professor and college president who met Washington on tour in Texas, where Riley was head of the state Anti-Saloon League. He soon afterward moved to Birmingham, where he asked Washington for advice on a book in progress that would call for a federal anti-lynching law and would answer the racial extremists.[81] When the product of Riley's labors appeared in 1910, it must have been a disappointment even to the thick-skinned Washington. Though a Negrophile in his fashion, Riley without a trace of irony called his book *The White Man's Burden* and portrayed blacks as children needing the kindly guidance of whites: "Where others would resist, he tamely submits, and where others would cherish malice and hatred, he returns a quiet good humor."[82] Yet, on Washington's invitation, Riley gave two addresses at Tuskegee and shared the platform with Washington at a New York City meeting in behalf of Tuskegee.[83] Washington also found passages he could approve in Riley's book. "What you say about the Negro in the South is the more impressive and important because it comes from a man who was born and raised in the South," Washington wrote; "one who knows the ties that bind the two races together; who sees the difficulties and the opportunities in the situation, and has the courage to say frankly and positively, what thousands of other white men know, but have been held back from saying heretofore. . . ."[84]

Washington's continuing friendship with Riley was not an alliance with southern dissent. It was instead a bizarre but genuine mutual admiration between a black and a white accommodator, for Riley could be called a southern dissenter only by comparison with outright Negrophobes. Washington encouraged Riley to write another book, to be entitled "The Real Situation in the South," to discuss such white wrongs as convict lease, peonage and other economic oppression, and the denial of civil rights, but also to present his belief that blacks were "disintegrating" through tuberculosis and venereal disease. Above all, however, Riley said in all earnestness that he would treat the subject of the Negro as a man. "Made in the image of God, and a sharer in redemption, he needs to be presented in this way, not by argumentation, but by direct assumption."[85] Once committed to "the presentation of the claims of humanity," Riley took his theme to lecture audiences all over the South. One type of reaction, however, puzzled him. "Some Negroes and others are distrustful of me," he wrote Washington, "and of my motives, most naturally, and I should be glad to show what you think of it. Please have it on your letter head." Washington replied that "there is no man in the South today who is inspired by a more sincere desire to be of help than yourself."[86] Soon after Washington's death Riley published a laudatory biography.

Willis D. Weatherford, southern-born secretary of the Young Men's Christian Association based in Nashville, more sophisticated than Riley, closer to the seams of southern society, also wrote a well-meaning but patronizing book, *Present Forces in Negro Progress* (1912). Weatherford catalogued as black racial traits such cultural features or southern social myths as fidelity, gratitude, kindliness, sense of humor, and special aptitude for music and religion. He minimized, on the other hand, black intelligence, self-mastery, industry and thrift.[87] The point, apparently, was to allay white fears by portrayal of the black as harmless and designed by nature's artfulness for subservience. Washington's only direct contribution to the book was information on eight Tuskegee graduates who had promoted agricultural progress as farm demonstration agents.[88]

Weatherford's racial views changed considerably in later decades.[89] The level of his racial thought about 1912, however, is suggested by his correspondence with Washington that year concerning a YMCA summer camp near Black Mountain, North Carolina. Weatherford planned a series of religious conferences there attracting white college men and women from all over the South. "Knowing that many of your girls have to work during the summer in order that they may put themselves through the winter," Weatherford wrote, "I thought that we might be able to use a number as waitresses and chambermaids in these buildings. I am very anxious to have a group of very high grade, industrially trained negro girls for two reasons. First, they will enable some two thousand of the most open-minded and best trained white people in the South to come into contact with the high grade of work which these girls, who have had genuine training, do." Also, it woud be "a great blessing to these girls to find how open-minded a group of college men and women can be and are. This would help on the other side in giving confidence to your girls in the best type of Southern white man." He proposed slightly higher than regular local wages.[90] Washington agreed to send fifteen or twenty students, but on the edge of summer Weatherford decided that, as he had not been able to secure a single other schoolgirl, it would be "impossible to use your girls."[91]

Even the most sympathetic white southerners believed in a hierarchical biracialism, a social structure that not only fitted the status quo but had the stamp of approval of current social science, and these men found in Washington's pragmatic accommodation and faith in evolutionary progress the only practical solution available to otherwise insoluble problems of equity in such a structure. Washington himself was inclined to find good in any white who did not actively attack blacks or betray hostility. Pressed by a New York journalist in 1907 to name some liberal southerners who could give the public some fresh and helpful words, Washington mentioned White, Northen, Bassett, and Ewing. He added two Tuskegee trustees, Belton Gilreath and R. O. Simpson; Harry Stilwell Edwards, who was actually a lily white Republican; and "a Mr. Percy," whose first name he could not recall.[92] At a later date he would probably have added the names of Weatherford and Riley, and Charles L. Coon, who had exposed the dishonesty of southern school appropriations and even considered joining the National Association for the Advancement of Colored People until Washington talked him out of it.[93]

Also on Washington's list in 1907 was a man he later denounced as a hostile witness in the black man's equity case. This was Alfred H. Stone of Dunleith, Mississippi, a planter and gentleman-scholar who managed a family estate crowded with black sharecroppers and who studied sociology and economics. The acquaintance began in 1903 when the Washington *Post* reported Stone as saying that men like Washington and Du Bois denied the significance of their white admixture "although in their heart of hearts they know and believe that the white strain does tell," and Stone wrote to deny that he had said it.[94] Washington believed Stone for a while and good-naturedly argued with him about his view that black tenants migrated frequently because of "lack of stability."[95] Stone had seemed so reasonable and open to suggestion in his letters that his articles and his book, *Studies in the American Race Problem* (1908), gave Washington a feeling of betrayal. Hearing that the Carnegie Institution had voted to subsidize Stone's research, Washington wrote Carroll D. Wright, director of economics and sociology at the institution, to protest. He had read most of Stone's work, said Washington, "and I think I am safe in saying that without exception there has been one conclusion to his investigations, and that is in plain words, to damn the Negro." He was "not the man to make such an investigation."[96] But Wright replied that Stone was working on the influence of the Negro on the economic development of the South, not on the Negro as such, that he had been carefully chosen, and that W. E. B. Du Bois and R. R. Wright, Jr., as his assistants, would guard against any bias.[97] For once, however, Du Bois agreed completely with Washington. He wrote Stone objecting to all of his writings as unfair to blacks.[98] Washington also wrote Stone urging him to reconsider his earlier conclusions that black education, and blacks as a race, had failed. He should visit Tuskegee and see for himself evidence of progress.[99] Stone brushed off this criticism as misunderstanding,[100] but when Stone's book appeared even the ambiguous secretary of the Southern Education Board, Edgar Gardner Murphy, thought "the sort of work he is doing is a real calamity."[101] Washington publicly ignored it, but he and Scott privately furnished some ammunition for a hostile reviewer.[102]

At the same time that Washington sought a modus vivendi with "the better class" of white southerners he groped by trial and error toward an understanding and fellow feeling with a special class of southerners, the Jews, who lived in considerable numbers in the cities and small towns of the South. Washington's discovery of Jews began in the 1890s with a faux pas, when in a national magazine he told the success story of a Jewish peddler and said "the blackest Negro in the United States" could succeed in business pure and simple the same as "a Jew or a white man."[103] Rabbi Isaac M. Wise retorted in the *American Israelite* that to distinguish between a Jew and a Caucasian was "a scientific blunder" and that Washington was "only exhibiting the secret malice that invariably marks a servile nature seeking to assume a feeling of equality with something higher, which it does not possess."[104] Washington also habitually sprinkled in his speeches mention of Jewish country storekeepers as oppressive usurers until a white adviser warned him. "I would leave out the Jew as distinct from others in cheating the people," wrote the Reverend R. C. Bedford. "He may have started it but others were quick and eager learners. I have always admired your addresses because of their freedom from any personal or race attack. This little tradition about the Jew I notice once in a while creeps in."[105]

Washington not only abandoned the rhetoric of anti-Semitism but generally excluded Jews from his anti-immigrant bias and found in their history of persecution and cultural nationalism a kinship with the black experience. He welcomed not only the philanthropists of the North but the Jews around him in the South. Washington and other Tuskegee faculty voted for a local Jewish man for sheriff.[106] He took a sympathetic interest in the victims of the Russian pogroms.[107] Rabbi Alfred G. Moses of Mobile, fascinated by a speech Washington delivered there, gave him works on Jewish history and put him in touch with his brother in New York.[108] Louis Edelman, a physician in Huntsville, treated Tuskegee students without charge for eye, ear, and nose ailments and lectured an audience of 1000 in the Tuskegee chapel on "The Jew: His Persecutions and Achievements."[109] Thus over the years gradually evolved a Jewish commitment, until Washington wrote in 1911 that "the majority of white people who come here for commencement are composed of Jews."[110] A good many of these were local merchants who did business with the institute. Two such merchants were Selig Gassenheimer and Charles F. Moritz of Montgomery, who gave small prizes to distinguished graduating students, and Gassenheimer also gave the money for a small building.[111]

Washington's own knowledge of what it meant to be a Jew broadened and deepened, particularly after he visited the East Side settlement houses of New York and the Jewish quarters of Warsaw and Cracow, but there were limits both intellectual and practical. Many important complexities of Jewish life and thought escaped his attention. And he was always the pragmatist in coping with southern society. He ordered the Tuskegee business office to buy supplies for the school whenever possible from Gentiles. "In looking over our bills from Montgomery," he wrote, "I very much fear that we are getting our trade too much centered in the hands of a few Jews. Wherever we can get equally fair treatment in prices and quality of goods from persons other than Jews, I prefer to have our trade scattered among them. In creating public sentiment in favor of the institution the Jews cannot be of much service." That this was Washington's judgment about southern power realities rather than anti-Semitism, however, is suggested by the exception he made. "Where all things are equal with our giving trade to Jews," he wrote the business agent, "I hope you will bear in mind Mr. J. Loeb. Quite a number of years ago when other wholesale merchants refused absolutely to deal with us and were threatened by boycott by the town merchants in case they did deal with us, Loeb paid no attention to our want of money and threatened boycott in town and stood by us and sold goods at wholesale prices. Of course, after he was brave enough to stem the tide for several months, others fell in line, but we owe him a great deal for helping us out in this way in our earlier days."[112]

In his ceaseless efforts to forge the solidarity of black followers, to find fresh allies for the black minority among the white majority, and to commit them to his program of inching along toward racial justice, Washington had in public speaking a more powerful weapon than in correspondence or one-to-one encounters. When he talked with a southern white man, he had to spend most of his time listening, and a large part of the remainder agreeing. When he wrote a letter he had to be on guard against misinterpretation. Somehow, an audience brought out his latent powers of persuasion. It was not that, all in all, his speeches were more challenging, but on the platform he lost a little of his formalism and dignity, scored points by humorous anecdote and inverted metaphor, played one part of his audience against another like a choir director, and evoked in each segment of his audience in turn the emotions of pride, hope, nostalgia, amusement, and mutual esteem. As a lay preacher he left his audiences feeling better than when he began, but the salvation he preached was of this earth.

Public speaking was the chief form of public entertainment in Washington's day, and he almost always put on a good show. Nearly all Americans, black and white, and certainly most southerners, wanted to see the famous Booker T. Washington at least once; and, having been entertained, many came back again. News that Washington was to speak could gather a crowd even at a crossroads hamlet, and his speeches at the largest halls of large cities drew packed houses with thousands milling outside waiting for him to come out and make a second speech to them. After some bad experiences with lecture bureaus in the 1890s, his speeches were generally open to the public without charge, except in a few cases of banquets, lodge gatherings, and other special invitations.

There was always an element of personal risk where aisles were packed and crowds pressed upon the doors. Washington had a vivid experience of just how dangerous this could be when he spoke at the black Shiloh Baptist Church in Birmingham in 1902. "Imagine, if you can," wrote an observer, "three thousand people jammed as closely as sardines in a box, all in the church; then three thousand on the outside packed just as densely, with only a passage way between these two assemblies 16 feet wide, and that being a stairway. . . . Now imagine this stairway, between the two brick walls of the building already packed until there was no more standing room. This stairway was the death trap." Washington had just finished addressing the National Baptist Convention there when two men began struggling over a vacant seat on the edge of the stage. A woman in the choir yelled "fight," but the crowd thought she had said "fire" and started a stampede through the only door into the stairway. Few if any who had been in the church were killed, but those who were on the stairway could not retreat against the unyielding crowd on the outside and became a human pavement for those in the house to walk out on. About a hundred persons lost their lives. In an interview afterward, Washington said, "[O]ne good sister whose name I did not learn, caught me firmly by the waist and held me throughout the excitement, saying 'Keep still.' "[113]

Washington was in no way responsible for the Birmingham disaster, however, and it was the only one of its kind. He found in public speaking not only a means of persuasion but a way to keep in personal touch with the local sponsors of his appearances, winning new friends and more tightly binding others to the Tuskegee Machine. Beginning in 1905 he began systematic speaking tours of one after another of the southern states, traveling with an entourage of black friends by train and speaking before mixed audiences in the various cities and towns along the route. Emmett Scott planned the itinerary of these state tours in correspondence with local members of the National Negro Business League, college presidents, ministers, and other local black bigwigs. The local sponsors usually found a mayor, judge, or other white dignitary to sit on the platform and say a few words, usually the most unpredictable part of the program. To meet his expenses and those of his entourage, Washington used the nominal salary the Southern Education Board paid him—so frustratingly without duties—and the railroads often gave special rates and schedules for the excursion train.

To describe one of these state tours is to describe them all. They were triumphal marches. The first was through Arkansas and the Oklahoma and Indian Territories in 1905. Washington took two Pinkerton detectives with him for safety, but they were unnecessary. At Little Rock he had the unique experience of "the colored people refusing seats, for the want of room, to white people," and wrote to Robert C. Ogden his impression "that the demagogue, like Jeff Davis and the radical press are fast losing their hold upon a certain class of the Southern white people."[114] In 1908, once again with Pinkerton detectives, he toured Mississippi under sponsorship of Charles Banks and the Mississippi State Negro Business League to challenge indirectly that state's leading racial demagogue, James K. Vardaman. Vardaman urged whites not to attend Washington's speeches, but they attended by the hundreds in Jackson and Vicksburg, with better results "than I even dared dream of," Washington wrote his white friend James H. Dillard, and a black sponsor wrote that the Southern Methodist Bishop James B. Galloway was "walking the streets denouncing Vardaman and openly pronouncing Dr. Washington the greatest living American."[115] Nevertheless, a Mississippi country newspaper called Washington "this saddle-colored accident of an evening's intemperance," and white ruffians hanged two blacks returning from a Washington speech along the side of the railroad in hope that Washington would see them as his train passed.[116]

The Mississippi tour was the model for three similar tours in 1909, stopping throughout South Carolina in the spring, throughout Virginia and West Virginia on the newly completed Virginian Railroad in the summer, and throughout Tennessee from Bristol to Memphis in the fall. Robert R. Moton became a standard member of the entourage. He led the singing of "the old plantation songs" as blacks "came by the thousands at the various railroad stations where we stopped and sang the songs under his leadership," Washington wrote. "It was a weird and interesting sight to see and hear them sing these songs often late in the night."[117] The tour over the Virginian Railroad in 1909 was a special case because of the promise Washington had made Henry H. Rogers before his death. Washington usually asked some member of his touring party to recount the tour in a magazine article. This time, however, he himself wrote the article, and to his great surprise Walter Hines Page turned it down for the *World's Work*. "I wonder if you know really how little you tell in that article," Page wrote. The public, he said, would regard it as simply "a puff of Mr. Rogers's road" because Washington had neglected to write about "the colored people and their problems & their progress."[118] This was a mistake Washington did not repeat.

Washington took only two days to speak in five cities in Delaware, but his usual state tour was a week to ten days. He spent a week covering North Carolina with an "all-star" aggregation of black notables in the fall of 1910. There Washington discovered the booming black business community of Durham. He even braved Wilmington, where twelve years earlier a race riot had climaxed the disfranchisement movement and caused the death of many blacks. Three thousand people, however, welcomed him at the railroad station, and the white owners of the Academy of Music threw its doors open to blacks, dividing the hall equally between the races, even the standing room being separate but equal. Washington's speeches managed to please both George Rountree, a leader of the white mob in the 1898 riot, and

Charles L. Coon, the liberal school man of Wilson, who said "the best white people in town have told me that your address was the very best ever made here."[119]

In 1911 Washington toured Texas, after elaborate preparations to protect him in that state famous for its violence, and Emmett Scott had the honor to introduce his chief to his former home town of Houston.[120] In 1912 Washington toured Florida. He spoke through Tidewater Virginia under Hampton Institute auspices in 1913, and he toured Louisiana in the spring of 1915. His health by then was failing, but the packed houses and the roar of the crowds seemed to rouse him to his usual vigor. Scott had insisted in the preparations for this tour that a rostrum be available for Washington to lean upon if he chose, but Washington was not much of a leaner.[121] About the only southern states where Washington did not organize statewide tours were the neighboring state of Georgia and his home state of Alabama, presumably because he spoke so often there that a special tour was unnecessary.

Throughout the two decades that followed the Atlanta Compromise of 1895 white southerners showed in word and deed their determination not only to subordinate but to humiliate their black neighbors. White solidarity in support of white supremacy increased in the South and spread in the North. Washington pragmatically adjusted his policies, utterances, and private actions to these circumstances. He put more stress on black long-range goals and the building of inner strength through self-improvement and sustaining black institutions, and correspondingly less stress on the good relationship with white neighbors that had been at the forefront of his Atlanta speech. He recognized that his early allies among southern conservatives and northern philanthropists of the Ogden type had been ineffective in restraining extreme white racism. While he avoided alienating these groups, he sought new allies among the more liberal southerners. The more Washington changed, however, the more he was the same, looking for the silver lining, taking advantage of disadvantages, finding examples of the golden rule, taking hope from one less lynching than the previous year.

CHAPTER 11

Provincial Man of the World

There are not a few Negroes who sometimes become discouraged and feel that their condition and prospects are worse than those of any other group of human beings. I wanted to see groups of people who are much worse off than the Negro, and, through detailing their condition, place such facts before the Negro in America as would make him feel and see that, instead of being the worst off, his condition and prospects are much better than those of millions of people who are in the same relative stage of civilization.*

BTW, 1912

BOOKER T. Washington's outlook throughout his life remained that of a provincial southern American, though he traveled widely and had a worldwide following. As his writings were translated into many foreign languages, he became the most famous black man in the world, and his fame drew foreigners to him like a magnet. All manner of men, American missionaries, European colonialists, African nationalists, Buddhist reformers, and Japanese modernizers sought to enlist his aid. On the one hand were whites who sought his aid in introducing plantation agriculture into colonial areas. On the other hand Africans and Asians hoped to find in Tuskegee industrial education and Washington's philosophy of self-help a source of strength to resist the political and cultural imperialism of the Europeans.

* From *The Man Farthest Down*.

Washington sought to accommodate all of these contradictory propositions, but he drew the line against back-to-Africa movements, took no part in the worldwide race conferences of his day, and never went to Africa, Asia, or the West Indies, though he found time for three trips to Europe. Washington was like the "cosmopolite" in O. Henry's story, who proclaimed himself a citizen of the world until someone criticized his home town.

Washington's substantial involvement in African affairs required little readjustment of his outlook, for the black role in American society was roughly analogous to that of black peoples in the African colonies. American blacks were a minority and the Africans a majority, but both were politically disfranchised, socially subordinated, and economically exploited. Both engaged in production of raw material by plantation agriculture or extractive industries. In African colonies as in America, Washington cooperated openly with white authorities and business promoters, while he sought through industrial education to encourage black self-reliance and the work-ethic, and privately gave encouragement to black nationalist movements, particularly in his effort to help independent Liberia survive in a colonialized continent through an American protectorate. As the years passed and Washington had many contacts with African students at Tuskegee and with African teachers, missionaries, and nationalist intellectuals, he gradually abandoned the white stereotypes of the benighted African, but his own experience in African affairs simply illuminated his essential conservatism, showing him as in a tailor's mirror, from new angles but in the usual stance.

Washington's first venture in Africa began on the first day of the twentieth century when a Hamburg freighter put ashore in the German colony of Togo three Tusekegee graduates and a faculty member, along with their educational equipment—plows, wagons, a steam cotton gin, and a cotton press. Their task was to interbreed local and American cotton to develop a hardy and commercially successful staple crop, and to train the local Africans in cotton culture. This enterprise was the outcome of a partnership Washington entered into with the *Kolonial-Wirtschaftliches Komitee* (Colonial Economic Committee), a private organization holding a concession from the German government to accelerate the economic growth of its colonies. If the Tuskegee cotton-growing experiment worked in Togo they planned to extend it also to Morocco and German East Africa.[1] The preceding fall, through arrangement with the German ambassador and the U. S. Secretary of Agriculture, a team of KWK experts visited Tuskegee, contracted with the graduating students, and raised the question whether the young men would find "the necessary authority towards the native population and . . . at the same time the necessary respect towards the German government official[s]." Washington reassured Baron Herman of the Komitee: "I do not think in any case that there will be much if any difficulty in the men who go from here treating the German officials with proper respect. They are all kindly disposed, respectful gentlemen. I believe at the same time they will secure the respect and confidence of the natives."[2] To make certain, however, James Nathan Calloway, a Fisk graduate and Tuskegee faculty member, accompanied the young men for the first year.

Togo had no real harbor, and the party of Tuskegeans stood on the beach with their pile of equipment, forty miles from their destination, without a beast of burden within 100 miles. The Africans who met them refused to draw the wagons over the rough roads, but offered to bear the wagons on their heads. This proved impracticable, and the Americans finally loaded only the most important items on 100 bearers and traveled inland for four days. Reaching their destination, they set up the Missahöhe experiment station. The draft animals they secured died of the tsetse fly, and locusts and drought plagued them. For lack of draft animals, they hitched four Africans to each plow and thirty-six Africans to the sweeps that turned the ginning machinery. In the first year they managed to grow, process, and ship to Germany a small cotton crop of twenty-five bales.[3]

Nine Tuskegeans in all went to Togo between 1901 and 1909. Four of them died. After 1903 only John W. Robinson, of the class of 1897, the hardiest and most talented, remained in Togo. He not only grew cotton with moderate success but established an agricultural school with some 200 African pupils. He died in 1909 while crossing a swift river on a move to a new experiment station and school farther inland.[4]

Throughout the German administration until World War I, cotton production climbed steadily but presented the German importers with problems because of its varying staple length. Washington gave German colonialism a sweeping endorsement while passing through Berlin in 1910. "I have followed with great care the policies and the plans according to which the German officials have dealt with the natives of

Africa," he said. "They do not seek to repress the Africans, but rather to help them that they may be more useful to themselves and to the German people. Their manner of handling Negroes in Africa might be taken as a pattern for other nations."[5] Actually, German colonial administration had been so arbitrary, exploitative, and disruptive of tribal traditions that the Africans had refused to cooperate. The German parliament instituted some reforms in 1907, but Togo administration was never "wholesome and constructive," as Washington described it without, of course, having visited the colony. As frequently in America, Washington construed white men's actions more favorably than they deserved.[6]

Tuskegee was the logical place for colonial developers of cotton culture to turn for expertise, and some Tuskegee graduates worked for British promoters in Nigeria and others in Belgian Congo. One of the pioneer developers of the cotton region of the Anglo-Egyptian Sudan was the American capitalist Leigh Hunt, who came to Tuskegee and picked three graduating seniors—a carpenter, an agriculturist, and a blacksmith—to organize a plantation in the Sudan and prepare the way for a larger colony of American blacks. He decided that they were "best adapted to assist in this pioneer work—to serve as model farmers, to train the natives and teach them how to make the best use of these lands."[7] Before the three young men left for Zeidab, on the banks of the Nile, Washington warned them that "a great many persons going to a warm climate, go to ruin from a moral standpoint." He hoped that they would not yield to the temptation, which would "do yourself, the school and the race the greatest injustice; but I feel sure you are going to stand up and be men."[8] The Tuskegeans proved to be effective workers, but Hunt soon pulled out of the syndicate that developed the Gezira irrigated cotton plantations and the Tuskegeans returned home.[9]

Washington's cooperation with colonialism extended also to southern Africa. When the British journalist W. T. Stead relayed to Washington a request that he tour Rhodesia and report to the British South Africa Company on the best methods to "raise, educate, and civilize the black man," Washington seriously considered it but decided he could not justify an extended absence from his institution or his leadership of American blacks. On the other hand, when the British were establishing the Union of South Africa following the Boer War, the commissioner of education in 1904 asked Washington a series of questions on the type of education the Africans needed. Washington's reply assumed that there was "no very great difference between the native problem there and the Negro problem in America." He proposed the same ambivalent formula of accommodationism and incentives to black self-help that characterized his racial philosophy in America. The government rather than missionaries should educate the blacks, he wrote, so that they would "be taught to love and revere that government better than any other institution." They should be taught English so as to provide them with a common language and an entrance into Western culture. Furthermore, they should have industrial training that would "fit them to go out into this rich country and be skilled laborers in agriculture, mining and the trades." Educated Africans should be accorded civil equality with Europeans, and tribal government "should gradually be replaced by an allegiance directly to the government of the land." Washington was thus seemingly on the side of the modernizers and the white elite. "Experience shows," he ended, "that the black, as other men, work better and more profitably when induced to this labor by reward and it is voluntarily performed. If proper inducements are offered these people they will labor more and more as their wants are increased by education."[10] The South African government took little heed of these suggestions, however, and Washington's attitude and impact on Africa was more ambivalent than these words of advice suggest. As in the United States, another thrust of his teachings was toward African independence through acquiring the immediately practical skills of survival, and toward keeping people "down on the farm" in an urbanizing, industrializing world.

Washington found a more congenial role in defending mistreated Africans in the Belgian King Leopold's Congo Free State. When the exposure of forced labor and police brutality in this supposedly model colony produced a worldwide scandal, Washington joined in efforts of the American wing of the Congo reformers by using his influence in Washington. He called personally on President Roosevelt and on members of the Senate foreign relations committee to urge American diplomatic pressure on the Belgian government. He took with him to the White House a protest committee of the National Baptist Convention which he had stirred into action. In 1904 the article "Cruelty in the Congo Country" appeared in *Outlook* under his name, though it was actually the first ghostwriting assignment Washington gave Rob-

Booker T. Washington and his children: Ernest Davidson Washington (standing left), Booker T. Washington, Jr., and adopted daughter, Laura Murray Washington. *Photograph by Frances Benjamin Johnston. Reproduced from the collections of the Library of Congress*

Margaret M. Washington, 1906. *Photograph by Frances Benjamin Johnston. Reproduced from the collections of the Library of Congress*

Dignitaries on reviewing stand during Tuskegee 25th anniversary celebration, 1906. Front row from left: (1st) Charles C. Thach; (3rd) Charles W. Eliot; (4th) William J. Schieffelin; (5th) Hollis B. Frissell; (6th) Isaac N. Seligman; (7th) Lyman Abbott; (8th) Wallace Buttrick; (9th) Robert C. Ogden; (10th) Andrew Carnegie. The tall man in back between Seligman and Abbott is J. G. Phelps Stokes. *Reproduced from the collection of the Library of Congress*

Cartoon showing Washington's success in tapping the wealth of Andrew Carnegie. Boston *Record*, April 25, 1903

Students stacking bricks at Tuskegee Institute, 1902. *Photograph by Frances Benjamin Johnston. From the Frances Benjamin Johnston Collection in the Library of Congress*

Music class at Tuskegee, 1906. *Photograph by Frances Benjamin Johnston. Reproduced from the collections of the Library of Congress*

Tuskegee class studying dairy products, 1906. *Photograph by Frances Benjamin Johnston. Reproduced from the collections of the Library of Congress*

George Washington Carver, 1906. *Photograph by Frances Benjamin Johnston. Reproduced from the collections of the Library of Congress*

Washington (seated) and his private secretary, Emmett Jay Scott (Tuskegee), 1906. *Photograph by Frances Benjamin Johnston (Booker T. Washington Papers, University of Maryland). Reproduced from the collections of the Library of Congress*

"BLAME THAT KNIFE ANYWAY! THAT MAKES TWICE I'VE CUT MYSELF!"

A cartoon depicting Theodore Roosevelt as inept in handling the "Negro Question," and thus alienating both southern whites and blacks. Denver *Post*, December 1, 1906

CLAIMS HE DIDN'T DESERVE BATTERING

A SOUTHERN CHUCKLE OVER A NORTHERN EVENT

A cartoon on the Ulrich incident, Anaconda *Standard*, March 22, 1911

BTW, with bandaged head, after being assaulted in New York City. Dayton *Herald*, March 23, 1911

Washington in Jacksonville, Florida, 1912

On tour in Louisiana, April 1915.
Photograph by A. P. Bedou

ert E. Park, the young sociologist who was then secretary of the Congo Reform Association. One of King Leopold's corrupt lobbyists offered Washington a free trip to Belgium to speak at a Congress on Economic Expansion, but Park warned him that "the King of Belgium hopes to win you over to his theory of dealing with the Blackman. It is part of his cynical view of things in general that everyone can be purchased with money or flattery." Park also remarked, "The difference between our colonial system and others consists in the fact that we are preparing the peoples we govern for citizenship, either in the United States or as independent states; other countries are interested only in the *economic development* (a vague term, which may be interpreted in many ways) of their possessions." Whether Washington believed in this distinction or not, he spurned all the temptations of Leopold's lobby, and he joined Mark Twain in a series of meetings for Congo reform.[11]

It was in Liberia, however, that Washington came closest to real influence in shaping African history. Liberia in 1908 was experiencing one of its many crises as a small independent state, and British and French colonial neighbors threatened territorial encroachments and creditors in both countries and Germany threatened forcible collection of Liberia's debts. A Liberian delegation sought out Washington, who escorted them to meetings with President Roosevelt, President-elect Taft, and members of the State Department, and then carried them to Tuskegee for a three-day private conference. While Washington threaded his way through potentially conflicting loyalties to his own government and to the African republic, President Roosevelt told Emmett Scott he hoped to settle the question "on the broad ground of the square deal to the Liberian Republic."[12] Since nobody in the American government had reliable knowledge about Liberia, Roosevelt decided to send a three-man commission to study conditions and recommend action. Roosevelt asked Washington to serve on the commission, but after much consideration he decided to stay at home to run his institution and advise incoming President Taft. Emmett Scott went in his stead. The other two commissioners were Roland P. Falkner, a former superintendent of education in Puerto Rico, and George Sale, a supervisor of Baptist missions in Puerto Rico and Cuba. Washington played some part in their selection.

The commissioners recommended and the administration and Congress approved what amounted to an American protectorate over Lib-

eria, including an all-American bankers' loan to refund the entire foreign debt of Liberia and thus free it of financial dependence on any
foreign power except the United States, and demanded in return an
American commissioner of customs and U. S. officers to command
and retrain the Liberian army that policed its borders and controlled
the tribal population of the interior. Washington threw the influence
of the Tuskegee Machine behind these arrangements to protect Liberia from foreign encroachments.

Washington saw three other essentials for a stable and progressive
future of Liberia, however, and worked for them as well. He wrote
President Daniel Howard of Liberia that "the whole future of Liberia
hinges upon its ability to get hold of the native population," for the
tribal Liberians had very real grievances against the minority of
Americo-Liberians, descendants of deported American slaves, who ran
the government and controlled the economy.[13] Another need was
economic development, not merely paying off old debts but capital
investment in goods for export. He tried to interest the banker Paul
M. Warburg, among others, in capital investment, and tried to induce
his black friend John S. Durham, who had managed a Cuban sugar
plantation, to consider a proposal for large-scale sugar planting in
Liberia. He wrote a Liberian editor in terms reminiscent of Henry
Grady's preachment of a New South, "Every time a Liberian eats a tin
of canned goods imported from any other country, it means poverty
for the Liberians; it means that the Liberians are paying somebody
else to manufacture the tin cans, and paying the freight upon the
cans, and all this of course means money taken out of Liberia."[14]
Washington saw also a third long-range need of Liberia, education,
and took some preliminary steps to deal with it. In 1908 Olivia E.
Phelps Stokes, whose anti-slavery ancestors had helped to found Liberia, began developing scholarships for both tribal and Americo-Lib-
erian students at Tuskegee; and she and Washington made plans for
what became, after the death of both, the Booker T. Washington Industrial Institute in Liberia.[15]

Washington influenced American-Liberian relations in the crucial
period from 1908 until World War I to a surprising extent for a black
man in an age of white supremacy, but his interracial diplomacy did
not affect any of the fundamental factors in the Liberian equation.
Liberia saved itself, but at the cost of protectorate status; it began to
get out of debt, but the wartime stagnation of African commerce put

it back into crisis again; it found in rubber its exportable commodity, but at the price of exploitation by the Firestone Rubber Company in the twenties and later; and it did not solve its problems of mass education.

All over Africa Washington had an influence through the translation and spread of his writings, particularly his autobiography. His industrial education program and social philosophy were clouded with such ambiguity that not only white missionaries but many Africans in search of independence embraced them. Africans showed little awareness that Washington's industrial education and accommodationism alike were challenged by Du Bois and his followers, who asserted the primacy of higher education and advocated verbal protest against white injustice. Missionaries and African nationalists saw industrial education, perhaps with some ambivalence, as a way of meeting immediate practical needs of survival of rural societies facing the challenge of the technologically advanced European settlers and mining corporations. Washington had correspondence or visits from those in charge of schools in West, East, and South Africa, and students came from all over Africa to attend Tuskegee.

Washington's most prominent African disciple was the Reverend John Langalabalele Dube, founder in 1901 of the Zulu Christian Industrial School at Ohlange, Natal. After missionary education and graduation from Oberlin College, Dube became a Congregational minister in New York in 1899. He visited Tuskegee and became a convert to its "education for life" through immediately practical industrial skills, and he modeled his school after Tuskegee and became known as "the Booker T. Washington of South Africa." The connection between Dube and Washington was not close, however, and most of Dube's funds came from American donors not connected with Tuskegee. In 1903, Dube founded a Zulu newspaper, and a few years later was one of the founders of the African National Congress, which became the focus of black political activity in South Africa. He had many of his model's qualities of ambiguity, strategic compromise, and underlying cultural nationalism. Dube eventually founded the Bantu Business League, modeled after the National Negro Business League.[16]

Washington's correspondence also includes requests for advice from a variety of African educational institutions, extending from the South African Native College at Fort Hare, and Lovedale Industrial School in the Cape of Good Hope to Church of Scotland missions in Nyasa-

land, the Lumbwa Industrial Mission in Kenya, and industrial institutes in the Gold Coast and Nigeria, as well as an experimental African Training Institute at Colwyn Bay, North Wales. Washington's
responses to these requests were largely perfunctory, since he had
never seen the institutions, and usually consisted of sending some of
his published writings and an invitation to visit Tuskegee. He certainly did not promote industrial education as a caste education suitable especially to Africans, as white men after his death did, particularly agents of the Phelps-Stokes and Jeanes Funds and colonial
administrators.[17]

It was the oracular nature of Washington's symbolic message that
attracted a diverse following related to Africa—black nationalists and
pan-Africanists, missionaries, colonial administrators, and the British
heirs of abolitionism. The West Indian black nationalist Edward W.
Blyden was a strong Washington supporter for awhile after the Atlanta Compromise address in 1895 because he equated Washington's
acquiescence in temporary segregation with nationalist separatism, but
turned sharply away from him after the dinner at the White House
showed that Washington did not elevate separation to a principle.[18]
Joseph Booth, the radical white missionary of East Africa, tried to
interest Washington in a plan to colonize American blacks in East Africa, but Park warned that Booth was a "little dinky missionary" who
would use any help "in fighting the English government in South Africa to whose policy he is opposed and by whom he is regarded as an
enemy of public peace." Washington disengaged himself from Booth.[19]

Washington had a more lasting intellectual influence on other African nationalist intellectuals, however. When he was in London in
1899 he took part in planning the Pan-African Conference there in
1900, though he did not attend the gathering nor adopt its militant
protest spirit in his American racial leadership. He corresponded with
J. E. Casely Hayford and his brother Mark C. Hayford of the Gold
Coast; with P. K. Isaka Seme, who visited Tuskegee while a student at
Columbia and continued to correspond with Washington after enroll-
ing at Oxford; and with other South African black nationalists, A.
Kirkland Soga and F. Z. S. Peregrino. He took an interest in the Pan-
African work of Duse Mohamed, editor of the *African Times and Orient
Review,* whose effort was to make his paper an international newslet-
ter on African affairs from the African viewpoint. What all of these
men saw in Washington was not so much his promotion of industrial

training or his compromises with the American *status quo* in racial subordination, but rather his promotion of racial solidarity and self-help, both in theory and in practice. Washington himself, however, in his outspoken criticism of white cruelty and oppression, particularly in the Congo and South Africa, was apparently motivated less by nationalistic fervor than by the effort to demonstrate the impracticality of American black emigration to a colonialized Africa as a solution of racial problems in the United States.[20]

Washington's growing interest in Africa culminated in an International Conference on the Negro at Tuskegee in 1912. He had attended none of the earlier international race conferences in 1895 in Atlanta and in 1900 and 1911 in London, possibly because his rival Du Bois was prominent in them. Robert E. Park seems to have conceived the 1912 conference, as in 1905 he asked Washington, "Would you be willing to write an article recommending that the Powers in Africa, the missionaries and educators, come together in an international conference to devise means for the systematic and harmonious extension of Industrial training in Africa[?]" Washington, or Park as ghostwriter, prepared such an article in the *Independent* the following year. Washington broadened the appeal to include "explorers, missionaries and all those who are engaged, directly or indirectly, in constructive work in Africa."[21]

Six years went by before Washington organized the conference. If jealousy of the prominence of Du Bois in the London race conference in 1911 inspired his decision, Washington did not acknowledge it. His call ignored the controversial themes of race and nationalism, however, and stressed "a more systematic development of constructive educational work on the part of missionaries and governments."[22] Invitations went to leading missionary societies and thousands of individual missionaries, and the U. S. Department of State at Washington's request publicized the conference among the colonial powers. Because of the type of publicity, the distance from Africa, and restrictions on travel of subject peoples, it is not surprising that most of the delegates were whites, nearly all of them connected with one of the twelve religious denominations represented, working in eighteen countries or colonies. Mark C. Hayford was the only black African known to have attended, though several black nationalists unable to attend sent letters expressing approval. These included J. E. Casely Hayford, Edward W. Blyden, and Duse Mohamed, who gave the conference sympathetic coverage in his *African Times and Orient Review*. These African nationalists did not emphasize industrial education, which they were beginning to view in the light of complex issues of "by whom," "to what end," and "how exclusively." Instead, they lauded Tuskegee Institute as an all-black institution, a "noble monument," as Blyden put it, to show "what the African can do for himself."[23] Blyden seemed forgetful of his earlier disapproval of Washington.

Among the whites at the conference Tuskegee also found approval from such diverse types as E. D. Morel, who had led the exposure of exploitation and inhumanity in the Congo, and Maurice S. Evans, a South African spokesman for white supremacy. Morel approved of a Tuskegee type of education as most likely to save African culture, which he did not patronize as primitive, from the onslaught of Western technology and its values. Evans, on the other hand, saw in Tuskegee the model of an education not designed exclusively for whites, but designed specifically for "a race of peasants living by and on the land." For nearly opposite reasons Morel and Evans both feared de-Africanization and saw in the Tuskegee ethos a model for African race pride that would preserve traditions and keep Africans in a separate sphere of activity. Morel would by this prevent Europeanization, while Evans would prevent the upheaval of black nationalism.[24] The conference reached no definite conclusions, but it planned to meet three years later, plans disrupted by the World War and Washington's death.

Washington thus exerted in his own lifetime a vague and even absent-minded but substantial impact on African developments, through his writings, technical assistance, protests against colonial exploitation, influence on missions though not himself an advocate of missionary activity, training of African students at Tuskegee, diplomatic activities notably in the case of Liberia, and international conferences. Washington frequently explained that industrial education was for black self-reliance and was not exclusive of higher education, but this was frequently misunderstood in Africa as in America. This was because he promoted industrial education in language that was so Delphic that in America and elsewhere there developed a mythic Washington who stood for special education of blacks that would relegate them to a lower caste serving white needs and allegedly suiting their racial character.

Tuskegee became a mecca for not only Africans but West Indians and Asians. Along with a few African students each year there were always, after the Spanish-American War, a score or more of Spanish-speaking Cubans and Puerto Ricans at Tuskegee. In addition there were Jamaicans and other English-speaking blacks from the British West Indies, and a sprinkling of Haitians.

The chief problems that Asians had with Tuskegee stemmed not from the school's policies but the anomalies of American racialism. "A Japanese student wants to come to us," the president of Fisk University wrote Washington. "Is the Japanese student a colored man or a white man?" He had stumped the city attorney of Nashville with the question, but Washington answered simply, "I see no objection on earth to your taking the Japanese student. We have had both Japanese and Chinese students and no adverse criticism has been made; in fact, a Japanese student graduated a few years ago."[25] Not only had Iwana Kawahara of Tokyo graduated in 1908, he also arranged for his sister and other Japanese to attend Tuskegee.[26] Japanese who had read *Up from Slavery* in translation saw in Tuskegee methods one of the means of overcoming their nation's technological lag behind the West. Washington wrote empathetically to one Japanese admirer: "Speaking for the masses of my own race in this country I think I am safe in saying that there is no other race living outside of America whose fortunes the Negro people of this country have followed with greater interest or admiration. The wonderful progress of the Japanese people and their sudden rise to the position of one of the great nations of the world has nowhere been studied with greater interest or enthusiasm than by the Negroes of America."[27]

Washington's autobiography found avid translators and many readers in India. "It dealt with so many of the problems that face us native Converts that I took the liberty to translate it into Urdu," wrote Lilavati Singh, a teacher in a Methodist school, Lucknow Woman's College, almost as soon as *Up from Slavery* appeared in 1901.[28] Not only Christians but Hindus, Sikhs, and Buddhists, responded to Washington's success story. In the far south of India K. Paramu Pillai, the Hindu headmaster of the Maharaja's High School in Quilon, Travancore, wrote that his Malayalam adaptation of the autobiography "has been adopted this year as a vernacular text book in one of the High School classes of this state. More than 700 boys and girls, between the ages of 12 and 16, are thereby likely to know something of your labours at Tuskegee, for your race, and I hope they will learn some lessons of self-help therefrom, and learn to recognise the dignity of manual labour and training."[29] He later reported that Madras University had adopted the book, and that he had begun to translate one of Washington's other books and publish it serially in a magazine he edited.[30] From another school in the same state, the headmaster asked for copies of four other of Washington's books and asked, "If you would allow us the privilege of keeping correspondence with you, we promise to keep you informed of the moral and mental need of the children here in the improvement of which your advice will be, I am far from flattering you, invaluable."[31] *Up from Slavery* was translated into Marathi and Telugu.[32]

Indian visitors to Tuskegee expressed hope of adapting its methods "all throughout length & breadth of India."[33] A Sikh who had spent four months in Japan learning pencil-making appealed to Washington to let him spend four months also at Tuskegee learning the school's methods and to help him get into an American pencil factory. "My object in so doing is to establish a school in my country on your plan," he wrote. "I appreciate the system of education which simultaneously trains up head, heart, and hand. If there is any salvation for my nation I see it in such a course."[34]

Probably the most influential of the south Asians adapting Washington's social ideas to fit their local situation was the Anagarika H. Dharmapala, a Sinhalese patriot and Buddhist reformer whose ideas about how his native Ceylon and India could best meet the onslaught of Western culture were a close parallel to Washington's emphasis on racial solidarity and self-help. Born David Hewartivarne in Colombo, the son of a well-to-do furniture manufacturer, he went to Catholic and Anglican schools and moved into the civil service, but by way of the Theosophical Society he found his way back from westernization to Buddhism and to Sinhalese nationalism. He became the leader of a movement for a pristine Buddhism free of the astrology and demonology that folk religion still clung to, and he sought to make this reformed, middle-class Buddhism an effective counterforce to the Christian missionary movements and Western cultural influences that accompanied colonial rule. His most important institutional achievement was the founding of the Maha-Bodhi Society to restore the ancient Buddhist shrines in India and to propagandize for Buddhism.

The Anagarika first attracted American public notice when newspaper reporters found him shivering in Chicago in the spring of 1903 clad in "garments fashionable about 250 B.C." and on his way to Tus-kegee. "I am an admirer of your Booker Washington," he said. "I expect to visit his institution during my stay here, and if I am success-ful I will pattern the Indian institutions after his."[35] Dharmapala's writings emphasized group solidarity, material advancement, self-help, and education. As one scholar has interpreted his message, he sought the "fusion of modern technology and economic methods with tradi-tional Buddhist values."[36] He also held up to his people the example of Meiji Japan, and probably for this Buddhist as well as for Hindus the appeal of Washington was his freedom from sectarian Christian-ity, his materialist progressivism, and perhaps also that he offered hope for improvement without direct challenge to a caste system.

The Anagarika made arrangements to spend two days at Tuskegee, hoping to find there the answer to the terrible poverty of India and Ceylon. "I love children and for their welfare I am working," he wrote Washington. "The missionaries that go to teach Christianity preach a post mortem salvation; but neglect the greater opportunity of making man happy in this world where he is to live, at any rate expected to live at least for a generation." He noted that Du Bois in *The Souls of Black Folk* took a different view, but said: "On the whole it is healthy that two parties are at work on two different lines; and there is no energy lost. The moral, political and industrial development are the three sides of a triangle."[37]

Washington had met Dharmapala in San Jose, California, but was not at Tuskegee when he visited there. "I have gained from my visit . . . an experience that I shall never forget," the Anagarika wrote Washington, "and when I saw the Tuskegee Institute with its mani-fold branches under enlightened teachers I rejoiced that you have made all this glorious work a consummation within a generation; and I thought of the Viceroy in India who with the millions of children starving for education and bread that he should waste in sky rockets and tomfoolery and vain show to please a few loafing lords who came from England last January six million dollars in thirteen days! He is not worth to loose the latchet of your shoe."[38]

It would be wrong, however, to exaggerate the significance of Washington's correspondence with extra-European nationalist lead-ers. His example and writings influenced them, or tended to confirm what they already believed, but they had little influence on him. His outlook was distinctively American and, beyond that, Europe-centered.

He was humanly receptive to the flattery of recognition by the nationalists, but instead of joining their movements he merely encouraged them to join his. He had as substantial a correspondence with white missionaries, nearly all of it initiated by them and eliciting from him only perfunctory response.

Washington's relationship with Marcus Garvey illustrates this one-way influence. This Jamaican black nationalist and back-to-Africa proponent reached the United States a few weeks after Washington's death and began the first black mass movement in America over the next decade. Temperamentally the opposite of the unexcitable Washington, and believing in a return to the African homeland that was anathema to Washington, nevertheless the two men shared—or Garvey borrowed—the philosophy of self-help, economic means, and racial solidarity. Garvey himself, hyperbolically, credited Washington with showing him his destiny during a stay in England from 1912 to 1914. "I read 'Up from Slavery,' by Booker T. Washington, and then my doom—if I may so call it—of being a race leader dawned upon me in London," he wrote. "I asked, 'Where is the black man's Government?' 'Where is his King and his kingdom?' 'Where is his President, his country, his ambassador, his army, his navy, his men of big affairs?' I could not find them, and then I declared, 'I will help to make them.' "[39]

Garvey began corresponding with Washington on his return to Jamaica in 1914, after forming the Universal Negro Improvement Association. He poured out his enthusiasm for the seminal influence of Washington's example and outlook, sending his promotional literature and an early copy of *The Negro World,* his Kingston newspaper that later became a New York daily. Washington responded with vague encouragement.[40] In the fall of 1915 Garvey renewed the correspondence, announcing, "I shall be writing you by next mail relative to my coming visit to America." He planned to visit Tuskegee and "furnish you and the American public with the best proofs of my integrity." Two Jamaicans had been attacking him in the press, he said, "one under the nom de plume of 'Progress' and an unknown dentist by the name of 'Mr. Leo: Pink.' These attacks have been rather personal, but as my integrity stands above malice and envy of these persons in Jamaica I am in no way affected."[41] Washington could certainly sympathize. He too considered attacks on him to be personal and had his own troubles with critics waving the banner of "Progress." It was Scott rather than Washington who replied, however, and when

Garvey wrote another letter within the month, Scott noted on the margin with evident exasperation: "Have already written this man."

In his next letter Garvey reiterated the story of his persecution by personal journalism. "The News Editor of the paper that has attacked me through inspired correspondence has allowed this because I happen to pass his paper over when giving advertisements out to the Press," he explained. "He is also among the coloured few who object to the name 'Negro' in connection with my Association. As I have explained to you already the difficulties in the development of the race rests with our own people as some do not like to call themselves 'Negroes' which will eventually lead them into an awkward position later on if they be allowed to continue in their blind ignorance." He promised to write later on his plan to tour the United States, giving addresses.[42]

Washington wished Garvey success in carrying out his plans but showed a misconception of Garvey's intentions, treating the Universal Negro Improvement Association as though it were a variant of the National Negro Business League. "This is the age of 'getting together,'" he wrote, "and everywhere we look, we see evidence of that constructive accomplishment which are [sic] the result of friendly cooperation and mutual helpfulness. Such, I am sure, is the object of your Association and I am only too sorry that I cannot afford the time just now to give more careful study to your plans so outlined."[43]

Europe was also secondary to America in Washington's pragmatic outlook, but unlike Africa, Asia, and the West Indies, Europe was a center of power, and Washington always paid his respects to power. He actively cultivated the acquaintance and goodwill of a variety of Europeans who put Tuskegee on their American itinerary or met Washington in New York or Boston, or who invited him to their houses and lecture halls on one of his several trips to Europe. They included such diverse men as the German sociologist Max Weber, the French journalist Jules Huret, the translators of *Up from Slavery* into the principal western European languages, the heirs of English abolitionism to whom Francis J. Garrison had given him letters of introduction when he first went to Europe in 1899, the novelist and social critic H. G. Wells, Ambassador James Bryce, Sir Harry H. Johnston the colonialist, and even royalty—Queen Victoria, Prince Henry of Prussia, and the King and Queen of Denmark. With Europeans as with Americans, Washington could almost always find some common ground.

In the fall of 1903 Washington made Europe his playground in one of the few genuine vacations he ever had, at the age of forty-seven. According to newspaper reports in late September, "broken down by overwork," Washington acted on his physician's advice by closing his summer home in South Weymouth, Massachusetts, made one last speech in Philadelphia, and planned to take ship for Europe without returning to Tuskegee for the opening of the fall term. "Mrs. Washington will take care of the work there," reported the New York *Tribune*. "He will do no lecturing abroad."[44] The report was in general accurate, but Washington denied that he was in broken health when he arrived the next day in New York to stay for a few days before sailing. "As a matter of fact," he said, "my general health was never better, but I have had no vacation, and a number of my friends have insisted that I take a short trip to Europe. I have yielded to their wishes, but shall return on the same ship I sail upon, and shall not be gone longer than three weeks altogether."[45]

More than half of Washington's entire vacation was spent at sea, aboard the North German Lloyd steamship *Kaiser Wilhelm II*. He probably slept much of the time and relieved his exhaustion, as he had an earlier voyage to Europe in 1899. After spending some days in Normandy, Washington turned up on October 1, in Paris, where French reporters besieged him for his views on the race question, on the mistaken assumption that his helping Leigh Hunt secure a few Tuskegee-educated cotton farmers for his experiment in the Sudan was part of a plan for wholesale emigration of blacks from the United States to Africa. Washington denied that rumor, pronounced the United States the best place for the Negro, and refused to discuss the prospects of future dinners at the White House.[46]

Washington then disappeared for a week, until his sailing on October 7. When he reached New York on the thirteenth, he explained: "When people heard I was in Paris invitations to speak at dinners and social functions began to pour in on me, and the only way I knew of to stop it was to change my name. I did that, and was known wherever I went as Homer P. Jones." Just what Washington did while footloose in Paris as Homer P. Jones he never explained. One thing he did not do was buy shoes. He told New York reporters, "I took my own supply of American shoes to Europe with me this time. You remember on my last trip I had but one pair along, and soon I needed new ones. The greater part of that trip was spent hunting for shoes, because none of the dealers had anything that would fit my large feet. I don't like European shoes, anyway." He also talked about his several days in Normandy. "I was much interested in the Normandy butter," he said. "It is superior to ours. I found that was due to the better pastur- age there and the grain which is given the cattle while they are in the stables." He said he planned to add to his observations all that he could learn from the literature in an effort to make Tuskegee's butter equal to that of Normandy.[47]

Washington had difficulty in establishing meaningful exchanges of ideas with continental Europeans, perhaps because of the language barrier or his own provinciality. With the English he had better rap- port, though generally in brief encounters for some special purpose of theirs or his. A case in point is H. G. Wells. Wells wrote Washing- ton that he was coming to the United States to write some articles on "The Future in America" and was "very anxious to meet & talk with one or two representative educated men of colour, upon the colour question." He had hoped to come to Tuskegee but found that the time and distance were too great for his schedule, and he asked Wash- ington to meet him in one of the cities he listed on his itinerary. "If there is any good typical negro quarter or community in Va within an easy run of Washington I shall go to see it," he wrote. "My own opin- ions (expressed pretty freely in *A Modern Utopia*) are against insur- mountable colour separations & I am happy to find my own precon- ceptions sustained by the experience of my friend Mr. Sidney Olivier, who was recently acting governor of Jamaica."[48] Washington ar- ranged to meet Wells in Boston for lunch, but wrote: "Let me express my sincere regret, however, that you do not see the Negro in the South where the whole problem of his future is to be worked out. To see the Negro in the North will not at all give you any adequate idea of the present conditions or of the progress made by him." He urged him to visit Tuskegee, or at least Hampton Institute, only a few hours from Washington, to see "the work of one of the notable schools doing its part in the solution of the Southern problem."[49] After their lunch together, Wells expressed disappointment that he was unable to "stop off at Cleveland this journey & to meet you again & hear you speak," but he invited Washington to visit him in England.[50]

Wells relied heavily on his interview with Washington in the chapter on "The Tragedy of Colour" in the book that resulted from his tour, *The Future in America* (1906). "Things are better in Jamaica and Barbadoes," Wells began on a note of patriotic weakness. Washington responded that things were much worse in South Africa. "Here we've got a sort of light. We know generally what we've got to stand. *There* —." Washington said he wanted Wells to hear him make a speech, when the words would come more easily, but Wells preferred to study his "rather Irish" face and hear his conversation in "the soft, slow negro voice." He compared Washington favorably with Du Bois, who "conceals his passionate resentment all too thinly" and "batters himself into rhetoric" against the walls of unjust exclusion. "But Mr. Washington has statecraft. He looks before and after, and plans and keeps his counsel with the scope and range of a statesman. I use statesman in its highest sense; his is a mind that can grasp the situation and destinies of a people."

Wells argued strongly over lunch against the view Washington seemed to hold that it was possible for black and white to live side by side without mingling and without injustice. He insisted that Washington must repudiate separation. "May we not become a peculiar people—like the Jews?" Washington replied. Wells concluded that Washington accepted white prejudice as the central fact of his life. "So he dreams of a coloured race of decent and inaggressive men, silently giving the lie to all the legends of their degradation. They will have their own doctors, their own lawyers, their own capitalists, their own banks—because the whites desire it so." Washington conceded that Jim Crow rules were unfair, saying, "I happen to be a privileged person, they make an exception of me, but the ordinary educated coloured man isn't admitted to a sleeping-car at all. If he has to go a long journey, he has to sit up all night. His white competitor sleeps." But the solution was not in agitation, he told Wells. "The only answer to it all is for coloured men to be patient, to make themselves competent, to do good work, to live well, to give no occasion against us." Wells did not agree, but he reported Washington fairly.[51]

Another Englishman with whom Washington had a longer, at first more promising, and in the end more frustrating acquaintance was Sir Harry H. Johnston. A little man of tremendous energy and broad interests—African explorer, colonial administrator, soldier, scholar and writer—Johnston came to the United States at the height of the Liberian crisis in 1908. The purpose of his visit was to write a book on blacks in the New World, but he was an expert on Liberia, having two years earlier published a book on its history. He was also a principal investor in the Liberian Development Company and thus an interested party in the scramble for Liberia's territory and wealth. Washington's friend Ernest Lyon, United States minister to Liberia, warned Washington not to trust Johnston, saying:

> Note: 1. Sir Harry is opposed to the American type of Negroes. 2. If he is to have any Negroes at all he prefers the West Indian type of British trained Negroes. 3. He has an unsavory reputation on the West Coast in his treatment of the Negro. 4. I am quite certain that Sir Harry will have nothing good to say of the Liberian Negro—whom he claims is American—but before Sir Harry should be taken seriously—the inside history of the Liberian Development Company and his part in the birth of the organization should be given by some one else.

Lyon hoped, however, that Washington would give Johnston some guidance in his study. "He must not study—if we can help it—the Negro from a palace car under the supervision of southern hospitality. —He should be made to see our best as well as our worst."[52]

Washington discounted Lyon's warning, however, when Johnston made the pilgrimage to Tuskegee under prestigious auspices. Johnston stopped by the White House to discuss East Africa with the outgoing President Theodore Roosevelt, who was planning an extensive hunting safari there as soon as he left office. Lord Bryce, the British ambassador to the United States, accompanied Johnston to Tuskegee, and Roosevelt gave him a letter of introduction to Washington as "the great English administrator, who in so many positions in Africa has shown such wise and intelligent sympathy with the native races. He is the kind of adviser and friend who is sorely needed by the colored race."[53] With such sponsors, Johnston was safe from such critics as Lyon, even though Washington's friend Bishop Isaiah B. Scott also wrote, calling Johnston "one of the smoothest propositions I ever met with" and "one of the hardest task-masters of our day," who "would not hesitate to advise the curtailment of the American Negro's privileges in every way possible."[54]

Johnston and Bryce traveled to Tuskegee with the Ogden party of northern visitors aboard Ogden's train of Pullman cars. The others moved on after two days at Tuskegee, but Johnston stayed for about a week, speaking twice to the faculty and twice to students on African history and anthropology. In his more formal talk in the chapel, he showed a number of stereopticon slides of the peoples of Liberia, both the native tribes and Americo-Liberians. "While he admitted that not near as much had been accomplished in Liberia as had been expected and hoped," according to a local review of his talk, "he believed that the country had a great future before it. Sir Harry himself has an experimental plantation in Liberia where he is trying to do somewhat the same sort of work as is carried on under the title of Demonstration Farming in Macon County." He stressed the need to develop the rich resources of Liberia which lay idle "for want of a practical system of education of the people."[55]

Even while he talked and answered questions about Africa, Johnston showed omnivorous curiosity about Tuskegee and closely questioned Washington, Carver, Monroe Work, and others. Washington, he observed, had "an odd look of an Italian about his eyes and face," and tried to attribute this and his middle name to an Italian overseer on the plantation where he supposed Washington was born. Washington introduced Johnston to his friend Joseph O. Thompson, who took the visitor to places where Washington could not, first to his plantation in rural Macon County, and then in buggy rides to isolated farmhouses as far away as southern Georgia, where time seemed to take a backward step to slavery days and southern ladies asked him for personal news of Queen Victoria as though she still reigned. Thompson even took him on a 'possum hunt, and then to the newer South of the Birmingham mines and steel mills.[56]

Completely taken in by Johnston's enthusiasm and flattering attention, Washington wrote his friend Lyon confidentially, "I am firmly convinced that Liberia has no warmer friends than Mr. Bryce and Sir Harry Johnston and that both of them are thoroughly committed to the policy of seeing to it that Liberia maintains her independence."[57] Washington should have listened more closely to the white superiority doctrines and social Darwinism that Ambassador Bryce more explicitly than Johnston expressed in endorsing the "sound, fertile, practical idea" of industrial training. "It is grounded in the history of the human race," he told the students. "Every family of mankind, whatever its color, has to begin, and the white race did begin from acquiring habits of steady and constant labor and from working out for itself a knowledge of the industries and arts on which civilization even in its simplest and rudest forms must rest. The white race had the advantage of beginning in comparatively cold climates. . . . you after thousands of years have to begin to learn what that stern mistress, Nature, taught us long ago."[58] As far as Liberia was concerned, Johnston's main point was that the two British companies to which the Liberian government owed some £100,000 must be repaid in any settlement of the Liberian question, and he warned that Germany might establish a protectorate to guard its investors if the United States acted too slowly.[59]

Never one to dawdle over a book, Sir Harry published in the London *Times*, January 1909, less than two months after his visit, his chapter on Tuskegee. It gave invaluable publicity to Tuskegee as "the greatest establishment existing in the United States for the higher and special instruction of the negro." Atlanta and Howard Universities and even Washington himself would have questioned Tuskegee as representing higher education, and all would have looked askance at the implications of "special instruction." Washington could not help being flattered, however, by Johnston's unstinted praise of every feature of the institute, from the kindergarten to the academic and industrial classes, the staff, the grounds, the drill of the student cadets, and the atmosphere of dedication to self-improvement that he found. Johnston seemed obsessed by the range of color that a race-obsessed America classified as black, from the blue-eyed and golden-haired through the red-haired and brown-eyed, to the brown-black; and he mistakenly attributed to Washington a condemnation of "any further intermixture in blood" and a desire to see "the existing types of negro and negroid . . . reunite and interfuse; thus possibly creating a new race altogether." This may have been Johnston's dream, but Washington treated intraracial color differences as unimportant.

Johnston did, however, truly depict the aim of Tuskegee Institute. "Many people who have not visited Tuskegee assume that the main object of that institution is to supply direct to the white or negro employer domestic servants, craftsmen, farm hands, &c," he wrote. "But while the students are perfectly free to do as they please when they have finished their course, and some of them do proceed direct to such service, the intention is rather that they may leave Tuskegee to become themselves employers or teachers in smaller communities; so that little by little there may be created a great class of intelligent negro farmers, negro tradesmen, and skilled artisans. In fact, Booker Washington's idea is the elimination of the negro loafer, sot, and ignoramus." Washington probably did not like being identified with the racist assumptions of that last statement, and Johnston also said, "The

South is emphatically the home for a coloured race in those districts and in those avenues of life especially suited to a negroid physique and to the negro's talents." Thus Washington and Tuskegee received the emphatic approval of a moderate but outspoken white supremacist, and for the very reason that Johnston assumed that they were preparing blacks for subordinate roles in society.[60]

Johnston had a personal impression of Washington at least as flattering as that of H. G. Wells. Not in his article, but a decade later in his autobiography, Johnston called Washington "a marvel" for his rise from the dregs of slavery and for his astounding range of knowledge. "He spoke English with comparatively little American accent," said Sir Harry, "and wrote it as any good English author might have done. He was witty—so witty that one never tired of hearing his public addresses, though they were in most cases impromptu." He also formed a high opinion of Margaret Washington. "She was rather a silent woman," he observed, "though quite able to converse in English as good as her husband's, when the subject interested her." As her husband had appeared Italian, she seemed an octoroon who "might have been mistaken for a Spanish woman of distinguished presence."[61]

Johnston bombarded Washington with advice on the organization of the American Commission to Liberia, and attempted to explain away an attempted British coup in Monrovia early in 1909. Washington, flattered by the *Times* article and the wide publicity it received in America, confided freely all the news about the commission, forgetful that Johnston had a different personal and national interst in Liberia.[62] Then Emmett Scott wrote from Liberia that Johnston was not to be trusted: "Liberia *is* in a bad way—but fortunately it is worse from without than from within. It is fearful—the treatment they have had at the hands of the British & Harry Johnston is clearly the worst of the lot! His conduct & treatment of this people has been fearful in its consequences."[63]

When the American Commission returned and began to work on its report, Scott with Washington's permission sent all of Johnston's confidential letters to the chairman. Essentially, Johnston argued that British aggression by land and sea was justified by the threat of a French protectorate. "The man seems to be fighting windmills, or perhaps it is a guilty conscience fighting against what he fears are to be revelations in the report of the American Commission," Scott commented.[64] The chairman replied: "I think you know my views in regard to the relative rascality of the British and the French. The only difference seems to be this: Great Britain attempts to cover her aggressions by a philanthropic interest in the poor native while the Frenchman frankly admits that he wants the land."[65] By that time more cautious about Sir Harry, Washington allowed Scott to write his reply to Johnston, stating that every commissioner carried Johnston's book with him aboard ship and was therefore familiar with his views, and that they intended "to take full note of any aggressions of the French, as well as of any other which may come under their notice."[66]

When the commission made its report and Washington sent Johnston a copy in the spring of 1910, Johnston complained bitterly of its strictures against his Liberian Development Company and a rubber company in which he had an interest, and when Emmett Scott at a conference on Africa and the Near East further remarked that these companies had "bamboozled" the Liberian government and exploited its people, Johnston shrilly denounced this as a slander, writing not only to Washington but to President Taft. Scott insisted that Johnston was protesting against revelation of the facts about his companies rather than the accuracy of his statements, and stood his ground.[67]

It was in this atmosphere that Washington reviewed Johnston's *The Negro in the New World* (1910) for the *Journal of the African Society*.[68] His review was in general favorable, as well it might be, since Johnston had concluded that the race problem would be solved not by protest or sympathy but by the Hampton-Tuskegee type of industrial education and by blacks making money as fast as they could, for money would overcome prejudice. Johnston read the proof of the review before publication, and took exception to only one remark therein, which revealed the depth of his racial bias:

> You call attention to my having given in the first chapter pictures of exaggerated negro types, exaggerated as regards their development of muscle and their homeliness of feature, and you seem to resent this a little. But my object was (as I think I explained in the text) not only to show the question in all its bearings, but to illustrate extreme features as well. For example, in my portraits of a typical Englishman and a typical Anglo-Saxon American, I selected faces altogether exceptional[,] remarkable for their beauty of outline or for the spirituality they conveyed, in order to show the White man at his best. I also wished to show the Negro at his worst, or, let us say, at his least developed; *not* from malice, but in some way to explain and partially excuse the White man's attitude of mind towards him, in the unreasonable guise in which it often appears.

Perhaps, also, I illustrated the best types of Anglo-Saxon to explain why the Negro has on the whole been so forgiving and so ready, over and over again, to 'put up with' the White man.

Johnston claimed that elsewhere in the book he had photographed "the Negro and Negroid at their *best*." He complained also that, though he had sent prepublication copies to other officers of Tuskegee none of them had reviewed the book or written to him.[69] Washington replied, "My statement that the Negro types used by you were exaggerated is, I find, confessed in your letter. Of course, it is a matter of one's personal judgment only as to whether he likes or does not like that kind of thing." He promised that someone would review Johnston's book in one of the school publications.[70] Thus ended an acquaintance of mutual usefulness that was, at the same time, disillusioning.

Washington took a journey of two months to Europe in the late summer and fall of 1910 for a specific purpose, to study the poorer classes of Europe in preparation for a book comparing them to the black people in the United States. A cynic would say, particularly if he knew Washington well, that he had written his conclusion before he left the United States. But he gave every evidence of conscientious intent, putting off all interviews, speeches, and offers of hospitality until near the end of the tour, with one notable exception, a visit to Skibo Castle, Andrew Carnegie's dream house in Scotland. "Bring your friend along," Carnegie wrote him. "Highland welcome awaits you."[71]

The friend who accompanied Washington throughout this European tour and played a large part in the book that followed it was Robert E. Park, Washington's chief ghostwriter and close white adviser. Park went to work for Washington after getting a Ph.D. at Heidelberg and a short stint with the Congo Reform Association, and soon after Washington's earlier white ghostwriter Max B. Thrasher died of a ruptured appendix. Washington used to taunt his college-trained faculty with the statement that he did not know what degrees Park had or whether he had any degrees, that he employed him because of what he could do. Working out of his house in Wollaston, Massachusetts, rather than Tuskegee, Park nevertheless threw his energies into the realization of Washington's purposes with a sense of vocation. "I was disgusted with what I had done in the University and had come to the conclusion that I couldn't do anything first rate on my own account," he later explained. "I decided the best thing to do was to attach myself to someone who was doing something first rate. Washington was not a brilliant man or an intellectual, but he seemed to me to be doing something real. So I went." [72]

Park researched, drafted, or revised most of Washington's writings for publication between 1905 and 1912, including his principal magazine articles and even many of his letters, particularly to foreigners. More importantly, Park took the book manuscripts that other ghostwriters had bungled and brought them into more polished and sophisticated condition, while retaining the distinctive Washingtonian plainness of style. Park completed the two-volume *Story of the Negro* (1910) after A. O. Stafford had failed to complete it in four years. [73] He also gave the final polish to Washington's life of Frederick Douglass after S. Laing Williams and T. Thomas Fortune had finished with it. "I think you will find the tone pretty thoroughly altered," Park wrote Washington, "with comparatively little modification of the text." [74] Park suggested the outline for *My Larger Education* (1911), a sequel to *Up from Slavery,* and orchestrated Washington's rough notes and the suggestions of Emmett Scott and the publisher Walter Hines Page into an episodic but reasonably coherent work. [75] In the course of this common effort Washington came to treat Park as an equal, something he rarely did. Park later said, "I think I probably learned more about human nature and society, in the South under Booker Washington, than I had learned elsewhere in all my previous studies." [76] As collaborators and travel companions, they were almost ideal.

Park preceded Washington to Europe in 1910 by several months, going by slow ship to save money, and planned their itinerary and accommodations before Washington crossed on the mail steamship *Carmania* of the Cunard line. [77] There are inconsistencies between Park's itinerary and Washington's journal notes, but apparently after London, Scotland, and Liverpool they went to Berlin, Prague, Vienna, Budapest, Belgrade, Sofia, and Constantinople by rail. They then traveled by ship through the Greek isles to Catania and Palermo, Sicily, thence to Naples. Two days later they were in Rouen, presumably by rail, thence to Berlin again, Copenhagen, and London. It was more than a month of fleeting travel and brief impressions. Visiting the farmlands of Hungary, Washington was impressed by the efficiency of cultivation and the employment of the latest agricultural science and technology by the large landowners, but he saw soldiers forcing barefoot Slavs to work, farm workers living in mud houses, and wide-spread farm strikes. Hungary, he concluded, was "improving land, trees & horses, but not the man furthest down." In Austrian and Russian Poland he saw filth, dirt floors, and solemn people in the farm villages. He discovered Jews without money in Poland, and in a Russian village "6 men eating out of one bowl in a farm house." Another vivid impression was of human degradation in the sulphur mines of Catania. There he noted in his journal that seven percent of the population voted, that robbers prayed to saints, that an entire family worked for 17¢ a day. In Naples fifty beggars followed them in the streets; he found a blacksmith shop in one bedroom and a poultry yard in another, and filth everywhere. These scenes were a contrast to clean Copenhagen, where the King and Queen entertained him at dinner.[78]

Both men took notes, discussed them, and then Washington would dictate a draft to a stenographer for Park to further refine by additional research. Washington could find no people of Europe at the bottom of society who were not worse off than American blacks—from the down-and-out of Liverpool to the Italian miner, the Slavic peasant to the East European Jew. "The Negro is not as a rule a degenerate," he wrote. "If he is at the bottom of America, it is not because he has gone backward and sunk down, but because he has never risen. . . ."[79] Park became rather disillusioned by Washington's chauvinism, which constantly got in the way of genuine curiosity. "When he was abroad," Park later wrote, "he was not interested in the common people as I thought he would be. They were just foreigners. He was an American and thought everything in America surpassed anything in Europe. He just wanted to get the dirt on them that was all, to discover for himself that the man farthest down in Europe had nothing on the man farthest down in the U. S."[80]

Washington tried to keep his focus on the poor of Europe, but both his standing as a celebrity and his own inclination interfered. Before he sailed he asked Scott for a list to carry with him of "all the prominent men both black and white, foreigners and Americans, I have met within recent years."[81] Reaching London he was, according to newspaper reports, "lionized here to such an extent that he had to refuse shoals of invitations to address meetings."[82] He spoke in Prague before a large audience, and in Berlin; in Vienna he turned down an offer to address the House of Parliament, but on his way home he spoke in London at the National Liberal Club, and again in Liverpool.[83] The highlight of his tour was not some vision of the people at their grimiest, but his dinner with the royal family of Denmark, which he later wrote was the biggest surprise of his life except for his Harvard honorary degree.[84]

Washington unfortunately became so carried away by his theme of blacks being better off in America than the lower classes were in Europe that his speeches in Europe reflected his overoptimism. This brought him sharp criticism from the white civil rights leader John E. Milholland of New York and London, who refused to attend a luncheon in Washington's honor by the Anti-Slavery and Aborigines Protection Society and published a circular letter giving his reasons.[85] Du Bois and other blacks calling themselves the National Negro Committee followed this by an open letter to the people of Europe denying the impression Washington had given "that the Negro problem in America is in process of satisfactory solution."[86] No such criticisms inhibited his welcome home to Tuskegee. Along the road from the train station at Chehaw "many of the colored people built bonfires," Scott reported to the Associated Press, "and as his carriage passed skyrockets and Roman candles were sent up." When he reached the campus the entire student body and faculty gathered with torches of pine knots. Some students unhitched the horses and pulled the carriage to his house, led by the institute band playing Hail to the Chief, Home Sweet Home, and Auld Lang Syne. Washington said briefly that in Europe he had found no place like home.[87]

In ghostwriting *The Man Farthest Down,* Park sought to tone down both Washington's optimism and the demand of the editors of the *Outlook,* where much of the book was serialized, for "the human side of things." "Outlook people very much afraid we will make them heavy and scientific," Washington warned.[88] Park succeeded so well that Washington preceded the articles and the book by acknowledging his debt to Park, saying "I could not have covered the ground or have made the observations that I did without the assistance of Dr. Robert E. Park."[89] Washington also assigned the copyright to Park.

Park soon afterwards, during Washington's conference on Africa, struck up a friendship with W. I. Thomas which led to his appointment on the faculty of the University of Chicago and to a distinguished career in sociology, but he and Washington continued to work together occasionally. Washington was so excited by their European tour that he almost immediately began to plan another, with Park again as his advance man and companion. This trip was to be devoted to speaking engagements in the leading European cities. Park suggested that he put it off for a couple of years.[90] "I am really in earnest about making a European trip," Washington reminded Park in 1913, "and want to be maturing it as soon as possible."[91] They brought John H. Harris of the Anti-Slavery and Aborigines Protection Society into their plans for the British portion of the tour. Then came the World War. "I suppose we will now have to wait until the majority of Europeans have succeeded in killing themselves off," Washington wrote Park. He took a certain wry relish in saying, "The more I see of the actions of these white people of Europe, the more I am inclined to be proud of the Negro race. I do not know of a group of Negroes in this country or in any other country who would have acted in the silly manner that these highly civilized, and cultured people of your race have acted."[92]

CHAPTER 12

Atlanta and Brownsville

Surely, Thou too art not white, O Lord, a pale, bloodless, heartless thing?*

W. E. B. DU BOIS, 1906

I have your letter of the 2nd instant. . . . You can not have any information to give me privately to which I could pay heed, my dear Mr. Washington, because the information on which I act is that which came out in the investigation itself.†

THEODORE ROOSEVELT, 1906

TWO events of the fall of 1906 shattered with their rifle bullets the Washingtonian rhetoric of accommodation and progress and the Rooseveltian promise of an open door of opportunity for blacks. The Atlanta race riot, in the very city that had given birth to the Atlanta Compromise, and President Roosevelt's wholesale dismissal of three companies of black regular troops on weak evidence that some of them were involved in the Brownsville shoot-out with white citizens, both showed that there was something systemically wrong with Booker T. Washington's formula for the assimilation of blacks into American society. In the case of the Atlanta riot, the forces of white enlightenment on which the Atlanta Compromise depended neither prevented the race riot nor brought it to an end until it had done

*"Litany of Atlanta," 1906.
†Letter to BTW, November 5, 1906.

terrible work of destruction to black lives, property, and hope. In Roosevelt's Brownsville decision, the very man who had invited Washington to dinner at the White House closed his ears to Washington's arguments and dismissed the black troops without even the formality of a court martial, an arbitrary action that would have been unthinkable if they had been white.

Atlanta had always had a double image. One face was that of the trade center facing the dawn of a New South, standing at the junction of two major railroads. But its Union Terminal, gateway to the South, required black people to use a separate entrance into a separate waiting room. Bustling, commercial Atlanta never found a place for blacks except as subordinates and pariahs. One reason for this paradox was that Atlanta was not fully urban. Many of its whites were in rather than of the city, displaced country persons who brought with them both the homely virtues of rural dwellers and also the attitudes that fired the lynch mobs in the surrounding country. The riot of 1906 was not Atlanta's first. There was a race riot in 1902, in which 3000 shots were reported, eight left dead—four whites and four blacks.[1]

The year 1906 began as one of promise for Booker T. Washington. In January he spoke in Nashville in its largest and most prestigious white Methodist church, completely packed with white men and women and with 500 turned away at the door. After his speech, the dean of the Vanderbilt University School of Theology invited Washington to lecture to his students on "How can the young Southern man help in the lifting up of the Negro race?"[2] In April, Tuskegee Institute held its twenty-fifth anniversary celebration amid the congratulations of the high and mighty. In the summer, Washington prepared to put his racial strategy of a decade to the test by returning to Atlanta to convene the National Negro Business League.

Hoping to avoid the racial friction that attended most Afro-American gatherings in southern cities, Washington wrote in advance of the NNBL meeting to his white friend, Charles A. Wickersham, general manager of the Atlanta and West Point Railroad that controlled the Atlanta terminal, to apprise him of the arrival of the businessmen from thirty to thirty-five states. "My especial point in writing you," he said, "is to see if some action can be taken by those in authority which will modify, during the days of the meeting of the Negro Business League, if possible, the rule now existing in the new depot which requires colored people to enter and leave the depot at a side door." This was certain to cause "much bitterness and, I fear, friction," he wrote. "No matter how well-intentioned the visitor may be, the arrangements are such that persons who have not lived in Atlanta and learned by experience where to enter and leave would [not] think of going to the side door." Washington said that as far as he knew Atlanta was unique in the southern states in routing black people through a side door.[3] Wickersham, however, refused to budge on the arrangements. There was no "General Main Entrance," he insisted, no front or side entrance, merely a "White Entrance" and a "Negro Entrance." His only concession, if it could be so called, was to put additional signs up to point out the "Main Colored Entrance." Emmett Scott noted on the margin of Wickersham's letter as he passed it on to his chief: "Will do more harm than good."[4] Washington urged Wickersham not to put up any more signs, and said that he would try to head off criticisms from the black newspaper editors and would also seek the help of Clark Howell, owner of the Atlanta *Constitution,* in minimizing white friction with the gathering.[5]

Washington arrived in Atlanta a few days before the NNBL meeting to prepare the way for it. He found the atmosphere of the city overheated by the recent primary campaign for the governorship, candidates Hoke Smith and Clark Howell having vied with each other in racial demagoguery in support of a disfranchisement amendment. A newspaper war between the older Atlanta dailies, the *Journal* and the *Constitution,* and a Hearst-owned newcomer, the *Georgian,* added fuel to the racial hostilities with daily reports of rape and rumors of rape in efforts to build up circulation. Washington gave the Atlanta newspapers advance copies of his annual address, apparently hoping that this would steer them away from any sensational reporting of the meeting. Headline writers of the *Constitution,* however, entitled the report of his speech: "LAW-BREAKING NEGROES WORST MENACE TO RACE: Booker Washington in Address to Business League Says South Is Best Place for Blacks Who Will Work." Before turning to the positive message of Washington's address, the *Constitution* reported: "That the worst enemies of the negro race are those negroes who commit crimes, which are followed by lynching, and that the south is after all the best place for black men who are willing to work, was the keynote of the address of Booker T. Washington to the National Negro Business League last night." The real keynote Washington tried to present was that the National Negro Business League, though recognizing injustice, "feels that the race can make progress and secure the greatest protection by its efforts in progressive, constructive directions, by constantly presenting to the world tangible, and visible evidences of our worth as a race." This was a familiar Washington theme and a debatable set of priorities, but it was a far cry from the emphasis on black crime that suited the white press of Atlanta.[6] Washington's black critics were quick to assume that his speech had been correctly reported, and even that he had allowed the Atlanta newspaper editors to persuade him to change his prepared speech.

The New York social worker Mary White Ovington, who was just beginning a lifetime of civil rights work, attended the Business League meeting as a reporter for the New York *Evening Post*. Writing to thank her for her helpful reports of the meeting, Washington explained his own course in Atlanta. "Aside from the time and strength which I had to give to the work of the Business League," he wrote, "I had to do considerable in the direction of trying to improve the sentiment existing between the colored and white people in Atlanta. When I first went down there, I found the tension very intense, and my first effort was to beard each editor in his den and have a frank talk with him, and I followed this up with other work in the same direction which I shall try to explain to you later. On the whole, I think our meeting not only accomplished good for the race as a whole but especially changed conditions there in Atlanta."[7] He also wrote to Ovington's editor, Villard, that racial tension was "almost to the breaking point" and blamed the state of feeling not only on the political campaign and the newspaper war but on "several outrages . . . committed by colored people on white women" in and near Atlanta. "One of the afternoon papers," he wrote Villard, "was advocating openly the formation of a Ku Klux Klan, another had offered a thousand dollars for the lynching of a colored man guilty of one of these crimes." All the newspaper editors had received him cordially, he said, "and all expressed the feeling that they needed help." Though they all gave the NNBL only perfunctory coverage, Washington felt he had eased tensions in Atlanta, for on the last day the *Journal* contained a protest against the Ku Klux Klan.[8]

Mary White Ovington was somewhat reassured but still skeptical about the atmosphere of racial hostility in Atlanta. "I was deeply impressed at the complete indifference to the League on the part of the white people whom I hoped to interest in it," she wrote Washington. "I did not hear any such encouraging talk in my hotel corridor as Mr. Fortune tells of in the Age, and I did hear much of the 'nigger' diatribe."[9]

The Atlanta race riot began when an armed mob of whites assaulted blacks on September 22, not quite a month after the Business League meeting. Five days of violence resulted in the deaths of at least ten black persons and one white, and many injuries and much property destruction in the black sections of the city. The riot started in the main black business district along Decatur Street, apparently on some vague assumption that the availability of liquor to blacks there had led to black crimes of violence. The white mob ignored pleas to desist by the mayor and the police commissioner. It attacked black persons on the streets as well as in restaurants and saloons and stopped streetcars to drag out and beat the black passengers. Some blacks fled from the city, but others resisted or took sanctuary on the campuses of black colleges or the houses of white employers. Black self-defense in the vicinity of Clark University held the white mob in check.[10]

As blacks in Atlanta responded in various ways to the white mob violence, those away from the scene offered advice. The outbreak brought out the latent radicalism of T. Thomas Fortune. "It makes my blood boil," he wrote Scott. "I would like to be there with a good force of armed men to help make Rome howl."[11] Washington, then in New York City, had a different reaction. He urged "the best white people and the best colored people to come together in council and use their united efforts to stop the present disorder." In a letter to the New York *World,* he especially urged the Atlanta blacks "to exercise self-control and not make the fatal mistake of attempting to retaliate, but to rely upon the efforts of the proper authorities to bring order and security out of confusion." The solution to disorder was "the inflexible enforcement of the laws against all criminals," and in this he urged all blacks to cooperate. Blacks should not be discouraged by this violent incident, he said, for "while there is disorder in one community there is peace and harmony in thousands of others."[12] Even in the dark cloud of race massacre Washington strained to see the silver lining. Many other blacks agreed with Fortune, who said, "I cannot believe that the policy of non-resistance in a situation like that of Atlanta can result in anything but contempt and massacre of the race."[13] He was glad to learn, however, that Washington was on his way to Atlanta, and he wired him that "it is the proper place for you, hope much from your presence and joint conferences."[14]

There is a myth that as soon as Washington learned of the Atlanta riot he took the next train to the stricken city, without regard for his own safety, to aid in the restoration of order and the work of reconstruction. Actually, he remained in New York until after the riot was over and order was restored, arriving in Atlanta on the evening of September 28. He did help in the work of reconstruction. A corollary myth is that Du Bois cowered at Calhoun School in Alabama while Washington braved the dangers of riot-torn Atlanta. Scott wrote an editorial to that effect to be published anonymously in the New York Age and other black newspapers.[15] Actually, Du Bois returned home to Atlanta University and his beleaguered family as soon as possible, and on the train composed the moving "Litany of Atlanta," with its haunting passage, "Surely, Thou too art not white, O Lord, a pale, bloodless, heartless thing?" To give both men their due, neither played the melodramatic hero, but each in his way sought to deal with the causes of the tragedy so as to work against its recurrence.[16] Du Bois believed that the white mob action was premeditated and that it could be countered most effectively by Niagara methods of protest, while Washington talked of the Golden Rule in race relations and practiced elaborate ritual negotiations with the Atlanta white leaders.

"I believe good in the end will result from the present trials through which, we as a race, are passing," Washington wrote his Atlanta friend J. W. E. Bowen during the riot.[17] Before leaving New York, he also arranged with Villard to send a white detective to Atlanta to investigate the causes of the riot. They first approached the Pinkerton Detective Agency, but its head suggested instead a federal secret service man. Villard rejected that idea as improbable, and even though Pinkerton finally agreed to furnish an agent, Villard wrote Washington that "he is so lukewarm and doubtful about the matter that I question very much whether we had better trust ourselves to them." He proposed instead George Kennan, a freelance reporter famous for his book on the Siberian exile system, but Kennan turned down the offer.[18]

Washington meanwhile began work in Atlanta by spending several hours on the campus of Clark University with President W. H. Crogman and J. W. E. Bowen. He publicly commended them for their leadership in self-defense efforts at Clark and at Gammon Theological Seminary. They "stood manfully and courageously at their posts," he wrote in a letter to the Houston *Freeman*.[19] Washington also took part in a meeting of twenty leading blacks with ten leading whites at the Colored Young Men's Christian Association, and reported hopefully to Wallace Buttrick of the General Education Board: "The colored people did not mince their words; they told the whites in no uncertain terms the way the colored people had been grievously injured. The whites were equally frank; they acknowledged their sins of omission and commission, and promised in most sincere terms amends for the future; in fact, their one dominant plea was to know what the colored people wanted." The leader of the white delegation was James W. English, a former Confederate captain and a banker, who at the outset of the riot had tried to calm the mob but was shouted down as a "nigger lover." The whites at the meeting proposed the closing of all black saloons, but the blacks insisted that if any saloons were closed, all must be. The most significant outcome of the meeting was "a permanent cooperating committee of ten of each race." Washington reported to Buttrick that the Atlanta whites seemed "thoroughly ashamed" and earnestly determined to end the lawlessness. "One is just as safe in Atlanta at present as in New York," he wrote three days after the riot had ended.[20]

Washington pinned his faith on the "reconstruction" of Atlanta through cooperation of leaders of both races. The "committee of safety" organized at the interracial meeting recommended measures to restore order. All the saloons in the city were closed for about ten days, and the police took strict measures against loiterers. Washington commended these steps in an article in the *Outlook* in December, but for more permanent improvement he counted on an organization founded by former Governor William J. Northen, president of the Atlanta Business Men's Gospel Union. Northen proposed to form under the auspices of his group a Christian League, to which approved members of both races would be eligible, who would agree to promote good citizenship, peace, and good will. The Christian League designated the second Sunday in December as a day when every minister in the city would preach a sermon in favor of law and order. In addition, the League held weekly interracial prayer meetings at the Colored YMCA. Northen proposed the spread of this organization throughout the South as a healer of racial discord.[21]

Two other efforts at the "reconstruction" of Atlanta gave Washington grounds for encouragement. An open letter in the Atlanta *Constitution* by the Interdenominational Union of Colored Ministers called for the extension of the public school system for blacks to include agricultural high schools in each rural congressional district and "a great central industrial school for negroes" in Atlanta and perhaps in other Georgia cities. This effort, Washington believed, was "favored by the white people," and about $30,000 was subscribed to support it. The third and perhaps most important effort was the one sponsored by Charles T. Hopkins, a white lawyer for Atlanta University and one of the heroes of the riot crisis, one of a group that raised money for aid to riot victims, a prominent member of the committee that had helped to restore order. Building upon this Committee of Safety, Hopkins organized a more permanent group known as the Civic League, founded on Thanksgiving Day 1906. The Civic League sent out a notice to some 5000 Atlanta citizens of both races urging them to join an organization dedicated to prevention of riots, lynchings, and other injustices and violations of law. Meanwhile, there was no action to bring to justice the hundreds of members of the white mob that had terrorized the black residents for days.

The Civic League took one step toward upholding its noble creed. Hopkins and two other attorneys for the League defended a black man accused of assault on a white woman who positively identified him. Convinced that the man was innocent, the three attorneys secured a relatively unbiased jury, brought twenty-five white neighbors to court as character witnesses, and secured an acquittal. Washington took hope from this "first time that a negro accused of this crime, who had been positively identified . . . ever escaped death." The lawyers bought the man a suit of clothes and a train ticket to a farm in Alabama where he could remain until the neighborhood quieted down. With his usual optimism, Washington found these organizations and their early steps promised "the most radical, far-reaching, and hopeful solution of the race problem that has ever been undertaken by Southern white people." [22]

Washington was premature in proclaiming the reign of the Golden Rule in Atlanta. There was little evidence of a change of heart among the whites. The disfranchisement of blacks endorsed by all gubernatorial candidates in the recent campaign was enacted. [23] Clark Howell wrote privately to Washington that he considered the remedy for future race riots depended not on the whites but on "the conservative and law abiding element of your race," who needed to drive lawbreakers from their midst. He praised Washington for "condemning the Northern hot heads and incendiaries who are endeavoring to incite the Negroes of the South" but was silent on the subject of the white incendiaries.[24] Not only fundamental white attitudes but the institutional features of white supremacy remained untouched by the cosmetic reforms. Atlanta continued, for example, to have no public high school for blacks, and excluded blacks from using the Carnegie library. The city refused to hire even a single black policeman, permitted a noisome slum district in the principal black residential area, and institutionalized residential segregation by a new muncipal ordinance. In less than a decade after the 1906 riot, Atlanta witnessed the lynching in 1915 of a local Jewish businessman after a lurid trial and conviction of the rape-murder of a Gentile girl, and in the same year the Ku Klux Klan was reborn at a cross-burning on nearby Stone Mountain.

Washington learned quite early that President Roosevelt felt he had no authority for sending federal troops to Atlanta to quell the riot.[25] Hearing that Roosevelt planned to discuss the riot in his next message to Congress, however, Washington sent him some suggestions. The message dealt mainly with lynching, and after Washington and a group of other black men went over the President's draft in a meeting at Whitefield McKinlay's house, Washington spent more than an hour with Roosevelt arguing for revision. "He did not take all the medicine which we prescribed for him," Washington wryly reported to McKinlay, "but he did take a portion of it." On one objectionable passage, Roosevelt "gritted his teeth and absolutely refused to budge a single inch."[26]

Washington hoped to turn the Atlanta disaster into some sort of good, however, by encouraging a muckraking journalist to study the riot and expose the forces that produced such explosions of racial hostility. He wrote to Villard of his disappointment with the Pinkerton Detective Agency, and warned him against sending any telegrams concerning the riot, for he had learned in Atlanta that "one of our leading colored men in that city had gotten into serious trouble through a telegram sent to New York by the telegraph authorities revealing the nature of his message."[27] He was referring to J. Max Barber's anonymous telegram to the New York *World,* which Washington described as "perhaps the most correct account of the Atlanta disgrace of anything that has been published."[28] After the telegraph operator's leak, some of Atlanta's leading citizens suggested to Barber that he leave town.

Ray Stannard Baker of the *American Magazine,* one of the nation's leading investigative reporters, took an interest in the Atlanta riot and began many months of broad-gauged study of the American race problem. Washington was eager to establish a close working partnership with Baker, for he learned that his Niagara Movement critics were repeating the charges that his National Negro Business League speech had helped to trigger the riot, and that it was written or revised by Atlanta whites. "The fact is," Washington wrote S. Laing Williams, "my speech was sent out to the Associated Press before I even went to Atlanta, and it was not altered in a single line or sentence after I got there."[29] What the Niagarites were emphasizing, however, was that by crediting the rumors of rape and taking a defensive stance, Washington had contributed to the chain of events leading to riot. Washington answered with his own innuendoes about Du Bois's late arrival and Barber's hasty departure.

Washington returned to Atlanta in December as principal speaker on Law and Order Sunday. Some 1200 persons, all the fire ordinance allowed, including many whites, crowded into Friendship Baptist Church while an equal number milled around outside. When Washington said that "social equality was not what blacks sought," the applause was "little short of a demonstration." Former Governor Northen, who shared the platform, called on both races to support his Civic League. Washington spoke again that night at his friend H. H. Proctor's First Congregational Church to another overflow crowd of both races.[30] But Franklin Clarkin, a reporter for the New York *Evening Post,* wrote Washington, "I can't find so much encouragement in the 'reconstruction' as you voiced," and he wrote his editor more frankly after a week's stay in the city: "A few men have dreamed a dream, that's all."[31]

When Ray Stannard Baker went south, his original idea for an article was a contrast between the ideas of Senator Benjamin R. Tillman of South Carolina and Booker T. Washington on the subject of racial violence, but as soon as he had heard Tillman's "unreasonable views" he abandoned that approach.[32] So he traveled through the South interviewing more broadly, seeking out the whole spectrum of white and Afro-American opinion on the nature of the race problem and its solution or insolubility. Washington, who was in the North at the time, urged Baker to stay in the South and meet with him at Tuskegee.[33] Baker remained at Tuskegee for several days, and spent about two weeks in Atlanta. Washington was so favorably impressed with him that he wrote Villard urging that Baker instead of Clarkin be the reporter selected for the searching study of the Atlanta riot.[34] Washington gave Baker a long list of persons he should interview in Atlanta and elsewhere in the South, and gave him letters of introduction to some of them. Black and white, they were Washington supporters to a man.

Meanwhile Ida Tarbell of the *American Magazine* staff had corresponded with her friend Mary White Ovington about Baker's plans. Ovington wrote Baker frankly that the blacks were sharply divided between those who believed in conciliation and those who protested against racial injustice. "The leader of the first group is, of course, as you know, Dr. Washington. Any men whom he introduces you to are likely to give you one-sided information. They will tell you of progress, but they will not show you in many ways what the real situation is. The other group of men could tell you a very great deal if they felt that they were safe in doing so." She gave Baker another list headed by Du Bois, a list that overlapped Washington's but included some of his radical critics.[35]

It was to Washington that Baker turned repeatedly for leads, however. "The farther I get into the subject the larger it looms and the more careful I feel that I should be before I begin to set anything down on paper," he wrote Washington, and asked for anything he could send him in the way of pamphlets and other literature.[36] By the end of 1906 Baker was viewing developments in Atlanta with Washington's optimism. "Letters & papers from there give the situation a most hopeful look," he wrote Washington. "It may be that the riot will be looked back upon as a blessing."[37]

Baker submitted to Washington a draft of his first article, a chronicle of the events leading up to and following the riot. Washington praised it but urged that Baker capitalize the word Negro "as much as Indian, Filipino, or any other of the race varieties." He said: "Self-respecting Negroes who are not ashamed of the term Negro are always very much disappointed when they find themselves treated as a common noun."[38] Baker, Du Bois, and a white Atlanta moderate,

Reverend C. B. Wilmer, engaged in a three-hour discussion of the race problem.[39] Nevertheless, as his series of articles developed, he returned again and again to Washington for suggestions, and Washington, Scott, and Robert E. Park read many of the articles before publication.

Du Bois was as pleased with Baker's first article as Washington was, but shrewdly observed that outsiders such as Baker never came to know blacks personally, as thinking, feeling men. They spoke of white southerners in the second person but regarded blacks in the third person.[40] If Baker did learn to use the second person with blacks, it was through Washington's persistent influence on him. Baker's articles read more and more like Washington's. This was partly because of his own publisher's plea for a noncommittal presentation. Observing that the articles were sold out everywhere in the South, John S. Phillips wrote Baker: "For the sake of effect we must keep the interest and friendliness of Southern readers. After all, they are the people whom we wish to reach and enlighten. I am glad that you went over the article for last examination from this standpoint."[41] During the two years that Baker devoted to his race study, he interviewed nearly everybody who claimed any expert knowledge. Dining with Washington at the Manhattan Hotel in New York, he recorded in his notebook Washington's remark that "The chief value of Tuskegee & schools of its class is that they teach the honor & dignity of labor." On the same day at New Haven, he interviewed the bedridden Edgar Gardner Murphy, who gave Baker the best argument of the "marry-my-daughter" variety that he had heard. Murphy said that if he invited Booker T. Washington to dinner even in New Haven, he would also have to entertain his wife, have to accept their return invitations, have to meet their relatives and friends, have to let one another's children visit back and forth. "Where do you draw the line?" he asked. "Can you draw it, unless you keep all negroes behind it? It comes hard, I admit, in exceptional men like Washington, though they work with great loyalty among their own people."[42] It is improbable that Baker disclosed that he had come to see Murphy after dining with Washington.

Emmett Scott feared that Baker's probing curiosity would lead him to the enemy camp. He asked Charles Banks to write Baker and ask him about the drift of his forthcoming articles. "It is due you to say," Scott wrote Banks, "that I have learned that the 'Trotterites' are seeking to guide Baker, so far as any favorable reference to Dr. Washington or Tuskegee is concerned, and I wish to find out from Baker himself, in this way, if this is true." He asked Banks not to mention his name, but simply to inquire of Baker whether he intended to discuss "Negroes' efforts at race building" and "Dr. Washington's part in keeping racial relations in the south in the pacific state."[43] Banks dutifully wrote Baker that Washington's policies were approved by both the blacks and "the best white people" of the South, whereas those who offered advice and remedy from a distance were often impractical.[44] John E. Bush and other Washington lieutenants wrote similar letters.

Washington and Du Bois both sent Baker the names of northern black men he should interview.[45] Washington also pointed out to Baker the southern racial injustices his articles had not seriously addressed, notably the convict lease system, the inequality of public school opportunities, and voting discrimination.[46] Du Bois also wrote, emphasizing voting rights as the heart of the problem.[47] If Baker was aware of the extent to which he was the object of a tug of war, his correspondence did not show it. Somehow, in a weak moment, probably after an interview with Edwin A. Alderman or some other southerner, Baker supported the desirability of the Jim Crow car.[48]

As he wandered along the color line, Baker learned from Samuel E. Courtney of Boston about the social world of the extremely light-skinned blacks, "the discussions of color, of the adventures of 'going over'" into the white world, of "pride of aristocracy—negro 400."[49] Bearding James K. Vardaman in his study in Greenwood, Mississippi, Baker asked him what he really thought of Booker T. Washington and noted his reply: "A fraud & a liar; a smart man; training social parasites; you never heard of a student of his school who ever did anything useful except teach school. BTW has one practice in South another in the North—showing him a hypocrite."[50]

When one of the articles put Washington in the center of the racial reform movement and Du Bois at one extreme and Senator Ben Tillman of South Carolina at the other, even Washington's friend R. R. Moton thought Baker went too far. The race needed champions of their rights such as Du Bois, even though he agreed with Washington's emphasis on duties, Frissell wrote Baker in explaining Moton's views. "He felt that the case placing in the same category Du Bois and men like Tillman, who are trying by every means to take away the rights of other people, was rather hard. But I tried to show him that you did not contend that they were alike in all respects but only in certain of their methods."[51]

Baker's articles and the book that grew out of them, *Following the Color Line* (1909), had a distinctly Washington tone. But Baker was a deeply ambivalent character, as shown by the fact that he wrote muckraking articles in his own name, and under a pseudonym wrote *Adventures in Contentment* and other books glorifying American small-town life.[52] Perhaps because Du Bois persuaded him that he advocated only "the barest sort of justice for Black men" and was naturally suspicious of all men who were not "upon that bare platform,"[53] Baker joined the National Association for the Advancement of Colored People and spoke at its second annual meeting. Immediately afterward, however, he wrote Washington: "The more I see of this whole matter, the more I feel sure that you are on the right track—that it is only by patient development and growth that the evils can be met."[54]

The Atlanta riot, instead of shaking Washington's faith in black progress through self-help and conciliation, actually seemed to reinforce it. He took occasion at the Alabama State Fair on Negro Day, about a month after the riot, to divide blacks into two classes, a large majority of "peaceful, law-abiding citizens" and the few lazy, immoral, drunken, or criminal blacks. He urged the whites to judge blacks by their majority. "Our people are making progress," he insisted. "Immense progress is being made. We want to be sure, however, that this progress is not retarded or halted by reason of any unwise action on our part. Let us hold up our hands and go bravely and wisely forward, and our course will meet with the approval of all men whose good will is worth possessing."[55] Washington had always lacked the capacity for the higher registers of indignation. He almost caricatured himself in a private letter to his longtime white friend and donor Emily Howland, saying that "the riot in Atlanta has resulted in an almost revolutionized condition there so far as the attitude of the white people toward the Negroes is concerned." Those who had let matters drift into the control of the irresponsible had now "taken the reins in their hands."[56] There is no evidence, however, that Washington wished for race riots elsewhere to accomplish similar "reconstructions." And he was not the only one to whistle Dixie in the crisis of Atlanta. From his consulate in Puerto Cabello, Venezuela, James Weldon Johnson wrote: "It is in the nature of things for one race to oppose and oppress another in which it sees a possible rival, and it will continue to do so until the under race becomes strong enough and powerful enough to render such opposition futile. The only way in which the Negro can *at once* put an end to all opposition is by stopping to make progress."[57]

Not long after the Atlanta riot came the President's dismissal without trial of three companies of black regular troops in Brownsville, Texas, an event that provided no grounds whatever for optimism about the progress of American race relations. It not only destroyed the benevolent image of Roosevelt and his party among blacks, but brought sharp criticism of Washington's ambiguous role in the dismissal.

Briefly stated, the Brownsville affray was a ten-minute shooting spree on the night of August 13, 1906, by unknown parties in the area of cafes and dance halls outside of Fort Brown in Brownsville. In the shooting, one white man was killed and a police official was wounded. The black infantry soldiers in the fort assumed that a white mob was attacking, and townspeople believed the black troops were attacking in retaliation for earlier assaults on individual soldiers. An armed mob demanded the punishment of the troops, who meanwhile signed affidavits denying participation in or prior knowledge of the shoot-out. War Department investigators concluded that the black soldiers had formed a "conspiracy of silence" to protect the guilty among them and demanded that they reveal the information that they denied possessing or face dismissal from the service. The soldiers steadfastly denied any knowledge, and the matter came before President Roosevelt for decision.[58]

Roosevelt summoned Booker T. Washington to the White House on October 30. Washington may have guessed that the subject on which the President wanted his advice was Brownsville, but it might also be the Atlanta riot, and Washington hoped that the President would link the two instances of violence as intolerable violations of law and order. He wrote his old friend McKinlay: "This is for your own eye and must not get out. The President is planning to take up the Southern riots in his message to Congress. I am to see him about the matter soon."[59] McKinlay convened at his house, probably on Washington's suggestion, a small group of prominent black men to consider whatever draft message the President might have prepared, in order to advise him on his treatment of riots and lynchings, but without any prior knowledge that he intended to act on the matter of the black troops.[60]

The President surprised Washington by his announcement that he intended to dismiss without trial three companies of the Brownsville regiment, except for their white officers. Only a few, if indeed any of the dismissed soldiers could have been guilty of the shooting. Washington urged the President not to dismiss them. As he soon afterwards told his friend Charles Anderson, he advised Roosevelt frankly that it was "in my opinion a great blunder" and "all the more regrettable because of his waiting until just the day after election before putting the order into effect."[61]

A few days after his audience with the President, Washington wrote him a letter reinforcing his plea, and asking him at least to postpone his decision. "If you possibly can avoid doing so," he wrote, "I very much hope you will not take definite action regarding the Negro soldiers in the Brownsville affair, until after your return from Panama. There is some information which I must put before you before you take the final action."[62] Just what that information was, it is impossible to say. Roosevelt took no heed. Always the man of decision, he either had no small voice of self-doubt to tell him that he was treating black soldiers in a different way from the way he would treat white soldiers, or else he refused to listen to the voice of indecision. He wrote to Washington with a hint of exasperation new to their correspondence: "I could not possibly refrain from acting as regards those colored soldiers. You can not have any information to give me privately to which I could pay heed, my dear Mr. Washington, because the information on which I act is that which came out in the investigation itself."[63]

Roosevelt had made the crucial decision of his administration with regard to black citizens. Now what could Washington do about it? If he denounced or publicly opposed the President's decision, it would be the end of his position as the President's black adviser, a role that he had found useful both to the race and to himself. He decided to swallow the bitter pill and try to minimize the importance of the decision. Though that was not much to say, he could certainly point to Roosevelt as a better friend of the black man than any president for decades of the recent past or in prospect for the near future.

"I have done my full duty in the matter," Washington wrote Charles Anderson, confidentially enclosing a copy of Roosevelt's curt letter.

With his usual pragmatism he remarked of the President: "He usually, however, comes out on top and I presume he will in this case, in the long run if not in the short run." The Brownsville decision posed more dangers for Washington's leadership of blacks than for the President's standing with his largely white constituency. Washington remarked to Anderson of his own predicament: "Of course I am at a disadvantage in that I must keep my lips closed. The enemy will, as usual, try to blame me for all of this. They can talk; I cannot, without being disloyal to our friend, who I mean to stand by throughout his administration."[64] Washington's continued reference to Roosevelt as "our friend" highlights the irony of his position as a presidential advisor. He had built his machine around the political power his closeness to Roosevelt gave him, and even after the patent injustice of Brownsville he could not bring himself to repudiate Roosevelt.

As soon as the dismissal order reached the public, Oswald Garrison Villard wrote a blistering editorial on the injustice the President had committed. Washington wrote Villard to express his private agreement. "I did my full duty in trying to persuade him from the course," he wrote Villard as he had already written Anderson. "I am not going to give up. As soon as he returns I expect to have a conference with him with a view of arranging some plan to do justice to innocent men. There is no law, human or divine, which justifies the punishment of an innocent man. I have the strongest faith in the President's honesty of intention, high mindedness of purpose, sincere unselfishness and courage, but I regret for these reasons all the more that this thing has occurred."[65] But Villard, unlike Anderson, was not Washington's personal friend, and he had lost all faith in Roosevelt's benign intentions toward blacks. He replied that Roosevelt was "the worst President we have had in 25 years."[66] Thousands of blacks—not just the Talented Tenth but many of the rank and file—felt betrayed by Roosevelt's action just as white liberals such as Villard did, and there were mass meetings in many cities to protest. Even the New York *World* called the action of dismissal without a court-martial "executive lynch law," and the generally loyal Anderson began to put quotation marks around "our friend" as a euphemism for the President.

John E. Milholland's Constitution League seized the opportunity to lead the protest movement. "Of course, the Milholland crowd are making the most of it," Anderson reported laconically from New York, "and are saying loudly, that if the order had been signed three days earlier, this state would have elected Hearst, and other Northern states would have gone democratic. They are even threatening to hold a public indignation meeting. I am doing my best to prevent this, and hope to succeed."[67] But Anderson did not succeed, and the indignation meetings in New York City and other centers began to broaden into movements for black political independence from the Republican Party in 1908.

Washington's belief in Roosevelt's sincerity probably rested on his private belief that some, at least, of the Brownsville soldiers were guilty of criminal violence. This was a belief which W.E.B. Du Bois publicly held all of his life,[68] and it was not an unreasonable assumption. Most of the Niagara men, their white sympathizers in the Constitution League, and Senator Joseph B. Foraker of Ohio believed, however, in the innocence of the troops and the racially biased arbitrariness of the President. Many Bookerites also were outraged at Roosevelt and upset at his wrecking their bid for race leadership. "Even Grover Cleveland would not have issued such an order," Bishop Abraham Grant complained. "Why don't you go see him and talk to him, and try to keep him a friend to the weak and helpless of the nation?"[69]

Washington may have had in mind some plan for softening the blow of Brownsville when he wrote the only black officer of the regiment involved, Captain Theophilus G. Steward, chaplain of the 25th Infantry. "Will you be kind enough," he asked, "to send me any information especially bearing upon the condition of individuals in the 25th Infantry that will help me to see that justice is done to the three companies which were dismissed?"[70] Whatever he had in mind seems to have been lost in the furor of public protest over the dismissal, the protest petitions, and independent and congressional investigations. Washington also saw the danger that the vacancy created by the dismissal would not be filled, thus reducing still further the black component of the regular Army. He wrote to Secretary of War William Howard Taft on November 20, 1906: "Will you not tell me whether it is the intention of the War Department to enlist additional colored soldiers to take the place of the three companies which were dismissed?" He also urged the Secretary to make some plans, by the time President Roosevelt returned from Panama, to mollify the black voters. "The race is not so much resentful or angry, perhaps, as it feels hurt and disappointed," he wrote. He did not presume to pass judgment on this attitude because he did not know all the facts on which the dismissal was based, he said, "but I am simply putting a condition before you," a condition further aggravated by the white aggression in the Atlanta riots.[71]

Washington apparently joined in the effort led by the Constitution League to persuade Secretary Taft to suspend the dismissal order until the President returned from Panama. Washington wrote to Kelly Miller during this period that he had written Roosevelt "two letters lately . . . putting the whole situation before him."[72] He may have been referring to the President's forthcoming message to Congress, however, rather than the dismissal order. At any rate, it was Mary Church Terrell who directly asked Secretary Taft to suspend the order, as did Charles Anderson's New York Negro Republican Club. Taft did suspend the order for the two days it took to exchange cables with the President, who insisted: "I care nothing whatever for the yelling of either the politicians or the sentimentalists. The offense was most heinous and the punishment I inflicted was imposed after due deliberation."[73]

Roosevelt was President and neither Taft nor Washington was inclined to question his executive authority or the sincerity of his motives. While those who had no stake in closeness to the President or who opposed his action on principle denounced the dismissal order and its author without restraint, Washington and Scott saw in the administration's political embarrassment an opportunity to seek some compensatory concessions. Scott undertook, with Washington's full knowledge and consent, to improve the lot of other black men in the military system. One area of patent and long neglected injustice was the Army's assignment of white bandmasters not only to all white regiments but even to the black regiments. The practice dated back to the establishment of those regular regiments during the Civil War and Reconstruction, where there was some truth in the claim that there were not enough blacks able to read and arrange martial music. But a reform was decades overdue, and Scott went to work on changing the policy.

Walter H. Loving presented an interesting case. He was an accomplished musician with every qualification, professional and personal, to be an Army bandmaster. A slim man of elegant demeanor, an honor graduate of the New England Conservatory of Music, he had served in the Army from 1893 to 1901, rising in rank from private to second lieutenant. When his volunteer regiment was mustered out, the Army rejected him as a candidate for bandmaster of a regular Army regiment. He therefore organized and conducted the all-Filipino band of the Philippine Constabulary. Washington probably met him for the first time when he and his Filipino band performed daily at the St. Louis World's Fair in 1904.[74]

Scott sought to take advantage of the War Department's embarrassment over Brownsville by writing to Secretary Taft in Loving's behalf. "I beg to call your attention to the fact that years ago white men were enlisted and appointed chief musicians," Scott began. "The custom is still in force, although the cause has long since ceased to exist." He pointed to the selection of white men for the posts as a case of closing "the door of opportunity, denying the best Afro-American talent a chance to rise and making it harder for the Army to recruit desirable black civilian musicians."[75] Taft, who fondly remembered his years as governor-general of the Philippines, recalled Loving as "an admirable leader." He referred the question to the General Staff of the Army, and sent a letter to the white colonels commanding black regiments expressing his wish that "ultimately we may have colored band leaders in the colored regiments."[76]

This small step forward was not in proportion to the giant step backward that the Brownsville dismissal represented, but it was the kind of action the Tuskegee Machine was designed for. The Indianapolis *Freeman* reproduced the correspondence with Taft and warmly praised Scott for thus taking advantage of the disadvantages of Brownsville. Thus encouraged, Scott put pressure on the Army at another vulnerable point. Reading in the black press of Scott's success with the bandmaster issue, Sergeant Major Presly Holliday of the 10th Cavalry Regiment wrote Scott from Fort Robinson, Nebraska, to suggest that he try to persuade the Army to establish regular black artillery units. The Army was about to expand the number of its artillery regiments, but it was a white racial assumption, Holliday observed, "that Colored men can not be found with sufficient intelligence to make good artillerymen. Indeed, I believe this theory is given out officially at the War Department." He said the theory was refuted by the fact that "wherever our men have had an opportunity to handle artillery they have given a good account of themselves, notably in serving the Hotchkiss gun battery at Las Guasimas in 1898."[77]

Scott brought this question to President Roosevelt himself. He asked Roosevelt to order that six batteries of field artillery and not less than eighteen companies of coast artillery be recruited with black men. In consideration of the population growth and progress of blacks since the Civil War, Scott argued, and a comparable growth in the size of the regular Army, the recent reduction in the number of black regular soldiers had produced a gross underrepresentation of blacks in the Army. He further noted that the desertion rate of blacks was lower than the white rate. "They possess sufficient intelligence," he asserted. "Many of the men at present in the army are especially intelligent, alert, and ambitious fellows. They do the most, or all, of the clerical work of their regiments."[78] Scott used the arguments Holliday had given him and added that Secretary Taft himself, in his address at Tuskegee a year earlier, had praised blacks for the great progress they were making "along intellectual and financial lines commensurate with the opportunities which have been offered them."[79] Scott was unsuccessful, however, in enlisting Washington in the effort to open the artillery to blacks. "I have several other matters to place before the President," he wrote Scott, "and I don't want him to think I am pushing too many matters at once."[80] A few days later, however, Washington did recommend Scott's proposal to Secretary Taft as a way to "stop much of the senseless and useless criticism that is now in the air."[81]

Scott gave an optimistic report to Holliday: "I think it may interest you to know that my suggestion to the President and the Secretary of War is being favorably considered by them, and it is quite likely that even before you receive this letter the proposed artillery branch of the service will be set apart."[82] Washington himself, after a long talk with Secretary Taft, gathered the impression that an order was impending to authorize a black artillery regiment. He gave Oswald Garrison Villard advance information to that effect, and Villard promised a supporting editorial.[83]

Ever the patronage broker, Washington began looking ahead to the time when the new black artillery regiment would need a black chaplain, and he saw in this an opportunity to cement an alliance with Bishop Alexander Walters, a politician as well as a spiritual leader of the African Methodist Episcopal Church, Zion. He gave Walters also advance notice of the new regiment and suggested that he and Bishop George Clinton have in readiness the name of a good, clean minister not over forty years old for the chaplaincy. "As you know," he wrote Walters, "the Ministers appointed heretofore have all been from the

A. M. E. Church and I have an idea that your church ought to be represented."[84] These two independent denominations contended with each other and with the Episcopalians and Presbyterians for the membership of the black elite.

Washington and Scott were premature, however, by several decades. The Army was moving away from opportunities for blacks, not opening them up. Sergeant Holliday sent Scott a copy of an order that made it clear that "nothing has been determined on so far towards organizing any Colored field artillery, and that it is the intention to organize the remaining unorganized batteries as white." The climate of white supremacy that pervaded the Army as much as the civil society it served was more powerful than guilt feelings over Brownsville, for behind the reluctance of white leaders to create black artillery units was not so much a doubt of their intelligence as an unspoken fear of black possession of the big guns.

Not even the black aspirants to bandmaster posts had clear sailing. The white commander of Holliday's own regiment, noting that no black man had applied for the position, reappointed his white bandmaster for a three-year term. The colonel had received the War Department order requiring black bandmasters for black regiments where available too late to secure a competent candidate, he reported to the War Department.[85] The human problems involved in the institutionalized discrimination in the Army were too complicated to be solved simply by promoting some black member of the band to chief musician and sending the white man he replaced to some white unit. "Now the trouble will be to get the right men for these positions that the bands may not degenerate by the loss of a good leader," Walter Loving remarked. He had taught his Filipino band to play orchestral as well as band numbers, and he was now a captain in the Constabulary and could not afford to take the loss in rank and pay to become a regular Army bandmaster. "Personally speaking," he wrote, "I do not know of a single man who is now in the service, who could successfully fill one of these positions."[86]

The chief musician probably should be a man unknown to the members of the band, who might not give proper respect to a man who had risen from their own ranks, Loving speculated. This had not been a problem as long as the bandmaster had been white. "You cannot expect to drink, folly, sleep and eat with a crowd of men and then after a quick ascension expect these men to pay you due respect," he said. Furthermore, promotion from within the ranks would play into the hands of unsympathetic white officers who would "pick out every little flaw to make good their objection to colored Bandmasters." Loving suggested that a search be made for four civilians of recognized musical talent to prepare for these new positions at a college of music for a period of six months. As things then were, the white colonels would not accept a man who could not outdo the incumbent bandmaster. "It would be too bad," he wrote Scott, "for you to work so hard to bring about this change and then have your work result in vain."[87]

One by one, however, blacks did become chief musicians of the black regimental bands. James A. Thompson, a black Army musician of fifteen years' experience, became chief musician of the 9th Cavalry in the fall of 1907 through a transfer of the white chief musician to a white cavalry regiment. Elbert Williams, a former Army musician who had been bandmaster at Tuskegee Institute for three years, took charge of the 25th Infantry band in the spring of 1908.[88] By the time of the election of 1908 only two black regimental bands were without black bandmasters.[89] Scott privately boasted that his enterprise and the exigencies of the administration had "just had a crimp put in the War Department machinations with regard to that bandmaster business."[90] He and his colleagues of the black press kept "close behind these fellows to keep them straight." Whenever a white bandmaster retired, the black newspapers clamored for the vacancy to be filled by some black bandsman in one of the black regiments.[91] President Roosevelt in 1908 strengthened their position by a supplementary order to expedite the appointment of black bandmasters. Before leaving office, he urged his successor to "carry out the spirit of the order I have already issued. As soon as it can be done without injustice, I wish all the colored regiments supplied with colored bandmasters."[92]

Scott's success in forcing this issue and his near-success on blacks in the artillery showed how Tuskegee Machine methods could score a few points against the inertia of the federal bureaucracy. But they also revealed Washington's psychological inability to comprehend the monstrous injustice of the President's action and the structural inability of the politics of accommodation to deal with outright betrayal by a white ally. When Washington learned early in 1909 that all of the six new regiments of light artillery had been staffed with whites, he could only express disappointment and urge Secretary Taft "at the proper time" to create a seventh regiment of black artillery. "Colored men as a rule are anxious to enlist in the service," he pleaded, "while I understand white men are difficult to get." [93]

Washington insisted on viewing President Roosevelt's action on the Brownsville affray as an unfortunate but honest mistake on the part of a long-established friend of blacks. He soon found that this view of Roosevelt was unacceptable to most articulate blacks and liberal whites, and that the minor concessions wrung from the Army did nothing to repair the damage Brownsville had done to his and Roosevelt's standing. Secretary of War Taft, who had held up the order for two days but then carried it out and defended it, came to be regarded by the critics of the Brownsville dismissal as Roosevelt's partner in injustice, and as he became Roosevelt's heir-apparent to the presidential nomination in 1908 he became increasingly the target of black outrage.

The Brownsville dismissal also took most of the pleasure if not the power from Washington's role as the President's adviser. "When Mr. Roosevelt requested you to act as his adviser and when you accepted that delicate responsibility," Kelly Miller reminded Washington, "the world may be expected to believe that he is guided by the advice of his own seeking. This, I know, often works an injustice to you, but it is exactly the kind of injustice that all leaders must bear. In the minds of many you are held responsible for the dismissal of the colored soldiers, although few fair minded men could believe that you counselled it." [94]

Compounding the indignity of the Brownsville dismissal, the President prepared his December 1906 annual message to Congress. In his opinion, it addressed the issues presented by the Atlanta race riot and the epidemic of racial lynching in the South. In his message Roosevelt made explicit the racial bias that his handling of the Brownsville issue had implied. This was the very message that Washington and his friends in the national capital had gone over in draft form. But the more they advised changing, the more Roosevelt clung to his racial premises, though he amended the language to give the speech a number of Booker T. Washington turns of phrase, so that the black adviser's mark was indelibly on a state paper that he did not really support and that many blacks condemned as a white supremacy document.

Kelly Miller had warned Washington in advance of the damage to his standing as a presidential adviser of the President's "proposed treatment of the Negro as a criminal race." Miller wrote of the draft message: "The Negro is held up as a race of criminals and rapists, banded together to uphold one another in crime, with only occasional individual exceptions. No further justification would be needed by those who despitefully treat us." The message would be more harmful than anything an avowed racist could say, branding the Negro "as a lecherous race, with the authority of the President of the United States."[95] Washington tried to reassure Miller that the effect of the forthcoming message would not be as bad as he feared. Some features of the message, Washington conceded, he would like to have changed and had tried to change, such as the passage urging blacks to hunt down criminals of their own race. "Of course, you must bear in mind that he has for his object the saying of something that will help to make life and property for the Negro in the South safer, and in order to do this he has, in a measure, placed himself in touch with the Southern people. I am now simply presenting his side of the case." Washington also said he wished he had been able to tone down the President's reference to speedy trials. "In all but those measures I got him to make modifications along the line of our advice."[96]

Roosevelt's message confirmed all Miller's fears. He began with the subject of rape, and in a tone of outrage that had something southern about it. Despite the dinner at the White House, the imperious closing of the Indianola postoffice, and the dogged insistence on a black collector of the port of Charleston, Roosevelt illustrated in his message how widespread the attitudes of white supremacy were in America. Perhaps his Georgia cousins and his aristocratic affinity with "southern chivalry" subconsciously colored his utterances, and he found Booker Washington attractive as an adviser just as many southerners did, because he was a conservative, who when he found himself at odds with the President did not reject his position but merely tried to modify it.

"The greatest existing cause of lynching is the perpetration, especially by black men, of the hideous crime of rape," wrote Roosevelt, "—the most abominable in all the category of crimes even worse than murder." In the President's calculus of rape, as among white southerners, the sexual union of white man and black woman was presumed to be consensual, whereas the union of black man and white woman was presumed to be rape. Having begun by establishing that rape was worse than murder, including lynching, the President noted that "when mobs begin to lynch for rape they speedily . . . lynch for many other kinds of crimes," and that many lynch victims were in fact innocent of any crime whatever. Then, in oblique reference to Brownsville, he urged "respectable colored people . . . not to harbor criminals." What was his solution for the lynching problem? To end black criminality. And how was that to be achieved? By the "best type of education for the colored man," the type offered by Hampton and Tuskegee and their offspring. Few of their graduates were guilty of crime, especially of "the form of that brutal violence which invites lynch-law."[97]

After reading the President's message, Fortune wrote Washington one of the last of his many helpful suggestions before cutting his close ties with the Tuskegee leader. "I am sorry that the President did not let you blue pencil his message, as far as it relates to us," he wrote, "and all the more so as he has employed throughout the message your phraseology and often your idioms. His advice that Afro-Americans who know nothing of their criminals shall help to hunt them down and his adoption of the lynch law method of slaying the innocent with the guilty are vile propositions calculated to do us great injury." Fortune also objected to Roosevelt's exclusive endorsement of industrial education, whereas Washington also approved of higher education of blacks. The President's endorsement, Fortune wrote, "will do the cause of industrial education no good whatever, in the estimation of Afro-Americans and especially those antagonistic to you, and as a general proposition to which you have subscribed the race needs the very sort of education that other Americans need." Fortune called on Washington to sever his connection with Roosevelt, and said that Emmett Scott, with whom he had recently had a long conversation, had agreed with him "that you have gone as far with [Roosevelt] as you can afford to."[98]

Instead, Washington decided he had gone as far as he could with Fortune. Emmett Scott as Washington's agent began acquiring stock in the New York *Age* early in 1907 and served as dummy stockholder. Fortune apparently believed that he would remain as editor, though Washington would control the business aspects, and he wrote the Tuskegean: "I feel now that I have justified to you the position I have always taken with you that it was very unsatisfactory to have you place money in a property in which you had no property interest."[99] Scott proposed to leave Fortune in control of the editorial page but to employ a "live business manager," increase the advertising, conduct a side business in job printing, improve the layout, and add new features.[100]

The changes Scott proposed increased strain on Fortune's precarious emotional health. He sought relief in sexual adventures, alcoholism, and an uncharacteristic religiosity. His health broke down completely in the fall of 1907, and he offered to sell his remaining shares in the *Age* to Fred R. Moore, who secured the money to carry out the transfer from Washington. Since Washington was aware of Fortune's emotional state, it was an act of moral callousness to buy him out at that time, and particularly so to do it in secret. Fortune soon recovered his balance sufficiently to try to return to Moore the small sum of $300 that had sealed the trade. Moore insisted, however, that he had a binding contract. Washington stood by Moore and continued to supply him with the money to buy Fortune's stock in installments. Moore claimed that a "white friend" had lent him the money, and Washington pretended to Fortune that he was unaware of the source of Moore's funds.[101] Washington also misled others as to his ownership and control of the *Age*. When Moore dismissed one of his feature writers, the man appealed to Washington as the owner. Washington replied: "I do not hold a single share of stock in connection with the *Age* and have no financial interest in it. I have made it a rule from the beginning not to own any part in colored newspapers."[102]

Under pressure from Tuskegee, Moore reversed the newspaper's editorial position on the crucial issue of Brownsville. This so enraged Fortune that he completely separated himself from both the *Age* and Washington. He even reported to the opposition papers that Washington now owned and controlled the *Age*. Fortune had "gone over, horse, foot, and dragoon to the enemy," Anderson complained.[103] Fortune left New York and spent many months in Chicago.

Fortune was only one of many black persons for whom the Atlanta and Brownsville episodes were turning points in their lives and in their perceptions of the white-dominated society around them. Many sensed a growing similarity between the whites in the South and those in the North on the issue of white supremacy. "Time is getting on," an anonymous white "Friend" wrote Washington. "Can't you see that the white people north and south are drawing closer every day on this race question?" The southern whites were not allowing blacks to vote, and the northern Republican newspapers were supporting disfranchisement. The writer urged Washington to bargain the black vote

for treaty rights for a black republic and the money for a mass emigration.[104] Passing this letter postmarked from Chicago to his lieutenant S. Laing Williams, Washington called it "one of the straws that
shows that the feeling between the Northern white people and the
Southern white people is more akin all the time." Washington blamed
"these frequent meetings held by these agitators" and expressed longing for black gatherings to found a bank or open a coal mine.[105] That
was hardly an adequate remedy, but for every emigrationist letter
Washington received two that advocated more vigorous efforts at assimilation. "Dont have nothing Jim Crowed," a black man wrote, "you
can see for your Self that Jim Crow politeness to one side have growed
to be Jim Crow everything, and if we Dont Change Jim Crow it will
finally be a Jim Crow death, it is already a Jim Crow life."[106]

The twin disasters of Atlanta and Brownsville showed the systemic
flaws of an accommodationist racial policy for any other purpose than
the survival of the minority group or the power of its accommodating
leader. At this moment, if ever, Washington had an option to change
course, not so much to join the protest movement as to give civil rights
a more central place in his own program. Washington might appear
better in the light of history if he had seized the moment, conceded
the inevitability of conflicting objectives of white and black, and challenged the rampant white supremacy of these two incidents. To do
that, however, he would have had to be someone other than Booker
T. Washington, schooled in slavery, trained to moderation, accustomed to compromise.

CHAPTER 13

Brownsville Ghouls

Another Brownsville and we will have everything.

JAMES A. COBB, 1908

W ASHINGTON could have walked out on Theodore Roosevelt and the whole political game after the Brownsville affair. He had said often enough that politics was no career for an ambitious black man. But Brownsville and the President's dismissal of the soldiers after a hasty and unfair investigation highlighted instead Washington's lack of one essential attribute for the leader of an oppressed minority—the capacity for righteous public anger against injustice. Washington could and did work with dogged persistence against a great variety of racial injustices that white men perpetrated. He could chide or cajole with great skill and subtlety. But somewhere back in his life the power to lose his temper with a white man had been schooled out of him. And Brownsville, the grossest single racial injustice of that so-called Progressive Era, was just the occasion for loss of temper. Instead, Washington thought of "taking advantage of our disadvantages" politically, as he had always advocated economically. Roosevelt was the white boss, and he said the incident was closed. Washington accepted that decision, used it to strengthen his machine, and became more than ever the black boss.

In the petty politics of black patronage, Brownsville actually helped Washington. His black critics scorned the pursuit of office in an administration they loathed, and they wanted no part of the campaign in 1908 of Roosevelt's chosen successor. Washington was therefore able to move into federal offices some of his lower echelon of followers to fill the vacuum left by the supporters of the Niagara Movement and of Trotter's newly organized Negro-American Political League.[1] President Roosevelt complacently remarked to Washington that "the Negro race had not acted near so badly over the Brownsville matter as the laboring element had acted over the Haywood affair."[2] That remark, however, probably reflected only Roosevelt's ignorance of the extent of black disaffection. Arthur I. Vorys of Indiana, whom Taft had already hired as the political manager of his campaign for the Republican presidential nomination a year later, warned Washington of "the serious and far reaching result" the Brownsville affair might have on black votes in the closely contested northern states. Washington answered that he was "doing some quiet and effective work with the colored newspapers" to try to defuse as yet unexploded editorial bombs.[3]

As the New York *Age*'s new owners, Washington and Scott reversed its earlier policy of denouncing the Brownsville dismissal. Even Fortune in his last days as editor had tempered his criticism of Roosevelt, at Washington's insistence, to such a degree that the Cleveland *Gazette* accused him of accepting Republican bribes.[4] Under the newly installed editor Fred R. Moore, however, the *Age* completely reversed itself. Washington and Scott had persuaded Moore to employ Ralph Tyler, who had had long newspaper experience, as a part-time editorial writer. Tyler wrote and the *Age* published the editorial "Brownsville Ghouls," attacking the critics of the dismissal action. These "ghouls," said Tyler, "raised the black flag of Race Discrimination and moved out in search, not of justice, but of the thirty pieces of silver coined for Judases." In other words, he implied that the protesters were simply demanding to be bought off.[5]

Fortune tried to publish a reply in the *Age*. Moore refused to publish it, so Fortune took it to the opposition newspapers. The real ghouls, he·said, were Roosevelt and Taft and the blacks who supported them.[6] Even Washington thought Tyler's editorial went too far, and privately chided him for his "boomerang."[7]

Washington and Scott saw early that Taft would probably be Roosevelt's successor and that he would be unpalatable to blacks. The Tuskegee Machine would have to support him, however, in the hope of entrenching itself in the Republican Party. Early in 1908, Scott sought to analyze the black complaints against Taft and consider how he should respond to them. First, it would be said that he had been instrumental in the order to dismiss the Brownsville soldiers. Scott thought Taft should not even reply to this. Second, it would be alleged that Taft had publicly endorsed the disfranchisement laws of the South and had opposed southern blacks holding federal office or participating in politics. Scott hoped that Taft would respond to that charge by unambiguously calling for "the equal treatment of the illiterate & propertyless classes" regardless of race.[8] Fortune had a more apocalyptic view, that blacks would repudiate not only Taft but Booker Washington for having abetted Roosevelt. Blacks, said Fortune, would no longer be satisfied "by the fact that the President entertained Booker Washington to dinner once, and never did it any more."[9] But there was dissidence in the dissenting ranks. Fortune favored an independent party; to Du Bois the best alternative seemed to be a vote— while holding his nose—for William Jennings Bryan.[10]

Washington insensitively concluded in 1908 that most blacks would remember that Roosevelt and Taft had "favored them in nine cases out of ten and the intelligent portion of the race does not believe that it is fair or wise to condemn such good friends as President Roosevelt and Secretary Taft because they might have done what is considered a mistake in one case, but in nine cases have done what they considered right."[11] Washington undertook to make the political defectors pay for their bolt. "Another Brownsville and we will have everything," said James A. Cobb, assistant district attorney and a member of the Tuskegee Machine.[12]

Meanwhile, the battle with the lily whites began again in the South, and the success that Washington's southern blacks had in getting Republican national convention seats would determine the standing of his lieutenants in the Republican campaign to follow.

Southern Republicanism was, as usual, a political swamp. In Alabama the two presidential referees, Charles H. Scott and Joseph O. Thompson, quarreled over the spoils, Scott accusing Thompson of coveting his national committeeman post, and Thompson saying Scott was conspiring with the lily whites. Roosevelt and Frank Hitchcock tried to restore peace by halving the patronage between the two, but Washington warned that this would mean "a permanent breach" and suggested getting them back into harmony instead.[13] "If a choice has to be made between the two men, Mr. Thompson is the man," he wrote Roosevelt.[14] The President liked Thompson too, and assurances reached Washington that Thompson would not be interfered with and would be considered the leader of the party in Alabama.[15]

The quadrennial battle of the factions began in February 1908 when the Alabama lily white state executive committee met without a single black member and endorsed an uninstructed delegation. Then Thompson's black-and-tan faction convened its executive committee and endorsed Taft by 30 to 2. Washington let the White House know that Charles Scott had "aligned himself pretty strongly with the 'lily white' element."[16] Each faction then held district conventions along the same lines. Many blacks in Alabama, outraged over Brownsville, considered joining the lily whites for lack of any other way of registering protest; and Washington had to work hard to prevent this.[17]

Alabama might be a pivotal state in deciding whether lily white delegations would be seated, since it came first in the alphabetical order, and Washington urged Thompson to make sure his lawyers had mastered every detail before the credentials committee. For example, they must be ready to show that state officials had given the lily whites an advantage by awarding them the party emblem on the ballot.[18] Washington arranged for northern blacks to talk with their national committeemen and to attend the sessions of the committee to make clear that northern blacks cared about the outcome. Washington won the Alabama contest by what Scott called a "knock-out," as the entire Thompson delegation was seated, the only vote against it being that of the lily white Charles H. Scott.[19]

Washington also cared about the Louisiana contest. In that state was a reversal of the Alabama line-up. The lily whites elected a delegation pledged to Taft, and Walter L. Cohen's delegation was uninstructed. Washington did everything in his power to change this, to get Taft and his manager Hitchcock to forgive it, to get Cohen to exact some pledge of loyalty to Taft from his delegation, but to no avail. Cohen said he had done the best he could, considering the bitterness over Brownsville. "To have a delegation composed of ex-office holders and a very large number of colored persons and for not a harsh word to be said against the administration is good work," he wrote Washington.[20] After 100-word telegrams to all the parties, Washington brought about a compromise. Cohen received half-votes for his delegation, the other half going to the lily whites, and a lily white remained as national committeeman while Cohen became state party chairman.[21]

Meanwhile, all through the first half of 1908, Washington was busy strengthening his hold on the party in the capital and the North. The first of his efforts was a complete but harmless fiasco. Learning that in February 1908 the boards of bishops of the three big black Methodist denominations were to meet at the same time in Washington, he saw that the firebrands among them, particularly Bishops Turner and Walters, were likely to lead a delegation to the White House to tongue-lash the President and then release their remarks to the newspapers. To head off any such embarrassment, he persuaded conservative Bishop Grant to head the delegation and to have it understood that neither the President's remarks nor their own were to appear in the press.[22] Washington also took the precaution to have Whitefield McKinlay and William Loeb, the President's secretary, present to "play the part of fool killers" if either Turner or Walters opened his mouth.[23] Just as Washington thought he had defused the bomb, however, the anti-Brownsville bishops refused to go to the White House without any mention of Brownsville, and somebody, probably Walters, started the rumor that Booker Washington had given Grant $500 to buy the silence of the dissident bishops.[24] Whether true or not, the rumor bluffed Grant into silence, and the meeting at the White House never took place.[25]

Washington meanwhile turned his attention to the more corruptible black press. He urged on Hitchcock and Vorys, the Taft managers, the "importance of getting hold of two or three of the strongest colored papers in your territory as soon as possible." These would "in a large degree control the utterances of the others."[26] He sent Hitchcock a list, grading them A, B, C, and so on, and omitting three or four "so unreasonable in their opposition to Secretary Taft and the President that I have not thought it well to name them at all."[27] He wrote Vorys, in charge of the Midwest, not to waste his time and money starting a new black newspaper but to encourage and strengthen established ones, particularly the Indianapolis *Freeman* and Chicago *Conservator*. "Neither of these papers have, so far, taken a definite position," he wrote, "that is, they have not gone far enough on the other side to prevent their being controlled." He suggested to Vorys that he "send for the men and have a personal conference with them." He did not write, however, exactly *how* to control the editors.[28]

A few weeks later, in early March 1908, Ralph W. Tyler went from Washington, D.C., to Chicago, Indianapolis, and other cities as the Republican Party bag man. Washington never touched any of the money that changed hands, but he knew every detail. "At Chicago I closed up with the Conservator," wrote Tyler, "and at Indianapolis brought the Freeman under our wing. At Chicago I mingled much with the natives up there, and scattered a lot of Taft sentiment."[29] He also had "a little seance" with Calvin Chase of the *Bee,* who promised thereafter "to run an administration paper." "I met Chase just at the psychological moment," Tyler wrote Scott, "and you know what that means in the career of a negro publication."[30] When some of Tyler's arrangements came unglued Washington was quick to suggest repairs. "Better get in close and immediate touch with Trice," he wired Tyler about the *Conservator*'s owner. "Plans may be thwarted and enemy get charge of paper unless you keep in close touch. May have to render little extra help."[31] "I sent Love a check for $50 yesterday, and wrote him that I would probably be able to duplicate it, for a like amount, in a short time," Tyler wrote of a Dallas editor. "Nick Child [Chiles], of the Topeka Plain Dealer was in to see me, and was willing to be taken care of," he added.[32] Trice, and presumably others, went to the well more than once.[33]

By special arrangement with Hitchcock and the Republican National Committee, Washington put the venerable black veteran of Reconstruction, P. B. S. Pinchback, on the circuit of the southern state conventions. "Gov. P. B. S. Pinchback will call to see you tomorrow," Washington wrote Hitchcock. "The Governor is one of the few old time politicians who still retain the entire respect and confidence of the Southern colored people and who has great influence on them. The mere fact that it is known that he favors Secretary Taft will count for much." At Washington's suggestion and at party expense Pinchback circulated quietly through the South. "He is a good 'mixer,' " Washington wrote Hitchcock, "and I strongly advise that he be permitted to spend as much money as you can afford in entertaining friends where he goes."[34] Pinchback roamed the South, occasionally spending a Sunday at Tuskegee to rest and report on his work.[35] He did yeoman service particularly in Georgia in reconciling the rival black factions.

None of Washington's efforts could lay the ghost of Brownsville or prevent the formation at Philadelphia in April 1908 of the National Negro-American Political League, led by Monroe Trotter. Its convention castigated Roosevelt and Taft and endorsed Joseph B. Foraker for President.[36] But Washington and the black Taft forces could at least send a spy. Ralph Tyler and W. T. Vernon by an understanding, or perhaps a misunderstanding, each gave W. Calvin Chase $25 to go to Philadelphia and report back.[37]

The only important result of this espionage was that it uncovered an act of petty venality by Vernon that led to his dismissal and replacement by a Washington lieutenant. Unknown to Tyler, Vernon had received $100 from Hitchcock to pay Chase's expenses. He paid only $25 to Chase, persuaded Tyler to give Chase another $25, and pocketed $75 from this sleight of hand. He even requested a blank receipt so that he could fill in an amount greater than he had paid Chase. At a meeting with Hitchcock, Tyler learned by accident of the $100, and quietly gathered the evidence. "I caught Mr. Vernon red-handed," Tyler reported gleefully to Scott. They waited until after the election, however, to present it to the administration. Meanwhile, Tyler privately diminished Vernon's dignity by derisive sobriquets such as "the eloquent one" and "Mr. Ego."[38]

In the spring of 1908 Washington worked assiduously to present the best possible image of Taft to the black public. Discovering that Taft's daughter taught a black Sunday school, he arranged for Scott and R. W. Thompson to publicize this in the black press.[39] He arranged for Taft to address a New York gathering in behalf of Hampton Institute and one in Nashville to dedicate the Carnegie Library at Fisk University. He went over both of these speeches in advance.[40] At Fisk Taft said that "with respect to a race like this you cannot have a system of education that is not in the form of a pyramid, with the best education, the highest education at the top, and a broad primary and industrial education to form the foundation of that edifice."[41] Washington privately called this speech "one of the best endorsements of college education from a public man I have seen."[42]

As the Republican national convention of 1908 approached, the Tuskegee Machine considered the question of a suitable black man to make the traditional seconding speech for Taft's nomination. This had proved a difficult problem four years earlier, but in 1908 it was an even more delicate one because of Brownsville. Tyler suggested to Vorys the name of J. McHenry Jones, president of the West Virginia Colored Institute.[43] But Washington thought Jones too dull a speaker and backed John E. Bush, receiver of public monies at Little Rock.[44] Taft himself more ambitiously favored William H. Lewis. "I believe it would be better to have a colored man from the north do it," Taft wrote Washington, "and I am sure he could not come from a better state than Massachusetts."[45] Washington accepted this, but apparently still harbored the memory of Lewis's scathing criticism of him a decade earlier. Washington confided to Charles Anderson that "there are several weak elements in his doing it, and some stronger man might have been selected, but I feared that if we did not clinch the matter at once with Lewis the fellow from Kansas [W. T. Vernon] might be selected which would have been disastrous, or if not him some other fellow who would have been untrustworthy or disloyal."[46] Anderson, who was himself out of the competition because his New York delegation supported Hughes as a favorite son, agreed with Washington that they "ought to defeat Vernon at all hazards."[47] Washington urged Taft to "stick to Lewis" but suggested Bishop Grant and Charles Banks as possible alternatives.[48] In the end no black man was invited to make a seconding speech, an omen of the troubles to come.

Washington possibly had some influence on the "Negro plank" in the party platform. He sent Taft some suggestions for the plank, commending Roosevelt's efforts for equal accommodations on the railroads, demanding equal protection of the laws, opposing the color line in voting, condemning the grandfather clause and the lily white movement. Washington wrote in a covering letter: "My own view is that something like the enclosed would do more good than the meaningless platform [of 1904] about reducing Southern representation."[49]

As in 1904, Anderson carried Washington's standard at the Republican national convention, and his chief aides were Scott, Tyler, and Pinchback. S. Laing Williams's Colored Taft League of Chicago organized a large meeting of blacks at Quinn Chapel. The Brownsville protesters also appeared in numbers, however, and the meeting was stormy. When the hosts arrived to light up the chapel, they found the wires cut, and the meeting began late. The crowd became restless and greeted Anderson, the first speaker, with "hisses, groans & some remarks." He persisted, however, until the crowd grew quiet, and Vernon and Pinchback followed.[50] "You see it always pays to be brave and frank like you always are," Washington wrote Anderson.[51]

To all of the black politicos who dealt with Frank Hitchcock as Taft's manager at the convention, he was evasive and uncooperative, as though he personally sympathized with the lily whites. As Tyler said,

"I am constrained to believe that none of us who were early and steadfastly in the game for Secretary Taft, will receive recognition if Mr. Hitchcock is chosen manager. I . . . think that he prefers to ignore the manly negro and prefers to recognize the obsequious negro." It was as easy, he said, to see the Czar of Russia as to see Hitchcock.[52] Washington shared this opinion, but he knew Hitchcock would be chosen regardless. The practice of accommodation had made him perfect at it, and he wrote to Hitchcock: "I have telegraphed Judge Taft at Hot Springs telling him that in my opinion it is the wish of the leading colored people throughout the country that you be placed in charge of his campaign."[53]

Washington asked Taft, if he said anything at all about the Negro in his acceptance speech, to let him look it over first.[54] He also suggested that Taft meet with a half-dozen representative blacks "and let it go out to the public that they had conferred with you at your invitation."[55] Taft agreed, and let Washington select the participants.[56] Soon Taft sent along a passage he proposed for his acceptance speech, and invited Washington to Hot Springs to discuss it. Washington sidestepped any visit to that southern spa, but gathered in New York with Tyler, Anderson, and Moore to review the document. "It was mighty lucky that I suggested to Secretary Taft to let me see what he was going to say on this subject," Washington wrote Scott, "otherwise he would have made a great bungle of it. What he proposed to say was in many respects very unhappily put, and his enemies would have simply gloated over his remarks."[57]

On the sensitive subject of disfranchisement, Taft wrote in his original draft:

It is to be taken as a step forward that the States in which there was originally fraud and violence have now sought to base their exclusion of Negroes on statutory law, which squares with the Federal Constitution, and thus, however much we may deplore the injustice now done to the Negro by unfair execution of such laws, I have strong hopes that the wisdom of the equal enforcement of the law will ultimately appeal to the Southern States in such a way as that the rules of eligibility will be enforced equally against black and white. The best friend of the Negro should be the Southern white man, and we ought to rejoice to see growing among the Southern people an influential element disposed to encourage the Negro in his hard struggle for industrial independence and assured political status.[58]

Washington and his conferees threw away that draft, which only made clear that Taft was not a genuine friend of blacks. Their draft, which Taft incorporated in his acceptance speech without change, stated:

> The Republican platform, adopted at Chicago, explicitly demands justice for all men without regard to race or color, and just as explicitly declares for the enforcement, and without reservation, in letter and spirit of the 13th., 14th. and 15th. Amendments to the Constitution. It is needless to state that I stand with my party squarely on that plank in the platform, and believe that equal justice to all men, and the fair and impartial enforcement of these amendments is in keeping with the real American spirit of fair-play.[59]

Emmett Scott, filing away the two drafts, commented to his chief: "Secretary Taft has in you a much better friend than he perhaps will appreciate."[60] The real question, however, was whether or not Taft could be made an ally and friend in spite of himself.

Washington promised Charles Anderson to talk straight to Taft, "that if he wants the support of the Colored people, a change of policy must take place—that you or some other Colored man must be recognized in a decent manner."[61] Anderson, however, predicted that the party would re-enact the parable of the prodigal son, "that the big folks will pay all of their attention to the men who have been fighting the party, and forget those who have been faithful."[62] He noted that while the candidate loafed at a southern resort all the black members were replaced by white southerners on the Republican National Committee, that no black had been asked to second the nomination, that the party had a chairman long friendly with the lily whites.[63] Washington had to agree that "we get nothing but what we fight for" and that "we will have to begin earlier and further back to agitate for what is wanted."[64]

As blacks were learning to expect less from the Republican Party, highly placed Republicans took a more complacent view of the black voter. Whitelaw Reid privately wrote that, "while I think him quite capable of taking Democratic money, I believe him still likely, when he gets into the polling booth, to select the Republican ticket!"[65] It was symbolic of the new era that a white man, William L. Ward of New York, headed the Negro Bureau.

Ward did, at least, take Washington's advice. R. W. Thompson went to meet Ward in early September as the Tuskegean's representative to settle on the black newspapers subsidies. Thompson reported that Ward had confessed he knew nothing of the black vote and was ready to take the advice of experienced blacks. Thompson wrote of his interview: "He asked if the papers and the amounts set opposite had been gone over by all of us in conference, and upon my assurance that the proportion and relative values had been approved by you and Mr. Tyler, with full knowledge of the influence wielded by each, he said the whole matter was endorsed by him and he would be guided solely by you and your assistants in handling the colored situation. Asked many questions, which I answered to the best of my ability, with due regard to caution and discretion about talking too much. He said he would 'take me on,' and an office will be provided for me in the building. . . ."[66]

Ward offered and Thompson accepted $50 a week. "That would enable me to take care of both ends and have a little to lay away for a 'rainy day,' " Thompson wrote Washington. He was aware, he said, that "upon my discretion depends much of the immunity you have from criticism of such people as the Boston Guardian," and promised to keep his political work as secret as possible by staying away from "the gang." He also told Washington that Tyler had volunteered "a personal missionary effort" with any of the black papers that needed the sort of persuasion he had used last spring.[67] In addition to these bribes to the black papers that Thompson and Tyler handled for Washington, the Tuskegee boss also sent Ward lists of blacks he should consult, others he should send to speak in the doubtful northern states, and black delegations that would give Taft a show of support along his campaign trail.[68]

All was not well at the white-run Negro Bureau, however. The sharp nose of Anderson detected there the smell of fatted calf. He called on Ward's headquarters to report on a speaking tour through Ohio, found Senator W. Murray Crane of Massachusetts closeted with Ward to discuss the black newspapers, and saw in Crane's hand a card bearing the names of Monroe Trotter of the *Guardian,* Clement G. Morgan of the Boston *Mirror,* and Charles Alexander of *Alexander's Magazine.* Crane urged Ward to send money to all three. "I at once protested," Anderson reported to Tuskegee. "I told them that Trotter and Morgan were both supporting Bryan, but urged Ward to help Alexander. We had quite a session, but at its conclusion Ward agreed to help

Alexander, but not Morgan or Trotter. I remained with him after
Crane left, and put a quietus on Mr. T. and Mr. M. What do you
think of this? It would surely have gone through had I not dropped
in."[69]

Washington prepared for Ward a fresh list of sixteen black newspapers in the East to receive subsidies of $625 a week, or $4525 for
the final seven weeks of the campaign.[70] Ward now insisted, however,
on deciding which papers would receive the available sums, passing
over several for their transgressions.[71] Thompson was to prepare the
Republican news and editorial handouts, but Ward decided that
Thompson should return to his Washington office to do this work,
handing out the Republican matter along with his regular syndicated
news service and without mention of his connection with the party.
For this clandestine service, Ward reduced Thompson's pay to $30 a
week.[72]

Thompson was never as discreet as he promised to be, and Scott
was "very much disturbed and surprised" to hear that Thompson was
carrying the list of bribed newspapers in his pocket and had shown it
to at least one person.[73] Either Thompson or Tyler also leaked word
of a confidential meeting at Washington's summer place on Long Island. "The only way Mr. Washington can do business with anybody,"
Scott warned, "is for them to keep in confidence all matters that are
agreed upon to keep in confidence." Tyler swore that he had kept "a
sphinx-like silence" and pointed his finger at Thompson, saying he
had met with him three times to "impress upon him the necessity of
absolute silence and confidence."[74]

Believing that Ward was mismanaging the Negro Bureau through
ignorance, Washington urged him to put trusted black men in charge
at Chicago, Indianapolis, and New York, "who might get among the
rank and file and give you first hand information as to what their
attitude is at present." In another letter on the same day, he sent
Ward evidence of Chicago blacks' "apathetic and sullen disposition
toward the Republican ticket" and the infiltration of the Republican
speakers' bureau there by "the organization known as the Niagara
Movement, which supports the Democratic party."[75]

A similar situation developed in New York, where the opportunistic
black national committeeman from Georgia, Henry Lincoln Johnson,
"hypnotized Ward, captured Hitchcock, and formed a close alliance
with Fortune." Anderson and his club refused to attend a meeting

Johnson organized without consulting Anderson, in Reverdy Ransom's church, with Pinchback in the chair. Ransom was one of Booker Washington's bitterest critics. Anderson organized his own meeting on the same night, where the President and Taft were vociferously endorsed. "At the other meeting, a riot was narrowly avoided," Anderson reported to Washington, "as Ransome had worked hard to pack the church with his kickers. Fortune tried to speak, but was hooted down. Moore tried also but was jeered at, I am told, but to cap the climax, Wetmore made the last speech of the night, in which he denounced you by name, called you a coward, and accused you of being responsible for the dismissal of the soldiers. As his friend Johnson was handled so roughly by the crowd, for stating that he believed the soldiers guilty, Wetmore changed the tactics, and instead of defending the President, he assailed him, and abused you. Poor Pinchback he had to grin and bear it."[76] J. Douglas Wetmore, whom Anderson despised, was a young lawyer formerly of Jacksonville. He was light enough to pass for white, and often did so. It became more and more evident that the white Republicans in charge of the black end of the campaign were wooing the disaffected at the expense of the loyal. Washington shook his head and declared that such things would never happen if Roosevelt were still in charge. "He is one of the few great men," Washington wrote Anderson, "who is not afraid to place power and responsibility in the hands of Colored people. He would not think of doing anything in New York without consulting you and getting your wishes."[77]

Despite the handicaps he worked under, Anderson did his usual superb organizational work. He created a campaign committee in New York City consisting of fifteen black members of the Republican county committee, eighteen election district captains, and three black ministers, "the men who do the work." He undertook to pack every black meeting in the city with "wildly enthusiastic and demonstrative" Republicans, and to put lithographs of Taft in the window of every black home in certain districts, in order to refute the claim that blacks were against Taft. "Any man passing through one of these black belts and seeing a Taft lithograph in every window of the colored tenement houses," he argued, "which are frequently five and six stories high, will surely be convinced that the alleged disaffection of the negro voters is all moonshine." Anderson started a school for campaign speakers at his club, telling them to avoid any reference to Brownsville. If someone in the audience brought it up, however, they were to refer to a bill sponsored by two Democrats to dismiss all the black soldiers in the army and to reject black enlistments. This, together with the silence of Democratic national and state platforms and candidate Bryan on the rights of blacks "ought to be a sufficient answer to any man who may have the nerve to ask about Brownsville, in a Republican meeting," said Anderson.[78]

The Brownsville affair had made a deep wound in the black psyche, however, and black voters were "growling quietly." The black Republican spellbinders became reluctant to address large crowds. "They do not seem to know just what to do or what to say," said R. W. Thompson.[79] Anderson believed a plot was hatching to get the Republicans to dump Booker T. Washington. He told Washington that Link Johnson "told Hitchcock that it would not do to have you control the colored end of things—that the colored people of the country were divided into two factions, the majority one being opposed to you, and that Mr. Taft would have every man against him, who is now opposing you, if your close connection with the campaign was not speedily ended." Anderson reported that Hitchcock then took Johnson to Ward and Herbert Parsons to repeat his allegations.[80]

Anderson apparently persuaded the Republican managers that Johnson was untrustworthy, for Hitchcock shipped him back to Georgia before the campaign was over. "Charley blanketed him, and Hitchcock sent him to the stable," as Tyler put it.[81] When candidate Taft himself spoke in New York at an A. M. E. Zion Church, Anderson handled the encounter with his usual éclat. Despite a torrential rain, the church was full and hundreds were forced into the basement and the street for overflow meetings. Even the street meeting in the rain had a large attendance, and Anderson proclaimed it "the largest and most enthusiastic demonstration of colored voters ever held in New York State." Taft emphasized black education and seemed especially anxious to leave the impression that he was in favor of higher education. Anderson reported to his boss that even Hitchcock, not usually generous toward him, had to give him credit for "delivering the goods."[82]

In the campaign of 1908 the Tuskegee Machine was reasonably effective, considering the albatross of Brownsville, the management of the Negro Bureau by ill-informed white men, and the general problem of supporting the old party and the status quo in a time of black unrest. Du Bois took pride after the election that "more Negroes voted against Mr. Taft than ever before voted against a Republican Candidate."[83] Actually, however, the great majority of blacks voted for Taft. They faced a choice between the party of hypocrisy and the party of outright racism, between a Taft carefully coached by Booker T. Washington and a Bryan who endorsed disfranchisement and lynching, and chose the lesser of evils.

Washington received help in his effort to deliver the black vote from Bryan and other Democrats, who undercut the appeal of Du Bois and Bishop Walters for defection from the Republican Party by their provocative white supremacy statements. Washington also outmaneuvered his black opponents by creating a liberal image of Taft, modifying his speeches at Hampton Institute, Cincinnati, and New York, and subsidizing the black editors to see a rainbow through a Republican prism. The "antis" could not claim in any state a shift in the black vote sufficient to carry it for Bryan. Taft got a smaller majority in Illinois, Indiana, and Ohio than the war hero Roosevelt had received in 1904, but these were traditionally swing states, where Bryan as a fellow midwesterner had more appeal than Parker had had in 1904.

The smallness of the immediate effect on the party balance, however, was largely a measure of the continually shrinking role of blacks in national politics. The scar of Brownsville was not on the Republican body but on the black soul. Even among blacks who were circumstantially Republican, who had no other place to go, Brownsville was an unforgettable shock. It erased any illusions about Roosevelt's benevolence created by the dinner at the White House and his vague promise of an open "door of hope." The end of Reconstruction, the persistent Republican refusal to challenge the southern white decision to make the black man voteless, had all led toward Brownsville. Those who bolted the party got nothing for their pains, but Washington, now that he had a monopoly of the black patronage, was to find the patronage itself slipping like sand through his fingers. Who needed a Wizard who could only change gold into dross?

CHAPTER 14

Black Politics in the Taft Era

. . . the best friend that the Southern Negro can have is the Southern white man.

WILLIAM HOWARD TAFT, 1908

. . . if the negroes want to vote for Roosevelt or a Democrat let them.

WILLIAM HOWARD TAFT, 1912

BLIGHTED as the last years of the Roosevelt administration had been by the Brownsville affair, they were only the prelude to the downhill slide of the black politicos in the Taft administration. Even before Taft entered office, he took two steps that signaled a change of climate. He forced the resignation of William D. Crum, and he prepared the worst inaugural address since Reconstruction in reference to black political rights. He removed most of the remaining black officeholders in the South and made only a few token appointments of blacks to federal offices in the North. By the time Washington cajoled and goaded Taft into a few appointments, it was too late to help the Republicans in the midterm elections. Washington helplessly watched the collapse of the little black political empire he had built, and yet he continued to work in the Taft camp for whatever he could gain or save.

Just after Taft had won the election of 1908, Walter Hines Page thought he saw a chance for some unofficial statesmanship by getting

Taft to commit himself at the outset to a liberal southern policy. Page offered to arrange an invitation to Taft to address the North Carolina Society of New York. He would edit every word the southerners said, while Washington would edit the President-elect's address.[1] Washington agreed, and wrote Taft: "The occasion can be made one to accomplish great good in liberalizing the South and starting matters off on a new basis."[2] He offered Taft "some suggestions, perhaps in the form of sentences," on equal justice as the basis for a strong Republican party in the South.[3] Every child, he urged Taft to say, should have a public school education, "reinforced, as far as possible, by thorough and practical industrial training," and higher education "in the degree in which it is needed." He prompted Taft also to speak of the moral harm that would result if the black man were made to feel that, regardless of property, education, or good character, "because of his color he will not be accorded the same privileges as other races."[4] Taft included all this in his good-humored address, but unfortunately he added some of his own thoughts, that the race problem was "largely a matter of industrial and thorough education," that "the best friend that the Southern Negro can have is the Southern white man," and that the "Federal Government has nothing to do with social equality." Even so, the Committee of Twelve under Washington's control printed and distributed 100,000 copies of the address, with the aid of $2000 from Andrew Carnegie.[5]

Taft sent word by Emmett Scott that he wanted Washington to advise him in the same way as he had Roosevelt, and Washington responded that he would gladly render this service but wanted no office. "One of the greatest satisfactions that has come to me during the administration of President Roosevelt," he wrote Taft, "is the fact that perhaps I have been of some service to him in helping to raise the standard of colored people holding office under him; in helping him to see that they were men of character and ability; in that way I am sure that President Roosevelt has helped the whole race. If I can in any degree serve you in the same manner I shall be most happy."[6]

Washington's first political errand for the President-elect, however, was not in the nature of advice. William D. Crum, collector of customs of Charleston, had symbolized all that was good about Rooseveltian race policy under Washington's advice, until Brownsville had blurred that image to obliteration. All that Taft saw in Dr. Crum was a political liability. As early as the autumn of 1908 Crum had sensed a coldness at Taft's campaign headquarters.[7] The party pointedly did not ask him to make any campaign speeches that year. Taft had decided that Crum must go even before the inauguration.

Anticipating that Taft would close the "door of hope," at least as far as her husband was concerned, Ellen Crum proposed as a compromise that he be appointed to an equivalent post in Washington. "What ever is Mr. Taft's attitude on this subject," she wrote the Tuskegee boss, "it might serve our best interests as a race, to procrastinate the finding out, instead of forcing the issue."[8] Unfortunately, however, it was Taft who forced the issue. He decided that if Crum did not gracefully resign, he would remove him. If Crum did resign, Taft promised a suitable place outside of the South at a suitable time. Washington wired Crum to meet him in Philadelphia. "Important. Let no one know you are making trip."[9]

Washington brought with him a draft letter of resignation already prepared for Crum's signature, saying in Washingtonian language: "I have had no unpleasant contact with any one in the city."[10] Washington took the precaution of asking Emmett Scott's opinion, and Scott thought Crum would make a "strategic mistake to resign," that he would be "severely criticized as relieving a situation not created by reason of any fault of his own."[11] But the "Big Chief" had decided otherwise, and Washington could see nothing Crum could gain by trying to hang on. He wrote Scott: "Mr. Taft positively will not renominate him. The only question is, whether he can serve his own interests by getting out gracefully or by being forced out. Mr. Taft feels most kindly toward him and is going to do his best to provide him something else, but he will feel more kindly to him if he gets out in the way suggested, that is, by resigning. Further than this, I find that people everywhere, even among our best friends, are tired of the Crum case."[12]

"He took it in good spirit," Washington wrote Taft after his meeting with Crum, "and went back home immediately to consult with his wife. I believe he is going to act in a sensible manner."[13] Crum resigned so early that his letter went to Roosevelt, and Taft entered office without the encumbrance of a high-ranking black officeholder dealing with the public in the cradle of the Confederacy. Taft's first offer of a reciprocal post was a medical appointment in the Canal Zone, but Crum did not take kindly to that. Crum wanted a Washington office, but after a year's delay Taft made him minister to Liberia.

This was a post of considerable importance because of the new American protectorate there, but segregated out of contact with white southerners. Crum's health, never robust, soon succumbed to a tropical fever, and he died in 1912.[14]

Washington met with Taft not long before the inauguration, and Taft gave him leave to speak frankly on any subject he thought important, not waiting until asked. "He said that he meant to lean on me heavily during his administration," Washington wrote Scott.[15] The opportunity for advice came earlier than expected, when Taft showed him a draft of the inaugural address. "Newspaper reports exaggerated contents," Washington wired Scott, "but Anderson, Major Moton and I went through it carefully and guarded it from misinterpretation."[16] Looking back several years later, Washington recalled that "if the inaugural address had gone out in the form it was when Mr. Anderson and I first saw it, it would have startled and discouraged the Negro one hundred per cent more than it did. Of course we cannot come out and say that the thing was pruned down and made many per cent less harmful than it was originally." The problem was that Washington could not put words or thoughts into the President's mind. All he could do was "advise him to say it in the least harmful and most helpful way."[17]

What Taft insisted on saying in his inaugural address, despite all of Washington's pruning, was that he would not appoint blacks to office in communities where this would cause race friction and thus reduce the efficiency of the office. This statement was, in effect, an open invitation to white protest not only wherever blacks were appointed but wherever they continued from earlier appointment. It became known as Taft's "Southern policy," for he had no other. As in the case of some of Roosevelt's messages, even Washington's improvements backfired on him, for the phasing was so clearly Washington's that blacks would recognize it and blame him for Taft's shortcomings. Meanwhile, as Washington's lieutenants took up the matter of the blacks' place in the inaugural parade, they hoped to "prevent it being said, as usual, that the Negro division is the one that passed after dark."[18]

Washington could advise Taft freely, but from the inaugural on Taft repeatedly ignored his advice. In his first six months he removed or announced the future removal not only of Crum but of Henry Rucker, the chief black officeholder in Georgia, and R. L. Smith,

Washington's lieutenant in Texas. Taft also withdrew the nomination of Oscar R. Hundley, a white protégé of Washington, who had served as a federal district judge in Alabama since 1907 but had not been confirmed, after Hundley courageously refused to reduce the sentences of men convicted of holding blacks in peonage in the Florida turpentine camps. Then Taft ignored Washington's alternate candidate for the judgeship to choose a man whose father had once done Taft a favor.[19]

Taft evaded Washington's repeated efforts to discuss with him the growing unrest among the black officeholders. Going to the White House with James A. Cobb in April 1909, Washington tried to get a few minutes alone with the President, explaining later to Cobb that "the big fellow is getting down to brass tacks now on you fellows and he wanted to ask me some important questions."[20] A few days later Washington asked Taft to set a date "when we could go over the whole situation so far as the colored men in office are concerned with a good deal of deliberation." Taft evaded on the ground that he did not have enough time at the moment.[21]

Taft not only made no new presidential appointments of blacks in the South but gradually reduced their ranks by refusal to reappoint black postmasters, many of whom had served acceptably since President Harrison's administraton. Local whites, encouraged by the signs that Taft would yield to pressure, began to oppose even those black officeholders they had not molested in the past.[22] As preparations began for the 1910 census, blacks did not receive their usual share of census enumerators, even in predominantly black districts.[23]

Washington tried to stem the tide in June 1909 by sending President Taft a list of the blacks who had disappeared from office, those whose terms were expiring unless they were reappointed, and those whose jobs were threatened in the near future. He expressed faith that Taft would in his own time and manner "let the colored people see that you are not inclined to decrease materially the number of Negroes holding office throughout the country," but he reported that blacks were watching events closely and were "not a little stirred up."[24] Taft responded that he had a plan, which he did not disclose, for redressing the balance, and he hoped that "circumstances will so adjust themselves that I can demonstrate it."[25]

Taft's black removal policy, coupled with his inaction on voting rights, confirmed the skepticism of blacks who had opposed him because of his involvement in the Brownsville dismissal, and the loyal Taft supporters who had been so jubilant between election and inauguration were now saying nothing.[26] When Washington in addressing a National Negro Business League audience of 3000 blacks referred to Taft in terms as complimentary as he could, "there was not a single handclap or a single move anywhere in the audience that indicated approval."[27] Washington at the first opportunity wrote Taft a frank letter reporting the mood of blacks, and Taft again implied something he had in mind that would please them.[28]

The conviction grew that Taft's plan was inaction. R. R. Moton saw Taft's letter to Washington and said it "does not answer the question." Taft, he said, "ought to be hammered at from every point and if he fails to 'make good' regarding the colored man, he cannot say that his friends did not warn him." Washington, however, had Scott counsel Moton against bombarding Taft with advice at that time.[29] In November Washington finally had his long talk with the President, and reported to Anderson: "I really think that I have put a little ginger into the situation. He seems to be on the point of doing something satisfactory."[30] When two weeks later there was still no action, Washington thought Taft "seems to be thoroughly stirred up on the importance of doing something for the colored people."[31] Apparently Taft intended some sort of promotion of William H. Lewis in Boston, but "matters miscarried again with our big friend," said Washington, and the year ended without Taft's having made a single major black appointment.[32]

Early in 1910 Taft did reappoint R. H. Terrell as District of Columbia judge, perhaps a harbinger that, after wholesale removal in the South, he would appoint blacks piecemeal in the North. He called in John C. Dancy, recorder of deeds of the District of Columbia, and told him there was great pressure to remove him. Washington urged Taft to retain Dancy on account of his powerful A. M. E. Zion constituency, his speaking ability, and his early and unhesitant support of Taft in 1908.[33] He wrote Anderson more pithily that "if Dancy goes out we are not sure of getting even as good a man in his place."[34]

Taft placed Washington in a dilemma by deciding against Washington's advice to replace Dancy with Henry Lincoln Johnson of Atlanta.[35] Johnson was no radical, but he was not part of the Tuskegee Machine either, and close enough to Atlanta University to feel its animus against the Tuskegean. Johnson had no obligations whatever to

Washington, and had recently betrayed the interests of his fellow black politicos by supporting the replacement of Henry A. Rucker as collector of internal revenue by a white man.[36] Dancy, however, hastened his own removal by an ill-considered retailing to the White House of charges of immorality and criminality against Johnson, contained in a "private and confidential" letter from Rucker.[37] Washington more wisely decided to keep his distance from the mudslinging. Since Taft "seems to have made up his mind to do this," he wrote Whitefield McKinlay, "I do not know that anything can be done to turn his head in a different direction."[38] Instead of a hopeless defense of Dancy, he had Scott prepare a memorandum bringing up to date all the removals and resignations of blacks replaced by white men, for the first anniversary of the Taft administration.[39]

P. B. S. Pinchback expressed the profound discouragement of the whole Tuskegee Machine: "Man! I am so mad I can scarcely write. It is all over the city that Dancy's defeat is Washington's defeat. I have had two quarrels already over the matter."[40] Washington tried to console Dancy with a philosophical reflection: "Everything in the way of a political office usually has an end, and that is one reason why I have emphasized so much as I have the importance of commercial development or business enterprise among our people. You will have now a rare chance to set an example in the way of commercial and business leadership and I very much hope that you will seize on to this opportunity."[41]

Behind the opposition of Washington's coterie to Link Johnson's appointment was their private fear that Johnson, already the "right-hand man" of Postmaster General Frank Hitchcock, would replace Washington as the administration's chief adviser. They also spoke of Johnson as "a cringing nig" who would acquiesce in the removal of other black officeholders.[42] Johnson did nothing to alleviate this fear by his air of independence and lack of deference to Washington.

As the midterm elections of 1910 approached and as Roosevelt returned from an extensive trip abroad, the Tuskegeans hoped that these developments would force some concessions toward a more liberal race policy from the Taft administration, and they privately resolved not to overpraise Taft for small accomplishments.[43] The time had come for frankness with the President, Washington wrote his lieutenants. "Unless one is perfectly frank with the President, he may go on feeling that the Negroes are satisfied, when they are not and when the time comes to expect their support, he will be disappointed, hence it is disloyalty for any person to deal in a manner that is not frank with the President."[44]

Amusingly, Taft's inaction permitted Washington to deny more convincingly than in the past the charges that he was a political boss. The fact was, he wrote the newspaperman Samuel Bowles, "that there have not been enough colored people appointed to take very much of the time of any one, certainly not enough to enable one to become a political boss even if he had the ambition." Taft had only appointed one black to office since he became President, and outside the city of Washington there were only about ten black men holding presidential appointments; "hence it would be impossible, if anyone desired to do so, to build up political influence, or any kind of reputation, or to give himself any kind of strength through the medium of helping to put colored people in office; besides anyone who has had any experience at all in public affairs knows that if one wants to make himself unpopular, the very way to do it would be to begin recommending men for office."[45]

The bad situation worsened. Washington's Nashville lieutenant James C. Napier was a candidate for register of the Treasury, the highest black office in Washington. But W. T. Vernon still clung to the post even though two years had passed since Tyler had caught him "red handed" with his hand in the till. This was because Hitchcock insisted that Vernon remain until after the 1910 election, for fear of black unrest in Kansas. Taft offered Napier instead the ministership to Liberia, but Washington urged Napier to refuse. "The climate, as you know, in Liberia is trying in certain seasons of the year," he wrote, and recommended Crum in Napier's stead. Be patient, he urged Napier, and remember that the really solid part of his life was his business career. "Taft in my opinion is a good, well meaning man, but it seems impossible for him to hold out against strong men, who want to use him for selfish purposes."[46]

"The anti's are jubilant at what they call the *fall* of one man power etc," wrote Pinchback. "To a bunch of them some time since I remarked—under the so called one man power you all got your places and the race some recognition. What are we getting now? Better one man power than no power at all. A dead silence for some moments."[47] Washington replied cryptically: "Strong forces are at work to bring about the removal of the main cause of our racial troubles. I think something is going to happen within the next few days or weeks. This is so important that I cannot put it in writing."[48]

Whatever the strong forces were that Washington alluded to, nothing happened in the next month except the relatively minor appointment of Whitefield McKinlay as collector of the port of Georgetown. McKinlay had turned down many earlier offers of office, and apparently accepted this one because it would not interfere substantially with his successful real estate business. Meanwhile, Washington learned from Charles Banks that Thomas I. Keys, black postmaster of Ocean Springs, Mississippi, was urged by the white presidential referee L. B. Moseley to resign. When Keys refused, Moseley had him summoned to Washington, where Postmaster General Hitchcock told him that "on account of so much opposition to such appointees in the South, he could not appoint him, but told him that Washington was a city where he could educate his children and if he would give up the candidacy for the Ocean Springs Post-office he would secure him a place in some of the departments in Washington with a salary of $1400.00 a year." Keys refused the offer, saying that there was no opposition to him at Ocean Springs and that he had the endorsement of the mayor, the white Methodist minister, and many other whites in the town.[49] Nevertheless, he was not reappointed.

Taft's subordinates thus took advantage of his inaugural statement to remove blacks and appoint lily whites in their places in the South, while Taft delayed the compensatory appointments in the North that he privately promised would make his southern strategy acceptable. The black press vented the race's disappointment and resentment. Washington was doubtless glad that he could escape the debacle for a while by a two-month trip to Europe. It was left to William H. Lewis to tell the truth to the White House staff. He told Charles D. Norton, the President's secretary, that "the trouble was that the President had not carried out his policy of making appointments in the North; if that had been done the criticism would perhaps have all quieted down, or there would have been no criticism, although there might have been some discontent among officeholders in the South; that nearly two years had elapsed and nothing has been done. . . ." Lewis reported to Scott that he had told Norton that "whatever was done ought to be done quickly and done long enough before the elections, before the colored people committed themselves or were put into the position of stultifying themselves. Those who are opposed should be given a chance to back up."[50] Lewis undertook in return for some action by the White House to persuade Fred Moore to moderate his attacks on Taft in the New York *Age* and to bring Moore and Norton together to try to reconcile their differences.[51] This was not difficult, in view of Washington's stock ownership and policy control of the *Age*.

Taft seemed to be genuinely puzzled by the black criticism. As Norton explained the President's position to Scott, the inaugural address had been "approved of before it was uttered" and did not bar blacks from office in the South completely. "It sets for them a higher standard perhaps of fitness for public office," wrote Norton, "but that is something that the race in my judgment should welcome, and will, just as white men should welcome it."[52] With Washington out of the country, a genuine rift was developing between Taft and the only blacks who had supported him in 1908.

Oswald Garrison Villard, sensing the President's indecision, wrote Norton that Booker T. Washington spoke for only one faction of blacks, that there was another and growing group who "consider him a traitor to the race." One cause of this opposition, he said, was that Washington had become through his friendship with Roosevelt and Taft "the office-broker for the race,—a position into which, as I have told Mr. Washington, frankly, no man ought to allow himself to be forced, however gratifying it may be, or how little he may have sought the honor." The black officeholders were all in Washington's camp, Villard wrote, but he would be glad to arrange a conference between the President and representative blacks "not merely of the job-hunting kind," men who did not measure the advance of the race by the number of offices it held.[53]

From the opposite end of the ideological spectrum, the lily white southern Republican William Garrott Brown commended "the practical acquiescence of the Republicans" in the disfranchisement of southern blacks, and praised Taft for his friendly remarks to southern white audiences and his removal of black officeholders. Brown observed: "Mr. Roosevelt did much in this direction, but the effect of it was largely marred by the Crum appointment, the Booker Washington dinner, and the Indianola incident," in which Roosevelt had closed the post office when local whites refused to accept a black postmistress. Negroes, he thought, would be better off if kept out of politics for some time to come. "But I should like to see a few good negroes put, with the consent of their communities, into inconspicuous places which would not bring them objectionably in contact with whites."[54] Brown's views fitted neatly with the President's plan to appoint blacks only in the North, but it was only at the eleventh hour of the 1910 campaign that he overcame his natural torpor and made the first of these appointments.

The appointment of William H. Lewis as an assistant attorney general was announced in late October 1910. This was the highest appointive federal office held by a black man until the New Deal era. "I shall use this to the very best advantage," Washington wrote Taft,[55] but it was then only a week before the election. It did not take effect until after the election, in fact not until March 1911. Nevertheless, the log jam on northern appointments had broken up. Scott, calling at the White House, found Norton happy over the reception both the black and the white press had given the announcement. Scott wrote his chief: "He told me that *Grief* will reign among our folks in the South soon however, as it is probable that no Negroes will be holding places soon: as the President is going to carry out pretty fully his program as to holding offices in the South. I told him we c'd not agree with [him] as to the program, but that [it] is better to have something to offset the feeling of the colored people in the way of these Northern appointments, as formerly we had *not* even them for an 'argument.' "[56] Robert R. Moton wrote less candidly to the President that the Lewis appointment would "strengthen the belief of a great number of colored people in your intentions to help them." He had just returned from a tour of North Carolina with Lewis and Washington, and he reassured Taft about Lewis's tact and judgment in delicate situations. "Mr. Lewis is not the kind of man who would embarrass the Administration or his friends in any social way."[57]

The Taft administration had alienated not only the blacks but other constituencies of the Roosevelt coalition, however, and the Democrats captured the lower house of Congress for the first time in more than a decade. Washington's judgment on this event was that "In the end it will do good and teach a great lesson." He confided to Charles Anderson his hope that "our friend, T. R.," would benefit. "I should not be surprised," he wrote, "if the seeming present defeat did not make him a strong candidate for 1912."[58] These words written in confidence suggest Washington's personal preference for Roosevelt as the Republican candidate in 1912. He not only admired Roosevelt as a winner but appreciated the personal directness and warmth that Roosevelt always brought to their consultations over political matters. Furthermore, Roosevelt took Washington's advice and acted upon it more readily than Taft. If Washington did prefer Roosevelt, however, he kept it a secret from his other lieutenants. He had committed himself, after all, to advise President Taft in Taft's interest, and in his own efforts to find places for his loyal followers there was obvious advantage in supporting the incumbent with an undivided loyalty. Furthermore, Taft finally began to warrant support by a loyal black Republican by some of his actions.

President Taft's standing among blacks continued to decline, as the ousted southern black officeholders began to work against him and his renomination. But he made a change in private secretaries from the cold and calculating Charles D. Norton to the more sympathetic Charles D. Hilles. Furthermore, Postmaster General Hitchcock, who had worked with the lily whites in 1908 and had zealously led the removal of black officeholders, fell from presidential favor after his mismanagement of the 1910 campaign. Then, with agonizing slowness, came the promised appointments in the North and in the capital. In February 1911 Vernon finally vacated and J. C. Napier of the National Negro Business League filled the office of register of the Treasury.[59] This was actually the first major black appointment of the Taft administration, almost two years after the inauguration. In the following month Taft formally made the already publicly promised appointment of Lewis as assistant attorney general.

The Senate confirmed Lewis without a contest in June 1911, after Washington and Scott headed off threatened opposition by some southern Senators. Soon afterward, Lewis and two other black lawyers, from Minnesota and Massachusetts, received nomination by their local bar associations for membership in the American Bar Association. Its executive committee approved pro forma. When their race became known, however, the ABA executive committee in 1912 proposed for the next annual meeting to rescind the membership on the ground that it was granted "in ignorance of material facts."[60]

"I took grave exception to the action of the Committee as unwarranted, unconstitutional and outrageous," Lewis wrote Washington. "I called upon the Attorney General to get the permission of the Department to fight the matter further. The Attorney General not only gave me permission to fight it to the finish, but took the matter in his own hands."[61] Attorney General George Wickersham, who surprised everyone by the zeal of his trustbusting campaign, also surprised Lewis and Washington by his egalitarian racial stance. "You do not know how deeply you have touched the hearts of the colored people throughout the country and how grateful they are to you for the generous and brave manner in which you have stood by Mr. William H. Lewis," Washington wrote.[62]

What Wickersham did was somewhat less than heroic. He headed off an acrimonious debate on the ABA's color line. As he wrote Washington after the meeting: "The things that really were accomplished, were first, the rebuke of the Executive Committee by the failure even to mention its report, and the complete abandonment of the effort to oust the three colored members; secondly, the recognition that under the constitution, although it had not been contemplated that negroes should be elected to membership, it was open to do so, and requiring that in case a local committee should nominate one for membership the fact of his race should be made known. No one, I think, could object to that. And third, the express recognition of the full status in membership of the three colored men who had been already chosen." Having done and said that much, however, Wickersham set a limit by adding: "The broader question of whether or not colored men should join that Association is one which will be fought out later and under better conditions than could have been done in a Presidential year."[63] And two months later, even after the presidential election, Wickersham invited all twenty-two attorneys connected with his department except Lewis to an official dinner in honor of a new solicitor general from Kentucky. "Ain't that hell?" asked Ralph Tyler. "Invited all the cubs below him in rank, but overlooked Lewis. Such gross discrimination is enough to make anarchists out of peaceful men."[64]

Washington meanwhile retained a minor influence on overseas appointments of blacks. W. T. Vernon—"the eloquent one," Tyler called him—must have had a strong following in Kansas and among white Republican leaders, for when he was unhorsed as register a movement immediately began to oust the competent incumbent minister to Haiti, W. H. Furniss, to make room for Vernon. Washington's lieutenants blocked this by reminders of Vernon's graft and Furniss's good record.[65] Vernon claimed there was bias against his dark color, and Huntington Wilson in the State Department privately urged: "The work in Haiti is so really difficult and important that I think, as I have said before, that a very able white man would be best for American interests."[66] Furniss remained, however, for lack of a suitable replacement. Other overseas posts included two in Liberia: Crum, as already mentioned, as minister, and William Bundy as secretary of legation. Charles A. Cottrill of Toledo went to Hawaii as collector of internal revenue. Taft made no change in the status of the five black consuls, but that was because they were under the civil service rules of the Foreign Service.

Vernon, kicked further downstairs, found his level as superintendent of federal Indian schools. Far from taking offense at his demotion, Vernon approached Washington with an offer to work in harmony with him in the future. Washington asked his lieutenants to give Vernon a chance. "Surely no harm can come of a good frank conversation," he wrote Tyler, "and perhaps much good will result. It is better always when one can do so with honor, to have a friend than an enemy."[67]

A little institution grew up with the grandiose name of "the Black Cabinet." It was simply an informal gathering of the Tuskegee coterie of black officeholders in the national capital. No significant administrative power or proximity to the President's ear distinguished this cabinet. It was just a daily gathering at Gray's Restaurant in Washington of Tyler, McKinlay, Cobb, Terrell, Napier, and Lewis. It excluded the common run of departmental clerks, but sometimes included marginal figures such as R. W. Thompson and Link Johnson, and unofficial peers such as Calvin Chase, Kelly Miller, and Pinchback. The news they shared was mostly bad.

Taft's southern policy of removal continued inexorably, and with it the crumbling of Washington's political machine. Cohen lost his place in the federal land office in New Orleans when the Department of the Interior consolidated his office with the one in Baton Rouge, and the Taft administration found no other place for him in New Orleans. He lost control of the Republican state committee to the lily whites. In Alabama, Joseph O. Thompson clung to his office, but the Republican Party machinery passed to another white Republican supported by the black members of the state executive committee.

Washington remained in the background during the latter half of the Taft administration, and it was Ralph Tyler who made two efforts to persuade Taft to abandon or revise his southern policy. Early in 1912 the President gave a hearing to five members of the Black Cabinet—Tyler, Lewis, Napier, Johnson, and McKinlay. They urged him to restate his position "so as to preclude misinterpretation either by subordinate white officials or members of our own race." Tyler reported to Tuskegee: "Practically all the time last evening was devoted to discussing his Southern policy, which we made plain to him was distasteful to every Negro. In addition to completing talk on his Southern policy tonight, we told him we wanted to take up Civil Service discrimination in the Departments, and Lynchings." They briefly discussed also Supreme Court appointments and railroad segregation. "Link went with us," Tyler wrote, "—behaved nicely and hit Southern policy hard blow—even rapped his master—Hitchcock, whom he is deserting now that he observes the signs." [68]

The talks adjourned to a second night, when Taft invited the black delegation into the White House library. Tyler informed Tuskegee that the delegation "told him that the Negroes could not defend his Southern policy as now carried out; could never defend it, and that in the South, with their elective franchise taken away, it made mere serfs of the Negro. We urged him to make a few Negro appointments in the South, and urged him to restate his Southern policy at the earliest opportunity so as to make it clear to subordinates that it did not mean positive exclusion of Negroes from offices everywhere in the South." The President seemed to take the criticisms in good spirit, and the black delegation pointedly referred to Washington as their "real leader." [69]

At President Taft's own suggestion Tyler submitted a draft of a speech the conferees hoped the President would deliver on some early occasion, perhaps to the alumni of Howard University. However, Taft scrawled on the draft: "I can't come out with such a speech. There is not much if anything I differ from." The President's secretary, Charles D. Hilles, evaded the issue for him by saying that the President's engagements would not permit him to attend the meeting. "We will have to let the question raised remain open for awhile because of this," he said. [70]

Two months later, in April 1912, Tyler tried again. He sent a revised draft and suggested that Taft incorporate it in a forthcoming speech. Tyler sought to commit the President not only to denial that he intended not to appoint blacks in the South, but to opposing Jim Crow car laws, lynching, and disfranchisement. This draft Taft initialed with the comment: "I am not going to say anything on many of the subjects here set out. I think it cheeky to ask it. What I have said

I have said and it can be quoted but if the negroes want to vote for Roosevelt or a Democrat let them."[71] Perhaps Tyler lacked some of Washington's gifts of tact, self-restraint, and persuasiveness as an adviser, but Taft's sharp reaction also showed the growing rift between the President and even the most loyal of his black supporters.

The only real gain from the White House talks was blocking Taft's intention of appointing Judge William C. Hook of Kansas to fill John M. Harlan's vacant seat on the Supreme Court. Taft had already appointed two ex-Confederates to the Court and had elevated a third to chief justice. The black conferees complained that Hook would be "very distasteful to the race."[72] William H. Lewis gathered the evidence that Hook was a racially discriminating judge and presented it to Taft. Hook had decided in an Oklahoma case that the railroad need not furnish separate sleeping cars, diners, or chair cars for blacks and could exclude blacks from such cars on the ground that they were luxuries not necessities, and therefore not among the requirements of the separate but equal rule.[73] Taft had already told a Hook supporter that he would send his nomination "right up," but Lewis, the Black Cabinet, and Washington himself arranged for a flood of black protest letters at the White House. "I do not see how any colored man after reading this decision could advocate the cause of Judge Hook," Washington wrote a black supporter of Hook. "It is a deliberate insult to a whole race of people. He goes further in trying to humiliate us than any Southern judge has ever done."[74] Lewis soon reported that President Taft had nominated another to fill the vacancy, and said simply, "It was not Hook and that sufficed."[75]

The 1912 presidential campaign presented Washington with a dilemma. Candidate Theodore Roosevelt was a member of the Tuskegee board of trustees and an old friend, but candidate Taft was a member of the board of the Jeanes Fund, and Washington had agreed at the beginning of Taft's administration to be his loyal adviser. When news reached him that Charles Banks was going to bolt to Roosevelt, Washington urged Banks not to do so. For Washington to openly endorse either good friend might alienate the other. "Sometime ago," he wrote a friend in June 1912, "members of our Trustee Board asked that I take no active part in the present political campaign, and I have refrained from doing so and intend to pursue that policy. I think no man would be quicker to disapprove of any active political effort on my part just now than would President Taft or ex-President Roosevelt."[76] Though Washington's papers furnish no direct evidence of how he voted, his continuance as Taft's private adviser and his discouragement of Banks's endorsement of Roosevelt even while he was still in the Republican Party suggest that he probably voted for Taft.

Washington simply used his board of trustees to conceal his position on an issue that would embarrass him either way. His friend George Myers, the Cleveland barber and black political savant, had a better explanation of Washington's position.

> Knowing that Mr Taft and Mr Roosevelt are both personal friends and your interests are indissolubly linked to each, as a friend I am writing to suggest that you consider well before expressing a preference for either. Loyalty is a trait admired by all. No one condemns a man for being loyal to his friends. You have been and are still loyal to each. . . . It is my personal belief that neither of them would seek to put you on record. Go ahead just as you have been doing and let us your friends fight the battle for Mr Taft. It should be an easy matter to line up the negroes of the North for him.

Scott passed on the Myers letter with the note: "Said you're car[ry]ing out plan he suggests."[77]

Some members of the Black Cabinet, leaderless, listless, and seemingly demoralized, did attend the Republican national convention in 1912. There they helplessly followed the lead of the southern black delegations endorsing the incumbent Taft. While Taft had decimated the ranks of southern black officeholders and had made only a few token appointments of northern Republicans, the memory of Brownsville was too fresh still to allow for any black enthusiasm for Roosevelt.

Ralph Tyler, one of the few blacks with an undiminished appetite for politics, took charge of the subsidizing of the black newspapers for the Republican Party, but he consulted with Emmett Scott about the details of his work in a way that suggests that Scott, at least, was far from neutral. Prior to the Republican national convention the Taft "literary bureau" gave Tyler $5000 to subsidize thirty selected black newspapers for the ten weeks before the choosing of delegates. Tyler asked Scott for his advice on the allotment of the funds, writing: "I figured on a sliding scale; that is, for instance a few would demand $50 per week while some could be got for $10 per week. If you suggest any of the above be eliminated and some others substituted, make the suggestion."[78] Scott proposed several changes. The largest subsidy, $175 a week, went to the *Age*.[79]

Washington had always stayed out of the foreground of political conventions, but in 1912 he was not even in the background. Taft won the Republican nomination, defeating Roosevelt, with the support of the southern delegations, and Roosevelt quickly formed the Progressive Party to support his candidacy. A few of Washington's political friends, notably Charles Banks, John C. Dancy, and Joseph O. Thompson, endorsed Roosevelt. Some members of the Black Cabinet apparently hoped that Roosevelt would win the Republican nomination, even though as officeholders they had to support the incumbent President.[80] But there was no place for blacks in the Progressive Party. Oswald Garrison Villard, who had always distrusted Roosevelt and had openly opposed him since the Brownsville dismissal, could not refrain from writing to Washington, "I told you so," after Roosevelt ejected the southern black delegations from the Progressive convention in what Anderson called "the discarding of the Spades." Washington had to concede to Villard "the deepest disappointment among the colored people."[81] None of the Tuskegee Machine could support the Democrats, however, for Woodrow Wilson was the candidate of "the enemy"—Du Bois, Trotter, and other militant blacks.

Though Woodrow Wilson had an aura of general nobility of purpose, nothing in his background encouraged blacks to expect him to be their champion. Though his adult career as educator and politician had been in the North, he was Virginia-born and his father had once been chaplain of the South Carolina legislature. Princeton under his presidency continued to be the only Ivy League school that excluded blacks, and when Booker T. Washington had attended Wilson's inauguration in 1901 as president of Princeton he was the only one among the honored guests not accommodated in a faculty house. Wilson's was the party of secession and white supremacy, with a stronghold in the Solid South, and when his election in 1912 swept his party into control of both houses of Congress, this meant that most of the committee chairmanships went to the most senior Democrats from rotten boroughs in the South.

The most militant blacks and their white liberal allies, however, rejecting Roosevelt and Taft on account of Brownsville, were able to secure from Wilson an assurance that they had "nothing to fear in the way of inimical legislation." Wilson carefully hedged his statement by refusing to commit himself on patronage or the use of his veto power.[82] In a public statement three weeks before the election, Wilson ex-

pressed his earnest wish for justice for blacks, "and not mere grudging justice, but justice executed with liberality and cordial good feeling." Blacks could "count upon me for absolute fair dealing and for
everything by which I could assist in advancing the interests of their
race in the United States."[83]

Washington's retreat from the campaign led to some anomalous behavior at Republican headquarters. For a time a white man headed
the Negro bureau. He was Joseph C. Manning, an ex-Populist from
Alabama who had joined the NAACP. Charles Anderson led a black
protest that ousted Manning and placed the black headquarters of the
party in Anderson's own Colored Republican Club in Harlem.[84] Tyler
tried to take credit for Manning's removal, but according to Anderson
Tyler at first sought to accommodate himself to Manning. "Men whom
I believed to be stout men, I found to be willing to sneeze whenever
a white-man took snuff," wrote Anderson.[85]

"Well, the fight is all over," Washington wrote his friend J. C. Napier after the election. "Matters have come out just about as I had
expected. The fact is the Republican party was completely split and
divided its votes between Mr. Roosevelt and Mr. Taft, while the Democrats remained solid for their ticket. Whether the old Republican
party will ever hold to pull itself together in an effective manner again
is quite a question. I am sincerely sorry for Mr. Taft. He, in my opinion, is a first-class, clean gentleman, meaning to do the right thing,
and I believe the time will yet come when the country will appreciate
his true worth."[86] These remarks strongly suggested that Washington
cast his own vote for Taft, despite the disappointments of four years,
but Washington could probably have said as much for Roosevelt, or
even for Wilson.

The "Black Cabinet" prepared to decamp, knowing that those covered by civil service would probably remain but the presidential appointees would go. Tyler whimsically suggested that a Carnegie "pension for the Black Cabinet will *not* be declined." "The 'Black Cabinet'
had a consolation stag at Gray's Thursday night," McKinlay wrote to
Pinchback, "feasting on 'possum and 'taters' sent by Dr. Washington
as consolation for our blasted hopes. We had a merry good time and
regret that you could not have been with us." McKinlay could only
hope that Wilson would be another Cleveland in race matters and
"keep the radical wing of his party in check."[87] Another question in
the minds of some of Washington's followers was whether he would

have any influence whatever on the Wilson regime. R. W. Thompson wrote Scott, either ironically or with unfounded optimism: "I daresay you and the 'Wizard' will have as much influence with this administration as you had with the Taft regime on the big questions."[88]

Meanwhile S. Laing Williams lost his office even before the Democrats could fire him. Washington asked Tyler and then Lewis to look into the reasons. Lewis found that of the three black Chicagoans holding legal positions under the Republican administration in Chicago, Williams was the only one who had stood by Taft, and that he was "getting the laugh at being turned out just after the election." One report Lewis heard was that the district attorney had "tried Mr. Williams on about everything in the office and that he was not competent." Gilchrist Stewart said, however, that the real reason was that Williams had taken a personal interest in the Jack Johnson morals case, attending court every day of the boxer's trial, and suggesting "the tip by which Johnson secured bail, by informing Johnson's friends that the U. S. Attorney had examined the bail proposed and found it O. K." If this report was true, Lewis concluded, the district attorney would consider it disloyalty warranting dismissal. Lewis believed, however, that Williams simply failed to make himself indispensable and depended on outside influence to keep him in his job.[89] As Washington succinctly summarized his whole experience with Williams, "It is pretty hard to help a man who has no ability to help himself."[90]

Washington had an interview with "the Colonel" not long after the election, and as he started to explain why he had not supported the Progressive Party, Roosevelt interrupted him to exclaim "that he considered my course the wisest one, that he should have been disappointed and chagrined if I had entered the movement, that it would have been the very worst thing that I could have done and he honored me for pursuing the course that I did pursue." In reporting this to Lewis, Washington added that Roosevelt seemed "a bigger man than I thought he was before."[91]

Washington noted with some amusement a few days before Wilson's inauguration that he was receiving as many applications from black Democrats for endorsement to office as he had received from Republicans.[92] In January 1913 he came reasonably close to a personal connection with President-elect Wilson. Learning that Wilson was to be in Chicago for a speech, he asked Julius Rosenwald if it would be worth while to try to arrange a side meeting with Wilson in behalf of Tuskegee.[93] When Rosenwald suggested a luncheon meeting, however, Washington backed away. "My idea is this," he wrote Rosenwald, "if you think it important that I be present at such a meeting the matter of the luncheon would bring up the old question of social equality and might embarrass Governor Wilson, and would certainly furnish the newspapers with a basis for some rather sensational reports. I think the Governor would be much more inclined to accept the invitation to meet and speak to a few selected people without the luncheon than he would to attend any affair of that character."[94] Washington decided not to make any overture.

A few days before the inauguration, Washington in an interview in the Nashville *Banner* said with characteristic hopefulness that he thought blacks would not suffer by the change of administration. According to the newspaper: "He stated that in his belief the next President of the United States is one of the best friends of negro education who has occupied the presidential chair, and that he will favor at all times all things that will prove beneficial to the people of his race. He said he had known President-elect Wilson for many years, and that he had great confidence in his willingness to hear any just cause that might be presented in behalf of the negro. Being Southern born, he had the knowledge of conditions in the South that would give him a thorough understanding of things that would tend to their advancement in the true sense."[95]

The newspaper reporter did not directly quote Washington, and possibly he put his own construction on what Washington said. But Washington did not repudiate the report, which was published throughout the country. He explained to Charles Anderson, "I tried to say as much as I could honestly say in his favor in the hope that it would induce him to be liberal in dealing with our people."[96] He gave Lewis a similar explanation, adding: "I fear the President's high-sounding phrases regarding justice do not include the Negro."[97]

CHAPTER 15

Washington and the Rise
of the NAACP

Mr. Villard, in my opinion, is a well-meaning, unselfish man, but he does not understand people. He has gathered about him a class of colored people, who have not succeeded, who are bitter and resentful and who, without exception, I think, live in the North. The white people who are with him . . . are dreamers and otherwise impractical people, who do not understand our conditions in the South.

BTW, 1910

He is a distinguished American and has a perfect right to his opinions. But . . . Mr. Washington's large financial responsibilities have made him dependent on the rich charitable public and . . . he has for years been compelled to tell, not the whole truth, but that part of it which certain powerful interests in America wish to appear as the whole truth.

THE NATIONAL NEGRO COMMITTEE, 1910

REPRESENTING the last generation of black leaders born in slavery in the Old South, and speaking for those blacks who had remained in the New South in an uneasy modus vivendi with the white southerners, Washington was able throughout his life to maintain his standing as the black boss because of the sponsorship of powerful whites, substantial support within the black community, and his skillful accommodation to the social realities of the age of segregation.

359

Nevertheless, he faced a fresh challenge in 1909 and thereafter from the National Association for the Advancement of Colored People. Growing out of a great national conference on civil rights, the NAACP was a coalition of Washington's black critics in the Niagara Movement with various whites concerned with social justice and able to bring fresh resources into the battle against white supremacy. These whites included neo-abolitionists, reform-minded social workers, socialist radicals, liberal Jews, and even a few southern mavericks. The NAACP was as diverse as the other reform coalitions of the Progressive Era, but the only one in that strangely callous epoch that dealt forthrightly with what W. E. B. Du Bois called "the problem of the twentieth century—the problem of the color line." The NAACP came to represent the future, and Washington the past.

It was a race riot in 1908 in Springfield, Illinois—Abraham Lincoln's home town—that precipitated the founding of the NAACP. White mobs there killed six blacks and drove 2000 others from the city. Booker T. Washington was as morally outraged by the riot as anyone, and when the city fathers invited him to speak the following year at the centennial of Lincoln's birth, his letter of refusal stated that "no man who hallows the name of Lincoln will inflict injustice upon a Negro because he is a Negro or because he is weak."[1] He relented a year later, however, when the sponsors assured him of "a great change of sentiment" in Springfield.[2] Thus, Washington worked in his own mediating way to erase the bloodstain of the Springfield riot. The founders of the NAACP, however, pursued a more unrelenting response to the riot's reminder that the way of the South had become the American way in race relations.

Oswald Garrison Villard, the initiator of the conference in 1909 that founded the NAACP, was the grandson of America's greatest abolitionist but also the child of a railroad baron, and he dreamed of joining the forces of Washington, whose work at Tuskegee he admired and supported, and W. E. B. Du Bois, the champion of human rights. Since he was virtually alone in his belief that the two leaders could be reconciled, it fell to him to write Washington and invite him to the NAACP organizing conference. "It is not to be a Washington movement, or a Du Bois movement," he wrote his old friend. "The idea is that there shall grow out of it, first, an annual conference . . . for the discussion by men of both races of the conditions of the colored people, politically, socially, industrially and educationally." Later, he hoped, a steering committee would follow up the discussion with action on legal and political rights. Villard explained to Washington that the organizers of the conference "do not wish to embarrass you; they do not wish to seem to ignore you, or to leave you out, or to show any disrespect whatever. On the other hand, they do not wish to tie you up with what may prove to be a radical political movement. Hence, they have not felt like urging you very hard to join the new movement, but have wanted you to know that you would be welcome at the conference, or if you decided you could not attend, the conference would least of all misrepresent your absence." Villard hoped that the new organization could at least count on Washington's sympathy and help, even if his educational affiliations caused him not to want to become closely allied with it.[3]

None of the blacks of the Niagara Movement, scarred by losing battles with the old chief, wanted Washington at the 1909 conference. And nobody except possibly Villard expected him to attend. Washington pleaded a prior engagement, but also said that his presence, "at the first session at least," would probably inhibit discussion and might even move the organization in directions it did not want to go. "I have always recognized," he wrote Villard frankly, "as I have stated to you more than once, that there is a work to be done which no one placed in my position can do, which no one living in the South perhaps can do. There is a work which those of us who live here in the South can do, which persons who do not live in the South cannot do. If we recognize fairly and squarely this, then it seems to me that we have gone a long ways." He reiterated his faith that it was "through progressive, constructive work that we are to succeed rather than by depending too largely upon agitation or criticism." He reassured Villard, however, that he would not feel bad at being left out of the conference.[4]

These formalities completed, Washington put Charles Anderson to work spying on the founding conference of the NAACP in 1909 in New York City. "One of their sessions is to be secret," Anderson found out in advance and reported. "I will find out as much about them as possible and let you know the facts."[5] "I am doing all I can to discredit this affair," Anderson promised as he passed on a newspaper item about the conference that he had placed in the New York *Sun*. "I think I have succeeded in defeating the dinner project to Du Bois, by asking all of my friends and yours not to subscribe to it. They will either have to drop it, or give him a small private dinner."[6] As the conference gathered he reported to Tuskegee that all of Washington's bitterest black critics of the Niagara Movement were in the secret sessions, along with Villard.[7]

Washington had a tendency to believe in conspiracy theories, and he apparently thought the secret sessions of the 1909 conference were for the purpose of building an engine to assault him. Actually, however, the white sponsors of the conference did all they could to avoid an obsession with Booker T. Washington. After the anthropologists and sociologists had read their formal papers, and the time came for practical organizing, someone suggested Washington for membership on the steering committee that would begin the work of the NAACP and plan the next annual conference. This suggestion produced such an outburst from the black delegates that Villard was taken aback. Mary White Ovington explained to him, however, that Washington's lieutenants had declared the entire conference out of bounds to loyal Washingtonians. Someone suggested that Washington's participation would make it easier to get financial support, and Villard mollified the gathering by reading aloud Washington's skillfully restrained letter explaining that he declined to attend in order not to inhibit its proceedings.[8]

Underneath his apparent equanimity, Washington was insecure about the effect of the new organization on his own power and role of leadership. Villard passed Washington's letter along to his Uncle Frank Garrison, who thought Washington's position "entirely reasonable," as his presence "would surely have invited the embittered attacks of the Trotter gang & so done infinite harm." He was glad to hear also that Du Bois was "satisfied with Washington's action in this case."[9] Washington knew, however, that Du Bois was far from satisfied with Washington's general stand on racial issues. Du Bois sharply attacked him in the course of an invitation to R. R. Moton to attend the Niagara Movement meeting that was to consider merger with the NAACP. Allen Washington, Moton's assistant commandant at Hampton, remarked after reading the letter: "If Dr. Washington needs anyone to help him kick Du Bois tell him to call on me and I shall be right at his elbow. Du Bois is hard to suit and very unruly."[10]

In public lectures as well, Du Bois spoke forthrightly against the Tuskegean on both educational and race leadership grounds. He had to write a letter to the Boston *Transcript* to explain one reference the reporter had garbled:

I said to the reporter, though not in my speech that Mr. Washington was the political boss of the Negro race in America. I used this word in its legitimate and clearly accepted sense because of these facts: Mr. Washington has long and earnestly counselled his race to let politics alone, acquiesce temporarily in disfranchisement and pay attention chiefly to industrial development and efficiency. I do not think this a wise programme, but it is a logical one and deserving of thought. In the face of this, however, Mr. Washington has for the last eight years allowed himself to be made the sole referee for all political action concerning 10,000,000 Americans. Few appointments have been made without his consent, and others' political policies have been deferred to him.

Du Bois asked what had been the result of giving preferment only to "those Negroes who agree with Mr. Washington's policy of non-resistance, giving up agitation, and acquiescence in semi-serfdom," and concluded that it amounted to "a substitution of monarchy for democracy among a population twice as large as that of all New England."[11]

Such attacks had often occurred in the Niagara years, but now Villard's influential New York *Evening Post* supported Du Bois's statement without even demurring at the charge of "acquiescence in semi-serfdom," and reminded its readers of "the extent of the cleavage" between Du Bois and Washington. While Du Bois focused on protest against wrong, Washington "subordinates everything else to the uplifting of the negro industrially and economically." By counseling submission to disfranchisement, said the *Evening Post,* Washington found welcome in the South and among conservatives in the North who believed the South should be let alone to work out the race problem. If Washington were simply to keep silent altogether, he could not be criticised. "It is his advice to his people to submit to government and taxation without representation that has hurt, and the fact that he has at the same time assumed or been forced into the place of a political boss of his race. The two positions are hopelessly inconsistent."[12]

Washington, who had been living comfortably with this inconsistency for years, did not reply directly. R. W. Thompson's news bureau, however, published the response of "a well-known educator, whose name is withheld at his request," probably Emmett Scott. This well-known unknown said: "It seems to me that it would be entirely out of place for Dr. Washington to enter into any discussion with a man occupying the place that Dr. Du Bois does, for the reason that

Dr. Washington is at the head of a large institution. . . . Dr. Du Bois, on the other hand, is a mere hired man, as it were, in an institution completely controlled by white people." Du Bois did not even own his residence, and instead of meeting a payroll as Washington did, "receives his salary month by month at the hands of a white person." Therefore, the argument would not be between equals.[13]

Washington continued his wary watch on the early growth of the NAACP. At its second annual meeting in Boston Peter J. Smith, well known as a local Washington supporter, was observed taking notes.[14] Information also reached Washington of the NAACP's efforts to establish branches in all the major black population centers. "Let not your heart be troubled," George Myers wrote after William English Walling, a young white socialist, came to Cleveland as an NAACP organizer. Charles W. Chesnutt, the black lawyer and novelist who criticized Washington's policies but remained his friend, came to Myers to ask for his support of a meeting with Walling, promising that it would not be anti-Washington. Myers suggested that the Cleveland Association of Colored Men would furnish Walling an appropriate audience. But Chesnutt soon returned to Myers to say that he was at a loss as to how to entertain Walling and his wife, "particularly so as they desired a mixed meeting and wanted to get in touch with the white people of the community who were friendly to the brother." Myers reported to Washington this difficulty in getting members of both races in the same meeting, and also quarrels within the Cleveland Association of Colored Men as to whether Washington should be criticized or not. He predicted that there would be no more NAACP meetings in Cleveland.[15] If Myers was candid with the Tuskegean, however, he misread the future.

Washington urged his northern lieutenants to challenge the NAACP in their cities. He received the encouraging news that the Reverend Adam Clayton Powell, Sr., had aroused himself and "openly declared himself as through with Du Bois and his crowd." Washington commended his sturdiest lieutenant Anderson for his bold and insistent speaking out on the issues that divided Washington from the NAACP, and he urged Fred Moore to do likewise. "We must not stand back and let the other fellows do all the fighting and secure all the prominent places at meetings," he wrote Moore. "We must go in and show them we are not afraid to battle for our side." When Washington found Ralph W. Tyler sidling toward the militants, he took steps to bring him back in line. Tyler had offered $50 for a Tyler Intercollegiate Prize Essay, to be awarded to the black college student writing the best essay on "The Negro's Place in the Present Industrial Development of the South," and included Du Bois along with Terrell and R. R. Wright, Jr., as judges. Seeing a copy of the circular announcing the contest, Washington wrote Anderson: "I find it mighty hard to find any of our fellows who do not want to sit on both sides of the fence and in the middle too. I suppose Tyler thought he would get the good will of Du Bois, Wright and their crowd by recognizing them in this way."[16] In almost no time, Washington heard from Calvin Chase, "Our friend, Ralph W. Tyler has written a strong editorial for this week's issue of The Bee in reply to your enemy Du Bois, and other critics."[17] Chase offered to send extra copies, and Scott put in an order for twenty.

By 1911 Washington began to worry about the influence of the *Crisis*, the NAACP monthly that Du Bois edited and gave his distinctive voice of black protest. Washington wrote Moore that the *Crisis* was getting a larger circulation than he realized and was beginning to compete with the *Age* itself. The *Crisis*, he said, was printing at least 15,000 copies a month, nearly the circulation of the *Age*. He suggested that Moore set a goal of 25,000 circulation by next fall, and develop an aggressive advertising campaign. "In several of the barber shops I noticed that The Crisis people have bright, attractive signs up advertising The Crisis," he wrote Moore, and suggested that he do likewise.[18]

A particularly disturbing puzzle to the Washington camp was the behavior of Mary Church Terrell. As an Oberlin graduate with a strong commitment to feminism and civil rights, she was a natural ally of the Talented Tenth, but the fact that her husband owed his judgeship and much more to Washington had restrained for years any impulse to join the militants. Anderson had been suspicious of her for a long time, and during the Brownsville crisis he had included her husband as well. Hearing that Judge Terrell had criticized the dismissal of the black troops, he wrote Washington that "Judge Terrell had better take a stitch in his tongue." The trouble with Terrell, he said, was that his term of office covered that of the President, "and he, therefore, feels that the Doctor can be of no more service to him. Hence, he is 'a Washington man' when the Doctor is around, and yet he manages to give his approval and support to all of his enemies."[19]

Anderson had a certain self-interest in casting suspicion on Washington's other lieutenants, but in Mary Church Terrell's case there were other grounds. She signed the call to the conference in 1909 that formed the NAACP, and took an active part in its annual meetings in 1909, 1910, and 1911. Washington ignored this at first, but by 1910 he was convinced that the NAACP was a hostile group, and he wrote her husband: "Not a few of your friends here [in New York] are nonplussed as to why Mrs. Terrell's name appears among the members of the executive committee and as one of the speakers on the program. This kind of thing is really embarrassing." The NAACP, he pointed out, was "likely to engage in wholesale abuse of the President of the United States as well as other friends of ours. . . . To have Mrs. Terrell's name appear on a program where the opposition is in charge not only makes it harder for your friends to help you when the time comes, but makes it embarrassing from every point of view. Of course I am not seeking to control anybody's action, but I simply want to know where we stand."[20]

Reading what his chief had written to Judge Terrell, Scott heartily approved. "The present attitude assumed by Mrs. Terrell is not one to be lightly passed over," he commented, "in view of the fact that they do not hesitate to call upon you whenever they are in trouble."[21] Terrell could simply have responded that his wife had a mind of her own, but the couple apparently came to an understanding about it. Mary Terrell undoubtedly wanted to guard and promote her husband's position, to which she owed some of her own standing. Learning that Washington was in New York during the NAACP Conference in 1910, she came by his hotel and left him a note on the Hotel Manhattan stationery: "I thought I would peep in here a minute to see if you were in the hotel. You probably divined my intention and fled. I want to talk with you about a matter connected with the Negro Conference just held."[22] The two apparently missed connection.

Washington seized every opportunity to win back followers who had strayed. Ray Stannard Baker, who had flitted like a moth between Washington and Du Bois during his writing of *Following the Color Line*, still could not quite make up his mind. After addressing the NAACP, he wrote Washington that his speech had had a cool reception by the radicals there and that, the more he thought of it, the more he supported Washington's gradual methods.[23] Washington replied that he knew most of the individuals in the meeting and that "Nothing that has real sense in it would be received with any degree of enthusiasm. What they want is nonsense." Furthermore, the blacks prominent in the organization were "not sincere," and their white allies were both gullible and insincere in persuading blacks "that they can get what they ought to have in the way of right treatment by merely making demands, passing resolutions and cursing somebody." He compared this approach to the race problem with offering candy instead of castor oil to a sick child.[24] He urged Baker to attend instead a National Negro Business League meeting and see the "men who are doing things."[25]

Baker continued to attend the NAACP meetings but declined an invitation to serve on one of its committees. While in New York for an NAACP meeting in 1915, he spent an evening with Washington at his hotel. "He is one of the comparatively few men I have met who always impresses me as being great—somehow possessing qualities beyond & above the ordinary," Baker confided to his notebook. A few days later, after listening to the oratory of the NAACP leaders, he jotted in the same notebook: "They emphasize rights, not duties & just as Washington attacks them in an indirect way, so they attack Washington. I find myself with them, too, though there are some aspects of their work I do not approve. Agitation for rights is necessary as well as emphasis upon duties. Probably Dr. Washington is attacking the problem from the South in the wisest way; & probably these people are doing the most useful thing here in the North. But always I find myself instinctively leaning toward those who teach duty and service. It is so easy to clamor for rights & so hard to earn or deserve rights."[26]

Washington's relationship to the NAACP took a sharp turn for the worse in the fall of 1910. What had begun with a mutual agreement to disagree and had progressed to indirect attack and competition for the hearts and minds of blacks became open, deep, and permanent rupture after the Milholland circular letter and the "National Negro Committee" Appeal to Europe.[27] Washington had ended his tour of continental Europe in the fall of 1910 with a visit to London to speak at a dinner sponsored by the Anti-Slavery and Aborigines Protection Society. John E. Milholland publicly refused an invitation, on the ground that Washington stood for "the inadequate education of his Race" and did not protest against the unconstitutional denial of rights.[28] Undeterred by Milholland's disapproval, Washington, according to a newspaper account of his address, said "there was wisdom, patience, forbearance, Christianity, and patriotism enough to enable each race to live side by side, working out its destiny with justice to the other."[29] Without utterly denying that wrongs were perpetrated on Afro-Americans, Washington stressed the hopeful signs. At a meeting at Liverpool before returning to America, he denounced lynching but said of the American newspapers, "If a negro burned down a house everyone heard of it, but if ten negroes built a house we never heard anything of it; if one white man killed a negro everyone knew of it, but if ten white men helped and encouraged a negro every day no one heard of it."[30]

Washington returned in October 1910 to large enthusiastic receptions in New York and Boston and then on to Tuskegee, where he mailed R. R. Moton confidentially a copy of Milholland's open letter. Moton had during Washington's absence worked hard to bring about an accord between Washington and the NAACP. In fact, he had sought a recognition by both factions of the other's legitimacy from the beginning of the NAACP. Washington wrote him, "I am wondering in view of Mr. Villard's protests and explanations to you . . . to the effect that their movement is not in opposition to me, if you would not like to send Mr. Villard this circular and call his attention to the fact that . . . in view of this circular the advantage would be rather to make anybody believe that the movement has not for its principal object the discouragement of the fundamentals of Hampton and Tuskegee and everything that we stand for."[31]

Before Moton could get a reply from Villard, however, another manifesto appeared, an open letter "To the People of Great Britain and Europe," signed by Du Bois and thirty-one other prominent Afro-Americans, most of them members of the NAACP. The first signature was that of J. Max Barber, but Du Bois in his autobiography claimed authorship.[32] The circular declared that "if Mr. Booker T. Washington, or any other person, is giving the impression abroad that the Negro problem in America is in process of satisfactory solution he is giving an impression which is not true." The circular eloquently detailed the indignities blacks met in America and said that "it is like a blow in the face to have one, who himself suffers daily insults and humiliation in America, give the impression that all is well. It is one thing to be optimistic, self-forgetful and forgiving, but it is quite a different thing, consciously or unconsciously, to misrepresent the truth."[33] The document's strength was in the truth of its observation of Washington's worst failing, his glossing over of patent evidence of deliberate white repression in order to find grounds for optimism. The statement's weakness, however, was that it went out on stationery headed "Headquarters, National Negro Committee, 20 Vesey St., New York, U.S.A." This was in fact the early name, recently changed, of the NAACP. Its address was 20 Vesey Street. Du Bois and his black co-signers had, in effect, used the NAACP's letterhead and address, without its permission, to attack Washington.

Washington's grievance against the circular of Du Bois and others was not that they criticized him, for he was constantly disparaging them and the NAACP in his own private correspondence. In fact, about this same time, the southern white Charles L. Coon wanted to move from agnosticism about white supremacy to a more positive commitment to racial equality and asked Washington if he thought he should join the NAACP. Washington advised against it, saying that Villard meant well but had gathered around him bitterly resentful blacks and white dreamers. "No one on earth knows what these people are likely to do," he warned Coon, "or likely to say at one of these meetings." Coon would do better "by speaking to the Southern white people than by speaking about them."[34]

What Washington resented most was the public nature of the Milholland and Du Bois criticism, contrary to Villard's earlier assurances. The Du Bois circular also conveyed the impression, whether deceptive or not, of NAACP sponsorship. Robert R. Moton also pointed out to Villard that the Milholland circular was inconsistent with the assurances Villard had given him that the NAACP would not attack Washington, Tuskegee, or Hampton, since Milholland was "one of the promoters of the movement and is at present an important officer in the Association."[35]

The most vulnerable signer of the Du Bois Appeal was William Pickens, because he was a teacher in a southern institution, Talladega College, and had been closely associated with Washington in the past. Washington asked him to send "a copy of anything that I actually said in London to which you object."[36] Pickens sought to dodge somewhat by insisting that the published version of the appeal was "not exactly the thing which I signed." He wrote that he had suggested "modifications in the protest, modifications which would tend to show that it was not the sense of the signers that Dr. Washington intended to give the impression" that blacks were progressing satisfactorily in America. "You know the advantage which the press takes of our words," he said, and promised to check again the wording of the original version he had signed.[37]

A little later upon reflection Pickens wrote that, while the signers of the Du Bois Appeal might have misunderstood Washington's intentions in his European utterances, the impression he gave the reporters for various London newspapers was that American injustices toward Afro-Americans had been exaggerated. In a tone almost obsequious, Pickens ended his letter: "I may be wrong in all this. I am a learner. I may change, if I learn better." He stood his ground, however, in saying: "It will not be well for us to alienate the sympathy of the outside world, and to have our protests against real wrong misunderstood as the exaggerated complaints of children."[38]

Washington protected his influence with his English friends by writing to Travers Buxton of the Anti-Slavery and Aborigines Protection Society that the Du Bois Appeal was also "engineered" by Milholland, and that most of the black signers were "ashamed of the race to which they belong and are angry because they are not white people." He said the reason they criticized him so sharply for claiming that blacks were making progress was because they themselves had "made failures in life and this has soured them against the world."[39]

Du Bois insisted to Moton, whom he would like to have wooed away from his alliance with Washington, that the Milholland circular and his own appeal were independent in origin, and that his statement was "not . . . an official publication of the Committee." Du Bois wrote acidly that he could not understand why Moton's efforts to "keep Mr. Washington . . . from well-merited criticism" were "greater than your eagerness to help the Negro race."[40]

Though Washington attributed the criticism to the carping of jealous men whose own careers had failed, he rather inconsistently wrote an English friend: "Signed to the circular there are more than half dozen lawyers, one Professor of Latin, several editors of magazines and newspapers, one Bishop, one President of a bank, one ex-member of Congress, and one ex-United States-Consul. It seems to me that a country where within 45 years of the enslavement of that race, there has been produced men who hold such positions as those men are represented as holding, is a country where the Negro has a chance and is making some progress, at least."[41]

Villard defended the NAACP and Du Bois as well as he could in response to Moton's complaint of broken faith. Villard reiterated his denial that the NAACP was anti-Washington, saying that the organization could not be held responsible for the individual opinions or actions of its members. He said that he himself agreed with Milholland that Washington's political activities were harmful, but he was no more opposed to Tuskegee than to Manassas, an industrial school that he had sponsored for many years on the Tuskegee model. He defended Du Bois's right to opinions of his own, and reassured Moton that the NAACP was not trying to "tear down" anything, but that this did not mean "that we shall be tongue-tied, like Dr. Washington, on the fundamental problems of negro citizenship, or that we shall even bear the appearance of acquiescing in monstrous injustice to the black man."[42] At this point Moton wrote Washington that he frankly doubted "whether we can do anything with these people." The appeal, he said, was clearly written by Du Bois, and "the contention of Mr. Villard and Dr. Du Bois that the Committee is not responsible for the actions of its members is all moonshine."[43]

Washington decided to make the signers of the appeal, and particularly Du Bois, as uncomfortable as possible. In a personal letter to Clark Howell, editor of the Atlanta *Constitution,* he wrote: "I think it is too bad that an institution like Atlanta University has permitted Dr. Du Bois to go on from year to year stirring up racial strife in the heart of the South. While Du Bois, as I understand it, has left Atlanta for New York, he is to come back to Atlanta in the spring and summer and conduct some kind of racial conference."[44] Members of the Tuskegee Machine also abandoned restraint in their editorial attacks on the signers. Tyler proudly sent to Tuskegee his editorial for the Washington *Bee* on the signers. Every movement that Du Bois had fathered, he said, "appears to have for its one object the pulling down of Dr. Washington from the high pedestal he occupies, and upon which the people placed him." As for the other signers, they were authors who earned no royalties, ministers lacking Christian charity, editors of sheets of billingsgate, "and a few human jokes who are but impecunious camp-followers, the whole lot forming a limited few iconoclasts."[45]

The controversy might have died away for lack of fuel, but for new information Washington obtained of dissension within the NAACP over the two documents. While in New York in December 1910 to

give one of her lectures in behalf of the NAACP, Mary Church Terrell once more made an effort to see Washington. She wrote him again
on Hotel Manhattan stationery while sitting in its lobby after finding
him out. "There are several things I should like to say to you which
can be spoken better than written," she wrote. Having thus piqued
curiosity, she added: "I feel as tho I must see you. . . . Mr. Villard
told me something yesterday which has pained me not a little and that
is why I want very much to see you. Don't fail to send me a telegram
or a special message letting me know when you can see me."[46] Nobody could have resisted such a letter, and least of all Washington,
who was no stranger to such brief encounters. He arranged to meet
her in his New York office the next afternoon.[47]

What Washington learned was well worth his time. "I have just had
a long talk with Mrs. Terrell," Washington wrote Villard the next day,
"and she tells me that your committee did not send out that circular
regarding my supposed utterances when I was in Europe." Mary
Church Terrell's information was a wedge that Washington managed
to drive between the white and the black members of the NAACP,
and it also confirmed his original judgment to have nothing to do with
the organization. He told Villard he was glad to learn that the NAACP
did not send out the circular because it was "so far at variance with
what you first wrote me regarding the purposes of the committee that
I confess I was greatly surprised when I saw it as coming from your
committee as I suppose." His supposition was a natural one, he said,
and shared by many others who saw the letterhead. "The use of the
word 'Negro' and 'Afro-American' instead of 'Colored' is a mere attempt to play on words and deceive," he added, "and I cannot see
how people who would thus try to deceive their friends and the public
can be trusted with the larger interests of the race." Moreover, with
all that needed to be done to punish lynchers, end peonage, gain an
equitable share of the school fund and an equal opportunity to vote,
"it is difficult to see how people can throw away their time and strength
in stirring up strife within the race instead of devoting themselves to
bringing about justice to the race as a whole."[48]

Washington dropped a line to Emmett Scott to say that "I am gradually coming around to the opinion that it is a valuable thing to have
Mrs. Terrell connected with that committee." Not only did she drop
several compliments of Tuskegee in her New York speech, but she

told him in private many things of interest about the NAACP. "One of her values is in this direction," he shrewdly observed:

She gets on the inside of things and is always capable of stirring up trouble in any organization that she has a part in. Of course all this is strictly confidential, as I have told her that her name would not be used. I can keep in close touch with her if her name is not quoted. She tells me that she and Du Bois have absolutely nothing to do with each other; they scarcely speak, and she did not see him during her stay in New York, but more important than this, she says, the European circular was an imposition on the committee, that Villard, a white woman and all the head people are disgusted and considerably torn up that such a circular should have been sent out presumably under the guise of the committee. . . . At any rate they seem to be in a pretty big row among themselves, and the circular seems to have caused it. Mrs. Terrell appears to be very much disgusted with the whole affair, and I think she will make matters pretty lively from now on.[49]

There is no evidence that Mary Church Terrell extended beyond this instance her career as a double agent. She continued to lecture for the NAACP before such groups as the New York Society for Ethical Culture and the white New York YMCA, and at a Swarthmore summer program. She was a member of a committee that presented to President Taft the NAACP resolutions against lynching. She gave every evidence of complete commitment to the NAACP, and if in private she told Washington anything further her name was not quoted. In 1912, after the incorporation of the NAACP, she became a member of its first board of directors.[50]

Meanwhile, Washington pressed his grievance against the signers of the Du Bois Appeal to the People of Great Britain and Europe. Villard replied rather lamely that he had been "on the point of writing you to tell you what Mrs. Terrell has already conveyed to you." He regretted, he wrote, that "in an unauthorized way the envelopes of the National Association were used in sending out the protest of the thirty-two colored men." His investigation had found that "it was absolutely accidental as far as this office was concerned." The circulars were not mailed from the office; the orders to erase the letterhead were not carried out "because the stenographer to whom they were submitted did not follow instructions." Having shifted to the passive voice and blamed an anonymous secretary, Villard proceeded once again to lecture Washington on the appropriateness of the complaint Du Bois and his co-signers had made, that Washington had misrepresented conditions in the United States. "Your optimism is leading you astray," he wrote. Washington was keeping silent about evils he should denounce. He should take heed of the evidence that "a greater and greater percentage of the intellectual colored people are turning from you and becoming your opponents, and with them a number of white people as well."[51]

Washington took some time to consider a reply to this half-hearted apology and renewal of criticism. He had been calling on his lieutenants to flood the newspapers with letters endorsing his position, as he believed Du Bois and his co-signers were doing on the other side. Now he sent Scott a telegram that the best policy would be to "discreetly advise our friends stop completely for considerable while giving attention to European circulars and other matters bearing upon Du Bois. He is getting a good deal of advertisement which he likes."[52] Four weeks passed before Washington answered Villard. He defied Villard to furnish "any specific utterance" he had made in Europe that was objectionable. He had only been trying to demonstrate, he said, that Villard's grandfather's labor for emancipation had been justified by black progress and self-help during freedom. Villard, Washington wrote, had the disadvantage "of not knowing as much about the life of the Negro race as if you were a member of that race yourself." Besides, he had surrounded himself with blacks who had failed and hence were sour and unhappy. Washington insisted to Villard that "both in my interviews and in my speeches I said the thing which I thought was right and which from the bottom of my heart I believed in. For this, I am sure I will have your respect, even though you do not agree with what I had to say."[53] As if to answer Washington's claim that he had said nothing objectionable in Europe, however, the next issue of the *Crisis* carried a comment from a London magazine: "Mr. Booker T. Washington recently gave us a glowing picture of the progress, industrial, intellectual and moral, made by his colored fellow-citizens in the United States during recent years."[54] The next month, it published the entire text of the National Negro Committee Appeal.[55]

In his correspondence with Villard, Washington had called Milholland untrustworthy and an outright liar for claiming that he had raised money for Tuskegee. He was probably pleased to hear from Villard that the NAACP and Milholland's Constitution League had separated. "I write this so that you may not in any way hold us liable for any actions taken by the Constitution League," Villard wrote, but Washington was so embittered by then that he did not believe the good news.[56] "This indicates one of two things," he wrote Anderson, "either that he and Milholland have broken, or that they have agreed between them to let the Constitutional League do the dirty work and use the other organization to inveigle our friends into believing in their sincerity."[57] As though to confirm the suspicion, Milholland reviewed *The Man Farthest Down,* Washington's book on his European trip, as a collection of "platitudinous, narcotic deliverances" designed to advocate living by bread alone.[58]

The correspondence between Washington and Villard had degenerated into a circular debate in which there could be no winner or loser, only a last word. Whereas Washington had personalized the issue and indicted the methods used to criticize his utterances, Villard sought to return the controversy to Washington's own misrepresentation of the state of race relations in America. Washington had presented "but half the case—the pleasant side," Villard wrote. As to Washington's claim that the blacks in the NAACP were failures, he replied that "there is nobody more successful than Dr. Du Bois." Their opposition was not to Washington personally, "but to the doctrines you advocate and the things you have said."[59] Washington finally agreed, with a parting shot at Milholland for "downright misrepresentation" in claiming to have raised money for Tuskegee, to abandon the futile correspondence.[30] Concluding that Villard was simply ill-informed about the real life of blacks, Washington instructed Emmett Scott to "have at our expense, if necessary, 12 of the strongest colored papers sent regularly to Mr. Villard, personally. Of course you will have to be very careful as to how this arrangement is made."[61] Scott did so, asking the editors not to use Washington's name.[62] Washington preferred to see his differences with Du Bois as a result of Du Bois's failure to realize that the chief work before the race at present was one of construction, not destruction.[63]

Washington was incapable, however, of keeping his differences with Du Bois and the NAACP for any length of time in any perspective but a personal one. He wrote of the NAACP to a Tuskegee graduate: "As a matter of straight fact, this organization is for the purpose of tearing down our work wherever possible and I think none of our friends should give it comfort."[64] As to Du Bois, he revived his old charges about Du Bois's conduct during the Atlanta riot in 1906. He wrote to T. Thomas Fortune, who was temporarily back on speaking terms, that "Du Bois did run away from Atlanta. All the time that the riot was going on, Du Bois was hiding at the Calhoun School in Alabama—a school which I was responsible for establishing some fifteen years ago. He remained there until the riot was over and then came out and wrote a piece of poetry bearing upon those who were killed in the riot." He followed this distortion by telling Fortune that the NAACP was simply the means by which "our friend Villard and John E. Milholland are attempting to run and control the destinies of the Negro race through Du Bois."[65] Fortune began on Washington's and Anderson's request a series of articles maligning Du Bois. "When we get done with Dr. Du Bois," he boasted, "I am sure that he will have some trouble in handing over the leadership of the race to white men."[66]

As the dispute over the National Negro Committee trailed off in an atmosphere of rancor and feelings of personal betrayal, the Cosmopolitan Club affair of 1911 occurred. This time it was Washington and Anderson who were the aggressors and deceivers, the employers of much more reprehensible methods than the National Negro Committee had used. Washington and his New York partner secretly directed newspaper ridicule on the little band of racial liberals with a savagery that cannot be explained by Washington's social philosophy, racial policy, or any other rational consideration. One might explain Washington's secret ruthlessness by the fact that he was still smoldering from the Milholland and Du Bois criticisms and Villard's apology for their methods. Washington's own private papers, however, reveal that he and Anderson had also secretly sabotaged an earlier Cosmopolitan Club dinner in 1908, when there was no such provocation.

The Cosmopolitan Society of America, founded in 1906 at Mary White Ovington's house in Brooklyn, was a meeting place for white liberals and members of the darker races for the purpose of dispelling racial stereotypes and gaining more sophistication through association with one another on a social basis. The club's significance was not in any great influence it had but in its uniqueness in treating race not as a problem but as a matter of human relations. After a number of meetings in private homes, the club decided in 1908 to meet for dinner at a midtown New York restaurant with about 100 guests, including Villard and Hamilton Holt, editor of the *Independent.* New York newspaper reporters learned of the meeting, appeared in force, and wrote stories that implied that the decorous gathering advocated not only social equality but intermarriage and socialism. They reported that "twenty white girls and women dined side by side at table with negro men and women." The publicity brought Miss Ovington such obscene letters that she had her male relatives open them.[67]

It is now clear from Washington's private papers that he and Anderson secretly arranged for the sensational press coverage of this dinner, and did so again in January 1911. Anderson sent Washington a copy of the invitation, remarking: "One needs only to glance over this invitation, printed as it is on yellow paper, and note the names of the speakers and the long-winded topics they are to discuss, to be convinced that they are a bunch of freaks. I shall do my best to see that the movement gets a full newspaper report. I would suggest that you do something along that line also. Much good can be accomplished by having the Associated Press, and other distributing news agencies send a full report of this meeting through the country."[68] Washington responded from Tuskegee: "Regarding black and white dinner be sure get hold of same reporter who reported for American year or two ago. Would see that copies of printed announcement reach all city editors in advance. Think New York Times will work in harmony with you."[69] Anderson replied that he was busy trying to get suitable press coverage. "I would like to get hold of the man who handled it before," he wrote Washington, "but unfortunately, I do not know his name. He was an artist. I shall leave no stone unturned to secure due publicity."[70]

Although Anderson failed to find the man who had handled the matter in 1908, he wrote Washington that "a 'good friend' on the Press took care of that end of it," and sent a sheaf of clippings. Anderson said he could not account for the failure of the New York *Times, Sun,* and *Herald* to cover the story, as they were all notified, but the New York *Press* and other yellow journals made up for that neglect, and he was hopeful that the City News Association and the Associated Press would further spread the news.[71]

The day after the dinner at the Cafe Boulevard, one edition of the New York *Press* carried the headline: THREE RACES SIT AT BANQUET FOR MIXED MARRIAGE. In another edition the story was headed: THREE RACES MIX AT BANQUET FOR MAN'S BROTHERHOOD: *Fashionable White*

Women Sit at Board with Negroes, Japs and Chinamen to Promote "Cause" of Miscegenation. The text of the news story made it clear that miscegenation had not actually been advocated, but the general tone of the coverage was that of innuendo:

> White women, evidently of the cultured and wealthier classes, fashionably attired in low-cut gowns, leaned over the tables to chat confidentially with negro men of the true African type. . . . the cosmopolitan chop suey . . . the broad smiles of the negroes as they leered surreptitiously across the room at their Caucasian friends made one feel their inner ecstasy over the unwonted social communion.[72]

The New York *World* carried a briefer account—"with proper sensational headlines," wrote Anderson. "Thus you see, the function was well handled by the papers."[73] Emmett Scott could scarcely contain his delight. He wrote Anderson: "Your 'special representative' seems to have served up for the New York Press a particularly savory article and I am sending it forward to the Doctor at Hotel Manhattan today. I am sorry that the 'artist' of The American was not also turned loose to describe this delectable function."[74]

Even Washington's sharpest critics, those who had recently embarrassed him by repudiating his utterances in Europe, never dreamed of his connivance with the biased white newspapermen to embarrass the white liberals of the NAACP. Miss Ovington, a very proper old maid, was still upset by the incidents of 1908 and 1911 when she wrote her memoirs in 1947. Still wondering who had tipped off the reporters, she spoke darkly of "the connivance of a few club members" and recalled with suspicion a Gallic twinkle in the eye of the Frenchman André Tridon, the club treasurer, when the reporters and photographers filed into the room.[75] Neither she—nor anyone but Anderson and Scott—had any idea of Washington's secret role.

If Villard and Du Bois could shabbily blame a stenographer for using the NAACP name to attack Washington contrary to promise, Washington's secret instigation of the Cosmopolitan Club affair surely went far beyond that in ruthlessness. Washington did not know that he was about to receive a rude, violent reminder that he himself was vulnerable to the tyranny of a man whose sole badge of superiority was a white skin.

CHAPTER 16

Night of Violence

He looked me right in the face and said, "Hello, sweetheart."

LAURA PAGE ALVAREZ

IT WAS about nine o'clock on Sunday evening, March 19, 1911. Booker T. Washington had arrived in New York the preceding day from Battle Creek, Michigan, and checked in at the Hotel Manhattan, a first-class, midtown hotel, without the usual accompaniment of his male stenographer. After giving talks at a black church and a white church, he returned to his hotel early Sunday evening, but instead of going to the dining room he made his supper out of a bag of peanuts bought on the street. Then he left the hotel, traveled uptown by subway, and entered the vestibule of an apartment building at 11½ West Sixty-third Street, a short distance west of the southern edge of Central Park. The building was near but not in the so-called Tenderloin, an "easy-morals" section of the city. There were enclaves of black residents nearby, but the building he entered was occupied entirely by whites, as were those on either side. A theater was across the street, and many of the inhabitants were connected with the theater in one way or another.

After scanning the directory Washington rang one of the bells, received no answer and, so he later said, thought the occupants might be at church and would return soon. While he studied the directory and considered whether to wait, a slim, attractive brunette about thirty years old left one of the first-floor apartments and passed him on her way out to walk her French bulldog. She later testified that he was peeping in a keyhole. Going out on the street to pace up and down the block while waiting, he passed the woman again. "He looked me right in the face," she later testified, "and said, 'Hello, sweetheart.' " Such a greeting would seem utterly out of character for Booker T. Washington, and he denied that he had spoken to man, woman, or child that night—or nodded, motioned, or bowed.[1] "I have been embarrassed on my visits to New York by being saluted by handsomely gowned, attractive women while I have been walking in the street," he told a reporter. "I could not remember whether I had met them in my work, although this may have been the case, so I did not respond to their salutations."[2]

Returning to the vestibule, Washington rang the bell again and received no answer. This time two young women, nineteen and twenty years old, passed him on the way into their apartment, but he did not speak to them. He returned to the sidewalk and resumed his walk, unaware that a white man, and then a second one, observed him from the shadow of the darkened theater entrance. When he had been in the neighborhood about an hour, he returned to the vestibule another time, put on his glasses, and leaned over to get a closer look at the names on the register.

Suddenly a stocky, powerful man about forty years old, five feet seven inches tall, charged into the vestibule from the street. He wore no coat, tie, or collar, and Washington later testified that the man appeared to be the worse for drink. "What are you doing here?" the man asked. "Are you breaking into my house? You have been hanging around here for four or five weeks."[3] The man later testified that Washington replied: "What do you want to know for? It is none of your business."[4] Washington said the man did not wait for a reply, but struck him with his fist on the side of his head. Washington then tried to explain why he was there, but the man hit him four or five more times. Washington then tried to defend himself, but at fifty-five and recently a patient at the Kellogg sanitarium in Michigan, he was no match for a powerful man fifteen years younger. The man later claimed that Washington had pleaded with him to let the matter drop, saying, "I know I have done wrong. Let me go."[5]

Washington managed, while fending off the assault, to open the outside door. He ran out into the street. The man followed, borrowed a heavy-headed walking stick from a bystander, and began to hit Washington systematically with it, striking him about a dozen times. "Don't beat me this way," Washington pleaded. "If I'm breaking the law call an officer and have him arrest me if I'm doing anything wrong." [6] When the assailant paid no heed, Washington ran down the street with the assailant and the owner of the cane close behind, beating him as they ran. Near the park Washington caught his foot in the trolley tracks, stumbled, and fell.

At the corner of Sixty-third Street and Central Park West was a plainclothes policeman, Chester A. Hagan, talking with a bank clerk named James Crowe, as Washington ran and stumbled toward them with the two men in pursuit. Washington fell to his hands and knees at the curb, almost at their feet. "Here's a thief," said Crowe, and by now Washington, his clothes torn and dirty, blood pouring from his head wounds, probably did look more like a thief than the educator and interracial diplomat that he was. Hagan grabbed Washington and showed his badge. The owner of the cane disappeared, but the principal assailant ran up, saying: "This man is a thief. I found him with his hand on the door-knob and his eye at the keyhole." [7]

Hagan put Washington under arrest, and a few minutes later when a uniformed policeman named Tierney arrived Hagan turned Washington over to him to be taken to the stationhouse on Sixty-eighth Street. "Officer, if you hadn't shown up I'd [have] knocked that black man's head off," Hagan later recalled the assailant saying.[8] When Officer Tierney questioned the plausibility of the burglary explanation of Washington's presence at the scene, saying that probably nobody would try to commit burglary through the front door, someone in the gathering crowd said that perhaps the black man was after the two young white women who had entered the building while he was in the vestibule. "Oh, that's so-and-so's daughters," the assailant said. "I wonder if I ought to change the charge to that." [9]

At the stationhouse the assailant identified himself as Henry Albert Ulrich, a resident of the apartment building. A carpenter by trade, he was currently making his living as proprietor of the West Side Dog Kennel. He had been charged but not convicted earlier in the year for the theft of a prize Pomeranian. "I was at dinner when my wife, who had been out calling, came in," he said. "She was very much excited and said that a negro was lurking about the front of the building. I went out, and on the first floor I saw a negro trying to 'peek' through a keyhole in the front door of Mrs. Revett's apartment. I asked him what he was doing and when I got no answer I started to throw him out of the building. He resisted and I gave him the best beating I could. I thought I was right at the time and I think so yet."[10] Ulrich claimed that Washington had hit him first with a hard blow to the jaw. He denied that he had beaten Washington with a stick or caused the two large gashes in Washington's head or his torn ear. In running outside, he said, Washington had stumbled and hit his head against a fire hydrant, and the other injuries came when he hit his head against the curb after stumbling on the streetcar tracks.

Lieutenant Robert Quinn decided to book the black man first and have his wounds attended to later. When Washington now gave his name for the first time, the lieutenant refused to believe him. Washington produced a calling card, but the officer was still skeptical. Rummaging through his pockets, Washington found a railroad pass in his name and a letter addressed to him. Finally convinced of Washington's identity and of the improbability of such a man's being a burglar, the lieutenant dismissed all charges against him and, to Ulrich's chagrin, entertained charges against him. Washington charged Ulrich with felonious assault, and he was held on $1500 bail. The lieutenant then summoned an ambulance from the nearby Flower Hospital, where in the emergency room the doctor closed Washington's wounds with sixteen stitches and released him. Washington returned to his hotel in the pre-dawn hours with a bandage around the entire top half of his head except the crown, where a skull cap covered the gauze and plaster. Before going to bed he called to his side three New York City black friends, Charles Anderson, Fred Moore, and Wilford Smith.[11]

Meanwhile, as Ulrich was on the way to the lockup, his wife rushed into the stationhouse and charged Washington with accosting her prior to the assault. "It is strange that a man cannot protect his wife and daughter from insult and keep out of jail," she said, "while the negro who insulted them is free." She went out and secured Ulrich's bail money.[12]

Finding the incident sensationally reported next morning in the New York papers, Washington sought help from the chairman of the board of trustees of Tuskegee Institute, Seth Low, the president of Columbia University and former mayor of New York. Low spent the entire day at Washington's side advising him. Washington sent his lawyer

Wilford Smith to secure a one-day delay in the court hearing on account of his physical condition. He gave out detailed interviews to the New York *World* and the New York *Evening Post,* denying that he had ever in his life used the expression, "Hello, sweetheart," and denying that he had been drinking.[13] He also gave an explanation of his presence at the scene of the assault. The night before at the hospital, while still affected by the shock and confusion of the assault, he had given reporters the impression that he had gone to that address in response to a telegram to meet Daniel Cranford Smith, the white man who audited the books of Tuskegee Institute for the trustees. Smith lived in Montclair, New Jersey, however, not in the New York West Side, and when reporters called his residence they learned that he was at Tuskegee and had been there for a month. When confronted with these discrepancies, Washington said it was a letter, not a telegram he had received, and not from Smith but from Scott, his private secretary. It was handwritten, he said, and no copy was kept. Unfortunately, Washington said, he had destroyed the letter after reading it in his hotel room because it contained confidential information about faculty members that he did not want lying about in his files for other officers of the school perhaps to see. As nearly as he could recall from memory, he told the reporters, Scott's message was: "I learned from Mr D. C. Smith a few days ago that he was finishing up his work here and that he is likely to be in New York about the same time you are. He said that he sometimes stopped with relatives or friends, the McCrarys—I think that name is right—at No. 11½ Sixty-third Street. I thought you might want to get in touch with him there regarding Mr. Low's matter."[14] The latter reference was presumably to a nine-page letter Low had recently written suggesting changes in Tuskegee's farm operations and accounts.[15]

Low also prepared over his own signature a press release stating Washington's version of the assault and read it over the telephone to Oswald Garrison Villard of the *Evening Post.* Low accepted a few changes Villard suggested and released the statement. Washington had convinced Low that there was nothing in the incident beyond unfortunate publicity in the yellow journals, but Villard wrote privately to his uncle Frank Garrison: "If he [BTW] should not be able to substantiate his story in court it would be a terrible thing, and I have been sick at heart over it because there are all sorts of stories already floating around among newspaper men that he really went to the place to

meet a white woman etc. This, of course, I cannot believe. The circumstances are most trying, and as Washington said to me, 'of course
the men are lying,' and trying to take advantage of his color to get
out of the assault upon him." [16]

Hundreds of black friends and well-wishers, and the merely curious
as well, were on hand when Washington arrived for the hearing. By
mistake Washington at first sat in the magistrate's seat, then laughed
and stepped down. He was in court for only a few minutes. He described his arrival in the city, the reading and destruction of Scott's
letter, the search for Smith at the home of the McCrary relatives or
friends, the assault with fists and cane, his flight and arrest. "I think,
to do him justice," he said of Ulrich, "that the man who struck me
made the mistake of thinking that perhaps I was a burglar." [17]

Ulrich's wife appeared in a "picture hat" to testify that Washington
had accosted her. Ulrich testified that he had observed Washington
for some time in the concealment of the theater entrance. When he
asked Washington what he was doing in the vestibule, Ulrich testified,
Washington said, "None of your d—n business," and hit Ulrich in the
jaw. He alleged that Washington had stumbled and fallen not because
he had hit him, but because he was drunk. Washington lowered the
charge against Ulrich from felonious assault to simple assault, but he
insisted that this did not mean that he felt Ulrich was justified in his
actions. Washington apparently believed that the arraignment of Ulrich was in effect a verdict of guilty. He sent telegrams to his two sons:
"Trial held this afternoon. Defendant afraid to go to trial and waived
examination which means practical guilt. Whole thing lasted about
three minutes. Judges, lawyers and everybody most kind." [18]

Messages, resolutions, and editorials all over the country supported
Washington. Andrew Carnegie visited his friend at his hotel and left
still believing him both the Moses and the Joshua of his people. [19]
Theodore Roosevelt, then traveling in the West, did not write until
nine days after the assault. His letter carried no ringing endorsement
when it did arrive, but urged the pressing of charges for the "utterly
wanton" assault. It was not made public. [20] President Taft, however,
made public a letter of support and faith. [21] Woodrow Wilson, while
campaigning a year later, on the other hand, indignantly denied that
he had sent any letter of support or condolence as southern conservative opponents of his nomination charged. [22]

Unfortunately it was not until three days after the assault that Emmett Scott arrived to serve as a buffer between Washington and the press corps.[23] Anderson, however, took some initial steps to shift public interest from suspicion of Washington to sympathy with him. Anderson gathered a crowd of some 500 blacks at the Bethel A. M. E. Church in New York and carefully shepherded the speakers. "I talked brass tacks to each speaker before the opening of the meeting," Anderson wrote Washington, "and cautioned them against any intemperance of language." He placed two well known fire-eaters so late on the program that the reporters had left before they began to speak. In his own address Anderson praised the press for its fairness. He did not really believe what he said, he wrote Washington, "but I thought I would hand it a little commendation in order to secure a favorable report of the meeting."[24] Similar meetings in the black communities across the country expressed in speeches and resolutions their sympathy for the stricken leader. The New York *Age* was "flooded with copies of resolutions of meetings."[25]

Even Washington's critics, Du Bois, for example, wrote sympathetic editorials. Monroe Trotter wrote in the Boston *Guardian:* "Our opposition to Mr. Washington because of his propaganda and methods, even to his method of treating reputable Colored men who get into trouble, as he has now, is well known, but we do not desire to take any advantage of his present troubles. We want to fight men when standing up."[26] The novelist Charles W. Chesnutt, often Washington's critic but always his friend, sent an ironic message. "I have more than once heard you say that if you were to be born over, and had your choice of races, you would select that of an American Negro," he wrote. "You have now had the opportunity of suffering physically for your faith—the blood of martyrs is the seed of the church."[27]

Washington worried intensely, however, about the southern white reaction. Ever since the Atlanta address had fixed his stereotype in the southern white consciousness, he had from time to time blurred the image, in dining with President McKinley and prominent southerners at the Peace Jubilee in 1898, in the dinner at the White House, in a sensationally reported dinner at Saratoga in 1905 with John Wanamaker and his daughter, and now in an ambiguous triangle with a white man and woman in New York. Washington hired a Pinkerton detective to ride on the same train when he returned to Tuskegee about a week after the incident. The only adverse remark the Pinkerton man reported overhearing on the train was made by a Bostonian.[28]

White southerners seemed in this age of disfranchisement and segregation to agree on the general principle of white supremacy, but differentiated as to its particular application to incidents outside the South, dividing according to class, temperament, and level of sophistication. The editor of the Richmond *Times-Dispatch* gave Washington fresh heart by writing of the Tuskegean that "if he were 'down in old Alabam' he would be able to prove his good character by his white neighbors."[29] Washington wrote the editor to express his gratitude with a touch of humor that showed he was regaining his equilibrium after the shock of the assault. He told the story of a black man from Georgia who settled in an Ohio town, but packed his bags again when a lynching occurred there. "He told them that he did not like to live in the Ohio town because of the recent lynching. The reply on the part of the white people was that the colored people were also lynched in Georgia. The colored man replied, 'Yes, I knows that, but if I'se lynched in Georgia I'll be lynched by my friends and not by strangers.' "[30] Washington found on his return home, however, that his white Tuskegee neighbors were not in a lynching mood. Many of them, he wrote his Richmond friend, "have simply poured out their hearts to me during this recent trouble in ways that I cannot describe."[31] Twenty leading white citizens of the town signed an expression of "utmost confidence in the truthfulness of your statements."[32]

The Triangle Shirtwaist Fire about a week after the assault took Washington, his assailant, and the unexplained circumstances out of the headlines. Washington's attorney arranged for the delay of Ulrich's trial before a three-judge municipal court until the following November. Washington returned to his usual routine and sought as far as possible to put the incident from his mind. After all, Ulrich was the one on trial. Actually, however, Washington was on trial in the court of public opinion, and what Ulrich had done was important only in so far as it cast a lurid light on the private life of Washington the public man. Among white supremacy extremists the New York incident became another item in the litany of his transgressions against accommodationism, and there was an undercurrent of dissatisfaction among his black militant critics at his unsupported explanation of what he was doing after nine o'clock at night in a neighborhood of tarnished repute. "They seem to think," a Tuskegee graduate living in New York wrote Washington, "that there was some particular and special motive of a character not explained to the public, i.e. there is an indefinite assumption that a laxity of morals was involved in looking for something or somebody."[33]

D. C. Smith, the auditor for Tuskegee Institute, did little or nothing to establish Washington's credibility. When asked in the court hearing two days after the assault how it happened that no one in the apartment building had ever heard of Smith, according to a newspaper report Washington hesitated a moment and then remarked: "We are expecting statements from Mr. Smith and from E. J. Scott, my secretary, both of whom are in Tuskegee, which will clear all of that up."[34] When Smith arrived in New York a few days later he did not go straight to his home in New Jersey, where reporters were camping at his doorstep, but at Washington's suggestion met him privately in New York before seeing the reporters.[35] Smith told a Hearst reporter that he had no knowledge of an appointment with Washington at 11½ West Sixty-third Street or anywhere else. "The letter which Secretary Scott wrote to Mr. Washington must have come from the secretary's own head—it certainly did not come from me," said Smith. When asked if he had ever met Washington at that address, he answered: "Never. We usually meet at one of my offices, for I am concerned with some twenty corporations. I met Mr. Washington Wednesday, on my arrival from the South, at the offices of the Oakland Chemical Company, No. 116 Liberty street. A careless blunder had been made on the secretary's part in sending that address or on Mr. Washington's part in memorizing it. You may think it strange that Mr. Washington destroyed the secretary's letter, but I, who am acquainted with his ways, think it quite natural."[36] Actually, the preservation and systematic filing of every scrap of correspondence was the regular practice of the Tuskegee principal's office, including many handwritten letters from Scott, usually when he was away from the office. If Washington even occasionally destroyed letters he received on the road, his papers show no evidence of it. Scott, after his arrival in New York, apparently prepared some sort of statement about sending a letter to be used if necessary in the trial, but Washington's lawyer never submitted it as evidence. References to the statement, but not the statement itself, appear in Washington's papers.[37]

To support his own account of his presence in the neighborhood, then, Washington had only his own word, the willingness of his loyal private secretary to corroborate it, and a lifetime of rectitude or extreme discretion. Furthermore, the prosecution of his assailant was in the hands of the district attorney's office rather than Washington's own attorney. Municipal judges would decide the case in a city noted for its corrupt political system, and they might favor a New York resident, a loyal son of Tammany, and a German-descended white man over a black stranger no matter how distinguished. Washington sensed his vulnerability and tried to strengthen his case in a variety of ways.

Washington undertook to damage the reputation of Ulrich and his principal witness, which proved surprisingly easy. The day after the hearing, Washington's lawyer Wilford Smith revealed that Mrs. Ulrich was not Mrs. Ulrich. She was Laura Page Alvarez, separated from a man of Spanish surname by whom she had a ten-year-old daughter, Dolores, who lived with her. Ulrich, who also lived with her, had a wife and young children in Orange, New Jersey. The real Mrs. Ulrich learned of her husband's whereabouts because of publicity of the assault. She was suing him in the New Jersey courts for desertion and non-support; she came to New York and offered to testify for the prosecution in the assault trial, while working also to have her husband extradited to New Jersey for trial. Smith also announced to the press that he had learned from residents of the apartment building that two or three weeks before the assault, the father of Dolores Alvarez and a black companion had tried to enter the apartment and kidnap the child from her mother. Smith implied that this would explain Ulrich's remarks and his misunderstanding of the reason for Washington's presence at the time of the assault.[38]

Washington wrote to Wilford Smith urging him to treat generously "old man Benton," father of the two young women who testified that they had passed Washington in the vestibule without molestation or other suspicious conduct on his part. Washington enclosed $10 "additional" for Benton. He also informed Smith that the Burns detective agency had offered him their services without charge, but he thought that more useful than a professional detective would be his white ghostwriter, Robert E. Park, whose talent for getting to the facts had been honed by a German Ph. D. in sociology and many years' experience as a journalist. It would be a good idea, he suggested, for Park to "nose around through the district of 63rd Street and get pretty well acquainted with this man and his wife as well as their friends and find out just what their state of mind and intentions are." He was reasonably sure Park would do this work and do it well. "He is an old newspaper man, besides he is a firm true friend." Washington feared that a detective might "string the thing out in order to get money and involve you in trouble." He distrusted most of them.[39] There is no evidence that Park did the detective work on the Ulrich case, but someone in Smith's employ did so.[40]

Washington and his advisers seriously considered using an undercover agent to persuade Ulrich and Laura Alvarez to retract publicly their statements that he was drunk and had made a sexual advance, after which Washington would drop the assault charge. Washington apparently decided against this. As Scott explained to Wilford Smith, "you certainly would not help matters if you let it appear that Mr. W. was paying out money for the sole purpose of bringing about a retraction." There was the danger of Ulrich "making capital out of the fact that he had been approached," or, even if he made a retraction, stating later that he had been paid or influenced to do so. "As we see it here," Scott wrote from Tuskegee, "a straight out retraction on the part of the woman and a straight out statement from the man to the effect that he is now convinced that he was mistaken in the object for which he thought Mr. W. was at the house and in regard to his actions will accomplish all that we can get accomplished."[41] Otherwise, as Washington wrote Seth Low, though he detested the publicity that would attend a court trial, "I see no way of disposing of the charges against me except by going forward with the trial."[42]

Washington secured from the ambulance surgeon who had attended him a certificate that he had "carefully observed his actions, speech and any odors which might suggest alcohol" and "could ascertain nothing which would pertain to alcoholism."[43] The emergency room physician corroborated this,[44] and Washington paid each the $10 they said was the regular charge for such affidavits among the interns at the hospital.[45] Washington took this course after hearing that Ulrich was "at work in an effort to secure manufactured and perjured testimony" that Washington had been drunk and that his actions resulting from intoxication had justified Ulrich's assault.[46]

Washington took heart from the report of his attorney that James E. Smith, the assistant district attorney in charge of prosecuting Ulrich, had reassured him that either before or at the trial "he has it in his power to make Ulrich make a statement either in court or out of court to the effect that he had no justification in assaulting me, and also to make him acknowledge that the woman's statement regarding me was false." Washington informed Low of this good news.[47] Not knowing what basis the assistant district attorney had for his optimism, however, and not entirely trusting any Tammany official, Washington asked Charles Anderson to find out who was "the backer of the District Attorney" and to "get into close personal touch with him something in the same way that you are with the other officials," but "without bringing up my case at all."[48]

Wilford Smith wrote Washington in late April that Ulrich's lawyer James I. Moore had come to him voluntarily to complain that Ulrich had not paid him and to propose settling the case out of court. A defense fund for Ulrich had been started immediately after his arrest, supported principally by white southerners, but most of the contributors withdrew their pledges when they learned that he was living with Mrs. Alvarez out of wedlock. For several months Washington engaged in elaborate bargaining with Ulrich through Paul D. Cravath, the distinguished New York attorney whom Washington knew well as a fellow-trustee of Fisk University. Cravath, Wilford Smith, and Washington prepared a statement for Ulrich to present either in open court or before the district attorney to the effect that the assault was a result of mistaken identity and therefore was unjustified. After that admission, Washington through his lawyers would withdraw the charge of assault. Assistant district attorney Smith agreed to this disposition of the case.[49]

Washington vacillated, however, about the propriety of this settlement out of court after months of delay. He wrote to Wilford Smith in the summer that both he and his friends and supporters were impatient with the inaction in the case. He had borne Ulrich no personal ill-will, he said, because he had always believed that on the night of the assault Ulrich was either drunk or otherwise confused and mistaken as to the reason Washington had called at the building. "For all these reasons I have been inclined to be lenient and patient," he wrote Smith, but the delay was exasperating and embarrassing. His friends were urging a change back to felonious assault. He was still inclined to the lighter charge if Ulrich would only "go into the courts and tell the straight truth in regard to the matter." If he would not, "we ought to fight this case to the bitter end."[50] In August, Washington made a final attempt through an intermediary, apparently a Pinkerton agent, to secure a statement from Ulrich that would clear Washington from any suspicion of impropriety.[51]

The case came to trial on November 6. Washington and Ulrich stood by their different versions of the incident. Mrs. Alvarez repeated her charge that Washington had looked straight at her and said, "Hello, sweetheart." The police officers Hagan, Tierney, and Quinn described the arrest and the events at the stationhouse. Ulrich denied using a cane to beat Washington, and no witnesses to the assault appeared. Washington, dressed in a blue serge suit and bow tie and showing no ill effects from the beating, testified that he was at the apartment building in search of D. C. Smith, whom he supposed to be visiting a family named McClure. He conceded that he did not find that name on the apartment directory but said he found a similar one and rang that bell. According to a newspaper report of the trial, "He could not, he said, remember the name of the people whose bell he rang."[52] The three judges retired to confer for five minutes and returned to announce the acquittal of Ulrich by a two-to-one vote.[53] The New York *Age* reported that the evidence introduced in court was so overwhelming that Ulrich had brutally beaten Washington with a cane that the audience was "astounded" by the acquittal.[54] The New York *World* account was more noncommittal, stressing Judge Lorenz Zeller's penetrating questions and Washington's vague answers as to why he was at the scene.[55] Smiling broadly at the verdict, Ulrich hurried from the courtroom, but in the hallway a policeman arrested him and took him to the Tombs to await extradition to New Jersey on the charge of desertion of his wife and children.[56]

Throughout the half-year ordeal Washington received criticism as well as support. James K. Vardaman made much of the ambiguities of the incident in his successful campaign for the U. S. Senate. Thomas Dixon, Jr., the white supremacy novelist, said: "There's a lie in it somewhere—either Booker Washington has lied or the man who accused him."[57] Even more sympathetic whites and blacks, who could understand how a black man's presence in a white neighborhood could be misconstrued, nevertheless wondered about the many unresolved questions and outright contradictions in Washington's version of the incident. Paradoxically, Oswald Garrison Villard saw in Washington's predicament and his vulnerability the opening he had sought for several years for Washington's reconciliation with the opposing black leaders that would bring Washington into the NAACP. Washington's

European speaking tour, the Milholland public letter, and the Du Bois Appeal to Europe had widened the factional split, but perhaps Washington's trouble might lead to a softening of attitudes on both sides.

A few days after the assault Villard wrote his uncle in Boston that Washington was "so overwhelmed by letters and telegrams of sympathy received from people whom he considered his worst enemies that he has come to the conclusion that 'this business of having a divided race' must cease, and he wants me to help him bury the hatchet and bring about a cordial union of both factions on a mutually satisfactory basis." The first step that Washington suggested to Villard was for the NAACP at its approaching annual meeting to appoint two or three delegates to the next National Negro Business League meeting. Villard also had in mind, however, persuading the NAACP to pass a resolution of sympathy and support for Washington.[58]

Washington wired his principal lieutenants for their advice on how to respond to such an olive branch. They urged him to accept rather than, as Anderson put it, "expose us to the charge of being narrow, and it would give the scoundrels on the other side an excuse for wielding the dirty weapons, which they know so well how to use."[59] Washington reached as far across the chasm as he could without losing dignity. He wired Villard, who was in Boston for the NAACP meeting: "I shall be glad to work in friendly cooperation with all the workers for the general advancement of the colored people especially in constructive directions." The time had come for laying aside selfishness and bickering and for keeping in mind "only rendering the service which will best promote and protect the whole race in all of its larger interests. In the last analysis I am sure that we all agree on more points than we disagree on." After suggesting that the NAACP send fraternal delegates to the NNBL meeting, he promised it would send a reciprocal delegation. "It will be a happy day for my race," he wrote, "when all of the forces and organizations while still remaining individually separate can sympathetically and heartily cooperate and work together for the larger good."[60] The Ulrich affair had not transformed Washington, but it had brought him to a state of sweet reasonableness.

The NAACP's resolution on the New York assault, however, was a minimal one, generous in expression of sympathy but ungenerous in its failure to give Washington a vote of confidence. The NAACP "Resolved that we put on record our profound regret at the recent assault on Dr. Booker T. Washington in New York City in which the Association finds renewed evidence of racial discrimination and increased necessity for the awakening of the public conscience."[61] The resolution was about the assault rather than Washington, and said not a word of faith in his rectitude. Even so, as Villard wrote Seth Low, "It was pretty hard work to get this resolution through."[62] It went beyond what Trotter wanted.[63] Villard wrote Washington that it seemed wisest not to make an issue of the delegates to the National Negro Business League. "Our people feel that as we have taken the first move it is your move next."[64]

One of the sources of continued friction was that the New York *Age*, whose part-ownership by Washington was an open secret, had only a few weeks before the Ulrich assault made a scurrilous editorial attack on a white NAACP officer, William English Walling, who was a defendant in a breach of promise case. The *Age* editorials were the result of Washington's direct instigation. He wrote Anderson: "I believe you are keeping up with the case of Mr. Wm. English Walling. He is a great fellow to become the leader of the colored race, to advise them along moral lines. . . . I wonder if you cannot get Moore to 'burn Walling up' in an editorial in his paper."[65] Moore was willing to oblige, and the *Age* remarked: "We hope that no colored man or woman will in the future disgrace our race by inviting Mr. Walling in their home or ask him to speak at any public meeting."[66] When Villard and R. R. Moton urged Washington to curb the *Age* attacks as a gesture of friendship for the NAACP, Washington denied that he had any control over the newspaper's policies, but he did try privately to moderate its tone.[67] He asked Moton to write to Moore, "telling him that he ought to assume a more friendly spirit toward the Association for the Advancement of Colored People. I have spoken to him in the same direction, and my words backed up by yours would help immensely."[68] Nevertheless, the proposed accord between the factions never came close to realization. Du Bois soon resumed his sharp criticism of Washington's philosophy and methods in the June 1911 issue of the *Crisis*, and Washington and the NAACP soon found fresh reasons for mutual disagreement and distrust.[69]

During the summer of 1911, while Washington's lawyers and agents were avidly at work privately to secure a confession from Alvarez and Ulrich that would permit settlement of the case in Washington's favor out of court, rumors spread among blacks and came to the surface in the black press that Washington was seeking to cover up some wrong on his part through out of court settlement. Francis J. Garrison was sympathetic to Washington and said he believed utterly in Washington's integrity, but he conceded to his nephew Oswald Villard that

> the word confidence is one we shall have to be wary of until W.'s statement shall be proven invincible. At present it does not fit closely. If he found a certain name & pressed a certain bell without getting a response, & then waited or walked around a bit, thinking the people might be at church, & came back again, the name should be shown to be in the Ulrich house door-directory. Scott's letter to W. should be found to have been sent. The cause for Smith's being at Tuskegee instead of N. Y. should be explained. I have an uncomfortable feeling that W. would rather not face the cross-examination he will have to if the case comes to trial, & that it is going to be settled out of court or quashed. And yet, as I have written, I cannot by the widest stretch of the imagination, think that W., after his thirty years of spotless life has suddenly made such a deflection from the path of virtue as is insinuated.[70]

Black men with less faith in Washington were coming to the same conclusion as to the importance of his case going to trial. "Dr. Washington will make the mistake of his life if he permits the prosecution to be dropped," Harry C. Smith wrote in the Cleveland *Gazette*. "If no good reason is given and he continues to refuse to prosecute Ulrich, as he certainly should, then, in common with thousands of others, black and white, the country over, we have a right to draw our own conclusions, and Dr. Washington's position in the public eye and mind, cannot help but be seriously injured, and as a natural result, harm will come to the race right where it can least afford it, at this time particularly."[71] After further reflection on the case, Smith wrote two months later that Washington would have to explain what he was doing in that "free and easy" neighborhood of New York at a late hour, "and on a Sunday, too."[72] Perhaps having forgotten his generous early reaction to the assault, William Monroe Trotter of the Boston *Guardian* in August could restrain himself no longer and, with two other black men, addressed an abortive open letter to Washington demanding a full public explanation. Apparently they failed to send a copy to Washington himself, but sent them to many black and white newspapers, and Washington received his from a friendly journalist. "In view of your great prominence as a colored man," they wrote, "this condition of affairs, by which you are actually suspected and accused by many white persons at least, of having been in the 'tenderloin' of New York City for improper reasons, with the charges of drunkenness and seeking after white women not followed up by the prosecution of the accuser, does great injury to the entire colored race."[73] Although 11½ West Sixty-third was not actually in the tenderloin prostitution district, it was nearby and only a little above it in reputation. If Washington explained anything, he would have to explain a great deal.

Meanwhile Washington went about his routine substantially without disruption, and his career did not wreck on the curbstones of New York. He continued to watch the minor details of Tuskegee Institute closely, raised more money than ever for his and other black institutions, spoke to cheering overflow crowds in the South and the North, and managed his Tuskegee Machine with his usual skill. There may have been a greater tendency of the faculty members he reprimanded to talk back to him, a response almost unheard of before 1911. He continued to dominate, but his dominance at Tuskegee was not quite so overwhelming as before.

An indication came to him, however, that things would never be quite the same again in New York. The Hotel Manhattan decided to forbid Washington its facilities. Washington wrote the owner, William S. Hawk, a pleading letter thanking the staff for its uniformly kind treatment in the past, noting that the hotel afforded conveniences for carrying on his office work that other hotels did not provide. While he had no immediate plans for staying at the Manhattan in the near future, he wrote, "I should not like to be compelled to stop at any other hotel in the near future because hurtful comment would be made upon the fact that I had been forced to change hotels." Thinking that Hawk might not care to write on this subject as frankly as he would talk, Washington gave the letter to his black friend John S. Durham of Philadelphia to carry to Hawk and receive his reply. Durham would understand Washington's predicament better than most because of his own travel experiences with his white wife. The original of the letter is today in Washington's papers, creased and worn as though carried in Durham's pocket.[74]

Seth Low also wrote the manager, who failed even to reply to his letter.[75] Washington was not without a place to stay in the New York area, for he had recently bought a house on Long Island, near Huntington, mainly as a summer residence. But he was never able to find another hotel in the downtown area as suitable as the Manhattan for his stays in the city in other seasons. In 1912 he stayed at the Astor House, but the following year it was closed for demolition. He moved to the Union Square Hotel, but it was apparently not to his liking. Falling into conversation on a train with Victor Fellner, maître d'hôtel of the McAlpin, an imposing structure in Greeley Square, Washington sent him a copy of his latest book and wrote: "One other thing. I am wondering if the management of your hotel would object to my stopping there sometime when I wish to do so when in New York. If necessary I could take my meals in my room. I should want a room with a bath." Apparently the answer was no, for Fellner's reply simply thanked him for the book.[76]

The Atlanta *Constitution* tried to accommodate the Ulrich affair in the general favor and sponsorship of Washington it had maintained since 1895. The trouble with Washington, said a *Constitution* editorial, was that "he is trying to do too much, with the help of the rich people of the north and east whom he has come in contact with. He goes about all over the country, flitting here and there like a butterfly, but what has he accomplished for the negro schools, except to raise money, some of which goes to the schools, and some does not?" Washington should stay home and devote his efforts to Tuskegee. "If he does this he will certainly not be found in New York, in the night time, 'hunting keyholes,' and attending police courts, with himself on the criminal side of the docket."[77] This was not very far from the view of Trotter, Du Bois, and other black critics.

The most persistent skeptic of Washington's version of events, however, was a Tuskegee trustee, Charles F. Dole of Jamaica Plain, Massachusetts, a Congregational minister and father of the Hawaiian pineapple millionaire. He had served Tuskegee Institute loyally if not with any particular distinction for nearly twenty years. Dole first unburdened his doubts in a letter to Seth Low, who told him he would simply have to accept Washington's word without evidence, in consideration of his lifetime of good behavior. Besides, said Low, Washington was too intelligent to have made up such a story, which depended on D. C. Smith being in New York, unless he thought he was certain that Smith was there.[78]

Dole persisted, however, in questioning Washington's explanations in a ten-page letter to Low. Why would Scott have written that Smith was coming north when he was not coming? Why would Smith have been in New York instead of at his own residence in the suburbs on a Sunday night? "How should this letter, the key-pin to the whole business, have been lost or destroyed, before the important address had been looked up. A man of affairs does not destroy such a letter, so as to be quite at a loss whether he has the right address." Furthermore, the "bad neighborhood" would not seem to be one that Smith would frequent or where his friends would live, so why would Washington persist in hanging about the place until 10 P.M.? What was the urgency of Washington's need to see Smith that warranted seeking him at a stranger's house on a weekend? "Moreover, in these days of telephones, before a late call at a stranger's house, upon the bare possibility of finding Mr. Smith, why should he not have used the telephone, & found once for all whether Mr. S. was there? Would not Mr. Smith's type of friends have had a telephone?" These were a few of Dole's many questions in his long letter.[79]

Dole held his letter for two weeks, in doubt of his own judgment, until Washington came to Boston and Dole met him at his hotel. "I talked very frankly with Dr. Washington," Dole wrote Low in a subsequent letter, "but it seemed to me that he was evasive rather than straightforward. Of course, he pleaded the advice of the lawyers not to talk about details, e. g. the Scott letter &c. But it puzzles me why an innocent man, who has good ground on which to stand, should decline himself, or be advised by any true friends to decline, to tell his story just as it was? This is the course which lawyers ask dubious characters to take. But I am shy of the lawyers & their roundabout methods."[80] Dole's questions had a rigid moral tone, but they were the questions neither Washington nor the historical evidence ever answered.

Washington undertook, in the way of a political boss, to reward those whose testimony or endorsement had aided him in his ordeal and to punish those who had not. There were rumors that one or more of the policemen involved in the arrest were saying that Washington was drunk at the time of his arrest.[81] Washington believed, however, that the plainclothes detective Chester A. Hagan had saved his life by arresting him and thus bringing Ulrich's assault to an end. Furthermore, Hagan expressed himself as willing to testify that Laura Alvarez's statement that Washington had accosted her was an afterthought to justify Ulrich's assault, trumped up after the burglary charge had collapsed. Washington tried to reward Hagan by bringing about his promotion. He urged his agent Charles Anderson to use discretion in this effort, lest the uniformed policeman involved should learn of the reward and become demanding or hostile.[82] Anderson was optimistic that something could be done for Hagan, for the chief of detectives was an old friend.[83] Washington spoke in Hagan's behalf to Police Commissioner James C. Cropsey. Unfortunately for his plan, however, a reformer named Rhinelander Waldo replaced Cropsey. Waldo was also a good friend of Charles Anderson, but Anderson explained to Washington that Waldo was, "as his name would suggest, an aristocrat, and a great stickler for merit promotions without allowing any other influences to affect them."[84] Hagan, now eager for promotion, urged Washington to take up the matter with Mayor William J. Gaynor himself.[85] Hagan offered Washington "to pay you back in any way I can," and even volunteered to go to Tuskegee and "explain to the students the true side of affairs."[86] Hagan hoped that Washington would see the mayor personally, as he had Cropsey, but instead Washington sent a letter after the trial, and Mayor Gaynor replied that all promotions in the police force were by competitive examination. He would do what he could, he said, but he could promise nothing.[87]

Washington also kept on Ulrich's case through Anderson. When he learned that the New Jersey authorities had applied to the governor of New York for Ulrich's extradition, Anderson got in touch with an old friend, the governor's secretary, and made him "fully aware of the antecedents of this scoundrel and of his villainous private character." Anderson also fully acquainted New Jersey officials with Ulrich's record, and promised Washington he would do his utmost "to see that there is not another miscarriage of justice in his favor."[88] At the county court in Orange, Ulrich pleaded guilty of desertion. He received a sentence of three years on probation, provided he furnished $1000 bond to pay $10 a week to the probation officer for the support of his wife and children.[89] Ulrich stubbornly refused to make bond, however, preferring to remain in the county jail rather than make the support payments.[90]

Washington soon terminated D. C. Smith's services to Tuskegee Institute in 1912 when Smith claimed that Tuskegee took too much of his time for the amount it paid him, but the parting was apparently a friendly one, and Smith went on to a career as one of the leading public accountants in the United States.[91] When Charles Dole continued to express his private doubts about Washington's actions, he ceased to be a trustee about 1913.[92]

Lorenz Zeller, one of the two judges who had voted to acquit Ulrich, became the object of a campaign to defeat him when he came up for re-election in 1913. Charles Anderson led Washington's New York friends in an elaborate attack on Zeller. Anderson first collected "all ascertainable facts about the Civil Rights cases which came before him and were decided against us." He placed this evidence before the president of the New York Bar Association. Anderson avoided mention of Washington by name or the Ulrich case in any of this material or in the campaign literature against Zeller, all of which he wrote. He did, however, privately discuss "the doctor's 'frame-up' " with the president of the Bar Association. Zeller had formerly been counsel for the local brewers' association, which also involved him in advocacy for bartenders, and Anderson proved that while on the bench Zeller had never ruled against a bartender or the proprietor of a hotel, restaurant, or saloon in the many cases involving refusal to serve black customers.[93] The New York Bar Association endorsed several other candidates on both tickets for judicial posts, but unanimously declared Zeller unfit to serve as a judge, both because of lack of adequate training and because of his discriminatory actions on the bench. Anderson used this non-endorsement to persuade black Tammany Democrats to vote against Zeller.

Anderson savored his revenge. A few days before the election, he wrote Scott at Tuskegee: "I am getting ready a little political requiem for old Zeller. He is never out of my mind these days. From the time I rise in the morning, which is quite early, until I retire at night, which is quite late, I am busy on Zeller. You will find a lot of good news in the New York papers of next Wednesday morning. Definite news ought to reach you Wednesday night, and when it does be sure to take a drink on the result, and be assured when you do it that there will be an answering hiccough from New York."[94] Anderson wrote the day after the New York election: "That old scoundrel got the worst drubbing that I have ever seen administered to a human being, not excluding the one that Mr. Jack Johnson handed out to Mr. Jeffries on that memorable day out West. The Tammany ticket was buried. Not a man was left alive to tell the tale."[95]

What conclusions can history reach about the Ulrich incident on the basis of such inconclusive and contradictory evidence? The court records in New York City for this period seem to have disappeared, and the principal reliance is on newspapers and their reporters notable for sensationalism and racial bias. Nevertheless, the Ulrich affair was of such importance to Washington's reputation that conclusions of some sort are imperative.

Ulrich was clearly not telling the truth. His charge that Washington was trying to burglarize an apartment was preposterous. The image of the "sage of Tuskegee" peeking through a keyhole seems equally absurd. Ulrich's claim that Washington was drunk, though implausible on the basis of what evidence exists on Washington's personal habits, cannot be categorically dismissed. Washington's private papers reveal occasional, even rare purchases of alcoholic beverages. These were of Glenlivet and Burnt Mill Scotch and expensive bourbon, the sort a host might buy to serve his guests rather than the cheaper brands a heavy drinker would usually buy for his own consumption. There is no direct evidence that Washington himself ever drank, and much hearsay evidence from his friends that he did not. His daughter Portia said that he drank, particularly in his later years, as ill health brought him pain. Just how *much* he drank, if at all, however, is an open question. He may have been a solitary drinker in his later years, but maybe not. It would be inconsistent with his advocacy of prohibition, but other prohibitionists lived with that inconsistency.

The claim of Laura Alvarez that Washington accosted her with the expression, "Hello, sweetheart," gains most of its plausibility from the seedy neighborhood near the Tenderloin where it occurred and by her own membership in the demimonde. It seems out of character for Washington to have said it, and particularly to a white woman, unless indeed he were drunk. And the plausibility is weakened by the fact that it was introduced after the arrest as a justification for her paramour's assault on Washington only after the initial justification of attempted burglary proved untenable. There is no doubt about the character of the neighborhood. Even the sympathetic Villard wrote his uncle that "it is, of course, as far as appearances are concerned very unfortunate that Smith should have been at Tuskegee and not where Washington sought him, particularly as this neighborhood where the house is is a very unsavory one, and the people largely of the class to which the Ulrich woman belongs." [96]

Nobody ever adequately explained Washington's presence at the apartment building, but in 1913, more than two years after the incident, he received a letter from a woman who asserted that she had been an eyewitness to the beating, and she confirmed Washington's version of the affray or at least the part of it that occurred after Washington had escaped to the street. She was Mrs. W. F. Behr of Santa Monica, California, she wrote, and had called on Laura Alvarez that night because their mothers had once been friends. The encounter, she said, "was all witnessed by me. I was in the apartment on the lower floor in the left hand side of the house at the time." She said of Ulrich: "He had no weapon when he left the house. The commotion in the hall we heard inside and a roomer who had the weapon hanging on the wall as an ornament of curiosity grabbed it, running out in his house sandals, following you down the steps and into the street. Between the two you were severely cut and beaten on the head, for no other reason whatsoever than because you were a Negro, presumably with no object other than looking for the name of a party in the reference rack which was located in the vestibule of the house."

After Washington's flight and arrest, wrote Mrs. Behr, she went to the police station, as did others in the neighborhood, but he had just left in an ambulance. She was horrified, on learning his name, knowing the good he had done and "knowing the nature of the weapon with which you were beaten (it being a very formidable looking object, having been sent from Africa)." She was "still more horrified to hear the lie—'He called me sweetheart' which I knew was spontaneously spoken to protect the man in the case." Why had she not come forward at the hearing or the trial? "For personal reasons I did not wish to be associated with the scandal," she wrote Washington, "as it had been a sorrow to me to know that my girlhood friend was living in such an atmosphere. For the sake of befriending her, however, I promised silence, and left New York state, battling with my sense of justice to come forward in your behalf." Since becoming a Christian Scientist, she wrote, she had reached the conclusion that it was her duty to vindicate Washington, whom she proclaimed "absolutely innocent."[97] She urged him, however, not to use her name. Washington sent a copy to Wilford Smith, saying that he did not plan to make any use of the letter at present but felt encouraged to "have the exact truth brought out." He added: "I think this is a genuine letter."[98]

If neither Ulrich nor Alvarez gave entirely convincing accounts, however, it does not follow that Washington was "absolutely innocent" or told the truth about his presence on the scene. In fact, Washington never gave credible answers to the many questions about his own part in the incident. Perhaps the questions were irrelevant to the assault itself, but they were imperatively demanded by his public in an Edwardian age that combined public standards of propriety with prurient interests.

It is possible that Washington had a more believable and creditable explanation that he did not feel at liberty to disclose, but if so there is not evidence of this in his most intimate correspondence. The notion that he might have been attempting to visit a woman donor to Tuskegee whose name he wished to keep out of the newspapers is blasted by the general character of the neighborhood. Why in a correspondence so rich is there so little documentation on this incident, and more particularly why is there no copy of Scott's letter alleged to have prompted this visit? It may have been that Washington's lifelong habit of duplicity, secretiveness, and mendacity in his public affairs caused him, in the shock of the beating and the panic of being arrested, to make up what seemed in his confused state a credible untruth instead of a less creditable truth. Deception had become for Washington almost a reflex action, much as a squid inks the waters, and the oft-quoted phrase seems appropriate, "Oh, what a tangled web we weave, when first we practice to deceive."

Whatever wounds, physical or psychic, that Washington suffered from the assault and the embarrassment of the trial, he bore them stoically and seldom referred to them. His health and his community standing seemed the same as before, and after about four days' rest he resumed his vigorous speaking and other public affairs. A whispering campaign about the Ulrich incident probably pursued him, but the financing of Tuskegee Institute and his other enterprises continued to prosper. If there were subtle pressures to explain himself, he resolutely dismissed them, but in his papers is a worn, dog-eared quotation he evidently carried in his wallet for moral support. It was a statement of Abraham Lincoln: "If I were to try to read, much less answer, all the attacks made on me, this shop might as well be closed for other business. . . . If the end brings me out all right, what is said against me won't amount to anything. If the end brings me out wrong, ten angels swearing I was right would make no difference." [99]

The Ulrich incident, nevertheless, was an event with historical consequences, and historians have considered it in the context of its period's civil rights and uncivil wrongs. Willard B. Gatewood, in the most extensive review of the affair, recognizes some of Washington's self-contradictions but sees him essentially in the framework of the Negro as victim.[100] C. Flint Kellogg found the incident relevant to a promising but abortive rapprochement between Washington and NAACP leaders.[101] Stephen R. Fox, the biographer of Monroe Trotter, counterposed his hero's generosity to a fallen foe to Washington's treatment of Trotter after the Boston Riot,[102] but Trotter not only opposed the mild resolution of sympathy the NAACP passed but badgered Washington before Ulrich's trial with a public letter. Clearly the Ulrich affair, like the Sphinx, belongs to history whether we can solve its riddle or not.

From a biographical perspective, the Ulrich affair, despite its ugly revelation of violence and racial bias, of blows struck against strangers in the anonymity of the city, does show Washington in all his fallibility as a human being. He was a man schooled to repress his feelings. His very dress—dark Victorian business suit and derby hat—was an understatement. In all the hundreds of thousands of his surviving letters there is not a single love letter, nor a cry of joy. Thrice-married, a conscientious family man who showed infinite care and concern for his children, he seemed incapable of passion or even affection, addressing his closest friends as "Mr. Anderson," "Mr. Fortune," "Mr. Scott." Enter Laura Page Alvarez, a sexually attractive young woman sweeping along the street behind a pair of dogs, later posing in her picture hat at the hearing as Ulrich's wife. It is possible that Washington had known her at some earlier time, between her life with the shadowy husband Alvarez and with the brutish Ulrich, that Washington addressed her as "sweetheart" not with the importunity of a stranger but with the recognition of an intimate friend. Such a hypothesis, however, would rest entirely on her unsupported allegation that he had accosted her, and without the admission of either that they had known each other. If she had known him earlier, surely she would have hesitated to make a scene at the stationhouse. In any case, the conflicting and self-contradictory stories of Ulrich, of Mrs. Alvarez, and of Washington himself seem to have been the hasty improvisations of a trio each of whom had different reasons for concealing the exact truth.

The only certain image that emerges from the Ulrich affair is the photograph of Washington as he appeared at the brief court hearing two days after the assault. His head swathed in bandages, he looked like Brer Rabbit finally cornered and mauled by Brer Bear.

If anything constructive came from this terrible assault that tore a scar across Washington's life, it was a revelation of what being a black man, even Booker T. Washington, really meant in a society dedicated to white supremacy. From that time forward, still in his persuasive rather than challenging way, Washington spoke out publicly, as he had long done privately, against the inhumanity of racial injustice.

Washington never admitted that he had ever been wrong about anything, and many in his own and later generations could believe that in his twenty years after the Atlanta Compromise with white supremacy in 1895 he had learned nothing. But after the New York incident came a succession of public statements on segregation in the federal government, residential segregation, the Jim Crow cars, and the stirring up of racial hostility. In addressing these broader issues of racial justice, Washington generally omitted his usual weasel words. His changed tone could be explained by a conjunction of many changes in the American racial scene. Washington's absence from the councils of the White House gave him more freedom. The Wilson administration ushered in an era of federal government promotion of white supremacy that was a slap in the face of every black person. The NAACP continued to challenge Washington's accommodation even as he modified it. All of these considerations must have affected his course of action, but surely the most vivid and recurrent was his self-recognition as he ran bleeding through the New York streets, that in the atmosphere of American racism even Booker T. Washington was lynchable.

CHAPTER 17

Outside Looking In

. . . like Nero, fiddling while Rome burns.

OSWALD GARRISON VILLARD, 1914

Anxious not to use word "protest"; nothing to be gained by giving that impression.

BTW, 1914

If the negro is segregated, it will probably mean that the sewerage in his part of the city will be inferior; that the streets and sidewalks will be neglected, that the street lighting will be poor, that his section of the city will not be kept in order by the police and other authorities, and that the "undesirables" of other races will be placed near him, thereby making it difficult for him to rear his family in decency.*

BTW, 1915

E VEN though the President of the United States no longer asked his advice, Booker T. Washington in his last years gave the outward impression of still being in charge of the Afro-American destiny, the black prince surrounded by his court, with much residual power and influence, still capable of wizardry, and still as busy as ever trying to be the all-purpose black leader. He kept up a grueling pace of

*"My View of Segregation Laws" (posthumous publication), *New Republic,* December 4, 1915.

public appearances, pulled the strings of philanthropy more than ever, and watched his campus as knowingly as the eye of God. He had a large following that believed his combination of accommodation and alternative routes could steer them through the age of segregation.

Two important changes were occurring, however. He rapidly aged and lost his energy. While he could puff himself up to full vigor on the lecture platform, he collapsed in repose. Scott took over more and more of his routine correspondence. Second, too little and too late to satisfy his critics, he became more outspoken in public and private against segregation and white racial extremism.

The incoming Wilson administration made short shrift of the Black Cabinet, which had only existed anyhow in the pretentious imagination of a small coterie of officeholders. The tallest heads were, with a few exceptions, the first to roll. Within two days after the inauguration the Georgia-born Attorney General William G. McAdoo asked for William H. Lewis's resignation as assistant attorney general. Lewis submitted it promptly and returned to Boston to leave politics alone for a great many years, he hoped. He had a brief dream of a corporation law practice through Washington's influence with Rockefeller and Carnegie, but nothing came of that.[1] Lewis noted with amusement that his resignation came as a surprise to the black Democrats, who had expected as a reward for their campaign support of Wilson to be consulted on black patronage matters.[2] They were to find soon that the administration would consult them very little on black appointments, there not being many. "It looks like a quick shoving of Ham down the chute," commented Ralph Tyler.[3]

One by one the black Bookerites lost their presidential offices. Fred R. Moore, an eleventh-hour Taft appointee as minister to Liberia, never had a chance to leave the United States. J. C. Napier returned to Nashville and Ralph Tyler to Columbus. James A. Cobb returned to his law practice and Whitefield McKinlay to his real estate business in Washington. All of these lieutenants of the Tuskegee Machine simply returned, with a few scars of political battle, to resume their successful careers. By June 1913, three months after the inauguration, the nation's capital was virtually cleared of black officeholders except the underlings covered by the civil service laws.

Washington explained to black supporters of Wilson, eager for his endorsement to replace the outgoing black officials, that he had endorsed no one to President Wilson, as indeed had been the case in the Republican administrations. If President Wilson should ask his advice about any individual, which he thought an unlikely prospect, he promised to respond.[4] He did make one exception, the endorsement of a Chicago physician for minister to Haiti, but was outraged to find that word of it had reached New York within hours of his private conversation with the candidate.[5] He viewed with outward calm, however, the decimation of black officeholders. He had always considered politics an uncertain calling and one that did little to advance the race, though he himself was closely involved with it. Now that he was disengaged he could probably agree with his friend P. B. S. Pinchback's farewell to a much longer political career. "Our friend, the enemy the south, is in the saddle and it looks like no negro need apply," Pinchback noted. "I am not sure that I will grieve over the situation. It may be a blessing in disguise."[6]

Two notable exceptions to the rule of summary black removal were Charles W. Anderson, who lasted for more than a year as collector of internal revenue in New York City, and Robert H. Terrell, who not only survived to the end of his term but found favor with the Wilson administration and gained reappointment. The explanation of Anderson's continuance was his exceptional competence, his popularity in the New York business community, and his high efficiency ratings. Before leaving office he successfully handled the administration of the new federal income tax law, whereas his inexperienced successor might have had more difficulty. Anderson quickly landed new employment in the Republican state administration where he had worked for many years before appointment to federal office. He had worked for the election of Charles S. Whitman as governor, and Whitman appointed him supervisory agent of the state department of agriculture in New York City, where he handled state marketing services and inspections within the city.[7]

Terrell's retention of his municipal judgeship in the District of Columbia, the only political triumph of the Tuskegee Machine during the Wilson era, can only partially be explained by his competence, though that certainly played a part. Always a man of mild address, in contrast to his fiery wife, Terrell took pains to behave in a nonpartisan way, not only on the bench but in private actions that ingratiated him with white members of the local bar association and with well-placed Democrats. Furthermore, Booker Washington reached an understanding with Bishop Alexander Walters, one of the leaders of the

Wilson movement among blacks in 1912. Walters agreed to represent Washington's interest in urging Terrell's reappointment and confirmation, while Washington remained in the background.

As early as April 1913, R. W. Thompson wrote to Emmett Scott the news that "Bishop Walters is extremely anxious to be on a 'working basis' with Dr. Washington, and begs me to assure him through you that he values the Wizard's friendship highly, and shall welcome suggestions along any line likely to be helpful to the race." Thompson had for years prided himself on his ability to play the loyal friend to both the Bishop and the Wizard, and he promised, "If a common ground can be found for the Wizard and the prelate, I shall be glad to see such eminent working forces working in concert for the good of all." [8] Washington saw in this overture an opportunity to have an influence on the Wilson administration while maintaining his dignity by not appealing directly in Terrell's behalf. Particularly after the racial policies of the new regime became public, he was glad to have Walters as a buffer between him and the Democrats. And Walters needed Washington if he was to achieve any success at all in placing blacks in office. Washington met with Walters at least once and perhaps more often on the Terrell appointment early in 1914. [9] Walters then had some part in persuading President Wilson to submit Terrell's name to the U. S. Senate. Walters wrote Terrell, "I am sure that your confirmation will open the way for other appointments of worthy colored men. If the nomination hangs fire let me know and I will come down and do what I can to help out." [10]

Though Terrell was irretrievably a Republican, Walters knew that the hopes of the black Democrats rode on his confirmation. Walters therefore wrote urgently to members of the Senate Judiciary Committee and other Senators in Terrell's behalf. [11] Once President Wilson had nominated Terrell, Washington also felt free to support him. He wrote President Wilson his appreciation, noting that years earlier he had recommended Terrell to President Roosevelt, and saying that "it has been a great satisfaction to know that he has lived up to the recommendation that was given him." [12] Washington also wrote Senator William E. Chilton, whom he had once known in West Virginia, urging the confirmation of Terrell. [13] One factor that Terrell's own wife threw into the balance in his favor may have been as decisive as his competent performance on the bench, mild personality, and non-partisanship in the white-supremacy climate of the Wilson era. That was his light skin color. Mary Church Terrell wrote to a Senator: "The fight waged against him in the Senate today is based solely on the slight infusion of African blood thought to be lurking in his anatomy . . . solely because he happens remotely to be identified with an oppressed and persecuted race."[14] The Senate confirmed Terrell, but the Democratic Senators showed how exceptional this was by blocking Wilson's appointment of a black man as register of the Treasury and by appointment of a white man as minister to Haiti.

While driving most of the high-ranking black officials from Washington, the Wilson administration also speeded up the segregation of the black civil servants who remained. These trends had already gathered some momentum in the preceding Republican administrations, as disfranchisement had signalled the political weakness of blacks. What had been practice now became policy, avowed by members of Wilson's cabinet and condoned by the President himself as a means of reducing racial friction within the federal government. The issue came up in a cabinet meeting on April 11, 1913, about a month after the Wilson term began, when Postmaster General Albert S. Burleson, a Texan, announced his plan to segregate the black employees in his own department, and there was no protest from the other cabinet members. The President remarked that he had made no particular campaign promises to blacks except to treat them justly, and he found no conflict between his promise and the segregation of offices and washrooms.[15]

Other cabinet members from the South followed Burleson's example. William G. McAdoo, Secretary of the Treasury, undertook to make the office of the register of the Treasury an all-black unit, and in the essentially southern city of Washington a voluntary popular movement developed to press for federal segregation. Ironically, it called itself the National Democratic Fair Play Association and dedicated itself to the proposition that no white secretary should be required to take dictation from a black man. The chief stumbling block in McAdoo's segregation plan was that Wilson could not secure confirmation of his black nominee as register because of the opposition of Senators James K. Vardaman, Hoke Smith, and Benjamin R. Tillman. The bureau of printing and engraving established separate toilets, the ones for blacks being in the basement. These were only a few of the incidents in a general and avowed policy of federal segregation.

Leading the chorus of protest against this policy were the militant

blacks and whites in the NAACP and in Trotter's National Independent Political League who had endorsed Wilson in 1912 and believed
that he had promised them racial justice. All of them felt betrayed,
and Trotter was particularly livid. The Grimké brothers organized
mass meetings of blacks in Washington and recruited vigorously to
enlarge the local NAACP chapter to take a lead in the black protest.
Oswald Garrison Villard castigated President Wilson in a New York
Evening Post editorial.

Washington did not feel the same sense of betrayal that those who
had voted for Wilson felt, but he was equally disappointed. He wrote
thanking Villard for his editorial. "You express the feelings of practically every Negro in the United States," he wrote; "I am glad to see
that a number of daily papers in other parts of the country have written editorials based upon yours." The appointment of a white man as
minister to Haiti was further evidence that "the present administration is hopeless."[16]

Villard asked Washington to allow him to enclose his letter in one
of his own to President Wilson urging a change of policy. Washington
decided instead to send another letter, one better calculated to persuade Wilson. "I have recently spent several days in Washington," he
wrote in this new version, "and I have never seen the colored people
so discouraged and bitter as they are at the present time." He expressed, however, "great faith in President Wilson" and recalled that
at the time of the inauguration he had said in a newspaper interview
that "I believed he would be just to the colored people." He could not
believe, he wrote Villard, that Wilson or his secretary Joseph P. Tumulty realized what harm the new discriminatory policy would do to
both races or "to what extent a lot of narrow little people in Washington are taking advantage of these orders and are overriding and per-
secuting the colored people in ways the President knows nothing
about." Washington warned particularly of the harm that vigilante
white clerks in the Democratic Fair Play Association were doing to
blacks. "If the President or somebody else could suggest that they
ought to attend to their own business in the departments and let the
President run the government it would help immensely."[17] Washington took no part in the demonstrations in northern cities against federal segregation, but this letter, which Villard sent on to President
Wilson, showed his thorough disapproval of the policy.

Obviously it was President Wilson's white colleagues, chiefly those who were southern or southern-born, rather than the blacks who had supported him after he vaguely promised a policy of fairness toward blacks who were responsible for federal segregation. Nevertheless, Washington and Scott could not resist the urge to blame the Trotter-Du Bois faction for opening the Pandora's box of a Democratic administration. They planted in the New York *Age* in November 1913 a communication ostensibly from Boston, reminding readers that "one Trotter, together with Dr. Du Bois, and Waldron, of Washington, was insistently active during the last campaign . . . for Woodrow Wilson. He urged them to put him in office because it was said that he would prove the savior of the Afro-American race. It was often stated to Hon. Trotter that he was making a mistake in giving this advice, but Mr. Trotter replied that he had read ancient history and that he was a graduate of Harvard University and that his advice ought to be taken." [18]

On the other hand, when the New York *Times* misquoted Booker Washington to the effect that he approved of the segregation of the federal offices, a black man replied that it was Washington's own past conduct and writings that had led to this misunderstanding. Washington had enjoyed the rewards of ambiguity; now he must pay its penalties. J. C. Waters wrote:

> The most prominent Negro in the world today, he is also the most pathetic figure in our national life. Slowly but surely the clouds of a race's indignation are gathering about Booker Washington's head and he may well wish to be dead before the storm breaks. For I give it as my most solemn belief that the day will come when Booker Washington's name will be cursed wherever an American Negro sets his foot, and the best that his most sanguine friends can hope for is that posterity will at least temper its judgment of him by conceding that he really and truly believed that the ends justified the means. [19]

The writer was of no prominence whatever, but he was a reasonably good prophet.

Washington's career as a political boss was ending not with a bang but with a chorus of whimpers. His lieutenants fell into petty quarrels with each other—Tyler with Anderson, Anderson with Moore, Cobb with Scott, and Calvin Chase with everyone. Washington, unable to bring himself to recommend black Democrats to a Democratic President, nevertheless could not bring himself to surrender his influence entirely, and worked to influence Wilson through the surrogate Bishop Walters. Washington's pathetic expressions of faith in Woodrow Wilson in the same breath with criticism of his administration's policy of segregation became a sort of parody of his earlier faith in Roosevelt and Taft.

Washington's only direct communications with President Wilson were a letter of condolence on the death of Wilson's first wife, an appeal with the Tuskegee trustees in behalf of the federal appropriation to Howard University, and a request to intercede against the closing of the campus branch post office at Tuskegee Institute. Some whites in Tuskegee, seeking to take advantage of having a Democratic administration in Washington, proposed to merge the institute post office with the one in town in order to be able to upgrade the postmastership there. Washington telegraphed the President. "For eleven years the Tuskegee Institute has had separate post office from the town of Tuskegee with postmaster appointed by the President. One of the objects for the separation was to prevent possible trouble by large numbers of colored students going into the Tuskegee town post office." To make a change now, he argued, would not only disrupt an arrangement that had increased the postal business but would also threaten the existing harmony of race relations. "Besides for the peace and good order of the school it is necessary that a postmaster be appointed who meets with our approval and who acts in accordance with the general policy and spirit of the institution. To make change would probably subject us to having a postmaster appointed who might not meet this qualification." Washington failed to mention that the chief qualification of the incumbent campus postmaster was that he was Washington's adopted brother. In a letter that followed the telegram, Washington argued further that there was "absolutely no objection" by white Tuskegeans to the separate office, that the sorting and handling of the Institute mail in town would occasion unnecessary delays. At least two other educational institutions, he noted, the University of Alabama and the University of Mississippi, had separate campus postal facilities.[20] Tuskegee Institute kept its separate post office.

Washington did nothing beyond his letter to Villard to protest federal segregation, in effect abdicating his leadership on this important issue. When the NAACP mass meetings of 1913–14 had no effect on government policy, Monroe Trotter decided to bring a black delegation to the White House to remonstrate with President Wilson against his betrayal of campaign promises. When the confrontation became heated Wilson abruptly terminated the interview, in effect ordering the black editor out of his office. Washington might have been secretly pleased to see his old enemy defeat his object by a loss of temper, but he was too dignified to side with President Wilson on the matter. Robert R. Moton, however, while writing to thank Wilson for a friendly letter that had been read at a black gathering, said he had taken the liberty of publishing the letter "to show your kindly feeling toward Negroes, as contrasted with the very unfortunate incident of Mr. Trotter, and I want to say that the Negroes, generally, do not in any way approve of Mr. Trotter's conduct at the White House."[21] Sending a copy to Washington, Moton added, "I did not, of course, mean to give the impression to him that I approved of segregation in Washington, but I think he is [in] such condition now that we may be able to make an impression on him."[22] Washington agreed rather cryptically that the President was "being 'pounded' so severely in various quarters that I imagine he was glad to have a word from some member of the race less stinging than some of those he is at present reading."[23] Scott, on the other hand, was unequivocally delighted to read the "unusually strong" editorial criticism of federal segregation that the Trotter incident had evoked. He wrote his chief: "I am not mentioning the matter as it relates to Trotter, but as it relates to *race!*"[24]

In his later years, without the albatross of responsibility for advising presidents, Washington began to address more directly several important questions of racial justice that came to the forefront as southerners came into power in Washington for the first time since the Civil War. Among these issues were the African exclusion bill, the unequal accommodations in separate cars and waiting rooms of southern railroads, increasing racial segregation in law and practice, and the baneful cultural impact of *The Birth of a Nation*, the pioneer motion picture by D. W. Griffith, based on a white supremacy novel.

The outbreak of war in Europe brought a halt to the heavy European immigration into the United States in 1914, but in January 1915 a general immigration restriction bill was before the United States Senate to prevent a large influx when the war was over. Senator James A. Reed, a Missouri Democrat, proposed and secured quick passage of an amendment to the bill to bar all immigrants of African descent, including blacks of the West Indies and elsewhere in the Americas. It was but one of many anti-black measures introduced when the Dem-

ocrats gained control of both houses of Congress and southerners because of their long tenure succeeded to most of the committee chairmanships. The difference with this amendment, however, was that
the Senate actually passed it and thus incorporated it in the bill that
went to the House of Representatives. There was no time to spare in
the campaign to keep it from passing also in the House.

This was an issue that united blacks all over the United States. With
less than a week in which to work, Washington marshaled a newspaper, letter, and lobbying campaign that defeated the bill. His first step
was a carefully worded but forceful statement of the argument against
the bill in letters to the editors of the New York *World,* Atlanta *Constitution,* and many other newspapers. Washington's main arguments were
that the bill was unnecessary because only a few thousand people of
African descent entered the country each year, that its total ban was
unreasonable because it put blacks in the same class as alien criminals,
and that it bottled up the growing populations of small island repub-
lics and thus put "an unnecessary hardship upon these smaller countries, which would not be done, in my opinion, if they were stronger."
He reminded readers that Jamaicans had been indispensable as laborers on the Panama Canal, and they should not be "slapped in the face
and told that they cannot enter this country even when they meet the
requirements of our Government." Black people had never been anarchists, and there was no political or sectional demand for this exclusion, which would be profoundly discouraging to American black people. "Certainly," he concluded, "we have enough to contend with
already without having this additional handicap and discouragement
placed in our pathway."[25]

Washington wrote or telegraphed to dozens of Tuskegee Machine
lieutenants in the national capital and other cities denouncing this
"unnecessary and unfair slap at the colored people." He called for
swift action "through Negro Business Leagues[,] colored newspapers
and through our various organizations that you can reach and bring
about the defeat of this unjust measure." He asked each to write his
Senators and Representatives.[26]

The lieutenants responded to the sense of urgency Washington
conveyed in his telegrams. Moton reported that he and Hollis B. Frissell were writing all the Hampton trustees as well as the Virginia congressmen, and that they had put Thomas Jesse Jones to work against
the bill and were sending another man to the capital "to pull every

possible string that can be pulled to defeat this unfortunate clause."[27] "Please keep close eye on immigration bill," Washington urged James A. Cobb of Washington. "Telegraph names of conferees both senate and house as soon as appointed." Meanwhile Scott spread to the black press copies of Washington's letter that had appeared in the daily newspapers and urged them to build up black concern for the issue.[28] Washington called on Kelly Miller, the Grimkés, Whitefield McKinlay, Daniel Murray, and W. Calvin Chase to go before the conference committee and "enter protest against exclusion of colored people."[29]

The lobbyists reported some initial resistance from conference committee members. McKinlay, Miller, and Archibald Grimké talked with Senator William E. Borah of Idaho and Congressman Martin B. Madden of Illinois, and McKinlay reported: "Borah favors amendment bill excepting students and merchants. Madden's objections kept bill from going to conference to-day and hopes to-morrow to eliminate measure. We plan to see other members to-morrow. . . . We feel hopeful but not sanguine."[30] Similarly Ernest Lyon of Baltimore, who appeared before the committee and called on some congressmen, was particularly discouraged that Congressman John L. Burnett of Alabama was chairman of the conference committee. "We must be prepared to carry our fight to the Pres. if the house refuses to eliminate it," he wrote.[31]

Washington succeeded because of the moral suasion of his public letter and the direct pressure he brought upon the congressmen through his lieutenants. On January 7 the House defeated the measure, 250 to 77. Washington warmly thanked his machine for its effective functioning after almost two years of inaction. "Grink [A. H. Grimké] and Miller deserves heartiest credit for their tireless fight," McKinlay wrote modestly, but most of Washington's other supporters gave Washington himself the chief credit for recognizing the crisis and seizing the moment.[32] Even Monroe Trotter found common cause with Washington for the brief time of lobbying against the bill. Washington learned of this indirectly through George Cleveland Hall, who wrote of Trotter's recent sojourn in Chicago: "When he left me he said that he hoped that through the immigration bill all factions might learn to stand on a common platform. He thought what a fine thing it would be for *you* DuBoise & *Himself* to appear in Washington arm in arm—fighting against the measure. He was willing to agree to an armistice until the fight was over, at least."[33]

Washington received many congratulations for this work, but doubtless the one he treasured most was signed by fifty-eight foreign-born teachers and students of Tuskegee. They wrote: "We do feel and believe, Sir, that the strength and force of your letter made a great impression on the minds of the legislators and thus helped considerably, if not altogether, in the defeating of the bill." They expressed the belief that the bill aimed at not only foreign blacks but the whole race, "and it is a consoling thought that the colored people can take care of themselves, whether in the United States, or in the most remote corner of the earth, that in you they have one who will always have the courage of your convictions to champion their cause."[34] Washington said in reply, "I was very glad to do this as the measure was thoroughly unreasonable and unjust. I think the matter will never come up again. It was my intention, if the bill had passed Congress, to have gone direct to President Wilson and ask him to veto the bill."[35] That would have been an interesting confrontation.

In this same period Washington systematically pursued another of his concerns, the inequality of separate facilities for blacks on the southern railroads. As always, he understated his protest, and lacked the tone of outrage that his critics wanted him to assume. He had said more or less the same thing since the 1880s, but around 1912 he redoubled the effort he put into persuading the railroads to change their ways. In a letter to Milton H. Smith, president of the Louisville and Nashville Railroad, for example, he expressed doubt that Smith knew of "conditions in the colored coaches." As an illustration, "On train Number 1, between Nashville and Montgomery, there is only one toilet room for both men and women, aside from this, there is no smoking room provided for colored men."[36] About the same time he asked the general passenger agent of the Atlanta and West Point Railroad if he knew that on No. 35 all of the coaches were unusually filthy. "The colored coach," he wrote, "the last time I came down from Atlanta, was so filthy that I went into the white car to see how it was and was surprised to find it was equally filthy."[37] Separate and equally filthy, however, was the exception rather than the rule. Washington complained to the officers of the tiny Tuskegee Railroad that ran the few miles from the town to Chehaw station. "We try to encourage the people all we can to travel over your road," he wrote, "but every excursion that comes experiences the same difficulty of being kept waiting at Tuskegee." Many excursioners from Montgomery and Birmingham complained that they could come from Chehaw in hacks in a shorter time than by train.[38]

Washington's article "Is the Negro Having a Fair Chance?" appeared in *Century* magazine in November 1912 and set the tone for his efforts in his last years to speak more forthrightly about racial discrimination. His conclusion was that blacks did not receive a fair chance any of a half-dozen measures of opportunity that he discussed. He discussed unequal educational facilities, convict lease, disfranchisement, and lynching, but some of the most telling passages in the article were on the Jim Crow cars, "the source of more bitterness" among blacks than any other one form of discrimination. "What embitters the colored people in regard to railroad travel," he said, "is not the separation but the inadequacy of the accommodations. The colored people are given half of a baggage-car or half of a smoking-car. In most cases, the Negro portion of the car is poorly ventilated, poorly lighted, and, above all, rarely kept clean; and then to add to the colored man's discomfort, no matter how many colored women may be in the colored end of the car, nor how clean or how well educated these colored women may be, this car is made the headquarters for the newsboy. . . . White men are constantly coming into the car and almost invariably light cigars. . . ." He quoted a conservative Texas black man to the effect that "the statement that the two races have equal accommodations is all bosh."[39]

After reading the article, Du Bois wrote in the *Crisis*, "We note with some complacency that Mr. Booker T. Washington has joined the ranks."[40] In fact, however, Washington was only saying with more urgency what he had said publicly for a quarter of a century, criticizing the inequality rather than separation itself. The article was not the end of his agitation. He pointed William H. Lewis's attention to a Mississippi sleeping car segregation case before the Supreme Court during Lewis's term as assistant attorney general.[41] He pressed the National Baptist Convention officers to influence their members to bargain with the L & N Railroad for improved conditions on trains going to their convention site.[42] "If you can get the time," he wrote Emmett Scott, "I wish you would write a letter to several colored papers with a Nashville date line describing the bad conditions that exist on the colored cars on the L. & N. road after leaving Nashville."[43]

Scott also sent to railroad officials and editors copies of an editorial probably written or inspired by him, "The Separate Car Law, as Operated: A Reflection upon the Business Sense of the Railroads," which appeared in the accommodationist black journal, *Southwestern Christian Advocate*.[44] He arranged for printing and distributing of 1000 copies of "Is the Negro Having a Fair Chance?"[45] Washington sent the article in pamphlet form to a long list of officials of southern railroads, with a letter saying, "I believe that improvement in the accommodations extended our race would help the railroads immensely as well as add to the comfort and happiness of our race and mutual friendship between white and black people."[46] Finding many of the replies encouraging, he wrote Frank Trumbull, a Tuskegee trustee and railroad investor, "I believe that the time will soon come when the railroads will begin to see that it is a matter of business to treat the Negroes better."[47]

Washington also launched a similar campaign to improve streetcar facilities for blacks. "Will you be good enough," he wrote his black New Orleans friend Robert E. Jones, "to let me have in the form of a letter the actual facts bearing upon the method of separating our race in the street cars of New Orleans? Also facts as to the humiliations to which they are subjected. Write me a letter that I can show to certain bankers who furnish the money. Also state if it is true, to what extent colored people refrain from riding on the cars because of the discrimination. Bring out especially the point that they do not have room enough."[48] He asked Jones later to come to New York. "I have done something in the direction of seeing those New York parties about the street car situation in New Orleans," he wrote, "but I find that in order to impress these people as they should be impressed it would help matters very much if you could be present when I see them again."[49] Apparently nothing substantial developed from these efforts.

In 1914 Washington developed a new method of bringing pressure on the railroads. He had Emmett Scott send to about 200 black newspapers the letters from railroad officials in answer to letters he had written them on the shoddy and unequal railroad accommodations for blacks. He followed this by a proposal to set aside a Sunday and Monday, June 7 and 8, to be known as Railroad Days. Washington suggested that all through the South on these days "various groups of our people, through churches, secret societies, business houses, Business Leagues, woman's clubs and other agencies organize themselves in a way to go directly to the railroad authorities and put before them the difficulties under which we labor in cases where there is existence of unjust treatment." A committee of two or three would accomplish more than a dozen or two in calling on railroad officials, he said, but he did not advise in detail what should be done in each community. He did stress three subjects each committee should bring up: "Proper accommodations in restaurants controlled by the railroads. Accommodation of the sitting rooms in the depots controlled by the railroads. Proper and just accommodations on street cars, steamboats and railroad trains." The black communities should take up the matter with vigor, directness, and frankness. The exact time was unimportant, but each community should concentrate its efforts in one day or at the most one week so that the railroad officials would be impressed with "the bigness of the occasion and the opportunity which is before them to increase their revenues by doing justice to nine or ten millions of their patrons."[50]

Response to the proposal was generally favorable, but Benjamin Daugherty of Pittsburgh, an obscure black man who said he had been working on the problem for some time as president of the Ethiopian Race Christian Brotherhood of the World, thought Washington was beginning at the wrong place, with the railroads rather than the state governments. He proposed an alternative, to collect signatures to a protest against the Jim Crow car laws in every state having such laws, "and at the same time do not support a man at the ballot box who will not pledge to our race, rights and liberty and happiness as all other races in said states. . . ." Scott replied for Washington that the Railroad Days campaign was against the inequality of accommodation rather than the separation that a disfranchised group could do nothing to change.[51]

Washington issued his call for Railroad Days two months in advance, and Scott was so zealous in keeping the idea before the black public in the interim that Washington telegraphed him: "Not my idea send out any more letters to colored papers on railroad situation over my signature. Would avoid impression of making protest but rather making request." This summarized the difference between Washington's style and that of the militants Trotter and Du Bois. When Scott demurred, Washington wired again: "Anxious not to use word 'protest'; nothing to be gained by giving that impression."[52] He wanted Scott to impress on the black delegations "the importance [of] *going to see* the R. R. officials, not merely talking *about* among themselves."[53]

A letter to the black editors suggested: "Little pointed paragraphs in your editorial or news columns from time to time will keep the people reminded of their duty."[54]

To add fuel to the campaign, the national organizer of the National Negro Business League sent Washington detailed accounts of sixteen trips he made over various southern railroads, naming the places, times, and in most cases the coach numbers where specific discriminations had occurred. The legislative enactment requiring accommodations "equal in all points of comforts and conveniences" hung in most Jim Crow cars, but the Business League organizer Ralph Tyler found not a single railroad running through the South complying with the laws, except for some of the trains of the Illinois Central and the Rock Island line. "Invariably the Negro coach—usually compartment," he reported, "was a wooden affair and attached immediately behind the baggage car (when not a compartment of the baggage car), a vantage point for all the engine smoke and cindars [sic], and a dangerous point in case of wreck."[55]

It is not clear how successful the Railroad Days campaign was in bringing about improvement of the Jim Crow facilities. Du Bois failed to mention in the *Crisis* any of the information Washington sent him about the campaign until after it was over, when he took brief, noncommittal notice of it in the July number.[56] A group in Selma, Alabama, led by the secretary of the National Baptist Convention brought a detailed petition to the local Southern Railway officials and sent a copy to the president of the company.[57] In Jackson, Mississippi, lawyer Perry W. Howard and a committee "took the matter up with the officials, were courteously received and promised full consideration on the matters set forth to them."[58] New Orleans, however, the junction of many railroads, had the most successful of the local efforts. R. E. Jones, editor of the *Southwestern Christian Advocate,* headed a general committee, and three-man subcommittees called on each railroad serving the city.

"This is one of the best days I have ever spent in the interest of the race, thanks to your leadership in promoting Railroad Days," Jones wrote after visiting the regional superintendent and the passenger agent of the L & N Railroad. "They were more than cordial and readily agreed to every request. It seems almost too good to be true." It probably was. The railroads apparently received the delegations as a public relations gesture. "I find that some of our people were fearful of the movement," Jones wrote Washington, "but there was not the least ground for their fear for the railroad people certainly met us half way." [59] Both the cordial atmosphere and the limitations of Railroad Days are explained by a clipping Jones enclosed from a New Orleans daily newspaper. "Believing entirely in the theory of the 'Jim Crow law,' but complaining of the lack of proper accommodations afforded members of their race on railroad trains in this part of the country, negroes of this city observed 'Railroad Day' Sunday in Central Congregational Church," the *Times-Picayune* reported. It quoted from the appeal against "second-class accommodations for first class fare," noticed that the black petitioners conceded that blacks were not without fault in the matter of littering the cars and that there was a "noisy, ill-mannered class" among blacks that warranted segregation. The petition insisted, however, that "no community can afford to force all men of any class down to the level of its lowest type. Self-respect, character and worth must be considered." [60]

The petitions of Railroad Days were not only non-protesting and non-threatening, but in the case of New Orleans tried to distinguish between classes of blacks. Washington was anxious to follow up the campaign with positive changes rather than confrontation. "It will not do," he wrote Charles Banks, "to have the railroad authorities get the idea that we are disposed to harrass them with suits for damages in connection with every little difficulty which may arise. I shall see what I can do toward discouraging such suits whenever opportunity offers." [61] He wrote a railroad official who had responded to an appeal: "I want to let you know how very much the colored people appreciate the provisions which have been made for them in the new car recently put on the West Point road; I refer especially to the separate toilet rooms." [62] Though he must have known that there was many a mile of Jim Crow travel ahead, Washington encouraged his followers, saying, "I feel quite sure we have set in motion forces which will be of incalculable service in the future." [63]

A terminal superintendent put the dialogue in a clearer perspective—that of triviality—when he wrote to ask Washington whether the inscriptions over waiting room doors in the new central station should read "Negro" or "Colored." "I beg to say that personally I have not the slightest objection to the word 'Negro,'" Washington replied, "but there are considerable numbers of our people who prefer the designation 'colored' for the reason that they feel that the word 'colored' takes in all the various shades of complexion. The latter designation then, I feel sure, will please a larger number of our people."[64] Washington wrote the general superintendent of the Pullman Company in Chicago to commend the courtesy of a particular conductor, and urged his black friends to do likewise. "I believe that it will strengthen the backbones of the conductors and make them stand up for us more satisfactorily," he wrote his campaigners, "if they know that the office in Chicago is backing them as is true in this case."[65]

The interchange with railroad officials soon evaporated, however, and Washington did not undertake a similar campaign the next year. In November 1914, when Washington and a party from Tuskegee were in Selma for a meeting, they tried to buy coffee at the railroad station lunchroom. On his return home Washington wrote the general manager in Atlanta and, after praising the clean, well-lighted, and well-heated Jim Crow car, reported:

> The only "fly in the ointment" was this, and I thought you might like for me to speak to you frankly about it. A number of us tried to get a cup of coffee at the lunch room near the station. The man in charge of the lunch room seemed to feel that it was his duty to drive patronage away from the railroad, instead of inviting it. He refused, of course, to let any colored person drink a cup of coffee on the inside of the lunch room, which was not surprising, but he refused to let anyone of the party bring a cup of coffee into the car where it might be drunk. Finally one of the party did succeed in paying a porter to permit the lunch counter keeper to let some coffee be brought out of the lunch room in a tin cup. I believe you will agree with me that if the same amount of time and energy were spent in trying to be courteous to people, instead of discourteous, it would serve a much higher purpose and bring about a greater degree of success on the part of individuals.[66]

One form of racial discrimination that gained rapid momentum in the Wilson years was residential segregation. Segregation was hardly a new phenomenon. It dated back to antebellum cities and to the patterns developed during Reconstruction. But residential segregation had a variegated pattern, including the alley dwellings of Washington, D.C., ownership of adjoining land in the rural areas, and the scattering of black residences among those of whites in many southern towns such as Tuskegee. Around the turn of the century clustering patterns were developing into ghettos of larger size, in the North as well as the South. In the town of Tuskegee there were two black residential areas, the

one around the campus of the Institute and another on the far side
of town. The court square was also segregated, with white stores on
one side of the courthouse and black stores on the other. An ingenious town planner arranged the through and dead-end streets in such
a way that the Institute students could travel into town only along a
single street. The black ghetto was developing as an all-American institution, bringing with it the pathology produced by discrimination
and neglect but also the black solidarity that proscription fed.

As residential segregation spread in the cities, it occurred to Clarence H. Poe, editor of the *Progressive Farmer,* and soon became his
obsession, that the rural areas also could and should be segregated.
Poe, a resident of Raleigh, was the son-in-law of Charles B. Aycock,
champion of the disfranchisement movement in North Carolina. Poe
expanded his magazine throughout the South, putting out a local edition in Birmingham. He felt that whites could purify the landscape of
the white men's country by refusing to sell land to blacks and refusing
to engage black tenants. Such a course he thought would improve the
social health of rural communities, even improve race relations by reducing the contacts between the races. It would give better schools to
both races, he claimed, and attract immigrants to the South as tenant
farmers. By the fall of 1913 Poe was waging an active campaign in
several state legislatures for "a simple law which will say that whenever the greater part of the land acreage in any given district that
may be laid off is owned by one race, a majority of the voters in such
a district may say (if they wish) that in future no land shall be sold to
a person of a different race," provided a judge or county commissioner ruled that such action would promote the peace, protection,
and social life of the community.

Washington was asked by a Winston-Salem lawyer, Gilbert T. Stephenson, who had recently written a book on racial distinctions in
American law, to state "the colored people's side" for his use in replying to Poe's editorials.[67] After consulting with Monroe Work and possibly with Robert E. Park, Washington replied at length. He did not
take the feasibility of the proposal seriously but deplored its implications as to white attitudes toward blacks.[68]

Washington wrote Stephenson that he knew of "no sentiment among
the substantial white landowners in this section of the South in favor
of such a proposition. The average Southern white man, as perhaps
you know, likes to have just as many black people in 'calling distance'

as possible." As for blacks, their only embarrassment was in not being able to buy all the land that whites were offering for sale. The Poe scheme he considered "utterly impracticable," and he thought the time and strength of both races should be spent on something more constructive. "If there is an attempt to carry the proposition into effect," he warned, "racial hatred, in my opinion, will be stirred up in a way that it has not been stirred up in the South since reconstruction days." The South's progress required racial harmony, he said. "I think we should learn a lesson along this line from what is taking place in Baltimore and in other cities where segregation has been attempted. So far as I have been able to ascertain, in every instance there has been a stirring up of racial hatred and, in some instances, rioting." Furthermore, he suggested, the handicap placed on blacks in securing land under such a scheme would retard the progress of the entire South.

Washington proposed a more constructive approach, to extend the agricultural cooperative movement, "such as where the white people and colored people have worked together in a county or community for better live stock, or a regional campaign for better school facilities for both white and black." His own observations of rural districts in the North and in Europe had led him to believe that "conditions that tend to make social life unsatisfactory are dependent more upon other things than they are upon the presence of two different races." Rather than turn over the important social question of improving the quality of rural life to legislators, he suggested "a Country Life Commission for the whole South," composed of fair and broadminded whites, which would make recommendations for local communities based on social surveys.[69]

Stephenson adopted most of Washington's arguments in an article against Poe's proposal but added an additional argument, that the issue involved fundamental legal rights. "Voting, for instance, is a privilege," he wrote; "but the right to hold property is inherent in citizenship and should not be tampered with without great caution." He proposed a commission to study rural race problems. "An impartial investigation may show that the white people are not leaving their farms because of the presence of the Negro or that segregation is not the best way of reducing race relations to a proper and permanent basis," he argued. Stephenson called for a careful diagnosis before applying a remedy, particularly "such a drastic remedy as rural segregation by legislation."[70] Reading the article in manuscript, Washington felt Stephenson had struck the right note. He wrote, "There is no hope for anything looking to a final settlement of racial questions except on a basis of justice and fair play between the races. Before we go far in segregating the Negro we should study the effects of segregation upon the Indian."[71]

Poe's particular proposal died when the North Carolina supreme court ruled that local subdivisions lacked the power to pass segregation laws. Poe was more significant than his scheme, however, as a bellwether of southern thinking in the Wilson era. He said his plan occurred to him when he read Washington's own boast that blacks were acquiring land in the South faster than whites. Washington defied him to find any such boast "in any of my writings over my signature or authorized by me." "I am just as happy," he added, "when a white man is making progress as when a black man is making progress, and I would certainly be the last one to feel that any real advance has been made in the way of civilization if black people are going back and white people standing still."[72] Poe seemed to Washington the only person interested in his proposal, and he told a northern researcher there was "not enough in that movement to warrant any serious or dignified attention. In fact, I think the more attention that is given to it, the more harm will be done."[73] Poe persisted, however, extended his efforts to a general stirring up of racial hostility, and attacked such practices as black ushers escorting whites to their seats at the meeting of the Southern Sociological Society. Though Washington had been minimizing Poe's impact in his land scheme, he wrote James H. Dillard in exasperation that Poe's most recent editorials showed "that the time has come in all these matters when we have got to take a position and stand by it. We cannot, in my opinion, without great loss to the cause, attempt to please everybody or attempt to straddle. The more this policy is followed the more we are going to get some of our best friends into an embarrassing position."[74]

While Washington was tilting with Poe's windmill, urban residential segregation by city ordinance was spreading. It appeared in December 1910 in Baltimore, and Washington inquired into the matter in correspondence with his Baltimore friends within two weeks of enactment. The editor of the *Afro-American* replied that he and his friends were trying to initiate a test case. "There does not seem to be much of a disposition on the part of our people in this state to do much,"

John Murphy wrote, but soon the local NAACP chapter took up the matter and succeeded in winning test cases against the act and a succeeding act in the state supreme court.[75] When the city council passed a third segregation ordinance, the NAACP national organization postponed a test case until after its victory against a Louisville ordinance before the U. S. Supreme Court in 1917.[76]

Though Washington did not play a central role in the struggle against urban residential segregation, he nevertheless took a keen interest in it. When Atlanta imitated Baltimore's ordinance, he wrote to Benjamin J. Davis of the *Independent*, "I see that the city government of Atlanta has just passed a segregation act. We are sure this act is wholly unconstitutional and cannot stand before any unprejudiced court. What are you all going to do about it? I advise that you hire the best lawyer you can get and fight the matter from now on. Let me know if you need any outside help and what your plans are." According to Washington's interpretation of the Atlanta statute, the very minute the population would shift and a black man's house was surrounded by a white majority, the whites could insist that he part with his property. "This, of course, would be robbery and no court would up-hold, in my opinion, such a law." Washington admonished Davis, "I should be greatly disappointed if the colored people of Atlanta do not begin to fight this unjust act and keep up the fight until victory has been attained even if it has to go to the United States Supreme Court."[77] If this did not put Washington in the forefront of the action, it showed his unequivocal concern about the effects of the segregation statutes.

Washington suggested to Carl Kelsey, a white sociologist at the University of Pennsylvania, that blacks needed to make public protest against segregation ordinances rather than relying on black votes, which would be insufficient to defeat them. "It is curious to note," he wrote, "that with one or two exceptions, the cities where segregation ordinances have been passed, are the cities where the colored people vote freely, but their ballot does not seem to protect them against these ordinances. This is notably true in such cities as Baltimore and Louisville where there has never been any question about the Negro casting his ballot and having it counted." Furthermore, he thought a campaign against segregation should have a constructive as well as negative emphasis—"for example, I think it ought to be constantly pointed out that colored people are treated very unjustly in most of the cities in the matter of providing them with proper streets, sewerage, lighting and other modern conveniences and necessities. I have found that the colored people are not so much opposed to living among themselves but they know by experience when they are shut off to themselves it means that they are to be provided with fewer of the necessities and safeguards of life, notwithstanding, in many cases, they pay a large proportion of the taxes that provide for the city government." [78]

Washington's efforts to combat residential segregation, however, were largely in private letters and through the agency of others. His critics in the NAACP assumed that he was doing nothing at all, and Joel E. Spingarn, chairman of the NAACP executive committee, bitterly attacked him in a Chicago speech as unfit to claim leadership of blacks. Oswald Garrison Villard felt not so much bitterness as regret. He wrote in the spring of 1914 to Roger Baldwin of St. Louis, nephew of Washington's trustee and adviser William H. Baldwin, Jr., sending a copy to Robert R. Moton:

> It is, however, very hard for us not to comment on the position in which Booker Washington finds himself. He is like Nero, fiddling while Rome burns. One right after another is being taken away from the colored people, one injustice after another being perpetrated, and Booker Washington is silent. There has developed in North Carolina the greatest menace yet, a movement under the leadership of Clarence Poe, which will undoubtedly result in legislation, segregating the Negro on the farm lands, thus giving the lie to Washington's advice to his people that if they will only be good and buy land they will be let alone and will flourish. He is silent about the segregation in Washington, in Baltimore and in nine other Southern cities, and then he believes that he is a leader of his people. It is pitiful beyond words, and pains me particularly as I have always been a loyal supporter of Tuskegee and of Washington, standing by him in his trouble here in New York [the Ulrich assault], and raising the Baldwin Fund [a Tuskegee endowment fund] for him. His name is getting to be anathema among the educated colored people in the country, and he is drifting further and further in the rear as a real leader. [79]

In part of what Villard wrote, he was misinformed. He seemed to have forgotten that Washington had given him a letter to send to President Wilson deploring federal segregation. He exaggerated the significance of the Poe rural segregation proposal and did not know that Washington had furnished arguments to Gilbert T. Stephenson,

Poe's leading challenger in North Carolina. He did not know of Washington's private concern about the segregation ordinances that were spreading from one southern city to another. He was right, however, in sensing that Washington, now that he had lost his political contingent in the capital, was drifting out of touch with the worsening racial situation. The times called for another approach than accommodation and self-improvement, and Washington met the changing times only part way.

Washington did in fact oppose residential segregation laws both publicly and privately, but he did so in a way radically different from that of the NAACP. The NAACP lawyers, carefully selecting a border city for their test case, challenged the Louisville ordinance and eventually in 1917 won a landmark Supreme Court decision outlawing restrictive covenants. Washington, on the other hand, used all his accommodationist tricks when he learned in the newspapers that Birmingham was considering a similar ordinance. He wrote privately to the president of the Birmingham board of commissioners, saying that while not a citizen of Birmingham he was deeply interested in the peace and welfare of both races there. Praising Birmingham for the "degree of harmony and friendship" between the races there, he added:

> This condition has been maintained very largely through the influence of a number of sensible, conservative colored people working in cooperation with the best white people. I am very anxious that nothing be done anywhere to disturb present relations between the races, and I very much fear that the passing of the law segregating the two races in Birmingham will stir up racial strife and bring about bitterness to an extent that will result in discouraging a number of the best colored people in the state.

The ordinance was unnecessary, he insisted, for blacks would not buy property in neighborhoods where they were not wanted. Custom in this matter was "stronger than a law." Instead of an ordinance, Washington suggested: "I believe if it were made known that certain things were desired in reference to the purchase of property in the future that the same results could be obtained as by passing a law which I very much fear will be misunderstood throughout the country and, I repeat, stir up racial strife."[80] The Birmingham official informed Washington a few days later that after a conference with leading Birmingham blacks "the ordinance is now in abeyance pending investigation of its working in other cities."[81]

Washington's methods were not nice, nor his results clean-cut. He flattered white Birmingham by pretending that race relations were good in that troubled city, suggested black self-segregation as an alternative to segregation by law, and led the white officials toward a bargain with black go-betweens. His action did, however, achieve his purpose of stopping the enactment of an ordinance that would have institutionalized residential segregation and would have put the power of the law in the hands of the discriminator. He also strengthened the intercessional role of the "sensible, conservative colored people" who represented the Tuskegee Machine in Birmingham.

Even while he was opposing the segregation laws, however, Washington continued to wrap himself in ambiguity. What he now advocated for Birmingham was the same black self-segregation that he and his colleagues at Tuskegee Institute had been practicing in their all-black school for more than thirty years. At Tuskegee the practice extended from the campus to Greenwood village, and in town to the segregated side streets of the courthouse square. It was one thing, however, for blacks to join together on terms that promoted group solidarity and quite another for the whites to herd them together on white terms and limits under laws imposed on the disfranchised blacks.

Though Washington worked privately against the segregation laws, his public silence made it possible for many newspapers, white and black, to publish a statement purported to be his that endorsed residential segregation laws.[82] Washington denied the attribution. What he actually did stand for, he wrote one inquirer, was "to urge our people not to become discouraged and disheartened in communities where they were segregated, but notwithstanding such segregation, to go forward and make progress. In a word, to overcome evil with good; to make so much progress in the beauty, comfort and convenience of their surroundings that those who have treated them unjustly will be made to blush with shame because of the progress that the colored people are making. In a word, I try to impress upon our people the idea that they should keep a cheerful heart and a strong will and not permit themselves to be continually on the defensive side of life. . . ." Lest he should seem to be questioning the appropriateness of protest, he added, "I realize fully the importance of condemning wrong—such wrongs as segregation," but constructive action should accompany the condemnation.[83]

Washington seized an opportunity to further the cause of equal access to residential property and to set the public record straight as to his views. In June 1915, when the editor of the *New Republic* received from Louisville a manuscript supporting residential segregation, he wrote Washington that he was "loath to publish such a paper without running at the same time an article which looks in another direction."[84] When Washington agreed to write such an article, the editor sent a copy of the first article but urged Washington to go beyond a mere criticism of it.[85] Washington delayed through a "tremendously busy" summer but sent in September a typescript with liberal corrections and additions in the hands of Robert E. Park and Emmett J. Scott.[86] Though he had collaborators and though the article appeared after his death, the work bore clearly the stamp of his authorship and his outlook. Furthermore, it was so much in harmony with the NAACP's views on the question that Du Bois reprinted part of it in the *Crisis* and the NAACP directors included it in a pamphlet they published on racial segregation.[87]

It was ironic that in "My View of Segregation Laws" Washington posthumously spoke more forthrightly than he had in life. He catalogued six reasons why "segregation is ill-advised": that it was unjust, invited other unjust measures such as failure to provide equal public services, would fail in its attempt "to make wrong right or seem to be right," was unnecessary, was inconsistent in placing no corresponding segregation on whites, and would widen the breach between the races. He said that in none of the recent cases of segregation ordinances had there been any spontaneous demand, that politicians had succeeded in passing them only after appealing to racial prejudices, but that once passed few whites would oppose them because they were "afraid of the stigma, 'negro-lover.'" As proof that the courts would eventually find the new segregation laws illegal, Washington expressed the certainty "that the courts in no section of the country would uphold a case where negroes sought to segregate white citizens. This is the most convincing argument that segregation is regarded as illegal, when viewed on its merits by the whole body of our white citizens." He regarded with amusement the argument that whites living next to black populations suffered physically, mentally, or morally, and pointed out that not only the President of the United States but five members of his cabinet and many leaders in Congress had been reared in the South, many of them having had black "mammies." This close proximity to blacks did not seem to have retarded their development.

"Right here in Alabama nobody is thinking or talking about land and home segregation," Washington noted. "It is rather remarkable that in the very heart of the Black Belt where the black man is most ignorant the white people should not find him so repulsive as to set him away off to himself." Besides, a segregated black community was "a terrible temptation to many white people" by allowing them the opportunity to do illegal or indecent things out of sight of their families and associates. "Now when a negro seeks to buy a house in a reputable street he does it not only to get police protection, light and accommodations, but to remove his children to a locality in which vice is not paraded." Washington ended his article with a plea for a spirit of justice and fair play and for a recognition that both races could only prosper together, for "in the gain or loss of one race, all the rest have equal claim."[88]

In the last year of Washington's life another public racial issue meteorically traversed the American scene—D. W. Griffith's epoch-making film, *The Birth of a Nation*. Washington at first tried to fit the film into the history of ten years of trouble with Thomas Dixon, Jr., author of the white supremacy novel *The Clansman* on which the film was based. Washington saw the issues involved much more complexly than did Monroe Trotter, who led the movement to ban the movie in Boston. Neither man was able to prevent the movie's box office success or its baneful impact on white popular attitudes toward blacks, but the history of Washington's involvement with the author and then the film provides a final illustration of the strengths and weaknesses of Washington's racial philosophy and leadership.

Dixon's novels portrayed blacks either as servile by nature or as subhuman beasts. He had once praised Washington's industrial education program in the belief, widely shared among southern whites, that it prepared blacks for subordination. Washington's dinner at the White House and with Wanamaker at Saratoga, his identity with the Ogden Movement, and his optimism about inexorable black progress, however, turned the South Carolinian against him. In an anonymous article Dixon accused Ogden of hugging Washington in the presence of 500 female employees of his New York department store. Dixon also wrote under his own name in the *Saturday Evening Post* of "some dangerous aspects of the work of Tuskegee," accusing Washington of training blacks not to serve whites but to compete with them, and thus bring on a race war that would exterminate the blacks.[89] "Such articles always carry their own refutation," Washington wrote privately in his refusal to reply.[90] Washington heard that Dixon planned to call the third volume of his trilogy "The Fall of Tuskegee," but decided that any protest would only increase Dixon's notoriety.[91] As if to confirm this, Dixon offered Tuskegee $10,000 if Washington would "give complete and satisfactory proof that you do not desire Social Equality for the Negro and that your School is opposed to the Amalgamation of the races." Washington told reporters: "I will make no answer whatever."[92] Dixon offered to debate Washington in the largest hall available, and even promised "not to refer to my play," but again Washington refused.[93]

When Washington first heard of the film, he associated it in his mind with Dixon rather than Griffith, and predicted to his friend Anderson that "it is Tom Dixon's plan over again. . . . He apparently wants to work the colored people into fever heat and reap the reward of the advertising."[94] Washington made his prediction while the film was in production, but Dixon soon confirmed it. Dixon, an enthusiastic Wilson man, arranged for a preview of the film at the White House. The President endorsed it as "history written with lightning."[95] Dixon promised the President's secretary that the movie would "transform every man in my audience into a good Democrat" and "a Southern partisan for life." Its only critics, he said, were "the members of Villards Intermarriage Society," whose disapproval only swelled the crowds, and "this opposition of fools is bringing all the motion picture interests . . . into an organization to fight for their rights of free speech."[96]

Washington was on an extended speaking tour in Louisiana in the spring of 1915 when the motion picture opened in Boston and members of his faction there wired for advice as to whether to join the boycott movement that Trotter had immediately launched. Washington's first advice was inaction. "Having not seen 'A Birth of a Nation' I hesitate to make suggestions, but from all that I can hear it is a vicious and hurtful play," he telegraphed a Boston donor to Tuskegee. "My fear is that any direct opposition will result in further advertisement of the play. Opposition is a thing which I think owners want.

Some years ago when the same people put on another play of the same nature they actually paid colored people to oppose it for the sake of the advertisement."[97] After further telegraphic correspondence he concluded that Dixon and Griffith had protected their investment by legal advice as to what they could do, but hoped they could be persuaded to tone down its depiction of blacks.

Washington changed his mind the next day, however, and wired his black supporter Samuel E. Courtney, sending a copy to the Boston *Transcript* for publication. "If it cannot be stopped it ought to be modified or changed materially," he wrote. "Best thing would be to stop it as it can result in nothing but stirring up race prejudice. Do not believe play will be permitted in its present form in any of our Southern cities. Glad to hear people in Boston are against play and hope their efforts to stop it will be successful." Being Booker T. Washington, he felt a need to end on a note of optimism, saying, "Particularly unfortunate to have this play at present time when we were entering upon era of good racial feeling throughout country such as we have not experienced lately."[98]

Though Washington himself at Tuskegee was far from the scene of the Boston struggle against the film, Courtney, William H. Lewis, and other Tuskegee lieutenants joined in the petitions to the mayor and state legislature and the picketing of the theater, though not to the point of arrest as Trotter did. Washington's friend George Foster Peabody condemned the film and perhaps influenced his friend Woodrow Wilson, whose secretary denied that the endorsement of the film was official. Chicago was the only large city that banned *The Birth of a Nation.* The opposition of Julius Rosenwald, as well as that of Mayor "Big Bill" Thompson and a united Chicago black community led to that result.[99] After that first day of hesitation, Washington was in fact so forthrightly against the showing of *The Birth of a Nation* that the NAACP quoted him in its 1915 pamphlet, *Fighting a Vicious Film.*

Washington was mistaken, however, when he wrote to a Boston friend, "We are taking measures to squelch it in all the Southern cities where it is possible to do so, and I believe we are going to succeed." In fact, the movie was a howling success in the South. At a showing in Houston, at the scene where a black man was depicted in pursuit of a young white girl, many whites sprang to their feet and yelled, "Lynch him. Lynch him."[100] Washington expressed the dream of many blacks, that "if this play can be put out of business in Boston, that no

other parties in the future will risk money in this kind of venture."[101]
The Birth of a Nation ushered in the big-business era of motion pictures, however, and for decades appeared annually at southern thea-
ters as the true history of Reconstruction, the answer to Yankee textbooks, and the justification for white supremacy. During the school
desegregation crisis in Little Rock in the 1950s, a photographer captured on his film a comic mispelling on a Little Rock marquee: "Want
Intergration? See The Birth of a Nation."

Washington had misgivings, however, about censorship as a means
of combatting unwholesome influences. When a reformer in 1910
asked him to help ban films depicting crime and immorality, he replied that the best remedy was "some provision for pictures that would
have a wholesome and uplifting effect."[102] Washington's friend Roger
Baldwin had similar inhibitions about censorship of *The Birth of a Nation* as a violation of the First Amendment. These were the inhibitions
that later led him, during the crisis of free speech in World War I, to
the founding of the American Civil Liberties Union.[103]

Both before and after the appearance of the film Washington and
particularly Emmett Scott tried several times to assist in the production of a film that would project a more positive image of black progress in America along the lines of Tuskegee Institute and Washington's racial ideology. In 1910 Washington and his school cooperated
with efforts of the Broome Exhibition Company of Boston, a black
firm, to produce a motion picture about Tuskegee Institute. It premiered at Carnegie Hall, but it was not a success.[104] The Anderson-
Watkins Company, another black enterprise, produced in 1913 a three-
reel film, *A Day at Tuskegee*, which premiered at Orchestra Hall in
Chicago to the accompaniment of folk music sent from Tuskegee.[105]
Though favorably reviewed in the black press, the movie failed financially, which one of the producers said was because the tickets were
fifty cents to a dollar, whereas "The 'brother' has been used to seeing
moving pictures for 5 & 10 cents."[106] In 1914 Washington and Scott
tried to interest two of the major white motion picture companies,
Edison and Paramount, in a movie version of *Up from Slavery* but without success.[107]

Thus, even before the appearance of *The Birth of a Nation* Washington had tried without success to promote an alternative film depiction
of black life. When one of his Boston supporters reported that D. W.

Griffith in a theater lobby had suggested making a film about Tuskegee, Washington did not take the offer seriously.[108] As *The Birth of a
Nation* proved so powerful an influence on racial attitudes, however,
outside script writers and Emmett Scott besieged Washington to approve of the filming of *Up from Slavery*. Washington lacked the energy
to follow through on the idea in the last few months of his life, however, and the experience of Hampton Institute also deterred him.
Hampton students had taken part in a prologue to *The Birth of a Nation* intended to moderate the impact of its racial stereotypes, but
Washington found that "the moving picture people are not keeping
faith with Hampton and do not show the Hampton pictures regularly."[109] Only a few days before Washington's death, Emmett Scott
was negotiating with Washington's publishers and a Chicago film company for production of a film version of *Up from Slavery*, while at the
same time the NAACP was considering a film to be entitled *Lincoln's
Dream*.[110]

Though Washington in his final years addressed many of the civil
rights questions that the NAACP was also actively concerned with, his
approach was radically different from theirs. Whereas the NAACP
from a northern base sought to challenge racial injustice, Washington
from a southern base sought to ameliorate it. The two factions continued to regard each other with suspicion. Ironically enough, it was
Villard, who had tried to make peace with Washington after the Ulrich assault, who renewed the friction with Washington. Villard in the
spring of 1913 organized a conference at the NAACP headquarters
that formed the Association of Negro Industrial and Secondary
Schools. Washington resented what he considered an NAACP invasion of his own bailiwick of education. He not only refused to attend
himself, on the legitimate ground of prior commitments, but persuaded at least one other industrial school head not to attend, and
refused to send anyone from Tuskegee unless Villard would move the
conference to some other place.[111] Villard went ahead with his conference and association, and held a second meeting the following year.
Villard insisted that the NAACP had always considered black education a part of its work and was therefore now doing what Tuskegee
should have been doing all along in organizing and strengthening the
black schools. "I have always dealt perfectly frankly with you," Villard
wrote Washington, "and I must say that I think your timidity is run-

ning away with you." [112] Washington finally consented for a Tuskegee faculty member to attend, but he was suspicious of the NAACP's hidden motives. He also thought it premature for the industrial schools to be organized before Thomas Jesse Jones completed his study, sponsored by the Phelps-Stokes Fund beginning in 1913, to determine which of these black secondary and industrial schools deserved support. [113]

Washington saw in the National Urban League, founded in 1910 by a coalition of other organizations, the kind of northern agency for the welfare of blacks that he could endorse more readily than the NAACP. The Urban League's membership was almost as diverse as that of the NAACP, but it included many supporters of Tuskegee and Hampton, and its chief founder was Ruth Standish Baldwin, widow of Washington's close advisor and trustee William H. Baldwin, Jr. Mrs. Baldwin herself continued to support and visit Tuskegee, and corresponded with Washington during the formative years of the organization. Its approach was one Washington would consider "constructive," as it was concerned with amelioration of the job opportunities and working and living conditions of the black working class in the northern cities. [114] Washington encouraged his lieutenants in the northern cities to join the Urban League, and he also gave friendly advice to its staff officers from time to time. [115] In 1914 he agreed to become a board member, and that year he made a series of speeches in Harlem in behalf of the league. "I think I might say something to them that would help them," he wrote Ruth Baldwin. "I do not mean the more prosperous or well-to-do men, but the down and out, discouraged and poorer classes." [116]

Washington seemed in his last years, after the rise of the NAACP, the Ulrich incident, and the reactionary racial policies of the Wilson era, to sharpen his criticism of racial injustice. The extent of the change should not be exaggerated, however. The main difference was an abandonment of his earlier optimism, and perhaps a recognition that he was running out of time. Washington remained what essentially he had always been, a southern-based political boss of a people still overwhelmingly southern and rural, ever conscious of the demands made upon him and other blacks by the white South that surrounded them, and willing to render unto Caesar that which was Caesar's, so long as blacks could bargain for economic and educational opportunity and the means of self-improvement. Washington was the last black leader born in slavery, and his policies of peasant conservatism reflected his origins as well as the New South spirit of materialism. He would have been out of place in the age that would follow, of migration to the cities and the struggle for civil rights.

CHAPTER 18

Gonna Lay Down
My Burden

Time and again on these trips in the North he would be carrying some
parcel or his travelling bags. When I would volunteer to carry these things
for him, he would always decline my invitation. He seemed never to want
other people to serve him; rather he wanted to save others any seeming
inconvenience. I recall but one exception to this general rule of his. This
was what proved to be his last visit to Chicago, in September. . . . I carried his travelling bags, sent his telegrams, answered his phone calls, ordered his carriages, bought his newspapers, and even carried his light
fall overcoat.

FRANK P. CHISHOLM, *ca.* December 1915

WORK was life to Booker T. Washington, and he worked without stint until he could work no longer, three weeks before his
death. But there were earlier warning signs and warning voices. He
had once collapsed before his thirtieth birthday, in 1885, and had to
spend ten days in bed and take a physical training course the next
summer at Harvard. But he quickly forgot his lessons of regular rest
and exercise. Not even the early deaths of his first two wives deterred
him from laboring day and night. Neither did the deaths in middle
age of his white father-figures, General Samuel Chapman Armstrong
and William H. Baldwin, warn him or stop his obsession with work,
for he had never learned to play. He was near collapse in 1899 when

the heavy sleep on an ocean voyage revived him, and he did the same thing in 1903.

On reaching middle age around the turn of the century, Washington lost his boyish figure and seamless face. He grew stocky though never fat, heavier also of face, his reddish hair receding slightly and turning more gray. He continued to drive himself as the layers of his activity multiplied. "You were very tired when you were at Bar Harbor," Tuskegee trustee William J. Schieffelin wrote him, after seeing Washington during his own vacation there. "I want to urge you to rest more and not do so much, and if you should break down, the loss would be far greater than missing now and then an opportunity to plead the cause."[1] The letter did not stop Washington from going on to Lake Mohonk and other resorts to catch millionaires at their leisure, but Scott wrote Schieffelin "to say that all of us at Tuskegee recognize the fact that Mr. Washington has worked very hard during the past year and is greatly in need of a somewhat extended vacation. This, of course, none of us expect him to take but I am very glad that you have written him a word of caution. . . ." He asked Schieffelin not to tell Washington he had written in this way.[2]

One of Washington's chronic ailments was indigestion, particularly when traveling. "Please send me five hundred Bell's Papayan tablets," he wired a pharmaceutical firm in 1909.[3] This protein-splitting enzyme extracted from unripe papayas was used to alleviate indigestion or tenderize meat. While he was in Boston in 1910 the newspapers reported him "quite ill earlier in the day in his room in the Parker House, suffering from an attack of indigestion." He felt better in the afternoon, however, and Nathan Hunt, who often traveled with him as his secretary, denied that he was in serious ill health.[4]

In mid-March 1911 Washington went to Battle Creek, Michigan, for several days at the Battle Creek Sanitarium, apparently both to test its curative regimen and to speak for Tuskegee. In fact, it was from Battle Creek that he went to New York, perhaps feeling his oats, as it were, only to suffer the assault of Henry Albert Ulrich. Dr. J. H. Kellogg, superintendent of the sanitarium, sent Washington at his request a telephone directory of Battle Creek and marked in it the men of means who might be interested in philanthropy. He deplored the assault, and said of Washington's visit: "You did as much for our people here as they did for you. I know of several people who have very different ideas now from what they did before with reference to your people and the work you are doing for them, not only in the South but in the whole country."[5]

Kellogg made a contribution of $500 to Tuskegee, and in April 1911 he sent there two of his assistants, a woman Dr. C. E. Geisel and a Miss Evans, who instructed the faculty and students on the elements of a healty diet. "We should be glad to welcome them back here at any time," Washington said. He had been compelled to be away during part of their stay, but said: "Mr. Snyder, in charge of our Boarding Department, tells me that a hundred students have applied to him to have vegetable tables. He also says that already the total expenditure on the part of the institution for meat has been greatly reduced."[6]

Sometime in 1911 Kellogg sent to Washington for his personal care a male nurse, William P. Crayton, who had served at Battle Creek since 1901. "I am glad to say that Mr. Crayton is rendering fine service in many directions here," Washington reported in 1912. "He is fast opening people's eyes to what your methods mean."[7] Returning to Battle Creek in 1914 to make an address, Washington said of Crayton: "Some three years ago I found myself almost out of commission physically. Without my knowledge or consent, my wife in some way got hold of a colored man trained here under Doctor Kellogg, by the name of Mr. Crayton. He came to Tuskegee, was installed in my home by my wife and for six months he had charge of me. At the end of that six months I was a new man, and not only a new man, but I knew more about living and enjoying life than I had ever known before. And so I want to express to you, Doctor Kellogg, my deep personal gratitude."[8]

The assault in New York was a close enough brush with the possibility of death to remind Washington to modify his will made in 1909 and to secure life insurance. His Last Will and Testament made his wife Margaret his executrix, mentioned that she had already acquired a separate estate sufficient for her support, and left her only the house and its furniture in Tuskegee. He left small amounts to his sister, brother, adopted brother, nephew Albert Johnston, secretary Emmett J. Scott ($400), his financial agent A. R. Stewart ($200), niece Laura Murray, and nephew Thomas J. Murray. He left his three children equal shares in his royalties and in the remainder of his estate.[9] The codicil he added in the summer of 1911 gave his wife the newly acquired house near Northport, Long Island, for her lifetime, then to pass to the three children equally. It also added Emmett J. Scott to the executors, John H. Washington and Warren Logan, in case of the death of the executrix, permitted the estate to be held intact for as long as three years if advisable, and provided that anyone contesting the will must bear all costs and expenses, to be deducted from that person's share of benefits.[10]

About the same time, Washington also arranged to take out a life insurance policy. In this era most old-line life insurance companies refused to write policies on blacks because their actuarial tables showed an earlier death rate, but Washington as usual was an exception. William H. Parker of Buffalo, an insurance agent, was anxious to insure Washington, and even went to New York City for a conference with William G. Willcox, the Tuskegee trustee, to get his approval.[11] Washington held back. He wrote Parker, "I do not think it wise to proceed further in this matter without taking the matter up fully and frankly with our trustees, that is with the responsible members." He explained: "People are much more likely to enter heartily into a scheme of this kind if they feel that they are responsible for the initiation of it than they are if they feel they are merely called on to give consent after something has been decided." [12] Parker said, however, that Willcox thought well of the plan but did not want to push on "without knowing positively that Life Insurance companies would grant you insurance." [13] The first step was for Parker's own physician to check Washington to see if he was physically insurable, and soon afterward Parker wrote that he was happy to report "a favorable opinion on your insurability by Dr Warner." [14] Apparently the life insurance policy was then issued.[15]

"A rumor comes to me that you are far from well," Ruth Baldwin wrote in 1911, urging him to "go a bit slow." [16] He replied: "I am glad to say that I am all right now. During the latter part of the summer I had considerable trouble." He had just completed a strenuous ten-day speaking tour of Texas in good shape.[17] George Foster Peabody also warned him about the same time to "let up in your quite too strenuous life" or else run the risk of breaking down as General Armstrong had.[18]

Washington ignored these warnings for a while. All of his life he had been so full of the work-ethic and purposefulness that he could not enjoy leisure and derived his pleasures from succeeding at his work. Emmett Scott somehow persuaded him, however, to join some of his more intimate black friends from around the country on a fishing trip to the coast at Mobile Bay in the early fall of 1913. They spent about two weeks in this relaxing atmosphere, and Washington responded so well to the rest that they repeated the expedition in 1914 and again in 1915. Dr. George Cleveland Hall, Washington's physician in Chicago, accompanied the party in 1914 and 1915 and took the occasion to observe and advise his patient.

Washington had always found water relaxing. On land he was always restless, but somehow on or near the water he could repress his inclination to be up and doing. He slept heavily on all of his ocean voyages, perhaps because of mild seasickness, but also because of cumulative fatigue. Often at his summer place on Long Island he would have the Tuskegee student who worked there for the summer row him up and down the harbor and bay. He was therefore receptive to Scott's suggestion of an outing in 1913. Both of them knew a Mobile undertaker and member of the National Negro Business League, Clarence W. Allen, but Scott had struck up a closer friendship. Allen, known locally as "the Admiral," and his wife "Miss Joe" conducted as a hobby or side-business a fishing camp at their summer place at Coden, on the west side of Mobile Bay. "The Doctor arrived at Coden Saturday P. M.," Allen wired Scott in September 1913. "Am with him. Wish you were here."[19]

Washington had expected to find heat, gnats, and mosquitoes, but the breeze off the water drove the pests inland and made the air so cool at night that it was sometimes necessary to use a blanket. He found something in the atmosphere that caused him to fall asleep as soon as his head met the pillow and to sleep soundly until the next morning. He wrote Anderson after the 1913 holiday that he had been "fishing with some very delightful people."[20] But it was the place as well as the companionship that had a tonic effect. At this point Mobile Bay had a string of bar islands and many bayous extending far inland, which made the fishing good not only in deep water but in the inlets. A short way from Coden the wrecked hulk of the last slave ship to America could be seen, the very ship on which some of the older black people of the vicinity had been brought from Africa.

In 1914 Dr. Hall and Emmett Scott accompanied the fishing party. "Admiral" Allen always went along to take care of all the accommodations, the boat, and any contingencies. Scott wrote back to Tuskegee from this visit: "Today Mr. [Victor] Tulane and I & our boatman caught more than 200 trout between us. What a pity some of it cannot be sent to Tuskegee."[21] In 1915 Washington, Hall, Scott, Allen, and five other friends spent twelve halcyon days at Coden.[22]

After his return from the 1915 excursion, Washington tried to capture the atmosphere of Coden in an article he never published, "A Paradise of Fish & Sea Food." "Aside from hunting and horseback-riding," he wrote, "nothing rests me more and delights my soul more than to get on some stream near an old-fashioned swimming pool, with the root of a tree close by and to spend as many hours as I can in fishing with the old-time pole and line." He had never had any luck with fresh-water fishing, however, and had concluded that the only true fisherman was St. Peter, who said, "We have toiled all night long and have caught nothing." Coden changed all that. "The whole atmosphere is one of sea-food." Shrimp, crabs, and the largest oysters he had ever seen were there in abundance, and the scenery as well was ever-changing. One could go to a new fishing place each day and catch different varieties of fish. "I caught so many," Washington reported, "that even the truth would be taken for the usual fish story."[23]

Most of the party at Coden in 1915 were connected with Tuskegee. They included Warren Logan, Major J. B. Ramsey, Dr. John A. Kenney, and Victor H. Tulane, a Montgomery merchant and a Tuskegee trustee.[24] Some idea of Washington's gradual relaxation on his vacation is conveyed by his letters. He wrote Edith, his son Dave's wife: "Tell Mrs. W. to let you have a lot of that corn and sweet potatoes for your pigs. Am doing well. Love to you and Dave. Tell Dave not to forget the garden. B.T.W."[25] He wrote Dave two days later: "We are having a great time, got up at 5 this morning. Caught 50 fish yesterday. Am keeping very well. Look out for my *garden* and chickens. Your Papa."[26] After his return to Tuskegee he wrote to C. W. Allen: "Every one who was there with me came away feeling that nothing was left undone to make our stay at your beautiful summer home in every way satisfactory and enjoyable."[27] He also thanked Allen's business partner for his courtesy in providing carriages to meet the train and for letting him go to his house and rest while waiting for the train.[28] In the last major speech of his life, at New Haven a few weeks later, Washington digressed for a few moments to pay tribute to the healing powers of the Mobile Bay shore.[29]

The annual vacation at Coden was a move in the right direction, but by the time Washington agreed to this change in the pace of his life it was too late. His faithful nephew Albert wrote him after his return from Coden that he needed a longer vacation, "at least a month's rest and the proper treatment." Such a course now would add years to Washington's life, he said. "It will be too late after you have completely broken down, and I must be truthful and say that you have shown many signs of giving out during the past year."[30] Albert Johnston had never before talked in that way to his Uncle Booker. It was a reversal of roles brought on by an obvious crisis in Washington's health. The older man appreciated the kind thought but said he was "not working very hard."[31] Washington's son Booker also expressed anxiety in a letter from Chambers County, Alabama, where he was working in the Tuskegee extension service. "Are you at the Bungalo?" asked young Booker. "I know that you are. But I want you to go to Battle Creek. Won't you please?"[32] The Tuskegee faculty members showed their concern about his health also by presenting him with a chair and a shotgun symbolizing the rest and recreation they thought he needed. He promised to use both of them as "the means of being additionally useful to the school and to our race."[33] Nevertheless, he plunged back into his usual routine of work, travel, and public speaking.

Obviously, friends, family and colleagues were all becoming increasingly concerned in the fall of 1915 about Washington's state of health, but little remains among Washington's papers that describes his physical condition. What was the nature of the illness that was to bring his death at the age of fifty-nine? His own papers supply not answers but clues, themselves contradictory. Emmett Scott and Lyman B. Stowe, in the first biography that appeared after his death, spoke of Washington in his last month as "wasted by disease and suffering almost constant pain,"[34] and again referred to "the insidious disease which was so soon to end his life."[35] Scott and Stowe were not explicit, and the evidence in the correspondence is less of the nature of the illness than of symptoms and attempted remedies. It is unclear whether Washington died of a curable disease or collapsed all at once like the one-hoss shay.

In 1914 Seth Bunker Capp, a philanthropically inclined acquaintance from Reading, Pennsylvania, asked Washington to sit for a portrait by the Bohemian artist Roman Hruska, and promised the black leader an opportunity to rest for a few days during the sitting.[36] Washington agreed to do so, and in the process of their conversations

Capp persuaded Washington to drink radium water as a possible cure of his digestive distress. This treatment may have been only harmless quackery, or may have contained a dangerous carcinogen. Washington wrote that he had "personally benefited" from the radium water received from Capp's friend Dr. John Ege. Capp immediately suggested that Washington try radium for his son Dave's eye affliction.[37]

Washington was seriously ill in August 1915 at the Boston meeting of the National Negro Business League. He was particularly nervous about this meeting because he remembered the Boston Riot twelve years earlier and feared another nearly all-black gathering in that city. He managed to make his annual address without attracting attention to the state of his health, however, and the meeting passed off without any trouble. It was not long after that that he made his last holiday at Coden.

Deciding that rest was not enough, Washington sought more expert medical advice. He wrote to George E. Vincent, president of the University of Minnesota: "It is probable that I shall want to go to Rochester [Minnesota] sometime within the next few weeks for a physical examination on the part of the Doctors Mayo and I am wondering if you will give me a personal letter of introduction to the Mayo brothers that I may use, in case I go there." Vincent promptly obliged Washington with a letter to William J. Mayo.[38] Washington then wrote Dr. George C. Hall, claiming to feel "fifty per cent better than I was when I was at Coden," and dreaming of the diamondback terrapins they would feast on in Chicago. But he asked Hall, "Would it be possible and practicable for you to go up to Rochester with me for a few days at my expense? This meets with the approval of Dr. Kenney and Mrs. Washington."[39] Dr. Hall said that, of course, he would go. "Let me hear from you regarding your future plans for your health and when you expect to come to Chicago." As soon as he knew, he would send to Coden for the diamondbacks. Hall shared Washington's delight in the fishing trip, and wrote: "I got a letter from the boy Mark Basage thanking me for a watch I sent him and he is sending me some oysters when I let him know. So I made a cracker friend out of him."[40]

Perhaps the Mayo brothers could have saved Washington's life, but he put off his visit there until he had met some other commitments, and his time ran out. Among these commitments was his last Sunday Evening Talk to the Tuskegee students in the chapel on October 17.

"Team Work," he said, had built the Panama Canal. It had also built the great Standard Oil Company. "A great many people think that it has been built up by one man, Mr. Rockefeller. That is far from true." When he was at West Point a few weeks earlier, he said, the adjutant had told him that what they strove most for was to bring about team-work. Tuskegee also needed teamwork, not only on the athletic field but in maintaining cleanliness, saving expenses, "doing honest work," and helping one another.[41]

In this same period, as though he sensed that time was short for saying what was on his mind, Washington wrote an article for the New York *Age* on the American occupation of Haiti. He explained that the indebtedness of Haiti to the warring Europeans precipitated the American occupation, and that the Monroe Doctrine legitimated it. But he warned that the United States needed to explain to the Haitians "the purposes we have in mind in taking over the control of their custom houses and their governmental affairs." He pointed out that the United States had a good opportunity to establish a tax-supported educational system, which Haiti had never had; and if that system should be developed he hoped that it would include agricultural and industrial education. The United States, he wrote, should also carefully select the right kind of white men for the administration of occupied Haiti, men who would not try to make Haiti a "white man's country." Only if they were willing to be "white men in a black man's country" and put themselves in the black man's place could they do any good with and for the Haitians.[42] It was one of the frankest articles he ever wrote, and summarized what he stood for in the United States as well—accommodating to white power, but calling for constructive programs and human understanding.

Washington went on to New Haven, where he was to make two speeches to large crowds. Yale University made plans for him to stay with John C. Schwab, the university librarian, with whom he had stayed during the Yale bicentennial in 1901, when he and Roosevelt had both been in the procession in cap and gown a few days after the dinner at the White House. Typical of the way he drove himself even at this precarious stage of his health was his itinerary for New Haven. He wrote Schwab that he would reach the city in midafternoon of October 25, meet with Anson Phelps Stokes, Jr., secretary of Yale, in the afternoon, then make two speeches that night, one at Woolsey Hall at Yale before the American Missionary Association and the National

Council of Congregational Churches, and later at a black church. He would go from the church to the boat from New Haven to New York, for he had an engagement in New York early the next morning.[43] Meanwhile, he put his visit to the Mayo clinic off for a while. "Since writing you a little while ago regarding my Rochester trip," he wrote Dr. Hall, "something has occurred which may delay my going to Rochester for a few days. This is confidential."[44] Emmett Scott was a little more explanatory. He wrote Hall: "I did not attempt to send you a night letter last evening for the reason that Dr. Washington is so greatly improved in every way that there really seemed nothing special to say aside from what you already know of his condition. I think he has been better the last week."[45]

On the very day that Washington spoke in New Haven, however, Dr. Hall wrote confidentially to Julius Rosenwald about Washington's health. He urged Rosenwald, as a friend and trustee of Washington, to arrange for him to be completely relieved of his work for six months to a year. "As you know I was with Dr. Washington 15 days last month, and during that time he had three severe attacks of kidney trouble—he is also suffering from high blood pressure—extremely high—and is taking a chance every time he exerts himself mentally as well as physically. In a confidential talk with me he indicated it would be a great relief to him if he could stay at home quietly and not have to worry about the running expenses of the school—and that he would be on the train and in the hotels ⅔ of his time . . . ."[46]

At Yale Washington unstintingly praised the work of the American Missionary Association. "You are maintaining more schools for the higher and secondary education of the Negro than any other board or association," he said. When it began its work among the freedmen about fifty years earlier, there were no such institutions, whereas in 1915 in the South there were fifty colleges, thirteen institutions for the education of black women, twenty-six theological schools, three law schools, four of medicine, two of dentistry, three of pharmacy, seventeen state agricultural and mechanical colleges, and over 200 normal and industrial schools. Even so, there was still great need for philanthropic work such as the A. M. A. was doing, for in the fifty colleges there were only 3000 students of collegiate grade. "At the present rate it is taking, not a few days or a few years, but a century or more to get Negro education on a plane at all similar to that on which the education of the whites is."[47]

This address proved once again that Washington was far from being opposed to higher education, however he might fear and hate the college-educated blacks who taunted him. "This proved to be the last public speech of Mr. Washington," the *Crisis* later reported, repeating a common error.[48] Despite the pain he must have been suffering, Washington went on to the A. M. E. Zion Church in New Haven and spoke again. A week later he heard from a black man who heard both speeches "and enjoyed them both immensely." The man asked Washington if he remembered that after he finished talking with ex-President Taft in the vicinity of Yale "a humble colored man addressed you saying; Mr. Washington please permit me to satisfy my ambition to shake the hand of the man whom he had been reading so much of and trying to follow the examples and teaching of him and remember also how readily you extended your hand and gave him that sincere grip which he will long remember and honor." William H. Jackson said: "Eloquent as your address was at Woosley Hall I enjoyed your heart to heart talk at Zion Church more. Why? Because you were among your own people and you could appeal direct to them in a confidential manner better than you could in a great meeting. . . . In this little place you could and did point out their fault and short comings in a manner in which they appreciated. You also prescribed a remedy which remedy I am sure will be followed until the last drop of the medicine has been taken." What Washington told his black audience was not about industrial education or the acceptance of their present lowly lot, but instead the failure of the blacks of New Haven to seize the opportunities for higher education that literally surrounded them. He said that in a city where colleges were open day and night, "where there are more than five thousand colored people . . . only two natives are attending Yale University." "Yes sir," wrote Jackson, a New Haven bartender, "those remarks of yours struck deep and I think fell on good soil and the results will be forthcoming."[49]

Washington took the boat to New York that night and wired his wife next day, "Spoke at two large meetings at Yale last night and felt no bad effects. Am getting on very well."[50] He went about business as usual. He wrote Logan that Anson Phelps Stokes had virtually promised money from the Phelps-Stokes Fund to enlarge Phelps Hall. He reported to J. H. Dillard, executive secretary of the Jeanes Fund, his conversation with Taft on Jeanes Fund business. He urged Tuskegee officers to keep expenses down.[51] "Other hotel so crowded have not been able to get rooms there," he wired Margaret Washington the next day, "so better send mail and telegrams to Herald Square Hotel."[52] She replied: "Letter sent you today Biltmore Hotel. Call for it. Be very careful what you eat."[53]

George Cleveland Hall wrote that he had followed his letter to Rosenwald with a long conversation about giving Washington a year or half-year rest, and that Rosenwald was "in perfect sympathy with the whole scheme and promised to take it up with the other trustees." He encouraged Washington to visit the Mayos as soon as he could. "They claim that they want to help you and you won't let them," he said of the trustees. "I have thrown the fear into them and you must not be so modest as to attempt to appear able to throw off these terrific attacks with out help."[54]

Washington had originally planned to return to Tuskegee for a visit by Julius Rosenwald and a Pullman car full of his relatives and friends, but Margaret Washington wired him, "Doctor Kenney and I both feel that you make a great mistake to make this extra trip to Tuskegee. Take the time to rest until you go to Virginia."[55] Washington decided to take that advice, and also to miss the inauguration of Fayette A. McKenzie as president of Fisk.[56] He had planned to give a speech in Petersburg, Virginia, before the Negro Organization Society of Virginia on November 5 because Robert R. Moton had absolutely insisted on it, not knowing how ill Washington was. Earlier in October, Washington had tried to secure a release, not on grounds of ill health which he and Scott kept a close secret, but in order to speak in North Dakota. He was probably trying to work his way toward the Mayo clinic, but Moton insisted on his obligation at Petersburg. "In the last analysis you must decide which is the more important meeting," Moton wrote, "one in Dakota among Northern white people or meeting in Petersburg among Southern white people and Negroes." Washington agreed to go, rather than admit he was ill, and Moton scheduled him for a ten-minute speech in the afternoon as well as the evening address.[57] On November 4 Washington finally had to admit to himself that he could not make the trip, and wired Moton, "It is perfectly exasperating and heartbreaking for me not to be with you tomorrow night."[58]

Meanwhile trustees Willcox and Low had a conference with Washington about his financial affairs, about which he was not seriously worried, and about his health. Washington had recently been relying,

Willcox reported to Rosenwald, largely upon Dr. Kenney at Tuskegee and thirty-one-year-old Dr. Edmund R. P. Janvrin in New York, both of whom felt that his condition had improved over the past several months. Willcox telephoned a specialist in abdominal diseases whom he knew well, Dr. Walter A. Bastedo, a Canadian-born graduate of Columbia University, associated with St. Luke's Hospital and a teacher of pharmacology at Columbia Medical School. Bastedo had in fact recently taught Dr. Janvrin and spoke well of him as a promising young man, but Willcox thought it wise to seek a second opinion on Washington's case and gladly accepted Bastedo's offer to examine his case himself, at St. Luke's Hospital.

"Dr. Washington has been there yesterday and again today," Willcox wrote Rosenwald, "and I have been just talking to Dr. Bastedo over the telephone, and he tells me that Dr. Washington has pretty serious kidney trouble and blood pressure of 215. He is making some further tests, and I shall have a more detailed report next week." At the suggestion of the distinguished Dr. Simon Flexner, director of laboratories of the Rockefeller Institute for Medical Research, Washington also went there to see Dr. Rufus Cole, director of the institute hospital and contributor of chapters on gonococcus infections, typhoid fever, and pneumonia in standard medical textbooks. Cole and Bastedo were to compare their findings with those of Janvrin. "I am afraid that his condition is more serious than any of us had suspected," Willcox confided to his fellow trustee, "and I think we must at least look forward to an almost complete cessation of his trips about the country and of public addresses."[59] Rosenwald replied that the discouraging report of Dr. Bastedo confirmed what Dr. Hall had told him, said he would be in New York directly after his visit to Tuskegee, and suggested an emergency meeting of the trustees there in mid-November.[60]

After the doctors had put their heads together, Washington wired Emmett Scott: "Tell Dr. Kenney doctors and trustees here want me to begin a new course of treatment. In order that he may understand how to carry it out they think important that he come here and stay three or four days. If he starts next Monday [November 8] will be satisfactory."[61] He also wired his wife to "come at once," "not later than Sunday."[62]

Restless in his inaction after a lifetime of compulsive activism, Washington fired telegrams to Tuskegee from his hospital bed, suggesting to Scott that he attend the Fisk inauguration in his place; to Clinton J. Calloway to be sure Rosenwald saw the Chehaw schoolhouse; to Albon L. Holsey, of the office force, to be sure to let the Greenwood families know when Rosenwald would speak at chapel; to Ezra C. Roberts of the academic department, "Remember Mr. Rosenwald likes to see how fully we coordinate the work"; to A. R. Stewart, his personal business agent, "Be sure my yard is well cleaned."[63] There was no time for letters, but the telegrams that reached Washington must have brought him some comfort. Moton wired after the Petersburg gathering: "Had fine meeting but missed you very much indeed. I am sure you did the wise thing. I hope you going to have a good rest. Count always on my loyalty."[64] From Stewart, whom he had asked for an up-to-date account of his estate, came a succinct telegram: "Macon County Bank eight thousand two hundred thirty two. Securities thirty four hundred. Property value forty thousand."[65] Washington had sworn to confidentiality all who knew about his health, but his brother John wired Margaret when she reached New York: "Please let me know condition of my brother. Many rumors here about his condition."[66]

The news of Washington's serious illness finally broke on November 10. "Suffering from a nervous breakdown," the New York *Tribune* reported, "Dr. Booker T. Washington . . . is confined in a private room in St. Luke's Hospital. Only his wife, his secretary and William G. Willcox, a trustee of the institute, have been allowed to see him." The secretary referred to was Nathan Hunt, who had traveled with him while Scott held the fort at Tuskegee. Washington had entered the hospital on the preceding Friday, the 5th, after the examination by Dr. Bastedo, who at that point took charge of his case. "Dr. Washington has been suffering from severe headaches for more than a month," Dr. Bastedo told reporters. "His condition became serious enough to alarm the trustees, who, I understand, have no successor in mind for the position of principal." Dr. Bastedo not only discussed matters outside of his competence but proceeded to reveal to the press intimate details about his patient. "At the request of Mr. Low and Mr. Willcox I made an examination of Dr. Washington a few days ago and found him completely worn out," he said. "We have thoroughly overhauled him and find that he is ageing rapidly. There is a noticeable hardening of the arteries and he is extremely nervous. Racial characteristics are, I think, in part responsible for Dr. Washington's breakdown. He is prone to worry under the strain of work, and while there is nothing to indicate that he is mentally unbalanced he is in no shape to go back to Tuskegee."

Dr. Bastedo not only violated the customary doctor-patient confidentiality, as often happens to public figures, but also ignored Washington's specific request when he entered the hospital that no information be given out to the effect that he was ill. Just what racial characteristics he presumed Washington to have, the doctor did not say. He may have meant what he went on to add, an alleged proneness to worry under stress. But the term "racial characteristics" made possible a whole circus of interpretation by press and public.

Seth Low, also interviewed, showed more discretion. "If he were well he would not be in a hospital," he said, "but I hope that he will soon be able to resume his duties as principal. We have not contemplated choosing a successor. I have not called on Dr. Washington yet, but I hope to do so next week."[67]

Dr. Hall, in Chicago while others had taken charge of his patient in New York, was upset by Bastedo's statement. "If his Doctor is quoted correctly," he wired Scott, "his future interviews should be censored. Headline Tribune Dr. Bastedo says he suffers from Racial characteristics which interpreted means specific nature. Show this to Mr. Rosenwald. Express our sympathy to family."[68] Hall was even more blunt in speaking to Rosenwald's secretary, William C. Graves. Graves wrote to Rosenwald: "Dr. George C. Hall is much put out because of the 'racial characteristics' statement as applied to the case mentioned and credited to Dr. Bastedo in attached clippings. That expression, Dr. Hall says, means a 'syphilitic history' when referring to Colored people and he declares a doctor making such a diagnosis in this case isn't the right kind to treat this patient."[69]

Later in the same day, Graves wrote Rosenwald again: "It occurred to me after I had sent you the bulletin about Dr. Hall that you might want to show same to Mr. Willcox and other Trustees in New York. Therefore, I am writing a substitute to be shown to them if you see fit. The original is a little too rough, although it accurately expresses Dr. Hall's feelings. In fact, for your private information, he was indignant about it and spoke of the publicity as an 'outrage' and said that at least 50 people, Colored and White, had seen that notice in the Tribune and had expressed to him their indignation. Dr. Hall felt that if Dr. Bastedo did give out that statement, he is not a fit man to have charge of our friend's case."[70]

Graves's new memorandum to Rosenwald perhaps toned down the rhetoric of the one earlier that day, but gave more specific information. He wrote: "Dr. Geo. C. Hall was surprised at the 'racial characteristics' statement attributed to Dr. Bastedo in two of the attached clippings. That expression, Dr. Hall said, was understood to mean, when a Colored man is the patient, 'a syphilitic history.' He was quite emphatic in voicing his distress of mind on account of this publication and expressed the opinion that, if correctly quoted, Dr. Bastedo had violated the code of medical ethics in talking for publication about a patient's private matters. Dr. Hall said so far as he was aware this patient had not had a Wasserman test (to detect whether syphilis was present) and did not need one and that his condition was due to other causes."[71]

Did Dr. Bastedo indeed mean to refer to syphilis when he spoke of "racial characteristics," or did he instead merely indulge in a white-supremacy stereotype of black nervous distress in the face of crisis? If he did signify syphilis, was the doctor on the scene, though indiscreet, more to be trusted than the discreet doctor far away, who had treated the patient for years but was a personal friend? Was it significant that the doctor consulted after Dr. Bastedo's examination was Dr. Rufus Cole, who happened to be an expert on gonococcus infections but also was the head of the Rockefeller Institute hospital? Not even the questions are clear, much less the answers. The voluble Dr. Bastedo's statement could be construed as a hint of syphilis but certainly not as a diagnosis of it, and it might in that race-obsessed era have been simply a white man's racial hyperbole. Furthermore, he apparently later retreated from it, for the *Tuskegee Student* after Washington's death quoted him as saying to reporters that Washington "was completely worn out, and in addition was suffering from nervous exhaustion and arteriosclerosis."[72]

Rosenwald wired from Tuskegee that he hoped Washington was convalescing rapidly, that his visit had been thoroughly enjoyable, and the chrysanthemum exhibit "most creditable." He said he was on his way to New York to see Washington.[73] Margaret Washington wired him, however, that they would miss each other, for the Washingtons would be going to Tuskegee while Rosenwald passed them on his way to New York. "Washington is very weak—very ill," she wrote. "The doctors all agree that I should go South at once. We wanted to see you but think we must go on—every day he is weaker and weaker. I am so glad that you were at Tuskegee. It is so hard for him to be away but he simply could not stand up another moment. It is terrible Mr. Rosenwald to see him so broken all at once it seems and yet he has not been well for a long time. Remember me to Mrs. Rosenwald and the rest of the family. We leave at 4:35 today."[74] She added a postscript, "Thank you again and again for what you are to us all."

It was November 12. At 1:45 that afternoon Margaret Washington sent a telegram to Scott: "We are leaving for home this afternoon. Will reach Chehaw on train due at nine o'clock Saturday Night. Please have two good autos meet train and wait if it is late. Also notify Booker and Portia."[75] Scott did these things, and wrote to Charles Banks, who wanted him to come to Mound Bayou and help him through the crisis of the cotton oil mill there, that "It is absolutely out of the question for me to think of leaving Tuskegee just now. . . . There is much that I can say about Mr. Washington's condition in person, that I must not write, but if I say to you that he is quite seriously ill, I think you will understand." He said of a clipping he sent referring to the "racial characteristics" statement: "I do not know what the man can be talking about, or referring to."[76]

The doctors at St. Luke's had given Washington only a few days or even hours to live, and he insisted on starting for home, even though the doctors warned him that he probably would not survive the journey. His response, which the Associated Press spread throughout the country, was, "I was born in the South, I have lived and labored in the South, and I expect to die and be buried in the South." The doctors, who had already pronounced it "uncanny to see a man up and about who ought by all the laws of nature to be dead," saw him once again pull himself upright and, with his wife's help, make his way to Pennsylvania Station. There a wheel chair awaited him but he spurned it, and leaning on the arms of his wife, Dr. Kenney and Nathan Hunt, he walked or tottered to his seat on the train.[77]

Washington's condition probably worsened en route, though in his biography Scott said it improved, for at Charlotte, North Carolina, Mrs. Washington wired ahead to Scott: "Send ambulance to Chehaw tonight nine o'clock with plenty blankets and sheets. Also send two automobiles. Wish you, Booker and J. H. Washington meet train."[78]

When the train reached the junction for Tuskegee, she awakened Washington, saying, "Father, this is Chehaw." He answered, roused himself with an effort and, when his son Booker, Jr., appeared, asked, "How is Booker?" meaning his grandson.

Then began the slow, careful ambulance trip to the institute, but, as a newspaper account delicately stated, "earth for Booker Washington was receding fast and soon unconsciousness came."[79] He apparently reached home alive, but at 4:45 the next morning he died in his bed, surrounded by members of his family, in the "city that Booker T. Washington built."

The sun rose that Sunday morning on a campus whose driving spirit had gone. "Mechanically, bells, calling the school to its duties, have been rung and routine work taken up," the Montgomery *Advertiser* reported, "but the heart is out of things. From the humblest pupil up through the faculty and the bereaved family at the institute, to the white and colored citizens of the town of Tuskegee, there is the feeling of personal loss. Nobody is hiding his tears. Nobody is free from gloom."[80] As the telegrams and then letters of condolence poured into the campus, they showed a sense of loss that was more than local. The Tuskegee trustees, largely white, would choose his successor as principal, but who would be his successor as head of the Tuskegee Machine? Would there indeed be a machine? His chief lieutenants were already demoralized by political defeat and the loss of office, and his personal dominance had not countenanced the raising of a successor. Melvin J. Chisum, who had been Washington's mole, hastened to make his own suggestion. "Peace to his ashes and I am hurt—shocked—overwhelmed with sorrow," he wrote Scott. "The King is dead and it seems to me that you must take his place. Long live the King."[81] A similar thought without a ready answer occurred to Capp Jefferson, a black realtor in Oklahoma City. He sent the Washington family an elegy that began:

> Comes now the question, no dispute
> Where can we find a substitute
> To carry out unfinished plans
> And fill the stead of this "Great Man"?[82]

Charles Anderson as usual said it best for those who loved and believed in Booker T. Washington when he wrote Scott that "I have become what steel becomes when it is demagnetized."[83] At Roscoe Conkling Bruce's suggestion and by order of the District of Columbia board of education, every school flag in the capital would be at half mast during the funeral and every teacher would tell the class of Washington's career.[84]

Washington's body lay in state in the chapel for a day before the funeral on Wednesday, three days after his death. One of the largest crowds in the history of the institute gathered in the chapel, black and white together, dignitaries and country folk, for a funeral ceremony marked by the same simplicity that Washington had shown in life, in his manner and his speaking and writing style. As the Tuskegee graduate Isaac Fisher described Washington's going out: "No labored eulogies; no boastings of his great work; no gorgeous trappings of horses; no streaming banners; no mysterious ceremonies of lodges—just the usual line of teachers, trustees, graduates, students and visitors which so often marched to the chapel just as it did Wednesday, and the simple and impressive—impressive because simple—service for the dead, said for the humblest, said so often for those who die, in all walks of life."[85]

As Washington's body lay in the open coffin an old black man, near his own sunset, came forward to touch a sleeve and ask, "Do you reckon they will let us see Booker? We have come so far jes' to see him de las' time."[86] Similar emotions stirred in Claude McKay, then working in a New Hampshire resort hotel but soon to be one of the songbirds of the Harlem Renaissance. He had been a Tuskegee student for only a few weeks in 1912 before deciding that industrial education was not for him, but he continued to admire the "subtle tact and power" of Washington, and wrote a memorial poem:[87]

> O how I loved, adored your furrowed face!
>   And fondly hoped, before your days were done,
> You would look in mine too with paternal grace.
>   But vain are hopes & dreams!—gone: you are gone;
> Death's hand has torn you from your trusting race,
>   And O! we feel so utterly alone.

Washington had asked to be buried in the little cemetery on campus beside the chapel, the gravestone to carry only his name and the years of his birth and death. This was done, but they chose a granite boulder as big as the rock of ages, dominating the graveyard as he had dominated the others buried there during their lives. Ironically, pick-pockets appeared to work the crowd at the railroad station, and soon after the funeral excitement a faculty member who had earlier suf-fered a nervous breakdown jumped to her death from a high window on the campus.[88]

NOTES

A Note on the Notes

The principal source cited in these footnotes is the Booker T. Washington Papers in the Division of Manuscripts of the Library of Congress, a rich collection of approximately a million letters, speeches, reports, newspaper clippings, and other documents. All unpublished sources and newspaper clippings cited in the footnotes *without a place reference* are from this collection. The Library of Congress has been engaged, since these notes were taken, in microfilming and rearranging the collection, and many of the items are now in different boxes from the ones in which I saw them. Occasionally, where a footnote cites two or more sources, the notation [LC] is used to differentiate these materials. Researchers should seek the assistance of the staff of the Division of Manuscripts in locating items in the Booker T. Washington Papers.

All other manuscripts cited are identified as to place, "LC" standing for the Library of Congress. Among these other collections is a smaller but substantial Booker T. Washington collection in the archives of Tuskegee Institute.

The principal published source is Louis R. Harlan and Raymond W. Smock, eds., *The Booker T. Washington Papers,* 11 vols. to date (Urbana: University of Illinois Press, 1972–   ). Documents in this source are cited as in *BTW Papers,* with volume and pages. Other published sources appear with full title at their first mention in any chapter and by short title thereafter.

Chapter 1

1. Cleveland *Plain Dealer,* Nov. 2, 1901, clipping.
2. William Jennings Bryan, editorial in *The Commoner* quoted at length in Jackson *Clarion-Ledger,* Nov. 5, 1901, clipping [LC]. See also New York *World,* Nov. 1, 1901.

3. Birmingham *Age-Herald,* Nov. 3, 1901, attributing to the Washington, D.C., correspondent of the Louisville *Courier-Journal* the report that an intimate of the President had said that Roosevelt said it was a luncheon during a business conference with Washington. The southern folklore surrounding the dinner, and particularly the luncheon version, is savored in detail in "The Roosevelt-Washington Dinner: The Accretion of Folklore," Chapter 2 in Willard B. Gatewood, Jr., *Theodore Roosevelt and the Art of Controversy* (Baton Rouge, 1970), 32–61.

4. Tuskegee *News,* Oct. 31, 1904.

5. "Trotter has been calling the President names for having *you* to dine with him." Samuel E. Courtney to BTW, Oct. 27, 1901, *BTW Papers,* VI, 280. For Councill's remarks, see New York *Times,* Nov. 9, 10, 1901. W. T. Andrews defended BTW against Councill's criticism in the Washington *Colored American,* Dec. 7, 1901.

6. Henry M. Turner to BTW, Nov. 5, 1901, *BTW Papers,* VI, 287. Turner, despairing of racial justice in America, was the leading advocate in his time of emigration to Africa, which BTW opposed.

7. Recent scholarly literature concerning Theodore Roosevelt's racial attitudes and behavior includes Richard B. Sherman, *The Republican Party and Black America from McKinley to Hoover, 1896–1933* (Charlottesville, 1973); Gatewood, *Theodore Roosevelt and the Art of Controversy;* George Sinkler, *The Racial Attitudes of American Presidents from Abraham Lincoln to Theodore Roosevelt* (New York, 1972); and Thomas G. Dyer, *Theodore Roosevelt and the Idea of Race* (Baton Rouge, 1980).

8. BTW to T. Thomas Fortune, Jan. 25, 1902, *BTW Papers,* VI, 383.

9. Scott to BTW, July 1, 1902, enclosing editorial in Atlanta *Constitution,* June 23, 1902, *BTW Papers,* VI, 491–92.

10. BTW to Fortune, Nov. 29, 1901.

11. Montgomery *Advertiser,* Aug. 3, 1902; Thomas R. Cripps, "The Lily White Republicans: The Negro, the Party, and the South in the Progressive Era" (Ph.D. dissertation, University of Maryland, 1967), 125.

12. Montgomery *Advertiser,* Aug. 15, 1902.

13. *Ibid.,* Sept. 12, 16, 17, 18, 1902.

14. BTW to Fortune, Sept. 15, 1902, *BTW Papers,* VI, 513.

15. BTW to Clarkson, Sept. 16, 1902, *BTW Papers,* VI, 515.

16. Clarkson to Roosevelt, Sept. 27, 1902, Theodore Roosevelt Papers, LC.

17. Clarkson to Roosevelt, Sept. 27, 29, 1902, *ibid.*

18. BTW to Roosevelt, Oct. 3, 1902.

19. Montgomery *Advertiser,* Oct. 26, 29, 30, 1902; John Tyler Morgan to Felix O. Dudley, Nov. 13, 1902.

20. BTW to Roosevelt, Nov. 4, 1902 [LC]; William F. Aldrich to BTW, Nov. 13, 1902 [LC]; Thompson to Clarkson, Nov. 15, 1902, James S. Clarkson Papers, LC.

21. BTW to the editor, Birmingham *Age-Herald,* Nov. 24, 1902, *BTW Papers,* VI, 590–92.

22. For biographical information on Wilson, see Mary Floyd Sumners, "Edgar Stewart Wilson: The Mississippi Eagle, Journalist of the New South" (Ph.D. dissertation, Mississippi State University, 1962); Gatewood, *Theodore Roosevelt and the Art of Controversy*, 66–68.

23. Wilson to BTW, Nov. 30, 1901.

24. BTW to Scott, Jan. 2, 1902, *BTW Papers*, VI, 372.

25. Quoted in Wilson to BTW, Jan. 16, 1902, *BTW Papers*, VI, 375.

26. Wilson to BTW, June 25, 1902.

27. Wilson to BTW, Oct. 6, 1902.

28. BTW to Roosevelt, Nov. 4, 1902 [LC]; Gatewood, *Theodore Roosevelt and the Art of Controversy*, 67.

29. *Ibid.* See the chapter on the Indianola affair, 62–89.

30. BTW to Roosevelt, June 19, 1906, in Emmett J. Scott and Lyman B. Stowe, *Booker T. Washington: Builder of a Civilization* (Garden City, N. Y., 1916), 120–21.

31. Ethan A. Hitchcock to BTW, June 13, 1903.

32. BTW to Scott, June 20, 1903(?).

33. Scott to BTW, June 21, 1903, *BTW Papers*, VII, 179–81; June 22, 1903 [LC]; BTW to Francis E. Leupp, June 22, 1903 [LC]; Roosevelt to Wilson, June 24, 1903, *BTW Papers*, VII, 184.

34. Quoted in Leupp to BTW, June 27, 1903, *BTW Papers*, VII, 185.

35. George W. Henderson to BTW, Jan. 29, 1902.

36. The lily whites used this against Cohen every time his reappointment was considered. See BTW to Cohen, Jan. 16, 1904, *BTW Papers*, VII, 393; Cohen to BTW, Jan. 20, 1904 [LC].

37. BTW to Roosevelt, Feb. 16, 1902, *BTW Papers*, VI, 404.

38. BTW to Cohen, Jan. 16, 1904, *BTW Papers*, VII, 393.

39. BTW to Roosevelt, Feb. 24, 1904, Theodore Roosevelt Papers, LC.

40. Roosevelt to BTW, Feb. 25, 1904 [LC]; Henderson to BTW, Feb. 29, 1904 [LC]; BTW to Roosevelt, March 7, 1904, with enclosure [LC]; BTW to Cohen, March 20, 1904, *BTW Papers*, VII, 476–77; Scott to Cohen, March 23, 1904 [LC].

41. BTW to Roosevelt, Dec. 14, 1901, *BTW Papers*, VI, 346–47. On Smith's background, see Lawrence D. Rice, *The Negro in Texas, 1874–1900* (Baton Rouge, 1971), 110–11.

42. George B. Cortelyou to BTW, Dec. 19, 1901.

43. McKinlay to BTW, Feb. 7, 1902, *BTW Papers*, VI, 393.

44. R. L. Smith to Scott, April 29, 1905.

45. Cortelyou to BTW, April 22, 1902.

46. See BTW to McKinlay, May 24, 1905, Carter G. Woodson Collection, LC.

47. Pledger to Scott, Jan. 31, 1903 [LC]. After this letter Washington and Scott cultivated Pledger more assiduously, lest he join their critics. See August Meier, *Negro Thought in America, 1880–1915: Racial Ideologies in the Age of Booker T. Washington* (Ann Arbor, 1963), 250–51.

48. Quoted in Scott and Stowe, *Booker T. Washington,* 314–15; see also Stephen R. Fox, *The Guardian of Boston: William Monroe Trotter* (New York, 1971), 26.

49. BTW to William H. Lewis, Oct. 1, 1901, quoted in Scott and Stowe, *Booker T. Washington,* 316.

50. BTW secured Terrell's appointment by sending his name along with those of five other black lawyers to the Attorney General at President Roosevelt's request, and then indicating that Terrell was his first choice. BTW to Philander C. Knox, Oct. 24, 31, 1901, *BTW Papers,* VI, 266–67, including n. 5. Evidence of Dancy's private services to Washington are Whitefield McKinlay to BTW, Dec. 14, 1901, Melvin J. Chisum to BTW, Feb. 26, 1906, *BTW Papers,* VI, 347–48, VIII, 534–35.

51. Biographical annotation in *BTW Papers,* IV, 154.

52. Eugene Levy, *James Weldon Johnson: Black Leader, Black Voice* (Chicago, 1973); see also J. W. Johnson, *Along this Way* (New York, 1933), his autobiography; and David L. Lewis, *When Harlem Was in Vogue* (New York, 1981), 143–49, 246–48, on Johnson's part in the Harlem Renaissance.

53. Anderson to BTW, Feb. 21, 1906.

54. Williams to BTW, May 17, 1903; BTW to Williams, Dec. 26, 1904.

55. Crum to BTW, Oct. 9, 1902; BTW to Roosevelt, Dec. 1, 1902, *BTW Papers,* VI, 542, 600. A detailed account of the Crum case, with a focus on Crum and Roosevelt rather than Washington, is in Gatewood, *Theodore Roosevelt and the Art of Controversy,* 90–134.

56. Different understandings of the conference agreement are discussed in *ibid.,* 98–99.

57. Roosevelt to James Adger Smyth, Nov. 26, 1902, in Elting E. Morison, ed., *Letters of Theodore Roosevelt* (8 vols., Cambridge, Mass., 1951–54), III, 383–85.

58. Montgomery *Advertiser,* Jan. 23, 1903.

59. BTW to Roosevelt, Dec. 1, 1902, *BTW Papers,* VI, 601.

60. James A. Lunn to Whitefield McKinlay, undated, *ca.* Feb. 1, 1903, Carter G. Woodson Collection, LC.

61. Cortelyou to BTW, Dec. 13, 1902, BTW to Roosevelt, Dec. 16, 1902, *BTW Papers,* VI, 612.

62. BTW to Roosevelt, Feb. 3, 1903, *BTW Papers,* VII, 28.

63. Gatewood, *Theodore Roosevelt and the Art of Controversy,* 115–16; Abbott to Roosevelt, Dec. 4, 1902, Theodore Roosevelt Papers, LC; BTW to Roosevelt, Feb. 3, 1903, *BTW Papers,* VII, 27–28; Baldwin to Albert Shaw, Feb. 5, 1903 [LC]; Ogden to BTW, Feb. 25, 1903, *BTW Papers,* VII, 97. Roosevelt told Whitefield McKinlay that Murphy had urged him to withdraw Crum's nomination. McKinlay informed BTW, who urged Roosevelt to stand firm. McKinlay to BTW, Feb. 14, 1903, *BTW Papers,* VII, 78; BTW to Roosevelt, Feb. 17, 1903 [LC].

64. McKinlay to BTW, Feb. 14, 1903, *BTW Papers,* VII, 78.

65. Pledger to BTW, Feb. 18, 1903.

66. McKinlay to C. B. Purvis, May 1, 1913, Carter G. Woodson Collection, LC.

67. McKinlay to BTW, Feb. 13, 1903, *BTW Papers,* VII, 75.

68. Crum to McKinlay, March 31, 1903, Carter G. Woodson Collection, LC.

69. F. L. McGhee to BTW, Jan. 12, 1904 [LC]; BTW to McGhee, Jan. 19, 1904, *BTW Papers,* VII, 399; BTW to Roosevelt, Jan. 20, 1904, Theodore Roosevelt Papers, LC.

70. Anderson to BTW, Feb. 18, 1904; Phil Waters to BTW, Feb. 13, 1904; BTW to P. B. S. Pinchback, Feb. 9, 1904.

71. McKinlay to BTW, Feb. 10, 1904.

72. BTW to Crum, Feb. 19, 1904, *BTW Papers,* VII, 444.

73. See undated list.

74. Crum to McKinlay, April 7, 1904, Carter G. Woodson Collection, LC.

75. Ellen Craft Crum to BTW, April 15, 1904, *BTW Papers,* VII, 482.

76. Gatewood, *Theodore Roosevelt and the Art of Controversy,* 120.

77. BTW to Roosevelt, April 21, 1904, Theodore Roosevelt Papers, LC.

78. BTW to Roosevelt, March 29, 1904, Theodore Roosevelt Papers, LC.

79. Addison Wimbs to BTW, May 13, 1904.

80. BTW to Pinchback, June 20, 1904 [LC]. See also Roosevelt to BTW, May 9, 1904, *BTW Papers,* VII, 497–98.

81. BTW to Roosevelt, Feb. 20, 1904, Theodore Roosevelt Papers, LC; BTW to Anderson, Feb. 24, 1904 [LC]; Anderson to BTW, July 23, 1903, Feb. 25, 1904, March 3, 11, 1904 [LC].

82. Anderson to BTW, April 25, 1904.

83. BTW to Anderson, June 7, 1904 [LC]; Cripps, "Lily White Republicans," 214–15.

84. Washington *Bee,* June 11, 1904; Cripps, "Lily White Republicans," 215.

85. BTW to Clarkson, June 8, 1904.

86. Typescript of plank and two earlier drafts, undated.

87. BTW to Clarkson, June 6, 1904, *BTW Papers,* VII, 523.

88. BTW to Humphrey, June 4, 1904, *BTW Papers,* VII, 521–22.

89. BTW to Anderson, June 16, 1904 [LC]; BTW to McKinlay, June 16, 1904 [LC]; BTW to Scott, Nov. 28, 1904, *BTW Papers,* VIII, 148.

90. See Kirk H. Porter, comp., *National Party Platforms* (New York, 1924), 263.

91. Ogden conferred with BTW before his speech. Ogden to Baldwin, May 6, 1903, Robert C. Ogden Papers, Southern Historical Collection, University of North Carolina. See also Montgomery *Advertiser,* Dec. 16, 1903; Boston *Guardian,* Dec. 19, 1903.

92. Lodge to Roosevelt, June 25, 1904, quoted in Horace Samuel Merrill and Marion Galbraith Merrill, *The Republican Command, 1897–1913* (Lexington, Ky., 1971), 177.

93. BTW to Roosevelt, July 29, 1904, *BTW Papers,* VIII, 34–35.

94. Roosevelt to BTW, Aug. 2, 1904, *BTW Papers,* VIII, 36.

95. Fortune to Scott, Feb. 22, 1904.

96. Anderson to BTW, May 27, 1904, BTW to Anderson, June 16, 1904, Scott to BTW, June 23, 1904, *BTW Papers*, VII, 514–16, 533, 541; C. F. Adams to BTW, June 27, 1904 and undated letter [LC].

97. Anderson to BTW, July 20, 1904, *BTW Papers*, VIII, 23–25. BTW and Anderson at first credited Clarkson's claim that he was refusing to deal with BTW's black rivals, but in September 1904 Anderson learned that Clarkson was to meet with W. Monroe Trotter of Boston. "I mean to drop in, quite by accident, and see what it means," he wrote BTW, but apparently he was unable to do so. Anderson to BTW, Sept. 21, 1904, *BTW Papers*, VIII, 72–73.

98. BTW to Scott, Aug. 15, 1904, *BTW Papers*, VIII, 49.

99. BTW to Anderson, Aug. 15, 1904, *BTW Papers*, VIII, 49–50.

100. BTW to Roosevelt, Aug. 27, Sept. 8, 1904, *BTW Papers*, VIII, 58, 64.

101. See, for example, BTW to S. A. Furniss, Sept. 18, 1904; W. L. Ward to BTW, Sept. 20, 1904; BTW to Harry S. New, Sept. 26, 1904.

102. J. C. Napier to BTW, Oct. 5, 1904; W. L. Cohen to Scott, Oct. 20, 1904; Anderson to BTW, Oct. 20, 1904.

103. BTW to Lyman Abbott, Oct. 17, 18, 1904 [LC]; BTW to Roosevelt, Oct. 31, 1904, Theodore Roosevelt Papers, LC: *Outlook*, LVIII (Oct. 29, 1904), 511–13, *BTW Papers*, VIII, 120–23.

104. BTW to Clarkson, Nov. 10, 1904, *BTW Papers*, VIII, 127–28.

105. Clarkson to BTW, Oct. 16, 1902, *BTW Papers*, VI, 550–52.

106. Belmont to Arthur P. Gorman, undated, *ca.* March 5, 1905, Theodore Roosevelt Papers, LC.

107. Scott to BTW, July 13, 1904, BTW to Scott, March 25, 1905, *BTW Papers*, VIII, 17, 242; Meier, *Negro Thought in America*, 237.

108. BTW to Roosevelt, Nov. 15, 1905, *BTW Papers*, VIII, 439–40.

109. Edward H. Morris to A. J. Hopkins, Dec. 9, 1905. See also Hopkins to Roosevelt, Dec. 12, 1905.

110. BTW to Williams, March 8, 1906.

Chapter 2

1. On BTW's contribution to secularization of black thought, see S. P. Fullinwider, *The Mind and Mood of Black America: 20th Century Thought* (Homewood, Ill., 1969), 66–67, 98–99.

2. Fortune to BTW, June 9, 1900.

3. Washington *Colored American*, May 26, 1900.

4. Cleveland *Gazette*, Sept. 15, 1900.

5. Indianapolis *Freeman*, July 6, 1901.

6. Clement to BTW, Jan. 2, 1898.

7. Fleischer to BTW, Feb. 11, 1903, *BTW Papers*, VII, 66–68.

8. BTW to Fleischer, Feb. 17, 1903, *BTW Papers*, VII, 81–83.

9. Samuel E. Courtney to BTW, Oct. 27, 1901, *BTW Papers*, VI, 280–81.

10. Quoted in Stephen R. Fox, *The Guardian of Boston: William Monroe Trotter* (New York, 1971), 29.

11. Bruce to BTW, Feb. 8, 1902, *BTW Papers*, VI, 396.

12. Bruce to BTW, Feb. 22, 1902, *BTW Papers*, VI, 409.

13. Fox, *Guardian of Boston*, 28–29.

14. Thomas J. Calloway to E. J. Scott, Jan. 12, 1903, *BTW Papers*, VII, 4–5. See also "The Ferris Wheel," in Washington *Colored American*, Jan. 17, 1903.

15. Thompson to Scott, Feb. 4, 1903, *BTW Papers*, VII, 33–35.

16. Interview of Robert W. Taylor in Washington *Colored American*.

17. Peter J. Smith to BTW, Feb. 8, 1903; BTW to William H. Moss, March 10, 1903.

18. The only detailed study of the organization is Emma Lou Thornbrough, "The National Afro-American League, 1887–1908," *Journal of Southern History*, XXVII (Nov. 1961), 494–512.

19. Peter J. Smith to BTW, July 3, 1902, *BTW Papers*, VI, 492.

20. Fredrick L. McGhee to BTW, June 27, 1902.

21. Scott to BTW, July 17, 1902, *BTW Papers*, VI, 497.

22. Washington *Bee*, July 26, 1902, quoted in Thornbrough, "The National Afro-American League," 505n.

23. Boston *Guardian*, July 26, 1902, quoted in Emma Lou Thornbrough, *T. Thomas Fortune, Militant Journalist* (Chicago, 1972), 229.

24. Walters to BTW, Feb. 21, 1903, *BTW Papers*, VII, 84–85.

25. BTW to Scott, April 6, 1903, *BTW Papers*, VII, 112.

26. Cyrus Field Adams to BTW, April 9, 1903 [LC]. See also BTW to William A. Pledger, April 6, 1903, *BTW Papers*, VII, 111–12.

27. Thornbrough, *T. Thomas Fortune*, 239–40.

28. Smith to BTW, Feb. 11, 1903.

29. BTW to Walters, Feb. 9, 1903, *BTW Papers*, VII, 62.

30. Moore to Scott, June 24, 1903.

31. BTW to Scott, June 26, 1903.

32. BTW to Fortune, June 26, 1903 [LC]. He also wired Fortune: "Greatest importance your opening address be of calm conservative nature." June 29, 1903, *BTW Papers*, VII, 186.

33. BTW to George L. Knox, June 28, 1903, and similar telegrams to W. A. Pledger, A. E. Manning, J. C. Napier, and Phil Waters.

34. Anderson to BTW, July 6, 1903, *BTW Papers*, VII, 195–96.

35. Fox, *Guardian of Boston*, 47–48; Louisville *Herald*, July 3, 1903, clipping.

36. BTW to Scott, July 1, 1903.

37. Louisville *Post*, July 2, 1903, clipping.

38. E. Davidson Washington, ed., *Selected Speeches of Booker T. Washington* (Garden City, N. Y., 1932), 92–99; Louisville *Evening Post*, July 3, 1903, clipping [LC].

39. Interview in Louisville *Herald*, July 3, 1903, clipping.

40. Louisville *Herald*, July 4, 1903, clipping.

41. Interviews in Louisville *Evening Post*, July 5, 1905, clipping.

42. Clarkson to James Loeb, July 7, 1903, Theodore Roosevelt Papers, LC.

43. BTW to the editor of the Brooklyn *Eagle,* July 9, 1903 [LC]. He also asked Fortune to write a similar letter minimizing the opposition, and the *Eagle* followed their lead in two editorials. BTW to Fortune, July 9, 1903, *BTW Papers,* VII, 203.

44. BTW to Scott, July 27, 1903, *BTW Papers,* VII, 225.

45. Trotter's questions were published in the Boston *Advertiser,* July 31, 1903, clipping [LC]. See also Fox, *Guardian of Boston,* 49–51.

46. See J. H. McMullen to the editor, Boston *Transcript,* Oct. 23, 1901, clipping.

47. See report of testimony in Trotter's trial, Boston *Record,* Aug. 5, 1903, clipping.

48. See BTW's statement in Boston *Globe,* July 31, 1903, *BTW Papers,* VII, 240–41.

49. Boston *Globe,* July 31, 1903, *BTW Papers,* VII, 229–40. See also Boston *Transcript,* July 31, 1903; Boston *Journal,* July 31, 1903; Boston *Record,* Aug. 5, 1903, clippings [LC]; Fox, *Guardian of Boston,* 49–52.

50. Montgomery *Advertiser,* Aug. 5, 1903.

51. Boston *Transcript,* July 31, 1903, clipping.

52. Reprinted in *Tuskegee Student,* XV (Aug. 15, 1903), 1.

53. Copy of resolution, July 31, 1903.

54. Atlanta *Constitution,* Aug. 9, 1903, clipping.

55. Hartford *Times,* July 31, 1903, clipping.

56. Washington *Bee,* Aug. 8, 1903 and Chicago *Broad Ax,* Aug. 8, 1903, quoted in Fox, *Guardian of Boston,* 54.

57. Typescript datelined at Boston, July 31 [1903], several copies.

58. Boston *Transcript,* Aug. 5, 1903, Boston *Record,* Aug. 5, 1903, clippings.

59. Judge Sherman, quoted in Boston *Colored Citizen,* Oct. 17, 1903, clipping.

60. BTW to Whitefield McKinlay, Aug. 3, 1903, Carter G. Woodson Collection, LC.

61. Baldwin to BTW, Aug. 10, 1903, *BTW Papers,* VII, 261.

62. BTW to Scott, Aug. 8, 1903, *BTW Papers,* VII, 257.

63. BTW to Scott, Sept. 12, 1903, *BTW Papers,* VII, 283.

64. Amos Joy statement, Boston, July [Oct.?] 15, 1903[?], typescript corrected in E. J. Scott's hand.

65. Fox, *Guardian of Boston,* 61–62.

66. BTW to Ogden, Oct. 21, 1903.

67. Ogden to BTW, Oct. 26, 1903.

68. Bumstead to Towns, Nov. 5, 14, Dec. 5, 1903, quoted in Fox, *Guardian of Boston,* 61–62; Bumstead to BTW, Dec. 5, 1903, enclosing reprimand of Towns by the trustees, *BTW Papers,* VII, 360.

69. BTW to Ogden, Oct. 20, 1903, *BTW Papers,* VII, 298.

70. Du Bois, *The Souls of Black Folk* (Chicago, 1903), chapter 3. Like Washington's *Up from Slavery,* it has remained in print ever since. After the book appeared, R. C. Bruce questioned the wisdom of paying the travel expenses of such a trenchant critic to the Tuskegee summer school and return, but

BTW insisted on paying them, saying: "If he chooses to be little we must teach him a lesson by bearing greater and broader than he is." BTW to Bruce, April 21, 1903, *BTW Papers*, VII, 124.

71. Ogden to Peabody, Nov. 9, 18, 1903, Robert C. Ogden Papers, LC.

72. Ogden to Peabody, Nov. 20, 1903, Robert C. Ogden Papers, LC.

73. Du Bois to Peabody, Dec. 28, 1903, George Foster Peabody Papers, LC.

74. Scott to BTW, July 13, 1904.

75. Thompson to Scott, March 21, 1905.

76. Undated typescript, *ca.* Feb. 1905.

77. Scott to C. N. Love, Jan. 22, 1906 [LC]; Meier, *Negro Thought in America*, 237.

78. Boston *Post*, Aug. 4, 1903; Boston *Advertiser*, Aug. 4, 1903, clippings.

79. Pickens to BTW, April 5, 1902.

80. Boston *Guardian*, May 9, 23, 1903, quoted in Fox, *Guardian of Boston*, 69.

81. See *ibid.*, 39, description of BTW in the *Guardian*.

82. J. C. May [Smith] to R. C. Black [Scott], Feb. 6, 1903.

83. J. C. May [Smith] to R. C. Black [Scott], March 2, 1903.

84. McAdoo [Smith] to Scott, June 9, [1903], telegram.

85. BTW to Smith, July 27, 28, 1903, telegrams.

86. Pickens to BTW, Sept. 1, 1903.

87. Smith to BTW, July 31, 1903.

88. BTW to Smith, Aug. 3, 1903.

89. J. C. May [Smith] to R. C. Black [Scott], Aug. 6, 1903.

90. William Pickens, "The Outlook for the Negro," an address before an A. M. E. church conference, in New Haven *Palladium*, Sept. 4, 1903, clipping.

91. Trotter to Towns, Oct. 28, 1903, quoted in Fox, *Guardian of Boston*, 69.

92. BTW to Pickens, Nov. 4, 1903, *BTW Papers*, VII, 328.

93. BTW to Smith, Nov. 4, 1903, *BTW Papers*, VII, 329–30.

94. BTW to Thompson, Nov. 12, 1903, *BTW Papers*, VII, 343–44. Scott wrote the statement that went out to newspapers under Thompson's name. Scott to BTW, Nov. 23, 1903 [LC].

95. Pickens to BTW, Feb. 3, 1904. See also Pickens to BTW, Jan. 15, 26, 1904; BTW to Pickens, Jan. 21, 26, 1904.

96. BTW complained to an official of the American Missionary Association about Pickens's criticisms, and it was only after Pickens left Talladega that its president sought BTW's intercession with the General Education Board. BTW to James W. Cooper, June 20, 1908; Cooper to BTW, June 30, 1908; M. P. Metcalfe to BTW, Aug. 6, 1914; BTW to Metcalfe, Aug. 15, Oct. 21, 1914. Pickens alighted briefly at Wiley College, but that was E. J. Scott's alma mater. The president of Wiley wrote Scott: "Many people will wonder why his stay here was so short—you know the reason why. After our talk on the train speeding through Louisiana I decided a change would be best. Aside from the reasons for a change exprest to you, I couldn't afford to keep one here who had arrayed himself against your interests and whom you deemed unfit." M. W. Dogan to Scott, June 25, 1914.

97. Scott to Fortune, Nov. 23, 1903.

98. Fortune to Scott, Nov. 25, 1903, BTW to Fortune, Dec. 18, 1903, *BTW Papers*, VII, 350–51, 375–76.

99. BTW to Scott, Nov. 11, 1903, *BTW Papers*, VII, 343.

100. Scott to BTW, Nov. 11, 1903, *BTW Papers*, VII, 343.

101. Scott to BTW, Nov. 14, 1903, *BTW Papers*, VII, 344.

102. Fox, *Guardian of Boston*, 65–66.

103. Chisum to Scott, May 18, 1903, magazine prospectus with Scott's marginal note dated June 17, [1903].

104. Scott to BTW, July 28, 1903, *BTW Papers*, VII, 228.

105. Galveston *New Idea*, Sept. 12, 1903, clipping.

106. "Trotter and Trotterism," draft of an editorial for the New York *Age, ca.* Sept. 1905, *BTW Papers*, VIII, 382–87. On the disappearance of the Chisum report, see Harry C. Smith to BTW, March 9, 1906 [LC]; Washington to Scott, July 5, 1906 [LC]; Scott to BTW, July 7, 9, Aug. 9, 1906, *BTW Papers*, IX, 40–41, 54.

107. BTW to Fortune, Sept. 10, 1903, *BTW Papers*, VII, 280.

108. Lewis to BTW, Sept. 16, 1903, *BTW Papers*, VII, 285–86. Lewis did have Chisum draw up an affidavit before a notary public, however, for future reference. Lewis to Chisum, Sept. 5, 1903, *ibid.*, VII, 278.

109. Fortune to BTW, Sept. 14, 1903, *BTW Papers*, VII, 283–84.

110. Lewis to BTW, Sept. 11, 1903.

111. BTW to W. H. Moss, March 10 [1903], telegram.

112. Smith to BTW, Feb. 8, 1903.

113. Smith to BTW, July 17, 1903, *BTW Papers*, VII, 211.

114. Scott to BTW, Aug. 8 [1903].

115. BTW to Scott, Sept. 10, 1903.

116. Scott to Smith, Oct. 8, 1903.

117. Smith to Scott, Oct. 26, 1903.

118. Smith to BTW, Dec. 31, 1903.

119. Smith's note and receipt, Dec. 31, 1903.

120. Smith to Scott, Jan. 15, 1904, Scott to Smith, Jan. 21, 1904.

121. Scott to Smith, Jan. 28, 1904.

122. Scott to Alexander, Jan. 19, 1904, *BTW Papers*, VII, 404. See also Scott to Alexander, Jan. 10, 1904; BTW to Alexander, Jan. 20, 28, 1904; Alexander to Scott, Jan. 18, 1904; Alexander to BTW, Jan. 22, 1904.

123. Scott to Alexander, Jan. 19, 1904, *BTW Papers*, VII, 404.

124. BTW to Alexander, Jan. 20, 1904.

125. BTW to Alexander, Feb. 29, 1904.

126. BTW to Alexander, May 3, 1904; July 4, 1904, *BTW Papers*, VIII, 3.

127. BTW to Smith, Feb. 9, 1904.

128. Alexander to BTW, Feb. 17, 1904.

129. Scott to Alexander, Feb. 28, 1904.

130. Quoted in Fox, *Guardian of Boston*, 73.

131. BTW to Garrison, May 17, 1905, *BTW Papers*, VIII, 279–83.

132. BTW to Alexander, March 9, May 16, 19, 1904, Scott to Alexander, May 5, June 8, 1904.

133. BTW to Scott, July 8, 1904.

134. BTW to Smith, April 25, 1904.

135. Fox, *Guardian of Boston*, 73–74.

136. On Plummer's double game, see W. H. Moss to BTW, June 9, 1903; June 28, 1903, *BTW Papers*, VII, 185; Boston *Evening News*, July 31, 1903, clipping.

137. See the correspondence of Sept.–Oct. 1904 between BTW and W. W. Bryant and R. W. Taylor; Courtney to BTW, Sept. 27, 1904; letters and telegrams in Sept.–Oct. 1904 between BTW, Scott, and Plummer. The quoted passage is from Plummer to BTW, Oct. 19, 1904.

138. Plummer to BTW, Dec. 22, 1904, *BTW Papers*, VIII, 156.

139. BTW to Bradley Gilman, Jan. 9, 1905, *BTW Papers*, VIII, 175.

140. BTW to Gilman, Oct. 14, 1904, *BTW Papers*, VIII, 92.

141. BTW to Roosevelt, Sept. 15, 1903, *BTW Papers*, VII, 284–85.

Chapter 3

1. BTW to Fortune, Sept. 11, 1900, *BTW Papers*, V, 637.

2. BTW to Du Bois, Feb. 12, 1903, *BTW Papers*, VII, 71.

3. BTW to Fortune, Feb. 13, 1903.

4. BTW to Alexander Walters, Feb. 13, 1903, *BTW Papers*, VII, 73–74. Similar letters went to the others invited.

5. Boston *Guardian*, Feb. 28, 1903.

6. Du Bois to Miller, Feb. 25, 1903, quoted in Herbert Aptheker, "The Washington–Du Bois Conference of 1904," in his *Toward Negro Freedom* (New York, 1956), 98–99. Aptheker's is the most detailed treatment of the conference, based on the Du Bois correspondence.

7. BTW to Du Bois, March 27, 1903, *BTW Papers*, VII, 108–9.

8. Scott to BTW, Nov. 2, 1903, BTW Papers, Tuskegee Institute.

9. Miller to R. C. Bruce, Nov. 2, 1903.

10. BTW to Fortune, Nov. 5, 1903, *BTW Papers*, VII, 333–34.

11. BTW to Lyons, Nov. 8, 1903, *BTW Papers*, VII, 338.

12. BTW to Du Bois, Nov. 8, 1903, *BTW Papers*, VII, 339–40.

13. See Du Bois to BTW, undated, in Herbert Aptheker, ed., *The Correspondence of W. E. B. Du Bois* (3 vols., Amherst, 1973–78), I, 54.

14. BTW to Du Bois, Nov. 14, 1903.

15. Scott to BTW, Nov. 15, 1903.

16. Du Bois to BTW, undated, in Aptheker, ed., *Correspondence of W. E. B. Du Bois*, I, 54.

17. BTW to Lewis, Nov. 19, 1903, BTW Papers, Tuskegee Institute.

18. Morgan to BTW, Nov. 28, 1903, BTW Papers, Tuskegee Institute.

19. BTW to Morgan, Dec. 4, 1903, BTW Papers, Tuskegee Institute.

20. Quoted without a clear reference in Elliott M. Rudwick, *W. E. B. Du Bois: Propagandist of the Negro Protest* (New York, 1968), 78.

21. BTW to Du Bois, Nov. 8, 1903, *BTW Papers*, VII, 339–40.

22. BTW to Morris, Nov. 19, 1903, BTW Papers, Tuskegee Institute.

23. BTW to Williams, Nov. 19, 1903, Williams to BTW, Nov. 21, 1903, BTW Papers, Tuskegee Institute.

24. Lewis to BTW, Nov. 30, 1903 [LC]; BTW to Lewis, Dec. 3, 1903, *BTW Papers*, VII, 355–56.

25. BTW to Du Bois, Dec. 4, 1903, BTW Papers, Tuskegee Institute.

26. BTW to Francis J. Grimké, Dec. 5, 1903, *BTW Papers*, VII, 359.

27. BTW to Lewis, Dec. 4, 1903, BTW Papers, Tuskegee Institute.

28. F. J. Grimké to BTW, Dec. 9, 1903, *BTW Papers*, VII, 363.

29. BTW to Morris, Dec. 20, 1903 [LC]; BTW to Durham, Dec. 12, 1903, BTW Papers, Tuskegee Institute.

30. BTW to Lyons, Dec. 13, 1903, BTW Papers, Howard University; BTW to McGhee, Dec. 26, 1903, BTW Papers, Tuskegee Institute.

31. Morgan to BTW, Dec. 23, 1903, BTW Papers, Tuskegee Institute.

32. McKinlay to BTW, Dec. 29, 1903.

33. BTW to Fortune, Jan. 2, 1904.

34. BTW to McKinlay, Jan. 2, 1904, *BTW Papers*, VII, 383–84. A similar but not so frank letter went to Du Bois on the same date [LC].

35. Fortune to BTW, Dec. 28, 1903, BTW Papers, Tuskegee Institute.

36. BTW to Roosevelt, Dec. 28, 1903, *BTW Papers*, VII, 381.

37. BTW to Buttrick, Nov. 27, 1903.

38. Fortune to BTW, Dec. 15, 1903, BTW Papers, Tuskegee Institute.

39. Du Bois to Francis J. Grimké, Dec. 28, 1903, in Carter G. Woodson, ed., *The Works of Francis James Grimké* (4 vols., Washington, 1942), IV, 89–90.

40. Boston *Guardian*, Dec. 26, 1903, quoted in Fox, *Guardian of Boston*, 84.

41. BTW to Du Bois, Jan. 2, 1904 [LC]. See also BTW to McKinlay, Jan. 2, 1904, *BTW Papers*, VII, 383–84.

42. Fox, *Guardian of Boston*, 84.

43. Rudwick, *W. E. B. Du Bois*, 80.

44. Du Bois to Miss A. P. Moore, April 2, 1907, quoted in Aptheker, *Toward Negro Freedom*, 101.

45. Baldwin to BTW, Jan. 7, 1904, *BTW Papers*, VII, 387–88.

46. Du Bois, *The Autobiography of W. E. B. Du Bois: A Soliloquy on Viewing My Life from the Last Decade of Its First Century* (New York, 1968), 246–47.

47. Rudwick, *W. E. B. Du Bois*, 81.

48. Courtney to BTW, Jan. 13, 1904.

49. Summary of the Proceedings of the Conference at Carnegie Hall, Jan. 6–8, 1904, *BTW Papers*, VII, 384–87.

50. John H. Washington to BTW, Jan. 9, 1900, *BTW Papers*, VII, 388–89.

51. BTW to Courtney, Jan. 10, 1904, *BTW Papers*, VII, 389.

52. Courtney to BTW, Jan. 13, 1904.

53. BTW to Lewis, Jan. 22, 1904, *BTW Papers*, VII, 407–8.

54. Anderson to BTW, Jan. 26, 1904, *BTW Papers*, VII, 413–14.

55. Anderson to Scott, Jan. 20, 1904.

56. Scott to Anderson, Jan. 23, 1904; Scott to Lewis, Jan. 29, 1904.

57. Anderson to Scott, Feb. 17, 1904.

58. Moton to BTW, Jan. 14, 1904.

59. BTW to Moton, Jan. 18, 1904 [LC]; Jan. 22, 1904, *BTW Papers*, VII, 407.
60. BTW to Baldwin, Jan. 22, 1904, *BTW Papers*, VII, 409–10.
61. Asbury to Hayes, Jan. 23, 1904.
62. Moton to BTW, Jan. 18, 1904.
63. BTW to Fortune, Jan. 19, 1904, *BTW Papers*, VII, 401.
64. Louis G. Gregory to BTW, Jan. 15, 1904, *BTW Papers*, VII, 391.
65. Bruce to Moton, Jan. 13, 1904.
66. Adams to BTW, *ca.* Jan. 18, 1904, *BTW Papers*, VII, 397–98.
67. W. Bruce Evans to Scott, Feb. 2, 1904.
68. Evans to Moton, Jan. 13, 1904.
69. Dancy to BTW, Jan. 22, 1904.
70. Evans to Moton, Jan. 13, 1904.
71. Washington *Bee*, Jan. 16, 1904.
72. Daniel Murray to BTW, Jan. 16, 1904.
73. Scott to Moton, Jan. 22, 1904.
74. BTW to Anderson, Jan. 21, 1904.
75. Anderson to BTW, Jan. 26, 1904, *BTW Papers*, VII, 414.
76. BTW to Du Bois, Jan. 27, 1904, *BTW Papers*, VII, 414–15.
77. This would cost very little, for Schurz had told Washington that a Massachusetts woman had given him $200 toward the cost of printing. Hugh M. Browne to BTW, Jan. 28, 1904; BTW to Browne, Feb. 23, 1904.
78. Du Bois to BTW, Jan. 30, 1904.
79. BTW, "Suggestions for Committee of Twelve," undated typescript, *ca.* Feb. 1904.
80. Du Bois, "Suggestions as to the Committee of Safety submitted to the sub-committee of organization," Feb. 20, 1904.
81. BTW to Browne, March 4, 1904, *BTW Papers*, VII, 459–60, paraphrasing what he had written to Du Bois.
82. Anderson to BTW, June 27, 1904.
83. Nina G. Du Bois to BTW, June 25, 1904.
84. See, for example, Scott to BTW, April 27, 1908, *BTW Papers*, IX, 511–12; BTW to R. A. Franks, Dec. 28, 1909 [LC].
85. Scott to BTW, July 14, 1904.
86. *Ibid.*
87. Copy enclosed in Browne to Du Bois, July 28, 1904, quoted in Aptheker, *Toward Negro Freedom*, 101–2.
88. BTW to Grimké, July 8, 1904, *BTW Papers*, VIII, 9.
89. Grimké to BTW, July 13, 1904, *BTW Papers*, VIII, 16–17.
90. Margaret L. Callcott, *The Negro in Maryland Politics, 1870–1912* (Baltimore, 1969), 101–38.
91. Cummings to BTW, Sept. 21, Nov. 3, 1905.
92. The Committee of Twelve printed 10,000 copies of the Grimké pamphlet on voting rights, and distributed them throughout the South. BTW to A. E. Pillsbury, Jan. 25, 1905.
93. BTW to A. B. Humphrey, Sept. 29, 1905, *BTW Papers*, VIII, 381.

94. Cummings to BTW, Nov. 8, 1905, *BTW Papers*, VIII, 436.

95. Cummings to BTW, June 22, 1909.

96. Scott to Harry T. Pratt, Dec. 6, 1909; W. M. Alexander to BTW, Dec. 28, 1909.

97. BTW to H. B. Frissell, Nov. 8, 1906, Hampton Institute Archives.

Chapter 4

1. *Voice of the Negro*, II (Jan. 1905), 677. Meier, *Negro Thought in America,* is the indispensable source on black ideologies of this period. See also William Toll, *The Resurgence of Race: Black Social Theory from Reconstruction to the Pan-African Conferences* (Philadelphia, 1979).

2. Louis R. Harlan, "Booker T. Washington and the *Voice of the Negro,* 1904–1907," *Journal of Southern History,* XLV (Feb. 1979), 50–51; BTW to J. W. E. Bowen, Dec. 27, 1904, *BTW Papers*, VIII, 167–68.

3. Du Bois to Villard, March 24, 1905, *BTW Papers*, VIII, 224–42.

4. Villard to Du Bois, April 18, 1905; also see Francis J. Garrison to Villard, April 9, 1905, Du Bois to Villard, April 20, 1905, Garrison to BTW, May 8, 1905, BTW to Garrison, May 17, 1905, *BTW Papers*, VIII, 251–52, 261–63, 265–67, 273–75, 279–83.

5. Williams to Scott, July 10, 1905, *BTW Papers*, VIII, 324–26.

6. Cox to BTW, July 6, 1905.

7. BTW to Cox, July 10, 1905, *BTW Papers*, VIII, 322. Apparently BTW also had two other spies at Buffalo, one known only as Crosby, and the other a friend of his wife, Mary Burnett Talbert. See BTW to Anderson, July 8, 1905, BTW to Margaret J. Washington, July 8, 1905, *BTW Papers*, VIII, 321.

8. Cox to BTW, July 11, 1905.

9. Plummer to BTW, July 12, 13, 1905, *BTW Papers*, VIII, 326.

10. Boston *Transcript* July 15, 1905.

11. Plummer to BTW, July 16, 1905, *BTW Papers*, VIII, 328–29.

12. BTW to Scott, July 17, 1905, *BTW Papers*, VIII, 329.

13. Scott to Thompson, July 18, 1905, *BTW Papers*, VIII, 331.

14. Thompson to Scott, July 20, 1905.

15. Scott to BTW, July 24, 1905, *BTW Papers*, VIII, 331–32.

16. BTW to Scott, July 27, 1905, *BTW Papers*, VIII, 332.

17. Cable to Thompson, undated, *ca.* Aug. 1, 1905.

18. BTW to Scott, Aug. 7, 1905, *BTW Papers*, VIII, 337–38.

19. See, for example, Scott to Thompson, Oct. 2, 1905; Charles R. Douglass to Scott, undated, *ca.* Nov. 1905; Scott to Douglass, Nov. 29, 1905.

20. Scott to Benjamin F. Allen, Dec. 21, 1905.

21. Du Bois, circular letter to members, June 13, 1906.

22. Spelling *sic.* See the discussion of Greener's experience as a consul in Allison Blakely, "Richard T. Greener and the 'Talented Tenth's' Dilemma," *Journal of Negro History,* LIX (Oct. 1974), 305–21.

23. Greener to BTW, July 31, 1906 and Scott's docketing note dated Aug. 2, 1906, *BTW Papers*, IX, 48.

24. BTW to Greener, Aug. 7, 1906, Greener to BTW, Aug. 11, 1906, *BTW Papers*, IX, 51, 55; BTW to Greener, Aug. 9, 1906 [LC].

25. BTW to Greener, Aug. 11, 1906, *BTW Papers*, IX, 55–56.

26. Greener to BTW, Aug. 23, 1906, *BTW Papers*, IX, 61.

27. BTW to Greener, Aug. 24, Oct. 20, 1906, Greener to BTW, Oct. 15, 1906.

28. Greener to BTW, Feb. 23, 1907.

29. BTW to William Loeb, Jr., June 12, 1907; Greener to BTW, June 23, 1907.

30. Greener to BTW, Aug. 31, 1907.

31. Cornelius B. Hosmer to Scott, April 20, 1912, written from an NAACP meeting.

32. BTW to James R. Wood Detective Agency, July 18, 1906.

33. James R. Wood, Jr., to BTW, July 19, 1906, *BTW Papers*, IX, 45–46.

34. BTW to Wood, Feb. 15, 25, 1907.

35. BTW to Anderson, Dec. 30, 1905, *BTW Papers*, VIII, 471.

36. See E. A. Johnson to BTW, Sept. 6, 26, Oct. 6, 9, 14, 1905, BTW to Johnson, Sept. 22, 29, Oct. 12, 1905; Robert H. Terrell to BTW, Sept. 24, 1905, BTW to Terrell, Sept. 29, Dec. 12, 1905; Johnson to BTW, Oct. 2, 1905.

37. Chisum to BTW, Feb. 16, 1906, *BTW Papers*, VIII, 522–23. Chisum reported that when Chase heard of a dinner in Washington's honor at which Washington was to speak, he said that "the niggers ought to have the thing published in the Bee," and that Chisum's reply was, "Get Busy Man."

38. Chisum to BTW, Feb. 19, 1906, *BTW Papers*, VIII, 526–27. See also Chisum to BTW, Feb. 17, 1906, 523–24.

39. Anderson to BTW, Feb. 21, 1906.

40. BTW to Chisum, Feb. 24, 1906, *BTW Papers*, VIII, 534.

41. For evidence of payment, see Chisum to BTW, Feb. 26, 1906, *BTW Papers*, VIII, 534–35.

42. Anderson to BTW, March 5, 1906, *BTW Papers*, VIII, 538.

43. BTW to Anderson, March 8, 1906, *BTW Papers*, VIII, 541–42.

44. Chisum to BTW, Feb. 17, March 28, 1906, *BTW Papers*, VIII, 523–24, 556–57.

45. Chisum to BTW, March 21, 1906, *BTW Papers*, VIII, 555–56.

46. Chisum to BTW, June 16, 1906, *BTW Papers*, IX, 31–32.

47. Chisum to BTW, July 12, 1906, *BTW Papers*, IX, 41.

48. BTW to Chisum, Aug. 4, 1906, *BTW Papers*, IX, 50. This was sent from a train in the Midwest en route to New York City.

49. Chisum to BTW, Oct. 11, 1906, *BTW Papers*, IX, 94.

50. Chisum to BTW, May 26, 1914.

51. Melvin J. Chisum's trail after the Washington years is obscure. See Wendell P. Dabney, *Chisum's Pilgrimage and Others* (Cincinnati, 1927); Pete Daniel, "Black Power in the 1920s: The Case of Tuskegee Veterans Hospital,"

Journal of Southern History, XXXVI (Aug. 1970), 368–88; William H. Harris, *Keeping the Faith: A Philip Randolph, Milton P. Webster, and the Brotherhood of Sleeping Car Porters, 1925–37* (Urbana, Ill., 1977), 15–16, 53–55.

52. Anderson to BTW, March 31, 1906; also see Anderson to BTW, March 23, 1906.

53. Anderson to BTW, April 3, 1906, *BTW Papers,* VIII, 560–61.

54. BTW to Anderson, April 10, 1906, *BTW Papers,* VIII, 574–75.

55. Anderson to BTW, Dec. 11, 1906.

56. BTW to Fred R. Moore, Nov. 5, 1907.

57. There are two good, complementary histories of early black Harlem, Gilbert Osofsky, *Harlem: The Making of a Ghetto, Negro New York, 1890–1930* (New York, 1966), and Seth M. Scheiner, *Negro Mecca: A History of the Negro in New York City, 1865–1920* (New York, 1965). Unfortunately, Constance McLaughlin Green, *The Secret City: A History of Race Relations in the Nation's Capital* (Princeton, 1967), does not offer the same depth of treatment or understanding of the black community of Washington.

58. In the latter half of her sensitive biography, *T. Thomas Fortune: Militant Journalist* (Chicago, 1972), Emma Lou Thornbrough furnishes many examples of Fortune's ambivalence and Washington's dominance until the Brownsville crisis precipitated a break between the two men.

59. Kenneth L. Kusmer, *A Ghetto Takes Shape: Black Cleveland, 1870–1930* (Urbana, Ill., 1976), 140. Elsewhere in the book Kusmer elaborates the interrelationship between changing business and occupational structure and black leadership. This closely parallels Meier, *Negro Thought in America,* 42–58, 139–57, in explaining the growing black solidarity in terms of changing class structure.

60. Furniss to BTW, Oct. 3, 1905, Grant to BTW, Nov. 1, 1905, *BTW Papers,* VIII, 390–91, 434; BTW to Furniss, Nov. 25, 1905 [LC].

61. Thompson to Scott, June 21, 1906.

62. An excellent history of blacks in Chicago in this period is Allan H. Spear, *Black Chicago: The Making of a Negro Ghetto, 1890–1920* (Chicago, 1967), which makes extensive use of the Booker T. Washington Papers to cast light on Chicago black affairs.

63. Sweeney to BTW, Dec. 4, 1905, Sweeney to Scott, telegram, Dec. 12, 1905, Scott to Sweeney, telegram, Dec. 12, 1905.

64. BTW to Sweeney, Dec. 4, 1905, and enclosure.

65. Clipping enclosed in Sweeney to Scott, Dec. 16, 1905.

66. Sweeney to Scott, Dec. 16, 27, 1905 [LC]; Sweeney to BTW, undated, *ca.* March 1906 [LC]; Sweeney to Scott, Dec. 25, 1905, BTW to Sweeney, Dec. 30, 1905, *BTW Papers,* VIII, 468–69, 470.

67. Fred R. Moore to Williams, telegram, Feb. 2, 1906, *BTW Papers,* VIII, 515.

68. Williams to BTW, Feb. 17, 1906, *BTW Papers,* VIII, 524–25. Another Chicago friend confirmed Williams's view that the *Conservator* could be purchased for a small sum. Robert T. Motts to C. W. Anderson, Feb. 16, 1906 [LC].

69. See Kealing to Scott, Dec. 29, 1906, Feb. 2, 1907, Scott to Kealing, Feb. 7, 1907.

70. BTW to Wilkins, April 17, 1907, *BTW Papers*, IX, 262.

71. D. H. Williams to Scott, April 20, 1907 [LC]. Scott was highly amused at Du Bois's recent reference to Wilkins as "an unpurchasable man." He wrote to BTW: "When he reads Wilkins' editorial of last week, I am sure he will have fits!" Scott to BTW, April 23, 1907, *BTW Papers*, IX, 265.

72. D. H. Williams to Scott, April 20, 1907.

73. Scott to D. H. Williams, July 31, 1907.

74. D. H. Williams to BTW, Jan. 12, 16, 1908, *BTW Papers*, IX, 441, 442–43.

75. Trice to BTW, Feb. 3, 1908.

76. Trice to BTW, Feb. 24, 1908.

77. BTW to Trice, March 2, 1908, *BTW Papers*, IX, 460.

78. Trice to BTW, March 4, 1908, telegram.

79. Trice to BTW, March 12, 1908, *BTW Papers*, IX, 466–67.

80. BTW to Trice, March 24, 1908, *BTW Papers*, IX, 479. The party referred to was Ralph W. Tyler, whom BTW had wired: "Better get in close and immediate touch with Trice. Plans may be thwarted and enemy get charge of paper unless you keep in close touch. May have to render little extra help." BTW to Tyler, March 21, 1908, *BTW Papers*, IX, 475.

81. The new editor was M. A. Majors. Trice to BTW, March 26, 1908, BTW to Trice, March 30, 1908.

82. Trice to BTW, March 28, May 15, 1908, BTW to Trice, May 28, 1908.

83. Meier, *Negro Thought in America*, 226.

84. Asbury to BTW, March 9, 1906.

85. Dancy to Scott, March 19, 1906.

86. Atlanta *Independent*, Aug. 25, 1906, clipping.

87. Davis to BTW, Sept. 3, 1906.

88. See, for example, Scott to John E. Bush, Sept. 24, 1906, telegram.

89. Asbury to BTW, Oct. 3, 1906, telegram.

90. BTW to Dancy, Oct. 4, 1906, telegram.

91. See, for example, BTW to R. H. Terrell, Oct. 4, 1906, telegram; J. E. Bush to BTW, Oct. 4, 1906, enclosing copy of telegram to Dancy.

92. BTW to Asbury, Nov. 15, 1906.

93. Asbury to Scott, Aug. 28, Sept. 29, 1908.

94. Whitefield McKinlay to BTW, Sept. 16, 1910.

95. Samuel E. Courtney to BTW, Nov. 29, 1907; Nelson P. Wentworth to BTW, Feb. 6, 1908.

96. Frederic S. Monroe to BTW, May 27, 1908, *BTW Papers*, IX, 543–44.

97. BTW to Monroe, June 5, 1908, *BTW Papers*, IX, 555–56.

98. The subject is treated in detail in Harlan, "Booker T. Washington and the *Voice of the Negro*, 1904–1907," 45–62.

99. *Voice of the Negro*, I (Jan. 1904), 33, 37–38.

100. Scott to Barber, July 23, 1904.

101. *Voice of the Negro*, II (Jan. 1905), 677.

102. Scott to Wilford H. Smith, Dec. 22, 1904, Smith to Scott, Dec. 26, 1904 [LC]; Scott to Smith, Dec. 31, 1904 [LC]; Philip A. Payton to *Voice of the Negro*, Jan. 4, 1905 [LC]; BTW to John A. Hertel, March 15, 1905, *BTW Papers*, VIII, 218.

103. BTW to Hertel, Aug. 7, 1905, *BTW Papers*, VIII, 338–39.

104. Hertel to BTW, Aug. 9, 1905, *BTW Papers*, VIII, 340.

105. Unsigned letter to the editor of the New York *Age*, Oct. 1, 1906, *BTW Papers*, IX, 82–83.

106. Scott to S. Laing Williams, Oct. 19, 1906.

107. BTW to John T. Emlen, June 13, 1908, *BTW Papers*, IX, 572–73.

108. Barber to Walter White, June 14, 1918, NAACP Archives, LC.

Chapter 5

1. *Tuskegee Student*, XIII (Sept. 28, 1901), 3.

2. Boston *Globe*, Oct. 20, 1901, clipping.

3. Alicia M. Keyes to BTW, April 21, 1902.

4. Katherine Coman to BTW, Jan. 22, 1902.

5. Boston *Globe*, Oct. 20, 1901, clipping.

6. Montgomery *Advertiser*, Nov. 6, 1902.

7. Caroline Hazard to the editor, in Boston *Transcript*, Nov. 10, 1902.

8. New York *American*, Nov. 4, 1902, clipping.

9. Boston *Guardian*, Oct. 4, 1902, quoted in Fox, *Guardian of Boston*, 39.

10. BTW to Julian L. Harris, Oct. 16, 1902, *BTW Papers*, VI, 549–50.

11. Fortune to BTW, Nov. 3, 1902, *BTW Papers*, VI, 571–72.

12. BTW to Fortune, Nov. 6, 1902, *BTW Papers*, VI, 577.

13. Portia M. Washington to BTW, Oct. 25, 1902.

14. Laura Knott to BTW, Nov. 11, 1902.

15. Editorial in the New York *Times*, Nov. 4, 1902; BTW to the editor, in New York *Times*, Nov. 15, 1902.

16. Boston *Guardian*, Nov. 22, 1902.

17. BTW to Baldwin, published in the New York *Age* and reprinted in Boston *Guardian*, Nov. 22, 1902.

18. Scott to Knott, Oct. 15, 1903.

19. BTW to Cora L. C. White, April 29, 1904, *BTW Papers*, VII, 491.

20. BTW to Portia M. Washington, Feb. 24, 1904.

21. Portia M. Washington to BTW, March 10, 1904.

22. BTW to Portia M. Washington, March 12, 1904.

23. BTW to Portia M. Washington, March 22, 1904.

24. Portia M. Washington to BTW, Oct. 23, 1904.

25. Portia M. Washington to BTW, Sept. 29, 1904.

26. Portia M. Washington to BTW, March 1, April 5, 1905.

27. Alice H. Luce to BTW, April 26, [1905].

28. BTW to Jane E. Clark, June 5, 1905.

29. BTW, Jr., to BTW, March 18, 1902.

30. Benner to BTW, May 30, 1903, *BTW Papers*, VII, 165–66.

31. *Ibid.*

32. Benner to BTW, Oct. 24, 1903, *BTW Papers*, VII, 309–10.

33. BTW to Benner, Jan. 20, 1904.

34. BTW to Benner, Feb. 29, 1904, *BTW Papers*, VII, 454.

35. BTW, Jr., to BTW, March 6, 1904.

36. Margaret M. Washington to Scott, April 19, 1904.

37. BTW to Benner, May 5, 1904, *BTW Papers*, VII, 495.

38. Hugh M. Browne to BTW, Aug. 19, 1904.

39. New York *World*, Oct. 23, 1904, *BTW Papers*, VIII, 105–7.

40. Hervey W. Laird to BTW, Nov. 10, 28, 1904.

41. BTW to Frank P. Glass, Nov. 8, 1904, BTW press release to Associated Press, Nov. 9, 1904 [LC]; BTW to Whitefield McKinlay, Nov. 8, 1904, *BTW Papers*, VIII, 124. Booker was also "accused" of attending the Massachusetts Institute of Technology. Tuskegee *News*, Nov. 17, 1904. BTW attributed these stories to partisan frenzy of the final days of the 1904 election campaign.

42. BTW to Dr. Frankle [or Frankel], April 13, 1905.

43. Lexa Calloway to Margaret M. Washington, Dec. 12, 1905.

44. BTW to W. D. Sprague, Dec. 28, 1905, Jan. 10, 1906.

45. *Tuskegee Student*, XIX (May 11, 1907), 2.

46. BTW to BTW, Jr., May 27, 1907, *BTW Papers*, IX, 273–74; BTW to Portia M. Washington, July 3, 1907 [LC].

47. J. W. E. Bowen to BTW, Sept. 3, 1907.

48. Birmingham *Ledger*, Oct. 7, 1907, and other clippings.

49. Harlan P. Amen to BTW, Nov. 7, 1907.

50. BTW to the editor of the Boston *American*, Oct. 7, 1907.

51. John F. Peck to Margaret M. Washington, Oct. 14, 1904.

52. BTW to Peck, Dec. 28, 1904.

53. Elwood T. Easton to Margaret M. Washington, Aug. 4, 1905; BTW to Edward E. Scott, Dec. 27, 1905.

54. BTW to Portia M. Washington, Jan. 9, 1906, *BTW Papers*, VIII, 490; BTW to E. Davidson Washington, Jan. 11, 1906 [LC].

55. BTW to Portia M. Washington, Nov. 15, 1906, *BTW Papers*, IX, 127.

56. BTW to Mary A. Elliott, Oct. 21, 1908, *BTW Papers*, IX, 666.

57. Jane E. Clark to BTW, Aug. 2, 1905.

58. BTW to Portia M. Washington, Feb. 25, 1906.

59. Interview with Portia W. Pittman, Jan. 15, 1967.

60. Portia M. Washington to BTW, June 29, 1906, *BTW Papers*, IX, 37–38.

61. BTW to Portia M. Washington, Nov. 15, 1906, *BTW Papers*, IX, 127.

62. Portia M. Washington to BTW, June 29, 1906, *BTW Papers*, IX, 37–38.

63. Portia M. Washington to BTW, June 27, 1906, *BTW Papers*, IX, 36–37.

64. R. W. Thompson to Scott, Dec. 30, 1906.

65. Engagement announcement in *Tuskegee Student*, XIX (Sept. 21, 1907), 1.

66. Los Angeles *Tribune*, Dec. 13, 1914, clipping [LC]; biographical annotation in *BTW Papers*, II, 236–37.

67. Wedding account in *Tuskegee Student*, XIX (Nov. 1, 1907), 1.

68. W. S. Pittman to BTW, Dec. 11, 1907.

69. BTW to W. S. Pittman, Dec. 12, 1907.

70. BTW to Fred W. Carpenter, Feb. 20, 1908, Carpenter to BTW, Feb. 22, 1908, William Howard Taft Papers, LC.

71. *Tuskegee Student*, XX (June 20, 1908), 1.

72. W. S. Pittman to BTW, April 28, 1909 [LC]; interview of Portia W. Pittman in Washington *Post*, Nov. 14, 1965, A15.

73. Interview with Portia W. Pittman, Jan. 15, 1967.

74. Obituary in Washington *Post*, Oct. 15, 1969, E6.

75. Roy L. Hill, *Booker T's Child: The Life and Times of Portia Marshall Washington Pittman* (Newark, 1974), *passim*.

76. BTW to Thomas W. Talley, Nov. 24, 1907, *BTW Papers*, IX, 409–10.

77. BTW to Herbert H. Wright, Jan. 29, 1909.

78. George W. Moore to BTW, Feb. 25, 1909.

79. "Booker T. Washington, Jr., Speaks," Nashville *Globe*, reprinted in *Tuskegee Student*, XXI (March 13, 1909), 1.

80. BTW, Jr., to BTW, May 13, 1909.

81. BTW to BTW, Jr., Dec. 28, 1909.

82. BTW, Jr., to BTW, Aug. 29, 1910.

83. BTW to Dora Scribner, June 28, 1911; Scribner to BTW, July 5, 1911.

84. BTW to Amen, Dec. 2, 1911.

85. BTW to Herbert H. Wright, June 20, 1913.

86. Margaret M. Washington to Mrs. Hancock, Jan. 3, 1914.

87. BTW to BTW, Jr., Feb. 7, 1914.

88. BTW to Professor Patterson, March 11, 1914.

89. BTW to BTW, Jr., June 16, 18, 1914.

90. BTW to Clinton J. Calloway, June 27, July 16, Aug. 8, 1914 [LC]; Hill, *Booker T's Child*, photograph following p. 38.

91. Obituary of Nettie Hancock Washington in Washington *Post*, Oct. 29, 1972; biographical annotation in *BTW Papers*, II, 361–62.

92. BTW to E. D. Washington, Sept. 25, 1910.

93. BTW to E. D. Washington, May 6, 1911; J. M. P. Metcalf to BTW, May 19, 1911.

94. Dr. John A. Kenney, statement on E. D. Washington's eye condition, Jan. 22, 1909.

95. Lester A. Walton to E. D. Washington, Jan. 25, 1913.

96. "Toney" to E. D. Washington, May 24, 1913.

97. Victoria M. Wheat to BTW, June 4, 1914.

98. Interview with Edith Washington Shehee, Aug. 25, 1968; E. J. Scott to E. D. Washington, Nov. 24, 1914; obituary in Norfolk *Journal and Guide*, Oct. 8, 1938, clipping.

99. See Louis R. Harlan, *Booker T. Washington: The Making of a Black Leader, 1856–1901* (New York, 1972).

100. William V. Chambliss to BTW, March 26, 1908, *BTW Papers*, IX, 480–81.

101. Photograph, 1906, in *BTW Papers*, VIII, facing p. 498.

102. BTW to Laura Washington, Dec. 7, 1914.

103. Laura Washington to BTW, Dec. 9, 14, 1914.

104. BTW to Laura Washington, Oct. 15, 22, 1915.

105. Montgomery *Advertiser*, July 16, 1925, clipping.

106. Wedding invitation, June 30, 1908.

107. BTW to Benjamin Johnston, June 15, 1908.

108. Amanda Johnston to BTW, Oct. 18, 1901. See also Clara Johnston to BTW, July 3, 1900; bill for house repairs, Oct. 18, 1901.

109. Amanda Johnston to BTW, Sept. 4, 1902, *BTW Papers*, VI, 508.

110. George M. Jones to BTW, Sept. 3, 1903; Amanda Johnston to BTW, Feb. 10, 1904.

111. BTW to G. W. A. Johnston, Feb. 25, 1905.

112. Amanda Johnston to BTW, April 10, 1905, BTW to Amanda Johnston, May 12, 1905.

113. Clara Johnston to BTW, Oct. 28, 1906.

114. BTW to Ruffner, Dec. 31, 1910, Jan. 24, 1911; Amanda Johnston to BTW, Aug. 27, 1911.

115. Clara Johnston to BTW, April 29, 1914. She added: "I notice my mothers talking a little absence minded Sunday night after service but laughed it off in a joke to her and paid no attention until eight o'clock Monday morning. I think she is a little better to day."

116. Byrd Prillerman to BTW, April 22, 1915.

117. BTW telegram to Clara Johnston, May 4, 1915, BTW to G. W. A. Johnston, May 6, 1915, Byrd Prillerman to BTW, May 6, 1915.

118. BTW to Prillerman, May 10, 1915 [LC]; see biographical annotation of Prillerman, *BTW Papers*, IV, 357–58.

Chapter 6

1. BTW, "The Higher and the Lower Life," *Southern Workman*, XXXVI (Sept. 1907), 478.

2. John D. Rockefeller, Jr., to BTW, Dec. 21, 1901, *BTW Papers*, VI, 357.

3. John D. Rockefeller, Jr., to BTW, June 24, 1903, *BTW Papers*, VII, 183.

4. *The General Education Board: An Account of Its Activities, 1902–14* (New York, 1915), table of subscriptions to colleges, 155–59.

5. Eastman to BTW, Jan. 2, 1902, *BTW Papers*, VI, 370.

6. Emery to BTW, Jan. 31, 1903.

7. BTW to Emery, Feb. 27, 1903, *BTW Papers*, VII, 100–101.

8. BTW, "H. H. Rogers as a Cash Giver," New York *Evening Post*, May 29, 1909, *BTW Papers*, X, 122–26.

9. *Ibid.*, 124.

10. *Ibid.*, 122; BTW to H. H. Rogers, Jr., June 7, 1909 [LC].

11. BTW to Rogers, Nov. 9, 1906.

12. On various aspects of the tour, see W. T. B. Williams, "With Dr. Wash-

ington through Virginia," *Southern Workman*, XXXVIII (Aug. 1909), 452–57; Calvin E. Henike to BTW, July 5, Oct. 7, 1909, BTW to Henike, July 7, 1909, BTW to Raymond Du Puy, Sept. 29, 1909, *BTW Papers*, X, 143–51, 177, 182–83.

13. Unsigned note, June 29, 1899.

14. Scott and Stowe, *Booker T. Washington*, 257–58.

15. William T. Eaton to BTW, Feb. 10, 1902 [LC]. On the description and cost of the building, see BTW to Carnegie, June 22, 1901, *BTW Papers*, VI, 158; BTW to Carnegie, May 1, 1902 [LC]; Indianapolis *Freeman*, May 3, 1902.

16. W. E. B. Du Bois, "Reminiscences," 150, Oral History Research Office, Columbia University.

17. Quoted in New York *Times*, April 15, 1903.

18. Ellen Collins to BTW, April 15, 1903.

19. Extracts from BTW's address, April 14, 1903, *BTW Papers*, VII, 113–19.

20. George McAneny, "Reminiscences," 30, Oral History Research Office, Columbia University.

21. Carnegie to Baldwin, April 17, 1903, *BTW Papers*, VII, 120.

22. BTW to Carnegie, April 19, 1903, Andrew Carnegie Papers, LC. Misfiled in 1907.

23. McAneny to Robert C. Ogden, April 24, 1903, Robert C. Ogden Papers, LC.

24. McAneny, "Reminiscences," 30.

25. Andrew Carnegie, *Autobiography* (Garden City, N. Y., 1923), 265–66. See also telegrams from BTW to Baldwin, April 21, 22, 1903, Baldwin to BTW, April 21, 22, 23, 24, 1903 [LC].

26. Quoted in New York *World*, April 24, 1903, clipping.

27. Baldwin to the Trustees of Tuskegee Institute, May 23, 1903, Baldwin to BTW, May 25, 1903, *BTW Papers*, VII, 154–58.

28. Boston *Record*, April 25, 1903, clipping.

29. Tuskegee *News*, May 14, 1903; New York *Age*, May 21, 1903, clipping; Indianapolis *Freeman*, May 30, 1903.

30. Washington aided the following schools, in approximately chronological order, to secure Carnegie grants: Wilberforce University. Snow Hill Normal and Industrial Institute, Livingstone College, Georgia State Industrial College, Wiley University, Biddle University, Alabama State Normal College in Montgomery, Fisk University, Howard University, Allen University, Christiansburg Normal and Industrial School, Mt. Meigs Colored Institute, Paine College, Rust University, Topeka Normal and Industrial Institute, Virginia Union University, Western University, Kentucky State University (Louisville), Prairie View Normal and Industrial Institute, Atlanta Baptist College, Lincoln University, and Calhoun Colored School. He also aided efforts to secure Carnegie branch libraries for blacks in Atlanta, Louisville, Montgomery, Jacksonville, New Orleans, Birmingham, Houston, Little Rock, and Liberia. He endorsed the efforts of several white institutions, notably the Girls Industrial School in Montevallo, Ala., Millsaps College, and LaGrange Female College.

He aided the efforts of C. B. Purvis of Howard University and G. M. P. King of Virginia Union University to secure Carnegie pensions. He secured an organ for Tuskegee's chapel and aided H. H. Proctor to get one for his church in Atlanta.

31. BTW to Carnegie, Dec. 15, 1910, Andrew Carnegie Papers, LC.

32. Carnegie to BTW, Nov. 30, 1906 [LC]; BTW to Carnegie, Dec. 7, 1906, Andrew Carnegie Papers, LC.

33. Bertram tt BTW, Jan. 30, 1910, BTW to Bertram, Feb. 1, 1910.

34. Jeannette E. Bertram to BTW, Dec. 30, 1910.

35. Typescript of Carnegie's address, April 5, 1906.

36. BTW to Hope, Dec. 13, 1906, *BTW Papers*, IX, 164–65.

37. BTW to Charlotte Thorn, April 11, 1913.

38. Scott to Bertram, July 21, 1910; typescript prospectus of a Carnegie Endowment for the Negro, undated; Park to Bertram, Feb. 13, 1913; Bertram to Park, June 2, 1915.

39. BTW to Carnegie, Nov. 26, 1913, Carnegie to BTW, Nov. 29, 1913.

40. Lillian D. Wald to Baldwin, May 11, 1903.

41. BTW to Baldwin, May 20, 1904.

42. Schiff to BTW, June 16, 1909, microfilm reel 677, p. 114a, Jacob H. Schiff Papers, American Jewish Archives, Hebrew Union College, Cincinnati.

43. BTW to Ruth S. Baldwin, Jan. 25, 1912.

44. BTW to Belton Gilreath, Feb. 5, 1912.

45. Rosenwald to BTW, May 31, 1912.

46. BTW to Rosenwald, March 29, 1912, Sept. 19, 1913.

47. Rosenwald to BTW, Aug. 5, 1912, Aug. 12, 1912.

48. Rosenwald to BTW, April 21, 1915, BTW to Rosenwald, *ca.* April 25, 1915.

49. BTW had tried at least once earlier to approach Ford. See E. G. Siebold, secretary to Henry Ford, to BTW, June 3, 1911. See Jacob G. Schmidlapp to Ford, June 24, 1915, enclosed in Schmidlapp to BTW, June 24, 1915.

Chapter 7

1. R. C. Bruce to BTW, Feb. 22, 1902, *BTW Papers*, VI, 408–11.

2. Among the general works on the theme of efficiency are Samuel Haber, *Efficiency and Uplift: Scientific Management in the Progressive Era, 1890–1920* (Chicago, 1964); Samuel P. Hays, *Conservation and the Gospel of Efficiency* (Cambridge, 1959); and Raymond Callahan, *Education and the Cult of Efficiency* (Chicago, 1962).

3. Report of J. H. Washington's committee to the executive council, June 10, 1903.

4. BTW to William H. Baldwin, Jr., Oct. 20, 1903, *BTW Papers*, VI, 299.

5. Petition of ten students to R. C. Bruce, Sept. 25, 1903.

6. Minutes of the executive council, Sept. 27, 1903.

7. Minutes of the executive council, Sept. 28, 29, 1903.

8. Minutes of the executive council, Oct. 20, 1903.

9. BTW to Baldwin, Oct. 20, 1903, *BTW Papers,* VI, 298–300.

10. BTW to Baldwin, Oct. 23, 1903, *BTW Papers,* VI, 306–7.

11. BTW to Baldwin, March 15, 1904, *BTW Papers,* VI, 467–68.

12. Bruce to the academic faculty, Jan. 10, 1905.

13. Hill to Bruce, Jan. 14, 1905.

14. BTW's handwritten draft of his annual report to the trustees of Tuskegee Institute, 1905.

15. BTW's annual report to the trustees of Tuskegee Institute, June 29, 1906.

16. Bruce to BTW, April 12, 1906.

17. BTW to Bruce, April 14, 1906.

18. Lee to BTW, Nov. 14, 1906.

19. BTW to Ruth Anna Fisher, Nov. 14, 1906, *BTW Papers,* IX, 125–26. See also the annotation recounting her subsequent career, BTW's letter to the president of Oberlin, and the angry protest of her father, 126–27, 128, 142.

20. Lee to BTW, Nov. 14, 1906.

21. BTW to Ella Flagg Young, May 17, 1907.

22. John C. Wright, "The Teaching of English at Tuskegee," undated typescript, *ca.* 1908.

23. BTW to Wright, April 5, 1910, *BTW Papers,* X, 311.

24. BTW to Lee, Nov. 7, 1912.

25. Lee to Scott, Nov. 8, 1913; BTW to Mrs. C. S. Smith, J. G. Jordan, and others, Feb. 13, 1915.

26. Undated salary list, *ca.* 1903.

27. Memorandum from the auditing department, May 31, 1908.

28. Bruce to BTW, undated, *ca.* June 1904.

29. See, for examples, BTW to James H. Van Sickle, Sept. 13 and *ca.* Sept. 20, 1904; BTW to Margaret P. Murrell, April 25, May 3, 6, 1904, Murrell to Secretary of the Board of Education of Washington, D. C., April 2, 1904; BTW to L. R. Wormley, July 28, 1905.

30. Scott to Bruce, July 28, 1904, Bruce to Scott, July 30, 1904.

31. Houston to J. Henry Duckrey, Sept. 28, 1904.

32. BTW to Bruce, Oct. 13, 18, 1904.

33. Houston to Duckrey, Sept. 28, 1906.

34. Houston to Duckrey, March 3, 1907; Houston to BTW, April 15, May 24, 28, 29, 1907.

35. Courtney to BTW, June 14, 1907.

36. Duckrey to BTW, June 15, 1907.

37. Courtney to BTW, July 12, 1907, *BTW Papers,* IX, 302.

38. Scott to BTW, July 24, 1907.

39. Houston to BTW, July 31, 1907.

40. BTW to Houston, Aug. 5, 1907, *BTW Papers,* IX, 330–31.

41. Houston to BTW, Aug. 6, 1907, *BTW Papers,* IX, 332.

42. BTW to J. H. N. Waring, Aug. 8, 1907. See also BTW to Waring, Aug. 7, 1907.

43. Scott memo to members of the office force, undated, *ca.* Nov. 1904.

44. Scott memo to the office force, April 22, 1905.

45. BTW to Scott, May 29, 1907, Julius R. Cox to Scott, May 31, 1907.

46. Josephine B. Bruce to BTW, undated, *ca.* 1902.

47. Carver to BTW, Sept. 13, 1902.

48. BTW to S. Helen Porter, Oct. 24, Nov. 7, 1913; Porter to BTW, Nov. 7, 1913.

49. Minutes of the executive council, Oct. 16, 1904; Scott to E. H. Gamlin, Jan. 6, 1905.

50. For example, BTW to Martha A. Hazard, Jan. 8, 1912.

51. BTW to R. C. Ogden, Nov. 25, 1905.

52. BTW to Marianna G. Brubaker, March 19, 1905.

53. *Ibid.*

54. Scott to BTW, March 17, 1905, *BTW Papers,* VIII, 219. Note also other reference in annotation there, and Scott to BTW, March 20, 1905.

55. John Massey to the Board of Trustees of Tuskegee Normal and Industrial Institute, May 23, 1905, *BTW Papers,* VIII, 290–91.

56. BTW to Massey, May 29, 1905, *BTW Papers,* VIII, 291–92.

57. BTW to R. C. Ogden, Nov. 9, 1906; BTW to Emmet Densmore, Oct. 23, 1906.

58. Scott to BTW, Nov. 2, 1906.

59. Hare to Ben de Lemos, Dec. 19, 1907.

60. These and other documents on the Penney investigation are in a container in the BTW Papers.

61. BTW to the young woman's father, Jan. 23, 1907.

62. BTW to Penney, Feb. 6, 1907, *BTW Papers,* IX, 212.

63. Penney to BTW, Feb. 6, 18, 1907, *BTW Papers,* IX, 212–13, 220–22.

64. Birmingham *Ledger, ca.* Feb. 8, 1907, clipping.

65. Penney to BTW, Feb. 18, 1907, *BTW Papers,* IX, 220–22.

66. Bumstead to BTW, March 1, 1907, *BTW Papers,* IX, 225–26.

67. BTW to Bumstead, March 27, 1907, *BTW Papers,* IX, 234–35.

68. Bumstead to BTW, April 10, 1907, *BTW Papers,* IX, 257–61.

69. BTW to Daniel Merriman, April 16, 1907; BTW to Bumstead, April 18, 1907, *BTW Papers,* IX, 263. He ended his exchange with Bumstead by saying that "my taking it up at all with a third party was simply through courtesy, and I ought not to be expected to continue explanations, defenses and discussions with another party." *Ibid.*

70. New York *Daily News,* Feb. 19, 1903, clipping [LC]; *Tuskegee Student,* XV (March 14, 1903), 1.

71. Washington *Colored American,* April 4, 1903.

72. Montgomery *Advertiser,* Nov. 30, 1902; *Tuskegee Student,* XIV (Dec. 6, 1902), 2–3.

73. Montgomery *Advertiser,* May 21, 25, 1902.

74. *Ibid.,* May 22, 1902.

75. *Ibid.,* May 23, 1902.

76. G. W. Craik to BTW, May 28, 1903. Craik was a railroad officer in Montgomery.

77. F. G. Blair to Wallace Buttrick, April 18, 1904.

78. BTW to W. H. Baldwin, Jr., May 24, 1904, *BTW Papers,* VII, 511–12. BTW was hypersensitive to any unfavorable comparison with Hampton Institute. See, for example, BTW to Thomas Wentworth Higginson, May 20, 1904.

79. BTW to J. B. Ramsey, Nov. 21, 1903.

80. Eliot to BTW, Sept. 7, 1906, *BTW Papers,* IX, 71–72. Eliot's relationship to BTW is explored in Jennings L. Wagoner, Jr., "The American Compromise: Charles W. Eliot, Black Education, and the New South," in Ronald Goodenow and Arthur White, eds., *Education and the Rise of the New South* (Boston, 1981), 26–46. When the Department of Superintendence of the National Education Association met in Mobile in 1911, many state and city superintendents visited Tuskegee in a body, and at BTW's request many wrote letters of evaluation. See three folders of correspondence [LC]; R. B. Teitrich to BTW, April 10, 1911, R. W. Hunelick to BTW, April 3, 1911 [LC].

81. BTW was absent when Max Weber visited, but the German sociologist expressed "high admiration" for Tuskegee, adding: "It was—I am sorry to say this—*only* at Tuskegee I found *enthusiasm* in the South at all." Weber to BTW, Nov. 6, 1904.

82. Kelly Miller, "A Tuskegee Visit," reprinted from Washington *Star* in the *Tuskegee Student,* XV (Aug. 29, 1903), 3–4.

83. Minutes of the Executive Council of Tuskegee Institute, March 19, 1906. On the occasion of President Theodore Roosevelt's visit, see *ibid.,* July 8, 1905.

84. Undated list of instructions, presumably for the commencement exercises in 1903.

85. Jesse Max Barber, news account of the Tuskegee 25th Anniversary, *Voice of the Negro,* III (May 1906), 315–22, in *BTW Papers,* IX, 15–24.

86. BTW to Ernest T. Attwell, May 15, 1906.

87. Logan to BTW, Aug. 13, 1903.

88. Montgomery *Advertiser,* Sept. 2, 1903.

89. Tuskegee *News,* Sept. 3, 1903.

90. Scott to BTW, Sept. 3, 1903.

91. Thompson to BTW, Sept. 4, 1903 [LC]. See also Thompson to BTW, Sept. 3, 1903; J. W. Adams to BTW, Sept. 5, 1903, *BTW Papers,* VII, 277.

92. Scott to BTW, Sept. 5, 1903, telegram; J. O. Thompson to BTW, Sept. 7, 1903.

93. BTW to Ernest W. Thompson, Dec. 15, 1906, *BTW Papers,* IX, 166–67.

94. J. O. Thompson to BTW, Dec. 17, 1906.

95. J. H. Washington to BTW, Jan. 2, 1907.

96. J. O. Thompson to BTW, Jan. 17, 1907.

97. Charles W. Hare to BTW, Jan. 16, 1907.

98. BTW to Braxton B. Comer, Jan. 17, 1907.

99. BTW to Comer, Jan. 19, 1907, *BTW Papers,* IX, 192–94.

100. Comer to BTW, Jan. 23, 1907, *BTW Papers,* IX, 201.

101. J. O. Thompson to BTW, Jan. 29, 1907.

102. Low to Ogden, Dec. 29, 1906, and press release quoting liberally from it.

103. BTW to Low, Feb. 8, 1907; also BTW to Ogden, Feb. 7, 1907.

104. Montgomery *Advertiser*, March 14, 1907; *Tuskegee Student*, XIX (March 16, 1907), 1.

105. BTW to Frank S. White, March 3, 1907.

106. Copy of the report in *Tuskegee Student*, XIX (Aug. 3, 1907), 1. See also Montgomery *Advertiser*, March 14, 1907.

107. Scott to BTW, July 17, 1907; Hervey W. Laird to BTW, July 17, 1907.

108. C. W. Hare, typed draft, undated, *ca.* July 24, 1907.

109. Report of debate in Montgomery *Advertiser*, July 27, 1907.

110. "An Educational Center for Colored People," undated pamphlet, *ca.* 1906; Scott to B. R. Ammons, Jan. 31, 1905; BTW to R. R. Taylor, Dec. 30, 1907.

111. BTW to R. R. Taylor, March 1, 1910.

112. BTW to Philip D. Newburn, July 7, 1910.

113. BTW to E. H. Gamlin, May 1, 1911.

114. Undated typescript, *ca.* 1903.

115. Gordon Macdonald, letter to the editor, in Washington *Post*, April 30, 1903, *BTW Papers*, VII, 132–35.

116. Max B. Thrasher and R. L. Stokes, report of interview with Gordon Macdonald, *ca.* May 25–June 3, 1903 [LC]. See also BTW to Erwin Craighead, May 15, 1903, *BTW Papers*, VII, 143–44.

117. Max B. Thrasher, report and annotated list of about thirty Tuskegee graduates in Montgomery, May 29, 1903.

118. BTW to Mrs. E. E. Brandon, Oct. 15, 1903. See also folder of letters in 1906–7.

119. Mobile *Herald*, Oct. 13, 1903, clipping.

120. Howell to BTW, Jan. 23, 1902.

121. BTW to L. W. Johnston, Sept. 30, 1907.

122. Hazlitt A. Cuppy to BTW, Dec. 21, 1908; BTW to Cuppy, Dec. 29, 1908.

123. BTW to T. J. Woofter, Jr., Feb. 1, 1914 [LC]; BTW to Mrs. M. L. Arnold, Jan. 13, 1915 [LC]. For his earlier consideration of this question, see BTW to Stella Scott Gilman, May 15, 1903, *BTW Papers*, VII, 145–46.

124. G. W. A. Johnston to BTW, Oct. 7, 1904, *BTW Papers*, VIII, 84–85.

125. Davis to BTW, Oct. 6, 1904, and undated fragment.

126. G. W. A. Johnston to Scott, Nov. 12, 1904, *BTW Papers*, VIII, 130.

127. Davis to BTW, Feb. 23, 1906, *BTW Papers*, VIII, 533.

128. BTW to Davis, Feb. 26, 1906, *BTW Papers*, VIII, 534; G. W. A. Johnston to BTW, Feb. 28, 1906 [LC].

129. BTW to J. D. D. Hall, May 25, 1907.

130. BTW to Davis, July 23, 1907, Davis to BTW, Aug. 19, Oct. 21, 1907, and undated.

131. BTW quoted in New York *World*, reprinted in *Tuskegee Student*, XXI (March 13, 1909), 1.

Chapter 8

1. BTW, address at the banquet of the Young Men's Forum of Cambridge, quoted in Boston *Globe,* Oct. 4, 1904, *BTW Papers,* VIII, 82.

2. BTW to Leslie Pinckney Hill, March 29, 1906, *BTW Papers,* VIII, 557–58.

3. BTW to Fortune, Nov. 3, 1903, *BTW Papers,* VII, 333.

4. BTW, *The Future of the American Negro* (1899), in *BTW Papers,* V, 331–35.

5. Harrison J. Pinckett to J. S. Clarkson, April 11, 1905; S. L. Williams to BTW, May 23, 1905.

6. Thirkield to BTW, March 9, 1907.

7. Thirkield to BTW, May 30, 1907, BTW to Thirkield, June 1, 1907 [LC]. A year earlier, in April 1906, the acting president and treasurer of Howard had attended Tuskegee's 25th anniversary celebration and had doubtless been impressed by BTW's influence on philanthropic men and organizations. Rayford W. Logan, *Howard University: The First Hundred Years, 1867–1967* (New York, 1969), 147. This visit may have made BTW's election as a trustee more palatable to the faculty, but it was Thirkield who sought out BTW and depended on his advice.

8. W. A. Sinclair to BTW, June 1, 1907.

9. BTW to Sinclair, June 4, 1907.

10. McKinlay to BTW, June 5, 1907.

11. BTW to Thirkield, Jan. 23, 1908.

12. Telegrams to Woodrow Wilson and members of Congress, Feb. 22, 1915.

13. Thomas S. Martin to J. P. Tumulty, Feb. 25, 1915; BTW to Seth Low, March 2, 1915.

14. W. P. Thirkield, "The Meaning and Mission of Education," typescript of address, Nov. 15, 1907. Logan, *Howard University,* 154–55, reports a charge in the Chicago *Conservator* that BTW would attempt to industrialize Howard, but finds no evidence to support it.

15. BTW to Thirkield, Aug. 15, 1909, *BTW Papers,* X, 156–57.

16. Du Bois to Francis, Aug. 31, 1909.

17. Scott to R. C. Bruce, Aug. 26, 1909.

18. Francis to BTW, Sept. 11, 1909.

19. James A. Cobb to BTW, Sept. 11, 1909.

20. Cobb to Scott, April 30, 1910, Scott to Cobb, May 3, 1910.

21. BTW to Thirkield, May 3, 1910.

22. Thirkield to BTW, May 7, 1910.

23. Terrell to Scott, June 9, 1911.

24. Miller to BTW, May 27, 1912.

25. BTW to Miller, May 29, 1912.

26. BTW to Miller, June 5, 1912.

27. Napier to BTW, May 6, 1915.

28. BTW to J. G. Merrill, April 26, 1904.

29. Merrill to BTW, Dec. 23, 1904.

30. BTW to Merrill, Dec. 31, 1904.

31. BTW to Merrill, March 14, 1905, *BTW Papers*, VIII, 216–17.

32. BTW to Whitefield McKinlay, March 14, 1905; BTW to J. C. Napier, March 14, 1905.

33. Napier to BTW, March 21, 1905.

34. Merrill to BTW, April 2, 14, 1905.

35. Scott to Merrill, Dec. 4, 1905, *BTW Papers*, VIII, 460.

36. BTW to Merrill, Dec. 14, 1905.

37. BTW to Merrill, Dec. 2, 1907, *BTW Papers*, IX, 410–11. BTW was in error as to the amount of Carnegie's offer, which was $20,000.

38. BTW to Bertram, Jan. 9, 1908, *BTW Papers*, IX, 436.

39. Bertram to BTW, Jan. 15, 1908. BTW promised to make no public mention of the "waiver." BTW to Bertram, Jan. 17, 1908, *BTW Papers*, IX, 443.

40. "Galileo Galilei" (1908), in W. E. B. Du Bois, *The Education of Black People: Ten Critiques 1906–1960*, edited by Herbert Aptheker (Amherst, 1973), 17–30.

41. Joe M. Richardson, *A History of Fisk University, 1865–1946* (University, Ala., 1980), 59–61.

42. Merrill to BTW, Oct. 26, 1908.

43. Merrill to BTW, Sept. 1, 1909.

44. BTW to Merrill, Sept. 7, 1909. See also BTW to Merrill, Oct. 8, 1909, *BTW Papers*, X, 183–84.

45. BTW to Gates, Oct. 25, 1909.

46. BTW to Paul D. Cravath, Nov. 16, 1909.

47. BTW to Gates, Jan. 15, 1910, *BTW Papers*, X, 264.

48. BTW to Gates, March 18, 1910, *BTW Papers*, X, 281–82.

49. BTW to Gates, Nov. 17, 1910, *BTW Papers*, X, 473–74.

50. BTW, "A University Education for Negroes," *Independent*, LXVIII (March 24, 1910), 613–18.

51. BTW to Robert R. Moton, March 24, 1910, *BTW Papers*, X, 283.

52. BTW to Gates, May 21, 1910, *BTW Papers*, X, 332–33.

53. Gates to BTW, May 13, 28, 1910.

54. H. L. Simmons to BTW, May 6, 1911, BTW to Simmons, May 15, 1911; undated list of contributions to Fisk, *ca.* 1913; Cravath to BTW, March 16, 1914; BTW to James Bertram, April 26, 1913 [LC]; Richardson, *History of Fisk University*, 68–69. The extensive correspondence in BTW's papers shows his strong commitment to the Fisk fund drive.

55. BTW to Haynes, June 27, 1914, Haynes to BTW, July 1, 1914.

56. BTW to Cravath, June 2, 1914, Cravath to BTW, Aug. 12, 1914.

57. See correspondence between BTW and Cravath, Nov.–Dec. 1914.

58. Richardson, *History of Fisk University*, 71–100; Lester A. Lamon, *Black Tennesseans, 1900–1930* (Knoxville, 1977), 274–92; Raymond Wolters, *The New Negro on Campus: Black College Rebellions of the 1920s* (Princeton, 1975), 29–69.

59. BTW to Frissell, Sept. 25, 1912.

60. Charles W. Dabney to Charles L. Coon, Aug. 27, 1903, Charles W. Dabney Papers, Southern Historical Collection, University of North Carolina.

61. Quoted in Dumas Malone, *Edwin A. Alderman: A Biography* (New York, 1940), 145–46.

62. Charles D. McIver, "Disfranchisement and Education," *Southern Workman*, XXX (Feb. 1901), 89–90.

63. BTW to Frissell, Aug. 19, 1901, *BTW Papers*, VI, 187.

64. BTW to Frissell, Nov. 1, 1901, *BTW Papers*, VI, 283–84.

65. Quoted in Baldwin to BTW, Nov. 6, 1901, *BTW Papers*, VI, 293–94.

66. Baldwin to BTW, telegram, Nov. 6, 1901.

67. Frissell to BTW, Nov. 9, 1901. See also Baldwin to BTW, Nov. 9, 1901, *BTW Papers*, VI, 311–13.

68. Ogden to BTW, Nov. 11, 1901.

69. BTW to Wallace Buttrick, May 6, 1902, *BTW Papers*, VI, 454–55; Buttrick's account of a tour of the South, May 19–June 2, 1902, J. L. M. Curry Papers, Alabama State Archives; Montgomery *Advertiser,* May 30, 1902.

70. W. D. Floyd to BTW, Feb. 1, 1903.

71. Alderman to Baldwin, Nov. 10, 1902 [LC]; see also BTW to Alderman, Nov. 16, 1902, *BTW Papers,* VII, 585–86.

72. Ogden to James H. Kirkland, Feb. 19, 1903, Ogden to Baldwin, May 27, 1903, Robert C. Ogden Papers, LC.

73. BTW to Ogden, Aug. 6, 1902, *BTW Papers*, VI, 499–500.

74. Baldwin to BTW, Aug. 11, 1902, *BTW Papers*, VI, 500–501.

75. BTW to Baldwin, Sept. 9, 1903 [LC]. See also Baldwin to BTW, Sept. 11, 1903, *BTW Papers*, VII, 282–83.

76. Dabney to Charles L. Coon, Aug. 27, 1903, Charles W. Dabney Papers, UNC.

77. R. F. Beasley to Eugene C. Brooks, Sept. 9, 1903, James Y. Joyner Papers, Southern Historical Collection, UNC.

78. Baldwin to BTW, Jan. 18, 1904.

79. Ogden to Baldwin, Feb. 28, 1904, Robert C. Ogden Papers, LC.

80. BTW to Baldwin, May 31, 1904.

81. Murphy to Ogden, March 8, 1904, Robert C. Ogden Papers, LC.

82. Murphy to BTW, Oct. 14, 1904.

83. Murphy to Ogden, April 8, 1904, Robert C. Ogden Papers, LC; Louis R. Harlan, *Separate and Unequal: Public School Campaigns and Racism in the Southern Seaboard States, 1901–1915* (Chapel Hill, 1958), 94–95.

84. BTW to Ogden, July 18, 1906 [LC]; BTW to Frissell, July 18, 1906, *BTW Papers,* IX, 43.

85. Minutes of Southern Education Board meeting, Aug. 6–8, 1906, Robert C. Ogden Papers, LC.

86. Charles L. Coon, *Public Taxation and Negro Schools* (Cheyney, Pa., 1909); BTW to Coon, April 21, 1909 [LC]. See also BTW to Buttrick, June 19, 1908, *BTW Papers,* IX, 583.

87. BTW to Frissell, July 8, 1909, Hampton Institute Archives.

88. BTW to Buttrick, July 23, 1909.

89. BTW to Peabody, July 30, 1909 [LC]. See also BTW to Frissell, Aug. 9, 1909, Hampton Institute Archives; BTW to Moton, Sept. 5, 1909 [LC].

90. BTW to Buttrick, June 13, 1910, quoted from the GEB archives in Raymond B. Fosdick, *Adventure in Giving: The Story of the General Education Board* (New York, 1962), 100.

91. Buttrick to BTW, June 18, 1910, *BTW Papers*, X, 340.

92. Actually, she posed this question in a letter, Jeanes to BTW, Feb. 25, 1905, *BTW Papers*, VIII, 201–2.

93. BTW to Jeanes, March 1, 1905, *BTW Papers*, VIII, 207.

94. BTW to Frissell, March 2, 1905, Hampton Institute Archives; BTW to Peabody, March 9, 1905, *BTW Papers*, VIII, 212.

95. Jeanes to BTW, March 25, 1905, BTW to Buttrick, April 11, 1905, *BTW Papers*, VIII, 243, 255–57.

96. Buttrick to BTW, Oct. 4, 1905.

97. Peabody to BTW, April 22, 1907.

98. Minutes of meeting of the Jeanes Fund board of trustees, Feb. 29, 1908, Robert C. Ogden Papers, LC.

99. BTW to Dillard, June 14, 1909.

100. J. H. Dillard, "Statement VII," Sept. 20, 1909. There is no adequate history of the Jeanes Fund.

101. BTW to Dillard, May 3, 1912.

102. See Tables 9 and 10 in Harlan, *Separate and Unequal*, 205, 207.

103. BTW to Buttrick, Jan. 6, 1915.

104. BTW to Rosenwald, Sept. 12, 1912; BTW to W. C. Graves, May 24, 1913.

105. Rosenwald to BTW, Dec. 26, 1912.

106. E. J. Scott, press release to black newspapers, June 18, 1914; BTW to Dillard, Aug. 5, 1914.

107. BTW to Rosenwald, Dec. 5, 7, 1914.

108. BTW to W. C. Graves, Dec. 26, 1914.

109. BTW to James L. Sibley, May 26, 1915.

110. BTW to Rosenwald, March 17, 1915, transcript, Julius Rosenwald Papers, University of Chicago.

111. BTW to Graves, Oct. 1, 1915.

112. BTW to Rosenwald, Oct. 15, 1915, Julius Rosenwald Papers, University of Chicago.

113. Anson Phelps Stokes, Jr. to BTW, May 2, 1911, *BTW Papers*, XI, 125.

114. BTW to Stokes, May 6, 1911, *BTW Papers*, XI, 129–30.

115. BTW to Stokes, May 15, 1911.

116. Stokes to BTW, Nov. 2, 1911, BTW to Stokes, Nov. 21, 1911, *BTW Papers*, XI, 354, 373–74.

117. BTW to Stokes, Dec. 1, 1911, *BTW Papers*, XI, 380–81; Stokes to BTW, Dec. 4, 1911 [LC]; BTW to Stokes, Jan. 11, 1913 [LC].

118. BTW to Stokes, Nov. 1, 1912.

119. BTW to Stokes, Nov. 9, 1912.

120. See Kenneth J. King, *Pan-Africanism and Education* (Oxford, 1971).

121. BTW to William G. Willcox, April 13, 1914 [LC]. See also BTW correspondence with Oswald Garrison Villard in 1914–15, in the forthcoming *BTW Papers*, XIII.

Chapter 9

1. John Spencer Bassett, "Stirring Up the Fires of Race Antipathy," *South Atlantic Quarterly*, II (Oct. 1903), 297–305.

2. BTW, "Chickens, Pigs, and People," *Outlook*, LXVIII (June 1, 1901), 291–300, in *BTW Papers*, VI, 134–41.

3. *Ibid.*

4. BTW, "The Best Labor in the World," *Southern States Farm Magazine*, V (Jan. 1898), 496.

5. BTW, *My Larger Education* (New York, 1911), reprinted in *BTW Papers*, I, 431.

6. Stenographic report of BTW's speech, Feb. 17, 1904.

7. Report of the Tuskegee Negro Conference in *Tuskegee Student*, XIX (March 2, 1907), 1.

8. Typescript of B. F. Riley's address at Tuskegee Institute, undated, 1910.

9. The declarations also urged raising more livestock and cultivating a garden. Declarations of the Tuskegee Negro Conference, Jan. 18, 1911, typescript.

10. Carver to BTW, Nov. 16, 1904.

11. *Tuskegee Student*, XVIII (April 21, 1906), 2; George R. Bridgeforth, report of the Jesup Wagon, June 5–9, 1906.

12. *Ibid.*

13. Bridgeforth's description, quoted in BTW to W. G. Johnson, Feb. 2, 1907.

14. BTW to Mrs. Morris K. Jesup, July 12, 1911.

15. Frederick T. Gates to BTW, May 24, 1905.

16. Minutes of the Executive Council of Tuskegee Institute, June 10, 1905.

17. Knapp to BTW, June 14, 1905, BTW to Knapp, June 19, 1905.

18. Knapp to BTW, Oct. 4, 1906.

19. Memorandum of agreement between Tuskegee Institute and the General Education Board, Nov. 9, 1906, *BTW Papers*, IX, 121–22.

20. BTW to Knapp, Dec. 27, 1907, Knapp to BTW, Dec. 30, 1907 [LC]. Charles Davis, "Early Agricultural Demonstration Work in Alabama," *Alabama Review*, II (July 1949), 176–88, presents evidence that most of the demonstration work was by white agents working with white farmers.

21. Thomas M. Campbell to Scott, Dec. 23, 1910.

22. Bradford Knapp to BTW, May 22, 1911.

23. *The General Education Board; An Account of Its Activities, 1902–1914* (New York, 1915), 35–40.

24. Russell to BTW, June 9, 14, 20, 1910 [LC]; BTW to the editor of the Washington *Post*, June 27, 1910, in *BTW Papers*, X, 346–47.

25. *Ibid.*, 347; William Watson Thompson to BTW, May 28, 1910, BTW to Thompson, June 1, 1910 [LC].

26. BTW to O'Neal, June 20, 1914.

27. Montgomery *Advertiser*, July 28, 1914, clipping; BTW to O'Neal, July 22, 1914; report of the special state commission on agricultural education at Tuskegee Institute, July 27, 1914.

28. BTW to O'Neal, July 22, 1914.

29. BTW to O'Neal, Aug. 6, 1914.

30. BTW to Thomas Jesse Jones, Nov. 25, 1914.

31. BTW to Jones, Nov. 30, 1914.

32. BTW to Jones, illegible date, *ca.* Dec. 1914.

33. T. J. Jackson to BTW, May 10, 1902.

34. "The Work of School Extension," *Tuskegee Student*, XVIII (April 28, 1906), unpaginated; Scott to G. H. Sandison, Dec. 11, 1906 [LC].

35. Calloway to BTW, Feb. 26, 1906.

36. BTW to Calloway, March 3, 1908.

37. See "Mr. Washington's speech at Brownsville school" (1909), "Dr. Washington and Party Make a Tour of Inspection in the Southern Part of Macon County" (1909), "Another Trip Through Macon County (1909); Joseph L. Sibley to BTW, Dec. 17, 1913, Jan. 24, Sept. 15, 1914.

38. BTW to Warren Logan, July 5, 1895, *BTW Papers*, III, 563–64.

39. "Southern Improvement Company," typescript, *ca.* 1907; BTW, description of Southern Improvement Company, *ca.* 1910.

40. BTW to Charles E. Mason, March 10, 1914.

41. BTW to the editor of the Montgomery *Journal*, Jan. 7, 1915.

42. BTW to Alonzo G. Chandler, June 4, 1915.

43. George R. Bridgeforth to C. J. Calloway, July 3, 1915, copy sent to BTW.

44. BTW to R. C. Bedford, March 21, 1905; see also BTW to Clyde, Aug. 1, 1904.

45. "Proposed Scheme for Hilton Head Settlement," undated typescript.

46. BTW to Powell, March 10, 1908.

47. BTW to J. R. E. Lee, March 28, 1908.

48. Lee to BTW, May 9, 1908.

49. BTW to Clyde, June 5, 1908.

50. Williams to BTW, March 8, 1909, Aug. 17, 1909, March 25, 1910.

51. W. P. Clyde, Jr., to BTW, May 3, 1910.

52. BTW, in *Tuskegee Student*, XXII (May 14, 1910), 3.

53. Williams to BTW, Feb. 28, 1911.

54. Williams to BTW, Aug. 12, 1911, BTW to Williams, Sept. 8, 1911; BTW to Powell, Oct. 15, 1912.

55. Powell to BTW, Nov. 18, 1912.

56. BTW to Robert E. Park, Dec. 7, 1912.

57. BTW to Powell, Dec. 27, 1912.

58. BTW to Powell, Feb. 20, 1913.

59. BTW to Powell, Feb. 25, 1913.

60. BTW to W. P. Clyde, Jr., April 11, 1913.

61. BTW, "Boley, A Negro Town in the West," *Outlook*, LXXXVIII (Jan. 4, 1907), 31.

62. This is the sound conclusion of August Meier, "Booker T. Washington and the Town of Mound Bayou," *Phylon*, XV (Winter 1954), 396–401, reprinted in August Meier and Elliott Rudwick, *Along the Color Line* (Urbana, 1976), 217–23.

63. Isaiah T. Montgomery, "The Negro in Business," *Outlook*, LXIX (Nov. 16, 1901), 733–34. The background of Montgomery and Mound Bayou is treated in Janet S. Hermann, *The Pursuit of a Dream* (New York, 1981).

64. Banks to Scott, Jan. 30, 1904.

65. Banks to Scott, Jan. 13, 1910.

66. BTW to Banks, Dec. 2, 1907. BTW also sent Tuskegee's independent auditor, D. C. Smith, to go over the books of the Bank of Mound Bayou. See Banks to Scott, Sept. 7, 1907.

67. BTW, "A Town Owned by Negroes, Mound Bayou, Miss.: An Example of Thrift and Self-Government," *World's Work*, XIV (July, 1907), 9125–34.

68. Banks to BTW, Sept. 16, 1907.

69. *Ibid.*

70. Banks to Scott, Feb. 10, 1910.

71. BTW to Walter Hines Page, March 5, 1910.

72. Banks to BTW, March 14, 1910.

73. Banks, press release, June 28, 1910.

74. Park's undated letter in reply to Scott to Park, Nov. 23, 1911.

75. Scott to Banks, Jan. 20, 1912.

76. BTW to Banks, March 28, 1912.

77. Meier, "BTW and the Town of Mound Bayou," 219. BTW also tried two years later to interest the Slater Fund and the Jeanes Fund in aiding the Mound Bayou school. J. H. Dillard to BTW, May 20, 1914, BTW to Dillard, May 23, 1914.

78. Montgomery to BTW, May 11, 1912.

79. Montgomery to BTW, July 3, 1912.

80. Montgomery to BTW, June 7, 1912, BTW to Montgomery, June 21, 1912.

81. Banks to BTW, Nov. 16, 1912.

82. BTW, extracts from address at Mound Bayou, Nov. 25, 1912.

83. Memphis *Commercial Appeal*, Nov. 27, 1912.

84. Rosenwald to Banks, Feb. 25, 1913, Banks to Rosenwald, March 1, 1913.

85. William C. Graves to BTW, Feb. 14, 1914; Banks to BTW, Sept. 30, 1915.

86. BTW to A. W. French, Feb. 24, 1913, and other letters to oil mill machinery officials.

87. Banks to BTW, telegram, Oct. 9, 1913.

88. Clement Richardson, in *Tuskegee Student*, XXV (Oct. 4, 1913), 1.

89. Meier, "BTW and the Town of Mound Bayou," 220.

90. Banks to Scott, Oct. 25, 1913.

91. BTW to Parsons, Feb. 24, 1913, Parsons to BTW, Feb. 28, 1913.

92. Banks to Scott, April 29, 1913, Scott to Banks, April 14, May 1, 1913.

93. Banks to BTW, May 29, 1913; Scott to Banks, April 21, 1914.

94. Scott to Banks, June 12, 1914; Banks to Rosenwald, June 16, 1914; Meier, "BTW and the Bank of Mound Bayou," 221.

95. Montgomery to BTW, Jan. 20, 1915.

96. BTW to Montgomery, Jan. 25, 1915.

97. Banks to BTW, April 14, 1915.

98. Banks to Scott, July 12, 1915.

99. Banks to Scott, Oct. 25, 1915.

100. Montgomery to BTW, Sept. 6, 1904, *BTW Papers*, VIII, 61–63; C. A. Buchanan to Montgomery, Aug. 30, 1904 [LC]. An excellent article on this wave of mob rule in Mississippi is William F. Holmes, "Whitecapping: Agrarian Violence in Mississippi, 1902–1906," *Journal of Southern History*, XXXV (May 1969), 165–85.

101. Theodore H. Price to BTW, Jan. 4, 1911.

102. Price to BTW, Jan. 13, April 15, 1911, Page to BTW, Jan. 17, 1910 (actually 1911), [BTW] to Price, April 22, 1911.

103. BTW to H. S. Bradford, Aug. 3, 1915.

104. Henry C. Davis to BTW, Feb. 5, April 30, May 26, June 17, July 13, 1900.

105. Coleman to BTW, June 18, 26, 1896 [LC]; Indianapolis *Freeman,* July 22, 1899; R. C. Simmons to BTW, July 7, 12, 1900 [LC]; Coleman to BTW, Nov. 3, 1903 [LC]; E. A. Johnson to BTW, May 28, 1904 [LC]; *Voice of the Negro,* I (Aug. 1904), 303.

106. R. P. Hallowell to BTW, March 8, 1902.

107. Wiley to BTW, Oct. 17, 1902; also see Dallas *Times–Herald,* May 31, 1903, clipping.

108. BTW to Warren Logan, July 29, 1904, Logan to BTW, Aug. 1, 1904.

109. James Mott Hallowell to BTW, Dec. 4, 1906.

110. Willcox to BTW, Aug. 30, 1911.

111. BTW to Wiley, Dec. 2, 1911.

112. BTW to Wiley, Feb. 2, 1912.

113. BTW to William Garrott Brown, June 20, 1904, *BTW Papers*, VII, 538.

114. N. B. Feagin to BTW, July 13, 1904, BTW to Feagin, July 22, 23, 1904.

115. BTW to W. S. Reese, April 3, 1904.

116. BTW to Feagin, July 22, 1904.

117. J. C. Thorpe to BTW, June 4, 1904; BTW to Feagin, July 23, 1904.

118. U. G. Mason to E. J. Scott, June 7, 1904, and attached newspaper clipping.

119. F. G. Ragland to BTW, June 15, 1904; BTW to Ragland, July 8, 1904.

120. Scott to BTW, June 18, 1902, *BTW Papers*, VI, 485; W. A. Hazel to J. B. Ramsey, April 7, 1914, Ramsey to BTW, April 16, 1914.

121. John C. Grant to BTW, Dec. 24, 1904.

122. Rosetta E. Lawson, report of engagements at Tuskegee Institute, November 1906.

123. BTW to Charles W. Hare, May 15, 1907.

124. BTW to S. S. McClure, Oct. 15, 1907.

125. BTW, "Prohibition and the Negro," *Outlook*, LXXXVIII (March 14, 1908), 587–89.

126. BTW to Baker, April 13, 1909.

127. BTW to W. H. Thomas, March 21, 1912.

128. BTW to W. H. Morgan, April 24, 1912.

129. BTW, "Negro Crime and Strong Drink," *Journal of the American Institute of Criminal Law and Criminology*, III (Sept. 1912), 384–92.

130. BTW, draft of an article or public letter, Dec. 12, 1913.

131. BTW, draft of an article for the *Congregationalist and Christian World*, enclosed in BTW to R. A. Bridgman, Aug. 4, 1914.

132. Tuskegee *News*, Dec. 3, 1908.

133. BTW to the Russell Sage Foundation, July 11, 1911.

134. BTW to Warren Logan, Jan. 10, 1914.

135. Montgomery *Advertiser*, Jan. 23, 1914.

136. BTW, extracts from an address at the Tuskegee Workers' Conference, Jan. 22, 1914.

137. BTW to Stokes, Oct. 26, 1914.

138. Stokes to BTW, Jan. 29, 1915, James W. McCulloch to BTW, Jan. 14, 1915.

139. BTW to Moton, Nov. 25, 1914, Moton to BTW, Nov. 28, 1914.

140. Correspondence and other documents on promotion of National Negro Health Week in 1915 fill almost an entire file box in the BTW Papers.

141. Richard W. Thompson, typescript of article, March 29, 1915.

142. BTW to Stokes, April 1, 8, 1915.

143. Howard J. Rabinowitz, *Race Relations in the Urban South, 1865–1890* (New York, 1978), particularly Chapter 6.

144. BTW to Stokes, Nov. 7, 1915.

145. Nancy J. Weiss, *The National Urban League, 1910–1940* (New York, 1974), 85–87. Another study incorrectly gives the Urban League credit for the initiation of National Negro Health Week but has some interesting information on its health campaign in New York City. Guichard Parris and Lester Brooks, *Blacks in the City: A History of the National Urban League* (Boston, 1971), 42, 66, 188.

Chapter 10

1. These dissenting white southerners will be discussed further on in this and a later chapter. Two recent studies of these men are Charles E. Wynes, ed., *Forgotten Voices: Dissenting Southerners in an Age of Conformity* (Baton Rouge, 1967), and Morton Sosna, *In Search of the Silent South* (New York, 1977), particularly pp. 1–41.

2. Montgomery *Advertiser,* Jan. 20, 1903; Francis J. Garrison to BTW, Feb. 8, 1903, *BTW Papers,* VII, 55–56.

3. BTW to Jelks, Oct. 9, 1906, Alabama State Archives; extracts from BTW's address, Oct. 27, 1906, *BTW Papers,* IX, 104–8.

4. Jelks to John T. Morgan, Oct. 31, 1906, John Tyler Morgan Papers, LC.

5. Jelks to Morgan, Nov. 8, 1906, John Tyler Morgan Papers, LC.

6. BTW to Jelks, Nov. 6, 1906.

7. Jelks to BTW, Nov. 22, 1906, *BTW Papers,* IX, 146–47.

8. BTW to J. K. Jackson, secretary of the governor, Dec. 12, 1906, *BTW Papers,* IX, 161–62.

9. Jelks to BTW, Dec. 12, 1906, *BTW Papers,* IX, 162–63.

10. Jelks to BTW, Dec. 18, 1906, *BTW Papers,* IX, 174–75.

11. The social forces of section, class and race, and the changing patterns produced by industrialization and urbanization are treated brilliantly in Horace Mann Bond, *Social and Economic Influences on the Public Education of Negroes in Alabama, 1865–1930* (Washington, 1939).

12. Thompson to BTW, Dec. 21, 1906.

13. Comer's address to the Colored Citizens' Club, in Birmingham *Age-Herald,* Jan. 2, 1907, clipping; BTW to Comer, Oct. 21, 1907, Comer to BTW, Oct. 22, 1907. On Comer, see above, Chapter 7.

14. Message of B. B. Comer to the Legislature of Alabama, Jan. 10, 1911, Alabama State Archives.

15. BTW to R. R. Taylor, Oct. 24, 1910. BTW apparently saw nothing incongruous in sending an M. I. T. graduate on such an errand.

16. BTW to Henry J. Willingham, Dec. 28, 1910, *BTW Papers,* X, 513.

17. BTW to O'Neal, June 17, 1911, Alabama State Archives.

18. O'Neal to BTW, Feb. 17, 1913.

19. *Tuskegee Student,* XXV (Nov. 29, 1913), 2.

20. BTW to J. H. Washington, April 28, 1914.

21. O'Neal to BTW, Nov. 23, 1914. BTW wrote a commendatory editorial for the *Outlook* and sent a copy to O'Neal. BTW to O'Neal, Nov. 25, 30, 1914.

22. Tuskegee faculty committee report on the Governor's visit on Jan. 5, 1915, and menu of the dinner, Jan. 9, 1915.

23. Typescript of a news item, Jan. 7, 1915.

24. See above, I, 297–98.

25. *Ibid.,* I, 300–303; letter of Thomas W. Coleman, former chief justice of the supreme court of Alabama and chairman of the suffrage committee in the constitutional convention of 1900–1901, in Birmingham *Age-Herald,* July 11, 1915, p. 9.

26. W. D. Jelks to J. T. Morgan, Jan. 10, 1902, John Tyler Morgan Papers, LC.

27. Montgomery *Advertiser,* March 14, 1902.

28. William Jenkins to BTW, March 22, 1902.

29. Wilford H. Smith to Scott, April 22, 1902.

30. Filipino [W. H. Smith] to "My Dear Friend" [Scott], June 17, 1902 [LC], Scott to BTW, June 18, 1902 [LC]; BTW to Scott, June 23, 1902, *BTW Papers,* VI, 487.

31. BTW to Scott, July 26, 1902, *BTW Papers,* VI, 498.

32. Apparently the earliest use of the new code names was J. C. May [Smith] to R. C. Black [Scott], Sept. 15, 1902, *BTW Papers,* VI, 514, and it mentioned receipt of a letter addressed to Miss Maybelle McAdoo, Smith's secretary. Correspondence under these pseudonyms continued into 1904 and involved not only the Giles cases but other legal and espionage matters in which Washington secretly engaged through the agency of Scott and Smith.

33. See, for example, J. C. May [Smith] to R. C. Black [Scott], Feb. 6, 1903, *BTW Papers,* VII, 38.

34. Washington could conceivably have raised the money from someone else, but if so it was at another layer of secrecy. Through Scott he took personal responsibility to "go to the limit" and meet the legal expenses. R. C. Black [Scott] to J. C. May [Smith], June 17, 1903, May to Black, June 18, 1903.

35. Montgomery *Advertiser,* Oct. 12, 1902.

36. *Ibid.,* June 11, 1902, April 29, 1903.

37. *Ibid.,* April 29, 1902.

38. Smith to BTW, Feb. 24, 1904.

39. BTW to Smith, Feb. 24, 1904.

40. BTW to Smith, March 3, 1904, *BTW Papers,* VII, 455–56.

41. BTW to Smith, July 16, 1904, Smith to Albert E. Pillsbury, July 20, 1904.

42. Smith to Scott, May 2, 1904, *BTW Papers,* VII, 492.

43. *Rogers* v. *Alabama,* 192 U.S. 226 (1904). On BTW's role, see the three-way correspondence between him, Scott, and Smith, sometimes using the code names; BTW to C. W. Anderson, Feb. 1, 1904.

44. Henry H. Proctor to BTW, April 18, 1900, *BTW Papers,* V, 487–88; Baldwin to BTW, Jan. 24, 1900, *ibid.,* V, 420; Lincoln to BTW, Feb. 6, 1900 [LC]; Proctor to BTW, July 6, 1900 [LC].

45. Baldwin to BTW, Jan. 24, 1900, *BTW Papers,* V, 420.

46. Baldwin to BTW, March 19, 1900, *BTW Papers,* V, 467–68.

47. Du Bois to BTW, Nov. 22, Dec. 4, 1902, Jan. 24, 1904, BTW to Du Bois, Jan. 27, Feb. 27, 1904, *BTW Papers,* VI, 590, 605, VII, 412, 414–15, 433; BTW to Du Bois, June 4, 1904 [LC]; Scott to Richard W. Thompson, Feb. 10, 1905 [LC].

48. Jackson to BTW, Oct. 5, 1900, Jan. 24, 1901, *BTW Papers,* V, 649–51, VI, 14–17; James H. Brewer, "The War Against Jim Crow in the Land of Goshen," *Negro History Bulletin,* XXIV (Dec. 1960), 53–57.

49. See BTW to Lincoln, Oct. 28, 1903, BTW to Baldwin, Oct. 28, Dec. 3, 1903, BTW to Napier, Nov. 2, 1903, BTW to Du Bois, Feb. 27, 1904, *BTW Papers,* VII, 312, 313, 324, 357, 453; BTW to Baldwin, Dec. 4, 1903 [LC], Jan. 18, 1904 [LC]; Napier to BTW, May 30, 1904 [LC].

50. A detailed account using these and other sources is Daniel W. Crofts, "The Warner-Foraker Amendment to the Hepburn Bill: Friend or Foe of Jim Crow?" *Journal of Southern History,* XXXIX (Aug. 1973), 341–58. See correspondence between BTW and his secret go-betweens in this affair, Kelly Miller,

Archibald H. Grimké, and Whitefield McKinlay, March–June 1906, and correspondence of BTW and Scott with Fortune, R. W. Thompson, J. A. Lankford, S. Laing Williams, and Andrew B. Humphrey in 1906 [LC]. Many of these are published in *BTW Papers*, VIII and IX.

51. BTW to Kelly Miller, Aug. 4, 1906, *BTW Papers*, IX, 49–50.

52. BTW to Villard, Aug. 9, 1910, *BTW Papers*, X, 364–65. See also Villard to BTW, Aug. 4, 12, 1910, *ibid.*, X, 362–63, 366.

53. A detailed review of the Franklin case is in C. Flint Kellogg, *NAACP 1909–1920* (Baltimore, 1967), 57–60.

54. See Pete Daniel, "Up from Slavery and Down to Peonage: The Alonzo Bailey Case," *Journal of American History*, LVII (Dec. 1970), 654–70; his book on peonage, *The Shadow of Slavery* (Urbana, 1972), 65–81; and the citations of sources in Louis R. Harlan, "The Secret Life of Booker T. Washington," *Journal of Southern History*, XXXVII (Aug. 1971), 403.

55. Garrison to BTW, Nov. 6, 1902, *BTW Papers*, VI, 579.

56. Buttrick to BTW, Jan. 27, 1903 [LC]. See also Sheats to BTW, Jan. 31, 1903, E. G. Murphy to BTW, Jan. 31, 1903, *BTW Papers*, VII, 15–17.

57. Sheats, quoted in *Report of the U. S. Commissioner of Education, 1896–97* (2 vols., Washington, 1898), II, 1287.

58. Jacksonville *Times-Union and Citizen*, Jan. 30, 1903, clipping.

59. BTW to Sheats, Jan. 31, 1904, Sheats to BTW, Jan. 31, Feb. 3, 1903, Sheats, W. R. Thomas, and W. M. Holloway to BTW, Feb. 4, 1903.

60. Thrasher to BTW, Feb. 4, 1903, Buttrick to BTW, Feb. 4, 1903.

61. BTW to Daniel Murray, Feb. 9, 1903 [LC], BTW to Lyman Abbott, Feb. 9, 1903 [LC]; article by J. Douglas Wetmore for the Indianapolis *Freeman*, Feb. 8, 1903, *BTW Papers*, VII, 56–60.

62. A thorough treatment is Arthur O. White, "Booker T. Washington's Florida Incident, 1903–1904," *Florida Historical Quarterly*, LI (Jan. 1973), 227–49.

63. *Ibid.*, 244–49.

64. Buttrick to Sheats, June 28, 1904.

65. Edward A. Johnson to BTW, Nov. 2, 1903.

66. Bassett, "Stirring Up the Fires of Race Antipathy," *passim*. In addition to the memoirs of Edwin Mims, Josephus Daniels, and others involved in the Bassett case, see Harry R. Jackson, "Reason against Racism: A Primer on Academic Freedom," *Duke Alumni Register*, L (Dec. 1964), 5–9, 22–27; and Earl W. Porter, *Trinity and Duke, 1892–1924* (Durham, 1964).

67. Montgomery *Advertiser*, Oct. 11, 24, 1903. The only serious scholarly attention that Ewing has received is a chapter in Wynes, ed., *Forgotten Voices: Dissenting Southerners in an Age of Conformity*, and unfortunately Wynes did not know at the time of the evidence in the BTW Papers.

68. Garrison to BTW, Dec. 27, 1905.

69. BTW to Garrison, Dec. 30, 1905.

70. Garrison to BTW, Jan. 3, 1906.

71. BTW to S. S. McClure, Jan. 11, 1906, *BTW Papers*, VIII, 496–97; Garrison to BTW, Jan. 15, 1906 [LC].

72. BTW to Ewing, Jan. 13, 1906, Ewing to BTW, Jan. 15, 1906.

73. BTW to Oswald G. Villard, Jan. 27, 1906 [LC]; BTW to Garrison, Aug. 8, 1906, *BTW Papers*, IX, 51–52.

74. BTW to Ewing, Feb. 18, 1914, Ewing to BTW, Feb. 23, 1914.

75. BTW to Emory Speer, July 12, 1904, BTW to Edward H. Clement, June 9, 1904.

76. BTW to George Foster Peabody, Jan. 21, 1907, L. G. Myers to BTW, Jan. 26, 1907, BTW to Northen, May 31, 1907.

77. J. Fred Rippy, ed., *F. M. Simmons, Statesman of the New South: Memoirs and Addresses* (Durham, 1936), 23, 29; Josephus Daniels, *Editor in Politics* (Chapel Hill, 1941), 318–24; Harlan, *Separate and Unequal*, 60.

78. White to BTW, July 15, 1904.

79. White to George Foster Peabody, June 10, 1907, George Foster Peabody Papers, LC. See also John E. White, "The Need of a Southern Program on the Negro Problem," *South Atlantic Quarterly*, VI (April 1907), 177–88; Sosna, *In Search of the Silent South*, 15. On other originators of the conference, see George B. Tindall, *The Emergence of the New South, 1913–1945* (Baton Rouge, 1967), 175–76.

80. Scott to White, July 31, 1915, Dec. 8, 1915.

81. Riley to BTW, Oct. 25, 1906, BTW to Riley, Oct. 31, 1906.

82. Quoted from George Fredrickson, *The Black Image in the White Mind* (New York, 1971), 289.

83. BTW to Riley, Jan. 21, 1910.

84. BTW to Riley, Feb. 20, 1911.

85. Riley to BTW, July 5, Aug. 7, 1911.

86. Riley to BTW, Jan. 31, 1912, BTW to Riley, Feb. 5, 1912.

87. Fredrickson, *Black Image in the White Mind*, 289–90.

88. Weatherford to BTW, Nov. 9, 1911, BTW to Weatherford, Nov. 17, 1911.

89. See Wilma Dykeman, *Prophet of Plenty: The First Ninety Years of W. D. Weatherford* (Knoxville, 1966).

90. Weatherford to BTW, April 20, 1912.

91. BTW to Weatherford, April 28, 1912, Weatherford to BTW, May 23, 1912.

92. BTW to Lyman Beecher Stowe, Oct. 19, 1907.

93. Coon to BTW, Nov. 8, 1910, BTW to Coon, Nov. 11, 1910, *BTW Papers*, X, 447–48, 454.

94. Washington *Post*, July 2, 1903; Stone to BTW, July 2, 1903, *BTW Papers*, VII, 192–93.

95. Stone to BTW, April 5, May 19, July 14, 1905, April 13, May 19, 1906, BTW to Stone, April 6, June 6, July 10, 1905, April 19, 1906. "He is a Southern white man, but a very fair and well meaning one," BTW wrote the manager of the Southern Improvement Company, asking him to supply Stone with information on the stability of farm labor where there was mutual trust and understanding. BTW to W. V. Chambliss, June 6, 1905.

96. BTW to Wright, March 26, 1907, *BTW Papers*, IX, 233–34; Wright to BTW, April 3, 1907 [LC].

97. Wright to BTW, April 15, 1907.

98. Du Bois to Stone, April 13, 1907, W. E. B. Du Bois Papers, University of Massachusetts, Amherst.

99. BTW to Stone, April 19, 1907, *BTW Papers,* IX, 263–65.

100. Stone to BTW, April 23, 1907. Washington responded that he wanted nothing either overstated or understated, "simply the facts, because in the last analysis, anything, other than the truth, at this time, would be more harmful than helpful." BTW to Stone, May 1, 1907.

101. Murphy to BTW, Aug. 26, 1908, Murphy to the editor of the *Outlook,* Aug. 26, 1908. BTW minimized the probable impact of Stone's book, saying: "It is hard to get up enthusiasm in connection with a funeral procession." BTW to Murphy, Aug. 29, 1908.

102. Memorandum for Daniel C. Gilman, Nov. 4, 1908, copy to R. R. Moton.

103. BTW, "Taking Advantage of Our Disadvantages," *A. M. E. Church Review,* X (April 1894), 478–83, in *BTW Papers,* III, 408–12.

104. *American Israelite,* XLI (July 26, 1894), 4.

105. Bedford to BTW, Jan. 14, 1896.

106. William Jenkins to BTW, Aug. 7, 1896, G. W. A. Johnston to BTW, Aug. 13, 1896.

107. BTW address in Little Rock, Ark., quoted in Boston *Transcript,* Dec. 4, 1905, clipping [LC]; BTW to Mrs. A. F. D. Grey, *ca.* June 5, 1903, *BTW Papers,* VII, 169. On this general subject, see Arnold Shankman, "Brothers across the Sea: Afro-Americans on the Persecution of Russian Jews, 1881–1917," *Jewish Social Studies,* XXXVII (Spring 1975), 114–21.

108. Alfred G. Moses to BTW, Jan. 2, 8, 1906, J. Garfield Moses to BTW, Jan. 14, 1906.

109. Typescript of Edelman's lecture, May 5, 1903; *Tuskegee Student,* XV (May 9, 1903), 2; Birmingham *News,* Sept. 5, 1903, clipping attached to BTW to W. H. Baldwin, Jr., Sept. 11, 1903.

110. BTW to Robert H. Terrell, April 4, 1911.

111. A. R. Stewart to BTW, June 14, 1909, BTW to Gassenheimer, June 16, 1909.

112. BTW to Lloyd G. Wheeler, Oct. 17, 1904. See also BTW to Ernest T. Attwell, April 4, 1911.

113. Birmingham *Age-Herald,* Sept. 20, 1902; J. A. Jones to the editor, in Indianapolis *Freeman,* Oct. 18, 1902; BTW to Roosevelt, Sept. 20, 1902, *BTW Papers,* VI, 525.

114. BTW to Ogden, Nov. 16, 1905, *BTW Papers,* VIII, 443.

115. Perry W. Howard to Scott, Oct. 13, 1908, BTW to Dillard, Oct. 21, 1911.

116. Eupora (Miss.) *Warden,* Nov. 5, 1908, clipping [LC]; Memphis *Commercial Appeal,* Oct. 12, 13, 1908, W. T. Montgomery to Scott, Oct. 14, 1908, *BTW Papers,* IX, 652–57.

117. BTW to George Foster Peabody, April 15, 1909 [LC]. See newspaper reports of the Tennessee tour, *BTW Papers,* X, 200–236.

118. Page to BTW, Aug. 3, Oct. 13, 1909.

119. See William H. Lewis's account of the North Carolina tour for the Boston *Transcript*, Nov. 12, 1910, Charles L. Coon to BTW, Nov. 8, 1910, *BTW Papers*, X, 447-48, 455-69.

120. See accounts of BTW's tour of Texas in October 1911, *BTW Papers*, XI, 322-30, 331-43.

121. On the Louisiana tour, April 13-16, 1915, see the thick folder, "Louisiana Tour—Dr. Robert E. Jones in charge," including an article for *Survey* by William A. Aery [LC]; Charles Vincent, "Booker T. Washington's Tour of Louisiana, April, 1915," *Louisiana History*, XXII (Spring 1981), 189-98.

Chapter 11

1. Louis R. Harlan, "Booker T. Washington and the White Man's Burden," *American Historical Review*, LXXI (Jan. 1966), 440-41; Mary E. Townsend, *The Rise and Fall of Germany's Colonial Empire* (New York, 1930), 256-59; on Tuskegee's assistance in Morocco and East Africa, see BTW to G. W. Carver, Sept. 11, 1910 [LC], Dr. Mathiesen, K.W.K., to BTW, Feb. 20, 1912 [LC].

2. Baron Herman, K.W.K., to BTW, Nov. [actually Sept.] 3, 1900; BTW to Herman, Sept. 20, 1900.

3. Harlan, "BTW and the White Man's Burden," 443-44; James N. Calloway, "Tuskegee Cotton-Planters in Africa," *Outlook*, LXX (March 29, 1902), 772-76.

4. Harlan, "BTW and the White Man's Burden," 444-46.

5. Quoted in *Tropenflanzer* (Berlin), sometime in 1910, reprint.

6. *Ibid.*; cf. J. D. Fage, *An Introduction to the History of West Africa* (3rd ed., Cambridge, Eng., 1962), 180; Harry R. Rudin, *Germans in the Cameroons 1884-1914* (New Haven, 1938), 212-13.

7. Hunt to George Roberts, Nov. 29, 1903, Hunt to BTW, Dec. 6, 1903, Sept. 24, 1904.

8. BTW to Cain Triplett, Poindexter Smith, and John P. Powell, Dec. 12, 1904, *BTW Papers*, VIII, 153-54.

9. Harlan, "BTW and the White Man's Burden," 447-48.

10. E. B. Sargant to Grace Lathrop Luling, Nov. 30, 1904, Luling to BTW, Jan. 17, 1905, BTW to Luling, Jan. 23, 1905.

11. BTW, "Cruelty in the Congo Country," *Outlook*, LXXVIII (Oct. 8, 1904), 375-77, in *BTW Papers*, VIII, 85-90; Park to BTW, undated, *ca.* May 1905 [LC]; BTW to Baron Moncheur, May 30, 1905 [LC]; Harlan, "BTW and the White Man's Burden," 449-52.

12. Quoted in Scott to BTW, undated [late Sept. 1908] [LI]; see the evidence, however, of white supremacy attitudes of Roosevelt, Secretary of State Elihu Root, and State Department officials in reference to Liberia, in Harlan, "BTW and the White Man's Burden," 454-55.

13. BTW to Howard, Feb. 6, 1912.

14. BTW to J. L. Morris, editor of Monrovia *Liberian Register*, Jan. 6, 1911 [LC]; Harlan, "BTW and the White Man's Burden," 457-59.

15. *Ibid.*, 459.

16. *Ibid.*, 459–60.

17. Tuskegee's brand of industrial education was always ambiguous enough to attract whites who wanted blacks to remain a "mudsill" caste at the bottom of southern society, but BTW maintained that its purpose was to create an independent small-business class. See Kenneth J. King, *Pan-Africanism and Education* (Oxford, 1971), 21–57, for an account of the use of industrial education as a means of African subordination, particularly under the leadership of Thomas Jesse Jones.

18. Harlan, "BTW and the White Man's Burden," 461–62.

19. Park to Scott, Nov. 8, 1913.

20. Harlan, "BTW and the White Man's Burden," 462–64; King, *Pan-Africanism and Education*, 13.

21. BTW, "Industrial Education in Africa," *Independent*, LX (March 15, 1906), 616–19, in *BTW Papers*, VIII, 548–52.

22. BTW, call for the International Conference on the Negro, April 17–19, 1912.

23. Blyden, quoted in King, *Pan-Africanism and Education*, 17. Blyden had died two months before the conference, but his letter of encouragement was read to the delegates.

24. *Ibid.*, 18–19. Evans, in *Black and White in South East Africa* (London, 1911), 112–13, 117, expressed the view that African education should avoid "overlapping of the races" in their "spheres of activity," and to accomplish this end preferred agricultural education to either industrial or literary education.

25. George A. Gates to BTW, Dec. 4, 1911, BTW to Gates, Dec. 7, 1911, *BTW Papers*, XI, 388–89, 400–401.

26. BTW to "whom it may concern," March 2, 1907; Malcolm Iwane Kawahara to BTW, May 23, 1908, Kawahara to Scott, June 9, 1908.

27. BTW to Nasichi Masaoka, Dec. 5, 1912 [LC]. See also Tuskegee *Southern Letter*, XXIX (Oct. 1913), 2.

28. Lilavati Singh to BTW, June 3, 1901.

29. K. Paramu Pillai to BTW, Jan. 24, 1905, April 25, 1906.

30. Pillai to BTW, April 25, 1906, June 12, 1908.

31. Rama V. Tampan, Parur, Travancore, to BTW, July 4, 1907, BTW to Tampan, Aug. 13, 1907.

32. N. V. Gunaji to BTW, May 15, 1914; C. V. Narasimham to BTW, June 3, 1913.

33. H. H. Pandya to BTW, May 6, 1914, BTW to Pandya, May 19, 1914 [LC]. On his visit, see *Tuskegee Student*, XXV (July 26, 1913), 2.

34. Saint N. Singh to BTW, July 7, 1906, BTW to Singh, July 31, 1906.

35. Quoted in New York *Herald*, May 10, 1903, clipping.

36. Balkrishna Govind Gokhala, "Anagarika Dharmapala: Toward Modernity through Tradition in Ceylon," in Bardwell L. Smith, ed., *Tradition and Change in Theravada Buddhism: Essays on Ceylon and Thailand in the 19th and 20th Centuries* (Leiden, 1973), 30–39.

37. Anagarika H. Dharmapala to BTW, June 20, 1903, BTW Papers, Tuskegee Institute.

38. Dharmapala to BTW, Dec. 26, 1903, BTW to Dharmapala, Dec. 31, 1903.

39. There has been since the 1960s a revival of scholarly interest in Garvey. In addition to the still useful work by E. David Cronon, *Black Moses* (Madison, 1955, 2nd ed., 1969), see Amy Jacques-Garvey, *Garvey and Garveyism* (Kingston, Jamaica, 1963), Tony Martin, *Race First* (Westport, Conn., 1976), and Theodore G. Vincent, *Black Power and the Garvey Movement* (Berkeley, 1975). Robert A. Hill is editing Garvey's scattered papers. See also Lawrence W. Levine, "Marcus Garvey and the Politics of Revitalization," in John Hope Franklin and August Meier, eds., *Black Leaders of the Twentieth Century* (Urbana, 1982), 105–38.

40. Garvey to BTW, Sept. 8, 1914, BTW to Garvey, Sept. 17, 1914. On Garvey's plans to tour the United States, including a visit to Tuskegee, see Garvey to BTW, April 12, 1915, BTW to Garvey, April 27, 1915.

41. Garvey to BTW, Sept. 11, 1915.

42. Garvey to BTW, Sept. 27, 1915.

43. BTW to Garvey, Oct. 2, 1915.

44. New York *Tribune*, Sept. 21, 1903.

45. *Ibid.*, Sept. 22, 1903.

46. New York *Times*, Oct. 2, 1903; Paris *Figaro*, Sept. 30, 1903; Paris *Temps*, Oct. 1, 1903.

47. New York *Times*, Oct. 14, 1903.

48. Wells to BTW, March 10, 1906, *BTW Papers*, VIII, 545–46.

49. BTW to Wells, March 24, 1906.

50. Wells to BTW, April 7, 26, 1906.

51. H. G. Wells, *The Future in America: A Search after Realities* (London, 1906), 259–81.

52. Lyon to BTW, Sept. 19, 1908, *BTW Papers*, IX, 625–27.

53. Roosevelt to BTW, Oct. 26, 1908, Theodore Roosevelt Papers, LC. On Roosevelt's friendship with Johnston, see Alex. Johnston, *The Life and Letters of Sir Harry Johnston* (New York, 1929), 264–68.

54. Scott to BTW, Oct. 23, 1908.

55. "Sir Harry Johnston's Visit," undated typescript [LC]; *Tuskegee Student*, XX (Nov. 21, 1908), 1, (Dec. 12, 1908), 1.

56. Sir Harry H. Johnston, *The Story of My Life* (Indianapolis, 1923), 390, 397.

57. BTW to Lyon, Nov. 12, 1908.

58. Text of Bryce's address, in *Tuskegee Student*, XX (Nov. 28, 1908), 1.

59. "Memorandum. File Sir Harry Johnston," undated typescript. This was apparently a record of an interview, either at Tuskegee or at the State Department in Washington, in November or December 1908.

60. Sir Harry Johnston, "The Negro in America, II. Tuskegee," London *Times*, Jan. 15, 1909. See also his article on Hampton Institute two days earlier.

61. Johnston, *Story of My Life,* 390–91.

62. Johnston to BTW, Jan. 19, April 29, May 9, July 20, 26, 1909, BTW to Johnston, Feb. 10, 28, April 13, May 22, 1909.

63. Scott to BTW, May 28, 1909, *BTW Papers,* X, 120–21.

64. Scott to Roland P. Falkner, Aug. 11, 1909.

65. Falkner to Scott, Aug. 19, 1909, State Department file 12083/288–289, National Archives. See also Falkner to Scott, Aug. 14, 1909 [LC].

66. BTW to Johnston, Sept. 1, 1909. BTW did not inform Johnston that he had shown his confidential letters confidentially to the American commission. BTW to Johnston, Aug. 11, 1909. For evidence of Scott's authorship of the Sept. 1 letter, Scott to Falkner, Aug. 26, 1909.

67. Johnston to BTW, April 29, July 30, Dec. 18, 1910 [LC]; Scott, "Memorandum in re: Sir Harry Johnston's Criticism of the Liberian Report," answering Johnston to BTW, April 29, 1910 [LC]; Scott to Johnston, Sept. 2, 1910 [LC]; Johnston to William H. Taft, Oct. 27, 1910, State Department file 882.51/128, National Archives; Scott to BTW, Nov. 29, 1910 [LC].

68. H. D'Egville, secretary and editor of *Journal of the African Society,* The Imperial Institute, London, to BTW, Oct. 17, 1910 [LC]. He allowed 6000 words for the review, or more if necessary. BTW's review, Jan., 1911, is in *BTW Papers,* X, 566–71.

69. Johnston to BTW, Dec. 18, 1910.

70. BTW to Johnston, Jan. 4, 1911, *BTW Papers,* X, 526–27. Monroe N. Work reviewed the book critically in *Tuskegee Student,* XXIII (Feb. 11, 1911), 1, 4.

71. Carnegie to BTW, Aug. 13, 1910, *BTW Papers,* X, 366. BTW played golf with Carnegie, probably for the first time in his life. BTW to Scott, Sept. 2, 1910, *BTW Papers,* X, 382.

72. Park, autobiographical fragment, quoted in Fred H. Matthews, *Quest for an American Sociology: Robert E. Park and the Chicago School* (Montreal, 1977), 62. Matthews devotes most of a chapter to Park's experiences with Washington and Tuskegee.

73. BTW to W. H. Page, May 18, 1904; Stafford to BTW, Aug. 10, Nov. 12, 1908; BTW to Park, May 2, Sept. 11, 1909.

74. S. L. Williams to BTW, June 7, Oct. 24, 1904; Park to BTW, undated, 1904 or 1905.

75. Park to BTW, Sept. 30, 1909, March 19, 1910, March 1, May 17, 1910; Scott to BTW, March 1, 1910; Page to BTW, June 6, 1910; BTW to Scott, Sept. 2, 1910.

76. "An Autobiographical Note," in Robert E. Park, *Race and Culture: Essays in the Sociology of Contemporary Man* (Glencoe, Ill., 1950), vii.

77. Park to BTW, July 5, 6, 1910.

78. Notebook of BTW's tour of Europe, Aug. 28–Oct. 7, 1910, *BTW Papers,* X, 368–76. The order suggested by the entries in the notebook, however, differs from the itinerary BTW sent Scott, Sept. 10, 1910 [LC].

79. BTW, *The Man Farthest Down: A Record of Observation and Study in Europe* (Garden City, N. Y., 1912), 19.

80. Robert E. Park, "Booker T. Washington," interview with Charles H. Thompson in 1942, quoted in Matthews, *Quest for an American Sociology*, 66.

81. BTW to Scott, Aug. 15, 1910.

82. New York *World* report from London, Sept. 2, 1910, quoted in *Tuskegee Student*, XXII (Sept. 10, 1910), 1.

83. BTW to Scott, Sept. 10, 1910.

84. BTW statement on his visit to Copenhagen, undated typescript, *ca.* 1910 [LC]. Cf., however, his account of the Danish rural schools, "How Denmark Has Taught Itself Prosperity and Happiness," *World's Work*, XXII (June 1911), 14486–94.

85. Milholland circular letter, Oct. 6, 1910, *BTW Papers*, X, 394–400.

86. Du Bois and others, open letter, Oct. 26, 1910, *BTW Papers*, X, 422–25. Another chapter treats events resulting from the letter.

87. Scott to Associated Press, Oct. 22, 1910.

88. BTW to Park, Oct. 20, 24, 1910 [LC]; Matthews, *Quest for an American Sociology*, 66.

89. BTW to Lawrence F. Abbott, Nov. 11, 1910; BTW, "The Man Farthest Down," *Outlook*, CXVIII (May 6, 1911), 21–26, *BTW Papers*, XI, 131–40.

90. BTW to Scott, Nov. 17, 1910; Scott to Park, Nov. 21, 1910; Park to Scott, Nov. 29, 1910.

91. BTW to Park, Nov. 22, 1913.

92. BTW to Park, Aug. 5, 1914.

Chapter 12

1. Montgomery *Advertiser*, May 18, 1902.

2. BTW to Robert C. Ogden, Jan. 9, 1906 [LC]; BTW to Francis J. Garrison, Jan. 10, 1906, *BTW Papers*, VIII, 491–92.

3. BTW to Wickersham, July 18, 1906, *BTW Papers*, IX, 42.

4. Wickersham to BTW, Aug. 3, 1906, BTW Papers, Tuskegee Institute.

5. BTW to Wickersham, Aug. 9, 1906, *BTW Papers*, IX, 53–54.

6. Atlanta *Constitution*, Aug. 30, 1906, *BTW Papers*, IX, 62–67.

7. BTW to Ovington, Sept. 6, 1906.

8. BTW to Villard, Sept. 6, 1906, *BTW Papers*, IX, 69–70.

9. Ovington to BTW, Sept. 10, 1906.

10. An excellent review and analysis of the riot is Charles Crowe, "Racial Massacre in Atlanta, September 22, 1906," *Journal of Negro History*, LIV (April 1969), 150–73.

11. Fortune to Scott, Sept. 25, 1906.

12. BTW to the editor of the New York *World*, Sept. 25, 1906, *BTW Papers*, IX, 74–75. The letter appeared in the *World* on Sept. 26, and in the New York *Times* on the same day.

13. Fortune to Scott, Sept. 28, 1906.

14. Fortune to BTW, Oct. 1, 1906.

15. Undated typescript of editorial, *ca.* Oct. 1906.

16. On Du Bois's whereabouts during the riot, see Rudwick, *W. E. B. Du*

Bois, 107. BTW spent "a part of two days" in Atlanta. BTW to Buttrick, Sept. 30, 1906, *BTW Papers,* IX, 78.

17. BTW to Bowen, Sept. 26, 1906, *BTW Papers,* IX, 76.

18. Villard to BTW, Sept. 27, 1906, *BTW Papers,* IX, 76–77.

19. Quoted in Houston *Freeman,* Nov. 9, 1906, clipping.

20. BTW to Buttrick, Sept. 30, 1906, *BTW Papers,* IX, 78–80.

21. BTW sent Northen a check for $100 to further this work. BTW to Northen, Jan. 11, 1907.

22. BTW, "The Golden Rule in Atlanta," *Outlook,* LXXXIV (Dec. 15, 1906), 913–16.

23. Dewey W. Grantham, Jr., *Hoke Smith and the Politics of the New South* (Baton Rouge, 1958), 147–62.

24. Howell to BTW, Oct. 22, 1906, *BTW Papers,* IX, 100–101.

25. Roosevelt to BTW, Oct. 8, 1906, *BTW Papers,* IX, 92.

26. McKinlay to BTW, Nov. 2, 1906, BTW to McKinlay, Nov. 8, 1906, *BTW Papers,* IX, 113–14, 119.

27. BTW to Villard, Oct. 1, 1906, *BTW Papers,* IX, 81.

28. BTW to Francis J. Garrison, Oct. 2, 1906, *BTW Papers,* IX, 84.

29. BTW to Williams, Oct. 25, 1906, *BTW Papers,* IX, 103–4.

30. Typescript press releases, Dec. 10, 1906 [LC]. See also extracts from BTW's address, Dec. 9, 1906, *BTW Papers,* IX, 158–61.

31. Clarkin to BTW, Dec. 10, 1906 [LC]; Clarkin to Villard, Dec. 10, 1906, Ray Stannard Baker Papers, LC.

32. Baker to BTW, Jan. 16, 1907.

33. Exchange of telegrams between BTW and Baker, Oct. 30–Nov. 7, 1906 [LC]; Baker to his father, Oct. 31, 1906, Ray Stannard Baker Papers, LC.

34. BTW to Villard, Nov. 9, 1906, *BTW Papers,* IX, 120.

35. Ovington to Baker, Nov. 12, 1906, Ray Stannard Baker Papers, LC.

36. Baker to BTW, Dec. 11, 1906.

37. Baker to BTW, Dec. 26, 1906.

38. BTW to Baker, Feb. 1, 1907.

39. A stenographic record of this conference, Jan. 31, 1907, is in the Ray Stannard Baker Papers, LC.

40. Du Bois to Baker, April 3, 1907, W. E. B. Du Bois Papers, University of Massachusetts, Amherst.

41. John S. Phillips to Baker, April 18, 1907, Ray Stannard Baker Papers, LC.

42. Baker's notebook J, 1907, entry for May 2, Ray Stannard Baker Papers, LC.

43. Scott to Banks, May 11, 1907.

44. Banks to Baker, May 13, 1907.

45. BTW to S. E. Courtney, June 19, 1907 [LC]; Du Bois to Baker, May 20, 1907, W. E. B. Du Bois Papers, University of Massachusetts, Amherst.

46. BTW to Baker, July 23, Aug. 21, 1907, *BTW Papers,* IX, 303, 333.

47. Du Bois to Baker, May 20, 1907, W. E. B. Du Bois Papers, University of Massachusetts, Amherst.

48. Villard to Baker, Aug. 29, 1908, Ray Stannard Baker Papers, LC.

49. Baker's journal of interviews, 1907, Ray Stannard Baker Papers, LC.

50. *Ibid.*

51. Frissell to Baker, May 1, 1908, Ray Stannard Baker Papers, LC.

52. See Baker's autobiography, *American Chronicle* (New York, 1945); introduction by Dewey W. Grantham, Jr., to the paperback edition of *Following the Color Line* (New York, 1964); and two good biographies, Robert C. Bannister, *Ray Stannard Baker: The Mind and Thought of a Progressive* (New Haven, 1966), 126–32; and John E. Semonche, *Ray Stannard Baker: A Quest for Democracy in America, 1870–1918* (Chapel Hill, 1969), 198–208.

53. Du Bois to Baker, May 6, 1909, Ray Stannard Baker Papers, LC.

54. Baker to BTW, May 13, 1910.

55. Extracts from BTW's address, Oct. 27, 1906, *BTW Papers*, IX, 104–8.

56. BTW to Emily Howland, Dec. 7, 1906.

57. J. W. Johnson to BTW, Feb. 14, 1907.

58. The best study of Brownsville is by the journalist John D. Weaver, *The Brownsville Raid* (New York, 1970). Ann Lane, *The Brownsville Affair: National Crisis and Black Reaction* (Port Washington, N. Y., 1971); James A. Tinsley, "Roosevelt, Foraker, and the Brownsville Foray," *Journal of Negro History*, XLI (Jan. 1965), 43–65; and Emma Lou Thornbrough, "The Brownsville Episode and the Negro Vote," *Mississippi Valley Historical Review*, XLIV (Dec. 1957), 469–83, emphasize the impact of the affair on black politics. Weaver's study had a decisive effect on the War Department's decision in the 1970s to change the dishonorable discharges to honorable, after all but one of the soldiers involved had died.

59. BTW to McKinlay, Oct. 25, 1906, *BTW Papers*, IX, 103.

60. BTW to Kelly Miller, Nov. 19, 1906, *BTW Papers*, IX, 113–14.

61. BTW to Anderson, Nov. 7, 1906, *BTW Papers*, IX, 118.

62. BTW to Roosevelt, Nov. 2, 1906, *BTW Papers*, IX, 113.

63. Roosevelt to BTW, Nov. 5, 1906, *BTW Papers*, IX, 118.

64. BTW to Anderson, Nov. 7, 1906, *BTW Papers*, IX, 118–19.

65. BTW to Villard, Nov. 10, 1906, *BTW Papers*, IX, 122–23.

66. Villard to BTW, Nov. 16, 1906, *BTW Papers*, IX, 129.

67. Anderson to BTW, Nov. 10, 1906, *BTW Papers*, IX, 123–24.

68. Lane, *Brownsville Affair*, 79; Du Bois, *Dusk of Dawn*, 55.

69. Grant to BTW, Nov. 7, 1906.

70. BTW to Steward, Nov. 10, 1906.

71. BTW to Taft, Nov. 20, 1906, *BTW Papers*, IX, 141.

72. BTW to Miller, Nov. 19, 1906, *BTW Papers*, IX, 138.

73. Roosevelt to Taft from Ponce, Puerto Rico, Nov. 21, 1906, quoted in Weaver, *Brownsville Raid*, 107. A recent study of Roosevelt's thought on race concludes that his summary dismissal was consistent with his belief that blacks were a "backward" race whose social control was essential to white "order." It was a logical extension of his behavior with black soldiers earlier in Cuba, where he maintained that blacks as a group must be "managed" though exceptional individuals could be treated individually. Dyer, *Theodore Roosevelt and the Idea of Race*, 114–15.

74. BTW to Taft, June 6, 1905 [LC]; Julia Davis, "Walter Howard Loving, Military Band Conductor," *Negro History Bulletin*, XXXIII (May 1970), 127.

75. Scott to Taft, Dec. 12, 1906, *BTW Papers*, IX, 163–64.

76. Taft to Scott, Dec. 17, 1906, Jan. 16, 1907, William Howard Taft Papers, LC.

77. Indianapolis *Freeman*, Feb. 23, 1907; Holliday to Scott, Feb. 24, 1907.

78. Scott to Roosevelt, March 8, 1907, *BTW Papers*, IX, 226–28.

79. *Ibid.*

80. BTW to Scott, March 11, 1907.

81. BTW to Taft, May 18, 1907.

82. Scott to Holliday, June 4, 1907.

83. BTW to Villard, June 9, 1907, Villard to Scott, June 4, 1907.

84. BTW to Walters, June 12, 1907.

85. Holliday to Scott, July 18, 1907; J. A. Augur to Military Secretary, U.S. Army, April 5, 1907.

86. Loving to Scott, April 5, 1907.

87. Loving to Scott, May 10, 1907.

88. Williams to Scott, March 19, 1908.

89. Scott to William Loeb, Jr., Oct. 16, 1908.

90. Scott to R. W. Thompson, Oct. 26, 1908.

91. Thompson to Scott, Nov. 27, 1908.

92. Roosevelt to Taft, Nov. 18, 1908, copy in correspondence of Scott with several black editors, Dec. 19, 1908.

93. BTW to Taft, Jan. 29, 1909.

94. Miller to BTW, Nov. 16, 1906, *BTW Papers*, IX, 131.

95. *Ibid.*, 130.

96. BTW to Miller, Nov. 19, 1906, *BTW Papers*, IX, 137–39.

97. See discussion of the message in Merrill and Merrill, *Republican Command*, 241–42; and for a more general discussion of Roosevelt's views on black crime, lynching, and race riots, see Dyer, *Theodore Roosevelt and the Idea of Race*, 109–17.

98. Fortune to BTW, Dec. 8, 1906, *BTW Papers*, IX, 156–58.

99. The incorporation of the New York *Age* is definitively discussed in Thornbrough, *T. Thomas Fortune*, 296–98. See also Scott to BTW, Jan. 18, 1907, *BTW Papers*, IX, 191–92.

100. Scott to BTW, Jan. 11, 1907.

101. Thornbrough, *T. Thomas Fortune*, 306–8; Anderson to BTW, Nov. 19, 1907, *BTW Papers*, IX, 403.

102. BTW to Fannie Barrier Williams, Sept. 16, 1907.

103. Thornbrough, *T. Thomas Fortune*, 314–16; Anderson to BTW, Nov. 19, 1907 [LC].

104. Anonymous Chicago white man to BTW, Nov. 28, 1906, *BTW Papers*, IX, 148–149.

105. BTW to Williams, Dec. 3, 1906, *BTW Papers*, IX, 152–53.

106. Anonymous letter to BTW, *ca.* 1908.

Chapter 13

1. On the origins of the Negro-American Political League, see Fox, *Guardian of Boston*, 110–12. It later changed its name to the National Independent Political League. See also Emma Lou Thornbrough, "The Brownsville Episode and the Negro Vote," *Mississippi Valley Historical Review*, XLIV (Dec. 1957), 469–93; James A. Tinsley, "Roosevelt, Foraker, and the Brownsville Affray," *Journal of Negro History*, XLI (Jan. 1956), 43–65.

2. BTW to Scott, June 9, 1907, *BTW Papers*, IX, 297.

3. Vorys to BTW, July 1, 1907 [LC]; BTW to Vorys, July 8, 1907, *BTW Papers*, IX, 301.

4. Thornbrough, *T. Thomas Fortune*, 301.

5. New York *Age*, Oct. 17, 1907; Thornbrough, *T. Thomas Fortune*, 314–15.

6. *Ibid.*, 316–17.

7. BTW to Tyler, Nov. 4, 1907, BTW to Fortune, Nov. 5, 1907, *BTW Papers*, IX, 395, 396–98.

8. Scott to BTW, March 6, 1908, *BTW Papers*, IX, 460–61.

9. Fortune, "Negroes in Revolt against Booker Washington," New York *American*, May 3, 1908.

10. Quoted in undated clipping, *ca.* June 23, 1908.

11. Quoted in Weaver, *Brownsville Raid*, 274–75.

12. James A. Cobb to Scott, undated, *ca.* March 27, 1908. Note also indecision of Anderson and Moore on the New York entertainment of the 10th Cavalry. Anderson to BTW, July 20, 1909.

13. BTW to Loeb, Feb. 3, 1908, *BTW Papers*, IX, 449–50.

14. BTW to Roosevelt, Feb. 7, 1908.

15. George von L. Meyer to BTW, Feb. 10, 1908; Thompson to Scott, Feb. 10, 1908, Scott to Thompson, Feb. 11, 1908.

16. BTW to Loeb, Feb. 24, 26, 1908; see also Scott editorial for Montgomery *Colored Alabamian, ca.* Feb 20, 1908; BTW to Meyer, Feb. 22, 1908; Nathan Alexander to BTW, March 11, 1908.

17. G. W. A. Johnston to BTW, March 17, 1908 [LC]. On the use of code names in their correspondence, see Scott to Thompson, March 7, 1908, *BTW Papers*, IX, 461–62.

18. BTW to Thompson, March 4, 1908.

19. BTW to Frank H. Hitchcock, April 22, 24, 1908 [LC]; BTW to Taft, June 5, 1908, *BTW Papers*, IX, 557. See also Scott to the editor of the New York *Age*, June 6, 1908 [LC]; Thompson to Scott, June 6, 1908 [LC]; Thompson to BTW, June 6, 1908, *BTW Papers*, IX, 558–59.

20. Cohen to BTW, March 6, 1908.

21. BTW to Cohen, June 8, 1908, Cohen to BTW, June 9, 1908.

22. BTW to Grant, Jan. 23, 1908, *BTW Papers*, IX, 443–44; Grant to BTW, Jan. 29, 1908 [LC].

23. BTW to McKinlay, Jan. 22, 1908, McKinlay to BTW, Jan. 30, 1908.

24. McKinlay to Scott, Feb. 16, 1908, Grant to BTW, Feb. 18, 1908.

25. BTW to Grant, Feb. 21, 22, 1908, McKinlay to BTW, Feb. 21, 1908 [LC]; BTW to McKinlay, Feb. 22, 1908, *BTW Papers*, IX, 455.

26. BTW to Frank H. Hitchcock, Feb. 21, 1908; BTW to A. I. Vorys, Feb. 21, 1908.

27. BTW to Hitchcock, March 3, 1908.

28. BTW to Vorys, Feb. 26, 1908.

29. Tyler to BTW, March 11, 1908.

30. Tyler to Scott, March 20, 1908.

31. BTW to Tyler, March 21, 1908, *BTW Papers*, IX, 475.

32. Tyler to Scott, March 31, 1908.

33. Tyler to BTW, April 20, 1908, *BTW Papers*, IX, 504–5.

34. BTW to Hitchcock, March 1, 1908, *BTW Papers*, IX, 458–59.

35. Pinchback to BTW, March 20, 24, 1908 [LC]; BTW to Hitchcock, March 23, 1908 [LC]. See also Pinchback to BTW, March 17, 1908, *BTW Papers*, IX, 473.

36. Pinchback to BTW, March 25, 28, 1908.

37. National Negro-American Political League, Address to the Country, April 8, 1908.

38. Tyler to Hitchcock, carbon to BTW, April 10, 1908 [LC]; Tyler to BTW, April 11, 1908, *BTW Papers*, IX, 497–98.

39. BTW to Scott, March 26, 1908, Scott to William Loeb, Jr., April 14, 1908.

40. BTW to Taft, March 9, 1908, *BTW Papers*, IX, 463–65.

41. Typescript of Taft's address at Fisk, May 22, 1908.

42. BTW to J. W. Cooper, June 20, 1908, *BTW Papers*, IX, 585.

43. Tyler to BTW, April 20, 1908, *BTW Papers*, IX, 504–5; Tyler to Scott, April 25, 1908 [LC]; Tyler to BTW, April 28, 1908 [LC].

44. Vorys to BTW, May 11, 1908, BTW to Vorys, May 19, 1908.

45. Taft to BTW, May 28, 1908, *BTW Papers*, IX, 544.

46. BTW to Anderson, June 3, 1908, *BTW Papers*, IX, 549–50.

47. Anderson to BTW, telegram, June 6, 1908, *BTW Papers*, IX, 559. See also BTW to Anderson, June 8, 1908, IX, 562–63.

48. BTW to Taft, June 6, 7, 1908, *BTW Papers*, IX, 558, 560–61.

49. BTW to Taft, June 4, 1908, with two enclosures, *BTW Papers*, IX, 550–52.

50. Scott to BTW, June 16, 1908, *BTW Papers*, IX, 581.

51. BTW to Anderson, June 19, 1908, *BTW Papers*, IX, 582–83.

52. Tyler to Scott, July 2, 1908.

53. BTW to Hitchcock, July 7, 1908 [LC]; see also BTW to Taft, July 7, 1908, *BTW Papers*, IX, 589.

54. BTW to Taft, July 9, 1908, *BTW Papers*, IX, 590.

55. BTW to Taft, July 8, 1908.

56. Taft to BTW, July 10, 1908 [LC]; Scott to BTW, July 13, 1908 [LC]; "Persons for Mr. Taft to invite," undated typescript, probably enclosed in BTW to Taft, July 18, 1908, *BTW Papers*, IX, 599–600.

57. Taft to BTW, July 19, 1908 [LC]; BTW to Scott, July 22, 1908, *BTW Papers*, IX, 603.

58. "Taft's Original Draft," typescript probably enclosed in BTW to Scott, July 22, 1908.

59. "New Draft," typescript probably enclosed in BTW to Scott, July 22, 1908; Taft to BTW, July 22, 1908.

60. Scott to BTW, July 25, 1908.

61. BTW to Anderson, June 22, 1908.

62. Anderson to Scott, June 27, 1908.

63. Anderson to Herbert Parsons, July 27, 1908, carbon to BTW.

64. BTW to Anderson, July 31, 1908.

65. Reid to Mrs. Cowles, Aug. 28, 1908, Whitelaw Reid Papers, LC.

66. Thompson to BTW, Sept. 6, 1908.

67. *Ibid.*

68. BTW to Ward, Sept. 6, 1908 [LC]. See also BTW to Ward, Sept. 8, 1908, *BTW Papers*, IX, 619–20, with enclosed suggestions.

69. Anderson to BTW, Sept. 10, 1908, *BTW Papers*, IX, 621–22.

70. BTW, undated memorandum for Ward.

71. Thompson to BTW, Sept. 15, 1908.

72. *Ibid.*

73. Scott to Thompson, Sept. 17, 1908, Thompson to Scott, Sept. 18, 1908.

74. Scott to Tyler, Sept. 17, 1908, Tyler to Scott, Sept. 18, 1908.

75. BTW to Ward, Sept. 30, 1908, two letters and enclosures.

76. Anderson to BTW, Oct. 2, 1908, *BTW Papers*, IX, 633–34.

77. BTW to Anderson, Oct. 3, 1908.

78. Anderson to BTW, Oct. 7, 1908.

79. Thompson to Scott, Oct. 8, 1908.

80. Anderson to BTW, Oct. 12, 1908, *BTW Papers*, IX, 649–51.

81. Tyler to Scott, Oct. 27, 1908, *BTW Papers*, IX, 669–70.

82. Anderson to BTW, Oct. 29, 1908.

83. Du Bois, in *Horizon*, Nov.–Dec. 1908, p. 11, quoted in Rudwick, *Du Bois*, 114.

Chapter 14

1. Page to BTW, Nov. 5, 1908, *BTW Papers*, IX, 687–88.

2. BTW to Page, Nov. 9, 1908, *BTW Papers*, IX, 690–91. BTW warned Page, however, that the southerners might "fall over themselves" to persuade Taft to abandon black education and political rights. BTW to Page, Nov. 12, 1908 [LC].

3. BTW to Taft, Nov. 19, 1908, *BTW Papers*, IX, 694.

4. BTW, "Memo for Mr. Taft," undated, early Nov. 1908. BTW sent the memo by Scott, who could find no hotel accommodations in Hot Springs, Va., but stayed at the house of the headwaiter. Scott to R. N. Smith, Nov. 27, Dec. 2, 1908.

5. Hugh M. Browne to BTW, Dec. 21, 1908 [LC]. A copy of the address in Committee of Twelve pamphlet form is in the William Howard Taft Papers, LC. See also BTW to Carnegie, March 12, 1909 [LC].

6. BTW to Taft, Dec. 1, 1908, *BTW Papers,* IX, 697.

7. Crum to Scott, Oct. 3, 1908.

8. Ellen Crum to BTW, Feb. 13, 1909, *BTW Papers,* X, 39–40.

9. BTW to Crum, Feb. 24, 1909, *BTW Papers,* X, 52.

10. Crum to Roosevelt, undated draft, *ca.* Feb. 27, 1909, *BTW Papers,* X, 57.

11. BTW to Scott, Feb. 24, 1909, Scott to BTW, Feb. 24, 1909, telegrams, *BTW Papers,* X, 53.

12. BTW to Scott, Feb. 25, 1909, *BTW Papers,* X, 54–55.

13. BTW to Taft, Feb. 28, 1909, *BTW Papers,* X, 58.

14. Gatewood, *Theodore Roosevelt and the Art of Controversy,* 133.

15. BTW to Scott, Feb. 25, 1909, *BTW Papers,* X, 54–55.

16. BTW to Scott, Feb. 24, 1909, *BTW Papers,* X, 53.

17. BTW to Tyler, Jan. 16, 1911, *BTW Papers,* X, 551–52.

18. Tyler to Scott, Jan. 27, 1908.

19. Birmingham *Age-Herald,* May 9, 1909, clipping; Edmund H. Dryer to BTW, May 10, 1909, BTW to Dryer, May 14, 1909.

20. BTW to Cobb, April 21, 1909, *BTW Papers,* X, 91.

21. BTW to Taft, April 23, 1909, *BTW Papers,* X, 91–92; Taft to BTW, April 26, 1909, William Howard Taft Papers, LC.

22. Charles Banks to Fred W. Carpenter, June 18, 1909.

23. Banks to Scott, Aug. 27, 1909.

24. BTW to Taft, June 18, 1909, enclosing a list of "Colored men who have disappeared from office since Mr. Taft became President," *BTW Papers,* X, 138–40.

25. Taft to BTW, June 24, 1909, *BTW Papers,* X, 140.

26. R. W. Thompson to Scott, Aug. 6, 1909.

27. BTW to Anderson, Aug. 20, 1909, *BTW Papers,* X, 157.

28. BTW to W. T. Andrews, Sept. 16, 1909; Taft to BTW, Aug. 25, 1909.

29. Moton to BTW, Sept. 9, 1909, Moton to Scott, Sept. 9, 1909, Scott to Moton, Sept. 25, 1909.

30. BTW to Anderson, Nov. 19, 1909.

31. BTW to Anderson, Dec. 5, 1909.

32. BTW to Anderson, Dec. 26, 1909.

33. BTW to Taft, Feb. 19, 1910, *BTW Papers,* X, 271–72.

34. BTW to Anderson, Feb. 19, 1910, *BTW Papers,* X, 270–71.

35. Taft to BTW, Feb. 22, 1910, *BTW Papers,* X, 273.

36. J. O. Thompson to BTW, July 31, 1909, reporting a conversation with Johnson.

37. Rucker to Scott, Feb. 24, 1910; Tyler to Scott, Feb. 26, 1910.

38. BTW to McKinlay, Feb. 24, 1910, Carter G. Woodson Papers, LC.

39. Scott, memorandum on "Changes affecting Colored people since Mr. Taft's Inauguration," March 4, 1910, *BTW Papers,* X, 275–77.

40. Pinchback to Fred R. Moore, March 1, 1910.

41. BTW to Dancy, March 10, 1910.

42. See, for example, Tyler to Scott, March 24, 1910.

43. BTW to Scott, March 14, 1910, Scott to BTW, March 17, 1910, R. W. Thompson to Scott, March 18, 1910.

44. BTW to James A. Cobb, April 1, 1910, *BTW Papers*, X, 306–8.

45. BTW to Bowles, April 5, 1910; see also BTW to Mr. O'Brien of the Boston *Transcript*, March 16, 1910.

46. BTW to Napier, May 24, 1910 [LC]; BTW to Taft, May 25, 1910, William Howard Taft Papers, LC.

47. Pinchback to BTW, June 19, 1910.

48. BTW to Pinchback, June 21, 1910.

49. Banks to BTW, July 28, 1910.

50. Lewis to Scott, Sept. 15, 1910.

51. Lewis to Fred R. Moore, Sept. 15, 1910, copy to Charles D. Norton, William Howard Taft Papers, LC.

52. Charles D. Norton to Scott, Sept. 15, 1910, *BTW Papers*, X, 384–85.

53. Villard to Norton, Sept. 20, 1910, *BTW Papers*, X, 385–87. See also Kellogg, *NAACP*, I, 73–74.

54. William Garrott Brown to Norton, Oct. 13, 1910, William Howard Taft Papers, LC.

55. BTW to Taft, Oct. 27, 1910, *BTW Papers*, X, 426.

56. Scott to BTW, Nov. 5, 1910, *BTW Papers*, X, 438–40.

57. Moton to Taft, Nov. 8, 1910, Hampton Institute Archives.

58. BTW to Anderson, Nov. 9, 1910, *BTW Papers*, X, 450–51.

59. BTW to Napier, Feb. 21, 1911, *BTW Papers*, X, 592.

60. Special Report of the Executive Committee of the American Bar Association and the Rescission Thereof, 1912, William Howard Taft Papers, LC.

61. Lewis to BTW, Feb. 21, 1912.

62. BTW to Wickersham, April 4, 1912 [LC]. The NAACP board of directors sent a similar note. Minutes of board meeting, March 5, 1912, NAACP Archives, LC.

63. Wickersham to BTW, Sept. 16, 1912.

64. Tyler to Scott, Nov. 19, 1912.

65. See particularly Tyler to Hilles, May 9, 1911, enclosed in Tyler to Scott, May 20, 1911.

66. Huntington Wilson to Taft, Sept. 11, 1912, William Howard Taft Papers, LC.

67. BTW to Tyler, June 21, 1911; also similar letter, BTW to McKinlay, June 21, 1911.

68. Tyler to Scott, Jan. 18, 1912.

69. Tyler to Scott, Jan. 19, 1912, *BTW Papers*, XI, 459–60.

70. Tyler to Taft, Feb. 9, 1912, Hilles to Tyler, Feb. 9, 1912, William Howard Taft Papers, LC.

71. Tyler to Hilles, and enclosed memorandum for Taft, April 6, 1912, William Howard Taft Papers, LC.

72. Tyler to Scott, Jan. 19, 1912, *BTW Papers*, XI, 459–60.

73. Boston *Herald*, Feb. 12, 1912, clipping, and attached typescript summary of Judge Hook's decision in the McCabe case, Feb. 10, 1911.

74. BTW to Blanche K. Bruce, Feb. 17, 1912, *BTW Papers*, XI, 466.

75. Lewis to BTW, Feb. 20, 1912.

76. BTW to Charles Banks, May 20, 1912, *BTW Papers*, XI, 539; BTW to John R. Lynch, June 7, 1912 [LC]. On southern politics in 1912, see Paul D. Casdorph, *Republicans, Negroes, and Progressives in the South, 1912–1916* (University, Ala., 1981), 23–92.

77. Myers to BTW, Feb. 26, 1912, *BTW Papers*, XI, 469–70. On the "late unpleasantness," see below, Chapter 14.

78. Tyler to Scott, Feb. 28, 1912.

79. Scott to Tyler, Feb. 28, 1912, Tyler to Scott, March 22, 1912.

80. See, for example, McKinlay to C. B. Purvis, May 1, 1913, Carter G. Woodson Papers, LC; Scott to Cobb, March 22, 1913 [LC].

81. Villard to BTW, Aug. 5, 1912, BTW to Villard, Aug. 29, 1912, *BTW Papers*, XI, 575, 586–87; Anderson to BTW, Aug. 7, 1912 [LC].

82. Wilson to Villard, Aug. 23, 1912, Ray Stannard Baker Papers, LC.

83. Wilson to Alexander Walters, Oct. 16, 1912, NAACP Archives, LC.

84. Anderson to BTW, Oct. 3, 1912.

85. Tyler to Scott, Oct. 3, 1912; Anderson to BTW, Oct. 28, 1912.

86. BTW to Napier, Nov. 7, 1912.

87. Tyler to Scott, Nov. 23, 1912 [LC]; McKinlay to Pinchback, Nov. 23, 1912, Carter G. Woodson Papers, LC.

88. R. W. Thompson to Scott, Nov. 15, 1912.

89. Lewis to BTW, Jan. 16, 1913; Tyler to BTW, Dec. 16, 1912. Stewart represented the Constitution League at the Johnson trial. Stewart to BTW, Dec. 16, 1912.

90. BTW to Lewis, Jan. 20, 1913.

91. *Ibid.*

92. BTW to Pinchback, Feb. 25, 1913.

93. BTW to Rosenwald, Dec. 24, 1912.

94. BTW to Rosenwald, Dec. 30, 1912. See also BTW to Rosenwald, Jan. 3, 1913.

95. Nashville *Banner*, March 1, 1913.

96. BTW to Anderson, March 24, 1913.

97. BTW to Lewis, March 21, 1913.

Chapter 15

1. BTW to James R. B. Van Cleave, Feb. 9, 1909, *BTW Papers*, X, 26–27.

2. Van Cleave to BTW, Feb. 14, 1910.

3. Villard to BTW, May 26, 1909, *BTW Papers*, X, 116–18.

4. BTW to Villard, May 28, 1909, *BTW Papers*, X, 118–20.

5. Anderson to BTW, May 29, 1909.

6. Anderson to BTW, May 30, 1909, *BTW Papers*, X, 126.

7. Anderson to BTW, May 31, 1909, *BTW Papers*, X, 127.

8. Rudwick, *Du Bois*, 123–24.

9. Garrison to Villard, June 6, 1909, Oswald Garrison Villard Papers, Harvard University.

10. Allen W. Washington to Moton, Aug. 9, 1909, Hampton Institute Archives.

11. Boston *Transcript*, March 19, 1910, clipping, George Foster Peabody Papers, LC.

12. New York *Evening Post*, April 1, 1910.

13. Thompson to Scott, April 9, 17, 1910, and clippings enclosed.

14. Garrison to Villard, May 18, 1910, Oswald Garrison Villard Papers, Harvard University.

15. Myers to BTW, Oct. 31, 1910, *BTW Papers*, X, 433–35.

16. BTW to Moore, Dec. 27, 1910; BTW to Anderson, Nov. 10, 1910.

17. Chase to BTW, Nov. 22, 1910.

18. BTW to Moore, July 15, 1911, *BTW Papers*, XI, 268–69. See also BTW to Moore, July 22, 1911 [LC].

19. Anderson to Scott, Feb. 25, 1907, *BTW Papers*, IX, 223–25; Meier, *Negro Thought in America*, 239–40.

20. BTW to R. H. Terrell, April 27, 1910, *BTW Papers*, X, 323.

21. Scott to BTW, April 30, 1910.

22. M. C. Terrell to BTW, May 24, 1910.

23. Baker to BTW, May 13, 1910.

24. BTW to Baker, May 24, 1910, *BTW Papers*, X, 333–34.

25. BTW to Baker, July 7, 1910, *BTW Papers*, X, 352–53.

26. R. S. Baker notebook, entries for Feb. 9, 13, 1915, Ray Stannard Baker Papers, LC.

27. A treatment of these interrelated circulars from the NAACP perspective is Kellogg, *NAACP*, I, 75–78.

28. Milholland, circular letter, Oct. 6, 1910, *BTW Papers*, X, 394–400.

29. Report of BTW's address, in London *Times*, Oct. 7, 1910, *BTW Papers*, X, 401–4.

30. Manchester *Guardian*, Oct. 8, 1910, *BTW Papers*, X, 404–5.

31. BTW to Moton, Oct. 24, 1910, *BTW Papers*, X, 416–17.

32. Du Bois, *Dusk of Dawn*, 229.

33. The text in full is in *BTW Papers*, X, 422–25.

34. Coon to BTW, Nov. 8, 1910, BTW to Coon, Nov. 11, 1910, *BTW Papers*, X, 447–48, 454.

35. Moton to Villard, Nov. 15, 1910, *BTW Papers*, X, 472–73.

36. BTW to Pickens, Nov. 15, 1910, *BTW Papers*, X, 471.

37. Pickens to BTW, Nov. 18, 1910, *BTW Papers*, X, 477–78.

38. Pickens to BTW, Nov. 24, 1910, *BTW Papers*, X, 489–91.

39. BTW to Buxton, Nov. 19, 1910, *BTW Papers*, X, 478–79.

40. Du Bois to Moton, Nov. 21, 1910, *BTW Papers*, X, 480–81.

41. BTW to T. Fisher Unwin, Nov. 16, 1910.

42. Villard to Moton, Nov. 23, 1910, *BTW Papers,* X, 487–89.

43. Moton to BTW, Dec. 2, 1910, *BTW Papers,* X, 498.

44. BTW to Howell, Nov. 23, 1910, *BTW Papers,* X, 483–84.

45. Tyler to Scott, Nov. 22, 1910, enclosing editorial; BTW to Tyler, Nov. 25, 1910.

46. M. C. Terrell to BTW, Saturday (Dec. 9, 1910).

47. BTW to M. C. Terrell, Dec. 10, 1910, two telegrams.

48. BTW to Villard, Dec. 11, 1910, *BTW Papers,* X, 502–4.

49. BTW to Scott, Dec. 12, 1910, *BTW Papers,* X, 504–5.

50. Minutes of National Negro Conference, Nov. 8, 1909, minutes of executive committee, March 7, June 6, 1911, Jan. 4, 1912, NAACP Archives, LC; Kellogg, *NAACP,* I, 304, 306.

51. Villard to BTW, Dec. 13, 1910, *BTW Papers,* X, 505–6.

52. BTW to Scott, Dec. 17, 1910, *BTW Papers,* X, 508. See also BTW to R. C. Simmons, Dec. 17, 1910 [LC].

53. BTW to Villard, Jan. 10, 1911, *BTW Papers,* X, 540–44.

54. *Crisis,* I (Dec. 1910), 15.

55. *Crisis,* I (Jan. 1911), 9–10, and comment, 10–11.

56. Villard to BTW, Jan. 19, 1911, *BTW Papers,* X, 554–55.

57. BTW to Anderson, Jan. 23, 1911.

58. *Crisis,* II (July 1911), 105–6.

59. Villard to BTW, Feb. 7, 1911, *BTW Papers,* X, 573–75.

60. BTW to Villard, Feb. 11, 1911, *BTW Papers,* X, 575–76.

61. BTW to Scott, Feb. 13, 1911, *BTW Papers,* X, 585.

62. Scott, letters to ten black editors, Feb. 24, 1911.

63. BTW to J. R. Barlow, March 1, 1911, *BTW Papers,* X, 608–9.

64. BTW to Isaac Fisher, March 1, 1911, *BTW Papers,* X, 609.

65. BTW to Fortune, Jan. 20, 1911, *BTW Papers,* X, 555–56.

66. Fortune to BTW, Jan. 23, 1911, *BTW Papers,* X, 556–57.

67. The 1908 Cosmopolitan Club dinner is treated in Harlan, "Secret Life of BTW," 413–14; Kellogg, *NAACP,* I, 71–72.

68. Anderson to BTW, Jan. 19, 1911, *BTW Papers,* X, 553–54.

69. BTW to Anderson, Jan. 21, 1911, *BTW Papers,* X, 556.

70. Anderson to BTW, Jan. 23, 1911.

71. Anderson to BTW, Jan. 25, 1911, *BTW Papers,* X, 558–59.

72. New York *Press,* Jan. 25, 1911, *BTW Papers,* X, 560–63.

73. Anderson to BTW, Jan. 26, 1911, *BTW Papers,* X, 563–64.

74. Scott to Anderson, Jan. 28, 1911, *BTW Papers,* X, 564.

75. Mary White Ovington, *The Walls Came Tumbling Down* (New York, 1947), 43–47; Harlan, "Secret Life of BTW," 414–15.

Chapter 16

1. Press release of an account of the assault by N. Barnett Dodson, black syndicated columnist, *ca.* March 22, 1911; New York *World,* Nov. 7, 1911, *BTW Papers,* XI, 28, 361.

2. BTW, interview in New York *World,* March 22, 1911.

3. Quoted in New York *Evening Post,* March 21, 1911.

4. Quoted in New York *Evening Post,* March 20, 1911.

5. Quoted in Philadelphia *Public Ledger,* clipping with dateline Nov. 6, 1911.

6. *Ibid.*

7. Quoted in New York *Evening Post,* Nov. 6, 1911.

8. Quoted in unidentified clipping, *ca.* Nov. 6, 1911.

9. *Ibid.*

10. Quoted in New York *Herald,* March 20, 1911, clipping [LC]. See also discussion of the theft charge against Ulrich in Willard B. Gatewood, "Booker T. Washington and the Ulrich Affair," *Phylon,* XXX (Fall 1969), 288.

11. A few weeks later while presenting resolutions of support for BTW before a black audience, the indiscreet Moore mentioned the three names. Anderson "stepped up and kicked him on the foot," and afterward explained that "as I was chairman of the meeting, and he presented the resolutions, and Smith was sitting by my side, the newspapers might look upon the movement as one engineered by the Doctor's three close friends, rather than as a spontaneous uprising of the colored people in his favor." Anderson to BTW, April 5, 1911, *BTW Papers,* XI, 82.

12. New York *World,* March 20, 1911.

13. New York *World,* March 22, 1911.

14. Quoted in New York *Evening Post,* March 21, 1911. Meanwhile, however, BTW had telegraphed Scott asking for a copy of a letter, and received, in the name of his traveling secretary Nathan Hunt, the following telegram: "Your telegram recd unable to understand from it what Copies of letters you wish. Please telegraph me definitely today to Fearing so he can be advised by friends." Scott to Hunt, March 20, 1911, *BTW Papers,* XI, 3. This suggests that Scott knew of no letter that would support BTW's account.

15. Low to BTW, March 9, 1911.

16. Villard to Francis J. Garrison, March 20, 1911, Oswald Garrison Villard Papers, Harvard University.

17. Quoted in New York *Evening Post,* March 21, 1911.

18. BTW to E. Davidson Washington, March 21, 1911 [LC]; BTW to BTW, Jr., March 21, 1911, *BTW Papers,* XI, 10.

19. Carnegie to W. H. Taft, March 25, 1911, Andrew Carnegie Papers, LC.

20. Roosevelt to BTW, March 28, 1911, *BTW Papers,* XI, 50.

21. Taft to BTW, March 21, 1911, see also BTW to Taft, March 22, 1911, *BTW Papers,* XI, 10, 16.

22. Arthur S. Link, *Wilson: The Road to the White House* (Princeton, 1947), 388. Several Democratic opponents of Wilson's nomination wrote to inquire whether Wilson had expressed sympathy. William E. Reynolds to BTW, May 22, 1912 [LC]; Luke Clancy to E. J. Scott, May 16, 1912 [LC].

23. Scott to Nathan Hunt, March 20, 1911, Scott to C. H. Fearing, March 22, 1911, *BTW Papers,* XI, 3, 18.

24. Anderson to BTW, March 28, 1911, *BTW Papers,* XI, 48–49.

25. Roscoe C. Simmons to BTW, March 30, 1911.

26. *Crisis*, I (April 1911), 11; Boston *Guardian*, March 25, 1911, quoted in Fox, *Guardian of Boston*, 134.

27. Chesnutt to BTW, March 22, 1911, *BTW Papers*, XI, 19.

28. BTW to Anderson, March 28, 1911, *BTW Papers*, XI, 46.

29. Richmond *Times-Dispatch*, March 21, 1911.

30. BTW to James C. Hemphill, March 28, 1911, Hemphill Family Papers, Duke University.

31. *Ibid.*

32. John Massey and others to BTW, March 23, 1911.

33. Gilchrist Stewart to BTW, March 28, 1911, *BTW Papers*, XI, 50–51. He added: "Unfortunately the first statement of a telegram, then a letter and the attorney holding out that the letter would be produced at trial, and then the subsequent statement, that the letter was destroyed, have all given rise to some doubt upon which a thousand interpretations have been stretched."

34. New York *Press*, March 22, 1911.

35. Nathan Hunt to Charles H. Fearing, March 21, 1911, Fearing to D. C. Smith, March 21, 1911, *BTW Papers*, XI, 11.

36. New York *American*, March 25, 1911.

37. Typed memorandum referring to "Scott interview," undated.

38. Augustus W. Abbott to Edward T. Devine, March 20, 1911, *BTW Papers*, XI, 8–9; New York *Herald*, March 22, 23, 1911; Washington *Post*, March 23, 1911, *BTW Papers*, XI, 31–32.

39. BTW to Wilford H. Smith, March 26, 1911, *BTW Papers*, XI, 40–41.

40. There are cryptic references to Smith's employment of "C" for some unexplained services of an investigative or clandestine nature in Scott to Wilford H. Smith, April 6, 1911, *BTW Papers*, XI, 87–88.

41. *Ibid.*

42. BTW to Low, April 9, 1911, *BTW Papers*, XI, 91–92.

43. John J. Reid to BTW, April 12, 1911.

44. Leland P. Botsford statement, April 8, 1911, enclosed in Botsford to BTW, April 10, 1911, *BTW Papers*, XI, 96–97. A distinguished New York physician who passed by after the arrest wrote that BTW, whom he did not recognize in his torn and bleeding condition, "presented a picture of dignity and reserve force in spite of his excitement and his bleeding face." George Livingston Peabody to Low, March 20, 1911, Seth Low Papers, Columbia University.

45. Botsford to BTW, April 19, 1911 [LC]; BTW to Botsford, April 22, 1911, *BTW Papers*, XI, 112–13.

46. BTW to Cravath, April 29, 1911, *BTW Papers*, XI, 119.

47. BTW to Low, April 16, 1911, Seth Low Papers, Columbia University.

48. BTW to Anderson, April 16, 1911, *BTW Papers*, XI, 104.

49. BTW to Low, April 27, 1911, BTW to Cravath, April 29, 1911, BTW to W. H. Smith, May 15, July 14, 1911, W. H. Smith to BTW, May 25, 1911, *BTW Papers*, XI, 117–18, 119, 156, 170, 267–68; BTW to Smith, June 1, 2, 1911, Smith to BTW, July 12, 1911 [LC].

50. BTW to W. H. Smith, July 22, 1911, *BTW Papers*, XI, 272.

51. Anderson to Scott, undated, *ca.* Aug. 8, 1911, Scott to Anderson, Aug. 10, 1911; BTW to Pinkerton's National Detective Agency, Sept. 1, Oct. 10, 1911.

52. New York *Evening Post,* Nov. 6, 1911.

53. BTW privately attributed the acquittal to the fact that Ulrich was a Tammany ward heeler, and to perjured testimony. BTW to F. K. Collins, Aug. 21, 1911 [LC]; BTW to Jennie E. Watson, Nov. 20, 1911, *BTW Papers,* XI, 372–73.

54. New York *Age* galley proof, *ca.* Nov. 6, 1911, *BTW Papers,* XI, 356–57.

55. New York *World,* Nov. 7, 1911, *BTW Papers,* XI, 359–62.

56. *Ibid.,* 361–62.

57. Thomas Dixon, Jr., letter to the editor, Kansas City *Post,* March 26, 1911, and reports of fund raising for Ulrich in Memphis and in Alabama, New York *Sun,* March 25, 1911, clippings.

58. Villard to Francis J. Garrison, March 24, 1911, Oswald Garrison Villard Papers, Harvard University; BTW to Villard, March 30, 1911, telegram [LC].

59. Anderson to BTW, March 29, 1911 [LC]; see also telegrams of Tyler, Anderson, Moton, and Williams to BTW, March 28, 29, 1911, *BTW Papers,* XI, 52–54. George A. Myers and W. H. Lewis also supported conciliation.

60. BTW to Villard, March 30, 1911, *BTW Papers,* XI, 54–55.

61. Villard to BTW, March 31, 1911, telegram.

62. Villard to Low, April 13, 1911, Oswald Garrison Villard Papers, Harvard University.

63. On the debate within the NAACP on the resolution, see Kellogg, *NAACP,* 80–83; Fox, *Guardian of Boston,* 135.

64. Villard to BTW, April 10, 1911, Oswald Garrison Villard Papers, Harvard University.

65. BTW to Anderson, March 3, 1911, *BTW Papers,* X, 614. BTW had instigated Moore's attacks on Walling earlier, in 1909. Kellogg, *NAACP,* 32–33, 79–80.

66. New York *Age,* quoted in *ibid.,* 80.

67. Villard to Moton, April 5, 1911, BTW to Villard, April 19, 1911, *BTW Papers,* XI, 83, 109.

68. BTW to Moton, April 10, 1911, *BTW Papers,* XI, 94.

69. Kellogg, *NAACP,* 84–86.

70. Garrison to Villard, March 26, 1911, Oswald Garrison Villard Papers, Harvard University.

71. Cleveland *Gazette,* April 8, May 20, 1911.

72. *Ibid.,* July 22, 1911.

73. William D. Johnson, M. Cravath Simpson, and William Monroe Trotter to BTW, copy sent to the editor of the Little Rock *State Republican,* Aug. 15, 1911, enclosed in John E. Bush to Scott, Aug. 31, 1911.

74. BTW to William S. Hawk, April 9, 1911, *BTW Papers,* XI, 92–93.

75. Low to BTW, April 13, 1911, *BTW Papers,* XI, 102–3.

76. BTW to Fellner, July 15, 1913, Fellner to BTW, Aug. 27, 1913.

77. Atlanta *Constitution,* Dec. 3, 1911.

78. Dole to Low, March 29, 1911, Low to Dole, March 31, 1911, *BTW Papers,* XI, 54, 69–71.

79. Dole to Low, April 11, 1911, *BTW Papers,* XI, 100–102.

80. Dole to Low, April 25, 1911, *BTW Papers,* XI, 115–16.

81. Villard to Garrison, March 22, 1911, Oswald Garrison Villard Papers, Harvard University.

82. BTW to Anderson, May 2, 1911, *BTW Papers,* XI, 124–25.

83. Anderson to BTW, May 5, 1911, *BTW Papers,* XI, 128–29.

84. Anderson to BTW, May 29, 1911, *BTW Papers,* XI, 176.

85. Hagan to BTW, May 18, 1911, *BTW Papers,* XI, 160.

86. Hagan to BTW, *ca.* June 3, 1911, *BTW Papers,* XI, 190.

87. W. H. Smith to BTW, Dec. 14, 1911 [LC]; William J. Gaynor to BTW, Jan. 15, 1912, *BTW Papers,* XI, 456.

88. Anderson to Scott, Dec. 5, 1911, *BTW Papers,* XI, 397–98.

89. A. W. Abbott to W. H. Smith, Dec. 9, 1911.

90. Fred R. Moore to Scott, Jan. 15, 1912.

91. BTW to D. C. Smith, June 21, 1912.

92. Stanley Yarnall to Hugh M. Browne, March 6, 1912, Browne to Yarnall, March 8, 1912, Herbert Welsh to Yarnall, March 21, 1912.

93. Anderson to Scott, Oct. 22, 24, 1913.

94. Anderson to Scott, Oct. 29, 1913.

95. Anderson to Scott, Nov. 5, 1913.

96. Villard to Garrison, March 22, 1911, Oswald Garrison Villard Papers, Harvard University.

97. Mrs. W. F. Behr to BTW, June 23, 1913 [LC]. Santa Monica city directories confirm a Behr family at the address she gave.

98. BTW to W. H. Smith, July 12, 1913.

99. Typescript, undated.

100. Gatewood, "Booker T. Washington and the Ulrich Affair," 286–302.

101. Kellogg, *NAACP,* 80–83.

102. Fox, *Guardian of Boston,* 134–35.

Chapter 17

1. Lewis to BTW, March 7, 1913. Scott suggested in BTW's absence that Lewis write instead to Henry W. Taft. Scott to Lewis, March 10, 1913, Lewis to Scott, March 12, 1913.

2. Lewis to Scott, March 14, 1913.

3. Tyler to Scott, March 7, 1913.

4. BTW to James H. Penn, April 11, 1913.

5. BTW to Delbert H. Anderson, April 11, 1913.

6. Pinchback to BTW, April 27, 1913.

7. Osofsky, *Harlem,* 166.

8. Thompson to Scott, April 18, 1913.

9. BTW to Walters, Jan. 18, 1914.

10. Walters to Terrell, Feb. 20, 1914, Robert Heberton Terrell Papers, LC.

11. Walters to Terrell, Feb. 26, 1914, Terrell Papers, LC.

12. BTW to Wilson, Feb. 25, 1914, Wilson to BTW, March 2, 1914 [LC].

13. BTW to Chilton, Feb. 25, 1914.

14. M. C. Terrell to Theodore E. Burton, March 29, 1914, Mary Church Terrell Papers, LC.

15. Diary of Josephus Daniels, April 11, 1913, quoted in Arthur S. Link, *Wilson: The New Freedom* (Princeton, 1956), 246–47. There are many articles but no definitive treatment of the Wilson administration policy toward blacks. See particularly Nancy J. Weiss, "The Negro and the New Freedom: Fighting Wilsonian Segregation," *Political Science Quarterly*, LXXXIV (March 1969), 61–79; August Meier and Elliott Rudwick, "The Rise of Segregation in the Federal Bureaucracy, 1900–1930," *Phylon*, XXVIII (Summer 1967), 178–84; and two articles by Kathleen Wolgemuth, "Woodrow Wilson and Federal Segregation," *Journal of Negro History*, XLIV (April 1959), 158–73, and "Woodrow Wilson's Appointment Policy and the Negro," *Journal of Southern History*, XXIV (Nov. 1958), 457–71. Stephen R. Fox, C. Flint Kellogg, and Constance M. Green also treat Wilsonian policies as reflected in the protest movements of Trotter and the NAACP.

16. BTW to Villard, Aug. 8, 1913, Oswald Garrison Villard Papers, Harvard University.

17. BTW to Villard, Aug. 10, 1913, BTW Papers, Tuskegee Institute. This was enclosed in BTW to Villard, Aug. 14, 1913, Oswald Garrison Villard Papers, Harvard University, granting Villard permission to show the Aug. 10 letter to the President or his secretary.

18. Special to the New York *Age*, Nov. 5, 1913.

19. J. C. Waters to the editor of the New York *Times,* undated clipping. Waters has not been identified.

20. BTW to Wilson, June 8, 1914.

21. Moton to Wilson, Nov. 16, 1914, copy to BTW.

22. Moton to BTW, Nov. 23, 1914.

23. BTW to Moton, Nov. 27, 1914.

24. Scott to BTW, Nov. 17, 1914.

25. BTW to the editor, in the New York *World,* Jan. 6, 1915. Among other versions of the letter are an undated typescript [LC], and BTW to the editor in Washington *Post,* Jan. 17, 1915.

26. Some examples are BTW to McKinlay, Jan. 3, 1915, Carter G. Woodson Papers, LC; BTW to George C. Hall, Jan. 2, 1915 [LC]; BTW to Moton, Jan. [3], 1915, Hampton Institute Archives.

27. Moton to BTW, Jan. 4, 1915.

28. Scott to George L. Knox, Jan. 5, 1915, for example.

29. BTW to Chase, Jan. 5, 1915.

30. McKinlay to BTW, Jan. 5, 1915.

31. Lyon to BTW, Jan. 6, 1915.

32. McKinlay to BTW, Jan. 7, 1915.

33. Hall to BTW, Jan. 6, 1915.

34. A. Henry May and others to BTW, Jan. 15, 1915.

35. BTW to A. Henry May and others, Jan. 18, 1915. In 1914–15 there were 68 Tuskegee students from the West Indies and Latin America. See typescript list.

36. BTW to Smith, Feb. 1, 1912.

37. BTW to J. P. Billups, March 30, 1912, also Oct. 10, 1912.

38. BTW to E. T. Varner, June 8, 1912.

39. BTW, "Is the Negro Having a Fair Chance?" *Century*, LXXXV (Nov. 1912), 46–55.

40. *Crisis*, V (Dec. 1912), 71.

41. Lewis to BTW, Jan. 23, 1913, BTW to Lewis, Jan. 28, 1913.

42. BTW to E. C. Morris, April 7, 1913, and similar letters to four other officers.

43. BTW to Scott, June 6, 1913.

44. Scott to Frank Trumbull, Aug. 2, 1913, Scott to Frank I. Cobb, Aug. 8, 1913, Scott to R. E. Jones, Sept. 11, 1913.

45. Scott to Trumbull, Aug. 2, 1913.

46. BTW to W. L. O'Dwyer, Oct. 16, 1913, and to a list of other railroad officials.

47. BTW to Trumbull, Oct. 23, 1913; some twenty replies from railroad officials.

48. BTW to Jones, Nov. 3, 1913. When Jones failed to reply, BTW wrote again and had Scott wire a rebuke. BTW to Jones, Dec. 4, 1913, Scott to Jones, Dec. 28, 1913.

49. BTW to Jones, Feb. 16, 1914. On earlier boycott efforts often led by BTW supporters, see "The Boycott Movement against Jim Crow Streetcars in the South, 1900–1906," in Meier and Rudwick, *Along the Color Line*, 267–89.

50. BTW to the editor of the New York *Age*, April 1, 1914.

51. Daugherty to BTW, April 19, 1914, Scott to Daugherty, April 23, 1914.

52. BTW to Scott, May 4, 5, 1914.

53. BTW to Scott, May 10, 1914.

54. BTW to John Mitchell, Jr., and other editors, May 17, 1914. He wrote the letters as *"Personal and Confidential."*

55. Tyler to BTW, May 28, 1914.

56. Charles F. Dole to BTW, June 2, 1914, BTW to Dole, June 5, 1914 [LC]; *Crisis*, VIII (July 1914), 116.

57. Copy of petition, June 8, 1914. BTW sent a copy to William Hayes Ward, editor of the *Independent*, July 14, 1914.

58. Charles Banks to BTW, July 9, 1914.

59. Jones to BTW, June 8, 1914.

60. New Orleans *Times-Picayune*, June 8, 1914, clipping.

61. BTW to Banks, July 16, 1914, replying to Banks to BTW, July 9, 1914.

62. BTW to Charles W. Wickersham, Aug. 5, 1914.

63. BTW to Jones, Aug. 10, 1914.

64. BTW to J. M. Walsh of the Yazoo and Mississippi Valley Railroad Company, Aug. 13, 1914.

65. L. S. Hungerford to BTW, Nov. 12, 1914; BTW to Jones, Nov. 18, 1914.

66. BTW to Charles A. Wickersham, Nov. 25, 1914. Albon L. Holsey of the Tuskegee party believed the lunch counter man showed discourtesy because the blacks did not remove their hats. Holsey memorandum for BTW, undated.

67. Stephenson to BTW, Sept. 25, 1913.

68. Work to BTW, Oct. 3, 1913; Park to BTW, July 17, 1912.

69. BTW to Stephenson, Oct. 7, 1913 [LC]. See also Stephenson, "The Segregation of the White and Negro Races in Cities," *South Atlantic Quarterly,* XIII (Jan. 1914), 1–18; Poe, "Rural Land Segregation Between the Whites and Negroes: A Reply to Mr. Stephenson," *ibid.,* XIII (July 1914), 207–12.

70. Stephenson, "The Segregation of the White and Negro Races in Rural Communities of North Carolina," *ibid.,* XIII (April 1914), 107–17.

71. BTW to Stephenson, March 5, 1914.

72. C. H. Moore to Scott, May 7, 1914, BTW to Poe, May 4, 1914.

73. BTW to Carl Kelsey, May 24, 1914.

74. BTW to Dillard, June 3, 1914. See also Dillard to BTW, Aug. 8, 1914, BTW to Dillard, Aug. 14, 1914.

75. John H. Murphy to BTW, Jan. 11, 1911 [LC]; Kellogg, *NAACP,* 183–84.

76. *Ibid.,* 183–87.

77. BTW to Davis, June 19, 1913.

78. BTW to Kelsey, May 24, 1914.

79. Villard to Baldwin, quoted in Villard to Moton, March 9, 1914.

80. BTW to George B. Ward, July 13, 1914.

81. Ward to BTW, July 16, 1914.

82. C. Elias Winston to BTW, Sept. 23, Oct. 9, 1914.

83. BTW to Winston, Oct. 2, 1914.

84. Herbert Croly to BTW, June 18, 1915.

85. Croly to BTW, June 28, Sept. 7, 1915.

86. BTW to Croly, Sept. 4, 13, 1915; copy of typescript with corrections, Sept. 13, 1915.

87. *Crisis,* XI (Feb. 1916), 126–27; NAACP minutes of meetings of the board of directors, Feb. 14, March 13, 1916, NAACP Archives, LC.

88. BTW, "My View of Segregation Laws," *New Republic,* V (Dec. 4, 1915), 113–14.

89. Ogden to BTW, June 1, 1905 [LC]; Baltimore *Manufacturers' Record,* June 15, 1905; Hugh C. Bailey, *Liberalism in the New South* (Miami, 1969), 90; Thomas Dixon, Jr., "Booker T. Washington and the Negro: Some Dangerous Aspects of the Work of Tuskegee," *Saturday Evening Post,* CLVIII (Aug. 19, 1905), 1–2.

90. BTW to the editor of the *Saturday Evening Post,* Aug. 21, Oct. 2, 1905.

91. Kelly Miller disagreed, and wrote a pamphlet, *As to the Leopard's Spots: An Open Letter to Thomas Dixon, Jr.* (Washington, 1905). See BTW to Dixon, Feb. 20, 1905 [LC].

92. Dixon to BTW, Jan. 22, 1906, *BTW Papers,* VIII, 508; New York *Times,* Jan. 23, 1906.

93. Dixon to BTW, Jan. 23, 1906, *BTW Papers,* VIII, 508–9; BTW to Dixon, Jan. 25, 1906 [LC].

94. BTW to Anderson, Nov. 12, 1914.

95. Dixon to Wilson, March 4, 5, 1915, Woodrow Wilson Papers, LC. On the campaign against the film, see Thomas R. Cripps, "The Reaction of the Negro to the Motion Picture *Birth of a Nation,*" *Historian,* XXV (May 1963), 344–62; Fox, *Guardian of Boston,* 188–98; Cripps, *Slow Fade to Black* (New York, 1977), 41–74.

96. Dixon to Joseph P. Tumulty, May 1, 1915, Woodrow Wilson Papers, LC.

97. BTW to Charles E. Mason, April 22, 1915.

98. BTW to Courtney, April 23, 1915, BTW to F. P. Hull of the Boston *Transcript,* April 23, 1915. He also wrote to Mason that he had become convinced that "every one ought to do all he can to have the play stopped or greatly modified. The best thing would be to stop it." BTW to Mason, April 23, 1915.

99. BTW to William C. Graves, June 1, 1915 [LC]; BTW to W. H. Thompson, June 3, 1915 [LC]; Cripps, "Reaction of the Negro . . .," 359. Washington heard later, however, that the film was to be shown in Chicago. BTW to Graves, June 16, 1915 [LC].

100. Scott to BTW, Oct. 28, 1915, enclosing a newspaper clipping.

101. BTW to J. Mott Hallowell of Boston, May 29, 1915.

102. H. J. Stuyckmans to BTW, March 2, 1910; BTW to Stuyckmans, undated draft, *ca.* March 4, 1910.

103. Report of Baldwin's attitude in May Childs Nerney to Kathryn M. Johnson, July 30, Sept. 21, 1915, NAACP Archives, LC.

104. New York *Age,* Jan. 20, 1910, clipping.

105. Louis G. Anderson to Scott, March 8, 1913, and leaflet.

106. Anderson to Scott, April 7, 29, 1913, Scott to Anderson, May 9, 1913. See also W. F. Watkins to Scott, May 18, 1913, Anderson to Scott, Jan. 21, 1914.

107. Scott to BTW, Feb. 11, July 9, Oct. 23, 1914, Scott to William Maxwell, Feb. 24, 1914, Scott to Paramount Picture Corporation, Oct. 12, 1914.

108. Philip J. Allston to BTW, April 12, 1915, BTW to Allston, April 19, 1915.

109. BTW to Charles E. Mason, May 28, 1915; Cripps, "Reaction of the Negro . . . ," 361.

110. Scott to S. A. Everitt, Oct. 26, 1915 [LC]; *Crisis,* XI (Nov. 1915), 8–9; folder on *Lincoln's Dream,* 1915, NAACP Archives, LC.

111. Villard to BTW, Feb. 1913, BTW to Villard, Feb. 27, March 21, 1913, Villard to Scott, March 8, 1913, Villard to Moton, March 31, 1913, Moton to Scott, April 3, 1913.

112. Villard to BTW, April 4, 1913.

113. BTW to William G. Willcox, April 13, 1914, Villard to BTW, May 21, June 3, 1914, BTW to Villard, May 27, 1914.

114. Nancy J. Weiss, *The National Urban League, 1910–1940* (New York, 1974), 47–70, finds in the league membership a blending of the BTW and Du Bois ideologies, with BTW's predominant. On BTW's early influence, see Ruth S. Baldwin to BTW, Oct. 2, 1911, April 15, 1912.

115. BTW to Anderson, Oct. 1, 1907, Eugene Kinckle Jones to BTW, Feb. 19, 1913.

116. BTW to George E. Haynes, Oct. 1, 1913, Baldwin to BTW, April 13, May 27, 1914, BTW to Baldwin, May 25, 1914.

Chapter 18

1. William Jay Schieffelin to BTW, Sept. 10, 1906.

2. BTW to Schieffelin, Sept. 18, 1906.

3. BTW telegram to Schoonmaker & Co., Jan. 12, 1909.

4. Boston *Post,* Dec. 18, 1910, clipping.

5. John H. Kellogg, M.D., to BTW, March 24, 1911; see also BTW to Kellogg, March 20, April 4, 1911.

6. Kellogg to BTW, April 10, 1911, BTW to Kellogg, May 1, 1911.

7. BTW to Kellogg, April 3, 1912, *BTW Papers,* XI, 510.

8. BTW, address at the First National Conference on Race Betterment, Jan. 8–12, 1914, in E. Davidson Washington, ed., *Selected Speeches of Booker T. Washington,* 218.

9. BTW, Last Will and Testament, May 25, 1909, *BTW Papers,* X, 112–16.

10. A Codicil to BTW's Last Will and Testament, June 13, 1911, *BTW Papers,* XI, 212–14.

11. Parker to BTW, July 31, 1911.

12. BTW to Parker, Aug. 5, 1911.

13. Parker to BTW, Aug. 8, 1911.

14. Parker to BTW, Aug. 16, 1911.

15. Neither the name of the insurance company nor the amount of insurance is revealed by the correspondence.

16. Ruth S. Baldwin to BTW, Oct. 2, 1911, *BTW Papers,* XI, 320.

17. BTW to Baldwin, Oct. 7, 1911, *BTW Papers,* XI, 321.

18. G. F. Peabody to BTW, Oct. 30, 1911.

19. Allen to Scott, Sept. 21, 1913.

20. BTW to Anderson, Oct. 2, 1913.

21. Scott to C. H. Fearing, Sept. 28, 1914.

22. BTW to Hall, Sept. 3, 14, 1914, July 30, 1915, Hall to BTW, Sept. 10, 1914.

23. BTW, "A Paradise of Fish & Sea Food," draft corrected in BTW's hand, undated, *ca.* October 1915.

24. Scott to Allen, Sept. 16, 17, 1915.

25. BTW to Edith M. Washington, Sept. 23, 1915, George Washington Carver Museum, Tuskegee Institute.

26. BTW to E. Davidson Washington, Sept. 25, 1915, George Washington Carver Museum, Tuskegee Institute.

27. BTW to Mr. and Mrs. C. W. Allen, Oct. 2, 1915.

28. BTW to L. E. Johnson, Oct. 6, 1915.

29. BTW address before the American Missionary Association and the National Council of Congregational Churches, Oct. 25, 1915, in E. D. Washington, ed., *Selected Speeches of Booker T. Washington,* 277.

30. G. W. A. Johnston to BTW, Oct. 4, 1915.

31. BTW to Johnston, Oct. 7, 1915.

32. BTW, Jr., to BTW, Oct. 6, 1915. Both his nephew and son suggested another sojourn at Battle Creek, but when BTW wrote to J. H. Kellogg at this time, it was to ask that Adella Hunt Logan, who had suffered a nervous breakdown, be admitted to the sanitarium. BTW to Kellogg, Oct. 4, 1915.

33. BTW to John H. Washington, Oct. 8, 1915.

34. Scott and Stowe, *Booker T. Washington,* 303.

35. *Ibid.,* 309.

36. Seth B. Capp to BTW, Sept. 9, 1914, BTW to Capp, Sept. 15, 1914.

37. Capp to BTW, Nov. 7, 1914.

38. BTW to Vincent, Oct. 11, 1915, Vincent to Mayo, Oct. 15, 1915, Vincent to BTW, Oct. 15, 1915.

39. BTW to Hall, Oct. 16, 1915.

40. Hall to BTW, Oct. 19, 1915.

41. BTW, "On Team Work," a Sunday Evening Talk on Oct. 17, 1915, *Tuskegee Student,* XXVII (Nov. 13, 1915), 1–2.

42. "Dr. Booker T. Washington on American Occupation of Haiti," New York *Age,* Oct. 21, 1915. The article also appeared in the *Outlook,* CXI (Nov. 17, 1915), 681.

43. BTW to John C. Schwab, Oct. 16, 1915.

44. BTW to Hall, Oct. 22, 1915.

45. Scott to Hall, Oct. 22, 1915. Scott also wrote to Fred R. Moore, Oct. 23, 1915, saying "I do not know how the rumor could have originated to the effect that Dr. Washington is seriously ill. It is certainly far from the truth. In fact, he is in better health now than he has been for several months. He is leaving today for New York City, and you will probably be meeting him within the next day or two."

46. Hall to Rosenwald, Oct. 25, 1915, Julius Rosenwald Papers, University of Chicago.

47. BTW, address before the American Missionary Association and National Council of Congregational Churches, Oct. 25, 1915, in E. D. Washington, ed., *Selected Speeches of Booker T. Washington,* 277–83.

48. *Crisis,* XI (Dec. 1915), 64.

49. William H. Jackson to BTW, Nov. 1, 1915.

50. BTW to Margaret Washington, Oct. 26, 1915.

51. BTW to Logan (two telegrams), Oct. 26, 1915, BTW to Dillard, Oct. 26, 1915.

52. BTW to Margaret Washington, Oct. 27, 1915.

53. Margaret Washington to BTW, Oct. 27, 1915.

54. Hall to BTW, Oct. 27, 1915.

55. Margaret Washington to BTW, Oct, 28, 1915.

56. BTW to Margaret Washington, Oct. 30, 1915, BTW to F. A. McKenzie, Nov. 8, 1915.

57. BTW to Moton, Oct. 10, 14, 1915, Moton to BTW, Oct. 11, 1915 [LC]; Moton to BTW, Nov. 1, 1915, Hampton Institute Archives.

58. BTW to Moton, Nov. 4, 5, 1915.

59. Willcox to Rosenwald, Oct. 10, 1915, Julius Rosenwald Papers, University of Chicago.

60. Rosenwald to Willcox, Nov. 1, 1915, Julius Rosenwald Papers, University of Chicago.

61. BTW to Scott, Nov. 4, 1915.

62. BTW to Margaret Washington, Nov. 5, 1915.

63. BTW to Calloway, Nov. 8, 1915, BTW to Holsey, Nov. 10, 1915, BTW to Roberts, Nov. 10, 1915, BTW to Stewart, Nov. 10, 1915.

64. Moton to BTW, Nov. 6, 1915.

65. Stewart to BTW, Nov. 10, 1915.

66. John H. Washington to Margaret Washington, Nov. 9, 1915. Punctuation supplied to this and other telegrams of this period.

67. New York *Tribune,* Nov. 10, 1915. The interview was quoted and reported in part by many other newspapers, though not always with reference to "racial characteristics." See Boston *Herald,* Nov. 10, 1915, clipping [LC].

68. Hall to Scott, Nov. 10, 1915. Scott, however, thought Hall had misconstrued Bastedo's statement, for the Birmingham *Age-Herald* had construed the phrase "to indicate that Dr. Washington is worrying under the strain of work, the implication being that this means that Negroes generally worry under the strain of work." Scott to Hall, Nov. 10, 1915.

69. William C. Graves to Ronsenwald, Nov. 1, 1915 (first letter), Julius Rosenwald Papers, University of Chicago. I thank Dr. Maceo Dailey for calling this telegram and the two letters which follow to my attention.

70. Graves to Rosenwald, Nov. 11, 1915 (second letter), Julius Rosenwald Papers, University of Chicago.

71. Graves to Rosenwald, Nov. 11, 1915 (third letter), Julius Rosenwald Papers, University of Chicago.

72. Quoted in *Tuskegee Student,* XXVII (Nov. 27, 1915), 1.

73. Rosenwald to BTW, Nov. 11, 1915. The chrysanthemum reference was to a show that Emmett Scott's wife had held each year for the past nine years, encouraging the neighboring people to compete.

74. Margaret Washington to Julius Rosenwald, Nov. 12, 1915, Julius Rosenwald Papers, University of Chicago.

75. Margaret Washington to Scott, Nov. 12, 1915.

76. Scott to Banks, Nov. 13, 1915.

77. Scott and Stowe, *Booker T. Washington,* 321–22.

78. Margaret Washington to Scott, Nov. 13, 1915.

79. Montgomery *Advertiser,* Nov. 15, 1915.

80. *Ibid.*
81. Chisum to Scott, Nov. 15, 1915.
82. An elegy by Capp Jefferson, Nov. 15, 1915.
83. Anderson to Scott, Nov. 16, 1915.
84. Bruce to Scott, Nov. 16, 1915.
85. Isaac Fisher's account, in Montgomery *Advertiser,* Nov. 16, 1915.
86. *Ibid.* A detailed account of the funeral is in the *Tuskegee Student,* XXVII (Nov. 27, 1915); see also *ibid.,* XXVII (Dec. 11, 1915).
87. Rhonda Hope [Claude McKay], "In Memoriam: Booker T. Washington," undated manuscript, *ca.* 1915, William Stanley Braithwaite Papers, Harvard University. This poem, sent with others to Braithwaite, was apparently never published. I wish to thank Wayne Cooper for a photocopy of the poem.
88. Alexander E. Manning to Scott, Nov. 20, 1915 [LC]; BTW to J. H. Kellogg, Oct. 4, 1915 [LC]; *Tuskegee Student,* XXVII (Dec. 25, 1915), 3.

Index

546   Index

Washington, Booker T. (*continued*)
riage, 119-20; care for BTW, Jr.'s
health, 115; concern about BTW,
Jr.'s grades, 114; concern for sister,
123-26; conscientious service as family member, 126-27; protects daughter from spiteful attacks, 110-11; relationship with wife, 107-8

INFLUENCE ON SOUTHERN WHITES: accommodationism, 203-5, 308-9; conciliation of governors of Alabama,
239-44; criticizes A. H. Stone, 259-
60; cultivation of conservatives, 239;
endorses cotton-picking machine,
226-27; endorses New South doctrine, 204; fondness for South, 202-
4; friendship with southern Jews,
260-61; helps to bring order after
Atlanta Race Riot, 299-304; methods
of interracial diplomacy, 238-39, 244,
261-62, 265; speaking tours of South,
262-65; supports prohibition movement, 230-33; tries to modify segregation at Atlanta railroad station,
296-97; turns from conservative to
more liberal whites, 251-61; whitecapping in Mississippi, 226

PERSONAL: acquires life insurance policy, 441; assaulted in New York City,
379-82; attunement to era of segregation, 436; buys summer residence
on Long Island, 395; called "the
Wizard," 15, 38, 39, 53, 56, 98, 357,
408; chronic ailments, 439-40; compared with Robert E. Lee, 203; conduct in Ulrich affair assessed, 399-
404; criticism of role in Ulrich affair,
393-97; death, 455; dinner with John
Wanamaker and daughter at Saratoga, 385; distrust of cities and intellectuals, 204-5; enters St. Luke's
Hospital, 450-51; final illness, 449-54;
follows Ulrich's later jail term, 398;
funeral, 456-57; guarded by Pinkerton detectives, 263, 385-86, 390-91;
H. G. Wells describes personality and
ideas, 283-84; H. H. Johnston describes, 288; hearing on Ulrich assault, 384; last public addresses, 446-
47; makes will, 440-41; more outspoken on civil rights after Ulrich assault, 404; nature of final illness, 450-
53; physical effects of Ulrich assault,
439-40; postpones visit to Mayo
Clinic, 445, 447, 449; question of use
of alcohol, 400; relationship to An-

drew Carnegie, 138-40; relationship
with white philanthropists, 142; returns to Tuskegee for last time, 453-
55; seeks retraction of Ulrich charges,
389; seeks to damage H. A. Ulrich's
credibility, 388; signs of aging and
tiredness, 438-39; southernness, 202-
5; summer home in South Weymouth, Mass., 44; tries to secure
promotion for detective in Ulrich
case, 397-98; Ulrich affair highlights
his secretiveness, 402-3; Ulrich trial
and acquittal, 391; under care of
physical therapist, 440; use of ghostwriters, 290-91; vacations on Mobile
Bay, 442-43; vice president of American Peace Society, 138; warned to
rest, 441-42

POLITICS: advises Taft on campaign
speeches (1908), 331; aids Taft to secure W. D. Crum resignation, 339-
41; aids Taft's nomination, 329;
chooses black presidential appointees, 6; coaches President-elect
Taft on southern policy, 339; com-
bats lily whites in South, 6-7; com-
mends Gold Democrats, 42; decline
of black voting power, 7; dinner at
White House, 3-5; directs Republican campaign in 1904 among blacks,
28; early support of Taft, 324-25;
expresses public optimism about
Wilson administration, 358; fights lily
whites in Texas, 14; finds Brownsville an advantage in politics, 323-24;
in Georgia, 15; keeps Roosevelt informed of black voter sentiment in
1904, 28; lieutenants in the North,
16-19; lieutenants in Washington,
D.C., 17-18; lobbies for confirmation
of W. D. Crum, 19-23; modifies
Taft's inaugural address, 341; Negro
planks in Republican 1904 platform,
25-26; opposes reduction of southern representation, 26-27; personally prefers Roosevelt in 1912, 348-
49; presents Brownsville dismissal as
honest mistake, 318; publicly dis-
avows deep involvement in politics,
10; relationship with Wilson administration, 412-13; remains loyal to
Taft but inactive in 1912, 353-54,
356; renewal of battle with southern
lily whites, 325-26; Republican National Convention of 1904, 23-26;
Roosevelt rejects advice on Browns-